SUPPLY CHAIN LOGISTICS MANAGEMENT

SUPPLY CHAIN LOGISTICS MANAGEMENT

Donald J. Bowersox

David J. Closs

M. Bixby Cooper

Michigan State University

Boston   Burr Ridge, IL   Dubuque, IA   Madison, WI   New York
San Francisco   St. Louis   Bangkok   Bogotá   Caracas   Kuala Lumpur
Lisbon   London   Madrid   Mexico City   Milan   Montreal   New Delhi
Santiago   Seoul   Singapore   Sydney   Taipei   Toronto

McGraw-Hill Higher Education

A Division of The **McGraw-Hill** *Companies*

SUPPLY CHAIN LOGISTICS MANAGEMENT

Published by McGraw-Hill/Irwin, an imprint of The McGraw-Hill Companies, Inc. 1221 Avenue of the Americas, New York, NY, 10020. Copyright © 2002 by The McGraw-Hill Companies, Inc. All rights reserved. No part of this publication may be reproduced or distributed in any form or by any means, or stored in a database or retrieval system, without the prior written consent of The McGraw-Hill Companies, Inc., including, but not limited to, in any network or other electronic storage or transmission, or broadcast for distance learning.

Some ancillaries, including electronic and print components, may not be available to customers outside the United States.

This book is printed on acid-free paper.

domestic   1 2 3 4 5 6 7 8 9 0 CCW/CCW 0 9 8 7 6 5 4 3 2
international 1 2 3 4 5 6 7 8 9 0 CCW/CCW 0 9 8 7 6 5 4 3 2

ISBN 0-07-235100-4

Publisher: *Brent Gordon*
Senior sponsoring editor: *Scott Isenberg*
Senior developmental editor: *Wanda J. Zeman*
Senior marketing manager: *Zina Craft*
Project manager: *Jill Moline*
Production supervisor: *Rose Hepburn*
Coordinator of freelance design: *Mary E. Kazak*
Supplement producer: *Erin Sauder*
Media producer: *Greg Bates*
Cover design: *Andrew Curtis*
Typeface: *10/12 Times Roman*
Compositor: *Shepherd Incorporated*
Printer: *Courier Westford*

Library of Congress Cataloging-in-Publication Data

Bowersox, Donald J.
    Supply chain logistics management / Donald J. Bowersox, David J. Closs, M. Bixby Cooper.
        p. cm.—(McGraw-Hill/Irwin series operations and decision sciences)
    Includes index.
    ISBN 0-07-235100-4 (alk. paper)—ISBN 0-07-112306-7 (international : alk. paper)
    1. Business logistics.   I. Closs, David J.   II. Cooper, M. Boxby.   III. Title.   IV.
Irwin/McGraw-Hill series. Operations and decision sciences
HD38.5 .B697 2002
658.7—dc21

                                                                                            2001054667

INTERNATIONAL EDITION ISBN 0-07-112306-7
Copyright © 2002. Exclusive rights by The McGraw-Hill Companies, Inc. for manufacture and export. This book cannot be re-exported from the country to which it is sold by McGraw-Hill. The International Edition is not available in North America.

www.mhhe.com

This book is dedicated to our families for their time, encouragement, and patience for it is the authors' families who ultimately pay the dearest price.

DONALD J. BOWERSOX is John H. McConnell University Professor of Business at Michigan State University where he has also served as Dean of the Business School. He received his Ph.D. at Michigan State and has worked with industry throughout his career. He is the author of numerous articles in publications such as the *Harvard Business Review, Journal of Marketing, Journal of Business Logistics,* and *Supply Chain Management Review.* Dr. Bowersox has led a number of industry-supported research studies investigating the best practices of logisticians in North America and around the world. He is a frequent speaker at industry and academic meetings.

DAVID J. CLOSS is Eli Broad Professor of Logistics at Michigan State University. He received his Ph.D. in marketing and logistics from Michigan State. Dr. Closs is the author and co-author of many publications in journals, proceedings, and industry reports. He was also a principle researcher for *World Class Logistics: The Challenge of Managing Continuous Change* and *21st Century Logistics: Making Supply Chain Integration a Reality* completed at Michigan State and published by the Council of Logistics Management. Dr. Closs' primary interests include logistics strategy and the development and application of computer models and information systems for logistics operations and planning. Dr. Closs is a frequent speaker at industry and academic conferences and presenter at executive education programs. Dr. Closs was the editor of the *Journal of Business Logistics.*

M. BIXBY COOPER is Associate Professor in the Department of Marketing and Supply Chain Management at Michigan State University. He is co-author of three texts on distribution and logistics, including *World Class Logistics: The Challenge of Managing Continuous Change* published by the Council of Logistics Management and *Strategic Marketing Channel Management* published by McGraw-Hill. His research has focused on logistics best practices in customer service and in performance measurement. He also served for four years on the Executive Board of the International Customer Service Association as head of the Research and Education Committee.

Over the last six decades, the discipline of business logistics has advanced from the warehouse and transportation dock to the boardroom of leading global enterprises. We have had the opportunity to be actively involved in this evolution through research, education, and advising. *Supply Chain Logistics Management* encompasses the development and fundamentals of the logistics/supply chain discipline. It also presents our vision of the future of business logistics and supply chain management and its role in enterprise competitiveness.

Although individually and collectively each of the three authors has written extensively on various aspects of logistics, the decision to write *Supply Chain Logistics Management* was motivated in part to acknowledge the significant change in logistical practice brought on by its examination and placement within the context of integrated supply chain management. *Supply Chain Logistics Management* represents the synthesis of many years of research, augmenting and, in many ways, supplanting earlier works of the authors published by McGraw-Hill. This union of ideas presented in this text provides a new supply chain framework for the study of the field of logistics, serves to expand the treatment of integrative supply chain management, by placing it firmly in the context of contemporary business, and highlights the increasing importance of logistics in global competitive strategy.

Logistics includes all the activities to move product and information to, from, and between members of a supply chain. The supply chain provides the framework for businesses and their suppliers that join to bring goods, services, and information efficiently and effectively to ultimate customers. *Supply Chain Logistics Management* presents the mission, business processes, and strategies needed to achieve integrated logistical management. We hope the text achieves three fundamental objectives: (1) presents a comprehensive description of existing logistical practices in a global society; (2) describes ways and means to apply logistics principles to achieve competitive advantage; and (3) provides a conceptual approach for integrating logistics as a core competency in enterprise strategy.

It would be impossible to list all the individuals who have made significant contributions to the contents of this book. Special thanks are due to Robert W. Nason, Chairperson of the Department of Marketing and Supply Chain Management at Michigan State University, for maintaining a collegial environment that fosters creativity and application of integrated logistics concepts. We also express our gratitude to Professor Emeritus Donald A. Taylor of Michigan State University, who has been a guiding force throughout our careers. In addition, for their specific suggestions regarding the manuscript, our appreciation goes to Frederick J. Beier, University of Minnesota; Mark L. Bennion, Bowling Green State University; Robert L. Cook, Central Michigan University; Patricia J. Daugherty, University of Oklahoma; Stanley E. Fawcett, Brigham Young University, Byron Finch, Miami University of Ohio; Satish Mehra, University of Memphis; Taeho Park, San Jose University; Alfred P. Quinton, College of New Jersey; Zinovy Radovilsky, California State University—Hayward; Powell Robinson, Texas A&M University; and Jay U. Sterling, University of Alabama; all of whom provided detailed reviews of the manuscript and offered numerous suggestions for improving the presentation.

We also want to acknowledge the staff at McGraw-Hill/Irwin for their guidance and efforts on behalf of the book: Scott Isenberg, Senior Sponsoring Editor; Wanda Zeman, Senior Development Editor; Jill Moline, Project Manager; and Erin Sauder, Supplement Producer.

As active members of the Council of Logistics Management, formerly the National Council of Physical Distribution Management, we have been the fortunate recipients of contributions by many council members to the development of this manuscript. In particular, we wish to acknowledge the assistance of George Gecowets, former executive director, Maria McIntyre, current executive director, and the CLM staff who maintain an open door to the academic community.

Over the past thirty-five years, business executives who have attended the annual Michigan State University Logistics Management Executive Development Seminar have been exposed to the basic concepts developed in the text and have given freely of their time and experience. We also acknowledge the long-standing support to Michigan State Logistics, through the funding of the endowed chair, provided by John H. McConnell, founder and chairperson of Worthington Industries.

The number of individuals involved in teaching logistics around the world expands daily. To this group in general, and in particular to our colleagues at Michigan State University, whose advice and assistance made it possible to complete and enhance this text, we express our sincere appreciation.

Teachers receive continuous inspiration from students over the years and, in many ways, the final day of judgment in a professional career comes in the seminar or classroom. We have been fortunate to have the counsel of many outstanding young scholars who currently are making substantial impact on the academic and business worlds. In particular, we appreciate the input of students who have used this text in manuscript form and made suggestions for improvement. We also acknowledge the contributions of current and former doctoral students, particularly Drs. Judith Whipple and Thomas Goldsby who participated extensively in case development and editorial support. Ann Cooper provided substantial help in documenting the Industry Insights. Luke Nieuwenhuis, Shubhendu Das, and Kathleen Kossen provided valuable assistance throughout manuscript preparation, managed the complex process of obtaining publication permissions, and guided development of the teaching manual and support material.

We wish to acknowledgment the contributions of Felicia Kramer and Pamela Kingsbury, for manuscript preparation on several earlier versions of this text. Cheryl Lundeen, who prepared many drafts of the manuscript, provided outstanding support for the last two editions. Without Felicia, Pam, and Cheryl, this long published text in its many variations would not be a reality.

With so much able assistance, it is difficult to offer excuses for any shortcomings that might appear. The faults are solely our responsibility.

Donald J. Bowersox
David J. Closs
M. Bixby Cooper

BRIEF CONTENTS

C O N T E N T S

PART III

OPERATIONS

11 Transportation Infrastructure and Regulation   328

12 Transportation Management   355

CASES

I   LOGISTICS IN SUPPLY CHAIN MANAGEMENT

Part I establishes the strategic importance of logistics to achieving business success by creating value throughout domestic and global supply chains. The initial chapter scopes the current business attention to supply chain collaboration. The supply chain provides the framework within which logistical strategies are developed and executed. Logistics, the primary topic of this book, is introduced in Chapter 2. The concept of lean logistics is developed by discussing the ways specific work tasks combine to support market distribution, manufacturing, and procurement. The third chapter describes the importance of customer accommodation to successful logistics. The value created by logistics can serve as a powerful driver of customer success. Chapter 4 is devoted to the challenges of servicing end customers. This chapter describes the complex issues related to supporting market distribution. Chapter 5 develops operational issues related to logistical support of procurement and manufacturing. While there are many similarities between consumer and industrial logistics, some distinct differences must be understood and accommodated to assure maximum value creation. The final chapter of Part I, Chapter 6, is focused on the challenges of internal integration of procurement, manufacturing, and market distribution operations. A model of enterprise integration is developed to generalize supply chain collaboration in the context of domestic and global business. Four strategic cases are presented at the conclusion of Part I.

1 21st-Century Supply Chains

As recently as the early 1990s, the average time required for a company to process and deliver merchandise to a customer from warehouse inventory ranged from 15 to 30 days, sometimes even longer. The typical order-to-delivery scenario involved order creation and transfer, which was usually via telephone, fax, Electronic Data Interchange (EDI), or public mail; followed by order processing, which involved the use of manual or computer systems, credit authorization, and order assignment to a warehouse for selection; followed by shipment to a customer. When everything went as planned, the average time for a customer to receive items ordered was lengthy. When something went wrong (as it most often did), such as inventory out-of-stock, a lost or misplaced work order, or a misdirected shipment, total time to service customers escalated rapidly.

To support this lengthy and unpredictable time to market, it became common practice to stockpile inventory. For example, inventories of identical products were typically stocked by retailers, wholesalers, and manufacturers. Despite such extensive inventory, out-of-stocks and delayed deliveries remained pervasive due to the large number of product variations.

These accepted business practices of the 20th century, as well as the distribution channel structure used to complete delivery, evolved from years of experience that dated from the industrial revolution. Such long-standing business practices remained in place and unchallenged because no clearly superior alternative existed. The traditional distribution process was designed to overcome challenges and achieve benefits that long ago ceased to be important. The industrialized world is no longer characterized by scarcity. Consumer affluence and desire for wide choice of products and services continues to accelerate. In fact, today's consumers want a wide range of options they can configure to their unique specifications. The desires of customers have shifted from passive acceptance to active involvement in the design and delivery of specific products and services. Transportation capacity and operational performance has increasingly become more economical and reliable, as today's transportation is supported by sophisticated technology that facilitates predictable and precise delivery.

Most of all, a massive change has occurred as a result of information availability. During the decade of the 1990s, the world of commerce was irrevocably impacted by computerization, the Internet, and a range of inexpensive information transmission capabilities. Information characterized by speed, accessibility, accuracy, and most of all relevancy became the norm. The Internet, operating at Web speed, has become an economical way to conduct transactions and launched the potential of business-to-business (B2B) consumer direct e-distribution. Driven by these fundamental forces, a global economy rapidly emerged.

What began during the last decade of the 20th century and will continue to unfold well into the 21st century is what historians will characterize as the dawning of the *information* or *digital age.* In the age of electronic commerce, the reality of B2B connectivity has made possible a new order of business relationships called *supply chain management.* Managers are increasingly questioning traditional distribution, manufacturing, and purchasing practices. In this new order of affairs, products can be manufactured to exact specifications and rapidly delivered to customers at locations throughout the globe. Logistical systems exist that have the capability to deliver products at exact times. Customer order and delivery of a product can be performed in hours. The frequent occurrence of service failures that characterized the past is increasingly being replaced by a growing managerial commitment to zero defect or what is commonly called six-sigma performance.[1] Perfect orders—delivering the desired assortment and quantity of products to the correct location on time, damage-free, and correctly invoiced—once the exception, are now becoming the expectation. Perhaps most important is the fact that such high-level performance is being achieved at lower total cost *and* with the commitment of fewer financial resources than characteristic of the past.

In this initial chapter, the supply chain management business model is introduced as a growing strategic posture of contemporary firms. The chapter reviews the development of the supply chain revolution in business practice. Next, the supply chain concept is presented in a strategic framework. The chapter then examines integrative

---

[1]Six Sigma performance reflects a level of achievement having an error rate of 3.4 defects per million or 99.99966 percent perfect. See Forrest W. Breyfogle, III, *Implementing Six Sigma: Smarter Solutions Using Statistical Methods* (New York, NY: John Wiley & Sons, 1999).

management, responsiveness, financial sophistication, and globalization as forces driving the emergence of supply chain logic. The chapter concludes with a review of contemporary issues related to supply chain management. The overall objective of Chapter 1 is to provide a framework describing 21st century supply chains in terms of logistical requirements. The supply chain is positioned as the strategic framework within which logistical requirements are identified and related operations must be managed.

The Supply Chain Revolution

What managers are experiencing today we choose to describe as the *supply chain revolution* and a related *logistical renaissance*. These two massive shifts in expectation and practice concerning the performance of business operations are highly interrelated, but they are significantly different aspects of contemporary strategic thinking.

 Supply chain (sometimes called the *value chain* or *demand chain*) **management** consists of *firms collaborating to leverage strategic positioning and to improve operating efficiency.* For each firm involved, the supply chain relationship reflects strategic choice. A supply chain strategy is a channel arrangement based on acknowledged dependency and relationship management. Supply chain operations require managerial processes that span across functional areas within individual firms and link trading partners and customers across organizational boundaries.

 Logistics, in contrast to supply chain management, is the *work required to move and position inventory throughout a supply chain.* As such, logistics is a subset of and occurs within the broader framework of a supply chain. Logistics is the process that creates value by timing and positioning inventory; it is the combination of a firm's order management, inventory, transportation, warehousing, materials handling, and packaging as integrated throughout a facility network. Integrated logistics serves to link and synchronize the overall supply chain as a continuous process and is essential for effective supply chain connectivity.[2] While the purpose of logistical work has remained essentially the same over the decades, the way the work is performed continues to radically change.

The fundamental focus of this book is integrated logistics management. However, to study logistics, a reader must have a basic understanding of supply chain management. Supply chain decisions establish the operating framework within which logistics is performed. As will be reviewed shortly, dramatic change continues to evolve in supply chain practice. Accordingly, logistics best practice, as described in this book, is presented as a work in progress, subject to continuous change based on the evolving nature of supply chain structure and strategy. Chapter 2, Lean Logistics, scopes the renaissance taking place in logistics best practice and sets the stage for all chapters that follow.

At first blush, supply chain management may appear to be a vague concept. A great deal has been written on the subject without much concern for basic definition, structure, or common vocabulary. Confusion exists concerning the appropriate scope of what constitutes a supply chain, to what extent it involves integration with other

---

[2]The Council of Logistics Management has developed the following definition: "Logistics is the process of planning, implementing and controlling the efficient, effective flow and storage of goods, services and related information from point of origin to the point of consumption for the purpose of conforming to customer requirements."

companies as contrasted to internal operations, and how it is implemented in terms of competitive practices. For most managers, the supply chain concept has intrinsic appeal because it visions new business arrangements offering the potential to improve customer service. The concept also implies a highly efficient and effective network of business linkages that can serve to improve efficiency by eliminating duplicate and nonproductive work. Understanding more specifically what constitutes the supply chain revolution starts with a review of traditional distribution channel practice.

To overcome challenges of commercial trading, firms developed business relationships with other product and service companies to jointly perform essential activities. Such acknowledged dependency was necessary to achieve benefits of specialization. Managers, following the early years of the industrial revolution, began to strategically plan core competency, specialization, and economy of scale. The result was realization that working closely with other businesses was essential for continued success. This understanding that no firm could be totally self-sufficient contrasted to some earlier notions of vertical ownership integration. Acknowledged dependence between business firms created the study of what became known as *distribution* or *marketing channels.*

Because of the high visibility of different types of businesses, the early study of channel arrangements was characterized by classification based on specific roles performed during the distributive process. For example, a firm may have been created to perform the value-added services of a wholesaler. Firms doing business with a wholesaler had expectations concerning what services they would receive and the compensation they would be expected to pay. In-depth study of specific channels quickly identified the necessity for leadership, a degree of commitment to cooperation among channel members, and means to resolve conflict. Those who conducted research in channel structure and strategy developed topologies to classify observable practice ranging from a single transaction to highly formalized continuous trading relationships.[3]

The bonding feature of channel integration was a rather vague concept that benefits would result from cooperation. However, primarily due to a lack of high-quality information, the overall channel structure was postured on an adversarial foundation. When push came to shove, each firm in the channel would first and foremost focus on its individual goals. Thus, in final analysis, channel dynamics were more often than not characterized by a dog-eat-dog competitive environment.

During the last decade of the 20th century, channel strategy and structure began to shift radically. Traditional distribution channel arrangements moved toward more collaborative practice that began with the rapid advancement of computers and information transfer technology and then accelerated with the Internet and World Wide Web explosion. The connectivity of the World Wide Web served to create a new vision.

Generalized Supply Chain Model

The general concept of an integrated supply chain is typically illustrated by a line diagram that links participating firms into a coordinated competitive unit. Figure 1-1 illustrates a generalized model adapted from the supply chain management program at Michigan State University.

---

[3]For example, see Louis W. Stern, Adel I. El-Ansary, and Anne T. Coughlan, *Marketing Channels,* 5th ed. (Saddle River, NJ: Prentice Hall, 1996).

FIGURE 1-1

Generalized supply chain model

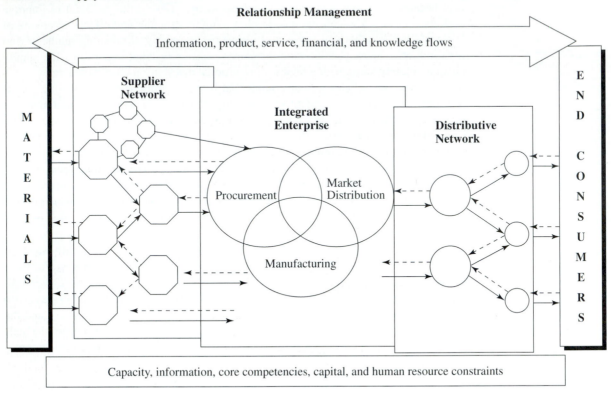

Source: Adapted from supply chain faculty. Michigan State University.

The context of an integrated supply chain is multifirm relationship management within a framework characterized by capacity limitations, information, core competencies, capital, and human resource constraints. Within this context, supply chain structure and strategy results from efforts to operationally link an enterprise with customers as well as the supporting distributive and supplier networks to gain competitive advantage. Business operations are therefore integrated from initial material purchase to delivery of products and services to end customers.[4]

Value results from the synergy among firms comprising the supply chain with respect to five critical flows: information, product, service, financial, and knowledge (see the bidirectional arrow at the top of the figure). Logistics is the primary conduit of product and service flow within a supply chain arrangement. Each firm engaged in a supply chain is involved in performing logistics. Such logistical activity may or may not be integrated within that firm and within overall supply chain performance. Achievement of logistical integration is the focus of this text.

The generalized supply chain arrangement illustrated in Figure 1-1 logically and logistically links a firm and its distributive and supplier network to end customers. The

---

[4]End customers are defined as destination points in a supply chain. End customers either consume a product or use it as an integral part or component of an additional process or product. The essential point is that the original product loses its unique configuration when consumed by end customers. This definition is developed in greater detail in Chapter 3.

TABLE 1-1   Successful Supply Chain Strategies

A recent Accenture study revealed six different, but equally successful, supply chain strategies.

• Market Saturation Driven: Focusing on generating high profit margins through strong brands and ubiquitous marketing and distribution.

• Operationally Agile: Configuring assets and operations to react nimbly to emerging consumer trends along lines of product category or geographic region.

• Freshness Oriented: Concentrating on earning a premium by providing the consumer with product that is fresher than competitive offerings.

• Consumer Customizer: Using mass customization to build and maintain close relationships with end consumers through direct sales.

• Logistics Optimizer: Emphasizing a balance of supply chain efficiency and effectiveness.

• Trade Focused: Prioritizing "low price, best value" for the consumer (as with the logistics optimizer strategy but focusing less on brand than on dedicated service to trade customers).

Source: Reprinted with permission, *Supply Chain Management Review,* March/April 2000, p. 29.

message conveyed in the figure is that the integrated value-creation process must be managed from material procurement to end-customer product/service delivery.

The integrated supply chain perspective shifts traditional channel arrangements from loosely linked groups of independent businesses that buy and sell inventory to each other toward a managerially coordinated initiative to increase market impact, overall efficiency, continuous improvement, and competitiveness. In practice, many complexities serve to cloud the simplicity of illustrating supply chains as directional line diagrams. For example, many individual firms simultaneously participate in multiple and competitive supply chains. To the degree that a supply chain becomes the basic unit of competition, firms participating in multiple arrangements may confront loyalty issues related to confidentially and potential conflict of interest.

Another factor that serves to add complexity to understanding supply chain structure is the high degree of mobility and change observable in typical arrangements. It's interesting to observe the fluidity of supply chains as firms enter and exit without any apparent loss of essential connectivity. For example, a firm and/or service supplier may be actively engaged in a supply chain structure during selected times, such as a peak selling season, and not during the balance of a year. To illustrate the complexity of such virtual supply chain arrangements, some observers choose to explain the resulting structure as being analogous to a ***value net.***[5] A value net description of supply chain complexity is illustrated in Industry Insight 1-1: Miller SQA. Table 1-1 identifies a wide variety of different supply chain strategies.

The overarching enabler of supply chain management is information technology. In addition to information technology, the rapid emergence of supply chain arrangements is being driven by four related forces: (1) integrative management; (2) responsiveness; (3) financial sophistication; and (4) globalization. These forces will continue, for the foreseeable future, to drive supply chain structure and strategy initiatives across most industries.

---

[5] The term was introduced by David Bovet and Joseph Martha, *Value Nets* (New York, NY: John Wiley & Sons, 2000). Ernst & Young describe such connected and complex supply chain networks as *value webs.* See Ernst & Young, "Supply Chain Management in the Connected Economy," *Advantage 99 Forum,* 1999.

INDUSTRY INSIGHT 1-1 MILLER SQA AS VALUE NET

Office furniture maker Herman Miller has created a new unit, Miller SQA, that provides an excellent example of value net design. Miller SQA, like its parent, makes office furniture, but with a twist. Its product and the entire furniture buying experience are designed to be "simple, quick, and affordable" (hence SQA).

- SQA's entire manufacturing and delivery system is customer aligned with the demands of specific purchasers: small businesses and others who value speed and simplicity more than unlimited choice. SQA also customizes the product for each buyer through a configure-to-order digital interface.
- Collaborative arrangements with suppliers allow Miller SQA to hold minimal inventory (1 to 2 days' worth in mid-1999), and supplier hubs located near SQA's manufacturing facility deliver components on a just-in-time basis. Activities occur in parallel rather than in sequence. As orders arrive, relevant information is transmitted to suppliers four times a day so that parts replenishment, order assembly, and logistics arrangements can begin simultaneously.
- Supply and manufacturing processes are geared to minimize handling and to maximize speed. Order-to-delivery time can take as little as 2 days, compared with the industry norm of 2 months.
- Digital information flows—between customers, SQA, and suppliers—orchestrate seamless production and allow the company to make firm delivery commitments at the time of order.
- SQA has kept its product line simple, ensuring that it is agile in matching customer demand.

The clarity of Miller SQA's vision, the value net design just described, and its exemplary execution have been hugely successful. Orders are being shipped 99.6 percent on time and complete. Profitability is excellent, and sales are growing at 25 percent a year.

SQA is not alone. Our interviews with more than 30 companies confirm that the value net concept is spreading. Some of the best examples we see are new, often Internet-based, companies that enjoy the luxury of creating their business designs on a clean slate. Others, like SQA, introduce the new concepts into a single division of a large corporation. But even entire enterprises with established supply chains can adopt a value net design to good effect.

Source: David Bovet and Joseph Martha, *Value Nets* (New York: John Wiley & Sons, Inc., 2000), pp. 8–9.

An in-depth discussion of the impact of information technology on logistical performance is reserved for Part II of this book. A brief discussion of each supply chain driver provides a foundation to understand the challenges supply chain management places on exacting logistical performance.

Integrated Management

Across all aspects of business operations, attention is focused on achieving integrated management. The challenge to achieving integrated management results from the long-standing tradition of performing and measuring work on a functional basis. Since the industrial revolution, achieving best practice has focused managerial attention on functional specialization.[6] The prevailing belief was the better the performance of a

---

[6]Frederick W. Taylor, *Scientific Management* (New York, NY: W.W. Norton, 1967).

specific function, the greater the efficiency of the overall process. For well over a century, this fundamental commitment to functional efficiency drove best practice in organization structure, performance measurement, and accountability.

In terms of management, firms have traditionally been structured into departments to facilitate work focus, routinization, standardization, and control. Accounting practices were developed to measure departmental performance. Most performance measurement focused on individual functions. Two examples of common functional measurement are the cost per unit to manufacture and the cost per hundredweight to transport. Cross-functional measurements and allocations were typically limited to costs common to all functional areas of work, such as overhead, labor, utilities, insurance, interest, and so on.

The fundamental challenge of integrated management is to redirect traditional emphasis on functionality to focus on process achievement. Over the past few decades, it has become increasingly apparent that functions, individually performed best in class, do not necessarily combine or aggregate to achieve lowest total cost or highly effective processes. Integrated process management seeks to identify and achieve lowest total cost by capturing trade-offs that exist between functions. To illustrate using a logistical example, a firm might be able to reduce total cost as a result of spending more for faster, dependable transportation because the cost of inventory associated with the process may be reduced by an amount greater than that being spent for premium transportation. The focus of integrated management is *lowest total process cost,* not achievement of the lowest cost for each function included in the process.

The concept of trade-off and the goal of lowest total cost have logical appeal. While deceptively simple, managers continue to find the identification, measurement, and implementation of a process to minimize total cost difficult in day-to-day operations. The unavailability of process performance data and cost measures capable of quantifying cross-functional trade-offs served to stimulate development of such integrative tools as Process Engineering and Activity-Based Costing (ABC).[7]

Three important facets of supply chain logic resulted from increased attention to integrated management: (1) collaboration, (2) enterprise extension, and (3) integrated service providers.

Collaboration

As discussed earlier, the history of business has been dominated by a desire to cooperate but always couched within a competitive framework. Whereas competition remains the dominant model guiding free market economies, the increasing importance of collaboration has positioned the supply chain as a primary unit of competition. In today's global economy, supply chain arrangements compete with each other for customer loyalty. Supply chains dominated by Sears, K-Mart, Target, and Wal★Mart are direct competitors in many markets. Similar supply chain alignments can be observed in industries ranging from entertainment to automobiles to chemicals. The global strategy of Limited Logistics Services (see Industry Insight 1-2) outlines the complexity of modern supply chain management.

---

[7]These integrative tools are discussed in Chapters 15 and 18, respectively.

INDUSTRY INSIGHT 1-2 BUILDING A SEAMLESS WORLD-CLASS SUPPLY CHAIN

Limited Logistics Services, a subsidiary of The Limited, has the complex and challenging assignment of providing supply chain support to The Limited's 11 retail businesses and their catalog operations. Its targeted mission is to effectively manage global supply chain complexity. This $9.2 billion specialty retailer operates more than 5,600 stores across North America. More than 4,500 associates companywide are involved in a process of sourcing goods from more than 60 countries and delivering them to the stores.

"We're constantly working to speed the flow of our fashion and specialty products from vendors in 60 different countries into our stores and to our catalog and e-commerce customers," explains Nicholas J. LaHowchic, president and CEO of Limited Logistics Services. "We're always asking ourselves, How do we add value to our brand initiatives? How do we use the supply chain as a competitive weapon? How can we take cycle time out of the process? How can we become more agile?"

Forging close relationships with other parts of the business is extremely important to LaHowchic because execution of the supply chain strategy is dependent upon integration of The Limited's major processes. These include store/catalog selling, logistics allocation, production, sales/volume planning, design and marketing, R&D, finance, information technology, and compliance management.

"Supply chain integration really begins with the goal of satisfying consumer demand," LaHowchic says. "This fundamental belief impacts everything we do in the supply chain. We seek to raise the level of quality throughout the chain to more effectively respond to consumer demand. And to do this, we need to optimize information and product flows through interdependent linked business processes—from the sourcing of raw materials all the way to the sale of the finished products."

Technology is an essential enabler of this supply chain integration process. Limited Logistics Services has implemented a transportation management system to handle the worldwide flow of goods and a warehouse management system for inventory management and replenishment operations. An advanced planning system also is integrated with The Limited's merchandising systems.

In LaHowchic's opinion, information systems will play an even more prominent role in enabling the organization's total supply chain capabilities in the years ahead. "We are quickly moving toward a full e-commerce interface with our core suppliers and logistics service providers," says the executive. "At the same time, more and more of The Limited's customers will be doing their shopping online. We want to reengineer our business systems to more efficiently serve all of our customers—regardless of how they shop."

One of LaHowchic's core beliefs is that supply chain management can add value in a number of important ways. These include:

- Profitable Growth—Supporting near-perfect flow execution through the supply chain; proactively participating in product go-to-market strategy and execution.
- Quality Maximization—Raising quality of product, processes, and services; accelerating cycle time throughout the pipeline to market.
- Reductions in Working Capital—Increasing inventory turns; minimizing days of supply needed in inventory.
- Fixed Capital Efficiency—Determining right number, size, and location of shipping points; productively and effectively utilizing fixed asset investment.
- Global Cost Optimization—Leveraging customs duty alternatives; leveraging quota alternatives.

By taking a value-added approach to supply chain management, Limited Logistics Services believes that it is raising overall quality—both in the product and in the processes that bring product to market. Raising quality also helps leverage the resources across The Limited's supply chain organization, which enables Limited Logistics Services to more intensely focus on building an organizational competency that manages seamlessly and effectively across the enterprise.

Source: Francis J. Quinn, "Building a Seamless World-Class Supply Chain," *Supply Chain Yearbook 2000,* pp. 43–44.

The general impetus to institutionalized collaborative working arrangements was the 1984 enactment of The National Cooperative Research and Development Act and was expanded in scope by the Production Amendments of 1993.[8] This national legislation and its subsequent modification signaled fundamental change in traditional Justice Department antitrust philosophy. The basic legislation, supplemented by administrative rulings, encouraged firms to develop collaborative initiatives in an effort to increase the global competitiveness of U.S.-based firms. Widespread realization that cooperation is both permissible and encouraged served to stimulate formation of supply chain arrangements.

While all forms of price collusion remain illegal, the collaborative legislation served to facilitate cross-organizational sharing of operating information, technology, and risk as ways to increase competitiveness. The response was a wide variety of new and innovative operating arrangements. One such development was the growing vision of the extended enterprise.

Enterprise Extension

The central thrust of **enterprise extension** expanded managerial influence and control beyond the ownership boundaries of a single enterprise to facilitate joint planning and operations with customers and suppliers. The fundamental belief is that collaborative behavior between firms that integrate processes will maximize customer impact, reduce overall risk, and greatly improve efficiency. Enterprise extension builds on two basic paradigms: information sharing and process specialization.

The **information sharing paradigm** is the widespread belief that achieving a high degree of cooperative behavior requires that supply chain participants voluntarily share operating information and jointly plan strategies. The scope of cross-enterprise collaboration should span beyond sales history to include plans detailing promotion, new product introduction, and day-to-day operations. See Industry Insight 1-3 for an example of lead supplier collaboration in the automotive industry.

It's important to emphasize that information sharing to support collaboration must not be limited to historical or even accurate sales data. Of greater importance is a willingness to share strategic information about future activities to facilitate joint planning. The guiding principle is that information sharing is essential among supply chain participants to collectively do the things customers demand faster and more efficiently.

The **process specialization paradigm** is commitment to focusing collaborative arrangements on planning joint operations toward a goal of eliminating nonproductive or non-value-adding work by firms in a supply chain. The basic idea is to design the overall supply chain processes in a manner that identifies a specific firm's responsibility and

---

[8]On October 11, 1984, President Reagan signed into law the National Cooperative Research Act of 1984 (Public Law 98-462) in an effort "to promote research and development, encourage innovation, stimulate trade, and make necessary and appropriate modifications in the operation of the antitrust laws." This law enables research and development activities to be jointly performed up to the point where prototypes are developed. The law further determined that antitrust litigation would be based on the rule of reason, taking into account all factors affecting competition. An extension to this act was signed into law by President Clinton on June 10, 1993. The extension, National Cooperative Production Amendments of 1993 (Public Law 103-42), allows joint ventures to go beyond just research to include the production and testing of a product, process, or service. This created a new act called the National Cooperative Research and Production Act of 1993 to replace the 1984 act. Furthermore, this new act established a procedure for businesses to notify the Department of Justice and the Federal Trade Commission of their cooperative arrangement in order to qualify for "single-damages limitation on civil antitrust liability."

INDUSTRY INSIGHT 1-3 MODULAR ASSEMBLY IN BRAZIL

DaimlerChrysler has built a small factory in Brazil, one of the potentially fastest-growing auto markets in the world. It is determined to show how a niche player in the auto industry can make money in a developing market.

The DaimlerChrysler factory is based on the concept of "modularity," in which suppliers assemble dozens of parts into dashboards or suspension units and the automaker then assembles the various modules. Industry experts calculate that this basic rethinking of auto manufacture could slash manufacturing costs by thousands of dollars a vehicle. DaimlerChrysler executives say their plant's flexible design allows it to respond quickly to shifts in the market, ramping up production or adding new models if needed.

At DaimlerChrysler's $315 million Brazilian plant, which makes Dakota pickup trucks, the most radical manufacturing innovation is known as the rolling chassis. At a plant about 2 miles down the road from DaimlerChrysler's, Dana Corp. of Toledo, Ohio, assembles the truck's frame, axles, brakes, and wheels—a total of 320 parts, complete with fully inflated tires—all within 108 minutes of getting an order by computer. Delivered in sequence with Daimler-Chrysler's line, the chassis roll into DaimlerChrysler's plant to mate with engines, transmissions, and bodies as workers push them across the plant floor on carts from the interior line. It is all part of a computer-choreographed dance that runs simultaneously at several factories in this part of Brazil as soon as DaimlerChrysler's workers begin taking the gray, metal body panels out of the cardboard boxes in which they are shipped from the U.S.

Dana's chassis accounts for about one-third of the value of the Dakota, a far larger share than any individual supplier-built unit would take up in traditional auto manufacturing. Daimler-Chrysler Chairman Robert Eaton says the company isn't considering using the rolling chassis in the U.S. yet, but he says that other elements of the modular assembly could be transferred.

In Brazil, the rolling chassis allowed DaimlerChrysler to hire fewer people and make its factory smaller, reducing upfront investment and shortening start-up time. The rolling chassis also provides DaimlerChrysler big discounts on import duties on parts, equipment, and the thousands of other vehicles it brings into Brazil from the U.S. Because Dana assembles the rolling chassis in Brazil, DaimlerChrysler can count the entire value of the unit as local, allowing it to import other parts, such as body panels, engines, and transmissions, from the U.S. If DaimlerChrysler made the chassis at its own plant, it could credit only the parts it actually made in Brazil as local.

DaimlerChrysler will start slowly, producing about 5,000 trucks this year and 12,000 next year. For an additional investment of less than $100 million, it could add another assembly line to bring capacity to 40,000 vehicles annually within a couple of years, but suppliers say current plans call for output of about 23,000 vehicles in 2002.

Source: Gregory L. White, "Chrysler Makes Manufacturing Inroads at Plant in Brazil," *The Wall Street Journal,* August 13, 1998, p. 1.

---

accountability to perform each element of essential work in a manner that maximizes overall results.

Firms participating in a supply chain have specific roles and share strategic goals. Sharing information and joint planning can reduce risk related to inventory positioning and increase movement velocity. Collaboration can eliminate duplicative or redundant work, such as repetitive quality inspection, by designating and empowering a specified member of the supply chain to be fully responsible and accountable. Such extended enterprise integration introduced new challenges regarding measurement, benefit and risk sharing, trust, leadership, and conflict resolution. It is clear that the challenges of collaboration and enterprise extension constitute new managerial horizons. A third contributing force to supply chain development is the rapidly changing managerial attitude toward integrated service providers.

Integrated Service Providers

As noted earlier, the origins of contemporary business were grounded in functional specialization. It is not surprising that firms developed the practice of outsourcing work to businesses that are specialists in the performance of specific functions. The two traditional logistics service providers are transportation and warehousing specialists.

The for-hire transportation industry consists of thousands of carriers who specialize in product movement between geographic locations. Over the years, a comprehensive carrier network has emerged providing shippers a broad assortment of services, utilizing all available forms or modes of transportation and related technology. The value proposition of for-hire transportation is based on specialization, efficiency, and scale economies. Value is generated by a carrier's capability to provide shared transportation services for multiple shippers. The transport alternatives for shippers are either to invest capital in transportation equipment and operations or to engage the services of specialized carriers. Naturally, a large number of firms develop transportation solutions that combine benefits of these alternatives.

In addition to transportation, a large number of service companies have traditionally provided warehouse services. Traditionally called *public warehouses,* these firms provide product storage supplemented with other specialized services. Two significant benefits are gained when shippers use public warehouses. First is elimination of capital investment in warehouse buildings. The second is the ability to consolidate small shipments for combined delivery with products of other firms who use the same public warehouse. Such multishipper consolidation achieves transportation efficiency not typically available when a firm ships from its own warehouse. Many firms combine private and public warehouses into a go-to-market distribution network.

In 1980 the landscape of for-hire services in the United States changed dramatically. Within a few short months, the economic and political infrastructure of transportation in the United States began to be deregulated as a result of the passage of the Motor Carrier Regulatory Reform and Modernization Act (MCA-80) and the Staggers Rail Act.[9] These regulatory changes served to initiate a trend toward a free transportation market that ultimately resulted in less government regulation for all forms of transportation. Over time, this trend extended worldwide to deregulate transportation in most free market industrialized nations.

In contrast to transportation, firms engaged in public warehousing had not been operationally regulated by federal or state governments. Most warehouse firms did not offer transportation services so as to avoid such regulation. However, with the deregulation of transportation, that practice soon changed. Overnight warehousing firms began to offer transportation services. Likewise, many transport carriers began to offer customers integrated warehouse services.

What occurred in the logistics service industry was a radical shift from single function to multifunctional outsourcing. Integrated service providers (ISPs) began to market a range of logistics services that included all work necessary to service customers, from order entry to product delivery. In many situations the foundation of transportation and warehouse services was augmented by the performance of a wide range of special services.[10] These customized services are typically described as *value-added services.* For

---

[9]Public Laws 96-296 and 96-488, respectively. These laws, as well as others briefly noted here, are discussed in greater detail in Chapter 12.

[10]For a comprehensive review of services offered by leading third-party logistics providers, see "Recognizing 3PL Excellence," *Inbound Logistics,* July 2000, pp. 47–49.

example, United Parcel Service (UPS) stocks Nike shoes and warm-ups at its Louisville warehouse and processes orders hourly. All related communication and financial administration are handled by a UPS call center in San Antonio. Thus, Nike has effectively outsourced basic logistics and related value-added service to UPS.[11]

The common name used throughout industry to describe ISPs is **third-party logistics providers.** In a general sense, third-party companies are commonly classified as being either *asset-* or *nonasset-based,* the distinction being that asset-based firms own and operate transportation equipment and warehousing buildings. In contrast, nonasset service firms specialize in providing comprehensive information services that facilitate supply chain arrangements. Such nonasset service providers arrange and integrate services using services of third-party asset operators on behalf of their customers.

The 2000 third-party logistics service market was estimated to be $56.4 billion with a projected growth of 24 percent to reach $70 billion by the year 2001.[12] The growth of integrated service providers makes both the formation and dismantling of supply chain arrangements easier. Thus, supply chain participants have the opportunity to engage the capabilities of what amounts to a virtual logistics network. Such outsourcing helps facilitate process-focused integrative management.

As discussed, the advent of collaboration, extended enterprise visioning, and the increased availability of integrated service providers combined to drive radically new supply chain solutions. The notion of collaborative benefits served to solidify the importance of relationships between firms cooperating in a supply chain. The extended enterprise logic stimulated visions of increased efficiency and effectiveness as a result of sharing information, planning, and operational specialization between supply chain participants. The deregulation of transportation served as a catalyst to develop integrated service providers. This development served to redefine and expand the scope of specialized services available to facilitate supply chain operations. In combination, these three drivers helped create integrated supply chain management. They served to identify and solidify the strategic benefits of integrated management. They combined to reinforce the value of core competency specialization and cast the challenges and opportunity of creating virtual supply chain arrangements. In Chapter 6, integrative management is examined in terms of individual firm, domestic, and global challenges.

Responsiveness

One could argue that the challenges and benefits of integrative management offered sufficient reason for the supply chain revolution. However, other basic drivers continue to make supply chain arrangements even more appealing. A fundamental paradigm shift in strategic thinking occurred as a direct result of information technology development. Information connectivity created the potential for developing response-based business models. To elaborate the far-reaching implications of this major development, it is useful to contrast traditional *anticipatory* business practice to the emerging time-based *responsiveness* business model.

Anticipatory-Based Business Model

Since the industrial revolution the dominant business model has encouraged anticipation of customer requirements. Because information concerning purchase behavior

---

[11]Kelly Barron, "Logistics In Brown," *Forbes,* January 10, 2000, p. 78.
[12]Robert V. Delaney, Twelfth Annual "State of Logistics Report," presented to the National Press Club, Washington, DC, June 4, 2001.

FIGURE 1-2

Anticipatory business model

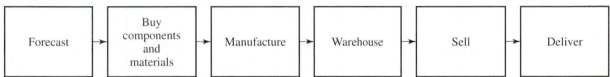

was not readily available and firms loosely linked together in a channel of distribution did not feel compelled to share their plans, business operations were driven by forecasts. The typical manufacturer produced products based upon a market forecast. Likewise, wholesalers, distributors, and retailers purchased inventory based on their unique forecasts and promotional plans. Since the forecast results were more often than not wrong, considerable discontinuities existed between what firms planned to do and what they, in fact, ended up doing. Such discontinuity typically resulted in unexpected inventory. Because of high cost and risk associated with conducting business on an anticipatory basis, the prevailing relationship between trading partners was adversarial; each firm needed to protect its own interest.

Figure 1-2 illustrates the typical stages in the anticipatory business model: forecast, purchase materials, manufacture, warehouse, sell, and then deliver. In nonmanufacturing firms, operations involved the anticipatory purchase of inventory assortments to accommodate expected sales. The key point is that almost all essential work was performed in anticipation of future requirements. The likelihood of misgauging end-customer requirements rendered the anticipatory business model highly risky. In addition, each firm in the distribution channel duplicated the anticipatory process.

Response-Based Business Model

The fundamental difference in anticipatory and response-based supply chain arrangements is timing. The response-based business model seeks to reduce or eliminate forecast reliance by joint planning and rapid exchange of information between supply chain participants.

The availability of low cost information has created *time-based competition.* Managers are increasingly sharing information to improve both the speed and accuracy of supply chain logistics. To illustrate, managers may share information to improve forecasting accuracy or even eliminate forecasts in an effort to reduce anticipatory inventory deployment. This transformation from anticipatory to response-based business is possible because today's managers can rapidly obtain and share accurate sales information and exercise improved operational control. When all members of the supply chain synchronize their operations, opportunities exist to reduce overall inventory and eliminate costly duplicate practices. More importantly, customers can be provided with products they want, fast.

Figure 1-3 illustrates a response-based business model that manufactures or assembles products to customer order. The fundamental difference is the sequence of events that drive business practice. Also notable, in comparison to Figure 1-2, are the fewer steps required to complete a response-based process. Fewer steps typically equate to less cost and less elapsed time from order commitment to delivery. The response-based sequence is initiated by a sale followed by a sequence of material purchase, custom manufacturing, and direct customer delivery. In many ways, this response-based business model is similar to the traditional build-to-order manufacturing. The primary

Figure 1-3

Response-based business model

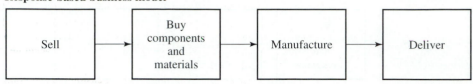

differences between modern response-based operations and traditional build-to-order are the time to execute and the degree of mass customization.

In terms of time to execute the order to delivery, the contemporary response-based system is substantially faster than the traditional build-to-order manufacturing. For example, custom-designed computers can be built and delivered to end customers in 3 days or fewer. It is becoming common practice to replenish retail store inventories of consumer products on a daily basis. Custom-built automobiles are being promised for delivery within 10 working days, with the goal to even further reduce the order-to-delivery cycle. Such compressed order-to-delivery cycles were not even imaginable a few years ago.

Perhaps an even more appealing attribute of response-based supply chains is their potential to uniquely customize products on smaller orders than typical of traditional build-to-order lot size manufacturing. The advent of direct connectivity with end customers via Web-based interactive communications is accelerating adoption of such customization. In most traditional anticipatory-based distribution systems, the customer was a passive participant. About the only power the customer had in the process was the decision to buy or not buy. Direct involvement of customers in a response-based process has three direct benefits. First, involvement provides comprehensive search capabilities that serve to expand the range of sources and choices a customer can consider when selecting a product or service. Second, customers are better informed about prices and, in some situations, are able to drive price advantage by virtue of bids and/or auctions. Finally, information-intense response-based systems provide innovation such as a *customer choiceboard* wherein customers design or customize their own product configuration.[13] Industry Insight 1-4 explores the benefits of choiceboards, both for suppliers and for consumers.

Postponement

At the heart of time-based competition is the capability to postpone manufacturing and the timing of logistical fulfillment. The concept of postponement has long been discussed in business literature.[14] However, practical examples involving postponement are directly related to advancements in information technology. Postponement strate-

---

[13]Adrian J. Slywotzky, "The Age of the Choiceboard," *Harvard Business Review,* January–February 2000, pp. 40–41; and Jarrus D. Pagh and Martha C. Cooper, "Supply Chain Postponement and Speculation Strategies: How to Choose the Right Strategy," *Journal of Business Logistics,* 19, no. 2 (1998), pp. 13–28.

[14]Wroe Alderson, *Marketing Behavior and Executive Action* (Homewood, IL: Richard D. Irwin, Inc., 1957), p. 426. For a modern discussion of postponement, see B. Joseph Pine, II, Bart Victor, and Andrew C. Boynton, "Making Mass Customization Work," *Harvard Business Review,* September–October 1993, pp. 108–19.

INDUSTRY INSIGHT 1-4 THE AGE OF THE CHOICEBOARD

Traditionally, customers have been presented with limited choices within a product category based upon the supplier's predictions of future demand. There may be some minor tailoring of features at the point of purchase, but generally the set of choices is fixed long before customers even begin to shop. If demand predictions prove to be inaccurate, suppliers must discount merchandise to dispose of it.

So why does a system that's bad for both customers and companies continue? Historically, there hasn't been an alternative. The slow, imprecise movement of information up the supply pipeline and of goods down it has meant that the manufacturing process must begin long before accurate information about demand exists. Our entire industrial sector operates on guesswork.

Thanks to the Internet, an alternative to the traditional unhappy model of supplier/customer interaction is finally becoming possible. In all sorts of markets, customers will soon be able to describe exactly what they want, and suppliers will be able to deliver the desired product or service without compromise or delay. This will be possible through the use of a choiceboard. Choiceboards are interactive, online systems that allow individual customers to design their own products by choosing from a menu of attributes, components, prices, and delivery operations. The customers' selections send signals to the supplier's manufacturing system that set in motion the wheels of procurement, assembly, and delivery.

Choiceboards are already in use in many industries. Customers today can design their own computers with Dell's online configurator, create their own dolls with Mattel's My Design Barbie, assemble their own investment portfolios with Schwab's mutual fund evaluator, and even design their own golf clubs with Chipshot.com's PerfectFit system. But the choiceboard model is still in its infancy. Despite its enormous benefits, it's involved in less than 1 percent of the $30 trillion world economy. Even where it's well established, such as in the PC business, it accounts for only a small fraction of overall industry sales. By the end of this decade, some experts anticipate that choiceboards will be involved in 30 percent or more of total U.S. commercial activity, as the economy moves from a supply-driven to a demand-driven system.

Because choiceboards collect precise information about the preferences and behavior of individual buyers, they enable companies to secure customer loyalty as never before. With each transaction, a company becomes more knowledgeable about the customer and hence better able to anticipate and fulfill that customer's needs. That knowledge can be used to tailor, in real time, the design of the choiceboard itself, customizing the options presented to the buyer and promoting up-selling and cross-selling. Moreover, once aggregated, the customer information can be used to guide the evolution of entire product lines and to spot new growth opportunities at their earliest stages. In such an environment, it becomes very difficult for a competitor, lacking the in-depth customer information, to displace the existing provider.

Eventually, choiceboards will be primarily information-collection devices and customer relationship-builders. Companies will use their choiceboards to actively solicit from customers information about their satisfaction levels, their buying intentions, and their requirements and preferences and they will use the information to predict customers' needs and behavior across virtually all product and service categories.

Source: Adrian J. Slywotzky, "The Age of the Choiceboard," *Harvard Business Review,* January–February 2000, pp. 40–41.

---

gies and practices serve to reduce the anticipatory risk of supply chain performance. As noted earlier, anticipatory arrangements require most inventory to be produced and deployed based on forecasts or planned requirements. Working arrangements, which allow postponement of final manufacturing or distribution of a product until receipt of a customer order, reduce the incidence of wrong manufacturing or incorrect inventory deployment. Two types of postponement are common in response-based supply chain operations: (1) manufacturing or *form* postponement; and (2) geographic or *logistics* postponement.

Manufacturing Postponement

The global competitive climate of the 21st century is facilitating the development of new manufacturing techniques designed to increase flexibility and responsiveness while maintaining unit cost and quality. Traditional practice has focused on achieving economy of scale by planning long manufacturing runs. In contrast, flexible and lean manufacturing logic is driven by a desire to increase responsiveness to customer requirements.

Response-based manufacturing stresses flexibility. The vision of **manufacturing or form postponement** is one of products being manufactured *one order at a time* with no preparatory work or component procurement until exact customer specifications are fully known and customer commitment is received. This dream of building to order is not new. What is new is the expectation that flexible manufacturing can achieve such responsiveness without sacrificing efficiency. To the degree technology can support market-paced flexible manufacturing strategies, firms are freed from forecast-driven anticipatory operations.

In actual practice, manufacturing lot size economics cannot be ignored. The challenge is to quantify cost trade-offs between procurement, manufacturing, and logistics. At this point, it is sufficient to understand that the trade-off is between the cost and risk associated with anticipatory manufacturing and the loss of economy of scale resulting from introducing flexible procedures.[15] Manufacturing lot size reduction requires a trade-off between line set-up, switch over, and associated procurement expense balanced against cost and risk associated with stockpiling finished inventory. In the traditional functional style of management, manufacturing schedules were established to realize the lowest unit-cost of production. From an integrative management perspective, the goal is to achieve desired customer satisfaction at the lowest total cost. This may require manufacturing postponement at some per unit cost sacrifice to achieve overall supply chain efficiency.

The operative goal of manufacturing postponement is to maintain products in a neutral or noncommitted status as long as possible. The ideal application of form postponement is to manufacture a standard or base product in sufficient quantities to realize economy of scale while deferring finalization of features, such as color or accessories, until customer commitment is received. Given a postponement-driven manufacturing scenario, economy of scope is introduced into the logistics equation by producing a standard or base product to accommodate a wide range of different customers. One of the first commercially viable examples of manufacturing postponement was mixing paint color at retail stores to accommodate individual customer request. Perfecting the in-store mixing process dramatically reduced the number of stockkeeping units required at retail paint stores. Rather than trying to maintain inventories of premixed color paint, retail stores stock a base paint and customize the color to accommodate specific orders.

In other industries, manufacturing practice is to process and store product in bulk, postponing final packaging configuration until customer orders are received. In some situations products are processed and packed in brite cans with brand identification labeling being postponed until specific customer orders are received. Other examples of manufacturing postponement include the increased practice of installing accessories at

---

[15]Greater detail related to manufacturing trade-offs is developed in Chapter 5.

automobile, appliance, and motorcycle dealerships, thereby customizing products to customer request at the time of purchase.

These manufacturing postponement examples have one thing in common: They reduce the number of stockkeeping units in logistical inventory while supporting a broad-line marketing effort and retaining mass manufacturing economies of scale. Until the product is customized, it has the potential to serve many different customers.

The impact of manufacturing postponement is twofold. First, the variety of differentiated products, moved in anticipation of sale, can be reduced, and therefore the risk of logistics malfunction is lower. The second, and perhaps the more important impact, is the increased use of logistical facilities and channel relationships to perform light manufacturing and final assembly. To the extent that a degree of specialized talent or highly restrictive economy of scale does not exist in manufacturing, product customization may be best delegated and performed near the customer destination market. The traditional mission of logistical warehouses in some industries has changed significantly to accommodate manufacturing postponement.

Geographic Postponement

In many ways **geographic** or **logistics postponement** is the exact opposite of manufacturing postponement. In fact, *acceleration* is a term often used to describe the dynamics of rapid fulfillment of customer requirements. The basic notion of geographic postponement is to build and stock a full-line inventory at one or a few strategic locations. Forward deployment of inventory is postponed until customer orders are received. Once the logistical process is initiated, every effort is made to accelerate the economic movement of products direct to customers. Under the concept of geographic postponement, the anticipatory risk of inventory deployment is completely eliminated while manufacturing economy of scale is retained.

An example of geographic postponement is Sears Store Direct Delivery System. Utilizing rapid-order communications, the logistics of an appliance is not initiated until a customer order is received. An appliance purchased on Monday could be installed in a consumer's home as early as Wednesday. The distinct possibility exists that the appliance sold on Monday was not manufactured until that night or early Tuesday.

Many applications of geographic postponement involve service supply parts. Critical and high-cost parts are maintained in a central inventory to assure availability for all potential users. When demand occurs, orders are electronically transmitted to the central service center and expedited shipments are made direct to the service center, using fast, reliable transportation. The end result is highly reliable customer service with reduced overall inventory investment.

The potential for geographic postponement has been facilitated by increased capability to process, transmit, and deliver precise order requirements with a high degree of accuracy and speed. Geographic postponement substitutes accelerated delivery of precise order requirements for the anticipatory deployment of inventory to local market warehouses. Unlike manufacturing postponement, systems utilizing geographic postponement retain manufacturing economies of scale while meeting customer service requirements by accelerating direct shipments.

In combination, manufacturing and geographic postponement offer alternative ways to refrain from anticipatory market distribution until customer commitments are received. The factors favoring one or the other form of postponement hinge on volume, value, competitive initiatives, economies of scale, and desired customer delivery speed and consistency. In a growing number of supply chains, both types of postponement are combined to create a highly responsive strategy.

Can you draw out the distinctions more clearly

Barriers and the Future

In reality, today's best supply chain practices do not reflect either extreme anticipatory or response-based design. Most established firms remain, to a significant degree, committed to anticipatory practices. However, response-based strategies are rapidly emerging. Perhaps the greatest barrier to adopting response-based arrangements is the need for publicly held corporations to maintain expected quarterly profits. This accountability creates expectations concerning continued sales and financial results. Such expectations often drive promotional strategies to "load the channel" with inventory to create timely sales. Conversely, it is never timely to make a major reduction in channel inventory. Efforts to lean or deload inventory to implement a more responsive operating posture require the ability to absorb a one-time sale reduction to supply chain partners. Start-up ventures such as e-commerce firms are ideally positioned to implement response-based fulfillment systems because they do not face the deload challenge.

strategy, breaking the rules, go 6, focused on long term not short term

A second barrier to implementing response-based operations is the need to establish collaborative relationships. Most business managers simply do not have training or experience in development of collaborative arrangements designed to share benefits and risks. While managers generally express a high degree of belief in the long-term potential for response-based alliances, they report considerable frustration concerning how to implement such supply chain arrangements.[16]

For the foreseeable future, most firms will continue to implement strategies that combine anticipatory and response-based supply chain arrangements. The trend toward increased involvement in response-based arrangements with specific customers and suppliers will continue to expand. A major force driving response-based distribution is Web-based commerce. The challenge is for firms to be simultaneously involved in a variety of delivery arrangements that combine the attributes of traditional and Web-based distribution. See Industry Insight 1–5 for an example of such a click and mortar strategy.

Financial Sophistication

Few managers question the benefits of applying the time-based strategies discussed above to supply chain operations. However, a valid question is, How fast is fast enough? Speed simply for the sake of being fast has little, if any, enduring value.[17] The answer concerning how much speed is desirable is found in the financial benefits that accrue. The process of creating value dictates that faster, more flexible, and more precise ways of servicing customers are justified as long as they can be provided at competitive prices. A third force driving competitive supply chain strategy is the ability to manage in a more timely manner to achieve financially attractive working arrangements.

The financial benefits of timely response are straightforward. Fast direct delivery translates to less inventory and reduced need for distribution facilities. Faster to customers means less working capital is required to support supply chain operations.

---

[16]Donald J. Bowersox, David J. Closs, and Theodore P. Stank, *21st Century Logistics: Making Supply Chain Integration a Reality* (Oak Brook, IL: Council of Logistics Management, 1999).

[17]George Stalk, Jr., and Alan M. Webber, "Japan's Dark Side of Time," *Harvard Business Review,* July–August 1993, pp. 93–102.

INDUSTRY INSIGHT 1-5 WEBWARD HO!

In the world of online retailing, Recreational Equipment Inc. (REI) stands out. The 60-year-old Seattle-based retailer of outdoor sports products has managed to keep pace with order fulfillment on sales made via the Internet. That's an impressive feat in view of its cyber sales volume. Almost 19 percent of its total sales resulted from the Internet last year, says Clark Koch, order fulfillment manager at REI. That figure represents a whopping 241 percent increase over 1997 Web sales.

REI has an advantage over many Web retailers in that it has years of experience handling individual customers' mail orders. In 1938, a group of Pacific Northwest mountaineers seeking quality climbing equipment founded REI. Although REI operates retail outlets, the company has handled mail order sales throughout most of its history.

To serve retail, mail, and online customers, REI relies on a 469,000 square foot distribution center in Sumner, WA. The warehouse employs somewhere between 35 and 40 workers during the nonpeak season. During the Christmas holiday in 1998, it added about 110 employees for a 3- to 4-week period. The building itself stores around 13,000 active stockkeeping units (SKUs) of recreational equipment.

The company hasn't changed its order picking procedure despite the increase in volume from Web sales. "When we get an order, we don't know if it's a phone, Internet, or mail order," explains Koch. Yet the company has managed to maintain a high level of order fulfillment accuracy and speed. Some 93 percent of all orders placed in 1998 went out the door in 24 hours, Koch says.

When a customer places an order on REI's website, it's processed automatically unless there's a problem. "If there's a discrepancy like a wrong bank card number, we have a staff of Internet people who can resolve the problems," says Koch. "If there's nothing wrong with the order, it goes right through electronically."

The company uses the same batch picking system for filling all individual customers' orders regardless of origin. Its computer systems process the orders and then group them into batches for picking. After the orders are selected, they are checked and then packed.

Interestingly, the company picks and packs individual orders without any automation although it does use bar codes for internal product tracking. "Our operation is very manual," says Koch. "We're not tied to automation. A lot of processes are the same processes that were in place when we started."

When it comes to shipping those orders, REI does business with a variety of carriers. The company uses UPS and the U.S. Postal Service for a majority of its ground domestic orders. It ships air domestic packages via FedEx. International shipments are split between DHL and the post office. Koch says REI does so much volume that FedEx and DHL both have personnel on-site in the retailer's warehouse. If products are shipped via FedEx or UPS, a customer can track an order online over those carriers' websites.

Koch says that Internet sales will be his company's largest source of growth over the next few years. As a result, REI is busy determining how it's going to handle that surge in volume, whether through automation, increased work area capacity, or more work shifts.

REI's experience demonstrates that companies with experience filling individual orders are well positioned to take on cyber sales. "We do have a clear advantage over other e-commerce businesses that don't have the back end established," Koch says.

Source: James Aaron Cook, "Web Commerce: Not Ready for Prime Time," *Logistics Management & Distribution Report,* 38, no. 3 (March 1999), pp. 59–63; http://www.manufacturing.net/magazine/logistic/.

Three aspects of financial sophistication are cash-to-cash conversion, dwell time minimization, and cash spin.

Cash-to-Cash Conversion

Cash-to-cash conversion refers to the time required to convert raw material or inventory purchases into sales revenue. Cash conversion is generally related to inventory turn: the higher the inventory turn, the quicker the cash conversion. A goal of supply chain design is to reduce and control order receipt-to-delivery time in an effort to accelerate inventory turns.

In traditional business arrangements, benefits related to cash-to-cash conversion have typically been enjoyed at the expense of business partners. Given typical purchase discounts and invoicing practices, it is operationally possible for firms to rapidly sell merchandise and still qualify for prompt payment discounts. To illustrate, terms of sale offering a 2 percent discount net 10-day payment (2% net 10) means that a prompt payment discount is earned if the invoice is paid within 10 days from time of delivery. Thus, if the invoice is $1000, a payment made within 10 days will earn a $20 discount. If the firm sells the product for cash before the invoice payment date, it, in effect, enjoys free inventory and may even earn interest by investing cash while awaiting the payment date.

In response-based systems, cash-to-cash conversion benefits can be shared by managing inventory transfer velocity across the supply chain. This ability to manage inventory velocity from origin to final destination has the potential to achieve greater efficiencies than attainable by a single firm. Coordinated operations may require that a designated firm in the supply chain serve as the principal inventory stocking location. Such practice means that risk and benefits related to inventory need to be shared by participating firms. To facilitate such arrangements, supply chain members often replace the discounts with **dead net pricing.**

Dead net pricing means that all discounts and allowances are factored in the selling price. Thus, incentives for timely payment are replaced by specific performance commitments at a specified net price. Invoice payment, based on negotiated net price, is completed upon verification of physical receipt. Such payment is typically in the form of Electronic Funds Transfer (EFT), thereby streamlining both the flow of physical goods and cash among supply chain partners. Managing supply chain logistics as a continuous synchronized process also serves to reduce dwell time.

Dwell Time Minimization

Traditional distribution arrangements typically involve independent business units loosely linked together on a transaction-to-transaction basis. A transaction view of traditional business operations results in a series of *independent* transactions buffered by inventory. In contrast, a supply chain has the potential to function as a synchronized series of *interdependent* business units.

At the heart of supply chain operating leverage is the willingness to transfer inventory on an as-needed basis, taking advantage of as much collaboration and information as possible. Such collaboration and information can be focused on maintaining the continued flow and velocity of inventory moving throughout the supply chain. The potential of such synchronization is a key benefit of supply chain connectivity.

A significant measure of supply chain productivity is **dwell time.** Dwell time is the ratio of time that an asset sits idle to the time required to satisfy its designated supply chain mission. For example, dwell time would be the ratio of the time a unit of inventory is in storage to the time that it is moving or otherwise contributing to achieving a supply chain's objectives.

To reduce dwell time, firms collaborating in a supply chain need to be willing to eliminate duplicate and non-value-adding work. For example, if three different firms perform identical processes as a product flows along a supply chain, dwell times will accumulate. Designating a specific firm to perform and be accountable for the value-added work can serve to reduce overall dwell.

Likewise, timely arrival and continuous inventory flow between supply chain partners reduce dwell. When a product flows from a supplier through a retailer's cross-dock sortation process without coming to rest or being diverted to warehouse storage, dwell time is minimized. A collateral benefit of reducing dwell time and the associated logistics cost is the ability to reduce investment in inventory and related assets.

Cash Spin

A popular term for describing the potential benefits of reducing assets across a supply chain is **cash spin,** sometimes referred to as **free cash spin.**[18] The concept is to reduce overall assets committed to supply chain performance. Thus, a dollar of inventory or the rent of a warehouse, if eliminated by a reengineered supply chain arrangement, represents cash available for redeployment. Such *free* capital can be reinvested in projects that might otherwise have been considered too risky.

Naturally, cash spin opportunity is not unique to the supply chain. The potential to spin cash applies to all areas of a firm. What makes the potential of supply chain cash spin so attractive is the opportunity to collaborate between firms.

The benefits flowing from fast cash-to-cash conversion, reduced dwell time, and cash spin combine to increase the financial attractiveness of effective collaboration. Another major force driving expansion of supply chain management is the growing involvement of most firms in international operations. Expanded global business is a result of two significant opportunities: market expansion and operating efficiency.

Globalization

A conservative estimate is that as much as 90 percent of global demand is not currently fully satisfied by local supply. Current demand coupled with a world population projected to increase by an average over 200,000 persons per day for the next decade equate to substantial opportunity. The range of product/service growth potential varies greatly between industrialized and emerging economies. In industrialized sectors of the global economy, opportunities focus on B2B and upscale consumer products. These more advanced economies offer substantial opportunities for the sale of products coupled with value-added services. While it is true that consumers in developing nations enjoy relatively less purchasing power than those in their industrialized counterparts, demand in such economies is huge in terms of basic products and necessities. Consumers in developing nations are more interested in quality of basic life than in fashion or technology. For example, the growing populations of India and the People's Republic of China offer huge market opportunities for basic products like food, clothing, and

---

[18]Gene Tyndall, et. al., *Supercharging Supply Chains* (New York, NY: John Wiley & Sons, 1998), p. 1.

consumer durables such as refrigerators and washing machines. Firms with aggressive growth goals cannot neglect the commercialization of the global marketplace.

In addition to sales potential, involvement in global business is being driven by significant opportunities to increase operating efficiency. Such operational efficiencies are attainable in three areas. First, the global marketplace offers significant opportunity to strategically source raw material and components. Second, significant labor advantages can be gained by locating manufacturing and distribution facilities in developing nations. Third, favorable tax laws can make the performance of value-adding operations in specific countries highly attractive.

The decision to engage in global operations to achieve market growth and enjoy operational efficiency follows a natural path of business expansion. Typically, firms enter the global marketplace by conducting import and export operations. Such import and export transactions constitute a significant portion of global international business. The second stage of internationalization involves establishment of local presence in foreign nations and trading areas. Such presence can range from franchise and licensing of local businesses to the establishment of manufacturing and distribution facilities. The important distinction between import/export involvement and establishment of local presence is the degree of investment and managerial involvement characteristic of stage two. The third stage of internationalization is the full-fledged conduct of business operations within and across international boundaries. This most advanced phase of international engagement is typically referred to as *globalization.*

The logistics of internationalization involves four significant differences in comparison to national or even regional operations. First, the *distance* of typical order-to-delivery operations is significantly longer in international as contrasted to domestic business. Second, to accommodate the laws and regulations of all governing bodies, the required *documentation* of business transactions is significantly more complex. Third, international logistics operations must be designed to deal with significant *diversity* in work practices and local operating environment. Finally, accommodation of cultural variations in how consumers *demand* product and services is essential for successful logistical operations. It is important to understand that successfully *going supply chain global* requires mastering the logistical challenge.

While logistics principles and the ideals of supply chain integration are essentially the same globally as they are domestically, the above characteristics make operating environments more complex and costly. The cost of logistics on a global basis exceeds $5 trillion a year.[19] Such expenditure is justified in terms of potential market expansion and operating efficiencies; however, risk exposure related to capitalizing on international supply chain management and its logistical components require integrated operating strategies and tactics.

Issues in Supply Chain Management

Facilitated by explosive information technology, the forces of integrative management, responsiveness, financial sophistication, and globalization have combined to clearly put the challenges of supply chain on the radar screens of most firms. Prior to moving to a discussion of lean logistics in Chapter 2, a review of issues related to supply chain implementation is appropriate.

---

[19] For details, see Chapter 6.

While the business press and seminar circuit abound with unbridled enthusiasm concerning the potential of supply chain management, little attention is directed to challenging issues and risks related to such collaboration. Issues and risks that have been identified by those critical of supply chain arrangements are based on implementation and social challenges.

Implementation Challenges

Whenever a business strategy is based on substantial modification of existing practice, the road to implementation is difficult. As noted earlier, the potential of supply chain management is predicated on the ability to modify traditional functional practice to focus on integrated process performance. Such changed behavior requires new practices related to internal integration as well as direction of operations across the supply chain. To make integrated supply chain practice a reality, at least four operational challenges must be resolved.

Leadership

For a supply chain to achieve perceived benefits for participating firms, it must function as a managed process. Such integrative management requires leadership. Thus, questions regarding supply chain leadership will surface very early in the development of a collaborative arrangement. At the root of most leadership issues are power and risk.

Power determines which firm involved in a potential supply chain collaboration will perform the leadership role. Equally important is the willingness of other members of a potential supply chain arrangement to accept a specific firm as the collaborative leader. A supply chain seeking to link manufacturers offering nationally branded consumer merchandise into a supply chain arrangement with a large mass merchandiser that has significant consumer store loyalty can represent substantial power conflict. Conversely, the linkage of tier one suppliers into an automotive assembly operation has a much clearer power alignment.

Risk issues related to supply chain involvement essentially center on who has the most to gain or lose from the collaboration. Clearly a trucking firm that provides transportation services within a supply chain has far less at stake than either the manufacturer or the mass merchant discussed above. Generally, risk drives commitment to the collaborative arrangement and therefore plays a significant role in determining leadership.

The issue of which firm leads and the willingness of other firms to collaborate under the guidance of such leadership rests at the heart of making the supply chain ideal work. Chapter 6 develops these challenging issues in greater detail.

Loyalty and Confidentiality

In almost every observable situation, firms that participate in a specific supply chain are also simultaneously engaged in other similar arrangements. Some supply chain engagements may be sufficiently different so as not to raise issues of confidentiality. For example, a firm as diverse as Dow Chemical can simultaneously participate in a variety of different supply chain arrangements without substantial overlap or fear of divided loyalty.

However, the more common situation is for firms to be engaged as members of supply chains that are direct competitors. For example, Procter & Gamble is a supplier of all major food retailers. Thus, when Kroger, Farmer Jack, Meijer, and several retail members of Spartan Stores, all operating stores in the same cities, develop collaborative arrangements with Procter & Gamble, the potential for conflict is very real. To further complicate the competitive framework, add the fact that these same retailers also collaborate with Procter & Gamble competitors such as Kimberly-Clark, Colgate-Palmolive, and Lever Brothers and the loyalty/confidentiality issues abound. Finally, add the complexity of other types of retailers such as Rite-Aid, Target, and Wal★Mart Stores, Inc., who sell the merchandise of these manufacturers in the same geographic market and the neat concepts of linear supply chain quickly dissolve into competitive complexity.

From within this maze of competitive interactions, collaborative initiatives must be launched, nurtured, and sustained if the potential of integrated supply chains is to be realized. Firms that simultaneously engage in supply chains that are competitive must develop programs to foster loyalty and maintain confidentiality. The name used to describe such arrangements is **partitioning.**

Partitioning involves the development of proprietary organization and information collaborations to accommodate the needs of specific relationships. In situations where the focus is on manufacturer-branded products and development of promotions with retailers, partitioning is often administered by using unique customer teams. In situations involving new product development, it may be necessary to create separate organizational units to deal with specific suppliers. For example, the Prince Group of Johnson Controls needs to maintain strict confidentiality as they simultaneously help design future automotive interiors for divisions of DaimlerChrysler, Ford, and General Motors.

The issues of how to maintain focused loyalty and confidentiality in organizations that simultaneously participate in competitive supply chains are of critical importance. Breaches in confidentiality can have major legal and long-term business consequences. Loyalty quickly comes into question during periods of short supply or otherwise threatened operations. To achieve the benefits of cross-organizational collaboration, these issues must be managed and prospective damage must be controlled.

Measurement

Unlike an individual business, supply chains do not have conventional measurement devices. Whereas an individual business has an income statement and balance sheet constructed in compliance to uniform accounting principles, no such universal documents or procedures exist to measure supply chain performance. The question of supply chain performance is further complicated by the fact that process improvements benefiting overall supply chain performance may reduce costs of one firm while increasing selected costs of other participating firms.

It is clear that the measurement of supply chain operations requires a unique set of metrics that identifies and shares performance and cost information between participating members. The union of multiple firms into a synchronized supply chain initiative requires measures that reflect the collective synthesis while isolating and identifying individual contribution. Likewise, it would be ideal to have supply chain benchmarks to proliferate collective best practices.

The rapid emergence of the supply chain format has helped identify measurement challenges. However, the development of meaningful metrics remains in its infancy. Chapter 18 reviews the current status of fledgling supply chain metrics knowledge.

Risk/Reward Sharing

The ultimate challenge is the equitable distribution of rewards and risks resulting from supply chain collaboration. To illustrate, assume a business situation wherein the leadership of a major manufacturer in collaboration with material suppliers and distributive organizations results in a superior product reaching market at improved profitability. The described scenario is the icon of supply chain success. The product is better than competitors' and is distributed on a more profitable basis. This scenario implies that waste, nonproductive effort, duplication, and unwanted redundancy across the supply chain have been reduced to a minimum while the product and its logistical presentation have reached new heights of achievement. The challenge in success or failure is how to share the benefits or risks.

In traditional practice, the method by which risk and reward are shared is the transfer price. Transfer pricing, guided by market forces, works in transactional driven business relationships. However, supply chain engagements require a higher level of collaboration involving risk and reward sharing. In other words, if the process innovation is successful, the collaborating firms must share benefits. Conversely, if the innovation fails, risks must be appropriately absorbed. While easy to frame in theory, risk and reward sharing arrangements prove extremely difficult to implement in practice.

Clearly without appropriate metrics, it is impossible to share risk or rewards. However, even with the metrics in place, appropriate allocation requires careful preplanning and assessment for sharing programs to work.

Limited Success

The preceding discussion raises some practical limitations regarding the reality of supply chains. The concept of collaborating for success is full of vitality and the notion of leveraging core competencies for efficiency is a compelling vision. The mechanics of how to make such complex relationships work on a day-to-day basis are not well understood. Successful supply chain arrangements need to be driven by a well-defined and jointly endorsed set of collaborative principles. Such implementation principles need to prescribe leadership, loyalty and confidentiality measurements, and sharing guidelines and agreements.

In today's world, most so-called supply chains do not enjoy the assumptive and policy framework essential for long-term success. In recent research completed by Michigan State University, it was determined that fewer than one out of five firms engaged in collaborative arrangements had developed and approved policies to guide their managers in the structure and conduct of such arrangements.[20] No firms reported or were willing to share cross-organizational collaborative agreements that extended beyond traditional performance contracts. Some such contracts did contain performance incentives and risk absorbing agreements; however, such agreements were not as much cooperative arrangements as they were statements of performance expectations.

The obvious conclusion is that end-to-end supply chain arrangements remain in their infancy. The landscape today is dotted with a number of sophisticated operating arrangements that extend and facilitate performance between two and sometimes three organizations. In a few situations, namely large retailers, consumer durable manufacturers' and high technology companies' supply chain strategies have been developed to the point where systemic benefits are reported. Less obvious is an in-depth understanding of whether these benefits are being shared across the full scope of supply chain participants or if they are being retained by the dominant or lead organization. However, beyond these well-publicized supply chain achievements, there appears to be a shortage of successful end-to-end collaborations.

---

[20] Donald J. Bowersox, David J. Closs, and Theodore P. Stank, *21st Century Logistics: Making Supply Chain Integration a Reality* (Oak Brook, IL: Council of Logistics Management, 1999).

Social Challenges

The previous discussion suggests a significant gap exists between the theory of supply chain collaboration and the reality of accomplishment. While some critics question the ability of managers to design and orchestrate supply chain collaborations, others question the social desirability of such arrangements. The critics of supply chain collaboration offer at least two lines of attack—antitrust and consumer value.

Antitrust Concerns

The antitrust challenge to supply chain collaboration rests on the doctrines of free market competition. During the early years of the industrial age, it became clear that business collaboration among large corporations could serve to the disadvantage of consumers and other less powerful business organizations. Firms that achieved near monopoly situations well were observed using their economic and monetary power to restrain trade and leverage unreasonable profits. The result was the passage and refinement of a series of antitrust laws, all of which defined acceptable behavior between firms and with respect to market and pricing practices.

The changing competitive nature of world markets and relative national industrial economic power, characteristics of the late 20th century, served to somewhat mediate these traditional antitrust doctrines. To compete on a global basis, U.S. firms needed to achieve a level competitive footing with the trading company structures of the Pacific Basin and the interlocking bank directorates of European industrial powers. What resulted was the passage of the Cooperative Research and Development acts discussed earlier. These acts served to encourage operational collaborations but did not enable or authorize any form of market collusion.

The critics simply feel that any form of collaboration will sooner or later serve to impact market offerings and prices. Such criticism, however, does not seem valid with respect to features and prices projected for the first round of collaboratively designed electric-powered automobiles. However, more questionable are practices related to retail gas prices and selected electronic components that have collaborative supply chain roots. Only time will tell if collaboration for quality ultimately becomes a pricing mechanism.

It is clear that a disproportionate balance of power in a supply chain arrangement could be used to the disadvantage of some participating firms. Critics point to the large number of former "suppliers of the year" who in subsequent years were forced into bankruptcy as examples of misuse of power in supply chain collaborations. While once again the events are factual, no evidence exists to directly link collaboration to the failure of such suppliers.

In a free market economy, any form of collaboration raises some concern regarding the potential misuse of power in terms of the consuming public or with respect to business partners. Most agree the potential to achieve cross-enterprise synergies justifies the risks and potential dangers associated with collaboration. However, actions by the Justice Department and the Federal Trade Commission concerning careful review of Internet-based trading alliances suggest that a new concern over the boundaries of collaboration is emerging. Others propose a form of combined collaboration and competition referred to as **coevolving.**[21] This form of cooperation proposes loose and constantly changing relationships between businesses in a supply chain. The perceived supply chain structure is a shifting web of relationships that sever deteriorating

---

[21]Kathleen M. Eisenhardt and D. Charles Galunic, "Coevolving: At Last a Way to Make Synergies Work," *Harvard Business Review,* January–February 2000, pp. 91–101.

arrangements while simultaneously generating fresh collaborations. Coevolving is discussed in greater detail in Chapter 17, dealing with organization.

Consumer Value Concerns

A somewhat more abstract but often cited potential downside of supply chain management could be labeled the dark side of collaboration. The argument is that the public does not benefit across the board from supply chain efficiency. Supply chain criticism comes in two parts.

First, the line of reasoning is that operating efficiency does not automatically translate to or guarantee lower consumer prices. Firms that collaborate may individually or collectively make larger profits and thereby generate large shareholder wealth. However, no mechanisms exist to guarantee that efficiencies will be passed on to consumers in the form of lower retail prices. In fact, the supporting logic is that as supply chains become the effective units of competition, a market structure will move from many competing firms to a few large supply chains. This shift to a more monopolistic structure is viewed by critics as having the potential to artificially elevate, not reduce prices. Exponents of this line of reasoning cite the Efficient Consumer Response (ECR) initiative in the food industry as an example of collaboration that offers no tangible evidence that consumer food prices were reduced as a result of widespread supply chain collaboration. However, no tangible evidence exists to support the contrary argument.

The second criticism of supply chain arrangements builds on the premise that operating efficiency may not always be socially equitable. The argument questions the benefits of more precise matching of supply to demand in terms of the overall reduction in surplus goods. To illustrate, if a precise quantity of dresses is sold at the top market price, then no overstocks or surplus garments are available to be marked down during a process that traditionally extends from clearance sales to bargain basement liquidations. The lady who purchases a final closeout garment at a below-cost price receives a benefit from the inefficiency of the marketing system. Precise supply chain collaboration would eliminate or significantly reduce such value opportunities. Assuming a reasonable profit can be made by firms that are not highly efficient and that low-end consumers realize superior values, the overall consuming public is viewed as being better off when inefficiencies occur. Similar lines of reason, justified or not, can be applied to the social benefits of grocery reclamation and new car rebates.[22]

These arguments, as presented and documented to date, are interesting but not persuasive. In terms of economic growth, initiatives aimed at reducing costs by elimination of waste, redundancy, and non-value-adding efforts remain appealing because they offer the potential to improve efficiency. The most serious concern may be the inability to effectively implement and manage comprehensive supply chain initiatives.

This is a biased view

Summary

The development of greater integrated management skill is critical to continued productivity improvement. Such integrative management must focus on quality improvement at both functional and process levels. In terms of functions, critical work must be performed to the highest degree of efficiency. Processes that create value occur both

---

[22]See James Aaron Cooke, "The Dark Side of the Supply Chain," *Logistics Management,* December 1997, p. 63.

within individual firms and between firms linked together in collaborative supply chains. Each type of process must be continuously improved.

The idea that all or even most firms will link together to form highly collaborative end-to-end supply chain initiatives at any time in the foreseeable future is quite unlikely. The dynamics of a free competitive market system will serve to harness such an end state. However, initiatives aimed at cross-enterprise integration along the supply chain are increasingly occurring and, to the extent successfully implemented, offer new and exciting business models for gaining competitive advantage. Once achieved, such supply chain integration is hard to maintain and is subject to continuous redefinition. What works today, may not work tomorrow. Conversely, what won't work today, may work tomorrow.

Thus, supply chain collaborations must be viewed as highly dynamic. Such collaborations are attractive because they offer new horizons for gaining market positioning and operating efficiency. Supply chain opportunities are challenges that managers in the 21st century must explore and exploit. However, supply chain integration is a means to increased profitability and growth and not an end in itself.

From the perspective of integrated logistics management, supply chain strategies scope the relevant operating framework. What must be logistically accomplished is directly linked to supply chain structure and strategy. When such structure and strategy are internationally positioned, logistics performance must embrace challenges related to globalization. In short, the supply chain strategy or lack of strategy and its related structure serve to shape the framework of logistical requirements. Chapter 2 introduces the challenges of lean logistics in greater detail.

Challenge Questions

1. Why can the current movement toward establishing supply chains be characterized as a revolution?

2. Compare the concept of a modern supply chain with more traditional distribution channels. Be specific regarding similarities and differences.

3. What specific role does logistics play in supply chain operations?

4. Describe "integrative management." Be specific concerning the relationship between functionality and process.

5. In terms of enterprise extension, describe the importance of the information sharing and process specialization paradigms.

6. Describe and illustrate an integrated service provider. How does the concept of integrated service provider differ from traditional service providers, such as for-hire transportation and warehousing?

7. Compare and contrast anticipatory and response-based business models. Why has responsiveness become popular in supply chain collaborations?

8. Compare and contrast manufacturing and geographic postponement.

9. Define and illustrate cash-to-cash conversion, dwell time minimization, and cash spin. How do supply chain strategy and structure impact each?

10. Discuss and support the following argument: "Supply chain arrangements may reduce consumer value."

2 LEAN LOGISTICS

No other area of business operations involves the complexity or spans the geography of logistics. All around the globe, 24 hours of every day, 7 days a week, during 52 weeks a year, logistics is concerned with getting products and services where they are needed at the precise time desired. It is difficult to visualize accomplishing any marketing, manufacturing, or international commerce without logistics. Most consumers in highly developed industrial nations take a high level of logistical competency for granted. When they purchase goods—at a retail store, over the telephone, or via the Internet—they expect product delivery will be performed as promised. In fact, their expectation is for timely, error-free logistics every time they order. They have little or no tolerance for failure to perform.

Although logistics has been performed since the beginning of civilization, implementing best practice logistics is one of the most exciting and challenging operational areas of supply chain management. Because logistics is both old and new, we choose to characterize the rapid change taking place in best practice as a renaissance.

Logistics involves the management of order processing, inventory, transportation, and the combination of warehousing, materials handling, and packaging, all integrated throughout a network of facilities. The goal of logistics is to support procurement, manufacturing, and market distribution operational requirements. Within a firm the challenge is to coordinate functional competency into an integrated operation focused on servicing customers. In the broader supply chain context, operational synchronization is essential with customers as well as material and service suppliers to link internal and external operations as one integrated process.

Lean logistics refers to the superior ability to *design and administer systems to control movement and geographical positioning of raw materials, work-in-process, and finished inventories at the lowest total cost.* To achieve lowest total cost means that financial and human assets committed to logistics must be held to an absolute minimum. It is also necessary to hold direct operational expenditures as low as possible. The combination of resources, skills, and systems required to achieve lean logistics are challenging to integrate, but once achieved, such integrated competency is difficult for competitors to replicate. Industry Insight 2-1 illustrates how Dell Computers has used lean logistics principles to gain competitive advantage.

This chapter focuses on the contribution of lean logistics to integrated supply chain management. First, cost and service are emphasized. Next, the logistics value proposition is developed. Then traditional business functions that combine to create the logistical process are reviewed. Finally, the importance of logistical synchronization to supply chain integration is highlighted in terms of performance cycle structure and dynamics.

The Logistics of Business Is Big and Important

It is through the logistical process that materials flow into the manufacturing capacity of an industrial nation and products are distributed to consumers. The recent growth in global commerce and the introduction of e-commerce have expanded the size and complexity of logistical operations.

Logistics adds value to the supply chain process when inventory is strategically positioned to achieve sales. Creating logistics value is costly. Although difficult to measure, most experts agree that the annual expenditure to perform logistics in the United States was approximately 10.1 percent of the $9.96 billion Gross National Product (GNP) or $1.006 billion.[1] Expenditure for transportation in 2000 was $590 billion, which represented 58.6 percent of total logistics cost. As further illustrated in Table 2-1, the logistics of business is truly big business!

Despite the sheer size of logistical expenditure, the excitement of lean logistics is not cost containment or reduction. The excitement generates from understanding how select firms use logistical competency to achieve competitive advantage. Firms that

---

[1]Robert V. Delaney, Twelfth Annual "State of Logistics Report," presented to the National Press Club, Washington, DC, June 4, 2001.

INDUSTRY INSIGHT 2-1 DELL GOES TO THE EXTREME

According to industry legend, Henry Ford's manufacturing philosophy was "You can have any color you want as long as it's black." The manufacturing strategy that has fostered unprecedented success for Dell Computers is the exact opposite of Ford's mindset: "Build every order to order." Essentially, it spawns the ultimate manufacturing oxymoron: mass customization.

The critical component to facilitate mass customization is a logistics program built upon a concept of "extreme warehousing" and a superior software platform. Ryder Integrated Logistics, a subsidiary of Ryder Systems, Miami, Florida, houses supplier-owned inventory for Dell at locations in Austin, Texas, and Nashville, Tennessee. The Austin facility is fed by 50 global suppliers and the Nashville site is fed by 60 vendors worldwide.

"Dell requires suppliers to respond with order fulfillment within two hours. The only way suppliers can meet this expectation is to utilize our logistics management," explains Dave Hanley, director of business development for Ryder. "Dell maintains less than six days of inventory, and turns work-in-process approximately 264 times annually. The company uses our services to minimize investment in inventory, and to abolish 'dead space,' or 'nonproductive storage areas.'"

"We replenish to kanbans and maintain a working inventory at the production facility," Hanley says. "Dell does an incredible job of estimating what products will be selling, and different products peak at various times. Laptops are big now and business machines are more popular in the first quarter of the year than in the last."

Currently, Ryder has responsibility for the inventory from the time it arrives at its facilities until it delivers to Dell. Hanley is confident that incorporating Ryder's processes and logistics management across all inbound shipments from suppliers, beginning at every point of origin, would bring tremendous additional value to Dell.

While he acknowledges Dell is the master of execution in manufacturing, Hanley says the software used by Ryder to manage the extreme warehousing requirements is one of the computer manufacturer's "top three critical success factors."

The software had to satisfy many requirements—from open architecture to a scalable platform that would grow with Dell. The solution has done precisely that, expanding with the Austin facility as it grew from 12,000 square feet in 1997 to more than 600,000 square feet by 1999.

"Extreme warehousing demands fast response and critical management," says Hanley. "There's a live customer waiting for the order, and a mistake today means a disappointed customer in just two days."

This rapid fulfillment doesn't allow recovery time for mistakes, so the WMS has to execute perfectly and flawlessly on every order, he notes. *Lack of flexibility*

Source: Anonymous, "Dell Goes to the Extreme," *Inbound Logistics,* January 2000, p. 122.

---

have developed world-class logistical competency enjoy competitive advantage as a result of providing important customers superior service. Leading logistical performers typically implement information technology capable of monitoring global logistical activity on a real time basis. Such technology identifies potential operational breakdowns and facilitates corrective action prior to delivery service failure. In situations where timely corrective action is not possible, customers can be provided advance notification of developing problems, thereby eliminating the surprise of an unavoidable service failure. In many situations, working in collaboration with customers and suppliers, corrective action can be taken to prevent operational shutdowns or costly customer service failures. By performing at above industry average with respect to inventory availability, speed and consistency of delivery, and operational efficiencies, logistically sophisticated firms are ideal supply chain partners.

TABLE 2-1   **U.S. Logistics Costs, 1980–2000 ($ Billions Except GDP)**

Year	Nominal GDP ($ Trillion)	Values of All Business Inventory	Percent of Inventory Carrying Rate	Inventory Carrying Costs	Transportation Costs	Administrative Costs	Total U.S. Logistics Cost	Logistics (% of GDP)
1980	$ 2.80	692	31.8	220	214	17	451	16.1
1981	3.13	747	34.7	259	228	19	506	16.2
1982	3.26	760	30.8	234	222	18	474	14.5
1983	3.54	758	27.9	211	243	18	472	13.3
1984	3.93	826	29.1	240	268	20	528	13.4
1985	4.21	847	26.8	227	274	20	521	12.4
1986	4.45	843	25.7	217	281	20	518	11.6
1987	4.74	875	25.7	225	294	21	540	11.4
1988	5.11	944	26.6	251	313	23	587	11.5
1989	5.44	1005	28.1	282	329	24	635	11.7
1990	5.80	1041	27.2	283	351	25	659	11.4
1991	5.99	1030	24.9	256	355	24	635	10.6
1992	6.32	1043	22.7	237	375	24	636	10.1
1993	6.64	1076	22.2	239	396	25	660	9.9
1994	7.05	1127	23.5	265	420	27	712	10.1
1995	7.40	1211	24.9	302	441	30	773	10.4
1996	7.81	1240	24.4	303	467	31	801	10.3
1997	8.32	1280	24.5	314	503	33	850	10.2
1998	8.79	1323	24.4	323	529	34	886	10.1
1999	9.30	1379	24.1	332	554	35	921	9.9
2000	9.96	1485	25.4	377	590	39	1006	10.1

Source: Robert V. Delaney, Twelfth Annual "State of Logistics Report," presented to the National Press Club, Washington, DC, June 4, 2001.

The Logistical Value Proposition

Thus far it has been established that logistics should be managed as an integrated effort to achieve customer satisfaction at the lowest total cost. Here we add that the modern challenge is to create *value*. In this section, the elements of the logistical value proposition, service, and cost minimization are discussed in greater detail.

Service Benefits

Almost any level of logistical service can be achieved if a firm is willing to commit the required resources. In today's operating environment, the limiting factor is economics, not technology. For example, a dedicated inventory can be maintained in close geographical proximity to a major customer. A fleet of trucks can be held in a constant state of delivery readiness. To facilitate order processing, dedicated communications can be maintained on a real time or Internet-enabled basis between a customer and a supplier's logistical operation. Given this high state of logistical readiness, a product or component could be delivered within minutes of identifying a customer requirement. Availability is even faster when a supplier agrees to consign inventory at a customer's facility, eliminating the need to perform logistical operations when a product is needed. The logistics to support consignment are completed in advance of the customer's need for the product. While such extreme service commitment might constitute a sales manager's dream, it is costly and typically not necessary to support most market distribution and manufacturing operations.

The key strategic issue is how to outperform competitors in a cost-effective manner. If a specific material is not available when required for manufacturing, it may force a plant shutdown resulting in significant cost, potential lost sales, and even the loss of a major customer's business. The profit impact of such failures is significant. In contrast, the profit impact of an unexpected 1- or 2-day delay in delivering products to replenish warehouse inventory could be minimal or even insignificant in terms of impact on overall operational performance. In most situations, the cost/benefit impact of logistical failure is directly related to the importance of service to the customer. The more significant the service failure impact upon a customer's performance, the greater is the priority placed on error-free logistical performance.

Creation and basic logistical performance is measured in terms of availability, operational performance, and service reliability.[2] The term *basic logistics service* describes the level of service a firm provides all established customers.

Availability involves having inventory to consistently meet customer material or product requirements. The traditional paradigm has been the higher inventory availability, the greater is the required inventory amount and cost. Information technology is providing new ways to achieve high inventory availability for customers without correspondingly high capital investment. Information that facilitates availability is critical to achieving lean logistics performance.

Operational performance deals with the time required to deliver a customer's order. Operational performance involves delivery *speed* and *consistency*. Naturally, most customers want fast delivery. However, fast delivery is of limited value if inconsistent from one order to the next. A customer gains little benefit when a supplier promises next-day delivery but, more often than not, delivers late. To achieve smooth operations, firms typically focus on service consistency first and then seek to improve delivery speed. Other aspects of operational performance are also important. A firm's operational performance can be viewed in terms of its *flexibility* to accommodate unusual and unexpected customer requests. Another aspect of operational performance is frequency of malfunction and, when such malfunction occurs, the required recovery time. Few firms can perform perfectly all the time. It is important to estimate the likelihood of something going wrong. *Malfunction* is concerned with the probability of logistical performance involving failures, such as damaged products, incorrect assortment, or inaccurate documentation. When such malfunctions occur, a firm's logistical competency can be measured in terms of *recovery time.* Operational performance is concerned with how a firm handles all aspects of customer requirements, including service failure, on a day in and day out basis.

Service reliability involves the *quality* attributes of logistics. The key to quality is accurate measurement of availability and operational performance. Only through comprehensive performance measurement is it possible to determine if overall logistical operations are achieving desired service goals. To achieve service reliability, it is essential to identify and implement inventory availability and operational performance measurements. For logistics performance to continuously meet customer expectations, it is essential that management be committed to continuous improvement. Logistical

---

[2]These basic measures of customer service are more fully developed in Chapter 3.

quality does not come easy; it's the product of careful planning supported by employee training, operational dedication, comprehensive measurement, and continuous improvement. To improve service performance, goals need to be established on a selective basis. Some products are more critical than others because of their importance to the customer and their relative profit contribution.

The level of basic logistical service should be realistic in terms of customer expectations and requirements. In most cases, firms confront situations wherein customers have significantly different purchase potential. Some customers require unique or special value-added services. Thus, managers must realize that customers are different and that services provided must be matched to accommodate unique requirements and purchase potential. In general, firms tend to be overly optimistic when committing to average or basic customer service performance. Inability to consistently meet an unrealistically high basic service target might result in more operating and customer relationship problems than if less ambitious goals had been attempted from the outset. Unrealistic across-the-board service commitments can also dilute a firm's capability to satisfy special requirements of high potential customers.

Cost Minimization

The focus of lean logistics can be traced to relatively recent developments of total costing theory and practice. In 1956, a classic monograph describing airfreight economics provided a new perspective concerning logistical cost.[3] In an effort to explain conditions under which high-cost air transport could be justified, Lewis, Culliton, and Steele conceptualized the total cost logistics model. Total cost was positioned to include *all* expenditures necessary to perform logistical requirements. The authors illustrated an electronic parts distribution strategy wherein the high variable cost of direct factory-to-customer air transport was more than offset by reductions in traditional inventory and field warehouse costs. They concluded that the least *total cost* logistical way to provide the desired customer service was to centralize inventory in one warehouse and make deliveries using air transportation.

This concept of total cost, although fundamentally basic, had not previously been applied to logistical operations. Probably because of the economic climate of the times and the radical departure in suggested practice, the total cost proposition generated a great deal of debate. The prevailing managerial practice, reinforced by accounting and financial control, was to focus attention on achieving the lowest possible cost for *each* individual function of logistics with little or no attention to integrated total cost. Managers had traditionally focused on minimizing functional cost, such as transportation, with the expectation that such effort would achieve the lowest combined costs. Development of the total cost concept opened the door to examining how functional costs interrelate and impact each other. Subsequent refinements provided a more comprehensive understanding of logistical cost components and identified the critical need for developing functional cost analysis and activity-based costing capabilities. However, the implementation of effective logistical process costing remains a new millennium challenge. Many long-standing practices of accounting continue to serve as barriers to fully implementing total cost logistical solutions.

---

[3]Howard T. Lewis, James W. Culliton, and Jack D. Steele, *The Role of Air Freight in Physical Distribution* (Boston, MA: Harvard University, 1956).

Logistics Value Generation

The key to achieving logistical leadership is to master the art of matching operating competency and commitment to key customer expectations and requirements. This customer commitment, in an exacting cost framework, is the **logistics value proposition.** It is a unique commitment of a firm to an individual or selected groups of its customers.

The typical enterprise seeks to develop and implement an overall logistical competency that satisfies customer expectations at a realistic total cost expenditure. Very seldom will either the lowest total cost or the highest attainable customer service constitute the fundamental logistics strategy. Likewise, the appropriate combination will be different for different customers. A well-designed logistical effort must have high customer response and capability while controlling operational variance and minimizing inventory commitment. And, most of all, it must have relevancy to specific customers.

Significant advances have been made in the development of tools to aid management in the measurement of cost/service trade-offs. Formulation of a sound strategy requires a capability to estimate operating cost required to achieve alternative service levels. Likewise, alternative levels of system performance are meaningless unless viewed in terms of overall business unit marketing, manufacturing, and procurement strategies.

Leading firms realize that a well-designed and well-operated logistical system can help achieve competitive advantage. In fact, as a general rule, firms that obtain a strategic advantage based on logistical competency establish the nature of their industry's competition. Industry Insight 2-2 illustrates industry leadership enjoyed by Cisco Systems as a result of logistical competency.

The Work of Logistics

In the context of supply chain management, logistics exists to move and position inventory to achieve desired time, place, and possession benefits at the lowest total cost. Inventory has limited value until it is positioned at the right time and at the right location to support ownership transfer or value-added creation. If a firm does not consistently satisfy time and place requirements, it has nothing to sell. For a supply chain to realize the maximum strategic benefit of logistics, the full range of functional work must be integrated. Decisions in one functional area will impact cost of all others. It is this interrelation of functions that challenges the successful implementation of integrated logistical management. Figure 2-1 provides a visual representation of the interrelated nature of the five areas of logistical work: (1) order processing; (2) inventory; (3) transportation; (4) warehousing, materials handling, and packaging; and (5) facility network. As described below, work related to these functional areas combines to create the capabilities needed to achieve logistical value.

Order Processing

The importance of accurate information to logistical performance has historically been underappreciated. While many aspects of information are critical to logistics operations, the processing of orders is of primary importance. Failure to fully understand this importance resulted from a failure to understand how distortion and dynamics impact logistical operations.

INDUSTRY INSIGHT 2-2 CISCO'S SINGLE ENTERPRISE STRATEGY

Cisco's sales were growing by 100 percent per year in the mid-90s. Employment was swelling to keep pace and supply chain costs were unacceptably high. Product life cycles continued to shorten. Demands for reliability, flexibility, and speed escalated at an alarming rate. To keep pace, Cisco undertook a wholesale revamping of its business processes, from design and forecasting to raw materials acquisition, production, distribution, and customer follow-up.

The creation of Cisco's global networked business model arose in multiple departments at the same time, out of a shared realization of the need for change. Within this model, Cisco views its supply chain as a fabric of relationships, rather than in a linear fashion. The goal was to transcend the internal focus of Enterprise Resource Planning (ERP) systems to embrace a networked supply chain of all trading partners. Primary goals were servicing the customer better, coping with huge growth, and driving down costs. Utilizing the Internet, it is pursuing a single enterprise strategy.

Today Cisco relies on five contract manufacturers for nearly 60 percent of final assembling and testing and 100 percent of basic production. Through strict oversight and a clear set of standards, Cisco ensures that every partner achieves the same high level of quality. All 14 of its global manufacturing sites, along with two distributors, are linked via a single enterprise extranet.

The quest for a single enterprise has tied Cisco to its suppliers in unprecedented ways. Product now flows from first- and second-tier suppliers without the documentation and notifications on which most supply chains rely. Instead of responding to specific work orders, contract manufacturers turn out components according to a daily build plan derived from a single long-term forecast shared throughout the supply chain. Items move either to Cisco or directly to its customers. Payment occurs automatically upon receipt; there are no purchase orders, invoices, or traditional acknowledgments.

In exchange for getting paid sooner, suppliers are required to aggressively attack their cost structures but not to the point where they can't make a profit. "It's not a partnership if you're putting the other guy out of business," says Barbara Siverts, manager of supply chain solutions within Cisco's Internet Business Solutions unit.

Cisco cites at least $128 million in annual savings from its single enterprise strategy. It has reduced time to market by 25 percent, while hitting 97 percent of delivery targets. Inventories have been cut nearly in half. Order cycle time has declined from 6 to 8 weeks 4 years ago to between 1 and 3 weeks now. Under a program known as dynamic replenishment, demand signals flow instantly to contract manufacturers. Inventories can be monitored by all supply chain partners on a real time basis.

Some 55 percent of product now moves directly from supplier to customer, bypassing Cisco altogether. This has removed several days from the order cycle. Direct fulfillment means reduced inventories, labor costs, and shipping expenses. Cisco pegs savings at $10 per unit, or around $12 million a year.

Working with UPS, Cisco took control of the outbound supply chain, allowing for time-definite delivery throughout Europe within 5 to 8 days, via a single point of contact. With Oracle's inventory control system hooked directly into UPS's logistics management system, Cisco now tracks product to destination on a real time basis. The extra measure of control allows it to intercept, reroute, or reconfigure orders on short notice. Through deferred delivery, Cisco ensures that a component won't arrive at the customer's dock until it's ready to be installed.

Cisco's outsourcing strategy took another step forward recently, with the decision to turn over shipping and warehousing functions to FedEx Corp. The air, ground, and logistics services provider will manage a merge-in-transit operation for direct shipment to end customers, resulting in the near elimination of Cisco-operated warehouses within 5 years.

Source: Robert J. Bowman, "At Cisco Systems, the Internet Is Both Business and Business Model," *Global Logistics & Supply Chain Strategies,* May 2000, pp. 28–38.

Figure 2-1

Integrated logistics

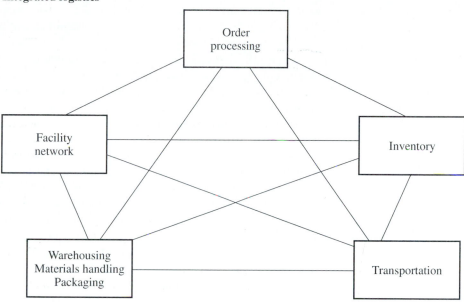

Current information technology is capable of handling the most demanding customer requirements. When desired, order information can be obtained on a real time basis.

The benefit of fast information flow is directly related to work balancing. It makes little sense for a firm to accumulate orders at a local sales office for a week, mail them to a regional office, process the orders as a batch, assign them to a distribution warehouse, and then ship them via air to achieve fast delivery. In contrast, data transmission or Web-based communication of orders direct from the customers' office combined with slower, less costly surface transportation may have achieved even faster overall delivery service at a lower total cost. The key objective is to balance components of the logistical system.

Forecasting and communication of customer requirements are the two areas of logistical work driven by information. The relative importance of each facet of operational information is directly related to the degree to which the supply chain is positioned to function on a responsive or anticipatory basis. The more responsive the supply chain design, the greater the importance is of accurate and timely information regarding customer purchase behavior. As established in Chapter 1, supply chains are increasingly reflecting a blend of responsive and anticipatory operations.

In most supply chains, customer requirements are transmitted in the form of orders. The processing of these orders involves all aspects of managing customer requirements from initial order receipt, delivery, invoicing, and collection. The logistics capabilities of a firm can only be as good as its order processing competency.

Inventory

The inventory requirements of a firm are directly linked to the facility network and the desired level of customer service. Theoretically, a firm could stock every item sold in every facility dedicated to servicing each customer. Few business operations can afford such a luxurious inventory commitment because the risk and total cost are prohibitive. The objective in inventory strategy is to achieve desired customer service with the minimum inventory commitment. Excessive inventories may compensate for deficiencies in basic design of a logistics system but will ultimately result in higher-than-necessary total logistics cost.

Logistical strategies should be designed to maintain the lowest possible financial investment in inventory. The basic goal is to achieve maximum inventory turn while satisfying service commitments. A sound inventory strategy is based on a combination of five aspects of selective deployment: (1) core customer segmentation, (2) product profitability, (3) transportation integration, (4) time-based performance, and (5) competitive performance.

Every enterprise that sells to a variety of different customers confronts uneven opportunity. Some customers are highly profitable and have outstanding growth potential; others do not. The profitability of a customer's business depends upon the products purchased, volume, price, value-added services required, and supplemental activities necessary to develop and maintain an ongoing relationship. Because highly profitable customers constitute the core market of every enterprise, inventory strategies need to focus on them. The key to effective logistical segmentation rests in the inventory priorities dedicated to support core customers.

Most enterprises experience a substantial variance in the volume and profitability across product lines. If no restrictions are applied, a firm may find that less than 20 percent of all products marketed account for more than 80 percent of total profit. While the so-called 80/20 rule or **Pareto principle** is common in business, management must avoid such outcomes by implementing inventory strategies based on fine-line product classification. A realistic assessment of the incremental value added by stocking low-profit or low-volume products is essential to avoiding excessive cost. For obvious reasons, an enterprise wants to offer high availability and consistent delivery of its most profitable products. High-level support of less profitable items, however, may be necessary to provide full-line service to core customers. The trap to avoid is high service performance on less profitable items that are typically purchased by fringe or noncore customers. Therefore, product line profitability must be considered when developing a selective inventory policy.

The product stocking plan at a specific facility has a direct impact upon transportation performance. Most transportation rates are based on the volume and size of specific shipments. Thus, it may be sound strategy to stock a sufficient range or assortment of products at a warehouse to be able to arrange consolidated shipments. The corresponding savings in transportation may more than offset the increased cost of holding the inventory.

A firm's degree of commitment to deliver products rapidly to meet a customer's inventory requirement is a major competitive factor. If products and materials can be delivered quickly, it may not be necessary for customers to maintain large inventories. Likewise, if retail stores can be replenished rapidly, less safety stock is required. The alternative to stockpiling and holding safety stock is to receive exact and timely inventory replenishment. While such time-based programs reduce customer inventory to absolute minimums, the savings must be balanced against other supply chain costs incurred as a result of the time-sensitive logistical process.

Finally, inventory strategies cannot be created in a competitive vacuum. A firm is typically more desirable to do business with, than competitors, if it can promise and perform rapid and consistent delivery. Therefore, it may be necessary to position inventory in a specific warehouse to gain competitive advantage even if such commitment increases total cost. Selective inventory deployment policies may be essential to gain a customer service advantage or to neutralize a strength that a competitor currently enjoys.

Material and component inventories exist in a logistical system for reasons other than finished product inventory. Each type of inventory and the level of commitment must be viewed from a total cost perspective. Understanding the interrelationship between order processing, inventory, transportation, and facility network decisions is fundamental to integrated logistics.

Transportation

Transportation is the operational area of logistics that geographically moves and positions inventory. Because of its fundamental importance and visible cost, transportation has traditionally received considerable managerial attention. Almost all enterprises, big and small, have managers responsible for transportation.

Transportation requirements can be satisfied in three basic ways. First, a private fleet of equipment may be operated. Second, contracts may be arranged with dedicated transport specialists. Third, an enterprise may engage the services of a wide variety of carriers that provide different transportation services on a per shipment basis. From the logistical system viewpoint, three factors are fundamental to transportation performance: (1) cost, (2) speed, and (3) consistency.

The **cost** of transport is the payment for shipment between two geographical locations and the expenses related to maintaining in-transit inventory. Logistical systems should utilize transportation that minimizes *total* system cost. This may mean that the least expensive method of transportation may not result in the lowest total cost of logistics.

Speed of transportation is the time required to complete a specific movement. Speed and cost of transportation are related in two ways. First, transport firms, capable of offering faster service, typically charge higher rates. Second, the faster the transportation service is, the shorter the time interval during which inventory is in-transit and unavailable. Thus, a critical aspect of selecting the most desirable method of transportation is to balance speed and cost of service.

Consistency of transportation refers to variations in time required to perform a specific movement over a number of shipments. Consistency reflects the dependability of transportation. For years, transportation managers have identified consistency as the most important attribute of quality transportation. If a shipment between two locations takes 3 days one time and 6 the next, the unexpected variance can create serious supply chain operational problems. When transportation lacks consistency, inventory safety stocks are required to protect against service breakdowns, impacting both the seller's and buyer's overall inventory commitment. With the advent of new information technology to control and report shipment status, logistics managers have begun to seek faster movement while maintaining consistency. Speed and consistency combine to create the quality aspect of transportation.

In designing a logistical system, a delicate balance must be maintained between transportation cost and service quality. In some circumstances low-cost, slow transportation is satisfactory. In other situations, faster service may be essential to achieving operating goals. Finding and managing the desired transportation mix across the supply chain is a primary responsibility of logistics.

Warehousing, Materials Handling, and Packaging

The first three functional areas of logistics—order processing, inventory, and transportation—can be engineered into a variety of different operational arrangements. Each arrangement has the potential to contribute to a specified level of customer service with an associated total cost. In essence, these functions combine to create a system solution for integrated logistics. The fourth functionality of logistics—warehousing, materials handling, and packaging—also represents an integral part of a logistics operating solution. However, these functions do not have the independent status of those previously discussed. Warehousing, materials handling, and packaging are an integral part of other logistics areas. For example, inventory typically needs to be warehoused at selected times during the logistics process. Transportation vehicles require materials handling for efficient loading and unloading. Finally, the individual products are most efficiently handled when packaged together into shipping cartons or other unit loads.

When distribution facilities are required in a logistical system, a firm can choose between the services of a warehouse specialist or operating their own facility. The decision is broader than simply selecting a facility to store inventory since many value-adding activities may be performed during the time products are warehoused. Examples of such activities are sorting, sequencing, order selection, transportation consolidation, and, in some cases, product modification and assembly.

Within the warehouse, materials handling is an important activity. Products must be received, moved, stored, sorted, and assembled to meet customer order requirements. The direct labor and capital invested in materials handling equipment is a significant element of total logistics cost. When performed in an inferior manner, materials handling can result in substantial product damage. It stands to reason that the fewer the times a product is handled, the less the potential exists for product damage and the overall efficiency of the warehouse is increased. A variety of mechanized and automated devices exist to assist materials handling. In essence, each warehouse and its materials handling capability represent a minisystem within the overall logistical process.

To facilitate handling efficiency, products in the form of cans, bottles, or boxes are typically combined into larger units. This larger unit, typically called the **master carton,** provides two important features. First, it serves to protect the product during the logistical process. Second, the master carton facilitates ease of handling, by creating one large package rather than a multitude of small, individual products. For efficient handling and transport, master cartons are typically consolidated into larger unit loads. The most common units for master carton consolidation are pallets, slip sheets, and various types of containers.

When effectively integrated into an enterprise's logistical operations, warehousing, materials handling, and packaging facilitate the speed and overall ease of product flow throughout the logistical system. In fact, several firms have engineered devices to move broad product assortments from manufacturing plants directly to retail stores without intermediate handling.

Facility Network

Classical economics neglected the importance of facility location and overall network design to efficient business operations. When economists originally discussed supply-and-demand relationships, facility location and transportation cost differentials were

assumed either nonexistent or equal among competitors.[4] In business operations, however, the number, size, and geographical relationship of facilities used to perform logistical operations directly impacts customer service capabilities and cost. Network
design is a primary responsibility of logistical management since a firm's facility
structure is used to ship products and materials to customers. Typical logistics facilities are manufacturing plants, warehouses, cross-dock operations, and retail stores.

Network design is concerned with determining the number and location of all
types of facilities required to perform logistics work. It is also necessary to determine
what inventory and how much to stock at each facility as well as the assignment of
customers. The facility network creates a structure from which logistical operations
are performed. Thus, the network integrates information and transportation capabilities. Specific work tasks related to processing customer orders, warehousing inventory, and materials handling are all performed within the facility network.

The design of a facility network requires careful analysis of geographical variation.
The fact that a great deal of difference exists between geographical markets is easy to illustrate. The 50 largest U.S. metropolitan markets in terms of population account for the
majority of retail sales. Therefore, an enterprise marketing on a national scale must establish a logistical network capable of servicing prime markets. A similar geographic dispar-
ity exists in typical material and component part source locations. When a firm is involved in global logistics, issues related to network design become increasingly complex.

The importance of continuously modifying the facility network to accommodate
change in demand and supply infrastructures cannot be overemphasized. Product assortments, customers, suppliers, and manufacturing requirements are constantly
changing in a dynamic competitive environment. The selection of a superior locational
network can provide a significant step toward achieving competitive advantage.

Logistical Operations

The internal operational scope of integrated logistics operations is illustrated by the
shaded area of Figure 2-2. Information from and about customers flows through the enterprise in the form of sales activity, forecasts, and orders. Vital information is refined
into specific manufacturing, merchandising, and purchasing plans. As products and materials are procured, a value-added inventory flow is initiated which ultimately results in
ownership transfer of finished products to customers. Thus, the process is viewed in
terms of two interrelated flows: inventory and information. While internal integrative
management is important to success, the firm must also integrate across the supply
chain. To be fully effective in today's competitive environment, firms must extend their
enterprise integration to incorporate customers and suppliers. This extension reflects the
position of logistics in the broader perspective of supply chain management. Supply
chain integration is discussed later in this chapter (see Logistical Synchronization).

---

[4]Alfred Weber, *Theory of the Location of Industries,* transl. Carl J. Friedrich (Chicago, IL: University
of Chicago Press, 1928); August Lösch, *Die Räumliche Ordnung der Wirtschaft,* (Jena: Gustav Fischer
Verlag, 1940); Edgar M. Hoover, *The Location of Economic Activity* (New York, NY: McGraw-Hill Book
Company, 1938); Melvin L. Greenhut, *Plant Location in Theory and Practice* (Chapel Hill, NC: University
of North Carolina Press, 1956); Walter Isard, et. al., *Methods of Regional Analysis: An Introduction to
Regional Science* (New York, NY: John Wiley & Sons, 1960); Walter Isard, *Location and Space Economy*
(Cambridge, MA: The MIT Press, 1968); and Michael J. Webber, *Impact of Uncertainty on Location*
(Cambridge, MA: The MIT Press, 1972).

FIGURE 2-2

Logistical integration

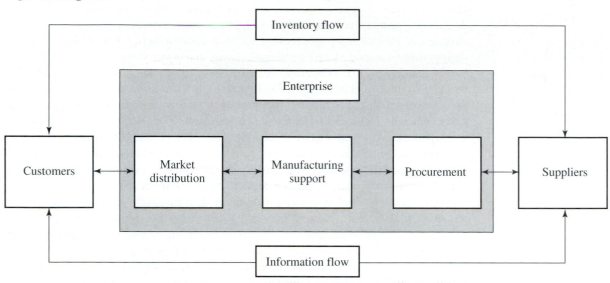

Inventory Flow

The operational management of logistics is concerned with movement and storage of materials and finished products. Logistical operations start with the initial shipment of a material or component part from a supplier and are finalized when a manufactured or processed product is delivered to a customer.

From the initial purchase of a material or component, the logistics process adds value by moving inventory when and where needed. Providing all goes well, materials and components gain value at each step of their transformation into finished inventory. In other words, an individual part has greater value after it is incorporated into a machine than it had as a part. Likewise, the machine has greater value once it is delivered to a customer.

To support manufacturing, work-in-process inventory must be properly positioned. The cost of each component and its movement becomes part of the value-added process. For better understanding, it is useful to divide logistical operations into three areas: (1) market distribution, (2) manufacturing support, and (3) procurement. These components are illustrated in the shaded area of Figure 2-2 as the combined logistics operational units of an enterprise.

Market Distribution

The movement of finished product to customers is **market distribution.** In market distribution, the end customer represents the final destination. The availability of product is a vital part of each channel participant's marketing effort. Even a manufacturer's agent, who typically does not own inventory, must be supported by inventory availability to perform expected marketing responsibilities. Unless a proper assortment of products is efficiently delivered when and where needed, a great deal of the overall marketing effort will be jeopardized. It is through the market distribution process that the timing and geographical placement of inventory become an integral part of marketing. To support the wide variety of marketing systems that exist in a highly commercialized nation, many different market distribution systems are available. All market distribution systems have one common feature: They link manufacturers, wholesalers, and retailers into supply chains to provide product availability.

Manufacturing Support

The area of **manufacturing support** concentrates on managing work-in-process inventory as it flows between stages of manufacturing. The primary logistical responsibility in manufacturing is to participate in formulating a master production schedule and to arrange for its implementation by timely availability of materials, component parts, and work-in-process inventory. Thus, the overall concern of manufacturing support is not how production occurs but rather *what, when,* and *where* products will be manufactured.

Manufacturing support is significantly different from market distribution. Market distribution attempts to service the desires of customers and therefore must accommodate the uncertainty of consumer and industrial demand. Manufacturing support involves movement requirements that are under the control of the manufacturing enterprise. The uncertainties introduced by random customer ordering and erratic demand that market distribution must accommodate are not typical in manufacturing operations. From the viewpoint of overall planning, the separation of manufacturing support from outbound market distribution and inbound procurement activities provides opportunities for specialization and improved efficiency. The degree to which a firm adopts a response strategy serves to reduce or eliminate the separation of manufacturing.

Procurement

Procurement is concerned with purchasing and arranging inbound movement of materials, parts, and/or finished inventory from suppliers to manufacturing or assembly plants, warehouses, or retail stores. Depending on the situation, the acquisition process is commonly identified by different names. In manufacturing, the process of acquisition is typically called *purchasing.* In government circles, acquisition has traditionally been referred to as *procurement.* In retailing and wholesaling, *buying* is the most widely used term. In many circles, the process is referred to as *inbound logistics.* For the purposes of this text, the term *procurement* will include all types of purchasing. The term *material* is used to identify inventory moving inbound to an enterprise, regardless of its degree of readiness for resale. The term *product* is used to identify inventory that is available for consumer purchase. In other words, materials are involved in the process of adding value through manufacturing whereas products are ready for consumption. The fundamental distinction is that products result from the value added to material during manufacture, sortation, or assembly.

Within a typical enterprise, the three logistics operating areas overlap. Viewing each as an integral part of the overall value-adding process creates an opportunity to capitalize on the unique attributes of each within the overall process. Table 2-2 provides a more exacting definition of the day-to-day work involved in each subprocess of logistics. The overall challenge of a supply chain is to integrate the logistical processes of participating firms in a manner that facilitates overall efficiency.

Information Flow

Information flow identifies specific locations within a logistical system that have requirements. Information also integrates the three operating areas. Within individual logistics areas, different movement requirements exist with respect to size of order, availability of inventory, and urgency of movement. The primary objective of information flow management is to reconcile these differentials to improve overall supply chain performance. It is important to stress that information requirements parallel the

TABLE 2-2   Specific Operating Concerns of Market Distribution, Manufacturing Support, and Procurement in Overall Logistics

Market Distribution

Activities related to providing customer service. Requires performing order receipt and processing, deploying inventories, storage and handling, and outbound transportation within a supply chain. Includes the responsibility to coordinate with marketing planning in such areas as pricing, promotional support, customer service levels, delivery standards, handling return merchandise, and life cycle support. The primary market distribution objective is to assist in revenue generation by providing strategically desired customer service levels at the lowest total cost.

Manufacturing Support

Activities related to planning, scheduling, and supporting manufacturing operations. Requires master schedule planning and performing work-in-process storage, handling, transportation, and sortation, sequencing and time phasing of components. Includes the responsibility for storage of inventory at manufacturing sites and maximum flexibility in the coordination of geographic and assembly postponement between manufacturing and market distribution operations.

Procurement

Activities related to obtaining products and materials from outside suppliers. Requires performing resource planning, supply sourcing, negotiation, order placement, inbound transportation, receiving and inspection, storage and handling, and quality assurance. Includes the responsibility to coordinate with suppliers in such areas as scheduling, supply continuity, hedging, and speculation, as well as research leading to new sources or programs. The primary procurement objective is to support manufacturing or resale organizations by providing timely purchasing at the lowest total cost.

actual work performed in market distribution, manufacturing support, and procurement. Whereas these areas contain the actual logistics work, information facilitates coordination of planning and control of day-to-day operations. Without accurate information the effort involved in the logistical system can be wasted.

Logistical information has two major components: planning/coordination and operations. The interrelationship of the two types of logistical information is illustrated in Figure 2-3. In-depth discussion of information technology is reserved for Part II, at which time the architecture of logistical information systems is developed in greater detail. The objective here is to introduce the framework that details information needed to manage integrated logistics.

Planning/Coordination

The overall purpose of planning/coordination is to identify required operational information and to facilitate supply chain integration via (1) strategic objectives, (2) capacity constraints, (3) logistical requirements, (4) inventory deployment, (5) manufacturing requirements, (6) procurement requirements, and (7) forecasting. Unless a high level of planning/coordination is achieved, the potential exists for operating inefficiencies and excessive inventory. The challenge is to achieve such planning/coordination across the range of firms participating in a supply chain to reduce duplication and unneeded redundancy.

The primary drivers of supply chain operations are **strategic objectives** derived from marketing and financial goals. These initiatives detail the nature and location of customers that supply chain operations seeks to match to the planned products and services. The financial aspects of strategic plans detail resources required to support inventory, receivables, facilities, equipment, and capacity.

FIGURE 2-3

Logistics information requirements

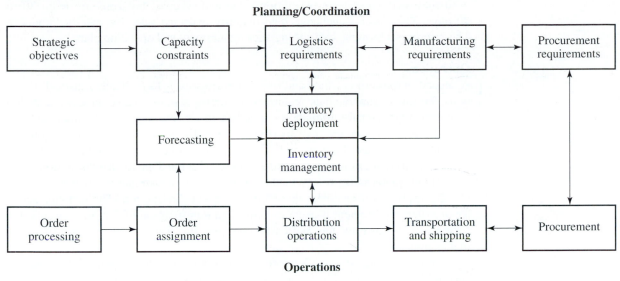

Capacity constraints identify internal and external manufacturing and market distribution limitations. Given strategic objectives, capacity constraints identify limitations, barriers, or bottlenecks within manufacturing and distribution facilities. It also helps identify when specific manufacturing or distribution work should be outsourced. To illustrate, whereas Kellogg owns the brand and distributes *Cracklin' Oat Bran,* all manufacturing is performed by a third party on a contract basis. The output of capacity constraint planning is time-phased objectives that detail and schedule facility utilization, financial resources, and human requirements.

Using inputs from forecasting, promotional scheduling, customer orders, and inventory status, **logistical requirements** identify the specific work facilities, equipment, and labor forces required to support the strategic plan.

Inventory deployment interfaces with inventory management between planning/coordination and operations, as shown in Figure 2-3. The deployment plan details the timing of where inventory will be positioned to efficiently move inventory through the supply chain. From an information perspective, deployment specifies the *what, where,* and *when* for the logistics processes. From an operational viewpoint, inventory management is performed on a day-to-day basis.

In production situations, **manufacturing requirements** determine planned schedules. The traditional deliverable is a statement of time-phased inventory requirements that is used to drive Master Production Scheduling (MPS) and Manufacturing Requirements Planning (MRP). In situations characterized by a high degree of responsiveness, Advance Planning Systems (APS) are more commonly used to time-phase manufacturing.

Procurement requirements represent a time-sequenced schedule of material and components needed to support manufacturing requirements. In retailing and wholesaling establishments, purchasing determines inbound merchandise. In manufacturing situations, procurement arranges for arrival of materials and component parts from suppliers. Regardless of the business situation, purchasing information is used to coordinate decisions concerning supplier qualifications, degree of desired speculation, third-party arrangements, and feasibility of long-term contracting.

Forecasting utilizes historical data, current activity levels, and planning assumptions to predict future activity levels. Logistical forecasting is generally concerned with relatively short-term predictions. Typical forecast horizons are from 30 to 90 days. The forecast challenge is to quantify expected sales for specific products. These forecasts form the basis of logistics requirement and operating plans.

Operations

A second purpose of accurate and timely information is to facilitate logistical operations. To satisfy supply chain requirements, logistics must receive, process, and ship inventory. Operational information is required in six related areas: (1) order processing, (2) order assignment, (3) distribution operations, (4) inventory management, (5) transportation and shipping, and (6) procurement. These areas of information facilitate the areas of logistical work outlined in Figure 2-1 and the related discussion.

Order processing refers to the exchange of requirements information between supply chain members involved in product distribution. The primary activity of order management is accurate entry and qualification of customer orders. Information technology has radically changed the traditional process of order management.

Order assignment identifies inventory and organizational responsibility to satisfy customer requirements. The traditional approach has been to assign responsibility or planned manufacturing to customers according to predetermined priorities. In technology-rich order processing systems, two-way communication linkage can be maintained with customers to generate a negotiated order that satisfies customers within the constraints of planned logistical operations.

Distribution operations involve information to facilitate and coordinate work within logistics facilities. Emphasis is placed on scheduling availability of the desired inventory assortment with minimal duplication and redundant work effort. The key to distribution operations is to store and handle specific inventory as little as possible while still meeting customer order requirements.

Inventory management is concerned with information required to implement the logistics plan. Using a combination of human resources and information technology, inventory is deployed and then managed to satisfy planned requirements. The work of inventory management is to make sure that the overall logistical system has appropriate resources to perform as planned.

Transportation and **shipping** information directs inventory movement. In distribution operations, it is important to consolidate orders so as to fully utilize transportation capacity. It is also necessary to ensure that the required transportation equipment is available when needed. Finally, because ownership transfer often results from transportation, supporting transaction documentation is required.

Procurement is concerned with the information necessary to complete purchase order preparation, modification, and release while ensuring overall supplier compliance. In many ways information related to procurement is similar to that involved in order processing. Both forms of information exchange serve to facilitate operations that link a firm with its customers and suppliers.

The overall purpose of operational information is to facilitate integrated management of market distribution, manufacturing support, and procurement operations. Planning/coordination identifies and prioritizes required work and identifies operational information needed to perform the day-to-day logistics. The dynamics of supply chain synchronization is discussed next.

Logistical Operating Arrangements

The potential for logistical services to favorably impact customers is directly related to operating system design. The many different facets of logistical performance requirements make operational design a complex task as an operating structure must offer a balance of performance, cost, and flexibility. When one considers the variety of logistical systems used throughout the world to service widely diverse markets, it is astonishing that any structural similarity exists. But keep in mind that all logistical arrangements have two common characteristics. First, they are designed to manage inventory. Second, the range of alternative logistics systems is based on available technology. These two characteristics tend to create commonly observed operating arrangements. Three widely utilized structures are echelon, direct, and flexible.

Echelon

Classification of a logistical system as having an echeloned structure means that the flow of products typically proceeds through a common arrangement of firms and facilities as it moves from origin to final destination. The use of echelons usually implies that total cost analysis justifies stocking some level of inventory or performing specific activities at consecutive levels of the supply chain.

Echelon systems utilize warehouses to create inventory assortments and achieve consolidation economies associated with large-volume transportation shipments. Inventories positioned in warehouses are available for rapid deployment to customer requirements. Figure 2-4 illustrates the typical echeloned value chain.

Typical echelon systems utilize either break-bulk or consolidation warehouses. A break-bulk facility typically receives large-volume shipments from a variety of suppliers. Inventory is sorted and stored in anticipation of future customer requirements. Food distribution centers operated by major grocery chains and wholesalers are examples of break-bulk warehouses. A consolidation warehouse operates in a reverse profile. Consolidation is typically required by manufacturing firms that have plants at different geographical locations. Products manufactured at different plants are stored in a central warehouse facility to allow the firm to ship full-line assortments to customers. Major consumer product manufacturers are prime examples of enterprises using echeloned systems for full-line consolidation.

Direct

In contrast to inventory echeloning are logistical systems designed to ship products direct to customer's destination from one or a limited number of centrally located inventories. Direct distribution typically uses premium transport combined with information technology to rapidly process customer orders and achieve delivery performance. This

FIGURE 2-4

Echelon-structured logistics

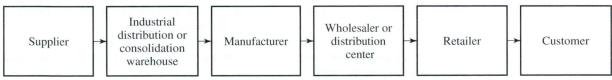

FIGURE 2-5

Echeloned and direct-structured logistics

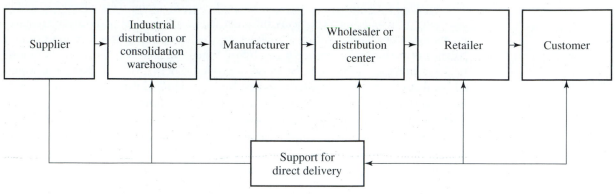

combination of capabilities, designed into the order delivery cycle, reduces time delays and overcomes geographical separation from customers. Examples of direct shipments are plant-to-customer truckload shipments, direct store delivery, and various forms of direct to consumer fulfillment required to support catalog and e-commerce shopping. Direct logistical structures are also commonly used for inbound components and materials to manufacturing plants because the average shipment size is typically large.

When the economics justify, logistics executives tend to desire direct alternatives because they reduce anticipatory inventories and intermediate product handling. The deployment of direct logistics is limited by high transportation cost and potential loss of control. In general, most firms do not operate the number of warehouses today that were common a few years ago and have been able to modify echelon structures to include direct logistics capabilities. Figure 2-5 illustrates direct logistics capability being added to an echeloned logistics structure.

Flexible

The ideal logistical arrangement is a situation wherein the inherent benefits of echeloned and direct structures are combined into a flexible logistics system. As noted in Chapter 1, anticipatory commitment of inventory should ideally be postponed as long as possible. Inventory strategies often position fast-moving products or materials in forward warehouses, while other, more risky or costly items, are stocked at a central location for direct distribution to customers. The basic service commitment and the order size economics determine the most desirable and economical structure to service a specific customer.

To illustrate, automobile replacement parts logistics typically distributes to customers utilizing a flexible logistics strategy. Specific parts are inventoried in warehouses located at various distances from dealers and retail outlets based on pattern and intensity of demand. As a general rule, the slower the part turnover is, the more erratic the demand is, and therefore the greater the benefit is of centralized inventory. The slowest or least demanded parts may only be stocked at one location that services customers throughout the entire world. Fast-moving parts that have more predictable demand are stocked in forward warehouses close to dealers to facilitate fast delivery.

A contrasting example is an enterprise that sells machine parts to industrial firms. The nature of this business supports a completely opposite flexible distribution strategy. To offer superior service to customers who experience machine failure and unexpected downtime, the firm stocks slow movers in all local warehouses. In contrast to the automotive firm, high-demand, fast-turnover parts in this industry can be accurately forecasted due to routine preventative maintenance. The least cost logistical methods for these fast movers are to ship direct from a centralized warehouse located adjacent to the parts manufacturing plant. These alternative logistics strategies, both of which use different flexible logistical capabilities, are justified based on unique customer requirements and intensity of competition confronted. The automotive manufacturer is the sole supplier of parts during the new car warranty period and must provide dealers rapid delivery of parts to promptly repair customer cars. Dealers require fast replenishment of parts inventory to satisfy customers while minimizing inventory investment. As cars grow older and the demand for replacement parts increases, alternative manufacturers enter the replacement parts market. During this highly competitive stage of the model's life cycle, rapid logistical response is required to be competitive. As a model ages, competition drops out of the shrinking aftermarket, leaving the original manufacturer as the sole supplier.

The industrial component supplier, in contrast to the automotive company, offers standard machine parts having a high degree of competitive substitutability. Whereas products used on a regular basis can be forecasted, slow or erratic demanded products are impossible to forecast. This enterprise forces a situation wherein customers measure suppliers in terms of how fast unexpected machine breakdowns can be remedied. Failure to perform to the level of customer expectation can open the door for a competitor to prove its capability.

Each enterprise faces a unique customer situation and can be expected to use a different flexible logistics strategy to achieve competitive superiority. The channel strategy that satisfies customer expectations at lowest attainable total cost typically utilizes a combination of echeloned and direct capabilities.

Beyond the basic channel structure, flexible capabilities can be designed into a logistical system by developing a program to service customers using alternative facilities. Flexible logistics capabilities can be designed to operate on an emergency or routine basis.

Emergency Flexible Structure

Emergency flexible operations are preplanned strategies to resolve logistical failures. A typical emergency occurs when an assigned shipping facility is out of stock or for some other reason cannot complete a customer's order. For example, a warehouse may be out of an item with no replenishment inventory scheduled to arrive until after the customer's specified order delivery date. To prohibit back-order or product cancellation, a contingency operating policy may assign the total order, or at least those items not available, for shipment from an alternative warehouse. The use of emergency flexible operation procedures is typically based on the importance of the specific customer or the critical nature of the product being ordered.

Routine Flexible Structure

A flexible logistics capability that has gained popularity as a result of improved communications involves procedures for serving specified customers developed as part of the basic logistical system design. The flexible logistics rules and decision scenarios specify alternative ways to meet service requirements, such as assignment of different shipping facilities. A strategy that exploits routine flexible operations may be justified in at least four different situations.

First, the customer-specified delivery location might be near a point of equal logistics cost or time for delivery from two different logistics facilities. Customers located at such points of indifference offer the supplying firm an opportunity to fully utilize available logistical capacity. Orders can be serviced from the facility having the best inventory positioning to satisfy customer requirements and the available capacity to achieve timely delivery. This form of flexible logistics offers a way to fully utilize system capacity by balancing workloads between facilities while protecting superior customer service commitments. The benefit is operating efficiency, which is transparent to the customer who experiences no service deterioration.

A second situation justifying routine flexible distribution is when the size of a customer's order creates an opportunity to improve logistical efficiency if serviced through an alternative channel arrangement. For example, the lowest-total-cost method to provide small shipment delivery may be through a distributor. In contrast, larger shipments may have the lowest total logistical cost when shipped factory direct to customers. Provided that alternative methods of shipment meet customer service expectations, total logistical cost may be reduced by implementing routine flexible policies.

A third type of routine flexible operations may result from a selective inventory stocking strategy. The cost and risk associated with stocking inventory require careful analysis to determine which items to place in each warehouse. With replacement parts, a common strategy mentioned earlier is to stock selected items in specific warehouses with the total line only being stocked at a central facility. In general merchandise retailing, a store or distribution center located in a small community may only stock a limited or restricted version of a firm's total line. When customers desire nonstocked items, orders must be satisfied from an alternative facility. The term *mother facility* is often used to describe inventory strategies that designate larger facilities for backup support of smaller restricted facilities. Selective inventory stocking by echelon level is a common strategy used to reduce inventory risk. The reasons for selective echelon stocking range from low product profit contribution to high per unit cost of inventory maintenance. One way to operationalize a fine-line inventory classification strategy is to differentiate stocking policy by system echelons. In situations following such classified stocking strategies it may be necessary to obtain advanced customer approval for split-order delivery. However, in some situations firms that use differentiated inventory stocking strategies are able to reconfigure customer orders for same time delivery, thereby making the arrangement customer transparent.

The *fourth* type of routine flexible operations results from agreements between firms to move selected shipments outside the established echeloned or direct logistics arrangements. Two special arrangements gaining popularity are flow through **cross-docks** and **service supplier arrangements.** A cross-dock operation involves multiple suppliers arriving at a designated time at the handling facility and is typically deployed in situations where storage and materials handling can be avoided. Inventory receipts are sorted across the dock and consolidated into outbound trailers for direct destination delivery. Cross-dock operations are growing in popularity in the food industry for building store-specific assortments and are common methods of continuous inventory replenishment for mass merchant and other retail stores.

Another form of routine flexible operations is to use integrated service providers to assemble products for delivery. This is similar to consolidation for transportation

FIGURE 2-6

Flexible direct echeloned structured logistics

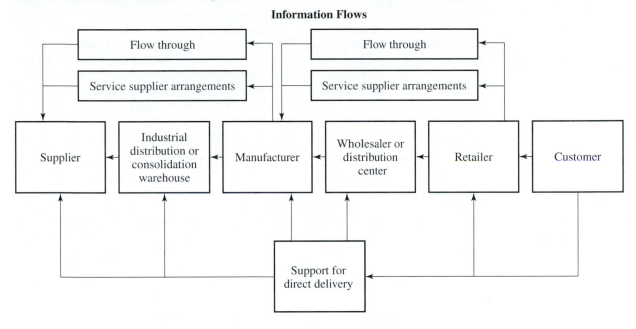

purposes discussed in the previous section of this chapter. However, as a form of flexible logistics, specialists are used to avoid storage and handling of slow-moving products through the mainstream of the echeloned logistics structure. Such service providers can also provide important value-added services. For example, Smurfit-Stone builds in-store point-of-sale displays for direct store delivery.

Figure 2-6 introduces flexibility to the logistical operating structures previously illustrated. A prerequisite to effective flexible operations is the use of information technology to monitor inventory status throughout the network and provide the capability to rapidly switch methods for handling customer orders. The use of flexible operations for emergency accommodation has a well-established track record. To a significant degree, an effective, flexible logistics strategy can substitute for the safety stock maintained in a traditional anticipatory-driven logistical system. As illustrated in Industry Insight 2-3, Biogen capitalized on flexible logistics and supply chain operations to secure a competitive edge.

The attractiveness of using integrated service providers is directly related to the designed flexibility of a firm's logistics strategy. If a firm elects to offer direct distribution, the services of highly reliable, fast transportation will be required. An echelon structure means that opportunities may exist for volume-oriented transportation and the services of firms that specialize in operating cross-docking facilities. A strategy that seeks the combined benefits of echeloned and direct logistics may be an ideal candidate for the integrated services of a third-party logistics specialist. It is important to keep in mind that the selected logistics strategy directly drives channel structure and relationships. To a significant degree, information technology is forcing reconsideration of long-standing practices regarding rigid ways of conducting business. These developments can be illustrated by an examination of managerial practices required to achieve internal and external integration of logistical operations.

Industry Insight 2-3 Biogen Unchained

When Biogen was founded in 1978, it had a simple, research-centered business model: its scientists would use biotechnology to discover compounds that might be used to create new drugs, and then it would license those compounds to big pharmaceutical companies. It had no need to build a manufacturing or distribution infrastructure because it didn't intend to actually produce drugs.

That business model was turned upside down in 1994 when the company received preliminary FDA approval to market Avonex, a breakthrough drug that could slow the progression of multiple sclerosis. Biogen suddenly had to find a way to get a product to customers quickly and dependably while building an efficient delivery system for the long term. The company embraced an entirely new way to organize and manage production and distribution. It would work with a network of partners to get its new product to market, becoming a virtual manufacturer.

The first step was to determine which tasks it would perform and which it would outsource. Biogen took a hard look at the four core tasks of drug production—bulk manufacturing, formulation, packaging, and warehousing and distribution—and determined that it could handle the bulk manufacturing at its existing facility. It would contract out everything else.

In choosing its partners, it looked for organizations that were big enough to accommodate rapid growth but small enough to give the Biogen account top priority. For formulation, which consisted of freeze-drying the drug and storing it at low temperatures, it chose Ben Venue Laboratories, a contract manufacturer in Ohio. Packaging Coordinators, a small but innovative company near Philadelphia, was given the job of packaging. And for warehousing and distribution, Biogen chose to partner with Amgen, which had a new distribution center in Louisville, Kentucky.

Biogen kept tight control over managing the network. It stationed some of its people at partners' sites, offered their staffs training and supervision, and installed new computer systems to manage the flow of shared information. It also set tough standards for the performance of the network, establishing world-class objectives for execution and quality and insisting on a goal of fulfilling every order without delay. The worst scenario would be to run out of the product. A shortage would not only hurt the patients who relied on the drug, but it would also undermine Biogen's profits. Because Avonex carried a high price—$1,000 for a month's supply—the cost of carrying inventory was tiny relative to the cost of a lost sale.

As the company waited for final FDA approval of Avonex, it worked with its partners to develop four detailed contingency plans for getting the drug to patients as quickly as possible.

Finally, at 11 AM on Friday, May 17, 1996, Biogen received FDA approval. The virtual organization worked seamlessly. The first shipments of Avonex reached pharmacy shelves within 35 hours—a new record for the pharmaceutical industry—and the drug was ready for dispensing by Monday morning. Within 6 months, Avonex had displaced Betaseron, another multiple sclerosis treatment drug introduced 3 years earlier, as the market leader, garnering more than 60 percent of new prescriptions.

The full value of the production and distribution network became apparent over time: between 1996 and 1999, the drug's production volume increased fivefold, and the virtual organization scaled up flawlessly to accommodate the growth. Avonex has never gone out of stock, and there have been no serious customer service problems or product recalls.

The outsourcing of key operational elements has enabled Biogen to achieve a competitive cost structure despite its limited production experience and small scale. It has also helped the company keep its fixed assets low, even when production volume increased dramatically. The required capital investment was modest relative to the size of the business, and much of the investment risk could be shared with partners.

Source: David Bovet and Joseph Martha, "Biogen Unchained," *Harvard Business Review,* May–June 2000, p. 28.

Logistical Synchronization

The previous discussion positioned logistics as an integrated management process within an individual firm. The challenge of supply chain management is to integrate operations across multiple firms that are jointly committed to the same value proposition. In an effort to facilitate logistical operations, supply chain participants must jointly plan and implement operations. Multifirm operational integration across a supply chain is referred to as **logistical synchronization.**

Logistical synchronization seeks to coordinate the flow of materials, products, and information between supply chain partners to reduce duplication and unwanted redundancy to an absolute minimum. It also seeks to reengineer internal operations of individual firms to create leveraged overall supply chain capability. Leveraged operations require a joint plan concerning the logistics work that each participating firm will perform and be held accountable for. At the heart of supply chain integration is the goal of leveraging member core competencies to achieve overall reduction of inventory dwell time.

As defined in Chapter 1, dwell time is the ratio of time inventory sits idle in comparison to the amount of time it is being productively moved to a desired location in the supply chain. To illustrate, a product or component stored in a warehouse is dwelling. In contrast, the same part moving in a transportation vehicle on the way to a customer is being productively deployed. Ideally, the shipment will arrive in a timely manner to be immediately used by the customer in a value-added process. The desire is to directly integrate inventory into the customer's value-adding process without product being placed in storage or otherwise restricting continuous movement. The benefits of synchronization serve to support the generalization that speed of performing a specific service or product movement is secondary to synchronizing the timing of supply with demand requirements.

Performance Cycle Structure

The performance cycle represents the elements of work necessary to complete the logistics related to market distribution, manufacturing, or support procurement. It consists of specific work ranging from identification of requirements to product delivery. Because it integrates various aspects of work, the performance cycle is the primary unit of analysis for logistical synchronization. At a basic level, information and transportation must *link* all firms functioning in a supply chain. The operational locations that are linked by information and transportation are referred to as **nodes.**

In addition to supply chain nodes and links, performance cycles involve inventory assets. Inventory is measured in terms of the **asset investment level** allocated to support operations at a node or while a product or material is in transit. Inventory committed to supply chain nodes consists of base stock and safety stock. Base stock is inventory held at a node and is typically one-half of the average shipment size received. Safety stock exists to protect against variance in demand or operational lead time. It is *at* and *between* supply chain nodes that work related to logistics is performed. Inventory is stocked and flows through nodes, necessitating a variety of different types of materials handling and, when necessary, storage. While a degree of handling and in-transit storage takes place within transportation, such activity is minor in comparison to that typically performed within a supply chain node, such as a warehouse.

Performance cycles become dynamic as they accommodate **input/output requirements.** The *input* to a performance cycle is demand, typically in the form of a work order that specifies requirements for a product or material. A high-volume supply chain will typically require a different and wider variety of performance cycles than a chain having fewer throughputs. When operating requirements are highly predictable or relatively low-volume throughput, the performance cycle structure required to provide supply chain logistical support can be simplified. The performance cycle structures required to support a large retail enterprise like Target or Wal★Mart supply chains are far more complex than the operating structure requirements of a catalog fulfillment company.

Supply chain *output* is the level of performance expected from the combined logistical operations that support a particular arrangement. To the extent that operational requirements are satisfied, the combined logistical performance cycle structure of the supply chain is effective in accomplishing its mission. Efficiency of a supply chain is a measure of resource expenditure necessary to achieve such logistical effectiveness. The effectiveness and efficiency of logistical performance cycles are key concerns in supply chain management.

Depending on the operational mission of a particular performance cycle in a supply chain structure, the associated work may be under the complete control of a single enterprise or may involve multiple firms. For example, manufacturing support cycles are often under the operational control of a single enterprise. In contrast, performance cycles related to market distribution and procurement typically involve multiple firms.

It is important to realize that transaction frequency and intensity will vary between performance cycles. Some performance cycles are established to facilitate a one-time purchase or sale. In such a case, the associated supply chain is designed, implemented, and abolished once the transaction is complete. Other performance cycles represent long-standing structural arrangements. A complicating fact is that any operation or facility in one logistical arrangement may simultaneously be participating in a number of other performance cycles. For example, the warehouse facility of a hardware wholesaler might regularly receive merchandise from multiple manufacturers and service competing retailers. Likewise, a motor carrier may participate in numerous different supply chains, spanning a wide variety of industries.

When one considers a supply chain of national or multinational scope that is involved in marketing a broad product line to numerous customers, engaging in basic manufacturing and assembly, and procuring materials and components on a global basis, the notion of individual performance cycles linking all participating firms' operations is difficult to comprehend. It is almost mind-boggling to estimate how many performance cycles exist in the supply chain structure of General Motors or IBM.

Regardless of the number and different missions of performance cycles a supply chain deploys to satisfy its logistical requirements, each must be individually designed and operationally managed. The fundamental importance of performance cycle design and operation cannot be overemphasized: *The logistics performance cycle is the basic unit of supply chain design and operational control. In essence, the performance cycle structure is the framework for implementation of integrated logistics across the supply chain.*

Figure 2-7 portrays an echeloned supply chain structure illustrating basic logistics performance cycles. Figure 2-8 illustrates a network of flexible performance cycles integrated in a multiecheloned structure.

Three points are important to understanding the architecture of integrated supply chain logistical systems. First, as noted earlier, the performance cycles are the fundamental unit for integrated logistics across the supply chain. Second, the performance cycle structure of a supply chain, in terms of link and nodal arrangement, is basically

FIGURE 2-7

Logistical performance cycles

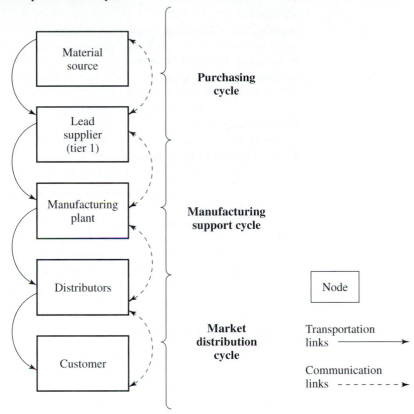

FIGURE 2-8

Multi-echeloned flexible logistical network

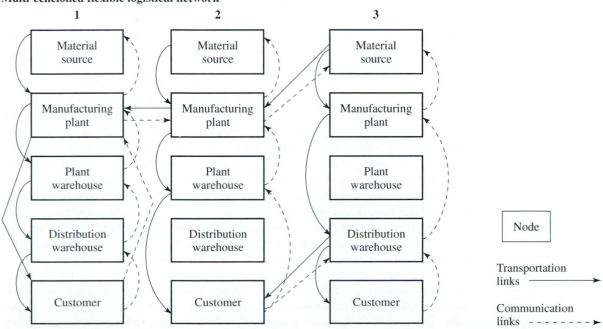

FIGURE 2-9

Basic market distribution performance cycle activities

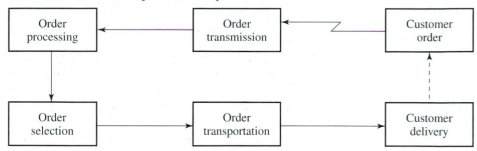

the same whether one is concerned with market distribution, manufacturing support, or procurement. However, considerable differences exist in the degree of control that an individual firm can exercise over a specific type of performance cycle. Third, regardless of how vast and complex the overall supply chain structure, essential interfaces and control processes must be identified and evaluated in terms of individual performance cycle arrangements and associated managerial accountability.

To better understand the importance of synchronization in supply chain integration, the similarities and differences in market distribution, manufacturing support, and procurement performance cycles are discussed and illustrated.

Market Distribution Performance Cycles

Market distribution operations are concerned with processing and delivering customer orders. Market distribution is integral to sales performance because it provides timely and economical product availability. The overall process of gaining and maintaining customers can be broadly divided into transaction-creating and physical-fulfillment activities. The transaction-creating activities are advertising and selling. The physical-fulfillment activities include (1) order transmission, (2) order processing, (3) order selection, (4) order transportation, and (5) customer delivery. The basic market distribution performance cycle is illustrated in Figure 2-9. From a logistical perspective, market distribution performance cycles link a supply chain with end customers. This interface can be conflictive.

Marketing is dedicated to satisfying customers to achieve the highest possible sales penetration. So, in most firms, marketing and sales impose liberal policies when it comes to accommodating customers. This may mean that marketing and sales will typically seek broad product assortments supported with high inventory or that all customer requirements, no matter how small or how profitable, will be satisfied. The marketing expectation is that zero logistical defect service will be achieved across the supply chain and customer-focused marketing efforts will be supported.

On the other hand, the traditional mindset in manufacturing is to achieve lowest possible unit cost, which typically is achieved by long, stable production runs. Continuous manufacturing processes maintain economy of scale and generate lowest per unit cost. Ideally, in continuous processing, a narrow line of products is mass-produced. Inventory serves to buffer and resolve the inherent conflict between these traditional marketing and manufacturing philosophies. The commitment of inventory to reconcile marketing and manufacturing has typically meant positioning it forward in the supply chain in anticipation of future sale. Products are shipped to warehouses based on forecasted requirements, acknowledging they might be moved to the wrong market and at the wrong time. The end result of such risky decisions is that critical inventory can be improperly deployed in an attempt to efficiently support customer service requirements. At this point, the important concept to keep in mind is that the market distribution performance cycle operates downstream in the supply chain forward from manufacturing and close to end customer. Inventories committed to market distribution, when correctly positioned, represent the maximum potential value that can be achieved by the logistical process.

The very fact that market distribution deals with customer requirements means that this facet of supply chain operations will be more erratic than either manufacturing support or procurement performance cycles. Attention to *how* customers order products is essential to reduce market distribution operational variance and simplify transactions. First, every effort should be made to improve forecast accuracy. Second, a program based on collaborative planning with customers should be initiated to reduce as much uncertainty as possible. Third, and finally, market distribution performance cycles should be designed to be as responsive as possible, which might include implementation of postponement strategies.

The key to understanding market distribution performance-cycle dynamics is to keep in mind that customers initiate the supply chain process when they order products. The agility and flexibility of response related to market distribution constitutes one of logistics' most significant competencies.

Manufacturing Support Performance Cycles

Manufacturing is the node in a supply chain that creates *form* value. To a significant degree, manufacturing efficiency depends on logistical support to establish and maintain an orderly and economic flow of materials and work-in-process inventory as required by production schedules. The degree of specialization required in market distribution and procurement can overshadow the importance of positioning and timing inventory movement to support manufacturing. Because customers and suppliers are not involved, manufacturing logistics is less visible than its counterparts.

The identification of manufacturing logistical support as a distinct operating area is a relatively new concept. The justification for focusing on performance cycles to support production is found in the unique requirements and operational constraints of flexible manufacturing strategies. To provide maximum flexibility, traditional manufacturing practices related to economy of scale are being reevaluated to accommodate quick product switchover and shorter production runs. Exacting logistical support between supply chain participants is required to perfect such time-sensitive manufacturing strategies. It is important to once again stress that the mission of logistical manufacturing support is to facilitate the *what, where,* and *when* of production, not the how. The goal is to support all manufacturing requirements in the most efficient manner.

Manufacturing support operations are significantly different than either market distribution or procurement. Manufacturing support logistics is typically captive within individual firms, whereas the other two performance areas must deal with the behavioral uncertainty across the supply chain. Even in situations when outsource contract manufacturing is used to augment internal capacity, overall control of a single enterprise is greater than in the other two operating areas. The benefits to be gained by exploitation of this control opportunity are the prime justification for treating manufacturing logistical support as a distinct operating area.

A recently introduced practice that is rapidly growing is to use **lead suppliers** to coordinate and facilitate the work of a group of related manufacturing suppliers. These related suppliers may produce similar or complementary products that are used to produce a subassembly that is part of a more complex product. The term *tier one* supplier is frequently used to describe the positioning of lead suppliers between a major manufacturer and suppliers of specific parts or components. The purpose of the lead supplier is to reduce the overall complexity of managing the supply chain. It is common for lead suppliers to be awarded contracts to perform subassembly operations, coordinate inbound movements, and oversee the work and quality of smaller suppliers. The lead supplier is delegated the responsibility of sorting, assembly, and sequencing subassemblies to support manufacturing. In such situations, the logistics of procurement and manufacturing are combined. The acronym JIT, which stands for Just-in-Time, evolved from an early effort at this type of supply chain synchronization by the Toyota Motor Car Company.[5]

Within a typical manufacturing organization, procurement has the responsibility to provide materials and outsourced manufactured components when and where needed. Once a firm's manufacturing operation is initiated, subsequent requirements for interplant movement of materials or semifinished products become the responsibility of manufacturing support. Manufacturing logistical support involves dock-to-dock movement and any intermediate storage required but typically does not include materials handling that is integral to in-plant assembly or production. When the manufacturing process is completed, finished inventory is allocated and deployed either directly to customers or to distribution warehouses for subsequent shipment to customers or customization. At the time of this movement, market distribution operations are initiated.

When a supply chain includes multiple plants that specialize in specific production activities, the manufacturing support system may contain a complex network of performance cycles. To the extent that specialized plants perform unique stages of production and fabrication prior to final assembly, numerous handlings and transfers may be required to complete the manufacturing process. It is the job of manufacturing logistics to perform this support process. In select situations, the complexity of manufacturing support may exceed that of market distribution or procurement.

Procurement Performance Cycles

Several activities or tasks are required to facilitate an orderly flow of materials, parts, or finished inventory along a supply chain: (1) sourcing, (2) order placement and expediting, (3) transportation, and (4) receiving. These activities, as illustrated in Figure 2-10, are required to complete the procurement process. Once materials, parts, or resale products are received, the subsequent storage, handling, and transportation requirements to facilitate either manufacturing or market distribution are appropriately provided by other performance cycles. Because of the focus on external supplies, this facet of procurement is referred to as *inbound logistics.* As shown in Industry Insight 2-4, Lands' End utilizes superior inbound logistics to achieve successful overall logistical performance.

With three important differences, the procurement performance cycle is similar to the market distribution cycle. First, delivery time, size of shipment, method of transport, and value of products involved are substantially different in procurement. Procurement often involves very large shipments, which may use barge, deep-water vessels, unit trains, and multiple truckloads for transport. Many materials and components

---

[5]See Richard J. Shonberger, *Japanese Manufacturing Techniques* (New York, NY: Macmillan Free Press, 1982); George C. Jackson, "Just in Time Production: Implications for Logistics Managers," *Journal of Business Logistics* 4, no. 2 (1983); and Richard J. Ackonberger, *Japanese Manufacturing Techniques, Nine Hidden Lessons in Simplicity* (New York, NY: The Free Press, 1982).

FIGURE 2-10

Procurement cycle activities

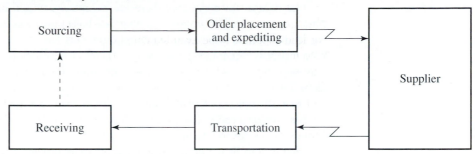

INDUSTRY INSIGHT 2-4 INBOUND OPERATIONS AT LANDS' END

Lands' End is one of the best-known mail-order companies because of its focus on high-quality merchandise, excellent product guarantees, and quick service. Serving a customer base of 6 million out of a 500,000 square foot distribution center in Dodgeville, Wisconsin, is not an easy task. Lands' End manages the extensive operation with two phone centers and 900 order operators. Much of its success is attributed to the company's inbound logistics system.

Lands' End works with some 250 suppliers that manufacture and merchandise products to meet specific, high-quality specifications. Furthermore, Lands' End has developed partnerships with inbound carriers as well. Lands' End produces 13 catalogs every year, which equates to one each month plus a special Christmas issue. Each catalog is filled with new products, seasonal items, and a variety of choices in clothing, luggage, bedding, and bath products.

To make this selection available, Lands' End sets strict operating goals for its procurement performance cycle. The main goal is to ensure that all merchandise offered in an upcoming catalog is available at the Dodgeville distribution center before final mailing of the catalog. This enables Lands' End to deliver customer orders within 24 hours, even on the first day the catalog arrives at the customer's home.

To achieve this goal, Lands' End concentrates on quality with its suppliers and carriers. In terms of supplier relations, Lands' End performs extensive quality inspection upon material receipt and sends teams to suppliers' facilities to assess their operations and offer suggestions for improvements. Furthermore, all suppliers are given a manual that explains Lands' End requirements and specifications for quality merchandise.

In terms of carriers, Lands' End controls all inbound transportation movements. This control allows it to develop partnership arrangements with key carriers to reduce costs by consolidating volumes and distances. In addition, Lands' End shares information by allowing electronic linkage between specific carriers and its Dodgeville distribution center.

Lands' End feels that its outbound success, achieved through a superior physical distribution system, is directly related to its successful inbound system. The efficient and cost-effective procurement process is maintained by concentrating on quality and partnerships with the inbound value chain.

Source: Deborah Catalano Ruriani, "Where Perfection Begins," *Inbound Logistics,* November 1992, pp. 20–23.

may be purchased internationally. While exceptions do exist, the typical goal in procurement is to focus on achieving inbound logistics at the lowest cost. The lower value of materials and parts in contrast to finished products means that a greater potential trade-off exists between cost of maintaining inventory in transit and time required to use low-cost modes of transport. Unless faced with an unexpected requirement, there is normally no benefit for paying premium rates for faster inbound transport. Therefore, performance cycles in purchasing are typically longer than those associated with market distribution of finished products.

Of course, for every rule there are exceptions. When high-value components are employed in manufacturing or in response-based business models, emphasis typically shifts to smaller purchases of exact requirements for arrival at precise times. Such precision logistics requires positive control. In such situations, the value of the material or component might justify the use of premium high-speed and reliable transportation delivery.

For example, a plant that manufacturers cake mix typically uses large quantities of flour in its production process. Since flour in bulk is relatively inexpensive, it makes sense for the firm to purchase flour in extremely large quantities that are shipped by rail. It would not make a lot sense to purchase small quantities, losing the bulk quantity price discount, and pay the high cost of small transportation shipments. In contrast, an automotive customizer buying electronic sunroofs might purchase on an as-required basis. Sunroof packages are significantly different for every car, and each package is relatively expensive. As such, the customizer is likely to order individual units to avoid holding inventory and be willing to pay premium transportation for fast delivery.

A second unique feature of purchasing is that the number of suppliers involved in a supply chain is typically less than the end-customer base it services. This difference was illustrated in Industry Insight 2-4. Lands' End has a customer base of over 6 million, but only deals with about 250 suppliers. In market distribution operations, each firm is only one of many participants in an overall supply chain. In contrast, the procurement performance cycle is usually more direct. Materials and parts are often purchased directly from either the original manufacturer or a specialized industrial wholesaler.

Finally, since the customer order processing cycle handles orders in response to customers' requirements, random ordering is a common situation in market distribution. In contrast, the procurement system initiates orders. The ability to determine when and where products are purchased serves to substantially reduce operational variance.

These three major differences in procurement, as contrasted to the market distribution order cycle, permit more orderly programming of logistical activities. The major uncertainty in procurement is the potential of price changes or supply discontinuity. A final feature of performance cycle synchronization critical to all facets of logistics is **operational uncertainty.**

Performance Cycle Uncertainty

A major objective of logistics in all operating areas is to reduce performance cycle uncertainty. The dilemma is that the structure of the performance cycle itself, operating conditions, and the quality of logistical operations all combine randomly to introduce operational variance.

Figure 2-11 illustrates the type and magnitude of variance that can develop in performance cycle operations. The performance cycle illustration is limited to finished goods inventory delivery. The time distributions, as illustrated, statistically reflect performance history for each task of a typical performance cycle. The diagram illustrates the minimum to maximum time historically required to complete each task and the related time distribution for the overall performance cycle. The vertical dashed line reflects the average time for performance of each task.

FIGURE 2-11

Performance cycle uncertainty

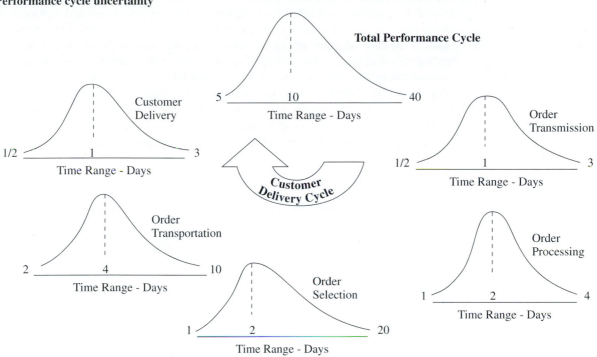

In terms of specific tasks, the variance results from the nature of the work involved. Order transmission is highly reliable when electronic transfer (EDI) or Web-based communications are used and more erratic when using telephone or routine mail. Regardless of the level of technology deployed, operational variance will occur as a result of daily changes in workload and resolution of unexpected events.

Time and variance related to order processing are a function of workload, degree of automation, and policies related to credit approval. Order selection, speed, and associated delay are directly related to capacity, materials handling sophistication, and human resource availability. When a product is out of stock, the time to complete order selection includes manufacturing scheduling. The required transportation time is a function of distance, shipment size, type of transport, and operating conditions. Final delivery to customers can vary depending on authorized receiving times, delivery appointments, workforce availability, and specialized unloading and equipment requirements.

In Figure 2-11 the history of total order-to-delivery time performance ranged from 5 to 40 days. The 5-day cycle reflects the unlikely event that each task is performed at the fastest possible time. The 40-day cycle represents the equally unlikely opposite extreme wherein each task required maximum time. The planned or target order-to-delivery cycle performance is to control combined variance so that actual operations meet a specific time goal as often as possible. Whenever actual performance is more or less than 10 days, managerial action may be necessary to satisfy customer requirements. Such expediting and de-expediting require extra resources and reduce overall logistical efficiency.

The goal of performance cycle synchronization is to achieve the planned time performance. Delayed performance at any point along the supply chain results in potential disruption of operations. Such delays require that safety stocks be established to cover variances. When performance occurs faster than expected, unplanned work will be required to handle and store inventory that arrives early. Given the inconvenience and expense of either early or late delivery, it is no wonder that logistics managers place a premium on operational consistency. Once consistent operations are achieved, every effort should be made to reduce the time required to complete the performance cycle to a minimum. In other words, shorter cycles are desirable because they reduce total assets deployed. However, speed is only a valid goal if it is consistent. Given consistency as the primary goal, faster order cycles reduce inventory risk and improve turn performance.

Summary

Logistics is the process that links supply chains into integrated operations. The cost of performing logistics is a major expenditure for most businesses.

Logistical service is measured in terms of availability, operational performance, and service reliability. Each aspect of service is framed in terms of customer expectations and requirements. Lean logistics is all about providing the essential customer service attributes at the lowest possible total cost. Such customer commitment, in an exacting cost framework, is the logistics value proposition.

The actual work of logistics is functional in nature. Facility locations must be established to form a network, information must be formulated and shared, transportation must be arranged, inventory must be deployed, and, to the extent required, warehousing, materials handling, and packaging activities must be performed. The traditional orientation was to perform each functional task as well as possible with limited consideration given to how one work area impacted another. Because the work of logistics is extremely detailed and complex, there is a natural tendency to focus on performing functions. While functional excellence is important, it must be supportive of overall logistical competency.

The functions of logistics combine into the three primary operational processes of market distribution, manufacturing support, and procurement. To achieve internal integration, the inventory and information flows between these areas must be coordinated.

In supply chain synchronization, the operational focus is the logistics performance cycle. The performance cycle is also the primary unit of analysis in logistical design. The performance cycle structure provides the logic for combining the nodes, levels, links, and allocation of assets essential to performing market distribution, manufacturing support, and procurement operations. Many similarities and a number of critical differences exist among performance cycles dedicated to these vital logistics operating areas. Fully understanding these similarities and differences is vital to planning and controlling overall supply chain integration. The basic proposition is that regardless of size and complexity, logistical integration is best understood and evaluated by the structure and dynamics of performance cycle.

The primary goal is to achieve consistency. The challenge is to design a supply chain capable of performing the required logistical work as rapidly but, even more important, as consistently as possible. Unexpected delays, as well as faster than expected performance, can combine to increase or decrease the elapsed time required to complete a performance cycle. Both early and late delivery are undesirable and unaccept-able from an operational perspective.

Chapter 2 has developed some important foundations of the logistical discipline and how it creates value in a supply chain context. These insights regarding the nature of logistics work, the importance of achieving internal operational integration through managing inventory and information flow, viewing the performance cycle structure as the basic unit of analysis, and the management of operational uncertainty combine to form a logically consistent set of concepts essential to supporting supply chain manage-ment. Chapter 3 focuses on customer requirements that drive supply chain performance.

Challenge Questions

1. Illustrate a common trade-off that occurs between the work areas of logistics.
2. Discuss and elaborate on the following statement: "The selection of a superior location network can create substantial competitive advantage."
3. Why are market distribution operations typically more erratic than manufacturing support and procurement operations?
4. How has transportation cost, as a percentage of total logistics cost, tracked since 1980?
5. Describe the *logistics value proposition.* Be specific regarding specific customer accommodation and cost.
6. Describe the fundamental similarities and differences between procurement, manufacturing support, and market distribution performance cycles as they relate to logistical control.
7. Compare and contrast a performance cycle node and a link. Give an example of each.
8. How does the "quest for quality" affect logistical operations? Does the concept of total quality have relevancy when applied to logistics?
9. Discuss uncertainty as it relates to the overall logistical performance cycle. Discuss and illustrate how performance cycle variance can be controlled.
10. What is the logic of designing echeloned logistical structures? Can echeloned and direct structures be combined?

3   CUSTOMER ACCOMMODATION

While in some ways it's an insight into the obvious, it is important to establish initially that logistics contributes to an organization's success by accommodating customers' delivery and availability expectations and requirements. What is not so obvious, however, is what exactly is meant by the term *customer*. The supply chain management concept requires careful consideration of just what is meant by the term and realization that there are many different perspectives.

From the perspective of the total supply chain, the ultimate customer is the end user of the product or service whose needs or requirements must be accommodated. It has historically been useful to distinguish between two types of end users. The first is a **consumer,** an individual or a household who purchases products and services to satisfy personal needs. When a family purchases an automobile to be used for personal transportation, that family is the consumer of the supply chain. The second type is an

organizational end user. Purchases are made by organizations or institutions to allow an end user to perform a task or job in the organization. When a company buys an automobile for a sales person or buys tools to be used by an assembly worker in a manufacturing plant, the company is considered to be a customer and the salesperson or assembly worker is the end user of the supply chain's products. A supply chain management perspective demands that all firms in the supply chain focus on meeting the needs and requirements of end users, whether they are consumers or organizational end users.

Another perspective of customer exists for a specific firm within the supply chain. This perspective recognizes that intermediate organizations often exist between the firm and end users. Common terminology generally recognizes these organizations as **intermediate customers.** Thus, in the Procter & Gamble (P&G) supply chain that provides Tide laundry detergent to ultimate consumers, Kroger and Safeway supermarkets are intermediate customers; they purchase Tide from P&G for the purpose of reselling to ultimate consumers.

Finally, for a logistician, a customer is any delivery location. Typical destinations range from consumers' homes to retail and wholesale businesses to the receiving docks of manufacturing plants and distribution centers. In some cases the customer is a different organization or individual who is taking ownership of the product or service being delivered. In many other situations the customer is a different facility of the same firm or a business partner at some other location in the supply chain. For example, it is common for the logistics manager of a retail distribution center to think of the individual stores to be serviced as customers of the distribution center, even though the stores are part of the same organization.

Regardless of the motivation and delivery purpose, the customer being serviced is the focal point and driving force in establishing logistical performance requirements. It is critical to fully understand customer needs that must be accommodated in establishing logistical strategy. This chapter details the nature of various approaches to accommodating customer requirements. The first section presents the fundamental concepts that underlie customer-focused marketing, with consideration of how logistics fits into a firm's overall marketing strategy. The second section describes the nature of the outputs of the supply chain to end users and how these outputs must be structured to meet their requirements. The sections that follow expand upon increasing levels of sophistication in accommodating customers. These levels range from traditional notions of logistics customer service to satisfaction of customers by meeting their expectations to the ultimate in accommodation—helping customers be successful by meeting their business requirements.

Customer-Focused Marketing

The basic principles of customer-focused marketing have their roots in the **marketing concept**—a business philosophy that suggests that the focal point of a business's strategy must be the customers it intends to serve. It holds that for an organization to achieve its goals, it must be more effective than competitors in identifying specific customer needs and focusing resources and activities on accommodating these customer requirements. Clearly, many aspects of a firm's strategy must be integrated to accommodate customers, and logistics is only one of these. The marketing concept builds on four fundamental ideas: customer needs and requirements are more basic than products or services; different customers have different needs and requirements;

products and services become meaningful only when available and positioned from the customer's perspective, which is the focus of logistics strategies; and volume is secondary to profit.

The belief that customer needs are more basic than products or services places a priority on fully understanding what drives market opportunities. The key is to understand and develop the combination of products and services that will meet those requirements. For example, if customers only require a choice of three different colored appliances, it makes little sense to offer six colors. It also makes little sense to try to market only white appliances if color selection is important from a customer's perspective. The basic idea is to develop sufficient insight into basic needs so that products and services can be matched to these opportunities. Successful marketing begins with in-depth study of customers to identify product and service requirements.

The second fundamental aspect of the marketing concept is that there is no single market for any given product or service. All markets are composed of different segments, each of which has somewhat different requirements. Effective market segmentation requires that firms clearly identify segments and select specific targets. While a comprehensive discussion of market segmentation is beyond the scope of this text, it is important to note that customers' logistical requirements frequently offer an effective basis for classification. For example, a contractor building new homes may place an order for appliances several weeks before needed for installation, while a consumer buying a replacement for a broken appliance may require immediate availability and delivery. It is unlikely that a company can operate in every market segment or profitably fulfill every possible combination of customer requirements; thus careful matching of capabilities with specific segments is an essential aspect of the marketing concept.

For marketing to be successful, products and services must be available to customers. In other words, the third fundamental aspect of marketing is that customers must be readily able to obtain the products they desire. To facilitate purchase action, the selling firm's resources need to be focused on customers and product positioning. Four economic utilities add value to customers: *form, possession, time,* and *place.* The product's form is for the most part generated in the manufacturing process. For example, form utility results from the assembly of parts and components for a dishwasher. In the case of a service such as a haircut, form utility is accomplished with the completion of specified activities such as shampooing, cutting, and styling. Marketing creates possession by informing potential customers of product/service availability and enabling ownership exchange. Thus, marketing serves to identify and convey the attributes of the product or service and to develop mechanisms for buyer–seller exchange. Logistics provides time and place utility requirements. Essentially, this means that logistics must ensure that the product is available when and where desired by customers. The achievement of time and place requires significant effort and is expensive. Profitable transactions materialize only when all four utilities are combined in a manner relevant to customers.

The fourth aspect of the marketing concept is the focus on profitability as contrasted to sales volume. An important dimension of success is the degree of profitability resulting from relationships with customers, not the volume sold. Therefore, variations in all four basic utilities—form, possession, time, and place—are justified if a customer or segment of customers value and are willing to pay for the modification. Using the appliance example, if a customer requests a unique color option and is willing to pay extra, then the request can and should be accommodated, providing a positive contribution margin can be earned. The final refinement of marketing strategy is based on an acknowledgment that all aspects of a product/service offering are subject to modification when justifiable on the basis of profitability.

Transactional versus Relationship Marketing

Traditional marketing strategies focus on obtaining successful exchanges, or transactions, with customers to drive increases in revenue and profit. In this approach, termed **transactional marketing,** companies are generally oriented toward short-term interaction with their customers. The traditional marketing concept emphasizes accommodating customers' needs and requirements, something few business organizations would argue with. However, as practiced in many firms, the result is a focus on creating successful individual transactions between a supplier and its customers. Further, the practice of segmentation and target marketing generally results in rather large groupings of customers, each having somewhat similar needs and requirements. In this approach to marketing *undifferentiated, differentiated,* and *niche* strategies are common.

An undifferentiated strategy views all potential customers as if they are essentially the same. While the organization may go through the process of segmentation, it ultimately *averages* the customers' needs and then tries to design a product and process that will meet the needs of the average customer. This allows the firm to streamline its manufacturing, market distribution, logistics, and promotional efforts to obtain cost efficiencies. For many years, Coca-Cola had only one cola product, Regular Coke, which was intended to satisfy the needs of all cola drinkers. For many years UPS followed a similar one-size-fits-all strategy in parcel delivery. Customers benefit from low-cost operations but many may not be fully satisfied due to the supplier's inability to satisfy unique requirements.

In a differentiated strategy, a firm targets multiple market segments, serving each with a product/service and market distribution process matched to more specifically meet that segment's unique needs and requirements. Coca-Cola today offers Diet Coke, Caffeine-free Coke, Cherry Coke, etc. When Federal Express entered the market for parcel distribution, UPS responded by developing a capability to meet the needs of shippers who required more rapid and controlled delivery. The result was different offerings to different market segments. While a differentiated strategy increases organizational complexity and cost, it allows a firm to accommodate more specifically the requirements of different customer groups.

A niche strategy is frequently utilized by small firms or new companies that choose to target one segment out of the overall market by offering very precise services. In the soft drink industry, Jolt Cola exists for those few customers who desire high sugar and high caffeine content. In parcel delivery, several small firms focus on customers who require same-day delivery.

Paralleling the development of the supply chain management concept, there has been a shift in philosophy regarding the nature of marketing strategy. This shift has generally been acknowledged as **relationship marketing.** Relationship marketing focuses on the development of long-term relations with key supply chain participants such as end users, intermediate customers, and suppliers in an effort to develop and retain long-term preference and loyalty. Relationship marketing is based on the realization that in many industries it is more important to retain current customers and gain a larger share of their purchases than it is to go out and attempt to attract new customers.[1]

The ultimate in market segmentation and relationship marketing is to focus on the individual customer. This approach, referred to as *micromarketing* or *one-to-one marketing,* recognizes that each individual customer may indeed have unique requirements.

---

[1]Thomas O. Jones and W. Earl Sasser, Jr., "Why Satisfied Customers Defect," *Harvard Business Review,* November/December 1995, pp. 88–99.

For example, although Wal★Mart and Target are both mass merchandisers, their requirements in terms of how they desire to interact logistically with suppliers differ significantly. A manufacturer who wants to do business with both of these major retailers must adapt its logistical operations to the unique needs of each. The best way to ensure long-term organizational success is to intensely research and then accommodate the requirements of individual customers.[2] Such relationships may not be feasible with every customer. It is also true that many customers may not desire this close relationship with all suppliers. However, one-to-one relationships can significantly reduce transaction costs, better accommodate customer requirements, and move individual transactions into a matter of routine.

There are four steps involved in implementing a one-to-one marketing program. The first is to identify the individual customers for the company's products and services. As simple as this may seem, many companies still tend to think in terms of groups of customers rather than individual customers.

The second step is to differentiate the customers, both in terms of value to the organization and in terms of their unique requirements. Clearly, all customers do not represent the same potential sales volume or profitability. Successful one-to-one marketers focus their efforts on those customers who represent the greatest potential return. Understanding differential customer needs provides the foundation for customization of products and services.

The third step involves the actual interaction with customers with the goal of improving both cost-efficiency and effectiveness. For example, cost-efficiency might be improved by automating routine interactions such as order placement or requests for information. Effectiveness can be improved by understanding that each interaction with a customer occurs in the context of all previous interactions.

Ultimately, one-to-one marketing is operationalized in the fourth step, customizing the organization's behavior. The company must adapt some aspect of its behavior to the customer's individually expressed needs. Whether it means customizing a manufactured product or tailoring services, such as customer packaging or delivery, the production and/or service end of the business must be able to deal with a particular customer in an individual manner.[3] Industry Insight 3-1 describes how Square D, a manufacturer of electrical equipment, has implemented relationship and one-to-one marketing with its key customers.

Supply Chain Service Outputs

Understanding customer-focused marketing in a supply chain context requires consideration of the services actually provided to end customers. Bucklin presented a long-standing theory that specifies four generic service outputs necessary to accommodate customer requirements: (1) spatial convenience, (2) lot size, (3) waiting or delivery time, and (4) product variety and assortment.[4] As discussed above, different customers may have different requirements regarding such service outputs. It follows that different supply chain structures may be required to accommodate these differences.

---

[2]For a comprehensive discussion of the one-to-one approach, see Don Peppers and Martha Rogers, *The One-to-One Manager: Real World Lessons in Customer Relationship Management* (New York, NY: Doubleday, 1999).

[3]Don Peppers, Martha Rogers, and Bob Dorf, "Is Your Company Ready for One-to-One Marketing," *Harvard Business Review,* January/February 1999, pp. 151–60.

[4]Louis P. Bucklin, *A Theory of Distribution Channel Structure* (Berkeley, CA: IBER Special Publications, 1966).

INDUSTRY INSIGHT 3-1   GETTING A SQUARE D-EAL

At Square D Co., a Palatine, Illinois-based manufacturer of electrical control products and unit of Paris-based Schneider Electric, VP of Marketing Chris Curtis enthusiastically promotes Square D's marketing approach toward its strategic accounts. These accounts, such as Daimler-Chrysler and IBM Corp., are high profile and generate significant sales. Square D uses a Relationship Management Process or RMP to market its products to these accounts. RMP stresses creating one-to-one marketing partnerships in which Square D customers are provided with exactly the products and level of service they want.

For example, Scott Chakmak is Square D's director of strategic accounts—DaimlerChrysler and spends his working days in DaimlerChrysler's Kenosha, Wisconsin, plant. This proximity to the customer allows Square D's sales staff to become well acquainted with DaimlerChrysler's needs. Prior to Daimler's acquisition of Chrysler, Mr. Chakmak realized that Square D's team could ease the workload of Chrysler's engineers by helping with the design of a new engine assembly line. He suggested that his team oversee the design of the electrical control system of each machine to ensure conformity. The consistency of the design would reduce training time and make Chrysler's employees more versatile.

After more than 2 years, Chrysler finally agreed to Square D's proposal and put its supplier in charge of the project. Communicating via the Internet with more than 80 other contributing suppliers around the world, Square D completed the project in 27 months, significantly shorter than the industry standard of 36 months, according to Mr. Chakmak.

Since that first project, Square D has overseen similar projects for various DaimlerChrysler plants around the world. "The first project took 2 years to sell," recalls Mr. Chakmak. "It took 9 months to sell the next time. Then it was 30 days. Since then, it's basically been a handshake."

Ultimately, RMP is about customer segmentation. If customers don't want or require value-added services, Square D simply sells them the products they need. For other customers, value-added services can be customized to meet their specific product needs. These extra efforts can be quite worthwhile for Square D, enhancing its value as a supplier to a strategic customer. For example, Square D is now the sole supplier of power supply equipment to IBM Corp.

Square D must adhere to rigorous standards in handling strategic accounts. Square D and its sister Schneider brand, Modicon, sell to IBM approximately $11 million in electrical control products annually under a 3-year pact signed last year. This pact ensures that IBM receives volume discounting, standardization across plants, prompt shipping, available inventory for essential products, and responsive service.

Mr. Curtis sums up Square D's RMP approach as an evolution of the total quality management movement of the 1980s. Instead of the manufacturing process, RMP scrutinizes Square D's relationship with its customers to better accommodate individual requirements and improve channel success.

Source: Sean Callahan, "Getting a Square D-eal," *Advertising Age's Business Marketing,* January/February 2000, pp. 3, 35.

Spatial Convenience

Spatial convenience, the first service output, refers to the amount of shopping time and effort that will be required on the part of the customer. Higher levels of spatial convenience are achieved in a supply chain by providing customers with access to its products in a larger number of places, thus reducing shopping effort. Consider, for example, the household furniture industry. Some manufacturers utilize a structure that includes department stores, mass merchandisers, and numerous chain and independent furniture specialty stores. Ethan Allen, on the other hand, restricts brand availability to a limited number of authorized Ethan Allen retail stores. This difference in the level of spatial convenience has major implications for the overall supply chain structure and for the logistics cost incurred in the supply chain. It is also clear that some customers are willing to expend greater time and effort than others as they search for a desired product or brand.

Lot Size

The second service output is **lot size,** which refers to the number of units to be purchased in each transaction. When customers are required to purchase in large quantities, they must incur costs of product storage and maintenance. When the supply chain allows them to purchase in small lot sizes, they can more easily match their consumption requirements with their purchasing. In developed economies, alternative supply chains frequently offer customers a choice of the level of lot-size service output. For example, consumers who are willing to purchase paper towels in a 12- or 24-roll package may buy at Sam's Club or Costco. As an alternative, they may buy single rolls at the local grocery or convenience store. Of course, the supply chain that allows customers to purchase in small quantities normally experiences higher cost and therefore demands higher unit prices from customers.

Waiting Time

Waiting time is the third generic service output. Waiting time is defined as the amount of time the customer must wait between ordering and receiving products: the lower the waiting time, the higher the level of supply chain service. Again, alternative supply chains offer consumers and end users choices in terms of the amount of waiting time required. In the personal computer industry, a consumer may visit an electronics or computer specialty store, make a purchase, and carry home a computer with, literally, no waiting time. Alternatively, the customer may order from a catalog or via the Internet and wait for delivery to the home or office. In a general sense, the longer the waiting time required, the more inconvenient for the customer. However, such supply chains generally incur lower costs and customers are rewarded in the form of lower prices for their willingness to wait.

Product Variety

Product variety and **assortment** are the fourth service output. Again, different supply chains offer differing levels of variety and assortment to consumers and end users. Typical supermarkets are involved in supply chains that provide a broad variety of many different types of products and an assortment of brands, sizes, etc., of each type. In fact, supermarkets may have over 35,000 different items on the shelves. Warehouse stores, on the other hand, offer much less product variety or assortment, generally stocking in the range of 8000 to 10,000 items, and usually offer only one brand and size of an item. Convenience stores may stock only a few hundred items, offering little variety or assortment as compared to supermarkets.

Supply chains provide additional service outputs to their customers. In addition to the four generic service outputs discussed above, other researchers have identified services related to information, product customization, and after-sales support as critical to selected customers.[5] The point to keep in mind is that there is no such thing as a homogeneous market where all consumers desire the same services presented in the same way. They may differ in terms of which services are most important and in terms of the level of each of the services desired to accommodate their needs. For example,

---

[5]V. Kasturi Rangan, Meluia A. J. Menzies, and E. P. Maier, "Channel Selection for New Industrial Products: A Framework, Method, and Application," *Journal of Marketing* 56 (July 1992), pp. 72–3.

some consumers may require immediate availability of a personal computer while others feel that waiting 3 days for a computer configured to their exact requirements is preferable. Additionally, customers differ in terms of how much they are willing to pay for services. Since higher levels of service generally involve higher market distribution costs, organizations must carefully assess customer sensitivity to prices relative to their desire for reduced waiting time, convenience, and other service outputs.

This discussion of generic service outputs focuses primarily on consumer or organizational end users in a supply chain. It has important implications for how supply chains are ultimately configured, what types of participating companies may be included to satisfy service requirements, and the costs that are incurred in the process. Attention is now focused on more specific considerations of customer accommodation in a *logistical* context. Three levels of customer accommodation are discussed: customer service, customer satisfaction, and customer success.

Customer Service

The primary value of logistics is to accommodate customer requirements in a cost-effective manner. Although most senior managers agree that customer service is important, they sometimes find it extremely difficult to explain what it is and what it does. While common expressions of customer service include "easy to do business with" and "responsive to customers," to develop a full understanding of customer service, a more thorough framework is required.

Philosophically, customer service represents logistics' role in fulfilling the marketing concept. A customer service program must identify and prioritize all activities required to accommodate customers' logistical requirements as well as, or better than, competitors. In establishing a customer service program, it is imperative to identify clear standards of performance for each of the activities and measurements relative to those standards. In basic customer service programs, the focus is typically on the operational aspects of logistics and ensuring that the organization is capable of providing the **seven rights** to its customer: the *right* amount of the *right* product at the *right* time at the *right* place in the *right* condition at the *right* price with the *right* information.

It is clear that outstanding customer service adds value throughout a supply chain. The critical concern in developing a service strategy is: *Does the cost associated with achieving specified service performance represent a sound investment?* Careful analysis of competitive performance and customer sensitivity to service attributes is required to formulate a basic service strategy. In Chapter 2, the fundamental attributes of basic customer service were identified as availability, operational performance, and service reliability. These attributes are now discussed in greater detail.

Availability

Availability is the capacity to have inventory when desired by a customer. As simple as this may seem, it is not at all uncommon for an organization to expend considerable time, money, and effort to generate customer demand and then fail to have product available to meet customer requirements. The traditional practice in organizations is to stock inventory in anticipation of customer orders. Typically an inventory stocking plan is based on forecasted demand for products and may include differential stocking policies for specific items as a result of sales popularity, profitability, and importance of an item to the overall product line and the value of the merchandise.

While the detail of establishing inventory stocking policies is covered in Chapter 10, suffice it to say at this time that inventory can be classified into two groups: base stock determined by forecasted and planned requirements, and safety stock to cover unexpected variations in demand or operations.

It should be clear that achieving high levels of inventory availability requires a great deal of planning. In fact, the key is to achieve these high levels of availability for selected or core customers while minimizing overall investment in inventory and facilities. Exacting programs of inventory availability are not conceived or managed *on average;* availability is based on three performance measures: *stockout frequency, fill rate,* and *orders shipped complete.*

Stockout Frequency

A **stockout,** as the term suggests, occurs when a firm has no product available to fulfill customer demand. Stockout frequency refers to the probability that a firm will not have inventory available to meet a customer order. For example, a study of retail supermarkets revealed that at any point in time during a week, the average supermarket is out of stock of approximately 8 percent of the items planned to be on the shelves. It is important to note, however, that a stockout does not actually occur until a customer desires a product. The aggregation of all stockouts across all products is an indicator of how well a firm is positioned to provide basic service commitments in product availability. While it does not consider that some products may be more critical in terms of availability than others, it is the starting point in thinking about inventory availability.

Fill Rate

Fill rate measures the magnitude or impact of stockouts over time. Being out of stock does not affect service performance until a customer demands a product. Then it is important to determine that the product is not available and how many units the customer wanted. For example, if a customer wants 100 units of an item and only 97 are available, the fill rate is 97 percent. To effectively consider fill rate, the typical procedure is to evaluate performance over time to include multiple customer orders. Thus, fill rate performance can be evaluated for a specific customer, product, or for any combination of customers, products, or business segments.

Fill rate can be used to differentiate the level of service to be offered on specific products. In the earlier example, if all 100 products ordered were critical to a customer, then a fill rate of 97 percent could result in a stockout at the customer's plant or warehouse and severely disrupt the customer's operations. Imagine an assembly line scheduled to produce 100 automobiles that receives only 97 of its required brake assemblies. In situations where some of the items are not critical to performance, a fill rate of 97 percent may be acceptable. The customer may accept a back order or be willing to reorder the short items at a later time. Fill rate strategies need to consider customer requirements for products.

Orders Shipped Complete

The most exacting measure of performance in product availability is **orders shipped complete.** It views having everything that a customer orders as the standard of acceptable performance. Failure to provide even one item on a customer's order results in that order being recorded as *zero* in terms of complete shipment.

These three measures of availability combine to establish the extent to which a firm's inventory strategy is accommodating customer demand. They also form the basis to evaluate the appropriate level of availability to incorporate into a firm's basic logistical service program. High levels of inventory have typically been viewed as the means to increasing availability; however, new strategies that use information technology to identify customer demand in advance of actual customer orders have allowed some organizations to reach very high levels of basic service performance without corresponding increases in inventory. These strategies are discussed more fully in Chapter 10.

Operational Performance

Operational performance deals with the time required to deliver a customer's order. Whether the performance cycle in question is market distribution, manufacturing support, or procurement, operational performance is specified in terms of speed of performance, consistency, flexibility, and malfunction recovery.

Speed

Performance cycle speed is the elapsed time from when a customer establishes a need to order until the product is delivered and is ready for customer use. The elapsed time required for total performance cycle completion depends on logistical system design. Given today's high level of communication and transportation technology, order cycles can be as short as a few hours or may take several weeks or months.

Naturally, most customers want fast order cycle performance. Speed is an essential ingredient in many just-in-time and quick-response logistical strategies as fast performance cycles reduce customer inventory requirements. The counterbalance is that speed of service is typically costly: Not all customers need or want maximum speed if it means increased total cost. The justification for speed must be found in the positive trade-offs; that is, the only relevant framework for estimating the value of service speed is the customer's perceived benefits.

Consistency

Order cycle consistency is measured by the number of times that actual cycles meet the time planned for completion. While speed of service is important, most logistical managers place greater value on consistency because it directly impacts a customer's ability to plan and perform its own activities. For example, if order cycles vary, then a customer must carry safety stock to protect against potential late delivery; the degree of variability translates directly into safety stock requirements. Given the numerous activities involved in performance cycle execution there are many potential sources of inconsistency in performance (review Figure 2-11).[6]

The issue of consistency is fundamental to effective logistics operations as it is becoming increasingly common for customers to actually specify a desired date and even specify a delivery appointment when placing orders. Such a precise specification may be made taking into consideration a supplier's performance cycle but that is not always the case. In fact, customers frequently place orders far in advance of their need for product replenishment. In such situations, it is very difficult for customers to understand why failure to deliver as specified occurs. Their viewpoint of supplier consistency in operational performance is whether the supplier delivered at the specified date and time. In such situations the definition of consistency must be modified. It is no

---

[6]See Figure 2-11, p. 63.

longer sufficient to evaluate in terms of planned time, such as 4 days to complete the cycle. It is essential to determine whether the performance cycle was completed according to the customer's specification.

Flexibility

Flexibility involves a firm's ability to accommodate special situations and unusual or unexpected customer requests. For example, the standard pattern for servicing a customer may be to ship full-trailer quantities to a customer's warehouse. However, from time to time, the customer may desire to have shipments of smaller quantities made direct to individual retail locations. A firm's logistical competency is directly related to how well it is able to accommodate such unexpected circumstances. Typical events requiring flexible operations are: (1) modification to basic service agreements such as a change in ship-to location; (2) support of unique sales or marketing programs; (3) new-product introduction; (4) product recall; (5) disruption in supply; (6) one-time customization of basic service for specific customers or segments; and (7) product modification or customization performed while in the logistics system, such as price-marking, mixing, or packaging. In many ways the essence of logistical excellence rests in the ability to be flexible.

Malfunction Recovery

Regardless of how fine-tuned a firm's logistical operations, malfunctions will occur. The continuous performance of service commitments on a day-in, day-out basis is a difficult task. Ideally, adjustments can be implemented to prevent or accommodate special situations, thereby preventing malfunctions. For example, if a stockout of an essential item occurs at a distribution facility that normally services a customer, the item may be obtained from an alternative facility utilizing some form of expedited transportation. In such situations the malfunction may actually be transparent to the customer. While such transparent recoveries are not always possible, effective customer service programs anticipate that malfunctions and service breakdowns will occur and have in place contingency plans to accomplish recovery and measure compliance.

Service Reliability

Service reliability involves the combined attributes of logistics and concerns a firm's ability to perform all order-related activities, as well as provide customers with critical information regarding logistical operations and status. Beyond availability and operational performance, attributes of reliability may mean that shipments arrive damage-free; invoices are correct and error-free; shipments are made to the correct locations; and the exact amount of product ordered is included in the shipment. While these and numerous other aspects of overall reliability are difficult to enumerate, the point is that customers demand that a wide variety of business details be handled routinely by suppliers. Additionally, service reliability involves a capability and a willingness to provide accurate information to customers regarding operations and order status. Research indicates that the ability of a firm to provide accurate information is one of the most significant attributes of a good service program.[7] Increasingly, customers indicate that advanced notification of problems such as incomplete orders is more critical

---

[7]Donald J. Bowersox, David J. Closs, and Theodore P. Stank, *21st Century Logistics: Making Supply Chain Integration a Reality* (Oak Brook, IL: Council of Logistics Management, 1999).

than the complete order itself. Customers hate surprises! More often than not, customers can adjust to an incomplete or late delivery, if they have advanced notification.

The Perfect Order

The ultimate in logistics service is to do everything right and to do it right the first time. It is not sufficient to deliver a complete order but to deliver it late. Nor is it sufficient to deliver a complete order on time but to have an incorrect invoice or product damage incurred during the handling and transportation process. In the past, most logistics managers evaluated customer service performance in terms of several independent measures: fill rates were evaluated against a standard for fill; on-time delivery was evaluated in terms of a percentage of deliveries made on time relative to a standard; damage rates were evaluated relative to a standard for damage; etc. When each of these separate measures was acceptable relative to standard, overall service performance was considered acceptable.

Recently, however, logistics and supply chain executives have begun to focus attention on zero-defect or six-sigma performance. As an extension of Total Quality Management (TQM) efforts within organizations, logistics processes have been subjected to the same scrutiny as manufacturing and other processes in the firm. It was realized that if standards are established independently for customer service components, even if performance met standard on each independent measure, a substantial number of customers may have order-related failures. For example, if orders shipped complete, average on-time delivery, average damage-free delivery, and average correct documentation are each 97 percent, the probability that any order will be delivered with no defects is approximately 88.5 percent. This is so because the potential occurrence of any one failure combined with any other failure is $.97 \times .97 \times .97 \times .97$. The converse of this, of course, is that some type of problem will exist on as many as 11.5 percent of all orders.

The notion of the perfect order is that an order should be delivered complete, delivered on time, at the right location, in perfect condition, with complete and accurate documentation. Each of these individual elements must comply with customer specifications. Thus, complete delivery means all product the customer originally requested, on time means at the customer's specified date and time, etc. In other words, total order cycle performance must be executed with zero defects—availability and operational performance must be perfectly executed and all support activities must be completed exactly as promised to the customer. While it may not be possible to offer zero defects as a basic service strategy across the board to all customers, such high-level performance may be an option on a selective basis.

It is clear that the resources required to implement a perfect order platform are substantial. Extremely high fill rates require high inventory levels to meet all potential order requirements and variations. However, such complete service cannot be achieved based totally on inventory. One way of elevating logistics performance to at least near-zero defects is to utilize a combination of customer alliances, information technology, postponement strategies, inventory stocking strategies, premium transportation, and selectivity programs to match logistical resources to core customer requirements. Each of these topics is the subject of detailed discussion in subsequent chapters. Suffice it to say at this time that firms achieving superior logistical customer service are well aware of the challenge related to achieving zero defects. By having a low tolerance for errors, coupled with a commitment to resolve whatever discrepancies occur, such firms can achieve strategic advantage over their competitors. Industry Insight 3-2 describes the importance of achieving perfect order performance, as well as the difficulties in the emerging industry of consumer-delivered groceries.

Basic Service Platforms

To implement a basic service platform, it is necessary to specify commitment level to all customers in terms of availability, operational performance, and reliability. The fundamental question, "How much basic service should the system provide?" is not easy to answer.

The fact is that many firms establish their basic service platforms based on two factors. The first factor is competitor or *industry acceptable practice*. In most industries, levels of minimum and average service performance have emerged. These acceptable levels are generally well known by both the suppliers and the customers throughout the industry. It is not uncommon to hear logistics and supply chain executives speak of customer service commitments in terms of "doing as well as competition" or "beating our major competitors' performance." The second factor derives from the firm's overall *marketing strategy*. If a firm desires to differentiate from com-

INDUSTRY INSIGHT 3-2 GROCERIES DELIVERED TO YOUR DOORSTEP

Several grocers are attempting to offer greater convenience to customers by offering electronic order placement and home delivery. This simple concept is quite complex to implement effectively.

The most important factor influencing consumer-direct channel adoption and customer loyalty is the ability to consistently pick and deliver perfect orders. However, it is complex and expensive to structure a low-cost logistics system to provide these desired service levels.

Consumer-direct logistics focuses on fulfilling demand at the household level through consistent delivery of perfect orders as it ensures a continuous supply of product at the lowest possible cost. A dedicated fulfillment center is preferred for greater picking accuracy, order customization, fill rates, and operational flexibility, but produces significantly higher operating margins than a traditional grocery store model.

Product fulfillment is the highest direct cost of processing an order, due to the goal of a consistent perfect order. This process typically includes household-level customization in high-impact perishable and prepared meat categories that mandate different temperature controls and date-management practices. For example, some consumers prefer green bananas to yellow bananas or rare roast beef sliced thin to the standard sliced product. Given an average 60-item order and a 99 percent picking accuracy at the individual item level, only 55 percent of all orders would be perfectly filled. The operator's challenge is to incorporate household-level specification in a high-volume, scalable operating environment where customers are ordering electronically.

Delivery capabilities involve the physical logistics of moving products directly to the customer's home. Most providers unitize products from across three temperature zones into a secure container and load it into a multitemperature vehicle to maintain proper temperatures across the home-delivery chill chain.

Unique characteristics of the grocery business (e.g., number of items per order, customer preferences within a given SKU, temperature maintenance requirements for different products) emphasize the difficulty of designing a logistics system to deliver perfect orders to each customer every time.

Source: Frank F. Britt, "The Logistics of Consumer-Direct," *Progressive Grocer*, May 1998, p. 39.

petitors based on logistics competency, then high levels of basic service are required. If the firm differentiates on price, then it likely will commit to lower levels of logistical service due to the resources required and costs related to high-level commitment.

The fact is that even firms with a high level of basic customer service commitment generally do not take a total zero-defect approach across the board for all customers. The common service commitment is to establish internal performance standards for each service component. These standards typically reflect prevailing industry practice in combination with careful consideration of cost and resource commitments. Typical service standards such as 97 percent fill rate or delivery within 3 days may be established and then performance would be monitored relative to these internal standards. While it is generally assumed that this strategic approach results in accommodating customers as well as or better than competitors, it does not assure that customers are, in fact, satisfied with either the overall industry performance or even the performance of an organization that performs above industry standard. In fact, there is only one way to be sure customers are satisfied—*ask them.*

Customer Satisfaction

Customer satisfaction has long been a fundamental concept in marketing and business strategy. In building a customer satisfaction program, however, the first question that must be answered is, What does it mean to say that a customer is satisfied? The simplest and most widely accepted method of defining customer satisfaction is known as **expectancy disconfirmation.** Simply stated, if a customer's expectations of a supplier's performance are met or exceeded, the customer will be satisfied. Conversely, if perceived performance is less than what the customer expected, then the customer is dissatisfied. A number of companies have adopted this framework for customer satisfaction and follow a commitment to meet or exceed customers' expectations. In fact, many organizations have gone further by speaking in terms of *delighting* their customers through performance which exceeds expectations.

While this framework for customer satisfaction is relatively straightforward, the implications for building a customer service platform in logistics are not. To build this platform it is necessary to explore more fully the nature of customer expectations. What do customers expect? How do customers form these expectations? What is the relationship between customer satisfaction and customer perceptions of overall logistics service quality? Why do many companies fail to satisfy customers, and why are so many companies perceived as providing poor logistics quality? If a company satisfies its customers, is that sufficient? The following sections provide some answers to these critical questions.

Customer Expectations

It is clear that when customers transact business with a supplier they have numerous expectations, many of which revolve around the supplier's basic logistical service platform; that is, they have expectations regarding availability, operational performance, and service reliability. Frequently, they have in place formal programs to monitor suppliers' performance with respect to each of these dimensions of logistical performance. However, in a pioneering study of service expectations and service quality, Parasuraman, Zeithaml, and Berry identified a set of 10 categories of customer expectations,

---

TABLE 3-1   Customer Expectations Related to Logistical Performance

---

Reliability: Reliability is one of the aspects of the firm's basic service platform. In this context, however, reliability refers to performance of *all* activities as promised by the supplier. If the supplier promises next day delivery and delivery takes 2 days, it is perceived as unreliable. If the supplier accepts an order for 100 cases of a product, it implicitly promises that 100 cases will be delivered. The customer expects and is only satisfied with the supplier if all 100 are received. Customers judge reliability in terms of all aspects of the basic service platform. Thus, customers have expectations concerning damage, documentation accuracy, etc.

Responsiveness: Responsiveness refers to customers' expectations of the willingness and ability of supplier personnel to provide prompt service. This extends beyond mere delivery to include issues related to quick handling of inquiries and resolution of problems. Responsiveness is clearly a time-oriented concept and customers have expectations regarding suppliers' timely handling of all interactions.

Access: Access involves customer expectations of the ease of contact and approachability of the supplier. For example, is it easy to place orders, to obtain information regarding inventory or order status?

Communication: Communication means proactively keeping customers informed. Rather than waiting for customer inquiries concerning order status, customers have expectations regarding suppliers' notification of status, particularly if problems with delivery or availability arise. Customers do not like to be surprised, and advance notice is essential.

Credibility: Credibility refers to customer expectations that communications from the supplier are in fact believable and honest. While it is doubtful that many suppliers intentionally mislead customers, credibility also includes the notion of completeness in required communications.

Security: Security deals with customers' feelings of risk or of doubt in doing business with a supplier. Customers make plans based on their anticipation of supplier performance. For example, they take risk when they schedule production and undertake machine and line setups in anticipation of delivery. If orders are late or incomplete, their plans must be changed. Another aspect of security deals with customer expectations that their dealings with a supplier will be confidential. This is particularly important in supply chain arrangements when a customer has a unique operating agreement with a supplier who also services competitors.

Courtesy: Courtesy involves politeness, friendliness, and respect of contact personnel. This can be a particularly vexing problem considering that customers may have contact with numerous individuals in the organization ranging from sales representatives to customer service personnel to truck drivers. Failure by one individual may destroy the best efforts of all the others.

Competency: Competence is judged by customers in every interaction with a supplier and, like courtesy, can be problematic because it is perceived in every interaction. In other words, customers judge the competence of truck drivers when deliveries are made, warehouse personnel when orders are checked, customer service personnel when phone calls are made, and so forth. Failure by any individual to demonstrate competence affects customer perceptions of the entire organization.

Tangibles: Customers have expectations regarding the physical appearance of facilities, equipment, and personnel. Consider, for example, a delivery truck that is old, damaged, or in poor condition. Such tangible features are additional cues used by customers as indicators of a firm's overall performance.

Knowing the Customer: While suppliers may think in terms of groups of customers and market segments, customers perceive themselves as unique. They have expectations regarding suppliers' understanding their uniqueness and supplier willingness to adapt to their specific requirements.

[handwritten margin notes: "I am said to say this is true, it should not be but it is." "Perhaps #1 in anyones book"]

each of which has implications for logistical management.[8] While their later research has focused on a reduced set of five determinants, Table 3-1 presents their original conceptualization with specific examples of logistical expectations that customers may have. These categories could, of course, be considered in the context of other marketing activities, such as expectations related to sales force performance.

---

[8]A. Parasuraman, Valerie Zeithaml, and Leonard L. Berry, "A Conceptual Model of Service Quality and Its Implications for Future Research," Report No. 84-106 (Cambridge, MA: Marketing Science Institute, 1984).

In a logistical and supply chain context, the notion of customer expectations is particularly complex because customers are usually business organizations made up of numerous functions and individuals.[9] Different personnel in a customer organization may prioritize the criteria of performance differently, or they may have different levels of expectation for the criteria. For example, some personnel may be most concerned with responsiveness and rapid handling of an inquiry regarding order status, while others may be more concerned with order completeness or meeting a delivery appointment. Meeting customer expectations requires an understanding of how these expectations are formed and the reasons many companies fail to meet those expectations.

Perceived Service Quality and Customer Satisfaction

Closely related to the concept of customer satisfaction is the concept of perceived service quality. Early on, one leading expert noted that *service quality* is "performance which results in customer satisfaction, or freedom from deficiency which avoids customer dissatisfaction."[10] In more recent research related specifically to logistics it was generalized that "The service quality approach is an attempt to understand customer satisfaction from the perspective of the differences between customer perceptions and actual service on various attributes."[11] While many authors do draw a distinction between customer satisfaction and service quality, the distinction is based primarily on the notion that satisfaction refers to a customer's evaluation of a single transaction, whereas service quality is an evaluation over multiple transactions. It is clear that the two concepts are sufficiently similar to warrant their being treated simultaneously.

A Model of Customer Satisfaction

Figure 3-1 provides a framework for understanding the process by which customers actually form their expectations of supplier performance. It also suggests that frequently a number of *gaps* exist which a supplier must overcome if it is to base its platform of customer accommodation on the satisfaction of customers.

There are several factors that influence customer expectations, both in terms of a prioritization of the criteria discussed above, as well as the level of expectation relative to each of the criteria. The first of these factors is very simply the customer's needs or requirements. At the heart of their own business strategies, customers have requirements, that depend on the performance of their suppliers. To a major extent, customers expect that these needs can and will be met by suppliers. Interestingly, however, customers' expectations are frequently not the same as their real requirements or needs. Previous supplier performance is a major factor influencing customer expectations. A supplier who consistently delivers on time will most likely be expected to deliver on time in the future. Similarly, a supplier with a poor record concerning performance will be expected to perform poorly in the future. It is important to note that previous performance experienced with one supplier may also influence the customer's expectation regarding other suppliers. For example, when Federal Express demonstrated the ability to deliver small packages on a next-day basis, many customers began to expect a similar performance capability from other suppliers.

---

[9]Logistics researchers have developed specific questionnaire scales to be used for assessment of satisfaction with logistics service. See, for example, John T. Mentzer, Daniel Flint, and John L. Kent, "Developing a Logistics Service Quality Scale," *Journal of Business Logistics* 20, no. 1 (1999), pp. 11–29.

[10]Joseph M. Juran, *Juran on Leadership for Quality: An Executive Handbook* (New York, NY: Free Press, 1980).

[11]John T. Mentzer, Daniel Flint, and John L. Kent, op. cit., p. 11.

Figure 3-1

Satisfaction and quality model

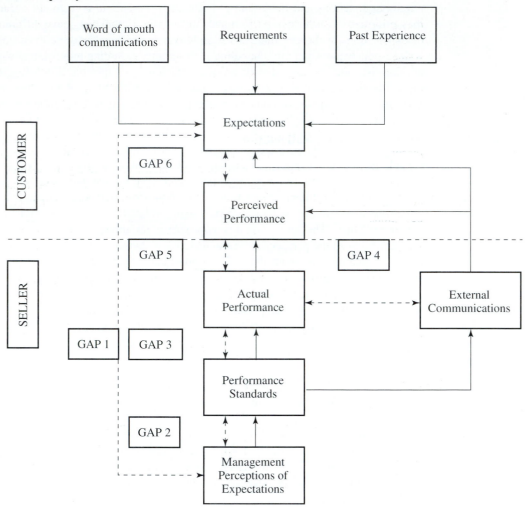

Source: Adapted from A. Parasuraman, Valerie Zeithaml, and Leonard L. Berry, "A Conceptual Model of Service Quality and Its Implications for Future Research," Report No. 84-106 (Cambridge, MA: Marketing Science Institute, 1984).

Related to a customer's perception of past performance is word-of-mouth. In other words, customers frequently communicate with one another concerning their experiences with specific suppliers. At trade and professional association meetings, the subject of suppliers is a common topic of discussion among executives. Much of the discussion may revolve around supplier performance capabilities. Such discussions help form individual customer expectations.

Perhaps the most important factor influencing customer expectations are the communications coming from the supplier itself. Promises and commitments made by sales personnel or customer service representatives, statements contained in marketing and promotional messages, even the printed policies and procedures of an organization represent communications that customers depend upon. These communications become a critical basis on which they form their expectations. The promise of meeting a delivery appointment or having full product availability becomes an expectation in the customer's mind. Indeed many suppliers may be guilty of setting themselves up for failure by overcommitting in an attempt to influence customer expectations.

Figure 3-1 also provides a framework for understanding what must be done by an organization to deliver customer satisfaction. The failure of many firms to satisfy their customers can be traced to the existence of one or more of the gaps identified in the framework.

Gap 1: Knowledge

The first and the most fundamental gap that may exist is between customers' real expectations and managers' perception of those expectations. This gap reflects management's lack of knowledge or understanding of customers. While there may be many reasons for this lack of understanding, it is clear that no beneficial customer satisfaction platform can be established without a thorough understanding of customer expectations, how they are prioritized, and how they are formed. Since sales typically has the major responsibility for customer interactions, knowledge regarding logistics expectations is often difficult to obtain.

Gap 2: Standards

Even if full understanding of customer expectations exists, it is still necessary to establish standards of performance for the organization. The standards gap exists when internal performance standards do not adequately or accurately reflect customer expectations. This is precisely the case in many organizations that develop their basic service platform based on examination of internal operating capabilities or on a superficial examination of competitive service performance.

Gap 3: Performance

The performance gap is the difference between standard and actual performance. If the standard is a fill rate of 98 percent, based on research with customers regarding their expectations, and the firm actually performs at 97 percent, a performance gap exists. It should be pointed out that many firms focus their efforts to improve satisfaction by eliminating the performance gap. It may be, however, that the dissatisfaction exists due to a poor understanding of customer expectations in the first place.

Gap 4: Communications

The role of communications in customer satisfaction cannot be overemphasized. As discussed previously, overcommitment, or promising higher levels of performance than can actually be provided, is a major cause of customer dissatisfaction. There should be no gap between what a firm is capable of doing and what customers are told about those capabilities.

Gap 5: Perception

It is true that customers sometimes perceive performance to be lower or higher than actually achieved. In logistics, many managers frequently lament, "We're only as good as the last order." Thus, although performance over a long time period has been very good, a late or incomplete or otherwise subpar delivery may result in a customer's expression of extreme dissatisfaction.

Gap 6: Satisfaction/Quality

The existence of any one or more of the above gaps leads to customer perception that performance is not as good as expected. In other words, these gaps result in customer dissatisfaction. When building a platform for delivering customer satisfaction, a firm must ensure that these gaps do not exist.

Increasing Customer Expectations

As an important component of TQM the notion of continuous improvement has been accepted by most organizations. As a corollary of continuous improvement, there has been a continued escalation of customers' expectations concerning supplier capabilities. Performance, which meets customer expectations one year, may result in extreme dissatisfaction next year as customers increase their expectations regarding acceptable performance levels.

To some extent, the increase in expectations can be traced to the dynamics of competition. As discussed previously, most industries traditionally have had explicit or implied levels of performance, which were considered to be adequate. If a firm wanted to be a serious competitor, it generally had to achieve these minimum industry service expectations. However, when one firm in the industry focuses on logistics as a core competency and provides higher performance levels, customers come to expect other suppliers to follow. Consider, for example, that after Federal Express introduced real time tracking of shipment status, UPS and other parcel delivery firms shortly followed suit.

Does achieving perfect order performance ensure that customers are satisfied? On the surface it would seem so. After all, if all orders are delivered with no defects, what basis exists for customers to be dissatisfied? Part of the answer to this question lies in the fact that perfect orders, as important as they are, deal with the execution of individual transactions and deliveries. Customer satisfaction is a much broader concept, dealing with many other aspects of the overall relationship between suppliers and customers. For example, a customer may continuously receive perfect orders but be dissatisfied with such aspects of the relationship as difficulty in obtaining information, long delays in response to inquiries, or even the perception that some supplier personnel do not treat the customer with proper courtesy and respect. Thus, satisfaction transcends operational performance to include aspects of personal and interpersonal relationships.

Limitations of Customer Satisfaction

Due to its explicit focus on customers, a commitment to satisfaction represents a step beyond a basic service platform in an organization's efforts to accommodate its customers. It is realistic to think that a firm satisfying customer expectations better than competitors will gain some competitive advantage in the marketplace. Nevertheless, it is important to realize some of the shortcomings and limitations of the customer satisfaction emphasis.

The first limitation is that many executives make a fundamental, yet understandable, mistake in their interpretation of satisfaction. In many organizations it is assumed that customers who are satisfied are also happy, maybe even delighted, with the suppliers' performance. That may or may not be the actual situation. It must be remembered that satisfaction is the customers' perception of actual performance in relation to expectation, not their requirements. Examination of Figure 3-2 may help explain this difference between satisfaction and happiness. The fact is that customers may have an expectation that a firm will not perform at a high level. If the customer has an expectation of a low level of performance and indeed perceives that the firm performs at this

FIGURE 3-2

Satisfaction is not the same as happiness

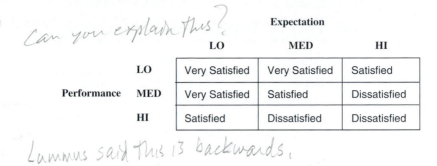

Can you explain this?

		Expectation		
		LO	**MED**	**HI**
Performance	**LO**	Very Satisfied	Very Satisfied	Satisfied
	MED	Very Satisfied	Satisfied	Dissatisfied
	HI	Satisfied	Dissatisfied	Dissatisfied

Lummus said this is backwards.

low level, it is clear that performance and expectation match. By definition, the customer is satisfied. The same is true at mid-level expectations and perceptions as well as high levels of each.

This notion that low levels of performance may be considered satisfactory can best be illustrated by example. Suppose a customer expects a supplier to provide, over time, a fill rate of 95 percent, or late deliveries 10 percent of the time, or damage of 2 percent. If the supplier in fact provides this level of performance, as is perceived by the customer, the customer is satisfied. Performance perceived to be poorer than the expectation level results in dissatisfaction. Is the satisfied customer necessarily happy about the supplier's fill rate or late deliveries? Of course not. While expectations may be met, indeed may be met as well as or better than competition, there is still no assurance that the customer will be happy. Even performance higher than that expected, while satisfying to customers, may not actually result in happiness. The focus on customer expectations ignores the fact that expectations are not the same as needs or requirements.

The second limitation to consider is actually related to the first: satisfied customers are not necessarily loyal customers. Even though their expectations are being met, satisfied customers may choose to do business with competitors. This can occur because they expect a competitor to perform at a higher level or at least as well as the organization in question. For many years, marketing and supply chain executives have assumed that satisfied customers are also loyal customers. Yet research has frequently shown that many customers, who report being satisfied that their expectations have been met, are likely to patronize and do business with competitors.[12]

A third limitation to customer satisfaction is that firms frequently forget satisfaction lies in the expectations and perceptions of individual customers. Thus, there is a tendency to aggregate expectations across customers and neglect the basic tenets of marketing strategy related to differences among customer segments as well as individual customers. Simply stated, what satisfies one customer may not satisfy other, much less all, customers.

Despite these limitations, customer satisfaction does represent a commitment beyond basic service to accommodate customers. It provides explicit recognition that the only way to ensure that customers are being accommodated is to focus on customers themselves. Firms that focus primarily on industry and competitor standards of basic service performance are much less likely to find that their customers are very satisfied or highly satisfied with their performance.

---

[12]Michael J. Ryan, Robert Raynor, and Andy Morgan, "Diagnosing Customer Loyalty Drivers," *Marketing Research* 11, no. 2 (Summer 1999), pp. 18–26.

TABLE 3-2   Evolution of Management Thought

Philosophy	Focus
Customer Service	Meet Internal Standards
Customer Satisfaction	Meet Expectations
Customer Success	Meet Customer Requirements

Note: Notice that the satisfaction model does not focus on *requirements*.

Customer Success

This is what God does what we should do.

In recent years, some firms have discovered that there is another commitment that can be made to gain true competitive advantage through logistical performance. This commitment is based on recognition that a firm's ability to grow and expand market share depends on its ability to attract and hold the industry's most successful customers. The real key, then, to customer-focused marketing lies in the organization's using its performance capabilities to enhance the success of those customers. This focus on customer success represents major commitment toward accommodating customers. Table 3-2 summarizes the evolution that customer-focused organizations have experienced. Notice that a customer service focus is oriented toward establishment of internal standards for basic service performance. Firms typically assess their customer service performance relative to how well these internal standards are accomplished. The customer satisfaction platform is built on the recognition that customers have expectations regarding performance and the only way to ensure that customers are satisfied is to assess their perceptions of performance relative to those expectations.

Customer success shifts the focus from expectations to the customers' real requirements. Recall from the previous discussion that customer requirements, while forming the basis for expectations, are not the same as expectations. Requirements are frequently downgraded into expectations due to perceptions of previous performance, word-of-mouth, or communications from the firm itself. This explains why simply meeting expectations may not result in happy customers. For example, a customer may be satisfied with a 98 percent fill rate, but for the customer to be successful in executing its own strategy, a 100 percent fill rate on certain products or components may be necessary.

Achieving Customer Success

Clearly, a customer success program involves a thorough understanding of individual customer requirements and a commitment to focus on long-term business relationships having high potential for growth and profitability. Such commitment most likely cannot be made to all potential customers. It requires that firms work intensively with customers to understand requirements, internal processes, competitive environment, and whatever else it takes for the customer to be successful in its own competitive arena. Further, it requires that an organization develop an understanding of how it can utilize its own capabilities to enhance customer performance. Industry Insight 3-3 describes how the customer success philosophy developed at Dow Plastics, a division of Dow Chemical.

Industry Insight 3-3   "We Don't Succeed Unless You Do"

In 1988, Dow hired the Anderson & Lembke ad agency, which is known for its cutting-edge creativity. Dow had just realigned its various plastics businesses into a single unit called Dow Plastics. Anderson & Lembke's tasks were to publicize the new entity and assist in its competitive positioning.

Dow's customers and its competitors' customers were surveyed. They ranked Dow a distant third behind industry leaders DuPont and GE Plastics. However, customers were unhappy with the service level they received from all three. "Vendors peddled resins as a commodity," says Hans Ullmark, president of Anderson & Lembke. "They competed on price and delivered on time, but gave no service."

These findings, confirmed by about 200 qualitative interviews, led to a positioning strategy that exceeded the standard customer service guarantee to promise customer success. This strategy, which began as a tag line for a division, grew in influence until it became the core of the parent company's mission statement: "We don't succeed unless you do."

It was concluded that whether a customer was using Dow plastics to manufacture grocery bags or complex aerospace applications, Dow Plastics needed to help them succeed in their markets. A campaign was developed which included print ads, direct-mail pieces, and supportive materials. The targeted communications promoted the different virtues of Dow Plastics' disparate products, but all carried the tag line "We don't succeed unless you do." This slogan and underlying philosophy tied the units together and created a brand identity for the division.

The campaigns were key in changing Dow Plastics from a sales-oriented company into a market-oriented company—from selling plastics to selling customer success. Dow has become the most preferred plastics supplier.

Dow's philosophy is so transformed that when a new product or market is encountered, they ask, "How does this fit in with 'We don't succeed unless you do'?"

Source: Nancy Arnott, "Getting the Picture," *Sales and Marketing Management,* June 1994, p. 74.

In many ways a customer success program requires a comprehensive supply chain perspective on the part of logistics executives. This is most easily explained by examining the relations depicted in Figure 3-3. The typical focus in basic service and satisfaction programs is that the firm attempts to meet standards and expectations of next-destination customers, whether they are consumers, industrial end users, or intermediate or even internal customers. How those customers deal with their customer is typically not considered to be a problem. A supply chain perspective and a customer success program explicitly recognize that logistics executives must alter this focus. They must understand the entire supply chain, the different levels of customer within that supply chain, and develop programs to ensure that next-destination customers are successful in meeting the requirements of customers down the supply chain. If all supply chain members adopt this perspective, then all members share in the success.

To ensure that a customer is successful may require a firm to reinvent the way a product is produced, market distributed, or offered for sale. In fact, collaboration between suppliers and customers to find potential avenues for success may result in the greatest breakthroughs in terms of redefining supply chain processes. The general topic of collaborative relationships and alliances is further developed in Chapter 4. It is enough to say here that such arrangements are not possible without significant amounts of information exchange between the involved businesses to facilitate an in-depth understanding of requirements and capabilities. However, one important way that many firms have responded to the challenges of customer success is through the development of value-added services.

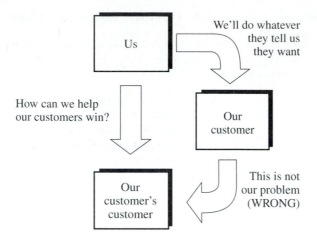

Value-Added Services

The notion of value-added service is a significant development in the evolution to customer success. By definition, **value-added services** refer to unique or specific activities that firms can jointly develop to enhance their efficiency and/or effectiveness. Value-added services help foster customer success. Because they tend to be customer-specific, it is difficult to generalize all possible value-added services.

When a firm becomes committed to value-added solutions for major customers, it rapidly becomes involved in customized or tailored logistics. It is doing unique things to enable specific customers to achieve their objectives. IBM's ability to produce and deliver customized personal computers and networks to individual customers is one example of adding value to a rather standard product. In a logistical context, firms can provide unique product packages, create customized unit loads, place prices on products, offer unique information services, provide vendor-managed inventory service, make special shipping arrangements, and so forth, to enhance customer success.

In reality, some of the value-added services that buyers and sellers agree to involve integrated service providers who are positioned to provide such services. Transportation carriers, warehouse firms, and other specialists may become intimately involved in the supply chain to make such value-adding activities a reality. At this point, a few specific examples of how they may work within a specific supply chain to provide value-added services are sufficient.

Warehouses, whether private or third-party, can be utilized to perform a number of customization activities. For example, a retail customer may desire a unique palletization alternative to support its cross-dock activities and meet the unique product requirements of its individual store units. Each store requires different quantities of specific product to maintain in-stock performance with minimum inventory commitment. In another situation, first-aid kits consisting of many different items are actually assembled in the warehouse as orders are received to meet the unique configuration of kit desired by specific customers. It is also common for warehouses to provide pick-price-repack services for manufacturers to accommodate the unique product configurations required by different customers.

Another form of value-added service involves the proper sorting and sequencing of products to meet specific customer requirements. For example, an auto assembly plant may require that components not only be received on time but also be sorted and sequenced in a particular manner to meet the needs of specific automobiles on the assembly line. The objective is to reduce assembly plant handling and inspection of incoming components. Meeting such exacting requirements for delivery is far beyond the basic service capability of many component suppliers. The use of third-party specialists is a necessity, especially when subcomponents from multiple suppliers must be integrated and then properly sequenced.

Value-added services can be performed directly by participants in a business relationship or may involve specialists. It has become more common in recent years to turn to specialists due to their flexibility and capability to concentrate on providing the required services. Nevertheless, regardless of how the specifics are organized and implemented, it is clear that logistics value-added services are a critical aspect of customer success programs.

Developing Customer Success: An Example

Customer success programs are typically focused on individual customers, as different customer organizations have unique requirements. Careful identification and selection of those customers who are most likely to respond to such efforts and who are willing to return loyalty to the supplier are essential to implementing success programs. In some instances, however, a firm may find it beneficial, or even necessary, to focus a success program on an entire segment of customers to ensure their long-term survival. Such a situation occurred in the wholesale drug distribution industry during the 1980s and 90s. Bergen Brunswig and other selected drug wholesalers revolutionized the independent, owner-managed segment of the retail drug industry. These retailers were faced with potential extinction due to the rise of chain and mass-merchant pharmacy operations but survived as a direct result of the wholesalers' success initiative.

Specifically, to enhance the business success of its retail drugstore customers Bergen Brunswig developed a classic four-stage model: cost-effectiveness, market access, market extension, and market creation. The long-term process is illustrated in Figure 3-4.

Overall, industry efficiency improvements were significant. Tailoring services to specific customers served to establish incentives for maintaining long-term alliances. The nature of Bergen Brunswig's initiative is reviewed below to illustrate how logistical competency can be used to achieve customer success and to gain competitive superiority.

Cost-Effectiveness
The first and most fundamental step was to gain cost-effectiveness. It was essential that the process and necessary related controls be in place to ensure that basic services

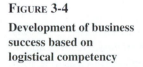

FIGURE 3-4

Development of business success based on logistical competency

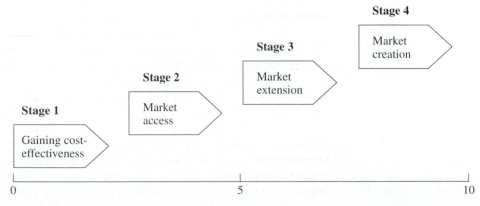

could be provided at a consistently high level of performance and in a cost-effective manner. From a managerial perspective, it is a prerequisite that a firm be able to efficiently perform the basic logistic services required by customers. Most firms that are serious about quality agree there is little room for basic operational error. Unless a firm is able to deliver basic service at reasonable cost, there is no reason for customers to commit additional business and there is limited possibility of moving forward toward a more exacting relationship.

Market Access

The market access stage consisted of higher-level commitments to customers who expressed a willingness to cooperate in efforts to achieve joint objectives. In other words, market access consists of buyers and sellers working together and sharing basic information to facilitate smooth joint operations. It is important to stress that no real level of customer selectivity was involved in market access. For example, Bergen Brunswig needed to establish a basic service commitment to all druggists who were willing to utilize it as a wholesale supplier. The only differential in the timing or level of service during the access stage was determined by the customer's purchase quantity. Once Bergen Brunswig offered retailers a specific service program, it became a principle of fundamental business fairness and legality that each druggist who purchased required volumes would receive equal basic services. For Bergen Brunswig, this commitment meant daily replenishment of exact inventory requirements within a consistent delivery schedule.

Market Extension

Market extension intensifies a business arrangement. Extension is based on moving toward zero defects and introducing value-added services in an effort to solidify and expand the business relationship. At this point the relationship became highly selective since the number of customers who were willing or able to participate was limited. In Bergen Brunswig's strategy, such value-added alliances consisted of a variety of programs to improve the competitiveness of selected customers who were willing to commit to Bergen Brunswig as almost a sole-source supplier. Typical of such value-added innovations were sophisticated bar coding, computer terminals for pharmacy checkout counters, point-of-sale encoding, shelf plan-o-gramming, immediate price change administration, profitability, and inventory turn reports. These innovations were designed to increase operating efficiency and extend overall competitiveness. Such value-added services were offered only to customers who committed to an extended business relationship.

Market Creation

The final stage, market creation, requires full commitment to a customer's success. While all previous stages contribute to competency, the final stage represents above-and-beyond initiatives to enhance success. In the case of Bergen Brunswig, one form of market creation consisted of researching and developing new and innovative ways to make relatively small druggists increasingly competitive with larger vertically integrated chains. For example, Bergen Brunswig pioneered and cooperatively tested such revenue-generating devices as selling cut flowers and carryout food. Creative arrangements also extended to the implementation of joint systems that electronically linked Bergen Brunswig to its retail customers for purposes of providing a full range of process control services.

The full impact of logistics is felt at every stage of the process. It is important to gain control and become cost-effective. High-level basic service is central to market access. During market extension, the commitment to perfect performance and value-added services solidifies the basic business arrangement. The relationship matures into a long-term situation wherein future growth is attained by helping the customer achieve the most successful business possible. The development of a business relationship built on such advanced principles takes time, as much as 10 years or more. The trust aspects of joint operations and free information exchange that are fundamental to such collaborations cannot be engineered and implemented in an untested, unseasoned business arrangement. The Bergen Brunswig model provides a classic illustration of the fusion of information technology and leadership collaboration required to achieve supply chain success.

Summary

The fundamental rationale for logistics is the need to accommodate customers, whether those customers are end users, intermediate, or even internal. The marketing concept provides the foundation for customer accommodation with its fundamental focus on customer needs rather than on products or services, the requirement to view and position products and services in a customer context, identification of market segments which differ in needs, and commitment that volume is secondary to profit.

Contemporary interpretation of the marketing concept suggests that it is more important to focus on the development of relationships with customers than to perfect individual transactions with customers. This interpretation focuses on the needs and requirements of individual customers as the core ingredient of one-to-one marketing. In a supply chain context, customer requirements related to spatial convenience, lot size, waiting time, and variety and assortment must be accommodated by logistical operations.

Organizations build their platform for accommodation on three levels of increasing commitment. The first of these is basic logistics customer service. To be competitive, a firm needs a basic service capability that balances availability, operational performance, and reliability for all customers. The level of commitment to each dimension of service requires careful consideration of competitive performance and cost/benefit analysis. The highest level of commitment is perfect order performance, which requires zero defects in logistics operations. Such high-level commitment is generally reserved for a firm's key customers.

Going beyond basic service to create customer satisfaction represents the second level of customer accommodation. Where basic service focuses on the organization's internal operational performance, customer satisfaction focuses on customers, their expectations, and their perceptions of supplier performance. Customer expectations extend beyond typical logistical operational considerations and include factors related to communication, credibility access, responsiveness, and customer-specific knowledge as well as reliability and responsiveness of operations. A firm can provide logistics service that is equal to or even better than competitors but still have dissatisfied customers. Failure to satisfy customers can arise from lack of knowledge about customer expectations, improper standards of performance, performance failure, poor communication, or incorrect customer perception of performance. As customer expectations escalate, logistics executives must continuously monitor customer satisfaction and improve logistics performance.

The highest level of customer accommodation is known as customer success. Where satisfaction programs seek to meet or exceed expectations, a success platform focuses on customer needs and requirements. Customer expectations are frequently different from needs and requirements. Achieving success requires intimate knowledge of a customer's needs, their operational requirements, and a commitment by the service provider to enhance a customer's ability to compete more successfully in the marketplace. Value-added services represent one way logistics can contribute to customer success. While customer success is normally associated with one-to-one marketing relationships, in isolated instances it may represent the most viable approach to ensuring the long-term survival of entire categories of customers. Bergen Brunswig and the retail pharmacy industry provide a classic example of how this approach worked.

Challenge Questions

1. Explain the differences between transactional and relationship marketing. How do these differences lead to increasing emphasis on logistical performance in supply chain management?

2. Why are the four primary service outputs of spatial convenience, lot size, waiting time, and product variety important to logistics management? Provide examples of competing firms that differ in the level of each service output provided to customers.

3. What is meant by availability in logistics customer service? Provide examples of the different ways to monitor a firm's performance in availability.

4. Compare and contrast speed, consistency, and flexibility as operational performance activities. In some situations, is one activity more critical than others?

5. Why is perfect order service so difficult to achieve?

6. Using the 10 categories of customer expectations in Table 3-1, develop your own examples of how customers might evaluate performance of a supplier.

7. Which of the gaps in Figure 3-1 do you think represents the major problem for most firms? How can a company attempt to eliminate the knowledge gap? The communications gap?

8. Compare and contrast the customer service, customer satisfaction, and customer success philosophies of supply chain management.

9. What is meant by value-added services? Why are these services considered essential in a customer success program?

10. How could a company use the four-stage process of cost-effectiveness, market access, market extension, and market creation to gain competitive superiority?

4 MARKET DISTRIBUTION STRATEGY

In the quest to accommodate customer requirements, no one activity is more important than any other and no one firm can be self-sufficient. This basic fact was discovered many years ago by no less than Henry Ford. Almost from the beginning, Ford envisioned an industrial empire, which was totally self-contained and relied on no other organization. He set out to develop the world's first totally vertically integrated firm.[1]

To support his auto manufacturing facilities, Ford invested in coalmines, iron-ore deposits, and steel mills. He bought land to grow soybeans used in the manufacture of paint and rubber plantations for tires. He owned railroads and ships for transporting materials and trucks for distribution of finished automobiles. He envisioned a network of automobile dealerships owned by Ford Motor Company and managed by his

---

[1]Henry Ford, *Today and Tomorrow* (Portland, OR: Productivity Press, 1926, 1988).

employees. The Ford Motor Company would be a highly integrated organization from raw material sourcing all the way to the final consumer.

Eventually, Ford found he needed help. Facing severe economic, regulatory, and labor barriers, he turned to a network of independent suppliers for needed materials, components, and services; for more effective marketing, a network of independently owned and operated dealerships. As time passed, Ford discovered that specialized firms could perform much of the essential work as well as or better than his own bureaucracy. The Ford strategy shifted from ownership-based control to one of orchestrating channel relationships.

This chapter is concerned with why and how firms develop and manage marketing channel distribution relationships. Chapter 5 deals with procurement, the activity that links a firm to its suppliers, and manufacturing, the activity that provides the form utility for customers. Throughout the two chapters, the focus is on the logistical integration of these activities to most effectively and efficiently accommodate customer requirements.

The study of marketing channels embraces a wide range of different ways that business operations are conducted. Supply chains are one of the popular marketing channel arrangements. The first section of this chapter deals with overall channel structure and the rationale for marketing channels in highly developed industrial economies. The second section deals with market distribution strategy, focusing on structure, channel design, and types of relationships among channel participants. Information technology, specifically electronic commerce, has had significant impact on market distribution strategy and is discussed in the third section of the chapter. The final section of the chapter focuses on the interrelationship of marketing strategy decisions related to pricing and logistics considerations.

Market Distribution in the Supply Chain

Imagine a society in which every individual is totally self-sufficient: each individual would produce and consume all of the products and services necessary for survival so there would be no need for any economic activity related to the exchange of goods and services between individuals. No such society can be found today. In reality, as individuals begin to specialize in the production of specific goods or services, a mechanism must arise for the exchange of those goods and services to satisfy the consumption needs of individuals. To do so efficiently and effectively, firms must overcome three discrepancies: discrepancy in *space,* discrepancy in *time,* and discrepancy in *quantity and assortment.*

Discrepancy in space refers to the fact that the location of production activities and the location of consumption are seldom the same. Consider, for example, the household furniture industry. Most household furniture in the United States is manufactured in a small geographic area in North Carolina and a great deal of office furniture is manufactured in western Michigan. Yet, where is furniture demanded? All over the United States! This difference between the location of production and the location of consumption is a fundamental problem that must be overcome to accomplish exchange. Overcoming this locational discrepancy provides customers the service output of spatial convenience discussed in Chapter 3.

Discrepancy in time refers to the difference in timing between production and consumption. Some products, agricultural commodities for example, are produced during short time periods but are demanded by customers continuously. On the other hand, many products are manufactured in anticipation of future customer demand. Since manufacturing often does not occur at the same time products are demanded, inventory and warehousing are required. The specific manner in which this discrepancy is overcome results in the service output related to waiting time discussed in Chapter 3. It should be noted here that much of the discussion in this text is devoted to the challenges firms face in more closely matching the rate of production with market consumption.

Discrepancy in quantity and assortment refers to the fact that manufacturing firms typically specialize in producing large quantities of a variety of items. Customers, on the other hand, typically demand small quantities of numerous items. This difference between the production and consumption sectors of the economy must somehow be reconciled to deliver the product variety and assortment to customers.

These basic problems of exchange are resolved by the overall market distribution process, through the mechanism typically referred to as the **channel of distribution.** A channel of distribution can be defined as a network of organizations and institutions that, in combination, perform all the functions required to link producers with end customers to accomplish the marketing task. An understanding of distribution channels is essential for logistics managers because it is within the channel that logistics strategy is actually executed to accommodate customer requirements. In this section, important elements of channel theory related to marketing functions, specialization, the sorting process, and channel separation are reviewed to highlight the interaction between marketing channel requirements and logistical accommodation.

Marketing Functions

Those who study marketing have long acknowledged that a number of specific acts or activities are essential to the successful completion of exchange. Although there are many ways to classify these functions, the traditional list includes selling, buying, transporting, storing, financing, standardization, market financing, risk bearing, and market information. In the typical channel arrangement, a function may alternately be performed by different channel members or it may be performed and duplicated numerous times.

Table 4-1 presents the traditional grouping of the eight universal functions into three subsets: exchange, logistics, and facilitation. The exchange functions represent

TABLE 4-1   Universal Marketing Functions Performed by Channel Arrangements

Group	Function
Exchange	Selling
	Buying
Logistics	Transportation
	Storage
Facilitation	Financing
	Standardization
	Risk
	Market information

the activities necessary for ownership transfer. Selling is necessary to cultivate product demand through development of products that satisfy market needs and through techniques of demand stimulation, such as advertising and personal selling. Buying involves the planning and acquisition of assortments so that proper quantities and qualities of products will be available to meet customer requirements. The logistics functions consist of getting the right products to the right place at the right time. In contemporary logistics the scope of concern is significantly broader than transportation and storage, encompassing all work related to inventory positioning, which may include aspects of satisfying form and possession requirements as well. The other four functions are collectively referred to as facilitation because their performance is necessary to complete the exchange and logistics activities.

Specialization

The need for functional performance leads directly to the economic concept of **specialization.** Specialization is a fundamental driver of economic efficiency. Manufacturers are specialists in the production of specific products. Wholesalers and retailers are specialists in the sense that they buy and sell specific assortments tailored to the requirements of the target markets they have chosen to serve. Warehousing and transportation firms are specialists in the performance of logistical functions. The logic of specialization is based on economies of scale and scope. When a firm specializes, it develops scale and scope to achieve operational efficiency. In fact, much of the economic justification for specialized channel participants lies in their ability to efficiently perform an activity.

The economic justification for using a specialist is challenged when a firm generates sufficient volume to consider performing the activity internally. Conversely, a firm may choose to spin off, or outsource, certain functions when it finds that it does not have sufficient economies of scale, or when it chooses to focus on other functions it deems more closely related to its core competency. The point is that essential functions may be shifted from one firm to another, absorbed, spun off, and the like.[2] Regardless of who performs the specific work, all functions must be performed to complete the distribution process.

Assortment

Product assortment is directly related to specialization and has received considerable attention in the business literature.[3] Market accommodation requires that distribution channels provide consumers and end users with their desired levels of product variety and assortment. In channel arrangements a number of independent businesses often cooperate to deliver the appropriate mix of products; at strategic positions in a distribution channel, products are concentrated, sorted, and dispersed to the next location in the overall supply chain. This process has four basic steps: concentration, allocation, customization, and dispersion.

---

[2]Rich literature exists concerning functional absorption and spin-off, based on the work of Bruce Mallen. For example, see Bruce Mallen, "Functional Spin-off: A Key to Anticipatory Change in Distribution Structures," *Journal of Marketing,* 37, no. 3 (July 1973), pp. 18–25.

[3]See Wroe Alderson, *Marketing Behavior and Executive Action* (Homewood, IL: Richard D. Irwin, Inc., 1957), chapter 7.

Concentration refers to the collection of large quantities of a product or of multiple products so they can be sold as a group. A manufacturer's consolidation warehouse, for example, brings the output of several different factories to a single location. Alternatively, an industrial distributor or wholesaler may purchase from several manufacturers and bring the items to a single location. One purpose of concentration is to reduce transportation cost. The cost reduction results from moving large quantities of product to the concentration location rather than each supplier individually shipping small quantities directly to customers.

Allocation refers to breaking down a homogeneous group of products into smaller and smaller lot sizes to more closely match customer requirements. Products received from suppliers in truckload quantities may in turn be sold in case quantities. Case quantities may be broken into individual product units. Allocation is also known as the process of breaking bulk.

Customization refers to regrouping the products into an assortment of items for resale to uniquely meet a specific customer's requirements. Manufacturers, through their consolidation facilities, allow wholesale and retail customers to purchase full truckloads of mixed products. Similarly, wholesalers build mixed assortments of products for retailers and retailers build assortments for consumers. For example, warehouse stores such as Costco may desire a unique product pack, such as two boxes of cereal wrapped together. Another retailer may require special promotional displays, which may even combine products from two different manufacturers. In contemporary supply chains, the ability to customize is vital.

Dispersion is the final step in assortment. It consists of shipping the customized assortments to customers when and where specified. A hypothetical example can illustrate the overall process of assortment and also provide insight into a critical economic principle of distribution: **the principle of minimum total transactions.** Figure 4-1(a) shows a simple structure with three manufacturers and six customers. The customers could be consumers or industrial users. For simplicity, assume the customers are retailers who are attempting to develop an assortment for resale to their consumer markets. In this figure, each retailer buys directly from each manufacturer, requiring a total of 18 separate transactions, each with its associated order placement, order processing, and order fulfillment cost, including the cost of transportation of relatively small quantities from the manufacturers to the individual retail locations.

Figure 4-1(b) introduces one wholesaler into the structure to accomplish the entire process of assortment. The wholesaler purchases the output of each manufacturer, which is delivered to one location. The wholesaler then breaks bulk and customizes quantities according to each retailer's specific requirements and transports these customized assortments to the individual retail locations. Using this intermediary, the total number of transactions is reduced to nine. Three transactions are required from manufacturer to wholesaler and six from wholesaler to retailer. The savings in order placement, processing, and fulfillment costs can be substantial. Furthermore, the cost of transportation is substantially reduced because there are only 9 transportation movements, each of large quantity, rather than 18 individual small quantity shipments. Of course, the intermediary must be compensated for the work performed. However, since both the manufacturers' and the retailers' costs are lower, the potential for a lower total cost system exists, even including the costs incurred by the intermediate wholesaler.

The assortment process provides considerable insight into the economics of market distribution. It also demonstrates how distribution channels provide different customers with their desired levels of product variety and lot-size requirements. It helps

FIGURE 4-1

Principle of minimum transactions

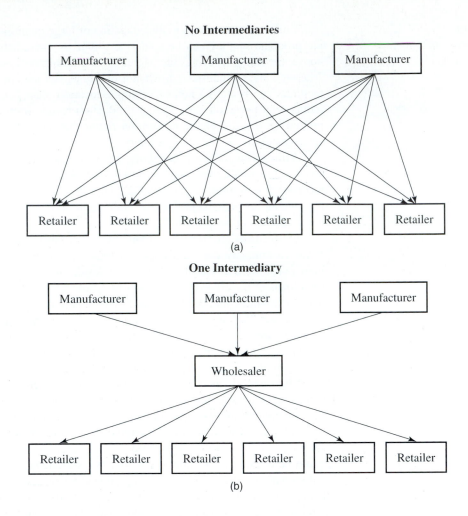

No Intermediaries

(a)

One Intermediary

(b)

explain why a manufacturer such as Kellogg would have a small grocery store purchase cereal through a wholesaler to obtain a wide assortment of food products. On the other hand, Kellogg might deal directly with large supermarket chains that purchase cereal in large volume quantities.

Channel Separation

The preceding discussion of specialization of functions and assortment leads to one other important concept in market distribution: **channel separation.** Separation usually focuses on isolating the buying and selling functions related to ownership transfer from the functions related to physical distribution or logistics. Although both sets of activities are necessary and must be coordinated, there is no requirement that they be performed simultaneously or even by the same businesses. A product may change ownership without physically moving or may be shipped and warehoused several times without changing ownership. Thus, the ownership, or marketing, channel consists of a network of firms engaged in buying and selling. It consists of intermediaries such as agents, industrial distributors, full and/or limited function wholesalers, sales representatives, and retailers, all of which are involved in negotiating, contracting, and administering sales on a continuing basis.

FIGURE 4-2

**Logistical and
marketing separation**

please explain this

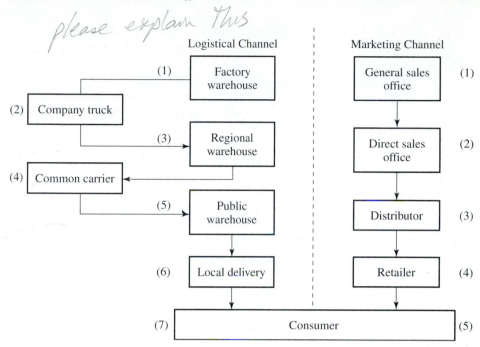

The physical, or logistics, channel represents a network of organizations involved with achieving inventory movement and positioning. The work of logistics involves transportation, warehousing, storage, handling, order processing, and an increasing array of value-added services concerned with achieving time, space, lot-size, and assortment requirements.

It must be noted that it is certainly possible that any given firm may participate in both the marketing and the logistics channels for a product. Wholesalers, distributors, and retailers typically do physically handle, store, and transport products, as well as participate in the marketing flows. It is very useful conceptually, however, to recognize that there is no requirement that a firm participate in both channels.

Separation in Practice

Figure 4-2 illustrates potential separation of the overall distribution channel for color televisions. The only time the marketing and logistics channels formally merge is at the manufacturer's factory and the consumer's home. Three specialists are employed in the logistics channel: a common transportation carrier, a public warehouse, and a specialized local delivery firm. In addition, three levels of logistics operations are performed by the manufacturer. Television sets are initially stored in the company's factory warehouse, transported in private trucks, and then stored in a regional warehouse facility before specialized intermediaries begin to participate in the logistics channel.

In the marketing channel, the distributor has legal title to the television sets from the time they are shipped from the manufacturer's regional warehouse. Retailers are served from the public warehouse. During the logistics process, the distributor never physically warehouses, handles, or transports the television sets. When the retailer sells a set, delivery is made to the consumer's home from the distributor's stock being held in the public warehouse. The retailer maintains limited stock for point-of-sale display. Sales are negotiated between the retailer and consumer, including a commitment to deliver a specified television set model directly to the consumer's residence.

Direct-to-home customer shipment is completed from a strategically located public warehouse, which may be many miles from the point-of-sale transaction and product delivery destination.

Structural separation, as illustrated, reflects common practice in a wide variety of industries such as furniture, appliances, and television sets. These businesses offer products with a variety of options, models, and colors. As such, it would be difficult for a retailer to stock the full range of products. Instead, the retailer limits inventory commitment to display items, keeping color swatches and option books on hand for customer demonstration. The benefits of logistical specialization result in low-cost delivery and effective marketing.

An additional example of separation is a factory branch sales office that carries no inventory. The office exists for the sole purpose of stimulating ownership transactions. The physical product exchange between seller and buyer may logistically move in a variety of combinations of transport and storage, depending on value, size, bulk, weight, and perishability of the shipment. Generally, no economic justification exists for locating warehouses and inventories at the same site as the branch offices. The network of branch sales offices is best designed to facilitate maximum marketing impact. The logistical structure should be designed to accomplish the required delivery performance and economies.

A final example of separation comes from the rapidly growing home shopping industry. An order placed by phone, at a local catalog desk, or via the Internet is typically fulfilled from a factory or distribution warehouse directly to the buyer's home. All direct marketing systems exploit separation to realize separation benefits.

Interdependence of Marketing and Logistics

While the emphasis in this text is on logistical flows, separation of marketing and logistics should not be interpreted to mean that either can stand alone. Both are essential to create customer value. The major argument favoring operational separation is increased opportunity for specialization.

Structural separation does not necessarily require outsourcing work to specialized service firms. A single firm may be able to internally satisfy all marketing and logistical requirements. The desired degree of operational separation depends on available service providers, economies of scale, resources, and managerial capabilities. The benefits of separation are independent of combining internal organization units with outside specialists. From an ownership transfer viewpoint, the customer value-creation process is not complete until logistical promises are fully performed. Depending on the products involved, the logistical operations may start in anticipation of, be simultaneous with, or follow actual sale. Logistical performance with respect to time, location, and terms of delivery must comply with specifications established during sales negotiation.

Market Distribution Strategy Development

The marketing channel is one of the least understood areas of business strategy. The diversity and complexity of channel arrangements make it difficult to describe and generalize the challenges managers face when developing a supply chain strategy. Marketing channels do not have uniform dimensions and often defy simple description. Some are very direct, linking manufacturers or growers of a product directly to consumers. Others contain many intermediate institutions with ownership transfer oc-

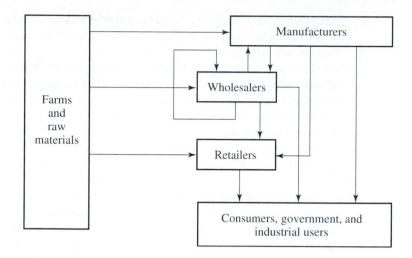

FIGURE 4-3

**Generic channels
of distribution**

curring many times. Complicating the subject is the fact that almost all firms are engaged in multiple channel arrangements as they seek the most effective means to penetrate many different market segments and meet the requirements of those segments they choose to serve.

Distribution Structure

Figure 4-3 illustrates an overall generic channel structure required to complete the marketing process. While its simplicity is misleading, it serves to illustrate the major types of institutions that may be involved in the overall process. Manufacturers are primarily involved in creating products. As the creators, they were traditionally considered to be the originators of channel arrangements and became the focal point for channel discussions. Comprehensive channel study, however, must include more than the manufacturer's perspective. To do otherwise would incorrectly position wholesalers and retailers as passive institutions.

In many channel situations, retailers are powerful and dominant in determining how the overall distribution process will be organized and what the management practices will be. As the institution closest to final customers, retailers have a great deal at stake in channel performance. Wholesalers are less visible in the process, but their role in orchestrating and coordinating the activities of many manufacturers with those of retailers cannot be ignored. Understanding the roles of the many types of channel participants is critical in developing market distribution strategy.

Channel Participants

Primary channel participants are those businesses that assume risk during the value-added distribution process. Below, the basic nature of each business type is reviewed. The purpose is to illustrate the extent, size, and complexity of potential distribution arrangements in an economy encompassing over 375,000 manufacturers, 450,000 wholesalers, and 1.1 million retail establishments.[4]

---

[4]All statistics related to number of firms and sales are from *1997 Census of Business,* U.S. Department of Commerce.

Manufacturers.   The process of combining materials and components into products is typically called **manufacturing** or **production.** Manufacturing firms are highly visible channel participants because they provide form utility by creating the products that become the primary concern of the overall distribution process.

Manufacturers take on significant risk with the creation of products. For example, General Motors, Ford, and DaimlerChrysler invest hundreds of million of dollars in developing, testing, and launching new styles, new options, and improved automobiles. Reputable manufacturers assume full responsibility for the quality of their products and their ultimate acceptance by customers. The most visible manufacturers are the firms that produce consumer products such as automobiles, appliances, food, pharmaceuticals, clothing, etc. These products, produced for mass consumption, often have highly advertised and publicized brands with high levels of consumer identification. But in reality, these firms represent only a small percentage of all companies engaged in manufacturing. The majority of manufacturing firms produce components, subassemblies, or ingredients that are sold to other business firms. Such business-to-business (B2B) marketing is critical to the overall performance of final-product manufacturing and distribution. It must be noted that while the extent of manufacturer's risk in the overall distribution process is considerable, it is limited to the specific products produced. Each specific manufacturer's products typically represent a small proportion of those handled by the other primary channel participants: wholesalers and retailers.

Wholesalers.   Perhaps the least understood and least visible channel participant is the **wholesaler.** Wholesalers are businesses that are primarily engaged in buying merchandise from manufacturers and reselling to retailers, industrial users, or business users. They may also act as agents in buying merchandise for or selling merchandise to companies. In 1997, there were over 450,000 wholesaling establishments in the United States with total sales exceeding $4 trillion!

The primary business of wholesalers is their specialization in performing assortment in a manner that reduces costs and risk for other channel members. For many years in many industries it has been thought that mergers, acquisitions, and continued concentration in both the manufacturing and retailing sectors of the economy would eliminate the economic justification of wholesalers. Yet, in many industries, wholesaling continues to flourish. Such firms as Super Value, True Value, Sysco, McKesson, Grainger, as well as many others, maintain their viability through innovative specialization in performing the assortment process for a large number of manufacturers and retailers. They do so by reducing risk, duplication of effort, and the number of transactions required to satisfy customer requirements. As described in Industry Insight 4-1, Valu Merchandisers developed a program for its retail customers that combines several product categories into a one-stop solution for nutritional and whole health products.

Retailers.   In simplest terms, **retail** is the business of selling goods and services to consumers who buy for their own use and benefit. In 1997, there were over 1.1 million retail establishments with total sales of over $3.8 trillion. Ranging in size and scope from such firms as Wal★Mart, Kroger, Toys R Us, and The Limited to individually owned and operated stores, retailers are clearly the most visible channel participant to consumers. They perform functions that combine to offer their target customers the right products, at the right place, at the right time, in the right quantity, and at the right price. The specific strategies employed by individual retail firms in providing these *rights* to consumers vary dramatically and range from mass merchandising to discounting, to super specialty, to focused service, and many

INDUSTRY INSIGHT 4-1 ONE-STOP SUPPLEMENTS

Valu Merchandisers, a Kansas City, Missouri-based wholesaler and subsidiary of Associated Wholesale Grocers, has developed Natural Solutions to offer consumers a convenient and complete whole health shopping experience. Natural Solutions incorporates frozen foods, dairy, books and magazines, bulk products, beauty care, and vitamins and herbal supplements into a whole health section. In addition, the Health Notes Online computer provides online access to additional health tips and a nutritional database with extensive reference materials. The section requires approximately 140 linear feet for optimal success. Industry information indicates that sales of related natural products can increase significantly when sections are merchandised correctly.

The Natural Solutions concept is consumer-driven. Generally, consumers desire to decrease their shopping time while saving money and choosing from a broad product assortment. According to Bob Carlson, director of nutrition centers for Valu, "Our position is that if we can offer a host of different products with the same theme in the same area, we can get consumers more interested in the overall section. That is going to boost traffic and it is going to boost sales. It's all about one-stop shopping."

The section concept is based upon shopping synergies. "We are trying to set a tone for the section and the overall store," says Carlson. "We don't want consumers to do the bulk of their grocery buying in our stores and then run across the street or down the block to a natural foods store for natural products. This strategy, we think, can keep the consumer in our store for all their purchases."

Source: Anonymous, "One-Stop Supplements," *Supermarket Business,* June 1999, pp. 67–8.

---

others. Retailing, in fact, is a dynamic industry that constantly changes as firms seek ways to appeal to and serve consumers.

The component of retail strategy of most concern to logistic operations is merchandise assortment. The investment in merchandise and resulting inventory risk assumed by retailers are substantial. The types and varieties of merchandise the retailer carries are defined by the specific consumer needs and wants it attempts to satisfy. Additionally, retailers make merchandise decisions regarding the depth of assortment concerning different brands, colors, sizes, styles, etc., to be offered to consumers. Along with decisions regarding fashion and quality level, these factors combine to shape retail decisions regarding supply and which distribution channels each retailer will include in their supply chain strategy. Thus, as large as Wal★Mart may be, it is not a participant in the supply chain of every potential supplier. Wal★Mart, in fact all retailers, must carefully craft supply chain relationships to effectively and efficiently serve targeted consumers.

Direct versus Indirect Structures

Figure 4-4 presents a range of potential channel structures that might be utilized to accommodate a particular consumer segment's requirements. The alternatives range from the extreme on the left of direct from manufacturer to consumer with no intermediary involvement, to the extreme on the right, which includes wholesale agents, wholesale merchants, and retail outlets. Should the channel be *direct,* involving no or very few intermediaries, or should it be *indirect,* involving several different intermediate institutions? This notion of direct versus indirect structure represents a fundamental strategic decision.

FIGURE 4-4

Typical channel structures

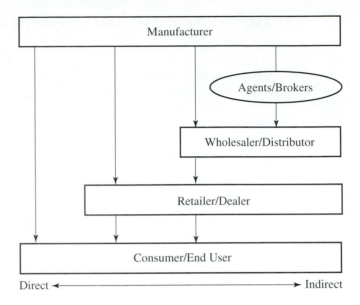

Earlier in this chapter the economies associated with intermediate stages of distribution were demonstrated. That discussion should not, however, be interpreted to mean that indirect distribution is always the appropriate solution. Furthermore, a question remains concerning the *degree of indirectness.* Which is the appropriate strategic choice? While no simple answer exists, the primary determinant lies in the consumer or end user's requirements. Recall from Chapter 3 that end-customer requirements were discussed in terms of lot sizes, variety and assortment, locational convenience, waiting time, and information. *As a general rule, as end-customer requirements for these outputs increase, the more likely it is that the required distribution structure will include intermediaries.* Several examples can be offered to demonstrate this point.

In Indonesia, and other developing countries, consumers with low discretionary income frequently purchase cigarettes one at a time from street vendors who purchase single packs from local wholesalers who purchase cartons from regional wholesalers. Because consumers desire to purchase in very small lot sizes, the distribution structure requires many intermediate levels. A direct manufacturer to consumer channel is infeasible. If consumers were willing to purchase in case lot quantities, however, a much more direct structure could be employed.

Perhaps a more comprehensive example can illustrate the nature of end-user requirements as the driver of channel structure. In the personal computer industry, Dell Computer pioneered the manufacturer direct-to-consumer distribution channel in the 1980s. Other PC manufacturers used, and most still use, a more indirect structure. The Dell channel is well suited for a particular type of consumer. A consumer who wants to buy one computer, who is willing to wait to receive the computer, does not desire to choose among several different brands, and has enough knowledge to intelligently specify all of the technical qualities desired can be well satisfied with the direct channel. Many other consumers, however, are not willing to wait days, or do not feel they personally have enough knowledge, or want to see an assortment of brands and models to compare features, quality, and prices. Their needs can only be satisfied through a structure that is less direct than that employed by Dell and which includes at least a retail intermediary.

As one thinks about the many different channel structures employed in the PC industry, it is worth also thinking about how each differs in the service requirements delivered to final consumers and end users. Gateway, for example, has a structure similar to Dell, with an important difference: the structure includes a retail level. In select markets, there are outlets called Gateway Country where potential customers can come to see, try out, and learn about Gateway computers. Customers can even buy a computer at Gateway Country. What they cannot do is take a computer home from a Gateway Country store. They still must wait for delivery. What is the advantage to Gateway of including this retail intermediary in its channel structure? The answer lies in the fact that it potentially satisfies a requirement of a number of customers—the requirement of information. Many consumers may feel that they do not have enough knowledge to make an intelligent choice of computers via the telephone or Internet. Gateway attempts to accommodate such information requirements through the Gateway Country retail store.[5]

Market Coverage

Related to the notion of channel structure is the decision concerning market coverage. Market coverage decisions involve choices concerning the relative intensity of outlets in any given geographic area so that the needs of existing and potential customers are adequately accommodated. Specifically, market coverage is most directly related to locational convenience for customers. Three basic market coverage alternatives exist: (1) intensive distribution, (2) selective distribution, and (3) exclusive distribution.

Intensive Distribution.   The placement of a product in as many outlets or locations as possible is known as **intensive distribution.** It is generally a logical choice for products that consumers purchase frequently and with minimal shopping effort, making locational convenience a key purchase requirement. Such products as soft drinks, candy, newspapers, gasoline, and aspirin represent just a few consumer products that are intensively distributed. For industrial end-users items such as maintenance, repair, and operating supplies (MRO), office supplies, and other industrial items may be intensively distributed.

On the surface it may seem that intensive distribution is the most logical alternative for all products and brands. After all, having a product available in many locations increases end-user convenience and, therefore, potential sales. Consider, however, what might happen to a manufacturer such as Sony if the decision were made to utilize intensive distribution. Sony might expand the number and types of outlets for televisions to include all mass merchandisers, discount stores, perhaps even drugstores and supermarkets, which frequently sell consumer electronics. As the number of outlets expands, Sony might increase market share in the short run, but several adverse consequences could also be expected. Some outlets might choose to sell Sony televisions at very low prices to attract consumers to their stores. This, in turn, might cause other outlets to reconsider their choice to participate in Sony's distribution channels. Some outlets could not provide the level of after-sales service necessary to support repair, and warranty, aggravating problems for those that do maintain such facilities. It is also likely Sony would take on more participation in marketing functions such as advertising, since many dealers who were once willing to promote Sony become reluctant to

---

[5]Robert Scally, "Gateway: The Crown Prince of Clicks-and-Mortar," *DSN Retailing Today,* May 8, 2000, pp. 75–6.

do so. While this discussion is, of course, speculative, it does demonstrate that intensive distribution is not the right choice for all products.

Selective Distribution.   The placement of a product or brand in a more limited number of outlets within a specific geographic area is called **selective distribution.** Of course, there can be many degrees of selectivity employed, ranging from almost intensive to almost exclusive. Again, the primary factor driving the choice is customer requirements for locational convenience and customers' willingness to spend time and effort to obtain the product. Sony televisions are, in fact, selectively distributed and made available through most electronics and appliance stores, and a limited number of other outlets, which will enhance its quality image and provide the level of support required for the brand.

Exclusive Distribution.   The exact opposite of intensive distribution, **exclusive distribution** involves placement of a brand in only one outlet in each geographic area. It is employed when consumers or end users are willing to expend considerable shopping effort and locational convenience is of little concern to them. It is also used when a firm wants to project an image of high quality, such as Rolex watches, or when very high levels of reseller support are required. Thus, construction and farm equipment, some brands of household furniture, designer fashion apparel, and similar products are exclusively distributed.

While certain types of products may seem to fit a particular market coverage alternative, generalizations can be misleading. It must be re-emphasized that companies choose which customers they will attempt to serve and that specific segments, or even individual customers, differ in their service requirements. Even in a product category such as candy, different choices have been made by competitive firms. Lifesaver mints, for example, are intensively distributed. Altoids, on the other hand, have more selective market coverage. Godiva is, for all practical purposes, available only through exclusive outlets. Finally, it should be noted that market coverage and channel structure are closely related. Intensive distribution generally necessitates indirect channels involving multiple intermediaries, whereas high selectivity and exclusivity may be supported through more direct channel structures.

Market Distribution Channel Design Process

The above discussion of structure and distribution coverage has emphasized the need to understand end-user requirements when developing market distribution strategy. As strategy is developed, the specific channel design must be defined. Two tools of significant assistance are channel mapping and a matrix approach to the design process. Each is explained below.

Channel Mapping
Figure 4-5 provides an example of channel mapping, the first of these tools. A **channel map** essentially is a flow diagram of the channels utilized by a specific firm. It is developed through careful research within an organization and discussions with numerous executives regarding how to go to market. As hard as it may be to believe, such research is an important step because, in most instances, very few people have a comprehensive understanding of the distribution channels utilized by their firm.

The purpose of mapping is to provide insight into current processes and establish a blueprint for change. Before channel design can be changed, or to decide whether

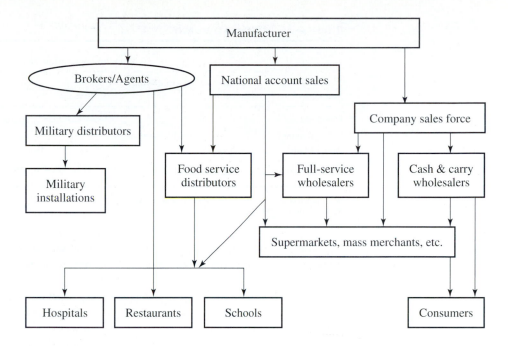

FIGURE 4-5

Channel map—food processor

change is appropriate, a full understanding of the current process is needed. Even when designing from scratch for a new company or a new product, mapping the industry and key competitors is useful.

Developing a channel map should begin with clear delineation of the market segments being served. Figure 4-5 illustrates a simplified map of the distribution channels for a food manufacturer. Three distinct market segments are identified: (1) consumers, (2) institutional users, and (3) military installations. A more comprehensive map could be drawn to illustrate distinct subsegments within each of these categories but would result in more complexity than is needed to explain mapping. The mapping process then proceeds backward from the markets being served to identify the different types of channel participants capable of serving their market distribution requirements.

Channel mapping does not end with construction of a diagram. It should also include specification of the volume of activity related to each link in the map. For example, what percentage of the total volume goes to the military, institutions, and consumers? Each link should also be examined closely to see what are the specific functions and activities performed by the channel participants and what are the economic characteristics of the transactions. For example, what are prices, expenses, and margins associated with each link in the map?

One result of the mapping process is the ability to pinpoint areas of potential duplication of effort, waste, and/or shifting of functions. It provides a *roadmap* that can be used to ask questions such as what shortcuts are possible. For example, could the food processor depicted in Figure 4-5 rearrange functional performance in such a way that overlap between wholesale intermediary activities is eliminated or at least reduced? It also provides a framework for understanding functional performance in each channel echelon and for raising issues concerning the appropriate financial implications. For example, are the costs and margins involved between broker and full-function wholesaler justifiable, given the functional performance and volume activity? Or, might some rearrangement provide a more effective and efficient design?

TABLE 4-2   **Matrix Approach**

	Demand Generation Tasks				
Sources	**Lead Generation**	**Qualifying Sales**	**Presales**	**Closing**	**Postsales Service**
Direct Sales			Large Lot-Size	Large Lot-Size	Large Lot-Size
Telemarketing		All Customers			All Customers
Direct Mail	All Customers				
Distributors			Small Lot-Size	Small Lot-Size	Small Lot-Size

Source: Adapted from Rowland T. Moriarty and Ursala Moran, "Managing Hybrid Marketing Systems." *Harvard Business Review,* November/December 1990, p. 151.

The channel map does not in and of itself provide answers to such questions. It does, however, provide insight into possible design flaws and potential changes in strategy or tactics. Ultimately, such maps help develop an understanding of which aspects of the current channel are working well and which are not.

Matrix Approach

A second tool for use in channel design is a simple, yet effective, matrix approach.[6] Because most companies serve several segments of consumers and end users, different structures and combinations of channel participants may be needed to serve each of those segments as efficiently and effectively as possible. The matrix approach involves extending the concept of separation discussed earlier in this chapter and provides insight into the most appropriate participants and structures to accomplish objectives. In fact, the matrix approach is based on the concept of channel separation and marketing functions discussed earlier in this chapter.

Extending Channel Separation.   The earlier discussion of separation demonstrated that marketing and logistics channels may have different firms and no firm *necessarily* has to participate in both. The matrix design approach extends this concept by suggesting that each function can be further subdivided into specific individual activities. Each activity could potentially be performed by different channel participants. For explanatory purposes, consider the selling function and its related activities. Keep in mind that the same approach could be employed for other functions.

Table 4-2 shows a matrix for design of the selling channel for a hypothetical firm. Across the top, specific activities of the sales task are individually specified: generating sales prospects, qualifying those prospects, presale negotiation, closing the sale, and providing postsales service. The rows of the matrix consist of alternative means, some internal and some external, of performing each of the necessary activities. In the example matrix, four alternatives are under consideration: (1) a direct sales force, (2) telemarketing, (3) direct mail, and (4) independent distributors.

Relating Activities to Participants.   The art of the matrix design process comes in most efficiently and effectively assigning activities to participants for specific customer segments. A hypothetical example is used to illustrate this process.

---

[6]For the original discussion of the matrix design process, see Rowland T. Moriarity and Ursala Moran, "Managing Hybrid Marketing Systems," *Harvard Business Review,* November/December 1990, pp. 146–55.

Suppose the company has targeted two market segments to be served. These segments have been defined as customers who purchase in large lot-size quantities and those who purchase in small lot-size quantities. In this hypothetical example, it would not be cost-efficient to generate sales leads or quality prospects for customers who purchase in small lot-size quantities through use of a direct sales force. The lead generation task might be assigned to direct mail and prospect qualification to telemarketing. Note that all potential customers fall into these two segments for these two tasks. After customers have been qualified, large lot-size customers are assigned to the direct sales force for negotiation and closing the sale. Small lot-size customers are assigned to distributors for those tasks. Postsales service is accomplished for certain service activities by telemarketing. Other activities may require direct sales or distributor participation.

The final distribution channel design comes from consideration of which activities can most cost effectively meet customers' requirements for completion of which tasks. In our simple example, two critical points are clear. First, no one channel has to perform all of the activities required to complete a function. Note that telemarketing was used only for prospect qualification and for certain postsales service activities. Second, no activity has to be completely performed by any given channel member for any market segment. The direct sales force and the distributor channels perform only those activities related to their specific segments.

Channel Relationships

Throughout this chapter, it has been stressed that channel structures, based on specialization of function and activities, typically result in arrangements of independent firms. Each firm is dependent upon the others for success in the marketplace. As such, dependency provides a useful framework for understanding the types of behavioral relationships observed in distribution. Three channel classifications are identified ranging from least to most open expression of dependence: (1) single-transaction channels, (2) conventional channels, and (3) relational collaborative arrangements (RCAs). True supply chain arrangements are characterized as selected forms of RCAs.

Each form of channel involvement reflects a different degree of commitment by its participants. Figure 4-6 provides a graphic illustration of arrangements based on acknowledged dependence. This classification also provides a distinction between transaction and relational structures. In transactional arrangements little or no acknowledged dependency exists. Participants feel no responsibility to each other. The laws and obligations that govern buying and selling operate as the sole foundation for ownership transfer. In relational channels, participants recognize dependency and feel committed to one another. While all types of channels have logistical requirements, those classified as relational offer the greatest opportunity for developing supply chain arrangements.

Managing these relationships to reduce conflict, avoid duplication and waste, and develop cooperative solutions to common problems is the true essence of supply chain management. Relationship management is discussed in detail in Chapter 17.

Single-Transaction Channels

A great many business transactions are negotiated with the expectation that the exchange will be a one-time event. Examples of single-transaction channels are real estate sales, stock and bond ownership transfer, and the purchase of durable equipment such as processing plants and heavy machinery.

While single-transaction channel engagements are not important in terms of relationship management, they are significant to the businesses involved. Requirements to

FIGURE 4-6

Classification of channel relationships based on acknowledged dependency

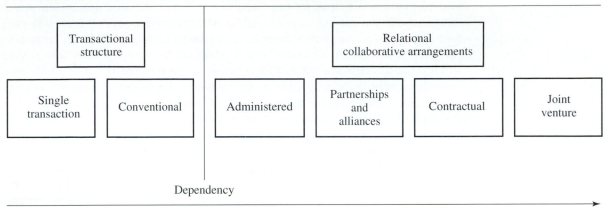

Increased formalization, information-sharing, and connectivity

complete promised delivery are often technical and difficult to accomplish. The movement of oversized equipment, such as a printing press, typically requires special permits and is often restricted to specific times of the day or year. In some situations, special transportation and materials handling equipment are required to accommodate size and weight of the products involved. If a firm deals primarily with single transactions, logistics performance is critical and typically represents a significant cost of overall operations. Failure to develop repetitive patterns of business with repeat buyers makes each logistical assignment a unique event. Even if the logistical activity proceeds without a glitch and all parties are highly satisfied, the likelihood of a repetitive transaction is minimal.

Conventional Channels

Conventional channels are best viewed as loose arrangements or affiliations of firms that buy and sell products on an as-needed basis, without concern for future or repeat business. The prime determinant of the timing and extent of transactions is selling price.

Firms involved in a conventional channel develop operational capabilities to provide services necessary to fulfill their own basic business missions. They have little or no loyalty to each other and little motivation to cooperatively improve the efficiency of the supply chain.

Activity in a conventional channel is conducted on a transaction-to-transaction basis. The typical transaction is adversarial in that the negotiation is price-dominated, creating an us-against-them posture. In other words, the involved firms fail to work out a formalized long-term relationship; either party is free to exit the relationship whenever it wishes. Involvement occurs until a better deal comes along. In fact, it is not uncommon for firms to start and stop doing business with each other several times within a single year.

Two points are significant concerning conventional channels. First, they are an important part of the overall business structure because of their sheer transaction volume. Second, because firms do not develop synergisms with trading partners, opportunities to gain efficiency by virtue of cooperation are sacrificed in favor of maintaining autonomy.

Relational Collaborative Arrangements

The distinctive feature of RCAs is that participating firms acknowledge dependency and develop joint benefits through cooperation to achieve industry superiority. To participate in such systems, each channel member must be willing to perform specific duties. In this way, the various forms of RCAs represent relationship management characteristic of supply chains.

The overall relationship of an RCA is typically orchestrated by a firm that is acknowledged as the leader. The leader is most often the dominant firm in the channel in terms of market share, size, or technical skills. The firm that provides leadership typically has the greatest relative power in the arrangement.

While acknowledged dependency is the cohesive force in RCA arrangements, it also creates conflict. Managers may feel that their firm is not getting a fair share of benefits or that they are being placed in an unnecessarily risky position. When potential or real conflict develops, it is essential that it be resolved to maintain channel solidarity. For an RCA to have stability the leader must resolve conflict situations in terms of the long-term interests of the overall channel. Finally, since RCAs are expected to exist for a substantial time period, it is important that the leader provide a vision of the future, facilitate joint planning, and change management as necessary to maintain competitive superiority.

In a broad sense, all channel systems that involve two or more independent firms have a degree of relationship structure. When relationships are managed to achieve joint goals and participating firms feel obligated to each other, the relationship becomes a supply chain. Four forms of RCAs are common: (1) administered systems, (2) partnerships and alliances, (3) contractual systems, and (4) joint ventures. As one would expect, the acknowledgment of dependency increases as the arrangement moves from administered system to joint venture.

Administered Systems.   The least formal RCA is the **administered system.** The interesting feature of an administered arrangement is that typically no formal or stated dependency is acknowledged on the part of participants. Usually a dominant firm assumes leadership responsibility and seeks cooperation of trading partners and service suppliers. While bordering on a conventional channel arrangement, an administered system seems to be guided by a mutual understanding that all independent companies will be better off if they work together and follow the leader.

On the part of the leader, it is essential that decisions be made in a manner that takes each channel participant's welfare into consideration. All channel members must view the relationship as fair and equitable. Operational stability is dependent on the leader sharing rewards as opposed to purely adversarial give-and-take negotiation that typifies a conventional channel. With enlightened leadership, an administered system can be maintained over an extended period of time. The firm providing leadership can operate at any channel level; however, most examples of administered systems are led by dominant retailers.

Many firms perceive the benefits possible from working together in the channel but are not comfortable with the lack of formalization that is characteristic of the administered arrangement. In some situations, two or more relatively powerful firms such as Wal★Mart and Procter & Gamble may desire to work closer but feel the need to develop a more structured relationship. When such formalization takes place, the dependency of the relationship becomes widely acknowledged and the participating firms form partnerships and alliances.

Partnerships and Alliances.   As firms desire greater clarity and longer-term commitment than typically provided in an administered system, they may seek to formalize their relationships. The typical extension is to form a nonlegal partnership and over time extend the relationship toward an alliance. In these arrangements, the firms give up some of their operational autonomy in an effort to jointly pursue specific goals. The expectation is that the arrangement will prevail for a substantial period of time.

A great many business arrangements are referred to by the participating firms as **partnerships.** Along with administered systems, the partnership working relationship is at the lower end of the dependency scale. While firms acknowledge mutual dependence, their tolerance to be led is minimal. In other words, the acknowledgment of a degree of loyalty tends to solidify repetitive business transactions as long as everything else is satisfactory. The commitment to the arrangement typically falls short of a willingness to modify fundamental business methods and procedures. Nevertheless, a true partnership reflects a dependency commitment far greater than an administered arrangement. At the very least, such partnerships build on the expressed desire to work together that typically involves an attitude of working out differences and, most of all, a level of information sharing. The weak link of many fledgling partnerships is the inability to resolve truly disruptive differences of opinion. A typical example of such conflict often involves price increases. If a firm's response to a supplier's requested price increase is to open the business to bid, then the quality of the partnership arrangement is doubtful. A true partnership arrangement must approach such routine adjustments in a problem-solving format. If such interorganizational compatibility exists, the partnership is moving toward an alliance.

The essential feature of an **alliance** is a willingness of participants to modify basic business practices. If managers feel that the overall business arrangement can benefit from best practice modification and they are willing to change, then the relationship is a true alliance. The motivation behind alliances is more fundamental than simply locking in the business. While repetitive business is important, emphasis on best practice is aimed at reducing duplication and waste and facilitating joint efficiencies. *In essence, the alliance goal is to cooperatively build on the combined resources of participating firms to improve the performance, quality, and competitiveness of the channel.* Such cooperation requires a commitment to information sharing and problem solving. The expected result is a win–win for all participants. This type of RCA format represents the channel arrangement most often referred to as a supply chain.

While partnerships are relatively easy to find, true alliances are more difficult to identify. Several high-profile alliances in the drug, garment, building supply, mass merchandise, and food industries have recently gained national publicity. Developing alliances has appeal because they can magnify the economic and market leverage of individual firms without financial investment. What results is the *power of cooperation.* The human and financial resources of alliance members are pooled to improve the overall competitiveness of the channel arrangement. Industry Insight 4-2 describes a unique partnership arrangement between two competitors, Ford Motor Company and DaimlerChrysler, and Exel Logistics, which resulted in substantial efficiency in distributing auto parts to dealers.

Contractual Systems.   As the name implies, many firms desire to conduct business within the confines of a formal contract. The most common forms of contractual agreements in distribution relationships are franchises, dealerships, and agreements between service specialists and their customers. The commitment to a contract takes

INDUSTRY INSIGHT 4-2 DAIMLERCHRYSLER AND FORD MOTOR COMPANY—PARTNERS?

Though the idea runs counter to competitive rivalries in the auto industry, DaimlerChrysler and Ford Motor Company, along with Exel Logistics, have built a successful partnership to improve service and reduce the cost of parts distribution.

The pilot program was tested with 11 dealers in northern Michigan. Dealerships were spread across a wide geographic area, requiring a large number of delivery vehicles; however, the capacity of these vehicles was underutilized. Under the arrangement, Ford paid a fee to place its parts on the dedicated fleet operated by Exel for the distribution of DaimlerChrysler parts. The test was a success and both companies expect to establish shared-service agreements with other auto companies in the future. They are considering a second phase of the test that could include 50 to 100 dealerships.

The pilot program created a template for developing future shared-service agreements. Both companies found that a third-party provider was key to implementing the agreement. Exel had resources that the automakers lacked, including time, personnel, and technology. It was also critical to create detailed protocols.

After the test in Michigan, DaimlerChrysler and Ford ran a similar test in Mexico. The geography and dealership dispersion throughout Mexico was conducive to the shared-service concept. The routes were relatively long and the freight density was relatively low, creating available freight space. Auto dealers outside Mexico City bought less than 50 percent of the parts sold in the country, but distribution to them accounted for 90 percent of the miles. Additionally, each of the partners stood to realize some significant benefits. DaimlerChrysler would realize savings from current rates; Ford would increase service levels to its dealers; and Exel would gain added revenue from the route.

Jerry Campbell, manager of North American logistics and customs for Ford's customer service division, says that the shared services idea is one way of meeting the constant cost pressure. "Optimally, we should [share services] within our own company, then extend it to other customers and providers." In fact, Ford's customer service division already shares services with Volvo, which Ford Motor Company owns, and with Mazda, in which it has a major equity stake.

What makes a shared-services project successful? According to Tim Flucht, Exel's account manager for the Ford/DaimlerChrysler projects, "The basic paradigm you have to get past is competition. People have in their minds that certain parts of the supply chain are a competitive advantage. That may or may not be true. If it is true, you have to consider it very carefully. It is less of an issue when it is only a perceived advantage." The managers of Ford and DaimlerChrysler agreed that the consumer had already made the purchase choice. Flucht states, "Now it was a matter of sharing costs or continuing to pay the full amount."

Other important factors in the success of shared-services partnerships are a large degree of trust and openness in considering how to implement the program.

Source: Anonymous, "Auto Pilot," *Logistics,* July 2000, pp. 89, 90, and 92.

———————————————

the relationship out of the pure voluntary framework that is characteristic of an alliance. In place of pure cooperation, the contractual arrangement establishes a set of legal obligations.

Many firms desire contracts because of the stability gained by formalizing commitment. In the case of a franchise or dealership, the formal agreement serves as guarantee concerning a firm's rights and obligations related to representing a service or product in a specific geographical area. The granting firm is ensured that conformance to specified ways of conducting business will occur and that a required minimum purchase will be made. Franchises and dealerships are most common in the marketing structure of automotive and fast food industries.

Many of the contractual arrangements are specifically directed to performance of the logistical activities necessary to complete distribution. For example, one of the most common forms of RCA contracting involves for-hire transportation. The most common contract between a shipper and carrier specifies the expected level of performance and establishes the fee or rate to be paid for the service. A typical example would be a carrier's agreement to regularly provide a predetermined amount of a specific type of equipment to a shipper. The shipper, in turn, may agree to load and position the equipment for efficient line-haul pickup by the carrier. The contract specifies the obligation of participating parties and the negotiated price.

The contract is a vital part of many logistical arrangements. Because many logistics relationships require extensive capital investment, participating company shareholders and financial providers desire contractual agreements to specify risk. Therefore, some degree of contracting is common throughout the range of voluntary relational arrangements.

Joint Ventures.   Some distribution arrangements are simply too capital-intense for development by a single firm. Therefore, two or more firms may select to jointly invest in an arrangement. The strictest **joint venture** involves two or more firms joined economically to create a new business entity. While such start-ups from scratch are not common, opportunities exist for future development.

The more likely joint venture scenario occurs when a shipper decides to fully outsource all of its logistics requirements—including facilities, equipment, and day-to-day operations—to a third-party or contract service provider. A logical way to arrange this outsourcing is to establish a joint venture between the shipper and service firm. The establishment of a business relationship where all management groups participate serves to reduce the risk, especially when broad-based exclusive arrangements are required.

E-Commerce Impacts on Market Distribution

Perhaps no single subject has received as much attention in recent literature as the explosive growth of electronic commerce throughout the world. Almost daily, articles appear in the general, business trade, and academic press concerning the volume of business transacted currently, projections for the future, and the fundamental change being created by electronic commerce. Many articles focus on the so-called new economy and how the firms involved in the old economy are being challenged, or even made obsolete, by the dynamics of the new economy.[7] While electronic commerce has many different forms, including fax and traditional EDI (Electronic Data Exchange), much recent discussion focuses on the Internet and its implications for how businesses go to market.

The pace of change makes it very difficult to generalize precisely what will be the long-term impacts on market distribution. Below, attention is first focused on the development of a new retail format, the so-called e-tailers, which began to emerge in the late 1990s. Of course, many disappeared by early 2001. Discussion then is directed to

---

[7]For example, see Barry Janoff, "New Economy," *Progressive Grocer,* June 2000, pp. 18–28.

new channel alternatives and relationships among channel participants fostered by electronic commerce. Finally, an assessment is offered as to how these developments will impact the logistics activities required to support increased complexity of marketing channels. The focus in this chapter is on e-commerce in the consumer sector of the economy. The changing nature of B2B relationships as impacted by e-commerce is discussed in Chapter 5.

The Emergence of E-Tailing

It is unclear today just who was the first so-called e-tailer. Who first decided to take advantage of the fact that the widespread availability of personal computers and usage of the Internet presented a new business opportunity to present consumers with an alternative means of shopping? As early as 1992, Internet Service Providers (ISPs) such as America Online began to offer customers the ability to enter virtual shopping malls where they could browse through merchandise offered by a number of virtual stores, and select and order merchandise for delivery direct to the house. The earliest efforts, however, met with limited success as consumers initially resisted the concept of online ordering. While these virtual malls reported rather large numbers of consumers browsing the merchandise, actual sales transactions were limited.

In 1995, Jeff Bezos founded Amazon.com. While perhaps not the first e-tailer, the success of Amazon.com in generating both publicity and sales revenue makes it a prime example of how e-tailing emerged as a channel alternative. Amazon.com and other e-tailers offer an alternative shopping format, which has both advantages and disadvantages relative to traditional land-based bricks and mortar stores. One significant advantage is locational convenience, for what can be more convenient than shopping from your own personal computer?

A second advantage arises from the assortment that can be offered to consumers from this format. Unconstrained by physical limitations of store space, the e-tailer can offer for sale a complete assortment of product that cannot be matched by any bricks and mortar store. Even before it branched into numerous other product categories, Amazon.com offered consumers over one million choices of book titles. A third advantage offered is information. Potential buyers can access book reviews by both professional reviewers and those written by other consumers and can easily find books related to subjects of interest or books written by favorite authors.

The most important disadvantages for the consumer shopping via e-tailing are waiting time, the inability to physically browse, handle, or try the merchandise, and concerns related to security. Once purchased, the consumer must wait at least 1 day, with waiting times extending to weeks in many instances, depending upon actual inventory availability. Additionally, consumers frequently want to physically handle merchandise, whether it is skimming the pages of a book or trying on clothing to ensure proper fit. Finally, concerns about security include the potential for credit card fraud and the ability of companies to amass considerable personal information about individual backgrounds, tastes, and habits. Despite the limitations, it is clear that e-tailing has appeal to a significant number of consumers. Consumer purchasing from e-tailers was estimated at $20 billion in 1999 and is projected to be as much as $180 billion by the year 2004.[8]

---

[8]"Shopping Online Opens Strong in 2000," *USA Today,* March 1, 2000, p. B-1.

New Channel Alternatives

Considerable speculation has developed that the Internet will open a new world of relationships among manufacturers and service companies and their final consumers. The Internet potentially provides a mechanism for suppliers to gain inexpensive direct access to customers. Alternatively, it has been suggested that consumers desire to gain direct access to firms that manufacture products. Regardless, the speculation is that there is reduced need for complex market channel relationships involving agents, wholesalers, or retail stores. After all, if consumers are willing to shop via the Internet, why not deal directly with product/service manufacturers, bypass existing channel arrangements, and bring a new era characterized by emergence of direct channels as the primary mechanism for the new economy?[9]

In fact, many examples of just such direct channel development exist. In the air passenger industry, almost every airline has established a website providing detailed information concerning routes, flights, availability, prices, etc. Consumers can perform their own search, by time or price, and execute their own flight itineraries. Simultaneously, the airlines have reduced commissions paid to travel agents who traditionally perform these searches. Many product manufacturers also have established websites where consumers can access volumes of information concerning products, product use, and demonstrations, and receive promotional offers. In such instances, it is easy to imagine the consumer simply placing an order directly with the manufacturer.

Given the widespread availability and the low cost associated with the marketing transactions via the Internet, many have projected that the future will be an era of role redefinition and shifting of marketing functions back to the originators of products and services. In short, they predict an era of widespread channel *disintermediation* whereby traditional marketing channels will no longer be necessary to close the gaps between producers and consumers. The result, as hypothesized, will be lower prices to consumers and higher profits to suppliers.

The fact is that consumers have shown great willingness to interact directly with manufacturers via the Internet, increasing manufacturers' participation in marketing flows, which traditionally were more likely to be completed by or shared with channel intermediaries. Research shows that a large number of consumers do visit manufacturer websites; they visit frequently and at several stages of the buying process. Table 4-3 presents data from one study of online consumers showing that many consumers use manufacturer websites for such purposes as researching product and purchase information. The data shows, however, that only 27 percent of the consumers had used the manufacturer's website to make a purchase.

Of course, a large number of manufacturers do not provide consumers with the ability to make online purchases. Their slow adoption of the Internet as a mechanism to complete direct sales transactions stems from three sources. First, most manufacturers are not capable of efficiently completing the logistical fulfillment required by consumer-direct transactions. Second, there is tremendous reluctance by many manufacturers to bypass established distribution channels and disrupt relationships with existing channel intermediaries. In a highly publicized event in 1999, The Home Depot sent a letter to its suppliers informing them that The Home Depot would no longer do

---

[9]See, for example, Robert Benjamin and Rolf Wigand, "Electronic Markets and Virtual Value Chains on the Information Superhighway," *Sloan Management Review,* Winter 1995, pp. 52–62; Debra Spar and Jeffrey Bussgang, "Ruling the Net," *Harvard Business Review,* May/June 1996, pp. 125–33.

TABLE 4-3   Empowered Consumers Look at Manufacturers as Retailers*

"When in the purchase process are you likely to visit a manufacturer's website?"

When not buying their products	*Awareness*	45%
When researching a product	*Consideration*	75%
After deciding what to buy and where to buy it	*Preference*	16%
To make a purchase	*Purchase*	27%
After deciding what to buy, but not where to buy it		42%
After buying, to find out about repair and service options	*Post-sale*	25%
After buying, for help installing and configuring a product		31%
After buying, to register a warranty		40%

"What kind of information have you looked for on the manufacturer's site within the last 6 months?"

Production information	79%	New product developments	37%
Product prices	79%	Warranty and guarantee information	35%
Where to buy specific products	49%	Installation and configuration info.	31%
Customer support	44%	General company information	31%
Accessory information about a product I already own	42%	How to connect with people with similar interests	4%

*Based on surveys from 8,842 online consumers. Data from Forrester's Technographics Online Retail & Media 2000 Field study (Forrester Research, Inc., Report: Channel Conflict Crumbles, March 2000, p. 2).

business with any manufacturer engaged in consumer-direct sales. Few manufacturers are willing to disrupt their relationships with established retail organizations. In the toy industry, Mattel discontinued efforts at online sales, and in the clothing industry, Levi-Strauss, which had been a pioneer in development of online capability, announced that it would stop selling jeans through its site.

Finally, it should be noted that while manufacturer direct-to-consumer sales via the Internet offer consumers many of the same advantages as e-tailing, it suffers a critical disadvantage. Manufacturers cannot offer the broad selection of products that can be offered by a retailer, whether a physical store or an Internet site. When consumers want a wide variety of product line and brand choices, direct transactions with manufacturers are not desirable. As a simple example, imagine trying to complete weekly grocery shopping via direct interaction with manufacturers.

Increased Channel Complexity

In contrast to disintermediation and channel simplification resulting from the Internet stands the potential for increased channel complexity. As existing businesses expand their activities in electronic commerce with consumers, and e-tailing gains in popularity with consumers, distribution relationships may proliferate and give rise to other forms of intermediaries. Many of these intermediaries were unheard of just a few years ago but currently play an important role in market distribution. Organizations with such names as affiliate sites, portals, and search engines have become an integral part of market distribution. Meanwhile, traditional wholesalers and retailers continue to operate, sometimes in conjunction with these new intermediaries. Consider, for ex-

INDUSTRY INSIGHT 4-3 CLICKS AS TRANSACTIONS

A simple, everyday example of Internet shopping will show how hypermediation works. Let's say that an occasional Web user—I'll call him Bob—becomes interested in the ubiquitous Harry Potter books. He thinks that he'd like to read them, but he wants to learn a little more about them. So he goes onto the Web and, since he's never bothered to change his browser's default home page, he ends up at the Netscape portal. In the search box he types the phrase "Harry Potter," and from a list of available search services he chooses, on a whim, GoTo.com. He's transported to the GoTo site, where his search results are posted. He chooses a promising-sounding site near the top called "Nancy's Magical Harry Potter Page."

Nancy's site, a personal home page with an unsophisticated but friendly design, is full of information that Bob finds useful. There are glowing reviews of the books by Nancy and a few of her friends, detailed plot summaries and character descriptions, and a discussion board where readers share their comments. There's also a link to a special Harry Potter page at eToys. Bob clicks on the link, and he finds that eToys is selling the first book in the series for just $8.97— 50 percent off its list price. He can't resist that kind of a bargain, so he takes out his Visa card and places an order. Three days later, the book is in his mailbox.

A fairly routine buying expedition on the Web, right? But consider the complex array of intermediaries that made money off Bob's modest purchase. There are the usual suspects, of course—the retailer eToys, the book distributor that eToys buys from, the bank that issued Bob's Visa card, the U.S. Postal Service. But there are less obvious players as well. First is Netscape. Netscape puts various search services on its home page and, in return, the services pay Netscape a penny or two every time a visitor clicks through to their sites. So when Bob was transferred to GoTo.com, Netscape received a little money. GoTo, for its part, auctions off its top search results to the highest bidders. Nancy, for instance, agreed to pay GoTo 1 cent for every searcher who clicks on her link. So when Bob chose Nancy's site, GoTo made a penny. GoTo didn't get to keep all of it, though. Because GoTo contracts with an outside provider, Inktomi, to conduct its searches, it had to pay Inktomi a fraction of that penny for processing Bob's search.

Then there's Nancy herself. Like thousands of other individuals who have personal Web pages, Nancy has signed up to be an affiliate of eToys. When she sends someone to eToys through a link on her page, the e-tailer pays her 7.5 percent of any resulting purchases. So Nancy made a cool 67 cents when Bob bought the book. What's more, eToys doesn't run its own affiliate program. It outsources the job to a company named Be Free. Be Free, in turn, takes a small cut on the purchases it administers. So it, too, got a little of Bob's money.

Add them up, and you'll find that no fewer than nine intermediaries had their fingers in Bob's $8.97 purchase. (And that doesn't even include the people who posted reviews on Nancy's site; they just haven't realized that they could be charging for their words.) In fact, every single time Bob clicked his mouse, a transaction took place: a little bit of value was created, and a little bit of money changed hands. Yes, the money usually amounted to only a penny or two, but it seems a safe bet that far more profit was made by the intermediaries that took those pennies than by eToys when it sold the book for half price. Bob's transaction is a microcosm of the emerging economic structure of e-commerce: the profits lie in intermediate transactions, not in the final sale of a good.

Source: Nicholas G. Carr, "Hypermediation: Commerce as Clickstream," *Harvard Business Review,* January/February 2000, pp. 46–7.

ample, that Barnes and Noble and Toys R Us have expanded their activities to include e-tailing. Rather than channel disintermediation, business-to-consumer e-commerce gives rise to what one author has called *hypermediation,* as channels of distribution adapt to the potential of the Internet.[10] Industry Insight 4-3 describes a consumer purchase of a book via the Internet and the many intermediaries involved in the purchase.

The most significant challenge posed by business-to-consumer electronic commerce is not the marketing and sales challenge; in fact, sales trends in 1999 and 2000 clearly demonstrate that some consumers are willing to shop and purchase electronically. Instead, the major challenge lies in the logistics process and efficient order fulfillment to satisfy consumer requirements. While e-commerce can significantly reduce marketing transaction costs related to generating and processing orders, it significantly impacts the economics related to physically picking, packing, and transporting those orders.

The business model on which a manufacturer's logistics process rests relies heavily on fulfillment of large orders shipped to a relatively small number of customer locations. Shipping truckloads to distribution centers is far different from shipping small parcels to consumer homes. E-distributors and e-retailers are not immune to the logistical challenges either. Preparing shipments of one or two items, documenting those shipments, tracing, and transporting within a very short time frame required to meet customer requirements and accomplishing these tasks in a manner which does not raise total costs to consumers is a primary concern of all Internet business-to-consumer organizations. In response to increasing customer requirements for fast delivery and increasing costs related to long-distance shipment of small parcels, Amazon.com embarked on a trail of building sophisticated distribution centers around the U.S. This strategy results in investment in facilities and equipment, not unlike that of traditional retail firms.

In fact, several alternative strategies for managing and accomplishing logistics exist for business-to-consumer e-commerce.[11] Some firms may accomplish fulfillment through a network of delivery centers in numerous markets where inventory is held in anticipation of customer orders. An alternative logistics strategy requires customer pickup at central locations, rather than home delivery. This approach has been called the *buy here/pick up there* strategy. In either case, such facilities could serve multiple sellers, providing some economies of scale. Another strategy may be to outsource the entire fulfillment process to partners who are specialists in physical fulfillment, especially third-party logistics firms that can consolidate operations for multiple sellers, provide flexibility in accommodating growth, and manage a more efficient flow of product from source to consumer destination. Sellers who have sufficient volume may choose to utilize dedicated fulfillment operations, as Amazon.com and Micro Warehouse have done.

Any strategic approach chosen will require careful examination of both cost and service level trade-offs. Each has implications for inventory investment, facility investment, transportation costs, and delivery to consumers. The analysis of these trade-offs is fundamental to logistical process design and is the subject of Chapter 16. Suffice it to say at this time that all organizations involved in business-to-consumer

---

[10]Nicholas G. Carr, "Hypermediation: Commerce as Clickstream," *Harvard Business Review,* January/February 2000, pp. 46–7.

[11]Fred R. Ricker and Ravi Kalakota, "Order Fulfillment: The Hidden Key to E-Commerce Success," *Supply Chain Management Review,* Fall 1999, pp. 60–6.

e-commerce are struggling to find the most appropriate logistics and fulfillment strategy for their firm.

Pricing and Logistics

Pricing is another aspect of marketing strategy that directly interacts with logistical operations. The terms and conditions of pricing determine which party has responsibility for performing logistics activities. A major trend in price strategy has been to *debundle* the price of products and materials so that services such as transportation, which were traditionally included in price, are now identified as separate items. Pricing practices have a direct impact on the timing and stability of logistical operations. In this section, several basic pricing structures are reviewed, followed by a discussion of pricing impact areas. No attempt is made to review the broad range of economic and psychological issues related to pricing decisions. The focus is on the relationship between pricing and logistical operations.

Pricing Fundamentals

Pricing decisions directly determine which party in the transaction is responsible for performance of logistics activities, passage of title, and liability. F.O.B. origin and delivered pricing are the two most common methods.

F.O.B. Pricing

The term *F.O.B.* technically means *Free On Board* or *Freight On Board.* A number of variations of F.O.B. pricing are used in practice. **F.O.B. origin** is the simplest way to quote price. Here the seller indicates the price at point of origin and agrees to tender a shipment for transportation loading, but assumes no further responsibility. The buyer selects the mode of transportation, chooses a carrier, pays transportation charges, and takes risk of in-transit loss and/or damage. In **F.O.B. destination** pricing, title does not pass to the buyer until delivery is completed. Under such circumstances, the seller arranges for transportation and the charges are added to the sales invoice.

The range of terms and corresponding responsibilities for pricing are illustrated in Figure 4-7. Review of the various sales terms makes it clear that the firm paying the freight bill does not necessarily assume responsibility for ownership of goods in transit, for the freight burden, or for filing of freight claims.

Delivered Pricing

The primary difference between F.O.B. and **delivered pricing** is that in delivered pricing the seller offers a price that includes transportation of the product to the buyer. In other words, the transportation cost is not specified as a separate item. There are several variations of delivered pricing.

Single-Zone Pricing. Under a single-zone delivered pricing system, buyers pay a single price regardless of where they are located. Delivered prices typically reflect the seller's average transportation cost. In actual practice, some customers pay more than their fair share for transportation while others are subsidized. The United States Postal Service uses a single-zone pricing policy throughout the United States for first-class letters and parcel post. The same fee or postage rate is charged for a given size and weight regardless of distance traveled to the destination.

Reprinted with permission from The Purchasing Handbook, *National Association of Purchasing Management.*

FIGURE 4-7

Terms of sale and corresponding responsibilities

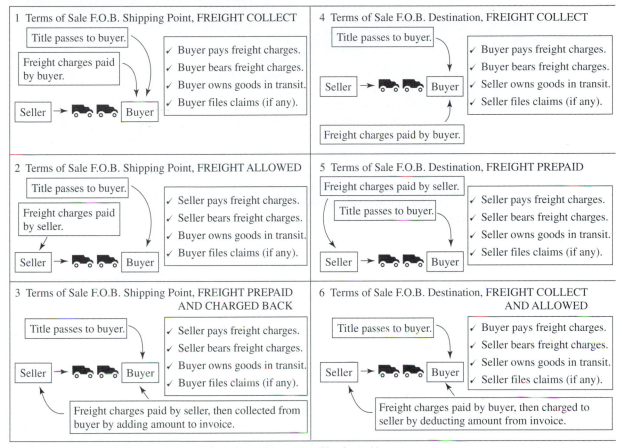

Single-zone delivered pricing is typically used when transportation costs are a relatively small percentage of selling price. The main advantage to the seller is the high degree of control over logistics. For the buyer, despite being based on averages, such pricing systems have the advantage of simplicity.

Multiple-Zone Pricing.   The practice of multiple-zone pricing establishes different prices for specific geographic areas. The underlying idea is that logistics cost differentials can be more fairly assigned when two or more zones—typically based on distance—are used to quote delivered pricing. Parcel carriers such as United Parcel Service use multiple-zone pricing.

Base-Point Pricing.   The most complicated and controversial form of delivered pricing is the use of a base-point system in which the final delivered price is determined by the product's list price plus transportation cost from a designated base point, usually the manufacturing location. This designated point is used for computing the delivered price whether or not the shipment actually originates from the base location.

Figure 4-8 illustrates how a base-point pricing system typically generates different net returns to a seller. The customer has been quoted a delivered price of $100 per

FIGURE 4-8

Base-point pricing

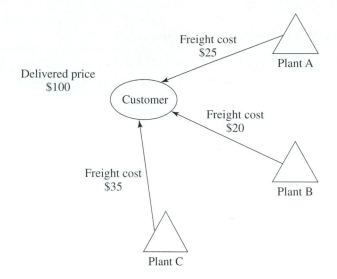

unit. Plant A is the base point. Actual transportation cost from plant A to the customer is $25 per unit. Plant A's base product price is $85 per unit. Transportation costs from plants B and C are $20 and $35 per unit, respectively.

When shipments are made from plant A, the company's net return is $75 per unit (the $100 delivered price minus the $25 transportation cost). The net return to the company varies if shipments are made from plant B or C. With a delivered price of $100, plant B collects $5 in *phantom freight* on shipments to a customer. Phantom freight occurs when a buyer pays transportation costs greater than those actually incurred to move the shipment. If plant C is the shipment origin, the company must absorb $10 of the transportation costs. **Freight absorption** occurs when a seller pays all or a portion of the actual transportation cost and does not recover the full expenditure from the buyer. In other words, the seller decides to absorb transportation cost to be competitive.

Base-point pricing simplifies price quotations but can have a negative impact on customers. For example, dissatisfaction may result if customers discover they are being charged more for transportation than actual freight costs. Such pricing practices may also result in a large amount of freight absorption for sellers.

Pricing Issues

Pricing practices are also integral to logistics operations in at least four other ways: potential discrimination, quantity discounts, pickup allowances, and promotional pricing.

Potential Discrimination

The legality of transportation pricing is an important consideration and must be carefully reviewed and administered to protect against potential discrimination. The Clayton Act of 1914 as amended by the Robinson-Patman Act of 1936 prohibits price discrimination among buyers when the practices "substantially lessen competition."

Zone pricing has the potential to be discriminatory because some buyers pay more than actual transportation cost while others pay less. Zone pricing systems are illegal when the net result is to charge different delivered prices for identical products to direct competitors. In recent years, determination of the legality of delivered zone pricing systems has centered around the issue of whether a "seller acts independently and not in collusion with competitors." The Federal Trade Commission is unlikely to take action unless there is clear-cut evidence of such conspiracy.

In the past, selected base-point pricing has been found illegal under both the Robinson-Patman Act and the Federal Trade Commission Act. The concern is whether it results in direct competitors having differential margins.

To avoid potential legal problems, the majority of firms use either F.O.B. or uniform delivered pricing policies. This strategy is generally preferable compared to defending average costing practices required in zone pricing or contending with the potential legal difficulties associated with base-point pricing. The following guidelines should be considered when establishing geographic pricing:

> Some of the geographic pricing strategies . . . may be illegal under certain circumstances. Three general principles can be used to guide policy in this respect. First, a firm should not discriminate between competing buyers in the same region (especially in zone pricing for buyers on either side of a zonal boundary) because such action may violate the Robinson-Patman Act of 1936. Second, the firm's strategy should not appear to be predatory, especially in freight absorption pricing, because such a strategy would violate Section 2 of the Sherman Act of 1890. Third, in choosing the basing point or zone pricing, the firm should not attempt to fix prices among competitors because such action would violate Section 1 of the Sherman Act.[12]

Quantity Discounts

Quantity discounts are generally offered by a firm as an inducement to increase order size or overall volume of business. To be nondiscriminatory, an identical discount structure must be available to all buyers. Under the Robinson-Patman Act, it is the responsibility of the seller to prove that the identical, noncumulative discounts are available to all qualified buyers. The quantity discount offered must be justifiable on the basis of direct cost saving.

The Robinson-Patman Act states that cost differences can be justified on the basis of savings in the manufacturing, delivery, or selling of goods. Quantity-related discounts based on reductions in manufacturing or selling cost are difficult to prove. Logistics-related savings are relatively easier to document since many are shipment-specific. Transportation and handling savings are often used to justify quantity discounts; thus, lower transportation rates for volume shipments are common.

In contrast to noncumulative discounts, cumulative discounts—based on consecutive purchases over some specified time period—are more difficult to justify. Cumulative discounts, by the very nature of their calculation base, favor large-volume purchasers while discriminating against smaller buyers. However, price discrimination can be proved only when potential or real injury to competition is determined.

Pickup Allowances

Pickup allowances are equivalent to purchasing merchandise on a F.O.B. origin basis. Buyers are given a reduction from the standard delivered price if they or their representatives pick up shipments at the seller's location and assume responsibility for transportation. A buyer may also use a for-hire carrier to perform merchandise pickup. In the food and grocery industry, which traditionally practiced delivered pricing, firms

---

[12]Gerard J. Tellis, "Beyond the Many Facets of Price: An Integration of Pricing Strategies," *Journal of Marketing* 50 (October 1986), pp. 146–60.

have realized significant savings by using private and for-hire carriers to pick up rather than purchasing merchandise on a delivered basis.

While some confusion exists concerning how to best establish a pickup allowance, a safe rule is that a seller should provide the same allowance to all directly competitive buyers. A uniform pickup allowance is often the price incentive offered to the customer closest to the shipping point. Other common policies offer pickup allowances equivalent to the applicable common carrier rate for the shipment.

The use of pickup allowances offers potential benefits for both the seller and the buyer. Shippers are required to deal with fewer small shipments, thereby reducing the need for extensive outbound consolidation. Buyers gain control over the merchandise earlier and are in a position to achieve greater utilization of captive transportation equipment and drivers.

Promotional Pricing

A final aspect of pricing that impacts logistical operations is the use of short-term promotions to provide incentives for purchases. Firms that pursue aggressive promotional strategies have a choice of designing their budgets to encourage consumers (via coupons) or wholesalers and retailers (via trade allowances) to purchase their products. For example, Procter & Gamble has an annual advertising and promotional budget that exceeds $2 billion. Marketing management must allocate these funds between media advertising focused on consumers and a combination of coupons and trade promotions. Budget dollars allocated to trade promotion push the purchase of P&G products and cause two results. First, the logistics systems of Procter & Gamble and its customers must handle increased product volume just before, during, and oftentimes immediately after a promotional period. Second, trade promotion spending lowers the effective price at which product is being sold. From a logistical perspective, the short-term increase in volume is of primary concern. Thus, while ultimate consumption may not demonstrate seasonal characteristics, logistical operations may have to deal with *seasonal surges* caused by promotional pushes.

The widespread practice of promotional pricing has traditionally been the way to provide an incentive for trade purchasing. Manufacturers establish list or sheet prices at an artificially high level with the expectation of reducing the effective price by trade promotion, consumer coupons, and new product slotting allowances. Administration of regular price changes usually involves advanced notification to customers, creating the opportunity for them to *forward buy*. This practice stimulates volume surges, which add excessive costs, and creates practices that do not add value. Forward buying involves purchasing merchandise beyond a customer's current needs. Sometimes these customers resell the extra product to other channel participants through the use of agents, a practice known as diverting. In effect, a firm is profiting by taking advantage of purchase incentives available to some channel participants and not others.

In an effort to stabilize promotional pricing, some firms have begun to develop coordinated programs. Manufacturers and retailers working together can negotiate *net prices* that are administered over a specific time horizon. The manufacturer and retailer jointly plan the promotion and advertising strategy for a product or merchandising category. A *dead net price* is determined that takes into account quantity purchase discounts, prompt payment discounts, and any other applicable price incentives. Finally, an agreement is reached concerning the duration of the negotiated price. These agreements also specify how performance will be measured during the operating period as a basis for future agreements.

The price negotiation framework described above has resulted in what is known as EveryDay Low Pricing (EDLP). Wal★Mart is generally credited with having created EDLP, the strategy around which it seeks to build customer loyalty. Other firms have developed EDLP purchase strategies with suppliers while following a promotional pricing format for consumer merchandising.

Few firms operate at the extremes of either EDLP or promotional pricing; however, most creative merchandisers develop a combination approach to stimulate consumer purchasing. While price or *loss leaders* are used to generate consumer traffic and encourage in-store impulse buying, few items are consistently sold as loss leaders, thereby reducing the risk of predatory pricing allegations.

In a more general sense, business in a free market society will and should engage in a wide variety of promotional and advertising activities. The challenge is to rationalize how such promotional efforts affect logistics. The timing and magnitude of promotional pricing need to be evaluated in terms of ability to consume and the capacity to efficiently handle volume surges. To a significant degree, *trade loading* practices result from end-of-period or end-of-year earnings pressures. This so-called Wall Street effect goes hand in hand with the use of promotional pricing to stimulate product flow so that sales can be booked during a specific time period. Such practices may offer short-term earnings relief but do little, if anything, to stimulate consumption. They are, however, guaranteed to increase logistics cost.

Menu Pricing

From a seller's perspective, a pricing program must be established to accurately and equitably charge customers for the products and services that they demand. Menu pricing is a technique used by many firms to accomplish this objective. An effective menu pricing system has three components: platform service price, value-added service specified costs, and efficiency incentives.

Platform Service Price

The first step in menu pricing is to establish the basic service platform to be offered to all customers and an appropriate price reflecting the costs related to providing that service level. The platform service price is expected to be paid by all customers, whether or not they require the service combination as specified. For example, the basic platform service price might be established for the following service level: "Full trailer of mixed products in unit load quantities on slip sheet from a distribution center for customer unload." The pricing quoted for this combination of delivery specifications, quantity, configuration, and unload requirements is the basis from which any additional charges or discounts are considered. Certain standard discounts may also be quoted as part of the basic service platform. For example, traditional quantity discounts and customer pickup allowances are typically considered to be a part of the basic platform price.

Value-Added Service Costs

The second aspect of menu pricing involves specifying charges for compliance to customer required additional activities. From the example above, an upcharge would be imposed for customized unit loading requested by a customer, such as layering products on the slip sheet in a specific order. A separate upcharge would be established for multiple stop-offs on the delivery, and a third upcharge would be

TABLE 4-4   Menu Pricing

Typical Value-Added Services Charges	Typical Efficiency Incentives
Using customer specified pallets	CHEP pallets
Multiple stop-offs	Expand receiving hours
Special packaging	Accept drop trailers
Sort/segregate loading	Timely unloading
Sequenced load	Flexibility on over/short/damage
Temperature control	Electronic ordering, invoicing, payment
Driver teams	Vendor-managed inventory
	Customer unload

established for delivery on pallets rather than slip sheets. This approach results in each customer paying for the specific combination of services it requires. Table 4-4 provides a listing of typical value-added services for which shippers frequently establish upcharges in their menu pricing programs. Of course, shippers may choose to offer some of these services as part of their basic service platform, in which case their basic price should include the appropriate charges.

Efficiency Incentives

The third step in a comprehensive menu pricing program is the establishment of efficiency incentives. Such incentives may be offered to encourage buyers to comply with specified requirements, which reduce logistics costs. The incentives provide a mechanism for sharing the benefits of such cost-reducing efforts. For example, a discount or allowance might be given to encourage ordering EDI, another incentive offered to receivers who guarantee truck unloading in 2 hours or less, and a third incentive for using CHEP pallets (CHEP pallets are specialized pallets which are bar-coded to allow constant monitoring and tracing of the pallet's specific location. CHEP pallets are leased on a per use basis rather than being purchased by a manufacturer.). Efficiency incentives frequently offered by shippers in a menu pricing program are listed in Table 4-4. Industry Insight 4-4 illustrates menu pricing as it is implemented at Campbell Soup Company.

Summary

No firm can be self-sufficient in meeting the requirements of its customers. Specialization in functions by organizations creates the need for a process to resolve the problems of efficient and effective exchange between those organizations. These problems relate to time, place, quantity, and assortment requirements. A market distribution mechanism must emerge to resolve these problems and create efficiency by minimizing the transactions required to meet customer demand. In fact, market distribution can be thought of conceptually as two separate structures: one to fulfill the buying and selling activities required and another to fulfill the logistical activities.

Developing market distribution strategy is a complex process. Alternative structural arrangements range from very direct between producer and consumer to very

INDUSTRY INSIGHT 4-4 CAMPBELL'S RECIPE FOR SAVINGS

Based in Camden, New Jersey, the Campbell Soup Company makes juices and sauces as well as the familiar red-and-white labeled cans of condensed soup. As a general rule, Campbell ships its product directly to U.S. retailers and grocery wholesalers from four plants located in Paris, Texas; Napoleon, Ohio; Sacramento, California; and Maxton, North Carolina. Campbell distributes its product via for-hire motor carriers to about 600 customers and more than 1,800 ship-to locations in this country. It shipped approximately 5.5 billion pounds of soups, sauces, and beverages in the United States last year.

Two years ago, the company began looking for ways to reduce its supply chain costs. Managers examined the operation, using the activity-based cost accounting method to establish the actual expense for specific logistics tasks. They identified factors such as pallet configuration, pallet type, shipment size, carrier unloading, and cash management practices that had a high impact on distribution costs. They concluded that customers that didn't order electronically and that ordered cases delivered via less than truckload transport were more costly to service than their counterparts that had automated their ordering procedures and ordered in truckload quantities.

In response, company executives decided to institute a strategic pricing program that would provide financial incentives for domestic customers to order product in full truckloads and in full pallets rather than in cases. The menu pricing program offers Campbell's customers a menu of pricing options—the choice of adopting certain practices and earning price reductions, maintaining their existing prices, or paying a higher price for additional services.

Customer orders get assigned to pricing brackets based on the cost Campbell incurs to service them. "If they order a certain percentage in full truckloads and full pallets, they qualify for different brackets," says Nicholas Bova, vice president for supply chain planning and logistics. "We also give them parameters around product unloading as well as electronic ordering and invoicing. In addition, customers are given allowances or price breaks for picking up the goods themselves and/or accepting direct plant delivery."

In the first 6 months of the program's operation, Campbell witnessed a significant change in its customers' buying practices. When the company launched the strategic pricing initiative, about 18 percent of Campbell's customers qualified for the best pricing bracket. Today, more than two-thirds of its customers meet the criteria for price discounts.

The program has enhanced the efficiency of Campbell's distribution operation. The company now consolidates more orders into full truckloads. Today, more than 90 percent of its domestic volume is ordered in full truckloads compared with 70 to 75 percent prior to the strategic pricing initiative. In addition, 85 to 90 percent of the volume moves on full pallets today compared with 70 percent in the past. Campbell exchanges electronic purchase orders and inventory information with about 90 percent of its customers as opposed to 60 to 65 percent when the program began.

Filling customer orders in the optimal way allows Campbell to improve its customer service, reduce distribution expenses, and share the savings with its trading partners. It now has fewer personnel and pays less overtime in its warehouse operation than in the past even though productivity has soared.

Campbell has been able to put into effect a 3-day processing time for standard orders from trading partners and a 2-day turnaround for customers in its continuous replenishment program. "If we move goods on full pallets, we have less handling," says Larry Venturelli, director of supply chain finance and customer logistics. "It shortens the amount of time it takes to fill an order. Because there's less handling, damage is reduced throughout the supply chain."

By motivating the customer to place more efficient orders, Campbell has realized major savings. Trading partners have also benefited through improved distribution and order handling practices, lowered transportation cost, upgraded warehouse and store service levels, and reduced administrative support.

Source: James Aaron Cooke, "Campbell's Recipe for Savings," *Logistics Management and Distribution Report,* March 2000, pp. 42–4.

indirect, involving various wholesale and retail intermediaries. End-user requirements form the basis for determining the appropriate structure. Their needs in terms of waiting time, lot-size purchase, locational convenience, and product assortment ultimately drive the decision concerning where and how producers must position their products. These decisions, in turn, influence the structure in terms of the number and types of intermediaries that should be included in the distribution process. A complicating factor is introduced by the fact that most companies attempt to serve multiple end-user segments. The best channel structure for one segment may not be best for all. Thus, most firms are engaged in multiple distribution channels.

Channel mapping is one tool used by organizations in designing distribution channels. A channel map outlines the alternative paths used to reach end customers, detailing the participants in each path as well as the functions performed and economic characteristics of each linkage in a path. A matrix approach, which details specific activities required to complete a function and alternative methods to complete each activity, can also be used to identify the most appropriate participants to meet specific customer requirements.

Different types of relationships are possible among channel participants. The basis for distinguishing among these relationships is the willingness of the members to acknowledge their mutual dependence. Ranging from single-transaction channels, which emerge for one-time exchange, to conventional channels, which operate with little recognition of dependency, to relational collaborative arrangements, such as partnerships and alliances, cooperation and information sharing among participants increase as the relationships become more formalized. Supply chains represent behavioral relationships that are advanced partnerships and alliances.

Perhaps no other development in recent years has as much potential impact on distribution channels as the Internet. Predictions for massive channel change such as the possibility that traditional retail stores will be replaced by e-tailers who have no store facilities, the disintermediation of channels as consumers interact directly with producers, and fundamental shifts of roles and responsibilities have dominated much of the discussion of the Internet's impact. It is too soon to actually determine what the long-term impact will be, but it is clear that logistical operations and fulfillment are a major concern for all businesses that interact with consumers directly via the Internet.

While price determination is not administered by logistics executives, pricing and logistics are highly interrelated. The continuum between F.O.B. and delivered pricing determines who controls logistics and how transportation expense is treated in price. Logistics also impacts such issues as price discrimination, discounts, allowances, and promotions. The development of menu pricing as a strategy allows a seller to most effectively charge for the actual services provided to a buyer.

Challenge Questions

1. Why is specialization so critical to distribution efficiency?
2. Describe how the process of assortment overcomes the problems created by specialization.
3. Given the principle of minimum transactions, explain why it is possible to have too many participants in a distribution channel.
4. What is the primary logic behind potential separation of marketing and logistics channel structure?

5. How does the risk related to inventory compare among manufacturers, wholesalers, and retailers?

6. Why wouldn't a manufacturer desire to always have intensive distribution coverage?

7. How could the matrix approach to design be applied to logistics activities?

8. Distinguish between the four types of relational collaborative arrangements. Provide an example of each.

9. What do you believe will be the impact of the Internet on market distribution by 2010?

10. What is a shipper's responsibility when terms of purchase are F.O.B. origin? F.O.B. destination? Why would a shipper prefer one over the other?

5 PROCUREMENT AND MANUFACTURING STRATEGIES

In Chapter 2, performance cycles were discussed as the foundation for integrated logistics in the supply chain. In fact, there are three performance cycles that must be linked through effective logistics. The *procurement cycle* links an organization with its suppliers; the *manufacturing support cycle* involves the logistics of production; and the *market distribution cycle* links the firm with its markets. As will be seen later in this chapter, manufacturing firms differ in their manufacturing strategies; thus, alternative approaches to procurement may be implemented to accommodate specific manufacturing requirements. Of course, all of this performance must meet customer requirements for quality products. This chapter begins, therefore, with a discussion of product quality from a customer's perspective and total quality management programs. Procurement and manufacturing are then each discussed with emphasis on alternative strategies employed. The chapter concludes with a discussion of logistical interfaces necessary to support an organization's chosen procurement and manufacturing strategies.

The Quality Imperative

An overriding concern of all organizations today is quality. In the competitive marketplace, no company dares to fall behind in providing quality to its customers, consumers, or end users. It has been argued that quality no longer provides an organization with an edge over its competitors but is a prerequisite for doing business in the global economy. Yet quality remains an elusive concept. In the end, quality rests in the eyes of customers and how they perceive an organization, its products, and its services. Many issues of quality were introduced in Chapter 3 with a perspective on the service expectations and requirements of customers. In this chapter, dealing with procurement of materials and manufacturing processes, critical issues of *product quality* are addressed. Much of the focus in supply chain management is ensuring product quality that meets customer requirements.

Dimensions of Product Quality

In the context of physical product form, quality is not as simple as it may first appear. In fact, the term *quality* means different things to different people. While everyone wants a quality product, not all may agree that a particular item or brand has the quality attributes desired. Eight different dimensions of product quality have been identified.[1]

Performance

Perhaps the most obvious aspect of quality from a customer's point of view is **performance,** or how well the product performs the task it was designed to perform. For example, personal computers may be judged with respect to their processing speed; audio components, in terms of sound clarity and lack of noise; or dishwashers, relative to how clean and spotless the dishes. Superior performance in a product is generally an objective attribute, which can easily be compared between items and brands. Of course, an item may actually have several performance dimensions, which complicates the comparison process. The personal computer is judged not only in terms of processing speed but also by such characteristics as internal memory, hard disk capacity, and numerous other aspects.

Reliability

Reliability refers to the likelihood that a product will perform during its expected life. It is also concerned with the number of breakdowns or repairs that a customer experiences after purchase. Consider, for example, Maytag's slogan "The Dependability People" and long-running advertising campaign featuring a company repairman as "the loneliest man in town." Maytag stressed that its products were more reliable than any other by showing that the Maytag repairman was never called to fix a broken appliance. Like performance, reliability is a characteristic of quality that can be objectively measured.

---

[1] David A. Garvin, "Competing on the Eight Dimensions of Quality," *Harvard Business Review,* November/December 1987, pp. 101–9.

Durability

While related to reliability, **durability** is a somewhat different attribute. It refers to the actual life expectancy of a product. An automobile with a life expectancy of 10 years may be judged by many consumers to be of higher quality than one with a life of 5 years. Of course, life span may be extended through repairs or preventative maintenance. Thus, durability and reliability are distinct but interrelated aspects of quality.

Conformance

Conformance refers to whether a firm's products actually meet the precise description or specifications as designed. It is frequently measured by looking at an organization's scrap, rework, or rate of defects. This quality measure is usually applied internally in an organization. For example, if 95 percent of a firm's products meet the specifications as designed, it has a 5 percent defect rate. The defective products may be scrapped or reworked to bring them into conformance. From a customer's viewpoint, conformance might be looked at as the number of "lemons." Suppose for example, that most of the automobiles sold by a manufacturer perform exactly as specified, have few breakdowns, and have a long life. However, if a small number of the autos are defective, the overall quality of the automobile may be judged as low.

Features

Customers frequently judge quality of specific products on the basis of **features**—the number of functions or tasks that they perform independent of aspects related to reliability or durability. For example, a television receiver with remote control, picture-in-picture, and on-screen programming is usually perceived to be of higher quality than is a basic model. But, in general, the more features a product contains, the greater is the likelihood that another quality attribute is lacking, particularly reliability.

Aesthetics

Aesthetics, the styling and specific materials used in a product, is an aspect used by many customers to judge quality. In clothing, cashmere sweaters are considered to be higher quality than polyester fabrics. In automobiles, the use of leather rather than cloth for seats, wood or metal rather than plastic, are aspects of style that imply quality. Included in aesthetics is the notion of *fit and finish* such as high-gloss paint on an automobile or seams that have no overlap. Product designs that are unique or innovative are also frequently regarded by customers to be of higher quality.

Serviceability

Serviceability, the ease of fixing or repairing a product that fails, is an important aspect of quality to some customers. Consider, for example, how some new appliances contain diagnostic capability, which alert users or service technicians that a failure is about to occur. Ideally, serviceability would allow the customer to fix the product with little or no cost or time lost. In the absence of such serviceability, customers generally consider those items or brands that can be repaired quickest with least cost to be better quality products.

Perceived Quality

As noted earlier, customers are the ultimate judges of product quality through their perception of how well the product meets their requirements. **Perceived quality** rests in customers' experiences before, during, and after the sale. Total product quality is a combination of the various dimensions, how they are blended by an organization, and how that blend is perceived. It is perfectly plausible that two different customers may perceive two different brands as being best quality, depending upon which blend of elements each considers to be most critical.

Total Quality Management

It is useful to remember that total quality encompasses much more than just the physical product. Of specific concern in this text are the elements related to service, satisfaction, and success discussed in Chapter 3. From the customer's perspective not only does the physical product have to incorporate the desired elements, but also the product must be available in a timely and suitable manner. Quality is, therefore, a responsibility of everyone in the organization.

Total Quality Management (TQM) is a philosophy and a system of management focused on meeting customer requirements in all aspects of their needs, from all departments or functions in the organization, whether the customer is internal or external, intermediate, end user, or consumer. While the specific tools and methodologies employed in TQM are beyond the scope of this text, the basic conceptual elements are: (1) top management commitment and support; (2) customer focus in product, service, and process design; (3) integration within and between organizations; and (4) commitment to continuous improvement.

Quality Standards

Establishing global standards for quality is extremely difficult due to different practices and procedures around the world. As a simple example, engineering tolerances in one country might be measured in millimeters, while in another, they are measured in tenths of an inch. Nevertheless, a set of standards has emerged from the **International Organization for Standardization (ISO)** and has gained worldwide acceptance.

In 1987, a series of quality standards was issued under the name ISO 9000. Incorporating several subsets (ISO 9001, 9002, etc.), these quality guidelines provide basic definitions for quality assurance and quality management. ISO 9001, for example, deals with the quality system in place for product design, development, production, installation, and service. Several organizations around the world are authorized to perform audits of companies and their practices and procedures for TQM. A company that meets the ISO guidelines can receive certification. In 1998, another set of guidelines, ISO 14000, was released. ISO 14000 deals with guidelines and procedures for managing a firm's environmental impact. Certification in both ISO 9000 and ISO 14000 would indicate that a company has in place both a world-class quality management and environmental management system.

Interestingly, the ISO certification process is accomplished by an audit of a firm's policies, systems, and procedures for quality and environmental management. It does not include actual testing of products or audits of customer satisfaction. Despite this limitation, ISO certification is an important indicator of a firm's commitment to TQM. It is also important because many companies and even the European Union are demanding that supply chain partners be ISO certified.

Another important quality standard, particularly for U.S. companies, is the **Malcolm Baldrige National Quality Award.** Established in 1987, the award is intended to recognize those companies that excel not only in quality management processes but also in quality achievement. Figure 5-1 lists the criteria for the award and the point values assigned to each. Notice that customer focus is critical not only in the third

[handwritten note in margin: That is a questionable statement. Many companies have an ISO 9000, etc certification and can't produce product of consistent quality.]

FIGURE 5-1

Malcolm Baldrige criteria and values

1 Leadership (120 pts.)
The **Leadership** Category examines how your organization's senior leaders address values and performance expectations, as well as a focus on customers and other stakeholders, empowerment, innovation, learning, and organizational directions. Also examined is how your organization addresses its responsibilities to the public and supports its key communities.

2 Strategic Planning (85 pts.)
The **Strategic Planning** Category examines your organization's strategy development process, including how your organization develops strategic objectives, action plans, and related human resource plans. Also examined are how plans are deployed and how performance is tracked.

3 Customer and Market Focus (85 pts.)
The **Customer and Market Focus** Category examines how your organization determines requirements, expectations, and preferences of customers and markets. Also examined is how your organization builds relationships with customers and determines their satisfaction.

4 Information and Analysis (90 pts.)
The **Information and Analysis** Category examines your organization's performance measurement system and how your organization analyzes performance data and information.

5 Human Resources (85 pts.)
The **Human Resource Focus** Category examines how your organization enables employees to develop and utilize their full potential, aligned with the organization's objectives. Also examined are your organization's efforts to build and maintain a work environment and an employee support climate conducive to performance excellence, full participation, and personal and organizational growth.

6 Process Management (85 pts.)
The **Process Management** Category examines the key aspects of your organization's process management, including customer-focused design, product and service delivery, support, and supplier and partnering processes involving all work units.

7 Business Results (450 pts.)
The **Business Results** Category examines your organization's performance and improvement in key business areas—customer satisfaction, product and service performance, financial and marketplace performance, human resource results, supplier and partner results, and operational performance. Also examined are performance levels relative to competitors.

Source: Obtained from the National Institute for Quality website at **www.NIST.gov.**

category but also in several other of the criteria. Other countries have also initiated their own quality award programs. While there is only one winner in each of three categories for the Baldrige award each year, many executives believe that the process of applying and being judged for the awards focuses an organization's attention on TQM. Some companies, such as Motorola, even insist that their suppliers at least apply for such awards as a mechanism to ensure that those companies are providing top-quality materials and services.

Procurement

Every organization, whether it is a manufacturer, wholesaler, or retailer, buys materials, services, and supplies from outside suppliers to support its operations. Historically, the process of acquiring these needed inputs has been considered somewhat of a nuisance, at least as compared to other activities within the firm. Purchasing was regarded as a clerical or low-level managerial activity charged with responsibility to execute and process orders initiated elsewhere in the organization. The role of purchasing was to obtain the desired resource at the lowest possible purchase price from a supplier. This traditional view of purchasing has changed substantially in the past two decades. The modern focus on supply chain management with its emphasis on relationships between buyers and sellers has elevated purchasing to a higher, strategic-level activity. This strategic role is differentiated from the traditional through the term **procurement,** although in practice many people use the terms purchasing and procurement interchageably.

The increasing importance of procurement can be traced to several factors. The most basic of these factors has been the recognition of the substantial dollar volume of purchases in the typical organization and the potential dollar savings from a strategic approach to managing the activity. The simple fact is that purchased goods and services are one of the largest elements of cost for many firms. In the average manufacturing firm in North America, purchased goods and services account for approximately 55 cents of every sales dollar.[2] By way of contrast, the average expense of direct labor in the manufacturing process accounts for only about 10 cents of every sales dollar. While the percentage spent on purchased inputs does vary considerably across manufacturing industries, it is clear that the potential savings from strategic management of procurement are considerable.

Related to the cost of purchased inputs is the emphasis on outsourcing, which has dominated many industries over the last two decades. The result is that the amount spent on procurement has increased significantly in many organizations. Firms today purchase not only raw materials and basic supplies but also complex fabricated components with very high value-added content. They spin off functions to suppliers to focus resources on their core competencies. This means that more attention must be focused on how the organization interfaces and effectively manages its supply base. For example, General Motors uses its first-tier supplier network and third-party logistics providers to complete subassemblies and deliver finished components on a just-in-time basis for incorporation into automobiles on the assembly line. Many of these activities were once performed by General Motors itself. Developing and coordinating these relationships are critical aspects of effective procurement strategy. The logistical requirements related to effective procurement strategy are identified below.

Procurement Perspectives

The evolving focus on procurement as a key capability in organizations has stimulated a new perspective regarding its role in supply chain management. The emphasis has shifted from adversarial, transaction-focused negotiation with suppliers to ensuring that the firm is positioned to implement its manufacturing and marketing strategies with support from its supply base. In particular, considerable focus is placed on ensuring supply, inventory minimization, quality improvement, supplier development, and lowest total cost of ownership.

Continuous Supply

Stockouts of raw materials or component parts can shut down a production plant and result in extreme cost to an organization. Downtime due to production stoppage increases operating costs and results in an inability to provide finished goods for delivery to customers. Imagine the chaos that would result if an automobile assembly line had all parts available but tires. The almost completed automobiles would have to wait until a supply of tires was received and, in fact, production would have to be halted until tires were available. Thus, one of the core objectives of procurement is to ensure that a continuous supply of materials, parts, and components is available for use.

---

[2]Shawn Tulley, "Purchasing: New Muscle," *Fortune,* February 20, 1995, p. 75.

Minimize Inventory Investment

In the past, downtime due to material shortages was minimized by maintaining large inventories of inputs to protect against potential disruption in supply; but maintaining inventory is expensive and utilizes capital that might be used elsewhere in the organization. One goal of modern procurement is to maintain supply continuity with the minimum inventory investment possible. This requires balancing the costs of carrying excessive materials against the possibility of a production stoppage.[3] The ideal, of course, is to have needed materials arrive just at the moment they are scheduled to be used in the production process, in other words, *just-in-time*.

Quality Improvement

Procurement can play a critical role in the quality of an organization's products. The quality of finished goods and services is obviously dependent upon the quality of the materials and parts used in producing those items. If poor-quality components and materials are used, then the final product will not meet customer quality standards.

Simply ensuring that each individual item purchased is of the appropriate quality level may not be sufficient. If a standard part is sourced from many different suppliers, and each supplier meets specified quality requirements, it is still possible that the final product may encounter quality problems. Industry Insight 5-1 describes the quality failures encountered by Tenant, a manufacturer of floor-cleaning machines. Ultimately, Tenant discovered that the key to improving quality of its products lay in a different approach to procurement.

Quality improvement through procurement also has substantial implications for cost in an organization. If defective materials are the cause of poor-quality finished products, the costs of scrap and rework in the production process go up. If the problems are not detected until customers receive the product, costs associated with warranties, guarantees, repair, and replacement increase substantially. Ultimately, procurement must maintain a quality perspective in dealing with suppliers to ensure that customer requirements are met in a cost-effective manner.

Supplier Development

In the final analysis, successful procurement depends on locating or developing suppliers, analyzing their capabilities, and selecting and working with those suppliers to achieve continuous improvement.[4] Developing good supply relationships with firms that are committed to the buying organization's success is critical in supplier development. The next step is to develop close relationships with those suppliers, working with them through sharing of information and resources, to achieve better results. For example, a manufacturer might share a production schedule with suppliers, which allows them to better meet the buyer's requirements for delivery. A retailer might share promotional plans to ensure that a supplier will be able to meet its needs for increased quantities at a specific time. This perspective on effective procurement stands in stark contrast to the traditional mode of purchasing which inherently created adversarial relationships with the supply base.

Lowest Total Cost of Ownership

Ultimately, the difference in perspective between traditional purchasing practice and contemporary procurement strategy can be summarized as a focus on **Total Cost of**

---

[3]James Carbone, "Suppliers as Strategic Business Partners," *Purchasing,* November 21, 1996, p. 23.

[4]Daniel Krause, "Suppliers Development: Current Practices and Outcomes," *Journal of Supply Chain Management,* Spring 1997, pp. 12–20.

INDUSTRY INSIGHT 5-1   SWEPT AWAY BY TENNANT

Tennant was experiencing severe oil leak problems in its floor sweepers and scrubbers. Quality checks found oil leaks in 1 out of every 75 hydraulic joints, or 2 per machine. To a floor-cleaning company a sweeper that leaked oil was the equivalent of a mortal sin. Fortunately, most leaks were caught before the machines were shipped from the plant, but rework was required. In 1979, Tennant was spending about 33,000 hours on manufacturing rework, at a cost of $2 million or 2 percent of revenues.

Investigating the cause of these quality problems revealed that purchasing was ordering hydraulic hoses and fittings from no less than 16 suppliers. Tennant switched between different suppliers based on price and availability. Consequently, parts didn't always fit together properly.

Douglas Hoelscher, Tennant's VP of operations, established a special multidisciplinary sourcing group for fluid connectors with the express purpose of selecting one hydraulic hose supplier. Eventually, Parker Hannifin was chosen and has been Tennant's only supplier of hydraulic hoses and fittings. As a result, Tennant was counting leaks per 100 joints in 1980; by 1985, it was down to 1 leak per 1,000 joints; and, by 1992, Tennant had quit counting altogether.

Tennant learned an important lesson from this experience. Quality could be greatly influenced by sourcing policies and relationships with suppliers. Consequently, Tennant gave Parker the opportunity to plumb an entire machine, which was previously done in-house. Tennant had always been reluctant to let outsiders see products still in the developmental stage. Now, the company routinely seeks suppliers' advice. "We saw the need to surround ourselves with suppliers that could provide engineering and design support, and that weren't just parts makers," says Don Carlton, Tennant's purchasing director.

Tennant has narrowed its supplier base to improve relations with its suppliers and improve quality. From 1,100 suppliers in 1980, active suppliers now number 250, with approximately 50 receiving the majority of Tennant's business.

Source: Ernie Raia, "Swept Away by Tennant," *Purchasing,* September 22, 1994, pp. 42–9.

Ownership (TCO) instead of a focus on purchase price. Procurement professionals recognize that although the purchase price of a material or item remains very important, it is only one part of the total cost equation in their organization.[5] Service costs and life cycle costs must also be considered.

Purchase Price and Discounts.   Whether established through competitive bidding, buyer–seller negotiation, or simply from a seller's published price schedule, the purchase price of an item is obviously a concern in procurement. No one wants to pay a higher price than necessary. Related to the price quote is normally a schedule of one or more possible discounts that the buyer may receive. For example, quantity discounts may be offered as an inducement to encourage buyers to purchase larger quantities or cash discounts may be offered for prompt payment of invoices.

Consideration of suppliers' discount structures immediately takes the buyer beyond simple quoted purchase price. Other costs associated with purchasing must be considered. For quantity discounts to be factored in, the buyer must also consider the costs associated with holding inventory. Larger purchase quantities increase inventory of materials or supplies. Size of purchase also impacts administrative costs associated

---

[5]Zeger Degraeve and Filip Roodhooft, "Effectively Selecting Suppliers Using Total Cost of Ownership," *Journal of Supply Chain Management,* Winter 1999, pp. 5–10. See also Lisa M. Ellram, "Total Cost of Ownership," *International Journal of Physical Distribution and Logistics,* August 1995, pp. 4–23.

with purchasing. Lot-size techniques such as **Economic Order Quantity (EOQ),** discussed fully in Chapter 10, can help resolve this rather simple cost trade-off.

Supplier terms of sale and cash discount structures are also an aspect of purchase price. A supplier offering more favorable trade credit terms is, in effect, impacting the purchase price from the buyer's perspective. For example, a discount for prompt payment of an invoice offered by one supplier must be compared with other suppliers' offers, which may have different percentages or time periods involved.

What normally is not considered in traditional purchasing practice is the impact of such pricing and discount structures on logistics operations and costs. For example, while traditional EOQ does include consideration of inventory carrying costs, it generally does not include such factors as the impact of order quantity on transportation costs or the costs associated with receiving and handling different size orders. Many of these logistical considerations had been ignored or given cursory consideration as buyers attempted to achieve the lowest purchase price of the goods and services acquired for the organization but there is now increasing recognition of the importance of these logistics costs.

Service Pricing and Debundling.   Sellers typically offer a number of standard services that must be considered in procurement. Additionally, a wide variety of value-added services must be evaluated as organizations attempt to find the lowest TCO. Many of these services involve logistical operations and the logistical interface between buyers and sellers.

The simplest of these services is delivery. How delivery will be accomplished, when, and to where are all aspects for cost consideration. As discussed in the previous chapter, in many industries it is standard practice to quote a price that includes delivery to the customer's plant, warehouse, or store location. Alternatively, the seller may offer the buyer a pickup allowance if the buyer picks up the merchandise at the seller's location and assumes responsibility for transportation. The buyer may be able to reduce total costs, not only through taking advantage of the allowance but also by more fully utilizing its own transportation equipment. The buyer may even find it beneficial to use a common carrier for these pickups, if the economics of the pickup allowance justify it.

There may also be different prices depending upon the destination preferred by the buyer. For example, delivery of a single large load to a retailer's distribution center might represent one level of service, whereas delivery of smaller quantities to individual store locations represents another. Each alternative service involves different costs for the seller and the buyer.

In Chapter 3, numerous other potential services were discussed, ranging from special packaging to preparation of promotional displays. Performance of subassembly operations in a supplier's plant or a third-party distribution center represents a further extension of potential value-added service. The point is that each potential service has a cost to the supplier and a price to the buyer. A key aspect of determining the TCO for purchased requirements is to consider the trade-offs involved in terms of value-added versus cost and price of each service. To do so, the purchase price of an item must be *debundled* from the price of services under consideration; that is, each of the services should be priced separately so that appropriate analysis can be made. In Chapter 4, this practice was referred to as *menu pricing.* Where traditional purchasing might overlook value-added services in seeking lowest possible purchase price, effective procurement executives consider whether such services should be performed internally, by suppliers, or at all. Debundling allows the buyer to make the most appropriate procurement choice.

FIGURE 5-2

Major categories for the components of total cost of ownership

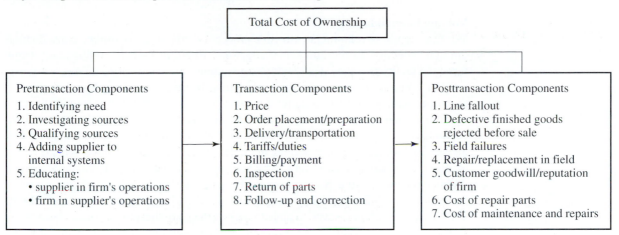

Source: Michel Leenders and Harold Fearon, *Purchasing and Supply Management,* 11 ed. (Chicago, IL: Irwin, 1997), p. 334. Reprinted with permission.

Life Cycle Costs.   The final aspect of lowest TCO includes numerous elements known as **life cycle costs.** The total cost of materials, items, or other inputs extends beyond the purchase price and elements of value-added service to include the lifetime costs of such items. Some of these costs are incurred before actual receipt of the items, others are incurred while the item is being used, and some occur long after the buyer has actually used the item.

One aspect of life cycle costs involves the administrative expense associated with the procurement activity itself. Expenses related to screening potential suppliers, negotiation, order preparation, and transmission are just a few of the administrative costs of procurement. Receiving, inspecting, and payment are also important. The costs related to defective finished goods, scrap, and rework, which are associated with poor supplier quality, must also be considered, as well as related warranty administration and repair of items that consumers have purchased. Even the costs associated with recycling or recovery of materials after the useful life of a finished product may have an impact on TCO.

Figure 5-2 presents a model of the various elements that comprise TCO. When each of these elements is considered in procurement, it is clear that numerous opportunities for improvement exist in most companies. Many of these opportunities arise from closer working relationships with suppliers than is possible when adversarial price negotiation dominates the buyer–seller relationship. When working cooperatively with suppliers several strategies may be employed to reduce both the buyers' and the sellers' costs, making the total supply chain much more efficient and allowing it to more effectively meet the requirements of downstream partners. Such strategies are discussed next.

Procurement Strategies

Effective procurement strategy to support supply chain management concepts requires a much closer working relationship between buyers and sellers than was traditionally practiced. Specially, three strategies have emerged: **volume consolidation, supplier operational integration,** and **value management.** Each of these strategies requires an increasing degree of interaction between supply chain partners; thus, they may not be considered as distinct and separate but rather as evolutionary stages of development.

Volume Consolidation

The first step in developing an effective procurement strategy is volume consolidation through reduction in the number of suppliers. Beginning in the 1980s many firms faced the reality that they dealt with a large number of suppliers for almost every material or input used throughout the organization. In fact, purchasing literature prior to that time emphasized that multiple sources of supply were the best procurement strategy. Numerous advantages were seen to this approach. First, potential suppliers were continually bidding for the buyer's business, ensuring that prices would be quoted as low as possible. Second, maintaining multiple sources reduced the buyer's dependence on any one supplier. This in turn served to reduce the buyer's risk should a specific supplier encounter problems such as a strike, a fire, internal quality problems, or other disruptions in ability to supply. For example, when UPS drivers went on strike in 1998, numerous shippers were unable to deliver their products to customers because of their extreme reliance on UPS for delivery service. Although other suppliers of package delivery service exist, none had the available capacity to cope with large volumes of shipments that had been handled by UPS. While other reasons for multiple supplier relationships exist, these reasons constitute the primary rationale.

By consolidating volumes with a reduced number of suppliers, procurement is able to leverage its share of a supplier's business. At the very least, it raises the buyer's negotiating strength in relationship to the supplier. More importantly, volume consolidation with a reduced number of suppliers provides a number of advantages for those suppliers. As working relationships with a smaller number of suppliers are developed, those suppliers can, in turn, pass these advantages to the buying organization. The most obvious source of advantage is that by concentrating a larger volume of purchases with a supplier, the supplier can gain greater economies of scale in its own internal processes, partially by being able to spread its fixed costs over a larger volume of output. In the example of Tennant cited in Industry Insight 5-1, reduction in hydraulic hose suppliers from 16 to 1 meant that the preferred supplier's increased sales to this one customer allowed economies in marketing, delivery, and production. Additionally, if a supplier can be assured of a larger volume of purchase, it may be more willing to make investments in capacity or in processes to improve customer service. When a buyer is constantly switching suppliers, no one firm has an incentive to make such investments.[6]

Clearly, when a single source of supply is used risk increases. For this reason, supply base reduction programs are almost always accompanied by rigorous supplier screening, selection, and certification programs. In many instances, procurement executives work closely with others in their organization to develop such preferred or certified suppliers. It should be noted that volume consolidation does not necessarily mean that a single source of supply is utilized for every, or any, purchased input. It does mean that a substantially smaller number of suppliers are used than was traditionally the case in most organizations. Even when a single source is chosen, it is wise to have a contingency plan in place.

The savings potential from volume consolidation is not trivial. One consulting firm has estimated that savings in purchase price and other elements of cost can range

---

[6]Matthew G. Anderson, "Strategic Sourcing," *International Journal of Logistics,* January 1998, p. 1–13.

from 5 to 15 percent of purchases. If the typical manufacturing firm spends 55 percent of its revenue on purchased items and can save 10 percent through volume consolidation, the potential exists to deliver a $5.5 million improvement on revenue of $100 million to bottom-line, pretax income!

Supplier Operational Integration

The next level of development in procurement strategy emerges as buyers and sellers begin to integrate their processes and activities in an attempt to achieve substantial operational performance improvement in the supply chain. The integration begins to take the form of alliances or partnerships with selected participants in the supply base to reduce the total costs and improve the operating flows between the buyer and the seller.

Such integration can take many specific forms. As one example, the buyer may allow the seller to have access to its sales and ordering information system, giving the seller early warning of which products are being sold and what future purchases to expect. Such information allows the seller to be better positioned to effectively supply requirements for materials at a reduced cost. Cost reduction occurs because the seller faces more certain demand from the buyer and can reduce the need for cost-inefficient practices, such as expediting.

Further operational integration can occur by buyer and seller working together to identify the processes involved in maintaining supply, searching for ways to redesign those processes. Establishing EDI linkages to reduce order time and eliminate errors is a simple form of such integration. More sophisticated efforts may involve eliminating redundant activities that both parties perform. For example, in some sophisticated relationships, activities such as buyer counting and inspection of incoming deliveries have been eliminated as greater reliance is placed on the supplier's capabilities. Many firms have achieved operational integration focused on logistical arrangements, such as continuous replenishment programs and vendor-managed inventory. Such integration has considerable potential for reducing TCO.

Some of the efforts in operational integration strive to reduce total cost through two-way learning. For example, Honda of America works closely with its suppliers to improve those suppliers' capability in quality management. Using its own personnel, Honda visits supplier facilities and helps identify ways that those suppliers can increase the quality of their output. Such improvements ultimately benefit Honda by reducing the suppliers' costs of rework and by providing Honda with higher levels of quality materials.

The primary objective of operational integration is to cut waste, reduce cost, and develop a relationship that allows both buyer and seller to achieve mutual improvements. The above examples are merely illustrative of some of the ways that integration can aid in this objective. Combined creativity across organizations can provide synergy that one firm, operating in isolation, would be unable to achieve. It has been estimated that operational integration with a supplier can provide incremental savings of 5 to 25 percent above the benefits achieved through volume consolidation.[8]

Value Management

Achieving operational integration with suppliers leads quite naturally to the next level of development in procurement strategy, value management. Value management is an

---

[7]Matthew Anderson, Les Artman, and Paul B. Katz, "Procurement Pathways," *Logistics,* Spring/Summer 1997, p. 10.
[8]Matthew Anderson, Les Artman, and Paul B. Katz, op. cit.

FIGURE 5-3

**Flexibility and cost
of design changes**

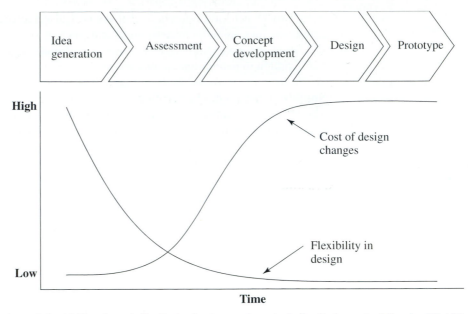

Source: Robert M. Monczka, et al., *New Product Development: Strategies for Supplier Integration* (Milwaukee, WI: ASQ Quality Press, 2000), p. 6.

even more intense aspect of supplier integration, going beyond a focus on buyer–seller operations to a more comprehensive relationship. Value engineering, reduced complexity, and early supplier involvement in product design represent some of the ways procurement can work with suppliers to reduce further the TCO.

Value engineering is a concept that involves closely examining material and component requirements at the early stage of product design to ensure that the lowest total cost inputs are incorporated into that design. Figure 5-3 shows how early supplier involvement can be critical in achieving cost reductions. As a firm's new product development process proceeds from idea generation through its various stages to final commercialization, the company's flexibility in making design changes decreases. Design changes can easily be accommodated in the early stages, but by the time prototypes have been developed, a design change is extremely difficult. The expense associated with a design change has the opposite pattern, becoming extremely high after a prototype is developed. The earlier a supplier is involved in the process, then, the more likely an organization is to capitalize on the supplier's knowledge and capabilities.

An example from an automobile manufacturer demonstrates the potential arising from early supplier involvement. In designing the front bumper for a new model, the design engineer was completing design of the bracket assembly for the bumper. During the process, an engineer from the assembly supplier, which had already been chosen even though production was still several years into the future, asked if the bracket location could be moved by about 1/2 inch. The design engineer, after some consideration, replied that it could be done with no impact on the final product. The design engineer was interested to know why the supplier's engineer requested the change. The answer was that by moving the bracket, the supplier would be able to use existing tools and dies to manufacture the piece. Under the original design, major capital investment would have been required for new tooling. The result was approximately a 25 to 30 percent reduction in cost due to the modification.

Clearly, value management extends beyond the procurement activity in an organization and requires close cooperation between numerous participants, both internal and external. Teams representing procurement, engineering, manufacturing, marketing and sales, and logistics as well as key supplier personnel attempt to find solutions to lower total cost, improve performance, or better meet customer requirements by investigating the cost and functionality of purchased inputs. Research by Mercer Management Consulting reveals that the potential payoffs from this approach vary widely in organizations but can be greater than the payoffs already achieved in volume consolidation and supplier operational integration.[9]

Purchase Requirement Segmentation

The Pareto effect applies in procurement just as it applies in almost every facet of business activity. In the procurement context, it can be stated simply: a small percentage of the materials, items, and services that are acquired account for a large percentage of the dollars spent. The point is that all procured inputs are not equal; however, many organizations use the same approach and procedures for procuring small items as they do for acquiring their most strategic inputs. One result is that they spend as much in acquiring a large $10,000 order of raw materials as they do for a $100 order of copying paper. Since all purchased inputs are not equal, many firms have begun to pay attention to segmented purchase requirements and prioritizing resources and expertise against those requirements.

It would be a mistake, though, to simply use dollar expenditure as the basis for segmenting requirements. Some inputs are strategic materials; others are not. Some inputs have potential for high impact on the business success; others do not. Some purchases are very complex and high risk; others are not. For example, failure to have seat assemblies delivered to an auto assembly line on time could be catastrophic, while failure to have cleaning supplies might be merely a nuisance. Obtaining a new computer order-processing system has major ramifications for the entire organization; purchasing a laptop for a new sales representative is a relatively simple task. The key is for the organization to apply the appropriate approach to procurement as needed. Volume consolidation and supply base reduction most likely can be justified for almost every material and service. The benefits described earlier from this approach can be gained for office supplies as well as raw materials. Because operational integration focuses heavily on improving the flow of products and information between organizations, it is particularly appropriate for inputs which have a high degree of logistical cost and potential value-added from logistics operations. A value-management approach should be reserved for the firm's most critical resource suppliers.[10]

E-Commerce and Procurement

The explosion in technology and information systems is having a major impact on the procurement activity of many major organizations. Much of the actual day-to-day work in procurement has traditionally been accomplished manually with significant amounts of paperwork, resulting in slow processes subject to considerable human

---

[9]Matthew Anderson, Les Antman, and Paul B. Katz, op. cit.

[10]An interesting approach to segmentation of supplier relationships is described in Rasmus Friis Olsen and Lisa M. Ellram, "A Portfolio Approach to Supplier Relationships," *Industrial Marketing Management,* March 26, 1997, pp. 101–13.

error. Applying technology to procurement has considerable potential to speed the process, reduce errors, and lower cost related to acquisition.

Basic Electronic Procurement

Probably the most prevalent use of electronic commerce in procurement is **Electronic Data Interchange (EDI).** EDI, as the term implies, is simply the electronic transmission of data between a firm and its supplier. This allows two or more companies to obtain and provide much more timely and accurate information. There are many types of data being transmitted directly, including purchase requisitions, purchase orders, purchase order acknowledgment, order status, and tracking and tracing information. The explosion in EDI usage during the late 1990s was a direct recognition of its benefits, including standardization of data, more accurate information, more timely information, shortening of lead times with associated reductions in inventories, and reduced TCOs.

At its most basic level, EDI is a major component of integration between buyers and sellers. At least in theory, buyers can communicate quickly, accurately, and interactively with suppliers about requirements, schedules, orders, invoices, and so forth. It provides a tool for transparency between organizations, which is needed to integrate processes in the supply chain.

Another basic application of electronic commerce in procurement has been the development of electronic catalogs.[11] In fact, making information available about products and who can supply them is a natural application for computer technology. Electronic catalogs allow buyers to gain rapid access to product information, specifications, and pricing. When tied to EDI systems, electronic catalogs allow buyers to quickly identify and place orders for needed items. Many companies have developed their own online electronic catalogs and efforts have also been devoted to developing catalogs containing products from many suppliers, which will allow buyers to compare features, specifications, and prices very rapidly. These tools potentially can bring significant savings in procurement, especially for standard items for which the primary criterion is purchase price.

The Internet and B2B Procurement

The real excitement in procurement related to e-commerce is the development of the Internet as a B2B tool. Even more so than in the business-to-consumer realm, the Internet and the World Wide Web are expected to have a major impact on how businesses interact with one another. As early as 1996, several major organizations, including General Motors and Wal★Mart, announced that suppliers who were not capable of conducting business via the Internet would be eliminated from consideration. Estimates of the future for B2B e-commerce vary even more wildly than business-to-consumer, but at least one respected authority predicts B2B Internet transactions could reach over $1 trillion by 2005.[12]

One advantage of the Internet relative to traditional EDI is that it overcomes some of the technical issues of compatibility of computer systems, which is required in EDI. The Internet itself provides capability for buyers and sellers to exchange files and information easily. General Electric created a "Trading Process Network" that turned a once completely manual process for procuring custom-designed parts into an elec-

---

[11]Doris Kilbane, "E-Catalogs Becoming Standard," *Automatic I.D. News,* August 1999, pp. 19–20.

[12]Reported in *USA Today,* May 10, 2000, p. B-1.

tronic system. The system sends requests for quotation along with drawings and specifications to vendors worldwide. GE reports that the system has reduced acquisition costs significantly and, perhaps more importantly, reduced cycle times by as much as 50 percent.[13]

Another example of how the Internet can transform B2B exchange is seen in the development of e-Chemicals. The company is known as an *infomediary* because it acts as intermediary, providing information between companies. Traditionally, purchasing small quantities of chemicals was extremely difficult both for the buyer and the seller. Chemical processors do not like to deal with numerous small orders, finding it very expensive from sales, marketing, and logistics standpoints. Small quantity purchasers likewise find that dealing with large chemical processors is difficult and costly. While there are industrial distributors in the industry, they are plagued by several problems, including maintaining inventories of a wide variety of chemicals from numerous manufacturers. E-Chemicals offers a solution to these problems via the Internet. It has developed relationships with major processors, which allows it to take orders of small quantities from numerous buyers. As illustrated in Figure 5-4, e-Chemicals takes these small orders, processes them, consolidates them into larger orders for the suppliers, makes arrangements with a third-party logistics provider for pickup and delivery, and conducts the invoicing and collection through an arrangement with a financial institution. Chemical suppliers benefit by no longer dealing with numerous small orders. Buyers benefit by receiving one shipment of items from several suppliers, receiving one invoice, making one payment, and having greater assurance of supply than is typically available from traditional distributors. Although e-Chemicals charges for its services, the cost reductions more than offset this expense. Developments similar to that of e-Chemicals have arisen in numerous industries, including steel, hardware, and farm equipment and supplies. Industry Insight 5-2 describes Farmbid.com, a website at which farmers can buy supplies.

Buying exchanges are another Internet-related development. While some companies have formed their own trading networks for dealing with their suppliers, buying exchanges represent cooperative efforts among companies, frequently competitors, to deal with their common base of suppliers. In the auto industry, General Motors, Ford, and DaimlerChrysler, each of which had initially formed separate trading networks, announced that they are forming a joint online buying exchange.[14] The auto companies will allow their suppliers to view requirements for parts and supplies, look at technical specifications, and even see production schedules. Since the auto manufacturers in many instances deal with common suppliers, these suppliers will be able to better plan their own production and delivery requirements by having access to information concerning all of their customers in one location. It is even considered possible that the buyers may pool some of their requirements for standard parts to achieve greater economies through volume consolidation.

The potential volume of procurement activity through buying exchanges is enormous. Exchanges have been developed in the aircraft parts industry, chemicals, steel building products, food distribution, and even retailing. For example, Sears and Carrefour, two of the world's largest retailers, formed GlobalNetxchange to combine their

---

[13]Richard Wough and Scott Eliff, "Using the Internet to Achieve Purchasing Improvements at General Electric," *Hospital Material Management Quarterly,* November 1998, pp. 81–83.

[14]Robert Simson, Farn Werner, and Gregory White, "Big Three Carmakers Plan Net Exchange," *The Wall Street Journal,* February 28, 2000, p. A-3.

FIGURE 5-4

E-Chemicals

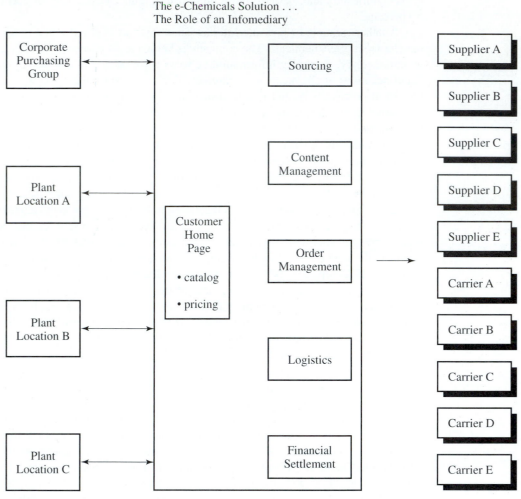

The e-Chemicals Solution . . .
The Role of an Infomediary

Source: e-Chemicals, Inc. Reprinted with permission.

joint $80 billion in purchases into one online network for dealing with suppliers.[15] Suppliers will be able to view the retailers' sales and inventory levels and better plan their production requirements. The entire procurement process, from request for quotes to purchase orders to invoicing and payment, can be conducted electronically via the website.

While numerous benefits are envisioned for trading exchanges and buying exchanges, there is a potential downside. Many suppliers fear that the exchanges will become a mechanism that ultimately will return procurement to focus strictly on purchase price. If buyers post their requirements and needs on the Web primarily for the purpose of soliciting bids from alternative suppliers, or use the technology to have suppliers enter into an auctioning process, it is feared that many of the advances in

[15]Calmetta Coleman, "Sears, Carrefour Plan Web Supply Exchange," *The Wall Street Journal,* February 29, 2000, p. A-4.

INDUSTRY INSIGHT 5-2 FARMING VIA THE INTERNET

Ted Farnsworth became frustrated as he searched the Internet for farming equipment for his brother-in-law's New York dairy farm. As a result, he has started his own farming website, Farmbid.com. Approximately 90,000 customers have registered to buy and sell seed, chemicals, machinery, and other agricultural products.

Farmbid is one of more than a dozen farming websites that have sprouted in recent months. Some auction cattle, pigs, sheep, and horses; while others sell everything from seed to animal vaccinations to farm insurance. These B2B sites are trying to cash in on the distance and isolation that many rural farmers face. By providing one-stop shopping, the sites hope to get a slice of the lucrative agricultural industry, estimated to be a $1 trillion market by 2004. Online agricultural transactions are expected to account for 12 percent, or $120 billion, in sales over the next 4 years.

The sites are welcome news for farmers, who are facing some of the lowest prices in history for their crops and goods. Farm sites allow customers to comparison shop among different manufacturers and have companies compete for their business. The digital marketplaces can lower prices as companies look to unload excess grain, seed, or equipment at relatively low prices. Farmers have traditionally bought products from catalogs, local dealers, and traveling salesmen. While the current system works, many farmers are restricted in what brand or type of product they can buy and don't always get the best prices.

The sites make money through advertising, transaction fees, or by taking a percentage of each sale executed over the site. Few sites are profitable, and most don't expect to be for at least a year.

Although there's a strong market for B2B farming sites, analysts say there's only room for two or three competitors. The industry is beginning to consolidate. Companies like DuPont and Cargill have strong relationships with farmers and other firms. To succeed, B2B sites need a critical mass of customers. But with only 1.9 million U.S. farms, the pool of available customers is limited.

Gary Carlson, CEO of Rooster.com, a soon-to-be-launched electronic mall, states that his site will be inclusive toward all agricultural companies. It will allow dealers to set up virtual storefronts where they can sell seed, chemicals, and other goods. However, according to Carlson, it will work "very closely" with agriculture dealers that already have established relationships with Cargill, Cenex, and DuPont and help them set up virtual shops.

Farmbid's Farnsworth expects a tough battle. But Farmbid "has advantages, such as having a lot of farmers signed up," he says. "We're building a Web site around the farmer and giving them everything they need," such as auctions, weather, classified, and even farm chat rooms.

The greatest hurdle for all the B2B players is the limited Internet access in rural areas. Few farms are served by high-speed Internet services, such as cable modems or digital subscriber lines (DSL). Most farmers can access dial-up Internet service providers, but often face long-distance charges. This curtails farmers' use of the Net and could limit the revenue of many sites, according to analysts.

Source: Deborah Solomon, "Farm B2Bs Find Fertile Soil on Net," *USA Today,* April 20, 2000, p. 1B.

---

supplier integration and value management will suffer. The future will show whether the result will be positive or negative.

In a supply chain management context, the link between a company and its external suppliers is critical. It provides for the integration of materials and resources from outside the organization into internal operations. Procurement is charged with the responsibility of ensuring that this transition is accomplished as efficiently and as effectively as possible. Much of the concern in procurement is focused on the logistical interface between the organization and its supply base. Ultimately, the purpose of procurement is to integrate material flow in accordance with manufacturing requirements. In the next section, alternative manufacturing strategies are discussed with a focus on their logistical requirements.

Manufacturing

A substantial number of firms in the supply chain are involved in manufacturing products. Whereas almost all business firms are engaged in procurement and market distribution operations, manufacturers add value by converting raw materials into consumer or industrial products. They create value by producing and marketing product/service bundles to either end customers or intermediate members of the supply chain. For example, retailers purchase a wide range of product from varied manufacturers to create an appealing assortment for consumers. This section reviews supply chain structure and strategy from a manufacturing perspective. Similar to the previous section that discussed procurement, the objective is to identify logistics requirements and challenges necessary to integrate and support manufacturing into supply chain operations.

Manufacturing Perspectives[16]

The range of products a firm manufactures evolves from its technological capability and marketing strategy. Firms perfect manufacturing competencies based upon market opportunity and willingness to take innovative risk. At the outset, a manufacturing firm creates or invents a new product assortment as its entry point as a value-added participant in a supply chain. Initial market success serves to define and clarify a firm's competency as perceived by customers and suppliers. A firm initiating manufacturing operations to produce automotive parts will be viewed by trading partners as being distinctly different from one that produces garments. While the products produced are clearly different, the real differentiator between firms is found in competencies related to knowledge, technology, process, and strategy. Once established, a manufacturing firm's image and focus are continuously modified in the eyes of supply chain partners as it conducts business, researches and develops new products, and performs agreed-to value-added services. Thus, the combination of capabilities and competencies that are exhibited by a manufacturing firm are dynamic. In terms of supply chain participation, the combination of products, services, capabilities, and competencies represents a firm's value proposition and provides dimension to its supply chain opportunities. A firm's manufacturing competency is based on **brand power, volume, variety, constraints,** and **leadtime requirements.**

Brand Power

Many manufacturers spend a great deal of promotional money to create brand awareness and acceptance among prospective buyers; as a result, they are typically identified by their product brands. The measure of a customer's purchase preference based on a manufacturer's reputation, product quality, and supply chain capabilities is known as brand power.

Buyers along the supply chain range from end customers to industrial purchasing agents. Under market conditions wherein a brand has high customer awareness, ac-

---

[16]This section draws upon Steven A. Melnyk and David R. Denzler, *Operations Management: A Value Driven Approach* (Chicago, IL: Richard D. Irwin, 1996).

INDUSTRY INSIGHT 5-3 THIRD-PARTY INNOVATION

Tradeteam is a joint venture of Exel Logistics, along with its parent company NFC Plc., and Bass Brewers to provide a national distribution network service to the U.K. beverage industry.

Tradeteam was developed in response to changing pressures and shifting market conditions in the industry. The beer market in the United Kingdom had been in long-term decline, with pub consumption shrinking at approximately 1 percent per year. Overall, the industry had been suffering from excess capacity and lower margins. On top of this, the government had required brewers to divest themselves of their interest in pubs, a directive with major marketplace implications. Between 1992 and 1999, for example, pub ownership by regional and national brewers declined from 74 percent to 33 percent. The end result was typical of low-growth industries: Brewers were consolidating and repositioning and were in need of a fresh approach to marketing and distribution.

As the United Kingdom's largest provider of brewery distribution services, Exel Logistics had a significant interest in protecting a business that was under pressure from individual brewers and emerging pub ownership groups. Exel's idea was to take over one major brewer's existing distribution infrastructure to achieve the critical mass associated with that company's market share. Leveraging that infrastructure, it would then offer cost-effective logistics services to other beverage suppliers. This concept led to the formation of the Tradeteam joint venture between Exel Logistics and Bass, which already was the industry's low-cost producer.

Tradeteam is now the U.K.'s leading independent logistics provider to the beverage industry. It has annual revenues of $200 million and delivers approximately 280 million gallons of beer and other beverages to more than 27,000 retail customers on behalf of a number of beverage suppliers. Uniquely situated as a multiuser distributor between the consumer and the supplier, Tradeteam has revolutionized the beverage industry supply chain.

Results to date have been encouraging. Tradeteam has enabled the brewers and beverage suppliers to reduce their operating costs, increase revenues through market expansion, and provide superior service levels to their customers. Market share for this innovative joint venture has reached the 40 to 50 percent range. In fact, this represents the largest outsourcing initiative yet undertaken in the United Kingdom.

Source: Anonymous, "One Example of Third-Party Innovation," *Supply Chain Management Review,* Fall 1999, p. 87.

---

ceptance, and preference, manufacturers can be expected to have a great deal of influence. As a general rule, *the stronger a firm's product brand image among buyers, the more leverage the manufacturing organization will have in determining supply chain structure and strategy.* For instance, Deere & Company dominates how farm machinery, as well as lawn and garden products, is sold, distributed, and maintained.

Independent of customer acceptance is the reality that a firm that brands and markets a particular line of products may not, in fact, be engaged in either the actual manufacturing/assembly or in the performance of supportive logistics services. It is common practice for an organization to outsource some or even all manufacturing and logistics operations required to market a specific product. The nature of the manufacturing process, cost, and next destination in the supply chain go a long way to determine the attractiveness of outsourcing. Logistical requirements in terms of inbound materials and finished product distribution are created by the geographical relationship between location of manufacturing operations and those of suppliers and customers. However, the power to determine the range of value-added services, physical product movement requirements, timing, and characteristics of flow along the supply chain is directly related to brand power. As illustrated in Industry Insight 5-3 a third-party supplier can help a firm develop effective brand power.

Volume

Manufacturing processes can be classified in terms of the relationship of cost per unit to volume of output. The traditional perspective is to treat volume in terms of the well-established principle of **economy of scale.** The scale principle defines a relationship wherein the average cost of producing a product declines as its manufacturing volume increases; that is, a product quantity should be increased as long as a per unit increase in volume decreases the average cost per unit manufactured. Economy of scale results from efficiencies generated by specialization of process, workforce, fixed asset utilization, procurement economies, and limited need for process changeover.

Economy of scale is extremely important in manufacturing situations involving high fixed cost machinery to convert raw material into finished products. Typical examples are found in the paper, steel, and refining industries. In fact, some petroleum processing firms have decoupled their refineries from their supply chain marketing structure and positioned them as independent external suppliers. The refineries are then able to sell in the open market to all potential buyers and fully exploit economy-of-scale advantage.

In volume-sensitive industries, high capital investment coupled with high cost of changeover tends to encourage extremely long production runs. In terms of logistical support, two considerations related to volume influence supply chain design. First, supply chain operations must accommodate the number of times a specific product is manufactured during a specific planning period. Such *manufacturing frequency* has a direct impact on both inbound and outbound logistical requirements. Second, the quantity or lot size typically produced during a specific manufacturing run determines the product volume that must be handled and warehoused in a supply chain structure.

Variety

In contrast to manufacturing situations dominated by scale, other production technologies feature flexibility. These manufacturing processes are characterized by relatively frequent product runs and high repetition of small lot sizes. As contrasted to economy of scale, manufacturing processes that feature variety rapidly switch production from one product to another while retaining efficiency are referred to as having **economy of scope.** Scope means that a manufacturing process can use varied combinations of materials, equipment, and labor to produce a variety of different products.

Variety refers to the *range* of product variations that are capable of being manufactured in a given manufacturing process. Such variation may result from the nature of how products are routed throughout a manufacturing plant and/or the use of general as contrasted to specialized equipment. The achievement of economy of scope is also directly related to the speed and cost of changeover from one product to another. In terms of logistical support, high variety translates to relatively small manufacturing lot sizes, flexible material requirements, and a broad range of product outputs. High manufacturing variety directly impacts the type of transportation and warehousing services required to accommodate flexible manufacturing.

Constraints

All manufacturing processes reflect a balance between economy of scale and economy of scope. Volume and variety drive logistical support requirements. Constraints interact with volume and variety to create manufacturing plans. The three primary constraints that influence manufacturing operations are *capacity, equipment,* and *setup/*

changeover. Each of these constraints forces compromise concerning ideal manufacturing operations. Such compromise planned in the context of forecasted sales and planned promotions reconciles into a production plan.

Capacity, as the name implies, is a measure of how much product can be produced per unit of time. Of particular interest is a firm's *demonstrated* capacity of quality production. Whereas a factory, process, or machine may have a *rated* capacity, the relevant measure is a firm's demonstrated ability to reach and maintain a specific level of quality output in a predictable time period. A measure of manufacturing competency is the speed to which a particular process reaches demonstrated capacity given an unexpected change in requirements.[17] Such scalability reflects a combination of manufacturing, procurement, and logistical agility.

Equipment constraints are related to flexibility concerning the use and sequencing of specific machines to perform multiple manufacturing tasks. Clearly the variety a factory can produce is constrained by the range of available equipment and the required sequence of work. However, some manufacturing requirements are more easily accommodated across a family of machines and by using variable work sequences than are others. In many situations, a specific machine or work task tends to constrain or act as a bottleneck to the overall manufacturing process. Likewise, logistical capability to accommodate different patterns of equipment utilization may serve to enhance or constrain flexibility of the manufacturing process. Manufacturing executives devote substantial time and resources to eliminating bottlenecks that serve to constrain operations. The structure for focusing managerial attention is captured in *theory of constraint* methodology.[18]

Setup/changeover constraints are directly related to the earlier discussion concerning variety. Substantial progress has been made in manufacturing management to speed up both process changeover time and the time required to reach demonstrated capacity. Whereas several hours and even days were once required for changeover, today the tasks are being performed in hours. For example, modular-manufacturing units, such as paint sprayers, are being set up and calibrated offline and then being inserted ready to flow into assembly lines. Of course all efforts to increase setup/changeover speed are directly dependent upon logistical support.

Leadtime

Manufacturing **leadtime** is a measure of the elapsed time between release of a work order to the shop floor and the completion of all work necessary to achieve ready-to-ship product status. Any given manufacturing process consumes operational and interoperational time.[19]

Operational time is the combination of setup/changeover and running or actual production time. In any manufacturing situation the greater the amount of total leadtime accounted for by actual production, the inherently more efficient is the conversion process. Efficient operational time must be traded off against the issues discussed earlier concerning volume and variety.

---

[17]Thomas G. Gunn, *21st Century Manufacturing* (Essex Junction, VT: OM NEO, 1992), Chapter 8.

[18]For origins of this logic, see Eliyahu M. Goldratt and J. Cox, *The Goal* (Croton on Hudson, NY: North River Press, 1984); and Eliyahu M. Goldratt and Robert E. Fox, *The Race* (Croton on Hudson, NY: North River Press, 1986).

[19]Steven A. Melnyk and R. T. Christensen, *Back to Basics: Your Guide to Manufacturing Excellence* (Boca Raton, FL: St. Lucie Press, 2000), pp. 15–17.

Manufacturing processes also encounter unexpected losses of time. During periods that a process, line, or machine is idle due to queuing, waiting, breakdown, or failure in logistical support, manufacturing efficiency is negatively impacted. All forms of unexpected delay represent serious bottleneck issues. For example, Melnyk and Christensen estimate that between 75 and 95 percent of all nonproductive delays result from unplanned queuing in manufacturing processes.[20] Needless to say, most manufacturing executives have little or no tolerance for unexpected production delays that result from late or damaged arrival of critical materials or components. Logistical delay on the part of a supplier who provides parts or materials can result in manufacturing failure to meet planned output. A firm's strategic impact is directly impacted by leadtime performance. As a general rule, firms that compress manufacturing leadtimes and control or eliminate unexpected performance variance exhibit greater flexibility to accommodate customer requirements while enjoying low-cost manufacturing.

Logistical operations committed to supporting manufacturing can impact operating efficiency in a variety of ways. The potential benefits of brand power are based on a firm's track record regarding timely performance of customer order-to-delivery commitment. Lot-size efficiencies related to manufacturing frequency and repetition are dependent on reliable logistical support. The decision to produce large manufacturing lot sizes directly creates need for logistical support. Economy of scale drives procurement best practice and average inventory investment across the supply chain. The decision to focus on variety in manufacturing impacts the logistics requirements by adding the complexity of frequent changeover. Logistical performance is also a key variable in managing constraints. Such constraints can be caused or resolved based on the quality and flexibility of logistical support. Finally, logistics is critical to achieving high levels of leadtime performance. In particular, logistical failure can increase manufacturing leadtime by introducing unexpected delays.

The above logistical interfaces, as well as all other factors that impact manufacturing performance predictability, serve to create operational gaps that are resolved by inventory. Inventory stocks occur, in part, when the timing of customer expectation exceeds a firm's, or its suppliers', ability to deliver the correct assortment of products to the right place at the right time. The management of these raw material and finished inventory stocks is a prime responsibility of logistics.

Manufacturing Strategy

The unique nature of each manufacturing process and the market served limit the practical range of alternative strategies. Manufacturing strategic range is constrained by both marketing and technological forces. Prevailing marketing practices serve to ground manufacturing strategy in terms of customer acceptability. Technology drives strategy to a manufacturing model that is competitive. For example, a manufacturer having a process dominated by economy of scale may desire to improve process flexibility. However, significant investment will typically be required to increase frequency and repetition.

Over time, the changing nature of the market and available technology serve to alter a firm's existing strategic posture. Consider, for example, the steel industry, which was long dominated by processes highly dependent on economy of scale. Recent years have witnessed market acceptance of a wide range of new steel-based materials combined with value-added services. The birth of the Steel Service Center has in-

---

[20]Steven A. Melnyk and R. T. Christensen, op. cit., p. 17.

troduced postponement as a way to increase customer accommodation. The nature of basic steel production has also undergone dramatic change. New process methods are being perfected that reduce long-time dependence on high-scale manufacturing processes. The combined impact of these changes in market and process has shifted the strategic posture of steel producers.

Matching Manufacturing Strategy to Market Requirements

In Chapter 3, typical marketing strategies were classified as being mass, segmental and focused, or one-on-one.[21] These strategies are differentiated, in part, in terms of the required degree of product and service accommodation. Mass marketing requires limited product/service differentiation. In contrast, one-on-one marketing strategy builds on unique or customized product/service offerings for each and every customer. The strategic marketing posture of a firm in terms of flexibility and agility to accommodate specific customer requirements is directly related to manufacturing capability. To a significant degree, a firm's manufacturing capability drives the feasible range of effective marketing strategy. For a manufacturing firm to effectively compete, it must be able to integrate manufacturing capability into a meaningful marketing value proposition.

Strategic Alternatives

The most common manufacturing strategies are **make-to-plan (MTP), make-to-order (MTO),** and **assemble-to-order (ATO).** It is also common to refer to MTP as **make-to-stock (MTS).**[22]

As a general rule, MTP strategies are characteristic of industries exploiting economy of scale that results from long production runs. Significant finished goods inventory is typically manufactured in anticipation of future customer requirements. The logistical requirement to support MTP is warehousing capacity to store finished product and to facilitate product assortment for specific customers. When flexible manufacturing is introduced to speed up switchover, the inventory lots produced are typically smaller in quantity. However, warehouses are still required for temporary storage and to facilitate product assortment.

In contrast, MTO manufacturing strategies seek to manufacture to customer specification. While MTO may not be as limited as the traditional job shop, exact quantities and configurations are produced in relatively small quantities. Logistical capacity may be required for temporary storage and to achieve outbound transportation consolidation, but most product produced in a MTO environment is shipped direct to customers.

In ATO situations, base products and components are manufactured in anticipation of future customer orders; however, the products are not fully assembled or customized until a customer's order is received. Such final assembly reflects implementation of the principle of manufacturing or form postponement.[23] The need for logistical capacity is critical in ATO operations. In fact, an increasing amount of ATO product finalization is being performed in distribution warehouses. The attractiveness of an ATO manufacturing strategy is that it has the potential to combine some facets of economy of scale typical of MTP with a degree of MTO flexibility. Full implementation of an ATO strategy requires that warehouse operations be integrated in the process to perform customizing and assembly operations. Industry Insight 5-4 illustrates the importance of logistically supporting an original equipment manufacturer.

---

[21]Chapter 3, p. 69.

[22]This general classification draws upon Robert H. Hayes and Gary P. Pisano, "Beyond World Class: The New Manufacturing Strategy," *Harvard Business Review,* January/February, 1994, pp. 77–86.

[23]See Chapter 1, p. 18.

INDUSTRY INSIGHT 5-4 CRITICAL PARTS DELIVERED WITHIN HOURS

Speed is increasingly a key supply chain differentiator, especially in the supply of critical parts, where customers expect delivery within hours, not days.

Two primary forces are driving development of this service niche. First, original equipment manufacturers have warranty contracts with their end users, which frequently include protections against downtime losses. Second, many parts supply operations are fragmented as companies generally have multiple service territories and different service providers for each. Faced with pressures to reduce inventory levels and associated investments, OEMs and other companies need greater visibility, not only to parts availability, but also to pipeline contents—a difficult challenge when responsibilities are spread across numerous networks.

"OEMs are always looking to improve their service to their end users, and having a service parts network with a high parts availability and rapid response time to their field engineers enables them to improve system uptime," says Scott Collins, VP of service parts logistics for Sonic Air, a division of United Parcel Service. Throughout the last decade Sonic Air, in conjunction with UPS, has focused on designing a service network to specifically meet the needs of these OEMs. "We give the OEMs a single point of contact, we use our own network, and we have systems connectivity across that entire network," states Collins.

Sonic owns a central parts distribution center with more than 1 million square feet of space within 3 miles of the UPS air hub in Louisville, an arrangement that enables Sonic to provide late-night processing of orders with delivery guaranteed by 10:30 A.M. the next day, or even earlier if customers use premium services. From that distribution center, Sonic replenishes its network of more than 400 field support bank locations worldwide. With the exception of a few dedicated sites, the field support banks are multiclient facilities.

Orders can come in to Sonic from customers by EDI, Internet, fax, or via one of several call centers Sonic operates, as late as 1 A.M. for next-day availability. Orders are routed to the appropriate dispatcher, who then alerts the respective branch operations that the particular part has to be pulled and dispatched for delivery. Parts can be sent overnight directly to certified engineers (CEs) in the field. Another option is a hold-for-pickup service at any of the 1,430 UPS service counters designated as sites where CEs can snag the parts as early as 7:30 A.M.

The Sonic strategy is to locate field support banks close to the end-user population of their customers to minimize the time from order entry to delivery. "Our network runs 24×7, and right now we can serve 68 percent of the U.S. business population within an hour, 88 percent in two hours, and 99 percent in four hours," says Collins.

Sonic also uses its Louisville distribution center to provide repair and refurbishment services, maintaining a staff of more than 300 technicians to provide rapid turnaround of equipment such as laptop computers, hard drives, monitors, and telecommunications devices, including the programming of cell phones.

Getronics (formerly Wang Getronics) is currently in the ramp-up phase of a new service program. Sonic technicians now perform 1,100 repairs a month for Getronics on a wide array of computer parts, peripherals, and point-of-sale equipment and Sonic expects to see that number rise from 6,000 to 8,000 as the program comes fully online.

Sonic also provides Getronics with end-of-runway central warehousing, which improves Getronics' efficiency and reduces some of the fixed and variable costs associated with the parts operation. "The Sonic/UPS relationship has allowed Getronics to enhance our overall logistics services to our customers by consolidating our freight services—ground, air, and next-flight-out, warehousing, and repair—in one central facility," says Richard Fogarty, VP of service delivery for Getronics. "This allows us to take advantage of freight savings and enables us to reduce our investments in parts by cutting the cycle time for returning defective parts to a serviceable condition. Getronics can also offer a higher level of logistics consulting services to our customers by using the Sonic nationwide network of parts distribution centers, which provide four-hour parts delivery in major business areas for our client base."

Sonic is reconfiguring its information systems. "By the first quarter of next year, we are going to have a fully integrated service parts system that ties together order entry, dispatch, order management, repair, inventory management, billing, and financials," says Collins. An inventory management system interconnecting the network will help identify which parts to store at particular locations, based on the frequency of failures experienced by the end-user population. "Hopefully, this visibility across the entire network will enable customers to do a better job planning and thus be able to reduce the total cost of the inventory in the pipeline," he adds.

Sonic provides much of this information on the Web. Using a browser, customers can pull tracking information on parts shipments and confirm deliveries, giving them visibility of a part from order entry through to delivery. "On the reverse side, where we have recovery operations for monitors and hard drives and laptops, the customer can track the reverse flow of those units through the pipeline and check the status of a particular repair as it moves through the shop floor in Louisville," says Collins.

Source: Kurt C. Hoffman, "With Critical Parts, Delivery is Counted in Hours, Not Days," *Global Logistics & Supply Chain Strategies,* June 2000, pp. 58–60, 62.

Total Cost of Manufacturing

The marketing and manufacturing strategies of a firm drive logistical service requirements. For example, MTO manufacturing strategies typically require less finished goods inventory than MTP and ATO strategies. However, MTO strategies typically require component inventory support and may result in high-cost market distribution. In light of such cost trade-offs, the design of a logistics support system should be based on the **Total Cost of Manufacturing (TCM).**

Total cost of manufacturing consists of production/procurement, inventory/warehousing, and transportation. All of the above costs are impacted by manufacturing strategy. As such, TCM represents the foundation for formulating a market distribution strategy. Figure 5-5 represents a generalized model of the TCM *per unit* ranging across strategic alternatives from MTO to ATO to MTP. Naturally, exact cost relationships will depend upon specifics related to each business situation. The design objective is to identify the manufacturing strategy that best fits the marketing opportunity confronted.

FIGURE 5-5

Total cost of manufacturing

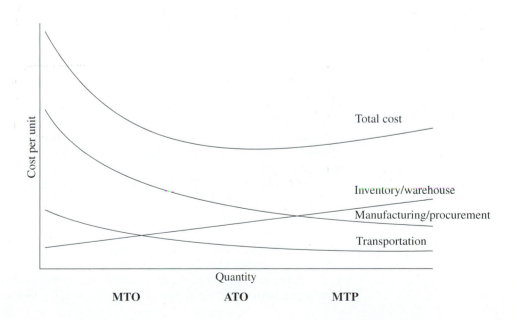

In Figure 5-5, the cost of manufacturing and procurement declines as quantity increases, reflecting economy of scale associated with MTP. Inventory and warehousing costs increase, reflecting the impact of larger manufacturing lot sizes. Transportation cost per unit decreases as a result of shipment consolidation. In contrast, MTO strategies reflect high per unit manufacturing and procurement costs which are, in part, offset by lower inventory and warehousing costs. In the MTO strategy, transportation cost per unit is higher, reflecting small shipment and/or premium transportation. The value of Figure 5-5 is to generalize relationships and visualize important trade-offs. The TCM results from functional integration of manufacturing, procurement, and logistics. From a perspective of integrated management it is important for manufacturing firms to design a supply chain strategy that achieves lowest total cost of manufacturing across the entire process.

Logistical Interfaces

The efficient and effective coordination of manufacturing strategy with the procurement of materials and components ultimately relies on logistics. Resource inputs must be procured and made available when needed for manufacturing operations. Whether the manufacturing strategy is MTO, ATO, or MTP, logistics links the supplier base with manufacturing processes. Clearly, the more seamless the interface, the better the opportunity is for achieving lowest cost of ownership and, ultimately, lowest total cost of manufacturing. Such operations only emerge when there is high-level supplier integration in both operations and in design. Just-in-Time, Materials Requirements Planning, and Design for Logistics represent three approaches to achieving desired coordination.

Just-in-Time

Just-in-Time (JIT) techniques have received considerable attention and discussion in recent years in every functional area related to supply chain management. Sometimes referred to as just-in-time production, often called just-in-time purchasing, and frequently referred to as just-in-time delivery, the goal of JIT is to time-phase activities so that purchased materials and components arrive at the manufacturing or assembly point just at the time they are required for the transformation process. Ideally, raw material and work-in-process inventories are minimized as a result of reducing or eliminating reserve stocks. The key to JIT operations is that demand for components and materials depends on the finalized production schedule. Requirements can be determined by focusing on the finished product being manufactured. Once the production schedule is established, just-in-time arrival of components and materials can be planned to coincide with those requirements, resulting in reduced handling and minimal inventories.

The implications of JIT are numerous. Obviously, it is necessary to deal with suppliers who have high and consistent levels of quality, as their components will go directly into the finished product. Absolutely reliable logistical performance is required and eliminates, or at least reduces, the need for buffer stocks of materials. JIT generally requires more frequent deliveries of smaller quantities of purchased inputs, which may require modification of inbound transportation. Clearly, to make JIT work, there must be very close cooperation and communication between a manufacturer's purchasing organization and suppliers. In JIT operations, companies attempt to gain the benefits of backward vertical integration but avoid the formal tie of ownership. They achieve many of the same ends through coordination and process integration with suppliers.

Originally, JIT was applied to manufacturing processes characterized as MTP, since the effective functioning of the system is dependent upon a finalized production schedule. However, as manufacturing strategies have evolved with more emphasis on flexibility, reduced lot-size production quantities, and quick changeovers, JIT concepts have evolved to accommodate ATO and MTO manufacturing as well. In many situations, lead suppliers are used by manufacturers to sort, segregate, and sequence materials as they flow into assembly operations. The goal is to reduce handling and facilitate continuous JIT.

Some organizations, seeing the benefits of JIT systems and recognizing the benefits of supplier integration, have gone so far as to bring their suppliers' personnel into their production plants. The supplier personnel are empowered to use the customer's purchase orders, have full access to production schedules, and have responsibility for scheduling arrival of materials. Originally introduced by the Bose Corporation, the term **JIT II** has been applied to these efforts to reduce leadtimes and cost.

Requirements Planning

In complex manufacturing organizations a process known as **Materials Requirements Planning (MRP)** is frequently used to aid in the interface between purchaser and supplier. MRP systems attempt to gain benefits similar to those of JIT, minimize inventory, maintain high utilization of manufacturing capacity, and coordinate delivery with procurement and manufacturing activities. Implementation of MRP systems requires a high level of technological sophistication. Software applications such as advanced planning and scheduling systems have been developed to deal with the complexity of information required, such as leadtimes, quantities on-hand and on-order, and machine capacities for literally thousands of materials across multiple manufacturing locations.

Design for Logistics

The logistics interface with procurement and manufacturing, as well as with engineering and marketing, can be greatly enhanced by incorporating a concept known as **Design For Logistics** into the early phases of product development. Recall that the objectives of JIT and MRP are to minimize inventories and handling, with materials and components being ready for assembly or transformation as they are needed. How a product is designed and design of the components and materials themselves can have a significant impact on this process. In particular, product packaging and transportation requirements need to be incorporated into the design process. For example, if inbound components are packaged in containers with a standard quantity of 50 but only 30 components are needed to meet production requirements, then waste will occur. Additionally, product and component design must have consideration of transportation and internal materials handling methods to ensure that cost-efficient, damage-free logistics performance can be achieved. Similar design considerations must be made for the finished product itself.

Table 5-1 summarizes the critical relationships between market distribution, manufacturing/procurement, and logistical requirements. The framework is useful in positioning how logistical requirements flow from the marketing and manufacturing strategy.

TABLE 5-1   Strategic Integration Framework

Market Drivers	Manufacturing Capabilities	Procurement	Logistics
Focused:	Make-to-Order:	B2B	Direct Fulfillment:
One-on-one strategies	Maximum variety	Discrete quantities	Time postponement
Unique product/service offerings	Unique configuration	Supplier VMI	Small shipment
Response-based	Flexible manufacturing		
	High variety		Form and Time
Segemental:	Assemble-to-Order:	B2B	Postponement:
Limited size	Wide variety	JIT	Warehouse ATO
Customer groups	Quick changeover		Combination direct and
Differentiated products	Product customization		warehouse fulfillment
Mixed response and anticipatory	High variety and volume		Consolidated shipment
Mass Marketing:	Make-to-Plan:	B2B	Warehouse Fulfillment:
Anticipatory	Long product runs	Commodity	Full stocking strategy
Little product differentiation	Focus low cost	Auction	Assortment mixing
	High volume/low variety	E-procurement	Volume shipment

Summary

Managing logistics in the supply chain requires an interface between logistics, procurement, and manufacturing strategies.

A primary concern of procurement and manufacturing is product quality, a prerequisite for any firm that desires to be a global competitor. In fact, product quality has several different dimensions. It can mean reliability, durability, product performance, and conformance to engineered specifications. From a customer's perspective it may also include aspects of product features, aesthetics, or serviceability. World-class companies have implemented Total Quality Management programs in all their activities in their efforts to achieve quality from their customers' perspective.

Procurement in an organization is charged with responsibility for obtaining the inputs required to support manufacturing and operation. The focus is multidimensional, attempting to maintain continuous supply, minimize leadtimes from suppliers and inventory of materials and components, and develop suppliers capable of helping the organization achieve these goals. Ultimately, modern procurement professionals focus on the Total Cost of Ownership of acquired resources, not just the purchase price of those inputs. This requires that they consider carefully the trade-offs among purchase price, supplier services and logistical capability, quality of materials, and how the materials affect costs over the life cycle of the product into which they are incorporated.

Procurement strategies today involve consolidation of the volumes purchased into a smaller, more reliable, number of suppliers. They include efforts to integrate supplier and buyer operations to achieve better and lower-cost logistics performance. Supplier integration in new product design represents another strategy to reduce total ownership costs.

In Chapters 4 and 5, strategic considerations related to market distribution, procurement, and manufacturing have been discussed in terms of their combined impact on logistical requirements. A number of important trade-offs were identified. We have seen that isolated optimization of any specific functional area without considering cross-functional impact will not likely result in maximum performance. Operational integration is the focus of Chapter 6.

Challenge Questions

1. Using television receivers as an example, how could three different brands be perceived by different consumers as being the best quality brand in the market?

2. Why does the contemporary view of procurement as a strategic activity differ from the more traditional view of "purchasing"?

3. How can strategic procurement contribute to the quality of products produced by a manufacturing organization?

4. Explain the rationale underlying volume consolidation. What are the risks associated with using a single supplier for an item?

5. How does lowest TCO differ from lowest purchase price?

6. What is the underlying rationale that explains why firms should segment their purchase requirements?

7. Explain how constraints in manufacturing are interrelated with a company's decisions regarding volume and variety.

8. Why would a company's costs of manufacturing and procurement tend to increase as the firm changes from an MTP to an MTO strategy? Why would inventory costs tend to decrease?

9. How does a firm's marketing strategy impact its decisions regarding the appropriate manufacturing strategy?

10. Explain how logistics performance is crucial to JIT.

6   OPERATIONAL INTEGRATION

The dominant theme of supply chain collaboration is the advancement of operational integration. The benefits attainable from collaboration are directly related to capturing efficiencies between functions within an enterprise as well as across enterprises that constitute a domestic or international supply chain. This chapter focuses on the challenges of integrative management by examining why integration creates value and by detailing the challenges of collaboration at the firm, domestic, and global levels of supply chain operations.

Why Integration Creates Value

The basic benefits and challenges of integrated management were introduced in Chapter 1. To further explain the importance of integrated management, it is useful to understand that customers have at least three perspectives of value.

The traditional perspective of value is **economic value.** Economic value builds on economy of scale in operations as the source of efficiency. Economy of scale seeks to fully utilize fixed overhead to achieve the lowest, total landed cost. The focus of economic value is efficiency of product/service creation. Economic value is all about doing things as well as possible. The customer take-away of economic value is *high quality at a low price.*

A second value perspective is **market value.** Market value is about presenting an attractive assortment of products at the right time and place to realize effectiveness. Market value focuses on achieving economy of scope in product/service presentation. The creation of multimerchant shopping malls, large-scale mass-merchandising retail stores and multivendor e-commerce fulfillment operations are all initiatives to achieve market value. The customer's take-away in terms of market value is *convenient product/ service assortment and choice.*

Realization of both economic and market value is important to customers. However, increasingly firms are recognizing that business success also depends upon a third perspective of value referred to as **relevancy.** Relevancy involves customization of value-adding services, over and above product and positioning that make a real difference to customers. Relevancy value means the right products and services, as reflected by market value, at the right price, as reflected by economic value, modified, sequenced, synchronized, and otherwise positioned in a manner that creates valuable segmental diversity. In a consumer context, for example, relevancy means transforming ingredients into ready-to-eat meals. In general merchandise retailing, relevancy means transforming products into fashionable apparel. In manufacturing and assembly, relevancy is achieved by integrating specific components into products to increase functionality desired by a specific customer. The customer's take-away in terms of relevancy is a unique *product/service bundle.*

The simultaneous achievement of economic value, market value, and relevancy value requires total integration of the overall business process and is known as the integrative management value proposition, as illustrated in Table 6-1.

Industry Insight 6-1 illustrates how the value proposition of traditional supermarkets is being challenged by alternative retail formats that offer greater value to customers.

TABLE 6-1   Integrative Mangement Value Proposition

Economic Value	Market Value	Relevancy Value
• Lowest total cost	• Attractive assortment	• Customization
• Economy-of-scale efficiency	• Economy-of-scope effectiveness	• Segmental diversity
• Product/service creation	• Product/service presentation	• Product/service positioning
Procurement/Manufacturing Strategy	**Market/Distribution Strategy**	**Supply Chain Strategy**

Industry Insight 6-1 Threats to Traditional Retail Food Supply Chains

Conventional supermarkets seek to simultaneously satisfy value drivers across many consumers. This initial supermarket strategy of trying to be all things to all shoppers may be its eventual downfall. Several retail formats now provide alternatives that focus on specific consumer value drivers, creating greater value.

A major and growing competitive threat to traditional supermarkets is meals prepared away from home. This segment represented 54 percent of the dollars spent for food in the U.S. for 2000 and is projected to enjoy the most future growth in food consumer expenditure. Heat-and-eat foods are available at a wide range of outlets, including supermarkets, or are available for home delivery. Restaurants are selling as many meals for carryout as they are for on-site consumption. This segment focuses on providing time and form value, giving customers what they want, when and where they want it.

The rapidly growing mass merchants pose the second threat to traditional supermarkets. Merely 5 years ago, Wal★Mart was not considered a player in food distribution. Today it is the second largest retailer of grocery products in the United States, outsized only by the merger of Albertson's and American Stores. Of course, Wal★Mart's entry into retail food stores is not unique. Many other mass merchandisers are following a similar strategy of focusing on a limited assortment of grocery products sold at the same stores with numerous nonfood products.

The convenience store format presents a third threat to the prominence of traditional supermarkets by creating value of time and place. Today, a growing variety of meal solutions are sold at convenience stores. These stores also provide a quick way to obtain select items, thereby avoiding a prolonged trip to the supermarket.

A final alternative to traditional food supply chains is home delivery. As early as the 1930s, A&P used bicycle delivery boys to deliver groceries direct to customer homes all over Manhattan. Grocery home delivery sales are not currently a serious volume threat to the conventional supermarket; nevertheless, all of the essential technology is in place to make home delivery a viable alternative format. Industry observers predict home delivery variations to range from 10 to 20 percent of total ingredient purchases in the first decade of the new millennium. The economics of this alternative are becoming more competitive. A total cost comparison of supermarkets and home delivery must quantify the "convenience cost" associated with shopping time and the reclamation cost of clearing unsalable product from the marketplace. The industry's $2 billion annual expenditure for reclamation is virtually nonexistent in the home delivery format. As long as the product is delivered within its expiration date, it will be consumed. Home delivery creates value through time and place.

Other competitive arrangements—such as vending machines—are also chipping away at the traditional supermarket's share of the consumer food dollar. All alternative formats build on the fact that the traditional supermarkets' custom of creating value through price and assortment does not offer sufficient *relevancy*. The success of these alternatives pressures supermarkets to reinvent themselves and streamline the supply chain. Selected companies are using efficient replenishment to counter alternative formats.

Source: Donald J. Bowersox et al., "Threats to Traditional Retail Food Supply Chains," *Supply Chain Management* (Washington, DC: Food Market Institute, 1999), pp. 59–60.

Systems Concept and Analysis

The **systems concept** is an analytical framework that seeks *total* integration of components essential to achieving stated objectives. The components of a logistics system are typically called functions. The logistical functions, as discussed in Chapter 2, were identified as order processing, inventory, transportation, warehousing, materials handling and packaging, and facility network design. **Systems analysis,** applied to logistics, seeks to quantify trade-offs between these five functions. The goal of systems analysis methodology is to create a whole or integrated effort, which is greater than the sum of the individual parts or functions. Such integration creates a *synergistic* interrelationship between functions in pursuit of higher overall achievement. In systems terminology, functional excellence is defined in terms of contributions a function makes to the overall process as contrasted to isolated performance in a specific area. Until the last few decades of the 20th century, process integration was generally neglected by managers who were trained to pursue functional excellence. Rapid advancement in information technology has increased the ability to identify and understand enhancement trade-offs to better facilitate logistics and supply chain initiatives.

When analyzed from a process perspective, the goal is balanced performance between functional areas within an enterprise and across the supply chain. For example, manufacturing economics are typically minimized by long production runs and low procurement costs. In contrast, integrated process management raises questions concerning the total cost and customer impact of such practices. A traditional financial orientation typically seeks to minimize inventories. While inventory should always be maintained as low as practical, arbitrary reductions below a level required to facilitate integrated operations typically increase total cost. Marketing's basic desire is to have finished goods inventory available in local markets. Inventory stocked in close geographical proximity to customers is believed to facilitate sales. Such anticipatory deployment of inventory is risky and may be in direct conflict with the least total cost process. In fact, e-commerce connectivity and fulfillment strategies are driving entirely different inventory stocking and fulfillment strategies.

In systems analysis, attention is focused on the interaction between components. Each component contributes a specific functionality essential to achieving system objectives. To illustrate, consider a high-fidelity stereo system. Many components are integrated for the single purpose of sound reproduction. The speakers, transistors, amplifier, and other components only have purpose if they contribute to quality sound. However, failure of any component will cause the output of the stereo system to fail.

Some principles can be stated concerning general systems theory. First, the performance of the total system or process is of singular importance. Components are only important if they enhance total system performance. For example, if the stereo system can achieve superior sound with two speakers, then it is unnecessary to include additional speakers. Second, individual components need not have best or optimum design. Emphasis is on the integrated relationship between components that constitute the system. Transistors, as an example, are hidden from view inside the stereo system. As such, they do not need to be aesthetically pleasing. To spend money and time designing an appealing transistor is not necessary in terms of system integration. Third, a functional relationship, called *trade-off,* exists between components that serve to stimulate or hinder total system performance. Suppose a trade-off allows a lower-quality amplifier to be used if an extra transistor is added to the system. The cost of the extra transistor must be justified in terms of savings in amplifier cost. Finally, components linked together as an integrated system may produce end results greater than possible through individual performance. In fact, the desired result may be unattainable without such integrated performance. A stereo system will technically operate without speakers, but audible sound is impossible.

The principles of systems analysis are basic and logically consistent. An integrated process with cross-functional integration can be expected to achieve greater results than one deficient in coordinated performance. In logistical systems, synergistic performance is targeted customer service at the lowest possible total cost. Although logical and indisputable in concept, effective application of systems integration is operationally difficult. In the final analysis, it matters little how much a firm spends to perform any specific function, such as transportation, as long as overall performance goals are realized at the lowest total cost expenditure.

Logistical Integration Objectives

To achieve logistical integration, six operational objectives must be simultaneously achieved: (1) responsiveness, (2) variance reduction, (3) inventory reduction, (4) shipment consolidation, (5) quality, and (6) life cycle support. The relative importance of each is directly related to a firm's logistical strategy.

Responsiveness

Responsiveness is concerned with a firm's ability to satisfy customer requirements in a timely manner. As noted repeatedly, information technology is facilitating response-based strategies that permit operational commitment to be postponed to the last possible time, followed by accelerated delivery. The implementation of response-based strategies serves to reduce inventories committed or deployed in anticipation of customer requirements. Responsiveness, as developed in Chapter 1, serves to shift operational emphasis from forecasting future requirements to accommodating customers on a rapid order-to-shipment basis. In a response-based system, inventory is not deployed until a customer commits. To support such commitment, a firm must have inventory availability and timely delivery once a customer order is received.

Variance Reduction

All operating areas of a logistical system are susceptible to variance. Variance results from failure to perform any expected facet of logistical operations. For example, delay in customer order processing, an unexpected disruption in manufacturing, goods arriving damaged at a customer's location, and/or failure to deliver at the right location on time all create unplanned variance in the order-to-delivery cycle. A common solution to safeguard against the detrimental variance is to use inventory safety stocks to buffer operations. It is also common to use premium transportation to overcome unexpected variance that delays planned delivery. Such practices, given their associated high cost, can be minimized by using information technology to maintain positive logistics control. To the extent that variance is minimized, logistical productivity will improve. Thus, **variance reduction,** the elimination of system disruptions, is one basic objective of integrated logistics management.

Inventory Reduction

To achieve the objective of **inventory reduction,** an integrated logistics system must control asset commitment and turn velocity. Asset commitment is the financial value of deployed inventory. Turn velocity reflects the rate at which inventory is replenished over time. High turn rates, coupled with desired inventory availability, mean assets devoted to inventory are being efficiently and effectively utilized; that is, overall assets committed to support an integrated operation are reduced.

It is important to keep in mind that inventory can and does facilitate desirable benefits. Inventories are critical to achieving economies of scale in manufacturing and procurement. The objective is to reduce and manage inventory to the lowest possible level while simultaneously achieving performance objectives.

Shipment Consolidation

One of the most significant logistical costs is transportation. Approximately 60 cents of each logistics dollar is expended for transportation. Transportation cost is directly related to the type of product, size of shipment, and movement distance. Many logistical systems that feature direct fulfillment depend on high-speed, small shipment transportation, which is costly. A system objective is to achieve **shipment consolidation** in an effort to reduce transportation cost. As a general rule, the larger a shipment and the longer the distance it is transported, the lower is the cost per unit. Consolidation requires innovative programs to combine small shipments for timely consolidated movement. Such programs require multifirm coordination because they transcend the supply chain. Successful e-commerce fulfillment direct-to-consumers requires innovative ways to achieve effective consolidation. Industry Insight 6-2 discusses logistics challenges of e-commerce to illustrate the importance of effective consolidation.

Quality

A fundamental operational objective is continuous **quality** improvement. Total Quality Management (TQM) is a major initiative throughout most facets of industry. If a product becomes defective or if service promises are not kept, little if any value can be added by the logistics process. Logistical costs, once expended, cannot be reversed or recovered. In fact, when product quality fails after customer delivery and replacement is necessary, logistical costs rapidly accumulate. In addition to the initial distribution cost, products must be returned and replaced. Such unplanned movements typically cost more than original distribution. For this reason, commitment to zero-defect order-to-delivery performance is a major goal of leading-edge logistics.

Logistics itself is performed under challenging conditions. The difficulty of achieving zero-defect logistics is magnified by the fact that logistical operations typically are performed across a vast geographical area during all times of day and night without direct supervision.

Life Cycle Support

The final integration design objective is **life cycle support.** Few items are sold without some guarantee that the product will perform as advertised. In some situations, the initial value-added inventory flow to customers must be reversed. Product return is common as a result of increasingly rigid quality standards, product expiration dating, and responsibility for hazardous consequences. Reverse logistics also results from the increasing number of laws encouraging recycling of beverage containers and packaging materials. The significant point concerning reverse logistics is the need to maintain maximum control when a potential health liability exists, such as a contaminated product. The operational requirements for reverse logistics range from lowest total cost, such as returning bottles for recycling, to maximum control in situations involving defective products. Firms that design efficient reverse logistics often are able to reclaim value by reducing the quantity of products that might otherwise be scrapped or sold at

Industry Insight 6-2 Delivering the E-Commerce Purchase

E-commerce companies that will survive growth will be those that achieve the best logistical support systems and the most dependable delivery. These goals are easily described, but not so easily accomplished.

Many e-commerce people fail to understand that the actual process of getting the product from factory to home remains the same, whether the customer has ordered through a retail store, an 800 number, a direct-mail catalog, or an e-commerce website.

The customer receiving the package doesn't know or care whether it originated at a warehouse, factory, or retail store but does care whether it arrives on time, is in good condition, and is the product ordered. The customer doesn't care whether it arrives via FedEx, UPS, USPS, or pony express as long as quality is maintained.

Home delivery is highly labor-intensive and most communities in the United States face a significant labor shortage. As a result, it is increasingly difficult to find a delivery service that shares the company's dedication to customer satisfaction. For some products, such as major appliances and furniture, proper delivery service includes final assembly; hooking up to water, gas, or electric lines; final quality check; and removal of the shipping carton. Finding a carrier with the skills and experience to do these jobs is not a simple task.

One potential solution is to subcontract the logistics function to a growing number of service providers who have targeted Internet vendors as a major new marketing opportunity. The best third-party providers understand the problems of home delivery; they have performed similar functions for other firms with similar operations. They have the trained staff, equipment, and software to handle the fulfillment process.

Consider these criteria when evaluating potential third-party providers:

1. Order acceptance and processing: Does the potential vendor have a state-of-the-art order acceptance system with satisfied users?
2. Assembly/packaging/value-added activities: Does the vendor have experience with home delivery and setup?
3. Credit card verification: If some deliveries are COD, can the vendor handle both credit cards and cash?
4. Returns handling: Is there a system in place to handle returns?

Sometimes a perfect delivery may be unacceptable to a customer. When the product is in the home, it may not have the color, feel, or look that was expected. Consequently, the customer wants to return it. This reverse logistics process is the least recognized and yet possibly the greatest challenge that faces the e-commerce industry.

Catalog sales companies have always experienced a higher return rate than other retailers, and it is probable that e-commerce will follow a similar pattern. Key planning questions include:

- What is the anticipated volume of returned goods?
- Are returned goods labeled or bar coded? If so, where is the coding?
- What are the returned goods procedures and the conditions of return goods authorization?

Reverse logistics is more complicated than normal outbound distribution; however, there are third-party specialists with substantial experience in the processing of customer returns. For example, one third-party reverse logistics company handles all of the customer returns for a major retail chain. When a customer returns an item to the store, the store sends it to a reclamation center in Indiana. At the center, each returned item goes through a grading process to determine whether the item can be locally repaired, repackaged, and returned to the vendor, or whether it must be destroyed. In some cases, substandard product is segregated and sold at a discount in an overseas market.

With the explosive growth of Internet vendors, there is a substantial opportunity for logistics specialists to provide support that these fast growth entrepreneurs desperately need.

Source: Alex Metz, "Where the Rubber Meets the Road . . . Delivering Your E-Commerce Purchase," *Hunt's Profiles in Logistics Management,* March/April 2000.

a discount. Sound integrative strategy cannot be formulated without careful review of reverse logistical requirements.

For some products, such as copying equipment, primary profit lies in the sale of supplies and aftermarket service to maintain the product. The importance of life cycle support is significantly different in situations wherein the majority of profits are achieved in the aftermarket. For firms marketing consumer durables or industrial equipment, the commitment to life cycle support constitutes a versatile and demanding marketing opportunity as well as one of the largest costs of logistical operations. Life cycle support requires *cradle-to-cradle* logistics. Cradle-to-cradle logistical support goes beyond reverse logistics and recycling to include the possibility of aftermarket service, product recall, and product disposal.

Enterprise Integration

The basic level of integration is the internal operations of individual firms. To inexperienced managers, the integration of functions under the managerial control of one enterprise might appear easy to achieve. In actual practice, some of the most challenging integration issues involve cross-functional trade-offs within a specific company. As noted earlier in the discussion of systems analysis, functional management is deeply embedded as best practice within most firms.

Internal Integration Barriers

Managers do not attempt to integrate operations in a vacuum. It is important to recognize barriers that serve to inhibit process integration. Barriers to internal integration find their origins in traditional functional practices related to organization, measurement and reward systems, inventory leverage, information technology, and knowledge hoarding.

Organization

The organization structure of a business can serve to stifle cross-functional processes. Most business organizations seek to align authority and responsibility based on functional work. In essence, both structure and financial budget closely follow work responsibility. The traditional practice has been to group all persons involved in performing specific work into functional departments such as inventory control, warehousing operations, or transportation. Each of these organizations has an operational responsibility, which is reflected in its functional goals.

To illustrate, transportation and inventory have traditionally been managed by separate organizational units. Created in isolation, goals for managing transportation and inventory can be contradictory. Transportation decisions aimed at reducing freight cost require shipment consolidation, but transportation consolidation typically causes inventory to increase.

Popular terms to describe such function myopia are a *sandbox* or *silo* mentality. The traditional managerial belief was that functional excellence would automatically equate to superior performance. In integrated process management, it matters little how much is spent to perform a specific function as long as process performance goals are achieved at the lowest total cost expenditure. Successful integration of processes, such as logistics, requires that managers look beyond their organizational structure and achieve cross-functional coordination. This may or may not require organizational change. Regardless, successful process integration requires significant traditional management behavioral modification.

Measurement and Reward Systems

Traditional measurement and reward systems serve to make cross-functional coordination difficult. Measurement systems typically mirror organization structure. Most reward systems are based on functional achievement. To facilitate internal process integration, new measures, increasingly called *balanced scorecards,* must be developed. Managers must be encouraged to view specific functions as contributing to a process rather than a stand-alone performance. A function may, at times, have to absorb increased costs for the sake of achieving lower total process cost. Unless a measurement and reward system is in place that does not penalize managers who absorb cost, integration will remain more theory than practice.

Inventory Leverage

It is a proven fact that inventory can be leveraged to facilitate functional performance. The traditional position is to maintain sufficient inventory to protect against demand and operational uncertainty. Stockpiling both materials and finished inventory leverages maximum manufacturing economy of scale. Such economy of scale can result in low per unit cost of manufacturing. Forward commitment of inventory to local markets can leverage sales. While such practices create functional benefits, they may be achieved at a cost, which is not typically allocated to that function. The integrative challenge is the cost/benefit balance of such leveraging and risks associated with potential inventory obsolescence.

Infocratic Structure

Information technology is a key enabler of process integration. A significant problem results from the fact that structure and availability of information have traditionally been based on functional organization requirements. As a result, information is typically formatted in terms of functional accountability. This early practice in formatting information has resulted in what is referred to as *infocratic structure.* The content and flow of available information follow long-standing functional organization. When managers attempt to reorganize to enable the cross-functional processes, the infocratic structure serves as an invisible force to maintain traditional functional practice. The impact of infocratic structure is one of the driving reasons why Enterprise Resource Systems (ERP) have great general management appeal. The infocratic structure also helps explain why ERP implementations are so difficult.[1]

Knowledge Hoarding

In most business situations, knowledge is power, so unwillingness to share and a general lack of understanding concerning how to best share knowledge are not uncommon. But by reinforcing functional specialization and by encouraging a workforce composed of experts, organizations inherently doom process integration. Consider, for example, the case when an experienced employee retires or for some other reason departs a firm. Replacement personnel must be given sufficient time to learn, but if information is concealed, all the time in the world may not help bring the new employee up to speed.

A more serious situation occurs when managers fail or are unable to develop procedures and systems for transferring cross-functional knowledge. Much process work

---

[1]See Chapter 8 for a detailed discussion of Enterprise Resource Systems.

FIGURE 6-1

The great divide: The challenge of managing across functional boundaries

is shared between jobs and is not restricted to a specific functional area, so transfer of knowledge and experience is vital.

The Great Divide

Clearly many obstacles make functional integration difficult. To some extent, the five barriers discussed above have contributed to a common situation in business referred to as the great divide. The great divide reflects an organizational condition wherein achieved integration is partial but not complete on an end-to-end process basis, as illustrated in Figure 6-1. The most common situation is when a firm achieves only partial integration of distribution/marketing on the outbound side of the enterprise and procurement/manufacturing on the inbound side. The paradox is that firms seem to be capable of achieving highly integrated operations with suppliers from whom they purchase materials and components. Firms also join operations in market distribution to service end consumers. Such initiatives reflect cross-functional integration that, in fact, extends beyond a single business enterprise. Despite these accomplishments, managers report considerable difficulty in linking these two types of external collaboration into an enterprisewide integrative process. In short, managers seem to achieve more successful integration with external business partners than they do with managers and departments within their own firm.[2]

The phenomenon of the great divide is interesting and challenging. The fact that such operational discontinuity is common among firms in many different industries supports generalization. First, integration appears to be easier with groups external to a firm, such as suppliers and distribution agents, at least in part because the balance of power is typically clear and integrative objectives such as sales and costs can be quantified. Second, senior managers in most organizations do not have a sufficiently clear vision of internal process requirements and related measures to drive across-the-enterprise integration. Finally, the barriers outlined earlier serve to render end-to-end integration a difficult, if not impossible, end state in most traditional organizations.

Several authors writing on the challenges of implementing integrative processes have concluded that the typical traditional organization cannot accommodate sufficient change to transform from a functional to process orientation.[3] This group advocates that successful implementation of integrative process management requires a major structural and philosophical shift in traditional command and control practice. Some go so far as to advocate the need to fully disintegrate traditional organization structure.

Most observers of current logistics practice feel significant inroads into improved process performance are being realized as a result of modifying and repositioning functional capabilities. The key is to align, focus, and measure functional performance in terms of process contribution. At stake in closing the great divide is commitment to

---

[2]Donald J. Bowersox, David J. Closs, and Theodore P. Stank, *21st Century Logistics: Making Supply Chain Integration a Reality* (Oak Brook, IL: Council of Logistics Management, 1999).

[3]Christopher Meyer and David Power, "Enterprise Disintegration: The Storm Before the Calm," *Commentary* (Lexington, MA: Barker and Sloane, 1999).

a single strategy, facilitated by well-defined processes, relevant measurement, common forecasting and planning, and a supportive reward system.

How Much Integration Is Enough?

The critical question concerning a firm's ability to participate in supply chain collaboration is, How much internal integration within a participating firm is necessary or desirable to achieve across-the-supply-chain collaborative success? This is a difficult question to answer. Any assessment must acknowledge two facts.

First, few, if any, existing supply chain arrangements are, in fact, end-to-end integrations. The more common examples reflect integration of cross-organizational processes involving either procurement and manufacturing or marketing and distribution. In other words, the separation of these cross-organizational processes serves to disrupt a firm's continuous supply chain operations. However, even limited integration appears to create value for the participating organizations. Therefore, one could conclude that limited collaboration offers sufficient benefits to justify supply chain initiatives.

Second, the number one reason given by executives to explain the limited scope of and high failure rate of such supply chain collaborations is the inability of participating partners to perform as promised. For example, collaborations fail because a firm's manufacturing cannot or does not produce the products marketing promised to customers. Likewise, collaborations fail because marketing does not provide manufacturers with timely and detailed promotional plans of market distribution partners. Of course collaborations also fail because logistics is not able to perform to the expectations of manufacturing and/or marketing. This second assessment point serves to support the insight that comprehensive across-the-supply-chain collaborations will not occur until participating firms achieve high levels of credible internal integration. In short, long-term supply chains' success will require that participating firms resolve their internal great divides.

Domestic Supply Chain Integration

Extending an enterprise across the supply chain requires a vision concerning how the firms involved in the collaboration will structure and manage their combined or joint affairs. The following discussion develops interorganizational behavior guidelines.

Supply Chain Competitiveness

A supply chain perspective shifts the relevant business model from a loosely linked group of independent businesses to a multienterprise coordinated effort focused on channel efficiency improvement and increased competitiveness. While not all supply chain collaborative arrangements involve logistics, most do. In such arrangements, attention shifts from firm-based logistical management to the coordination of supply chain performance. Two beliefs facilitate this drive for efficiency and competitiveness.

First, the fundamental belief is that cooperative behavior will reduce risk and greatly improve efficiency of the overall logistical process. To achieve a high degree of cooperation it is necessary for supply chain participants to share strategic information. Such information sharing must not be limited to transaction data. Equally or more important is a willingness to share information concerning future plans so participating firms can jointly develop the best way to satisfy customer requirements. Collaborative information is essential to positioning and coordinating participating firms to jointly do the right things faster and more efficiently.

The second belief is the opportunity to eliminate waste and duplicate effort. As a result of collaboration, substantial inventory deployed in a traditional channel can be eliminated. Supply chain collaboration can also eliminate or reduce risk associated with inventory speculation. Significant inventory can be eliminated. One grocery industry study concluded the average dry grocery product requires 104 days to reach the supermarket checkout counter from the time it is packaged by a food processor.[4] The average inventory in the health care industry ranges between 12 and 18 months' supply.[5] The notion of supply chain rationalization is *not that inventory is bad* and should be totally eliminated; rather, inventory deployment should be driven by economic and service necessities and not tradition and anticipatory practices.

In the mass-merchandise industries, retailers like Wal★Mart, K-Mart, J.C. Penney, Target, and Walgreens are facilitating supply chain arrangements aimed at improved competitiveness. Using a combination of internal resources and collaboration with suppliers, these firms have positioned their logistical competency as a core business strategy. Their record in terms of retail growth and profitability speaks for itself.

Several manufacturers are facilitating supply chain collaborations in such diverse industries as chemicals, textiles, building supplies, and household tools. Firms such as DuPont, Levi-Strauss and Company, Owens-Corning Fiberglass, and Black & Decker are implementing revolutionary new strategies to improve the value processes of their specific supply chains.

At the wholesale level, drug suppliers such as McKesson and Bergen Brunswig have moved from near extinction to dominant suppliers in their industry. Food wholesalers and cooperatives such as Sysco, Spartan Stores, Fleming, and SuperValu are revolutionizing traditional logistics practices in their industries. Similar developments can be observed in the paper and supplies industry by firms such as Unisource and ResourceNet International. Likewise, Ace in the hardware business and W.W. Grainger in industrial supplies have revolutionized conventional logistics practice in their respective industries.

This diverse list of firms that have increased supply chain competitiveness exhibit several similarities. First, their collaborative practices are technology driven. Second, their business solutions achieve competitive superiority. Finally, most initiatives combine the experience and talents of key supply chain participants blended with a combination of third-party service providers. At the heart of several of the firms highlighted is a solid commitment to creating and maintaining a unique supply chain culture. Such cultures are forged on a fundamental understanding of risk, power, and leadership.

Risk, Power, and Leadership

Dependency is a primary driver of supply chain solidarity. To the degree that participating enterprises acknowledge mutual dependency, the potential exists to develop collaborative relationships. Dependency drives a willingness to plan functional integration, share key information, and participate in joint operations. The concepts of

---

[4]"Efficient Consumer Response: Enhancing Value in the Grocery Industry," Kurt Salmon Associates, Inc., New York, NY, January 1993.

[5]"Efficient Healthcare Consumer Response," CSC Consulting, Inc., Cleveland, Ohio, November 1996.

risk, power, and *leadership* are essential to understanding acknowledged dependency and how it makes supply chain integration work.

Risk

Enterprises that participate in supply chain arrangements must acknowledge they have responsibility for performing specific roles. They must also believe that their business will be better off in the long run as a result of collaboration. Each enterprise must be positioned to specialize in an operational area or function based on its unique core competency. The driving force behind supply chain integration is to leverage these core competencies.

As a general rule, a supply chain member whose competency is highly specialized will assume comparatively less risk with respect to overall performance. Conversely, firms that have a great deal at stake will be positioned as the prime facilitators and will confront the most risk in the supply chain arrangement. Firms with unique specialization, more often than not, will participate in multiple supply chains. For example, a wholesaler incurs risk as a result of stocking products for a specific manufacturer. The traditional practice among wholesalers is to hedge such risk by offering customers an assortment of many different manufacturers' products, thereby reducing reliance on any supplier.

In contrast, a manufacturer with a limited product line may be totally captive to a few supply chain arrangements. In essence, the manufacturer may be betting the business that the collaboration will be successful. For manufacturers, commitment to supply chain arrangements can be risky business. The disproportionate risk among channel members is of primary importance because it structures dependency relationships and determines how the collaboration will be managed. Some participants have a deeper dependence on supply chain success than others. Therefore, participants with the most risk can be expected to assume active roles and shoulder greater responsibility for facilitating collaboration.

Power

In a practical sense, the prerogative and even the obligation to spearhead collaboration rests with the supply chain participant who enjoys the greatest relative power. In many situations, that participant will also be the firm having the greatest risk. Over the last decade significant power shifts have occurred in business. One of the most significant is the increased power of retailers, which resulted from four somewhat independent developments.

First, the general trend of retail consolidation translated into fewer but more dominant retailers with more extensive market coverage. Second, the proliferation of point-of-sale data, frequent shopper programs, and credit card use provide retailers with easy access to vital market information. As a result, consumer trends can be rapidly identified and accommodated. Many mass merchants even maintain in-store computers and continuous satellite transmission to keep merchandise buyers fully involved in developing market trends. A third factor favoring retailers is the increasing difficulty and high cost manufacturers confront in developing new brands. The fact is that many private label products owned by retailers have greater category penetration than so-called national brands. For example, the Gap and The Limited almost exclusively distribute private branded merchandise. Finally, as noted earlier, the process of logistical replenishment has shifted to a more response-based posture. The exact timing and sophisticated orchestration of a high-velocity market-paced logistics system are ideally driven from the point of consumer purchase. When consumers purchase products, the final or ultimate value of the supply chain is a reality.

While the above noted forces are a modern reality, not all forces are shifting power forward in the supply chain. One major countervailing force has been the rapid development of Internet-based purchase sites that allow direct consumer involvement with manufacturers. In the not so distant past, marketing channels were structured to accommodate product line. Today's scrambled merchandising environments result in products increasingly being cross-channel distributed to accommodate specific markets that are volatile and rapidly changing. New retail formats, both Web-based and traditional brick and mortar, are blurring channel arrangements. The result is that manufacturers confront new supply chain arrangements for distributing their products.

As a substitute for full reliance on traditional brand power, selected manufacturers have reengineered their operations to become the dominant supplier for selected consumer product or categories. The movement toward category dominance allows manufacturers to offer greater value to their prospective supply chain partners. In addition to superior brands at competitive prices, dominant category position can involve several key operational capabilities that increase a firm's attractiveness as a supply chain participant.

The drive to establish dominant category positioning involves the following capabilities: (1) willingness to develop collaborative arrangements; (2) manufacturing and logistical flexibility to accommodate a wide range of supply chain requirements; (3) rationalization and supplier integration to assure accommodation of frequent schedule changes; (4) segmental or custom marketing and merchandise programs; (5) availability of information connectivity to accommodate cross-organizational operations; and (6) short, responsive, flexible, and reliable order cycles to facilitate rapid replenishment of customer requirements. Of course it goes without saying that the ideal supplier will perform at or below average industry logistics cost.

Because both manufacturers and distributors have repositioned traditional operations, the potential exists to leverage collaboration. *As a general rule, powerful firms tend to link together in the development of supply chain arrangements.* For the arrangement to be successful the dominant parties to the cooperative arrangement need to agree to a leadership model.

Leadership

Just as individual organizations need leaders, so do supply chains. At the present stage of supply chain maturity no definitive generalization can be made concerning how firms gain leadership responsibility. In many situations, specific firms are thrust into a leadership position purely as a result of their size, economic power, customer patronage, or comprehensive product portfolio. In other arrangements, for less obvious reasons, there is a clear presence of leadership on the part of one enterprise, which is acknowledged in the form of mutual dependency and respect on the part of other participating supply chain members. In other situations leadership appears to gravitate to the firm that initiates the relationship.

The essence of channel leadership is to orchestrate the core competencies of participating firms into integrated performance. Constructive leadership is necessary to stimulate and reward collaborative behavior. Maintaining an overall supply chain perspective is particularly important. The leadership role involves creating function spin-off and absorption agreements between businesses participating in the arrangement. The role also requires problem-solving negotiation and mediation of risk and reward sharing. Such fusion between participating firms can be facilitated by the supply chain integrative framework.

FIGURE 6-2

Supply chain flows

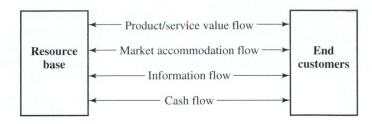

Supply Chain Integrative Framework[6]

A supply chain integrative framework is required to identify the range and continuity to achieve comprehensive collaboration. Such a framework requires that capabilities and competencies essential to integrating supply chain logistics are identified and implemented. The creation of value related to supply chain integration is best achieved by simultaneous orchestration of the four critical flows shown in Figure 6-2: product/service, market accommodation, information, and cash.

The product/service value flow represents the value-added movement of products and services from the raw material source to the end customers. Product value increases as it flows along the supply chain as a result of physical modification, packaging, market proximity, customization, service support, and related activities that enhance end-consumer desirability of the product.

While the product/service flow generally moves from the resource base to end customers, as noted earlier, supply chain arrangements must also accommodate critical reverse flows such as product recalls, reclamation, and recycling. The market accommodation flow provides a structure to achieve postsales service administration. Market accommodation also involves information exchange concerning sales patterns and product usage essential for supply chain planning. Examples are product customization requirements, point-of-sale (POS) data, end-customer consumption, and warehouse releases. This information provides supply chain members with channel visibility concerning the timing and location of product consumption. Planning and operations can be better synchronized when all participants share a common understanding of demand and consumption patterns.

The information flow is bidirectional exchange of transactional data, inventory status, and strategic plans between supply chain participants. Typical examples of this aspect of collaboration are forecasts, promotional plans, purchase orders, order acknowledgments, shipping and inventory information, invoices, payments, and replenishment requirements. Information exchange initiates, controls, and records the product/service value flow. Historically paper-based, an increasing amount of the information flow is now being exchanged via EDI and Web-based connectivity.

Cash typically flows in the reverse direction of value-added activities. However, in arrangements involving promotion and rebate, cash flows to facilitate product and service movement. Cash flow velocity and asset utilization are critical to superior supply chain performance.

Naturally, these four flows must occur between channel participants even when the supply chain is not integrated. However, situations characterized by low coordination and integration between supply chain participants typically result in delay, redun-

[6]Donald J. Bowersox, David J. Closs, and Theodore P. Stank, op. cit.

FIGURE **6-3**

Supply chain framework

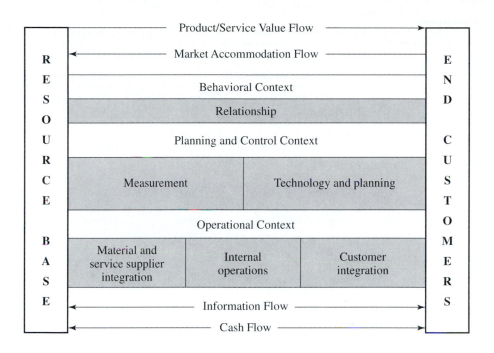

dancy, and inefficiency. To facilitate effective and efficient supply chain flows, competencies and their supporting capabilities must be integrated.

Framework Constructs

The supply chain integrative framework illustrated in Figure 6-3 encompasses a broad range of capabilities and competencies. The framework serves to facilitate operations into a supply chain context by integrating basic work, functions, capabilities, and competencies.

A job or *basic work,* such as order picking or truck driving, is the most visible part of the logistical operations. Jobs are often industry- or firm-specific in content; however, they are usually grouped into organizational units to facilitate control. For example, all the jobs related to warehousing are often grouped. Another common grouping is to organize all jobs related to transport into a transportation department. These functional groupings are significant because they are highly visible elements of an organization. Departments have traditionally been the focal point for financial budgeting, performance measurement, and operational control. Functional work arrangements constitute the drivers of logistical best practice. It is the functions or drivers that combine to create value. The critical shift in operational thinking is to view functional excellence in terms of process performance that enhances *overall* supply chain integration.

To achieve integration, functional value should be focused in terms of universal capabilities. A **capability** is the knowledge and achievement level essential to developing integrated performance. Capabilities relate to *why work is being performed* as contrasted to a functional perspective concerning *how it is performed.* The capability reflects the value contribution of the work. Inherent in a capability is the application of integrative principles that allow multiple functions to be synchronized into value-creating competencies. Whereas jobs and functions may be highly relevant to specific industries and work situations, capabilities are universal. Capabilities span the supply

TABLE 6-2   Supply Chain Context, Competencies, and Supportive Capabilities

Competencies	Operational Context			Planning and Control Context		Behavioral Context
	Customer Integration	Internal Integration	Material/Service Supplier Integration	Technology and Planning Integration	Measurement Integration	Relationship Integration
Supportive Capabilities	Segmental focus	Cross-functional unification	Strategic alignment	Information management	Functional assessment	Role specificity
	Relevancy	Standardization	Operational fusion	Internal communication	Activity-based and total cost methodology	Guidelines
	Responsiveness	Simplification	Financial linkage	Connectivity	Comprehensive metrics	Information sharing
	Flexibility	Compliance	Supplier management	Collaborative forecasting and planning	Financial impact	Gain/risk sharing
		Structural adaptation				

chain and are equally applicable to suppliers, manufacturers, wholesalers/distributors, and across the full range of retail formats. Capabilities also transcend industries, nations, and even cultural boundaries. Furthermore, they are observable and most importantly measurable within firms of all sizes. Research has firmly established that capabilities reflecting best logistics practice are to some degree observable in all firms that participate in a supply chain.

Examples of capabilities include the ability to (1) identify and accommodate the needs of specific customers; (2) work with supply chain partners to achieve integrated operations; (3) effectively share operating and planning information between supply chain partners; (4) measure and understand overall supply chain performance; and (5) share benefits and risks.

The fusing of capabilities results in universal **competencies.** Table 6-2 details the capabilities related to each of the six integrative competencies grouped in terms of their supply chain context. The operational context includes traditional processes related to procurement, production, and market distribution. The planning and control context incorporates information technology and planning systems, as well as measurement competency. The behavioral context relates to how a firm manages internal and external relationships among supply chain entities.

The Operational Context

Operations involve the processes that facilitate order fulfillment and replenishment across the supply chain. To achieve leading performance in an operational context, firms must be customer-focused, must achieve interorganizational coordination, and must excel in functional and process performance.

Customer integration builds on the philosophies and activities that develop intimacy and is the competency that builds lasting competitive advantage. Firms have always paid attention to the needs of customers but only recently have begun to identify and consider their differences in terms of capable operational segmentation. Any firm seeking supply chain integration must also demonstrate strong commitment to the supportive capabilities of relevancy, responsiveness, and flexibility.

Internal integration focuses on the joint activities and processes within a firm that coordinate functions related to procurement, manufacture, and market distribution. Many firms have attempted to integrate internal functionality but, as discussed earlier, anecdotal and quantitative evidence strongly indicates there are significant gaps. Managers often report more success in coordinating with customers than with their own manufacturing, logistical, and marketing operations. The capabilities that support internal integration are cross-functional unification, standardization, simplification, compliance, and structural adaptation.

Supplier integration focuses on capabilities that create operational linkages with material and service providing supply chain partners. While the customer is the overriding focal point or supply chain driver, overall success also will depend on strategic alignment, operational fusion, financial linkage, and supplier management. Competency in supplier integration results from performing the capabilities seamlessly in internal work processes. Firms that desire to excel must blend their operating processes with those of supply partners to meet increasingly broad and demanding customer expectations.

It is not insignificant that the thirteen capabilities that support customer, internal, and supplier integration can be identified, quantified, and organizationally learned.

The Planning and Control Context

Operational excellence must be supported by integrated planning and measurement capabilities. This involves joining technology across the supply chain to monitor, control, and facilitate overall supply chain performance.

Planning and control integration concerns the design, application, and coordination of information to enhance purchasing, manufacturing, customer order fulfillment, and resource planning. This competency includes database access to enable sharing of appropriate information among supply chain participants. It also concerns transaction systems to initiate and process replenishment and customer orders. In addition to information management, it is essential that capabilities related to internal communication, connectivity, and collaboration be developed.

Measurement integration is the ability to monitor and benchmark functional and process performance, both within the firm and across the supply chain. Because each firm is unique, the collaborative effort must define, operationalize, and monitor standard or common measures. Competency in measurement requires the capabilities of functional assessment and activity-based methodologies. Comprehensive metrics and financials impact assessment.

The Behavioral Context

Effective relationship management is the final competency essential in supply chain engagements. Successful implementation of supply chain strategy rests on the quality of the basic business relationship between partners. In general, managers are far more experienced in competition than they are in cooperation.

Whereas guidelines exist for the development of meaningful and distinctive supply chain relationships, no two situations are identical. No shortcuts or substitutes exist for the detailed commitment necessary to build and develop successful long-term relationships. In dealing with customers, suppliers, and service providers, firms must specify roles, define guidelines, share information, share risk and gains, resolve conflict, and, when necessary, be able to dissolve an unproductive arrangement. The managerial skill sets required for successful supply chain integration require development of an interorganizational culture. This is particularly true since the dynamic environment in which firms compete requires regular review of assumptions, processes, and measures to

Industry Insight 6-3 The Eight I's to Creating Successful We's

The characteristics of effective intercompany relationships challenge many decades of Western economic and managerial assumptions. For example, most Westerners assume that modern industrial companies are run most effectively by professional managers operating within limited, contractual Western obligations. And most Westerners assume that any person with the requisite knowledge, skills, and talents can be a manager in the modern corporation. Although smaller companies, family businesses, and companies that are operating in developing countries have retained "premodern" characteristics, the "rational" model has been considered the ideal to which all organizations would eventually conform.

Intercompany relationships are different. They seem to work best when they are more familylike and less rational. Obligations are more diffuse, the scope for collaboration is more open, understanding grows between specific individuals, communication is frequent and intensive, and the interpersonal context is rich. The best intercompany relationships are frequently messy and emotional, involving feelings like chemistry or trust. And they should not be entered into lightly. Only relationships with full commitment on all sides endure long enough to create value for the partners.

Indeed, the best organizational relationships, like the best marriages, are true partnerships that tend to meet certain criteria:

Individual Excellence. Both partners are strong and have something of value to contribute to the relationship. Their motives for entering into the relationship are positive (to pursue future opportunities), not negative (to mask weaknesses or escape a difficult situation).

Importance. The relationship fits major strategic objectives of the partners, so they want to make it work. Partners have long-term goals in which the relationship plays a key role.

Interdependence. The partners need each other. They have complementary assets and skills. Neither can accomplish its goals apart from the other.

Investment. The partners invest in each other (for example, through equity swaps, cross-ownership, or mutual board service) to demonstrate their respective stakes in the relationship and each other. They show tangible signs of long-term commitment by devoting financial and other resources to the relationship.

Information. Communication is reasonably open. Partners share information required to make the relationship work, including their objectives and goals, technical data, and knowledge of conflicts, trouble spots, or changing situations.

Integration. The partners develop linkages and shared ways of operating so they can work together smoothly. They build broad connections between many people at many organizational levels. Partners become both teachers and learners.

Institutionalization. The relationship is given a formal status, with clear responsibilities and decision processes. It extends beyond the particular people who formed it, and it cannot be broken on a whim.

Integrity. The partners behave toward each other in honorable ways that justify and enhance mutual trust. They do not abuse the information they gain, nor do they undermine each other.

Source: Rosabeth Moss Kanter, "Collaborative Advantage: The Art of Alliances," *Harvard Business Review,* July/August 1994, p. 100.

---

assure those relationships remain relevant. Industry Insight 6-3 summarizes research that identified the *Eight I's* that are essential to achieving a supply chain *We.* Tables 6-3 and 6–4 summarize success factors and common obstacles directly related to supply chain integration.

Finally, ample evidence suggests that managers must plan for the ultimate dismantling or renovation of supply chains. While some arrangements may encounter a natural death as a result of losing momentum, others may persevere to the point that they no longer embody leading edge practice. Thus, like most managerial concerns, supply chain integration is a dynamic situation that must be continuously re-evaluated.

TABLE 6-3   Factors Increasing Likelihood of Supply Chain Relationship Success

Retailers	Manufacturers
• High level of cooperation	• Information sharing
• Similarity of goals/objectives	• Recognition of mutual benefits
• Clear communications	• Controlled implementation
• Senior management support	• Joint task force
• Control of inventory	• Commitment/resource dedication
	• Benefits realization

Source: Reprinted by permission of Accenture Consulting.

TABLE 6-4   Common Obstacles Confronted When Creating Supply Chain Relationships

Retailers	Manufacturers
• Low-volume stockkeeping units (SKUs)	• Lack of communication
• Resistance of manufacturers to change	• Trust level
• Information systems	• Noncompatible systems
• Noncompatible data formats	• Understanding of technical issues
	• Resistance of customers to change
	• Readiness of retailers

Source: Reprinted by permission of Accenture Consulting.

Integration and Logistical Competency

Three points are significant concerning supply chain logistical competency. First, when an overall integrated process becomes one of the most admired and differentiating proficiencies between supply chains, it has the potential to become the strategic cornerstone. Logistical core competency is common in today's competitive environment.

Second, from an academic viewpoint, the abstraction of logistics from function to capability to competency in a supply chain context forms the constructs of a viable theory. The identification of capabilities offers the first level of generalization. The fusing of capabilities into universal competencies serves to blend the specific discipline of logistics into the sum of the business. The positioning of logistics as a core competency expands the value generation of supply chain integration.

Third, logistics is the operationally based process across the supply chain that must be truly integrative for the supply chain to provide overall customer value.

Global Supply Chain Integration

Whereas an effective logistics system is important for domestic supply chain integration, it is absolutely *essential* for successful global manufacturing and marketing. Domestic logistics focuses on performing value-added services to support supply chain integration in a somewhat controllable environment. Global logistics must accommodate operations in a variety of different national, political, and economic settings while also dealing with increased uncertainties associated with the distance, demand, diversity, and documentation of international commerce.

The operating challenges of global logistics systems vary significantly within different operating regions of the world. The North American logistics challenge is one of open geography with extensive land-based transportation and limited need for cross-border documentation. The European logistician, in contrast, is confronted by relatively compact geography involving numerous political, cultural, regulatory, and language situations. The Pacific Rim logistical challenge is island-based, requiring extensive water or air shipment to transcend vast distances. These different perspectives require firms that have global operations to develop and maintain a wide variety of capabilities and expertise. Industry Insight 6-4 illustrates the complexity of introducing change in a global context.

In the past, an enterprise could survive by operating with a unique North American, European, or Pacific Rim business strategy. While regionalization remains viable for some firms, those which desire to grow and prosper are facing the challenges of globalization. Strategic business initiatives must change as a firm and its supply chain become progressively more globalized.

Logistics in a Global Economy

Global operations increase logistics cost and complexity. Estimated 1997 logistics cost for industrialized nations exceeded $5 trillion, or 13.4 percent of estimated global Gross Domestic Product (GDP). Table 6-5 lists GDP and estimated logistics cost by country. In terms of complexity global operations, in contrast to domestic, are characterized by increased uncertainty and decreased ability to control. Uncertainty results from greater distances, longer lead times, and decreased market knowledge. Decreased ability to control results from the extensive use of international service firms coupled with potential government intervention in such areas as customs requirements and trade restrictions.

These unique challenges complicate development of an efficient and effective global supply chain strategy. Fortunately, there are forces that both drive and facilitate globalization and necessitate borderless logistics operations.

Stages of International Development

The continuum of global trade perspectives ranges from *export/import* to *local presence* to the concept of a *stateless enterprise.* The following discussion compares conceptual and managerial implications of strategic development.

Export/Import: A National Perspective

The initial stage of international trade is characterized by exporting and importing. A participating organization typically is focused on internal operations and views international transactions in terms of what they will do for domestic business. Typically, when firms are committed to an export/import strategy they use service providers to conduct and manage operations in other countries.

A national export/import business orientation influences logistical decisions in three ways. First, sourcing and resource choices are influenced by artificial constraints. These constraints are typically in the form of use restrictions, local content laws, or price surcharges. A **use restriction** is a limitation, usually government imposed, that restricts the level of import sales or purchase. For example, the enterprise

Industry Insight 6-4 Virtual Europe

Because of the complexity, it took a team of KPMG consultants 2.5 years to successfully develop and implement centralized Customs clearance in the European Union (EU). They used a virtual warehousing strategy supported by the European Commission and individual national Customs authorities.

Initially, the pilot targeted Belgium and Finland. Now other countries are giving the idea serious attention. The hope is it's a first step toward a reformed, centralized, and simplified Customs accounting and revenue collection process within the EU. Multinational companies operating in Europe can expect to see improved compliance and greater efficiency from the audit-based Customs reporting systems. The ultimate goal—a single European authorization—is within reach.

In practice, this virtual warehouse exists only on paper (or the Web), but it earns the same duty determent benefits as a Customs warehouse. Just as important, it lets all goods imported into the EU clear Customs at a single point. That means all Customs activities can be conducted with a single Customs authority even though goods may be received in several countries. If the company meets the requirements for constant stock control, goods can be stored in a number of locations.

Information systems replace physical Customs control over stock inventories. It's all done with computers, but those computer data must measure up to EU Customs standards. Most importantly, they must accurately tally the taxes due each EU member country from participating companies.

It's been legal to pick your Customs authority since 1985, but figuring out how to do it was the challenge. In fact, figuring out how to slice the money collected was the main reason the initial pilot project took so long. "We worked with Belgium, Finland, Germany, and UK to reach agreement for the pilot projects," says Terry Shaw, partner with KPMG in charge of trades and customer practice in Europe. Shaw also was the partner responsible for the KPMG virtual warehouse team. "We went live in May 1998—it has taken all that time to work it out."

Cooperation of participating countries is fundamental and there are still some issues, says Shaw. In the short term, he insists companies will need an intermediary. It is absolutely essential that participants have a good stock tracking system and a clear understanding of current Customs procedures. Centralized stock control is critical to acceptance of centralized reporting to a single Customs authority.

Shaw claims the virtual warehouse uses a versatile reporting system so it can customize different aspects of Customs reporting for various scenarios. A company might export, then reimport product which could be entitled to re-enter duty-free. For example, a wheel manufacturer in Europe exports wheels to a U.S. automotive manufacturer, then reimports the car to several countries in Europe. They might qualify for relief from the full Customs duty for the wheel.

To make this intricate system work, data have to be forwarded in the right format to be used by the Customs authority. Goods arrive physically in two or three countries. When they're ready for free circulation, the main controller is notified. This triggers a notice to Customs and the goods are freed to move.

The virtual warehouse concept does not eliminate the need for visual inspection, however. Customs will always have the right to inspect all goods to control smuggling, regardless of where goods are stored or cleared.

If successful, the virtual warehouse will grant new freedom to U.S. companies who now may be restricted as to which ports they can use to funnel goods through and distribute from.

Source: Anonymous (within article written by Helen Richardson), "Virtual Europe," *Transportation & Distribution*, March 2000, p. 42.

TABLE 6-5   Sizing 1997 Global Logistics Expenditures ($U.S. in Billions)

Region	Country	GDP	Logistics ($)	Logistics (%GDP)
North America	Canada	658	$ 80	12.1%
	Mexico	695	106	15.3
	United States	8,083	849	10.5
	Total	9,436	1,035	11.0
Europe	Belgium/Lux.	240	27	11.4
	Denmark	123	16	12.9
	France	1,320	158	12.0
	Germany	1,740	228	13.1
	Greece	137	17	12.6
	Ireland	60	8	14.0
	Italy	1,240	149	12.0
	Netherlands	344	41	11.9
	Portugal	150	19	12.9
	Spain	642	94	14.7
	United Kingdom	1,242	125	10.1
	Total	7,238	884	12.2
Pacific Rim	PRC	4,250	718	16.9
	India	1,534	236	15.4
	Hong Kong	175	24	13.7
	Japan	3,080	351	11.4
	Korea	631	78	12.3
	Singapore	85	12	13.9
	Taiwan	308	40	13.1
	Total	10,063	1,459	14.5
South America	Brazil	1,040	156	15.0
	Venezuela	185	24	12.8
	Argentina	348	45	13.0
	Total	1,573	225	14.3
Remaining Other Countries		9,690	1,492	15.4
TOTAL		38,000	$5,095	13.4%

Sources: Donald J. Bowersox, David J. Closs, Theodore P. Stank, *21st Century Logistics: Making Supply Chain Integration a Reality* (Oak Brook, IL: The Council of Logistics Management, 1999); and Donald J. Bowersox and Roger J. Calantone, "Executive Insights: Global Logistics," *Journal of International Marketing* 6, no. 4 (1998), pp. 83–93.

may require that internal divisions be used for material sources even though prices or quality are not competitive. **Local content laws** specify the proportion of a product that must be sourced within the local economy. **Price surcharges** involve higher charges for foreign-sourced product imposed by governments to maintain the viability of local suppliers. In combination, use restrictions and price surcharges limit management's ability to select what otherwise would be the preferred supplier.

Second, logistics to support export/import operations increases planning complexity. A fundamental logistics objective is smooth product flow in a manner that facilitates efficient capacity utilization. Barriers resulting from government intervention make it difficult to achieve this objective.

Third, an export/import perspective attempts to extend domestic logistics systems and operating practices to global origins and destinations. While a national perspective simplifies matters at a policy level, it increases operational complexity since exceptions are numerous. Local managers must accommodate exceptions while remaining within corporate policy and procedure guidelines. As a result, local logistics management must accommodate cultural, language, employment, and political environments without full support and understanding of corporate headquarters.

International Operations: Local Presence

The second stage of international development is characterized by establishment of operations within a foreign country. Internal operations include combinations of marketing, sales, production, and logistics. Establishment of local facilities and operations serves to increase market awareness and sensitivity. This is often referred to as gaining **local presence.** At the outset of a local presence strategy, foreign operations typically use parent company management and personnel, and practice home country values, procedures, and operations. However, over time, business units operating within a foreign market area will adopt local business practices.

This adoption typically means hiring host country management, marketing, and sales organizations and may include the use of local business systems. As local presence operations expand, the host country philosophy will increasingly emerge; however, the company headquarters' strategic vision remains dominant. Individual country operations are still measured against home country expectations and standards.

Globalization: The Stateless Enterprise

The stateless enterprise contrasts sharply to operations guided by either an export/import or international perspective. The stateless concept was originally popularized in a *Business Week* article describing enterprises that effectively make decisions with little or no regard to national boundaries.[7]

Stateless enterprises maintain regional operations and develop a headquarters structure to coordinate area operations. Thus, the enterprise is stateless in the sense that no specific home or parent country dominates policy. Senior management likely represents a combination of nationalities. Denationalized operations function on the basis of local marketing and sales organizations and are typically supported by world-class manufacturing and logistics operations. Product sourcing and marketing decisions can be made across a wide range of geographical alternatives. Systems and procedures are designed to meet individual country requirements and are aggregated as necessary to share knowledge and for financial reporting.

Consider an enterprise that has its historical foundations in Germany, Japan, or the United States, but with a high percentage of its sales, ownership, and assets maintained and managed in China, for example. China is estimated to be the world's third largest economy, but it very much remains a third-world country in many respects—including logistics and supply chain infrastructure. China has poor communications, no intermodal systems, no boxcar or container location tracing, no cargo airlines, and virtually nonexistent roads outside major cities. For these reasons, a stateless enterprise operating in China would rely on local management that fully understands underdeveloped business systems, the rapid rate of change, and exploding trade volume.

---

[7]"The Stateless Corporation," *Business Week,* May 14, 1990, p. 98.

Examples of firms that fit the specification of stateless enterprises are ABB (Switzerland), Dow Chemical (United States), ICI (Britain), Hoechst (Germany), Nestlé (Switzerland), and Philips (Netherlands).

While most enterprises engaged in international business are operating in stages one and two, a truly international firm must focus on the challenges of globalizing operations. Such globalization requires a significant level of management trust that transcends countries and cultures. Such trust can only grow as managers increasingly live and work across cultures. Table 6-6 provides a comparison of characteristics of firms that operate at different stages of global supply chain integration.

Managing the Global Supply Chain

To meet the challenges discussed above, management must evaluate the complexity of global supply chains and focus on five major differences between domestic and international operations: (1) performance cycle structure, (2) transportation, (3) operational considerations, (4) systems integration, and (5) alliances.

Performance Cycle Structure

The performance cycle length is the major difference between domestic and global operations. Instead of 3- to 5-day transit times and 4- to 10-day total performance cycles, global operational cycles are measured in weeks or months. For example, it is common for automotive parts from Pacific Rim suppliers to take 60 days from replenishment order release until physical order receipt at a U.S. manufacturing facility.

The reasons for a longer performance cycle are communication delays, financing requirements, special packaging requirements, ocean freight scheduling, slow transit times, and customs clearance. Communication may be delayed by time zone and language differences. Financing causes delays since international transactions often require letters of credit. Special packaging may be required to protect products from in-transit damage since containers typically are exposed to high humidity, temperature, and weather conditions. Once a product is containerized, it must be scheduled for movement between ports having appropriate handling capabilities. This scheduling process can require up to 30 days if the origin and destination ports are not located on high-volume traffic lanes or the ships moving to the desired port lack the necessary equipment. Transit time, once the ship is en route, ranges from 10 to 21 days. Port delays are common as ships wait for others to clear harbor facilities. Customs clearance may further extend total time. Although it is increasingly common to utilize electronic messaging to preclear product shipments through customs prior to arrival at international ports, the elapsed performance cycle time is still lengthy.

The combination and complexity of the above factors causes international logistics performance cycles to be longer, less consistent, and less flexible than is typical in domestic operations. The reduced consistency, in particular, increases planning difficulty. The longer performance cycle also results in higher asset commitment because significant inventory is in transit at any point in time.

Transportation

The U.S. initiative to deregulate transportation during the early 1980s has extended globally. Three significant global changes have occurred: (1) intermodal ownership and operation, (2) privatization, and (3) cabotage and bilateral agreements.

Historically, there have been regulatory restrictions concerning international transportation ownership and operating rights. Transport carriers were limited to

TABLE 6-6   Characteristics of Global Development

Three Stages of Development	Typical Characteristics					
	Product Focus	Marketing Strategy	Supply Chain Strategy	Management	Information and Decision Support	Human Resource Development
Export/import	Domestic production and distribution	Specific customers	Agents and third-party logistics service providers	Transportation driven with integrated financials	Home country focused with limited EDI	Management with "home country" focus and limited international experience
International operations; local presence	Local market customization supported by postponement or local production	Focused specific market areas which may cross national boundaries	Subsidiaries and local distributors with specific business charters and visible local presence	Decentralized management of local operators and strategic alliances with local profit responsibility	Independent database and decision support	Limited top management with international experience and strong "home country" decision focus
Globalization; the stateless enterprise	Global brands	All economic regions	Worldwide flow of key resources to leverage global sourcing and marketing advantages	Centralized planning with locally flexible distribution supported with common systems	Integrated database and decision support	International training and experience required for all upper-level management with some requirements for mid-level management

operating within a single transportation mode with few, if any, joint pricing and operating agreements. Traditionally, steamship lines could not own or manage integrated land-based operations such as motor or rail carriers. Without joint ownership, operations, and pricing agreements, international shipping was complicated. International shipments typically required multiple carriers to perform freight movement. Specifically, government rather than market forces determined the extent of services foreign-owned carriers could perform. Although some ownership and operating restrictions remain, marketing and alliance arrangements among countries have substantially improved transportation flexibility. The removal of multimodal ownership restrictions in the United States and in most other industrialized nations served to facilitate integrated movement.

A second transportation impact on global operations has been increased carrier privatization. Historically, many international carriers were owned and operated by government in an effort to promote trade and provide national security. Government-owned carriers often subsidize operations for their home county businesses while placing surcharges on foreign enterprises. Artificially high pricing and poor service often made it costly and unreliable to ship via such government carriers. Inefficiencies also resulted from strong unionization and work rules. The combination of high cost and operating inefficiencies caused many government carriers to operate at a loss. A great many such carriers have been privatized.

Changes in cabotage and bilateral service agreements are the third transportation factor influencing international trade. Cabotage laws require passengers or goods moving between two domestic ports to utilize only domestic carriers. For example, water shipment from Los Angeles to New York was required to use a U.S. carrier. The same cabotage laws restricted Canadian drivers from transporting a backhaul load to Detroit once a shipment originating in Canada was unloaded in Texas. Cabotage laws were designed to protect domestic transportation industries even though they also served to reduce overall transportation equipment utilization and related efficiencies. The European Community has relaxed cabotage restrictions to increase trade efficiency. Such reduced cabotage restrictions will save U.S. corporations 10 to 15 percent in intra-European shipping costs.

Operational Considerations

There are a number of unique operational considerations in a global environment. First, international operations typically require multiple languages for both product and documentation. A technical product such as a computer or a calculator must have local features such as keyboard characters and language on both the product itself and related manuals. From a logistics perspective, language differences dramatically increase complexity since a product is limited to a specific country once it is language-customized. For example, even though Western Europe is much smaller than the United States in a geographic sense, it requires relatively more inventory to support marketing efforts since separate inventories may be required to accommodate various languages. Although product proliferation due to language requirement has been reduced through multipurpose packaging and postponement strategies, such practices are not always acceptable. In addition to product language implications, international operations may require multilingual documentation for each country through which the shipment passes. Although English is the general language of commerce, some countries require that transportation and customs documentation be provided in the local language. This increases the time and effort for international operations since complex documents must be translated prior to shipment. These communication and

---

TABLE 6-7   Common Forms of International Logistics Documentation

---

- *Export irrevocable commercial letter of credit.* A contract between an importer and a bank that transfers liability or paying the exporter from the importer to the (supposedly more creditworthy) importer's bank.
- *Bank draft (or bill of exchange).* A means of payment for an import/export transaction. Two types exist: transaction payable on sight with proper documents (*sight draft*), and transaction payable at some fixed time after acceptance of proper documents (*time draft*). Either type of draft accompanied by instructions and other documents (*but no letter of credit*) are a documentary draft.
- *Bill of lading.* Issued by the shipping company or its agent as evidence of a contract for shipping the merchandise and as a claim to ownership of the goods.
- *Combined transport document.* May replace the bill of lading if goods are shipped by air (*airway bill*) or by more than one mode of transportation.
- *Commercial invoice.* A document written by the exporter to precisely describe the goods and the terms of sale (similar to a shipping invoice used in domestic shipments).
- *Insurance certificate.* Explains what type of coverage is utilized (fire, theft, water), the name of the insurer, and the exporter whose property is being insured.
- *Certificate of origin.* Denotes the country in which the goods were produced to assess tariffs and other government-imposed restrictions on trade.

---

documentation difficulties can be somewhat overcome through standardized electronic transactions.

The second operational difference in global commerce is unique national accommodations such as performance features, power supply characteristics, and safety requirements. While they may not be substantial, the small differences between country requirements may significantly increase required SKUs and subsequent inventory levels.

The third operating difference is the sheer amount of documentation required for international operations. While domestic operations can generally be completed using only an invoice and bill of lading, international operations require substantial documentation regarding order contents, transportation, financing, and government control. Table 6-7 lists and describes common forms of international documentation.

The fourth operating difference is the high incidence of countertrade and duty drawback found in some international situations. While most established firms prefer cash transactions, countertrade is important. Countertrade, in essence, is when a seller agrees to take or purchase products from the buyer as part of a sales agreement. While such agreements have financial consequences, they also have major implications for logistics and marketing in terms of disposal of goods received as payment.

For example, Pepsi supplies syrup to the Soviet government, which bottles and markets the soft drink with practically no control from Pepsi. In return, Pepsi is paid for the syrup by receiving exclusive rights to distribute Russian Stolichnaya vodka in the United States. This exclusive right requires marketing and logistics support.

Systems Integration

Few firms currently enjoy global systems integration. Since firms typically globalize by acquisition and merger, the integration of systems typically lags. Operational integration requires the ability to route orders and manage inventory requirements electronically throughout the world. Development of supportive technology integration represents substantial capital investment. The overall process was significantly facilitated by the global initiative to achieve Y2K compliance. However, there remain few enterprises that have integrated global systems.

Alliances

A final difference in international operations is the extended role of third-party alliances. While alliances with carriers and specialized service suppliers are important in domestic operations, they are essential in international commerce. Without alliances, it would be necessary for an enterprise operating internationally to maintain contacts with retailers, wholesalers, manufacturers, suppliers, and service providers throughout the world. International alliances offer market access and expertise and reduce the inherent risk in global operations. The number of alternatives and the complexity of the globalization require increased use of alliances.

Globalization is an evolving frontier that is increasingly demanding supply chain integration. As international business develops, the demand for logistical competency increases due to longer supply chains, less certainty, and more documentation. While the forces of change push toward borderless operations, supply chain management still confronts market, financial, and channel barriers. The barriers are exemplified by distance, demand, diversity, and documentation. The challenge is to position an enterprise to take advantage of the benefits of global marketing and manufacturing by developing world-spanning logistical competency.

Summary

Operational integration is a managerial challenge at the level of individual enterprises, across domestic supply chains, and for the conduct of international business. Operational integration creates value as a result of coordinated cross-functional efficiency. The application of systems analysis and assessment of total cost provides a methodology to integrate functions into a productive process. Integrated processes offer distinct cost and service benefits.

At the individual firm level operational integration is difficult. Barriers exist and serve as obstacles to internal operational integration. This resistance to integration can be traced to long-standing functional management practices and related information systems and reward practices. Conventional measurement practices and metrics serve to reinforce functionalism. The resistance to process integration is sufficiently strong and can be universally observed. The commonly observed phenomenon referred to as the great divide reflects the common difficulty in achieving enterprise end-to-end integration.

The paradox is that many firms successfully integrate with customers and/or suppliers. Thus, firms often integrate more outside their specific enterprise than they do internally. This means that many attempts at extending the enterprise across the supply chain are, at best, partial solutions. However, many such limited supply chain engagements appear to be valuable arrangements for their participants. It remains unclear just how much internal integration is necessary for a firm to be a viable supply chain participant. Of course, the risk is that failure to achieve internal operational integration may cause a firm to be unable to meet supply chain commitments.

The reason that partial supply chain integration achieves value is directly related to the significant potential to reduce waste, duplication, and operational redundancy. In particular, collaboration offers ways to reduce inventory investments and related risk for participating firms. Successful supply chain integration requires cross-organizational programs to facilitate operations, technology and planning, and relationship management collaboration. While few, if any, across-the-supply-chain collaborations exist today, the potential benefits of such holistic integration are staggering.

As a supply chain strategy moves into the international arena, new complexities are encountered. These complexities result from longer distances, difference in demand, cultural diversity, and complex documentation. Firms will increasingly confront the need to expand operations into the global arena. Strategies to achieve a share of the rapidly expanding world market range from export/import to local presence to true globalization. Regardless of the strategic focus, success will, to a large extent, be dependent upon a firm's logistical capabilities.

Challenge Questions

1. Compare and contrast economic, market, and relevancy value.
2. Illustrate the differences in product/service creation, presentation, and positioning.
3. Explain the following statement: "The methodology is systems analysis and the theoretical framework is the systems concept."
4. Why is variance reduction important to logistical integration? Illustrate in terms of logistical operations.
5. What is the meaning of the phrase *cradle-to-cradle* logistics? Discuss the operational differences of original versus reverse logistics.
6. How do reward systems serve as barriers to enterprise integration?
7. In your words, describe and illustrate the *great divide*. Do you believe the great divide phenomenon is as widely experienced as the text indicates? Support your position with an illustration.
8. What creates power in the context of supply chain collaboration? Why do many observers feel power is shifting forward or closer to end consumers in many supply chain arrangements?
9. Demonstrate your understanding of the relationship between logistical capabilities and competencies by tracing the evolution of logistical work to universal competencies. Does this logic have any practical application in understanding logistical sophistication? If so, what is the practical benefit?
10. Compare and contrast export/import operations to local presence. What are the logistics ramifications of each stage of international development?

II TECHNOLOGY STRUCTURE

The impact of technology upon the development of logistics and the rapid expansion of supply chain collaboration has been profound. In Part II we discuss in depth how technology drives logistics and facilitates supply chain integration. First, Chapter 7 provides a broad framework of information networks that support logistical integration. Then, Chapter 8 explores the functionality of Enterprise Resource Planning (ERP) systems and provides a general description of execution systems, often referred to as bolt-ons, that provide logistical functionality and integration. Finally, Chapter 9 discusses Advanced Planning Systems (APS) that are essential for planning logistical operations in a supply chain setting. All three chapters emphasize the need for enterprise and supply chain *integration* to achieve competitive advantage and maximize resource effectiveness.

7 INFORMATION NETWORKS

Supply chain information systems initiate activities and track information regarding processes, facilitate information sharing both within the firm and between supply chain partners, and assist in management decision making. This chapter describes these comprehensive information systems as a combination of communication networks, transaction systems, and decision support systems. All component systems must be integrated to provide comprehensive functionality for analyzing, initiating, and monitoring supply chain operations.

Information System Functionality

From its inception, logistics focused on product storage and flow through the distribution channel. Information flow and accuracy was often overlooked because it was not viewed as being critical by customers. In addition, information transfer rates were limited by the speed of paper. There are four reasons why timely and accurate information has become more critical for effective logistics systems design and operations. First, customers perceive information about order status, product availability, delivery schedule, shipment tracking, and invoices as necessary elements of total customer service. Customers demand access to real time information. Second, with the goal of reducing total supply chain assets, managers realize that information can be used to reduce inventory and human resource requirements. In particular, requirements planning using the most current information can reduce inventory by minimizing demand uncertainty. Third, information increases flexibility with regard to how, when, and where resources may be utilized to gain strategic advantage. Fourth, enhanced information transfer and exchange capability utilizing the Internet is changing relationships between buyers and sellers and redefining channel relationships.

Supply chain information systems (SCIS) are the thread that links logistics activities into an integrated process. The integration builds on four levels of functionality: (1) *transaction systems,* (2) *management control,* (3) *decision analysis,* and (4) *strategic planning.* Figure 7-1 illustrates logistics activities and decisions at each level of information functionality. As the pyramid shape suggests, management control, decision analysis, and strategic planning enhancements require a strong transaction system foundation.

A **transaction system** is characterized by formalized rules, procedures, and standardized communications; a large volume of transactions; and an operational, day-to-day focus. The combination of structured processes and large transaction volume places a major emphasis on information system efficiency. At the most basic levels, transaction systems initiate and record individual logistics activities and functions.

FIGURE 7-1

Information functionality

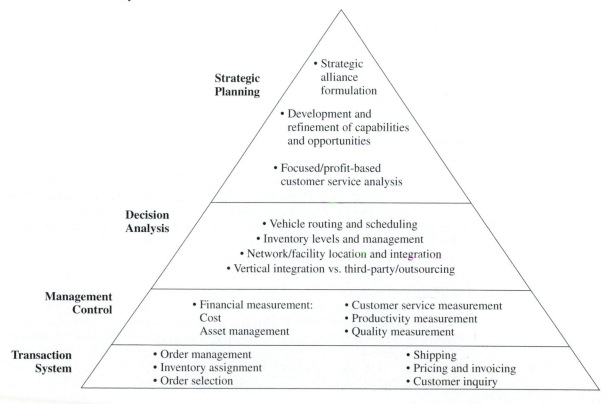

Transaction activities include order entry, inventory assignment, order selection, shipping, pricing, invoicing, and customer inquiry. For example, customer order entry represents a transaction that enters a customer request for product into the information system. The order entry transaction initiates a second transaction as inventory is assigned to the order. A third transaction is then generated to direct warehouse operations to select or pick the order from the warehouse storage location. A fourth transaction initiates transport of the order to the customer. The final transaction develops the invoice and records an account receivable. Throughout the process, the firm and customer expect the availability of real time information regarding order status. Thus, the customer order performance cycle is completed through a series of information system transactions.[1]

The second SCIS level, **management control,** focuses on *performance measurement and reporting.* Performance measurement is necessary to provide management feedback regarding supply chain performance and resource utilization. Common performance measures include cost, customer service, productivity, quality, and asset management measures. As an example, specific performance measures include transportation and warehousing cost per pound, inventory turnover, case fill rate, cases per labor hour, and customer perception.

While it is necessary that SCIS report historical system performance, it is also necessary for the system to identify operational exceptions. Management exception information is useful to highlight potential customer order or operational problems. For example, proactive SCIS should be capable of identifying future inventory shortages based on forecasted requirements and planned inventory. Management exception reporting should also be capable of identifying potential transportation, delivery warehouse, or labor requirements that exceed capacity limitations.

While some control measures, such as cost, are well defined, other measures, such as customer service and quality, are less specific. For example, customer service can be measured internally, from the enterprise's perspective, or externally, from the customer's perspective. While internal measures are relatively easy to track, external measures are more difficult to obtain since they require monitoring performance regarding specific customers.

The third SCIS level, **decision analysis,** focuses on software tools to assist managers in identifying, evaluating, and comparing supply chain and logistics strategic and tactical alternatives for improved effectiveness. Typical analyses include supply chain design, inventory management, resource allocation, routing, and segmental profitability. Decision analysis SCIS must also include database maintenance, modeling, analysis, and reporting over a wide range of potential logistics situations. Similar to management control, decision analysis includes some tactical analysis considerations such as vehicle routing and warehouse planning. Decision analysis applications are also being used to manage customer relationships by determining the trade-offs associated with having satisfied and successful customers, as discussed in Chapter 3. Because decision analysis is used to guide future operations and needs to be unstructured and flexible to allow consideration of a wide range of alternatives, users require more expertise and training to benefit from its capability.

Strategic planning, the final SCIS level, organizes and synthesizes transaction data into a wide range of business planning and decision-making models that assist in evaluating the probabilities and payoffs of various strategies. Essentially, strategic

---

[1]For a review of performance cycle structure and dynamics, see pp. 55–64.

FIGURE 7-2

SCIS usage, decision characteristics, and justification

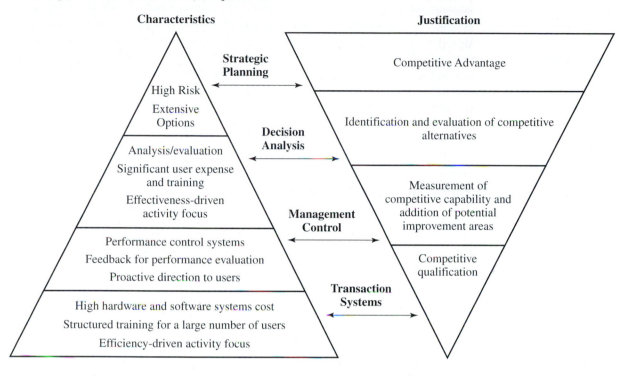

planning focuses on information support to develop and refine supply chain and logistics strategy. These decisions are often extensions of decision analysis but are typically more abstract, are even less structured, and have a longer-term focus. Examples of strategic planning decisions include the desirability of strategic alliances, development and refinement of manufacturing capabilities, and market opportunities related to customer responsiveness.

The relative shape of Figure 7-2 illustrates relative SCIS development costs and benefits. The left side of the figure illustrates development and maintenance characteristics while the right side reflects benefits. Development and maintenance costs include hardware, software, communications, training, and personnel expenses.

In general, a solid base requires significant SCIS investments for transaction systems. Transaction system costs are high due to the large number of system users, heavy data communications requirements, high transaction volume, and significant software complexity. Transaction systems costs are also relatively well defined and exhibit more certainty and limited payoff with respect to benefits or returns. A comprehensive transaction system does not provide a substantial competitive advantage in today's environment; it is a competitive requirement. Virtually all firms that are still in business have made substantial investments to achieve transaction system efficiency. Therefore, while the investment is substantial, the relative return is often quite small. Higher level systems such as management control, decision analysis, and strategic planning typically require fewer hardware and software resources but often involve greater uncertainty and risk with regard to potential system benefits.

Management control and decision analysis systems, on the other hand, focus on providing insight into problem processes and alternatives. For example, benchmarking management control systems can identify processes where a firm lags competitors while external customer service audits may identify opportunities for selective, customer-focused programs. Finally, strategic planning systems with the ability to assess supply chain design, customer/product profitability, segment contribution, or alliance benefits can have a major impact on enterprise profitability and competitiveness even though they are not particularly hardware or software intensive.

In the past, most systems development focused on improving transaction system efficiency. While these investments offered returns in terms of speed and lower operating costs, anticipated cost reductions have often been elusive. SCIS development and implementation now focus on enhanced supply chain system integration and more effective decision making.

Comprehensive Information System Integration

A comprehensive information system initiates, monitors, assists in decision making, and reports on activities required to complete logistics operations and planning. There are many components that must be combined to form an integrated information system, and there are many ways to organize and illustrate the combined components.

The major system components include: (1) Enterprise Resource Planning (ERP) or legacy systems, (2) communication systems, (3) execution systems, and (4) planning systems. Figure 7-3 offers one illustration of these components and their typical interfaces.

ERP or Legacy Systems

The **ERP** or **legacy systems** highlighted in Figure 7-4 are the backbone of most firms' supply chain information systems. This backbone maintains current and historical data and processes transactions to initiate and track performance. Legacy systems refer to the mainframe applications that were developed prior to 1990 to automate transactions such as order entry, order processing, warehouse operations, inventory management, transportation, and related financial transactions. For example, systems related to customer orders were often labeled Order Management Systems (OMS) since they managed the order fulfillment process. In addition to order information, legacy systems typically maintain information regarding customers, products, inventory status, and facility operations. In many cases, these legacy systems represent independently developed software modules that lack integration and consistency; consequently, problems with data reliability and integrity abound. These problems are further complicated by the fact that multidivisional firms often use different legacy systems for each division or country.

During the 1990s, many firms began to replace legacy systems with ERP systems designed as integrated transaction modules with a common and consistent database. ERP systems facilitated integrated operations and reporting to initiate, monitor, and track critical activities such as order fulfillment and replenishment processing. In addition to data integrity and consistency, ERP systems gained rapid popularity as a way to minimize potential problems with the Year 2000 millennium bug. ERP systems also incorporate an integrated corporatewide database, sometime referred to as a data warehouse, along with appropriate transactions to facilitate logistics and supply chain operations. Typical transactions can accommodate order entry and fulfillment, procurement, and production transactions. Beyond these operational applications, ERP

FIGURE 7-3

Integrated supply chain system modules

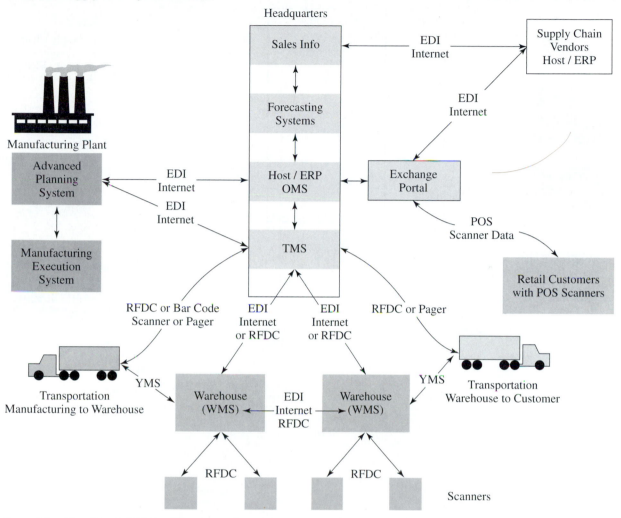

Source: Adapted from Cahner's Publishing, "The Information Flow Across an Integrated Supply Chain," *Logistics Online* (**www.manufacturing.net/scl/yearbook/**). Used with permission.

systems typically include financial, accounting, and human resource capability. Table 7-1 lists the traditional and emerging capabilities characteristic of ERP systems, and Industry Insight 7-1 describes how one company (Cisco) has used ERP systems to facilitate tremendous growth, support acquisitions, and develop superior customer service.

To capitalize on the benefits of integration, headquarters systems are beginning to include two other system components, forecasting and Customer Relationship Management (CRM), as illustrated in Figure 7-3. The CRM or sales management system is one of the newer applications designed to facilitate information sharing between the sales force and operational management. CRM provides sales representatives and customers with current information gained through the ERP system regarding sales history, shipment history, order status, promotional summary, and shipment information. The history and current status information, combined with information regarding

FIGURE 7-4

Enterprise resource planning

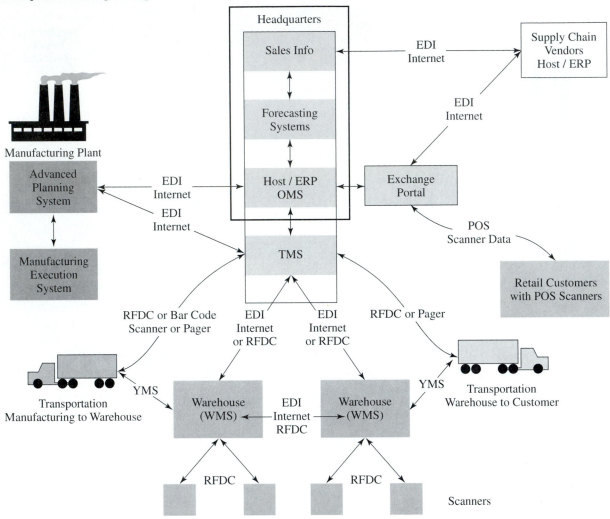

Source: Adapted from Cahner's Publishing, "The Information Flow Across an Integrated Supply Chain," *Logistics Online*
(**www.manufacturing.net/scl/yearbook/**). Used with permission.

product development, pricing, and promotion, allows CRM to forecast customer orders that will maximize customer success as discussed in Chapter 3. Such timely and
accurate information exchange between a firm and its customers increases the likelihood that product sales and promotion plans will be supported with available product.

Communication Systems

The communication module facilitates information flow between functional areas
within the firm and between supply chain partners. Figure 7-5 highlights the major
communication components required for supply chain operations. Logistics information consists of real time data on company operations—inbound material flows, production status, product inventories, customer shipments, and incoming orders.

TABLE 7-1   Capabilities of ERP Systems

What do you get with ERP?

As monolithic as ERP may sound, it isn't. In fact, the software is composed of many different modules (as many as 60) that connect to the company's financial system. That collected data is then used to project the performance of key corporate financials. This enterprise-centric model of ERP is now being expanded to include new modules that allow ERP to be part of the planning process by the company and its suppliers and customers.

Traditional Capabilities:
- Bill of materials
- Accounts payable and accounts receivable
- General ledger
- Inventory control
- Order entry
- Purchasing
- Project requirements planning
- Routings
- Capacity requirements planning

Emerging Capabilities:
- Enterprise application integration
- Visibility
- Collaborative planning, forecasting, and replenishment
- Customer relationship management
- Web-enabled applications
- Hosting

Source: Gary Forger, "ERP Goes Mid-Market," *Modern Materials Handling,* January 2000, p. 71. Reprinted with permission.

From an external perspective, firms need to make order, shipment, and billing information available to suppliers, financial institutions, transportation carriers, and customers. Internal operating units must be able to share and exchange information on production schedule and status. Typical supply chain communication technologies include bar coding, scanning, Electronic Data Interchange (EDI), satellite communication, radio frequency, and the Internet. Standards and formats to exchange data are discussed later in this chapter.

Execution Systems

Enterprise execution systems work in conjunction with the firm's ERP to provide specific functionality to support logistics operations. While some ERP systems include reasonable logistics functionality, many lack the capabilities to facilitate contemporary warehouse and transportation operations. Figure 7-6 highlights selected execution system modules. Most execution systems are "bolted-on" or integrated into the ERP system to facilitate data exchange. In addition to facilitating standard warehouse management functionality such as receiving, storage, shipping, and warehouse automation, Warehouse Management Systems (WMS) typically include management reporting, support for value-added services, and decision support capability. The Transportation Management System (TMS) typically includes routing, load building, consolidation, and management of reverse logistics activities as well as scheduling and documentation. Yard Management Systems (YMS) track inventory in vehicles stored in facility yards. Chapter 8 provides a more detailed discussion of logistics execution systems.

Planning Systems

The final information system components are the planning systems highlighted in Figure 7-7. While the ERP system processes transactions to execute specific logistics

INDUSTRY INSIGHT 7-1   ACHIEVING INTEGRATION THROUGH DECENTRALIZATION

Since its founding in 1984, Cisco has always seemed to be able to look a bit further over the horizon than its competitors. It concentrated on networking when the rest of the world was point-to-point. It specialized in the enhanced functionality of routing when most people thought switches were all they'd ever need. And it moved rapidly to put a large portion of its sales operations online before most people thought this was practical.

As a result, Cisco now manages 75 percent of its revenues through its website: $25 million per day, $8 billion per year. This is believed by many industry observers to be the largest electronic commerce site in the world.

Despite Cisco's indisputable record of success, the journey hasn't always been an easy one. Growth was one reason. By 1994, Cisco had rapidly outgrown its application systems. "We were experiencing growth rates of more than 70 percent per year," says Andy Starr, IS Manager. Revenues had reached nearly $1 billion, but Cisco was still operating on applications meant to support a company half that size. To remedy the situation, Cisco embarked on an aggressive ERP implementation using an Oracle database and applications. In 1995, after only 9 months, the company went live with a big bang implementation—a complete switch of all worldwide transactions systems. Five thousand orders in backlog were converted in just one weekend. Peter Solvik, Cisco's CIO, says, "The applications provided the architecture on which we could very, very rapidly grow, adapt, and scale the company."

Acquisitions were another reason. In 5 years Cisco has acquired 27 companies. When acquiring a company, systems integration is critical to support the 60- to 90-day closing period applied by Cisco. The goal is to take orders for that company's products on Cisco's information system the day the deal is closed. The acquired firm's legacy systems are then replaced quickly, creating a common worldwide ordering environment. "We wouldn't have acquired these companies if we didn't have the ability to integrate them fluidly. They wouldn't provide value to our customers or our shareholders," says Solvik.

Cisco's ERP framework has grown from a single server into three U.S.-based servers and one in the Netherlands. This network of servers coordinates Cisco's manufacturing and order fulfillment processes, providing immediate response to requests and better availability of products to its customers.

For example, an order loaded into the Amsterdam server is scheduled for delivery using the U.S. Available-to-Promise (ATP) server. The ATP server schedules according to the supply said to be available by the U.S. manufacturing server. The customer order is then built and shipped from one of five manufacturing sites and invoiced from the Amsterdam server. All of these servers combined provide Cisco with four benefits: increased reliability, reduced risk of server failure, enhanced flexibility and scalability of the ERP system, and a reduction in lead times from 4 weeks to 1.

Solvik states that Cisco's entire Internet commerce initiative is based on a simple truth: "customers prefer self-service." To achieve a higher degree of self-service, Cisco was the first company to integrate its website with an Oracle Applications ERP infrastructure. The Cisco Connection Online (CCO) Internet site offers customers and suppliers global communications with 49 pages of country- or region-specific support services and product and contact information translated into 14 different languages. It operates with dedicated server links located in Australia, China, France, Hong Kong, Japan, the Netherlands, and South Korea that support 200 offices in 54 countries around the world.

Within the CCO is the "Internet Product Center" where customers can configure and place orders; look up pricing, lead times, and order status; and access invoicing information. This has reduced order entry cycle time from 1 week to less than 3 days. It has also reduced order acknowledgment cycle time from 12 hours to 2 hours, with the goal of achieving real time acknowledgment in the next 6 months. Cisco has the unique ability to process billing in multiple currencies and manage tax and regulatory issues in every country where it conducts business, yet consolidate financial performance based upon U.S. currency. "The CCO allows the salesperson to focus on the strategic aspect of the relationship," says Solvik, "and improves responsiveness to the customer through automation of mundane tasks."

Thanks to the capabilities of its Oracle ERP infrastructure, Cisco has been able to add out-sourced manufacturing to its operations over the last 4 years. "Over 50 percent of the units shipped are untouched by a Cisco factory or a Cisco employee," Solvik says. "We run our worldwide out-source factory across almost 50 suppliers entirely on Oracle Manufacturing Applications."

Cisco has also extended its communications throughout the supply chain to about 100 suppliers. "Now our component suppliers can bid against each other on a new product over the Internet," says Solvik. Changes in Bills of Materials are broadcast to suppliers through the CCO site. "We've reduced the engineering change order cycle time from 25 to 10 days within the last four years. This improves quality significantly and reduces inventory write-offs," says Solvik.

Most important, Solvik can appreciate the benefits of a good relationship in dollars and cents. "By adding together the benefits of electronic commerce, electronic self-service, manufacturing initiatives, and a few [benefits] offered by the Internet, the annual contribution to the company amounts to over $550 million from these top areas alone."

Source: **http://www.oracle.com/customers/sia/cisco.html.**

FIGURE 7-5

Communication modules

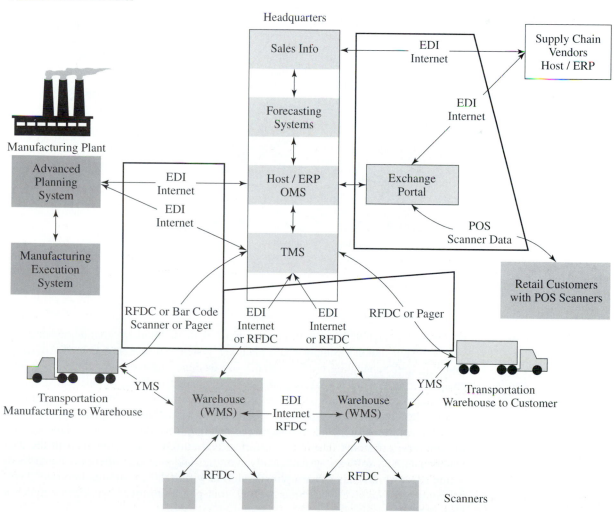

Source: Adapted from Cahner's Publishing, "The Information Flow Across an Integrated Supply Chain," *Logistics Online* (**www.manufacturing.net/scl/yearbook/**). Used with permission.

FIGURE 7-6

Execution modules

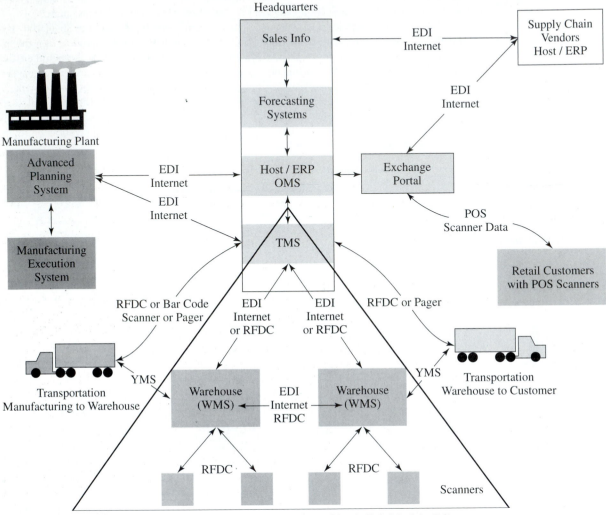

Source: Adapted from Cahner's Publishing, "The Information Flow Across an Integrated Supply Chain," *Logistics Online* (**www.manufacturing.net/scl/yearbook/**). Used with permission.

activities, transaction systems in general don't evaluate alternative strategies or assist with decision making. Supply chain planning systems, now being termed Advanced Planning and Scheduling (APS) systems, are designed to assist in evaluating supply chain alternatives and advise in supply chain decision making. Sophisticated supply chain planning systems are becoming increasingly common to allow for consideration of complex alternatives under tight decision time constraints. Typical supply chain planning applications include production scheduling, inventory resource planning, and transportation planning. Using the historical and current data maintained in the data warehouse, APS software systematically identifies and evaluates alternative courses of action and recommends a near optimal solution within the constraints imposed. Typical constraints involve production, facility, transportation, inventory, or raw material limitations.

FIGURE 7-7

Advanced planning and scheduling components

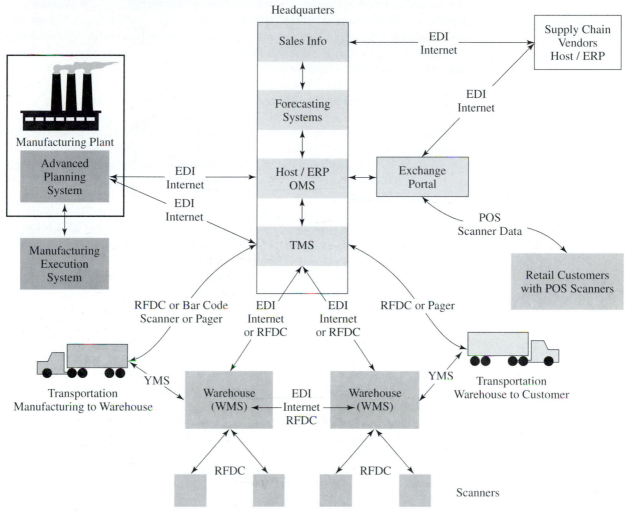

Source: Adapted from Cahner's Publishing, "The Information Flow Across an Integrated Supply Chain," *Logistics Online* (**www.manufacturing.net/scl/yearbook/**). Used with permission.

Planning systems can generally be grouped into two categories, strategic and tactical. Strategic planning systems are designed to assist in analyses where there is a large number of alternatives and data outside the range of current history is required. Examples of strategic planning applications include supply chain network design and structural analyses such as which combination of supplier, production, and distribution facilities should be used and how product should flow between existing or potential facilities.

Tactical planning focuses on operational issues as constrained by short-term resource constraints such as production, facility, or vehicle capacity. The information support for tactical planning is typically available from a firm's data warehouse. Tactical planning processes evaluate customer requirements and identify an operational combination of production, inventory, facilities, and equipment utilization that can be applied within capacity constraints. The result is an action plan to guide short-term operations.

Accessing Supply Chain Applications

The maintenance of comprehensive information system technology can be extremely expensive. The hardware is extensive, and the software is complex. The hardware typically includes a network of servers and personal computers to provide the computing power and storage capacity to track a large number of customers, products, inventory, and order transactions. The software must allow for a wide range of options for users that are frequently located throughout the world. In addition, both the hardware and the software must incorporate substantial security and redundancy to prevent loss of critical capabilities and information if either the software or the hardware fails. Hardware and software also require substantial human expertise for both implementation and ongoing maintenance. Although smaller firms may not require the same level of system scale, redundancy, and globalization, the required operational functionality is essentially the same. There are three ways firms obtain access to necessary hardware, software, and support.

The first is through *direct ownership*. The firm purchases the hardware and software for implementation within its facilities. While the initial cost can be substantial, the direct ownership route offers high security and low variable cost. Firms can reduce capital investment by leasing equipment or software from vendors or a third-party financing company. However, there are also risks associated with the direct ownership plan. The firm must employ or contract individuals who can provide the expertise to implement, modify, and maintain both the hardware and the software. Management and financial support of information technology resources may use capital and talent that are needed to develop core competency of a firm. In addition, direct ownership of information technology resources must carefully evaluate redundancy requirements. SCIS require that global operations be supported 24 hours a day, 7 days a week.

A second strategy is to *outsource* information management to a third party with the competency and expertise to implement, maintain, and manage such technologies. Firms such as International Business Machines (IBM), Electronic Data Systems (EDS), and Accenture provide comprehensive information technology outsourcing and consulting. The hardware and software can be dedicated or shared with other clients of the service provider. In either case, both the hardware and the data are reasonably secure. The benefits of outsourcing are that operational responsibility is assigned to a specialist that has extensive resources to focus on both hardware and software implementation and operations. In addition, such management firms typically offer backup services by sharing substantial resources across a number of clients. The major disadvantage of using a third-party service provider is increased variable cost. To provide the service, a profit margin must be added to the cost of equipment and software. However, the cost differential may be more than justified since the service provider should be in a position to achieve economies of scale by sharing resources and personnel across multiple clients.

The third strategy is the use of an *Application Service Provider* (ASP). An ASP is a relatively new type of service provider that has emerged via the Internet. ASPs are third-party service firms that own and maintain computer hardware and software which they rent to clients on a usage or transaction basis. With an ASP, the hardware and software are typically limited to a personal computer, a Web browser, and an Internet connection. The ASP owns websites that offer a variety of software and client computer files. In what is coming to be called *Apps on tap,* the ASP maintains and upgrades the computer software and database and makes it available to the firm. The

TABLE 7-2   Application Service Provider Benefits and Risks

Benefits	Risks
Cost savings: Not necessary to purchase or upgrade software	Security: Proprietary information possibly vulnerable due to ASP failures
Time savings: Firm can focus on core business	Infrastructure: ASP requires high-speed Internet connection
Staffing: ASP provides technical staff to support implementation and maintenance	History: No clear business model yet.
Flexibility: Client can remotely access software with a Web browser	

Source: ASPNews.com. Cherry Tree & Co. Reprinted with permission.

ASP is responsible for the security, redundancy, and integrity of the website. Table 7-2 lists major ASP benefits and risks.

In most cases, firms will employ a combination of the three strategies to accommodate information technology requirements. The basic order entry and management software may be acquired and operated by a firm using internal computers to minimize cost and provide security. More complex software such as planning systems may be rented from ASPs. In any case, the combination of the ownership and access methods provides firms with the capability to create a comprehensive information system without extensive in-house expertise and significant initial funding.

Communication Systems

Information technology is also critical for information sharing to facilitate logistics and supply chain planning and operations. Historically, coordination of logistics has been difficult since logistics activities are often performed at locations distant from information technology hardware. As a result, information was not available at the location of essential work in terms of both time and content. The past decade has witnessed remarkable advances in logistical communication systems capability. EDI, the Internet, Extensible Markup Language (XML), and satellite technology exist to facilitate communication between firms and facilities. Radio frequency allows short-range communication within facilities such as warehouses. Image, bar coding, and scanner technologies allow communication between supply chain information systems and their physical environment.

Electronic Data Interchange

While the phone, fax, and direct computer connection have enabled information exchange in the past, EDI and the Internet are quickly becoming the standards for effective, accurate, and low-cost information exchange. EDI is defined as intercompany computer-to-computer exchange of business documents in standard formats to facilitate high-volume transactions. It involves both the capability and practice of communicating information between two organizations electronically instead of via the traditional forms of mail, courier, or even fax.

Direct EDI benefits include increased internal productivity, improved channel relationships, increased external productivity, increased ability to compete internationally, and decreased operating cost. EDI improves productivity through faster information transmission and reduced redundancy. Accuracy is improved by reducing repetitive data entry and interpretation. EDI impacts logistics operating cost through (1) reduced labor and material cost associated with printing, mailing, and handling paper-based transactions; (2) reduced telephone, fax, and Telex; and (3) reduced clerical cost. The graphics industry has found that EDI can eliminate up to 90 percent of paper-based systems, can reduce receipt processing time by 50 percent, and can save $8.00 per invoice document.[2] In another example, Texas Instruments reports EDI has reduced shipping errors by 95 percent, field inquiries by 60 percent, data entry resource requirements by 70 percent, and global procurement cycle time by 57 percent.[3]

While EDI has made significant inroads into logistics communication, its penetration is beginning to plateau at about 50 percent of the transactions. Large manufacturers, distributors, and retailers have adopted EDI as a means to exchange information with major trading partners, but the substantial setup costs and expertise required have limited its application by medium and small firms. Annual surveys of logistics firms by The Ohio State University indicate the majority of EDI activity is with vendors and key accounts.[4]

Communication and information standards are essential for EDI. Communication standards define technical characteristics so that the computer hardware can correctly perform the interchange. Communication standards deal with character sets, transmission priority, and speed. Information standards dictate the structure and content of the message. Standards organizations have developed and refined two general standards as well as numerous industry-specific standards in an effort to standardize both communication and information interchange.

Communication Standards

The most generally accepted communication standards are ANS X.12 (American National Standards Committee X.12) and UN/EDIFACT (United Nations/Electronic Data Interchange for Administration, Commerce, and Transport). X.12 is promoted as the U. S. standard, while EDIFACT is promoted by the United Nations as more of a global standard.[5] Each organization has defined a structure for exchanging common data between supply chain partners. Experts indicate that the most likely migration path is to EDIFACT standards.[6] Table 7-3 illustrates the difference between paper and electronic communications. The left side of the table illustrates the line item detail necessary to communicate a four-line order. The specific data include the quantity, unit-of-measure, item number, description, and unit price. The table's right side illustrates the information in coded form with field separators. Note that this approach is limited as fields must be transferred in a commonly accepted and understood sequence because the X.12 format does not include a variable definition. Lack of consistency in variable definition and interpretation has further reduced the adoption rate for EDI and

---

[2]Anonymous, "EDI Benefits Are Seen in the Dealer Channel," *Graphic Arts Monthly,* March 1999, p. 20.

[3]Clay Youngblood, "EDI Trial and Error," *Transportation and Distribution,* April 1993, p. 46.

[4]The Ohio State University, "Careers Patterns Survey," 1998; available under "careers" at the Council of Logistics Management website, **www.clm1.org.**

[5]Gregory B. Harter, "What Can We Expect," *Transportation and Distribution* 34, no. 4 (April 1993), p. 42.

[6]Ibid.

TABLE 7-3   Comparison of Communication Transaction Formats

Quantity	Unit	No.	Paper Format Description	Price	ANS X.12 Format
3	Cse	6900	Cellulose sponges	12.75	IT1•3•CA•127500•VC•6900 N/L
12	Ea	P450	Plastic pails	.475	IT1•12•EA•4750•VC•P450 N/L
4	Ea	1640Y	Yellow dish drainer	.94	IT1•4•EA•9400•VC•1640Y N/L
1	Dz	1507	6″ plastic flower pots	3.40	IT1•1•DZ•34000•VC•1507 N/L

Source: Mercer Management, Inc. Reprinted with permission.

TABLE 7-4   Primary Logistics Industry EDI Standards

UCS (Uniform Communication Standards): grocery

VICS (Voluntary Interindustry Communication Standards Committee): mass merchandisers

WINS (Warehouse Information Network Standards): warehouse operators

TDCC (Transportation Data Coordinating Committee): transportation operators

AIAG (Automotive Industry Action Group): automotive industry

motivated the advancement of XML, a flexible computer language discussed later in this chapter.

The National Institute of Standards and Technology (NIST) and automotive experts are further driving information integration by experimenting with approaches to exchanging data for the entire business cycle. The program, known as STEP (Standard for the Exchange of Product Model Data), was designed for exchanging design and engineering data between supply chain partners. STEP should allow users to integrate business and technical systems data involving all elements of the business cycle including design, analysis, manufacturing, sales, and service.[7]

EDI Transaction Sets

Communication standards are implemented via transaction sets. A transaction set provides a single common standard to facilitate information interchange between partners in any industry and country. Table 7-4 lists the common logistics-related industry transaction standards. For each industry, the transaction set defines the types of document that can be transmitted. Documents cover common logistics activities such as ordering, warehouse operations, and transportation. Table 7-5 lists the transaction set usage matrix. The transaction set consists of a transaction code (or ID) and is followed by the required data. The transaction code indicates whether the electronic communication is a warehouse shipping order (code 940) or a warehouse stock transfer receipt (code 944), for example. In addition to the transaction code, a warehouse transaction contains warehouse number, item number, and quantity.

While applications are migrating toward common standards, there is still conflict regarding the ultimate goal. A single common standard facilitates information

[7]Amy Zukerman, "Standards, Technology, and the Supply Chain," *Transportation and Distribution,* May 2000, p. 44.

TABLE 7-5   **Transaction Set Usage Matrix**

TS ID	Transaction Set Name	UCS	VICS EDI
102	Associated Data		✓
180	Return Merchandise Authorization and Notification	✓	✓
204	Motor Carrier Load Tender	✓	
210	Motor Carrier Freight Details and Invoice	✓	
214	Transportation Carrier Shipment Status Message	✓	
753	Request for Routing Instructions		✓
754	Routing Instructions		✓
810	Invoice	✓	✓
812	Credit/Debit Adjustment	✓	✓
816	Organizational Relationships	✓	✓
818	Commission Sales Report	✓	
820	Payment Order/Remittance Advice	✓	✓
824	Application Advice	✓	✓
830	Planning Schedule with Release Capability	✓	✓
831	Application Control Totals	✓	✓
832	Price/Sales Catalog		✓
846	Inventory Inquiry/Advice	✓	✓
850	Purchase Order	✓	✓
852	Product Activity Data	✓	✓
853	Routing and Carrier Instructions		✓
855	Purchase Order Acknowledgment	✓	✓
856	Ship Notice/Manifest	✓	✓
857	Shipment and Billing Notice	✓	
860	Purchase Order Change Request—Buyer Initiated		✓
861	Receiving Advice/Acceptance Certificate		✓
864	Text Message	✓	✓
867	Product Transfer and Resale Report	✓	
869	Order Status Inquiry		✓
870	Order Status Report		✓
875	Grocery Products Purchase Order	✓	
876	Grocery Products Purchase Order Change	✓	
877	Manufacturer Coupon Family Code Structure	✓	
878	Product Authorization/De-Authorization	✓	
879	Price Information	✓	
880	Grocery Products Invoice	✓	
881	Manufacturer Coupon Redemption Detail	✓	
882	Direct Store Delivery Summary Information	✓	✓
883	Market Development Fund Allocation	✓	
884	Market Development Fund Settlement	✓	
885	Store Characteristics	✓	
886	Customer Call Reporting	✓	
887	Coupon Notification	✓	
888	Item Maintenance	✓	
889	Promotion Announcement	✓	✓
891	Deduction Research Report	✓	
893	Item Information Request	✓	✓

TABLE 7-5   Continued

TS ID	Transaction Set Name	UCS	VICS EDI
894	Delivery/Return Base Record	✓	
895	Delivery/Return Acknowledgment and/or Adjustment	✓	
896	Product Dimension Maintenance	✓	
940	Warehouse Shipping Order	✓	✓
944	Warehouse Stock Transfer Receipt Advice	✓	
945	Warehouse Shipping Advice	✓	
947	Warehouse Inventory Adjustment Advice	✓	✓
997	Functional Acknowledgment	✓	✓

Source: Deborah Faraqher, Uniform Code Council, Inc., 1995.

FIGURE 7-8

Value-added networks (VANs). The VAN collects transaction messages and information from a manufacturer and then translates those messages and information into appropriate industry-specific communication standards.

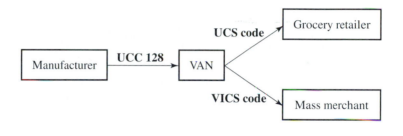

interchange between partners in any industry and country, but many firms believe that strategic advantage can be achieved only with proprietary EDI capabilities. Proprietary capabilities allow a firm to offer customized transactions that efficiently meet information requirements.

Additionally, a standard transaction set would have to accommodate the needs of all types of users and, as a result, would be more complex. For example, the grocery industry requires a 12-digit universal product code (UPC), while the electrical supply industry requires a 20-digit item code. Standardized logistics EDI transactions would have to accommodate both.

Many firms resolve this dilemma through the use of value-added networks (VANs). A VAN, illustrated in Figure 7-8, is a common interface between sending and receiving systems. The VAN adds *value* by managing transactions, translating communication standards, and reducing the number of communication linkages. Transaction management includes broadcast of messages to subsets of suppliers, carriers, or customers and receipt of messages from customers using different communication standards.

The Uniform Code Council (UCC), in partnership with EAN International, is the organization responsible for international numbering standards and is committed to developing common global standards for products and transaction sets. Information regarding the status of their current initiatives can be found on their website at **www. uc-council.org.** Another source documenting the evolving commercial standards is the Voluntary Interindustry Commerce Standards (VICS) at **www.vics.org.**

Internet

The widespread availability of the Internet and standardized interfaces offered through Internet browsers such as Netscape and Internet Explorer have substantially expanded the opportunities and capability to exchange information between firms of all sizes. The Internet is quickly becoming the supply chain information transmission tool of choice for forecasted requirements, orders, inventory status, product updates, and shipment information. In conjunction with a PC and an Internet browser, the Internet offers a standard approach for order entry, order status inquiry, and shipment tracking. The Ohio State University survey predicts the Internet will carry 20 percent of customer orders by the year 2010.[8] Industry Insight 7-2 describes how OshKosh B'Gosh uses document templates along with the Internet to provide inventory and transportation visibility.

The increasing availability of the Internet has also enabled the development of the exchange portal, a communication medium that has significant supply chain implications. An exchange portal is an *infomediary* that facilitates horizontal and vertical information exchange between supply chain partners. Figure 7-9 illustrates an exchange portal of a firm designed to facilitate communication between the firm's customers and suppliers. The firm can provide information regarding raw material requirements, product availability, or price changes and allow the marketplace to react by placing bids or orders based on the most timely information. It is projected that 60 percent of Fortune 500 firms will have exchange portals by 2003 to facilitate communication with key customers and suppliers.[9] While a single firm site might provide good Internet advertising, it does increase complexity, as all the partners have to contend with multiple, unique interfaces resulting in high transaction cost.

A second type of exchange portal is industry-based. It facilitates communication between all supply chain partners within an industry and can substantially reduce transaction costs. Figure 7-10 illustrates the exchange portal that the automobile industry has developed to facilitate communication between the original equipment manufacturers and their multiple tiers of suppliers. This portal offers a common framework for exchanging information including design information, proposal requests, commodity availability, bids, and schedules. While the information can be made available to all interested parties, it is also possible to restrict information availability. There is increasing fear that industry portal collaborations might increase the potential of monopolistic practices and trade restraints. The Federal Trade Commission (FTC) can be expected to play an increasing role in the evolution of the exchange portals, particularly for B2B activities.[10]

A third type of exchange portal is cross-industry-based and is designed to facilitate communication between firms that have common interests in commodities and services. Figure 7-11 illustrates a cross-industry exchange portal for manufacturers, suppliers, service providers, and customers. When one of the member firms has a need for raw material, product, or service, it can access the exchange portal to determine availability and potential price. Similarly, when one of the member firms has excess product or service capacity, such availability can be posted on the portal to solicit interest or a possible bid by one of the exchange members. Industry Insight 7-3 provides a detailed description of the Tradematrix.com exchange portal.

---

[8]The Ohio State University, "Careers Patterns Survey," 1998; available under "careers" at the Council of Logistics Management website, **www.clm.org.**

[9]Sanjiv Sidhu, "Harvesting Value in the Eye of the Hurricane," presented at the Planet 2000 Conference, San Diego, CA: October 9, 2000.

[10]Kim S. Nash, "Really Check," *Computerworld,* June 5, 2000, pp. 58–9.

INDUSTRY INSIGHT 7-2 USING THE INTERNET SAVES TIME AND MONEY

From its base in White House, TN, OshKosh B'Gosh's logistics management activities extend to the nation's borders and beyond. To manage the inevitable paperwork that accompanies international shipping, logistics managers have implemented a number of steps to streamline operations. "We've taken all of our documents and made templates," says Dennis Defnet, OshKosh's corporate transportation manager. This allows the company to send import documentation to its Customs brokers via the Internet, eliminating the use of faxes. Not only does that improve speed and reduce the amount of paper, it has been a hit with Customs officials, who appreciate the clarity of the documents. "It's done tremendous things for accuracy, speed, and pre-clearing shipments," Defnet says. In addition, he reports, the cost per document using the Internet versus EDI is significantly lower.

By linking its systems with suppliers' and carriers' systems, OshKosh also has the information it needs to manage inbound shipments. Gaining visibility of inbound shipments is crucial, explains Joe Burgert, the company's director of distribution. OshKosh has a large number of contractors shipping from Asia. The distribution center may receive 20 or more ocean containers per day. Knowing what product is in each container allows distribution center managers to locate seasonal product quickly and determine the best unloading sequence.

For those international shipments, OshKosh relies on shipment arrival information provided by its Customs brokers. "We have visibility as to the contractor, the seasonality, and the number of units and cartons," Burgert says. "We have all the information sent to the receiving department at White House." The data, provided electronically, are loaded into spreadsheet files, which OshKosh managers can use for planning.

Defnet adds that knowing the time of arrival allows the company to manage warehouse space and time for unloading air and ocean shipments. "We know exactly where our shipments are, when they clear Customs, when the trucking company is notified, and so on," he says.

Source: "Big Results From Small Packages," *Inbound Logistics*, November 1999.

FIGURE 7-9

Single-firm exchange portal

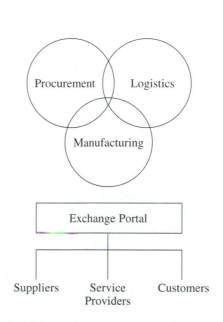

FIGURE 7-10

Automobile industry exchange portal

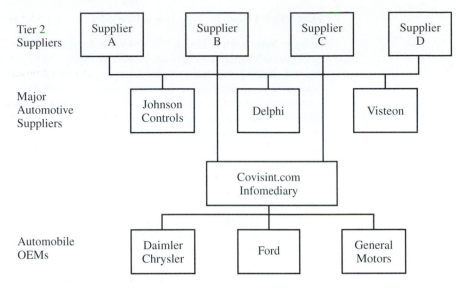

FIGURE 7-11

Cross-industry exchange portal

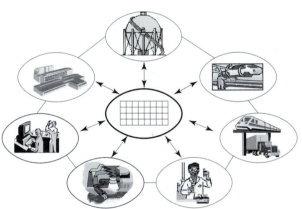

The Internet and the exchange portal have advanced supply chain communication from one-to-one or limited capability to a one-to-many environment capable of being extended to a many-to-many capability. The result is that extended Internet communication is a reality that offers substantial challenge in terms of exploiting widely available information.

One of the major challenges to the wide adoption of exchange portals is the definition and acceptance of online catalogs. Much like the paper version, an online catalog contains a listing of the products and services offered along with their descriptions and specifications. A catalog that is consistent across participating firms is critical to facilitate effective comparison of products and services across firms. For example, a firm desiring to purchase a simple T-shirt from a portal would like all the T-shirt suppliers on that portal to have a similarly formatted entry describing the shirt, its coloring, its contents, as well as other minute details so that the customer can make an effective comparison. While customers prefer consistent catalogs, suppliers prefer to use a catalog as a differentiator and are thus reluctant to deviate from their proprietary format. To facilitate information sharing and exchange, the Voluntary Interindustry Commerce Standards (VICS) and Collaborative Planning, Forecasting, and Replenishment (CPFR) are actively promoting common and consistent catalog definitions and standards.

INDUSTRY INSIGHT 7-3 AN INFOMEDIARY FOR SUPPLY CHAINS

TradeMatrix.com is an e-business platform that enhances design, operations, and evaluation of B2B marketplaces to better meet consumer demands. This electronic marketplace allows firms to focus efforts on key customers, determine segmental profitability, and accelerate time-to-market.

The TradeMatrix concept is to allow firms to build, launch, and service Internet marketplaces that facilitate very focused customer relationships. The Internet becomes the central trading system for major manufacturers and service providers. For example, participating firms can now instantly check the inventory—and the production capacity—of all their major suppliers at the same time to determine how quickly orders can be delivered. Such information sharing can substantially reduce supply chain uncertainty and results in less inventory and shorter, more consistent performance cycles. The visibility can also assist in new product development by allowing suppliers, manufacturers, and even customers to design, refine, and source components prior to initiating production.

A cross-industry trade portal supported by the collaboration of a number of supply chain product and service providers, TradeMatrix includes the application functionality to support procurement, marketing, fulfillment, planning, product development, and customer care. While many of the participating firms offer e-business services, through TradeMatrix they are also providing the hardware and software infrastructure to allow other firms to initiate e-business activities. TradeMatrix provides the complete suite of software, tools, and services to facilitate design and launch of an electronic marketplace and improve trading with supply chain partners.

The establishment of an online marketplace like TradeMatrix requires a combination of shared technology services and e-marketplace management. Shared technology services provide a set of guidelines and standards to facilitate applications design, deployment, runtime operations, and monitoring. The e-marketplace management provides the managerial and technical expertise for system hosting, catalog management, personalization, billing, profile management, relationship management, and services management.

Sun Microsystems and IBM applied the TradeMatrix concept to their own supply chains. Sun operates in a fabless (no internal component manufacturing) environment with contract manufacturers who produce its electronic components. With this model, Sun must oversee and coordinate the business processes of several component suppliers, their contract manufacturers, and third-party logistics providers. The system has allowed Sun to address some of its most critical business challenges, including large fluctuations in forecasted product mix, long product lead times through the supply chain, long collaborative planning lead times with suppliers, and balancing inventory turns with customer satisfaction.

IBM Personal Systems Group focused its efforts on reducing channel inventory while enhancing service levels. IBM enhanced communications with distribution channel partners by using POS data provided using EDI along with other data to create a recommended forecast. The channel partners collaboratively edit the forecast and provide it back to IBM planners. The resulting forecasts then form the input to an integrated planning process for supply/demand matching and allocation. The collaboration reports increased customer service levels to near 100 percent availability, reduced channel inventory by 80 percent, and reduced order scheduling time from 10 to 3 days.

Source: **www.TradeMatrix.com** and **www.i2.com/marketspaces/case_studies/index.htm.**

Extensible Markup Language

Extensible Markup Language (XML) is a flexible computer language that facilitates information transfer between a wide range of applications and is readily interpretable by humans. It was published in 1998 by the World Wide Web Consortium to facilitate information transfer between systems, databases, and Web browsers. Since EDI is very structured, the setup cost and required expertise are relatively high, limiting applications to situations involving high transaction volumes. XML is emerging as the information transfer medium between firms and service providers that do not have transaction volumes to justify EDI. XML is facilitating communication by breaking down many information technology barriers that have constrained EDI adoption.

A basic XML message consists of three components: the actual information being transmitted, data tags, and a DTD (Document Type Definition) or schema. The data tag is a key feature as it defines the data being transmitted. For example, in a shipment XML, the tag for address would be "address" and might appear <address>123 Main St.</address>. The tags tell computers what the data between the brackets are and where the data should go in a database or Web page. The use of common terms and the lack of sequencing requirements make XML transactions much easier to use than EDI. The XML DTD or schema tells the computer what document format to refer to when decoding a message. A DTD is essentially a template that maps out a standard form, its tags, and their relation to a database. For example, there would be separate schema for customer orders, advanced shipping notifications, or transportation documentation.

In situations characterized by low volume, XML is superior to EDI for three reasons. First, it is not expensive to install. It is easy to design an application and requires much less time to implement. Second, XML is easy to maintain because it can be easily converted to HTML (HyperText Markup Language), the language of Web browsers. This makes it much easier to modify and share data between applications. Finally, XML is more flexible, allowing for broad applications and quick definition and extension of standards.[11] One of the major challenges for the growth of XML is the definition of industry standards. Launched in 1998, Rosettanet, a consortium of over 60 companies, has begun developing common definitions for business practices and products as well as standards for using XML to transmit information through the supply chain.[12] Such a common vocabulary is necessary to enable supply chain participants to communicate with each other and have the confidence that the information exchange is secure.

Satellite Technology

Satellite technology allows communication across a wide geographic area such as a region or even the world. The technology is similar to microwave dishes used for home television in areas outside the reach of cable. Figure 7-12 illustrates two-way communication between corporate headquarters and both vehicles and remote locations such as stores.

Satellite communication provides a fast and high-volume channel for information movement around the globe. Schneider National, a nationwide truckload carrier, uses communication dishes mounted on its trucks to enable two-way communication between drivers and their dispatchers. Such real time interaction provides up-to-date information regarding location and delivery information and allows dispatchers to redirect trucks based on need or congestion. Retail chains also use satellite communication to quickly transmit sales information back to headquarters. Wal★Mart uses daily sales figures to drive store replenishment and to provide input to marketing regarding local sales patterns.

[11]For more detail, see Gordon Forsyth, "XML: Breaking Down IT Barriers in Logistics," *American Shipper*, June 2000, pp. 20–6.
[12]James Aaron Cooke, "New Wave," *Logistics*, January 2000, pp. 67–70.

FIGURE 7-12

Logistics satellite communication applications

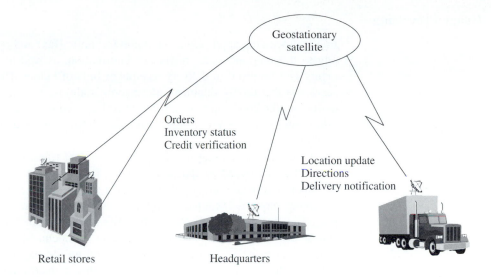

Retail stores   Headquarters

Radio Frequency Exchange

Radio Frequency Data Communication (RFDC) technology is used within relatively small areas, such as distribution centers, to facilitate two-way information exchange. A major application is real time communication with mobile operators such as forklift drivers and order selectors. RFDC allows drivers to have instructions and priorities updated on a real time basis rather than using a hard copy of instructions printed hours earlier. Real time instructions to guide work flow offer increased flexibility and responsiveness and have the potential to improve service using fewer resources. Logistics RFDC applications also include two-way communication of warehouse selection cycle count verification and label printing.

Advanced RFDC capabilities in the form of two-way voice communication are finding their way into logistics warehouse applications. Instead of requiring warehouse operations personnel to interface with a mobile or handheld computer, voice RFDC prompts operators through tasks with audible commands and waits for verbal responses or requests. United Parcel Service uses speech-based RFDC to read zip codes from incoming packages and print routing tickets to guide packages through their newer sortation facilities. The voice recognition systems are based on keywords and voice patterns of each operator. The primary benefit of voice-based RFDC is easier operator interface; since keyboard data entry is not required, two hands are available for order picking.[13]

Radio Frequency Identification (RFID) is a second form of radio frequency technology. RFID can be used to identify a container or its contents as it moves through facilities or on transportation equipment. RFID places a coded electronic chip in the container or box. As the container or box moves through the supply chain, it can be scanned for an identifying code or even for the list of contents. Retailers are beginning to use RFID to allow entire cartloads of merchandise to be scanned simultaneously. The U.S. Department of Defense uses RFID to list the contents of pallets so that they can be tracked as they are loaded on transportation equipment or move through facilities.

---

[13]Patti Satterfied, "Voice-Directed Systems Boost Warehouse Picking," *Parcel Shipping & Distribution*, September 1999, pp. 22–4.

Image Processing

Image processing applications rely upon facsimile (fax) and optical-scanning technology to transmit and store freight bill information, as well as other supporting documents such as proof of delivery receipts or bills of lading. The rationale for this new service is that timely shipment information is almost as important to the customer as delivering the goods on time. As freight is delivered to customers, support documentation is sent to image processing locations, electronically scanned, and logged into the system.

Electronic images of the documents are then transmitted to a main data center where they are stored on optical laser disks. By the next day, customers can access the documents through computer linkages or a phone call to their service representative. Customer requests for a hard copy of a document can be filled within minutes by a facsimile transmission. Customer benefits include more accurate billing, faster response from carrier personnel, and easy access to documentation. The carrier also benefits because the system eliminates the need to file paper documents, reduces the chance of loss, and provides improved credibility with customers.

Satellite technology, RF, and image processing require substantial capital investment prior to obtaining any returns. Experience has shown, however, the primary benefit of these communication technologies is not lower cost but improved customer service. Improved service is provided in the form of more timely definition of tasks, quicker shipment tracing, and faster transfer of sales and inventory information. There will be increased demand for these communication technology applications as customers observe the competitive benefits of real time information transfer.

Bar Coding and Scanning

Auto Identification (ID) systems such as bar coding and electronic scanning were developed to facilitate logistics information collection and exchange. Typical applications include tracking receipts at warehouses and retail sales. These ID systems require significant capital investment for users, but necessarily replace former paper-based information collection and exchange processes that were error-prone and time-consuming. In fact, increased domestic and international competition is driving shippers, carriers, warehouses, wholesalers, and retailers to develop and utilize Auto ID capability to compete in today's marketplace.

Auto ID allows supply chain members to quickly track and communicate movement details with a low probability of error, so it is fast becoming a fundamental service requirement for freight tracking by carriers. Both consumers and B2B customers expect to be able to track the progress of their shipment using the Web-based system offered by carriers such as United Parcel Service and FedEx.

Bar coding is the placement of computer readable codes on items, cartons, containers, pallets, and even rail cars. Most consumers are aware of the Universal Product Code (UPC) that is present on virtually all consumer products. UPC bar codes, used first in 1972, assign a unique 12-digit number to each manufacturer and product. Standardized bar codes reduce errors when receiving, handling, or shipping product. For example, a bar code distinguishes package size and flavor. European Article Numbering (EAN) is the European and United Nations standard for bar coding of items. It is likely that the UPC and EAN systems will become more harmonized due to pressures of global trade.

While UPC/EAN symbology is suitable in the consumer goods industry, some supply chain members desire more comprehensive information. Shippers and carriers, for example, are concerned with contents of pallets or containers. Therefore, a need exists for bar codes to identify cartons, pallets, or containers of products, rather than an individual retail item. Although it is possible to have a paper document listing pallet contents, the document may be lost or damaged in transit. A computer readable code that contains information regarding shipper, receiver, carton contents, and any special instructions and can be attached to an in-transit shipment is necessary; however, incorporating this amount of information into a bar code overwhelms the capability of a 12-digit UPC/EAN code. The basic problem is that marketers do not want bar codes to take up valuable space on packages because it reduces product information and advertising design space. On the other hand, including more information within existing space would make the codes too small and increase scanning errors.

To resolve these problems, bar code research and development have proceeded in a number of directions. There are now other symbologies that are particularly relevant for logistics. These include Code 39, Code 128, Interleaved 2 of 5, and PDF 417.

Code 39 was developed because some industries needed to encode alphabetic as well as numeric data into a bar code. Code 39 is typically the nonfood standard bar code and is used for identification, inventory, and tracking purposes in various industries, such as manufacturing. Code 39 produces relatively long bar codes and may not be suitable if label length is a consideration.

Code 128 evolved when the need for a wider selection of characters arose than Code 39 could provide and is used in the shipping industry when label size is an issue. Code 128 is gaining wide acceptance as the international standard container code, as it uniquely identifies each container in a shipment and improves routing and traceability. Code 128 allows manufacturers and distributors to provide container identification from production to point of sale. UCC 128 is used in conjunction with an EDI Advance Ship Notice (ASN) that precisely identifies carton contents.

It is projected that over 90 percent of all shipments in the medical, retail, apparel, and wholesale drug industry will use Code 128 symbology to track expiration dating, lot numbers, and production dates.[14]

Interleaved 2 of 5 is another symbology commonly used in the shipping industry. It is a very compact symbology that is widely used on corrugated boxes for shipment to retailers. The Interleaved 2 of 5 is a one-dimensional code that records a 10-digit numeric value.

PDF 417 is a two-dimensional, high-density, nonlinear symbology that has substantial data capacity. The PDF is really a Portable Data File as opposed to being simply a reference number. PDF 417 utilizes a stacked matrix design that can store 1800 characters per inch.

Table 7-6 presents an overview of common bar codes along with their relative strengths and weaknesses. Bar code development and applications are increasing at a very rapid rate. Table 7-7 summarizes the benefits and opportunities available through Auto ID technologies. While the benefits are obvious, it is not clear which symbologies will be adopted as industry standards. Standardization and flexibility are desirable to accommodate the needs of a wide range of industries, but they also increase cost, making it more difficult for small- and medium-size shippers, carriers, and receivers to

---

[14]For a discussion of bar coding and scanning trends, see Rick Gurin, "Scanning Technologies Adapt to Changing Times," *Automatic I.D. News,* December 1999, p. 28.

TABLE 7-6   **Comparison of Common Bar Codes**

Background	Strengths	Weaknesses
Datamatrix (Datacode)		
• Developed for small-item marking	• Readable with relatively low contrast • Density for small numbers of characters	• Limited error correction capability • Proprietary code • Not laser readable • Only readable with expensive area scanner
Codablock 39/128		
• Developed in Europe	• Straightforward decoding based on one-dimensional symbology • Public domain	• No error correction • Low density • Does not support full ASCII
Code 1		
• Most recent matrix code	• Best error correction capability of matrix codes • Public domain	• Limited industry exposure • Not laser readable • Only readable with expensive area scanner
Code 49		
• Developed for small-item marking	• Readable with current laser scanners • Public domain	• No error correction • Low capacity
Code 16K		
• Developed for small-item marking	• Readable with current laser scanners	• No error correction • Low capacity
PDF 417		
• Developed to represent large amounts of data in small physical areas • Reduces reliance on EDI (knowledge travels with the labor)	• Dramatically increased capacity • Error correction capability • Reads information vertically and horizontally • Public domain	• Requires technological development to reduce scanning cost • Testing required for highly advanced applications

Notes: *Capacity* refers to the number of characters that can be coded within a specific area.
Public domain means that the code can be used freely without paying royalties.
Error correction means that coding errors can be identified and corrected.

implement standardized technologies. Finally, while continued convergence to common standards is likely, surveys indicate that select industries and major shippers will continue to use proprietary codes to maximize their competitive position.

Another key component of Auto ID technology is the **scanning process,** which represents the eyes of a bar code system. A scanner optically collects bar code data and converts it to usable information. There are two types of scanners: handheld and fixed position. Each type can utilize contact or noncontact technology. Handheld scanners are either laser guns (noncontact) or wands (contact). Fixed position scanners are either automatic scanners (noncontact) or card readers (contact). Contact technologies require the reading device to actually touch the bar code. A contact technology reduces scanning errors but decreases flexibility. Laser gun technology is the most popu-

---

TABLE 7-7   Benefits of Automatic Identification Technologies

Shippers	Warehousing
Improve order preparation and processing	Improved order preparation, processing, and shipment
Eliminate shipping errors	Provide accurate inventory control
Reduce labor time	Customer access to real time information
Improve record keeping	Access considerations of information security
Reduce physical inventory time	Reduced labor costs
Carriers	**Wholesalers/Retailers**
Freight bill information integrity	Unit inventory precision
Customer access to real time information	Price accuracy at point-of-sale
Improved record keeping of customer shipment activity	Improved register checkout productivity
Shipment traceability	Reduced physical inventory time
Simplified container processing	Increased system flexibility
Monitor incompatible products in vehicles	
Reduced information transfer time	

---

lar scanner technology currently in use, outpacing wands as the most widely installed technology.[15]

Scanner technology has two major applications in logistics. The first is Point-of-Sale (POS) in retail stores. In addition to ringing up receipts for consumers, retail POS applications provide accurate inventory control at the store level. POS allows precise tracking of each Stock Keeping Unit (SKU) sold and can be used to facilitate inventory replenishment. In addition to providing accurate resupply and marketing research data, POS can provide more timely strategic benefits to all channel members.

The second logistics scanner application is for materials handling and tracking. Through the use of scanner guns, materials handlers can track product movement, storage location, shipments, and receipts. While this information can be tracked manually, it is very time-consuming and subject to error. Wider usage of scanners in logistical applications will increase productivity and reduce errors. The demand for faster and less error-prone scanning technology drives rapid changes in the marketplace for applications and technology.[16]

Summary

Supply chain information systems link logistics activities in an integrated process based on four levels of functionality. The transaction system provides the foundation by electronically taking the order, initiating order selection and shipment, and completing appropriate financial transactions. Management control systems record functional and firm operating performance and provide appropriate management reporting.

---

[15]For more detailed information regarding bar coding processes, hardware, and cases, see the Symbol Technology website at **www.symbol.com.**

[16]Rick Gurin, op. cit., pp. 28–9.

Decision analysis systems assist management in the identification and evaluation of logistics alternatives. Strategic planning systems provide top management with insight regarding the impact of strategic changes such as mergers, acquisitions, and competitive actions. While the transaction system provides the foundation, management control, decision analysis, and strategic planning systems are becoming critical for high-performance supply chain management.

ERP or legacy systems are the backbone of most SCIS because of their integrated database capabilities and modular transactions. The communication systems facilitate information exchange internally within the firm's functions as well as externally across global sites and with other supply chain partners. The execution systems are becoming more critical for controlling warehouse and transportation operations. Supply chain planning systems will likely become the critical competitive differentiator for the future as firms strive to improve their asset productivity through reduced inventory and physical assets.

There are three alternative approaches for obtaining supply chain hardware, software, and support. While direct ownership remains common, outsourcing and the use of ASPs are becoming increasingly popular. Outsourcing turns over the entire information technology responsibility to an outside service provider, while an ASP uses the Internet to access key software applications, particularly for communications and planning.

Remarkable advances have been made to facilitate logistical communication both within a given firm and among its supply chain partners. EDI, satellite, and more recently XML continue to enable quicker and more consistent communication between supply chain partners. Other technologies, such as bar coding, scanning, and radio frequency, are substantially enhancing the communication effectiveness between logistics information systems and the physical environment in which they must operate.

The increasing accessibility and capabilities of these information and communication systems substantially increase the availability and accuracy of supply chain information. Communication technology advances have dramatically reduced the uncertainty between large firms, but substantial opportunities remain for improved communications between smaller firms which make up the majority of supply chain participants. While further communication system improvement will continue to reduce uncertainty, it is likely that major opportunities for future performance enhancers will be through supply chain analysis and strategic planning systems.

Challenge Questions

1. Compare and contrast the role of ERP systems and planning systems in enhancing firm performance and competitiveness.

2. Compare and contrast the role of ERP systems and logistics execution systems.

3. Compare and contrast the role of supply chain ERP systems and advanced planning and scheduling systems in enhancing firm and supply chain competitiveness.

4. How can smaller firms remain competitive in the exchange of logistics information?

5. Discuss and compare the role that EDI and the Internet will play in facilitating communication between supply chain partners.

6. Compare and contrast the role of EDI and the Internet for logistics and supply chain information exchange.

7. Describe and contrast the role of RFDC and RFID for logistics and supply chain applications.

8. Discuss the relative benefits of software purchase, use of third-party providers, and use of application service providers.

9. Compare and contrast the benefits and risks of firm level, industry level, and cross-industry trade portals.

10. Discuss the relative differences between contact and noncontact scanning.

8   Enterprise Resource Planning and Execution Systems

Enterprise Resource Planning (ERP) and enterprise execution systems are the major software components of logistics information systems. ERP provides the database and the transaction capability to initiate, track, monitor, and report on customer and replenishment orders. ERP systems provide firms with information consistency, economies of scale, and integration. ERP system design includes the central database and application modules to facilitate supply chain, financial, and human resource management. Supply chain system design includes components for planning/coordination, operations, and inventory deployment. The planning/coordination component manages firm and supply chain resources including production, storage, and transportation resources. The operations component controls transaction processing to initiate, manage, fulfill, and ship both customer and replenishment orders. Inventory deployment manages firm and increasingly supply chain inventory resources.

Enterprise execution systems provide the interface between the ERP and the day-to-day operations with the customer, transportation, and the warehouse. Customer relationship management systems offer insight regarding the firm's activity level and performance with key customers. Transportation management systems initiate shipments and record movements to monitor the firm's transportation performance and cost. Warehouse management systems initiate warehouse activities, control material handling equipment, monitor labor performance, and report warehouse performance levels and cost.

Rationale for ERP Implementation

When firms introduced extensive computing to control and monitor operations and financials in the early 1970s, much of the development was completed piecemeal. The financial and accounting systems were typically introduced first, followed by some type of sales and order management system. When additional functionality was needed, other applications were developed or purchased. These added modules frequently used inconsistent processes, conflicting assumptions, and redundant data. In some cases functional systems were developed internally by the firm to fit internal work processes. The result was a series of *legacy* systems that incorporated much of the firm's history regarding processes and information but was unique in terms of processes, capabilities, and features. Since processing and storage hardware were often very expensive at the time these legacy systems were introduced, their developers often used sophisticated and complex programming techniques to minimize storage and run-time requirements. As an example, many of these legacy systems included programs with the *Year 2000 Millennium Bug* (Y2K) embedded into the operating logic. By only storing two digits of the year, less disk storage was required to store dates, thus reducing the cost of the technology. This combination of events relating to legacy systems along with the availability of relatively inexpensive information-storage technology caused firms to reinvest in their enterprise systems during the 1990s. Firms were also looking to enhance their internal integration. While the capabilities of the new technologies are certainly well beyond those of the original legacy systems, the costs of implementation are quite substantial—exceeding millions or tens of millions of dollars in some cases. At this point, most if not all of the Fortune 1000 firms either have implemented or are in the process of implementing an ERP system and there is substantial growth potential in the market for ERP systems for small and mid-level firms. Regardless of the size of the firm, such investments are typically rationalized through three factors: consistency, economies of scale, and integration.

Consistency

As discussed earlier, many firms or divisions of firms developed legacy systems to meet their own specific requirements and processes. This was also true for international divisions as the firm extended markets and operations globally. Similarly, the many acquisitions and mergers that occurred during the 1980s and 1990s brought together firms with incompatible legacy systems. The result was many different systems that provided different and, in many cases, inconsistent processing. One manager from

TABLE 8-1   Typical Legacy System Status

	Region/Division A	Region/Division B	Region/Division C	Region/Division D
Financial	FS1	FS2	FS3	FS4
Human Resource	HR1	HR2	HR3	HR4
Order Management	OM1	OM2	OM2	OM3
Warehouse Management	WM1	WM1	WM2	WM3
Materials Planning	MP1	MP1	MP2	MP2

a consumer products multinational reported that he had to look into 15 different computer systems to determine the sales and inventory situation for their South American subsidiaries![1] Table 8-1 illustrates a situation in which each division or region has a different financial (FS), human resource (HR), order management (OM), warehouse management (WM), and materials planning (MP) system. The table indicates how each region or division might have a different software or hardware platform for various supply chain and other applications. Region A has implemented Financial System 1 while Region B has implemented Financial System 2 because of its currency capabilities. Similarly divergent systems decisions are often made for other regions or divisions. The table illustrates the situation in many firms where some system components are common across multiple divisions while others, such as order management, are unique for each division.

The result is inconsistent and conflicting information and multiple systems that are difficult to maintain and complex to interpret as the timing and processes may be different for each.

Thus, the first major ERP objective is to create a system that utilizes consistent data and processes for firm regions and divisions globally. In the typical application, the data is resident in a common data warehouse that can be accessed globally. In addition, the data can be modified with appropriate security and controls using transactions available in multiple languages. The transactions to initiate a specific supply chain activity are implemented using common assumptions and timing. Likewise, consistent processes allow global customers to use the same order entry procedure, for example, regardless of where they enter the order. Such a unified perspective offers senior management a consistent integrated view of the firm and operating management and ease of use by customers.

Economies of Scale

As firms merged and expanded globally, management made increasing demands to take advantage of global scale economies through resource rationalization. Similarly, customers began looking for suppliers that could provide product globally using consistent system capabilities and interfaces to take advantage of scale economies. ERP offers firms potential economies of scale in several ways. First, a

---

[1]Discussion with a Johnson & Johnson logistics manager.

single centralized processor or network of decentralized processors with common configured hardware offers the potential for substantial procurement and maintenance scale economies.

Second, the centralized ERP approach offers significant software scale economies since only a limited number of software licenses are necessary with all divisions and regions using the same application. While the initial software license cost might be substantial, the license and maintenance fees for the single ERP application should be less than the multiple copies required for each division or region. However, the real scale economy benefits result from the reduced personnel required to implement and maintain a common ERP system. Multiple divisional or regional systems require many individuals with varying hardware and software expertise to implement, maintain, and modify each application. Since some knowledge has limited transferability across hardware and software platforms, the expertise of the individuals typically cannot be used effectively. While potential scale economies for ERP expertise do exist, they may not be apparent today as relatively few individuals have developed extensive skills and they are highly sought after as employees.

Finally, the centralized ERP approach increases the potential for a multidivisional firm to implement shared resources and services across divisions or even regions. The ability to review the production, storage, or transportation resource requirements of multiple divisions in the common system increases the potential for sharing of critical resources. The integrated information facilitates use of common suppliers, production facilities, storage facilities, or transportation equipment, resulting in substantial potential for negotiating and operating economies.

While there is not adequate evidence that current ERP implementations are yielding these scale economies, the benefits will likely begin to accrue as the relatively recent implementations stabilize.

Integration

The final ERP benefit is enhanced system integration both within the firm and enterprise and between suppliers and customers. Internal integration results from a common integrated database and implementation of common processes across divisions and regions. Typical common processes included in ERP are order entry, order processing, warehouse management, invoicing, and accounting. Such commonality offers the capability to merge processes and provide major customers with a common and consistent interface with the firm. Such integration also results in standard financial practices across business units. The standardized interfaces offered by many ERP systems also facilitate external communication with supply chain partners. For example, many firms in the automobile and chemical industries are standardizing on the ERP system offered by SAP. The major manufacturers are then asking their suppliers to interface with their SAP database to obtain requirements data and to provide release schedules. Such information and process integration substantially enhances supply chain information sharing, which reduces uncertainty within the firm and between supply chain partners.

Most industry analysts believe that an ERP system should be thought of as a necessary cost of doing business. One ERP provider noted:

> I think most people would have a hard time providing an ROI number for an ERP system. A fact of business is that you might be able to run a $10 million company on a PC, but if

you want to grow to be a $50 million company, you need an ERP. The trick is to purchase a system that will scale up as you grow.[2]

The growth in ERP implementations has slowed among large firms as most absorb and refine what they have implemented. In contrast, smaller firms are just beginning their investment and implementation.

A new generation of ERP systems is evolving to provide additional integration, particularly with customers. These systems, identified as ERP II, integrate traditional ERP along with a Customer Relationship Management (CRM) system to better integrate the requirements of key customers with the firm's supply chain plans. The major improvement offered through ERP II is the external connectivity that is so critical for supply chain collaboration. It is also becoming more common for these integrated applications to be accessed via the Internet, thus providing a common global interface.[3]

ERP System Design

Figure 8-1 illustrates an ERP system's major modules. The center of the system is the central database or information warehouse where all information is maintained to facilitate access to common and consistent data by all modules. Surrounding the database are the functional modules that initiate and coordinate business activities. Although total ERP benefits can best be achieved when all functions are integrated into a common application, many firms elect to implement systems using a modular approach to spread resource requirements and minimize risk as a limited number of firm functions are in transition at any time.

Central Database

The **central database** is the relational information repository for the entire ERP system. The central database is described as relational because it relates or links information regarding operational entities so that there is minimal information redundancy in the database. Over time, information redundancy usually leads to inaccuracy because one reference to a data item is eventually changed without a comparable change in the other reference. For example, if a customer address is contained in two different locations in the database, it is likely that eventually one reference will be changed if the customer moves but the second reference will be forgotten. At that point, the database would no longer be consistent and all references to the second address would be incorrect.

Some ERP applications use a proprietary data structure that limits access. In these cases, all communication with the database must be accomplished through the ERP. Having the ERP system act as an interface doesn't have to be a problem, but it may reduce flexibility and data consistency. In most cases, however, the database structure uses one of several *open database architectures* that can be accessed by other systems. An open database architecture means that the interface is publicly defined and documented and can be used by a range of other applications. Public definition means that the software developer has publicly documented the database structure and contents so

---

[2]Anonymous, "Who's Using ERP," *Modern Materials Handling* 54, no. 13 (November 1999) pp. 14–18.
[3]Michel Roberto, "ERP Gets Redefined," *Information Technology for Manufacturing,* February 2001, pp. 36–44.

FIGURE 8-1

ERP architecture

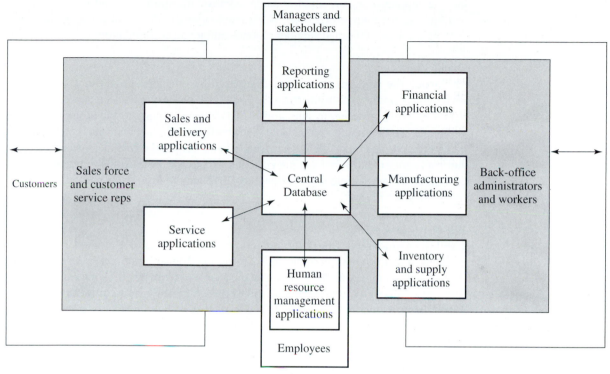

Source: Thomas H. Davenport, "Putting the Enterprise into the Enterprise System," *Harvard Business Review,* July/August 1998, p. 124. Reprinted with permission.

that other software providers can access, change, and report the data in the central database. Although the central database is extensive and can contain millions of data items in numerous files, eight major data files are critical to logistics operations: (1) customer file, (2) product file, (3) supplier file, (4) order file, (5) bill-of-materials file, (6) purchase order file, (7) inventory file, and (8) history file.

Customer File

The **customer file** contains information describing the firm's customers. Each entry defines one customer, including name, address, billing information, ship-to location, company contact, price list, terms of sale, and special instructions. A common customer file is helpful particularly when multiple divisions of the firm serve the same customer.

Product File

The **product file** contains the information describing the products and services offered by the firm. Specific entries include product number, description, physical characteristics, purchase source or manufacturing location, references to equivalent products or updates, and standard cost data. The price file or related file also contains information regarding prices and quantity breaks. Product file maintenance is increasingly challenging due to shorter product life cycles and more frequent price changes.

Supplier File

The **supplier file** lists the firm's suppliers for materials and services. Specific entries include supplier number, supplier name, address, transportation and receiving information, and payables instructions. A common supplier file is critical to achieve purchasing economies through supplier rationalization and consolidation.

Order File

The **order file** contains the information regarding all open orders that are in some stage of processing or fulfillment by the firm. Each order represents a current or potential request by a customer to ship product. The order file contains the customer number and name, the requested receipt date, and the list of products and quantities that are being ordered. The order file is increasingly being required to include special shipping and packaging requests for unique customers. The system must also increasingly accept orders from multiple sources including EDI and the Internet as well as by internal order entry.

Bill-of-Materials File

The **bill-of-materials file** describes how raw materials are combined for finished products. For example, a simple bill-of-materials for an automobile would indicate that one car requires one body, one chassis, four seats, one engine, one transaxle, and four tires. Although these product relationships are typically used in manufacturing, it is becoming increasingly important for logistics as well. Logistics operations are beginning to use bills of materials to facilitate packaging, customization, and kitting in distribution center operations.

Purchase Order File

The **purchase order (PO) file** is roughly comparable to the order file except that it contains the records of purchase orders that have been placed on suppliers. The purchase order may be for raw material to support product or for MRO (Maintenance, Repair, and Operating) supplies necessary to support operations and administration. MRO items are not directly included as finished products sold by the firm. Specific purchase order file information includes purchase order number, supplier number and name, request date, ship-to location, transportation mode and carrier, and a list of the items to be purchased and the corresponding quantity. Other critical requirements of the PO file are the product specifications, delivery requirements, and contracted price.

Inventory File

The **inventory file** records the physical inventory or quantity of product that the firm has available or may be available in the future based on current production schedules. The file also documents the physical location of the product within the material storage and facility; the product status in terms of available to ship, damaged, quality hold, or on-hold for a key customer; and lot numbers for products that must be tracked. Specific inventory file information includes product number, facility location, storage location, and inventory quantity for each product status.

History File

The **history file** documents the firm's order and purchase order history to facilitate management reporting, budget and decision analyses, and forecasting. In essence, this file contains summaries of the customer orders that have been filled and the purchase orders that have been received.

Supply Chain Applications

The ERP supply chain applications include the modules labeled *inventory and supply applications, manufacturing applications,* and *sales and delivery applications* in Figure 8-1. These three modules support supply chain activity, including raw materials acquisition, production, and customer order fulfillment. These modules incorporate the transactions and processes that initiate the entire range of supply chain activities. The specific processes and activities are discussed following this modular overview.

Financial Applications

The financial module incorporates the transactions necessary to maintain the firm's financial and accounting records. Specifically, the module maintains the contents and references to the firm's general ledger and tracks payables and receivables. The module also facilitates the development of standardized income statements and balance sheets for divisions, geographic regions, or for the entire global operation. The typical transactions include accounts receivable and payable, invoicing, financial accounting, and management reporting.

Service Applications

The service module supports postsales product service and warranty support. Customers of expensive capital equipment such as manufacturing, medical, communication, or transportation equipment require strong after-sales support for maintenance and repair. The system has to track equipment types and versions to ensure that the correct repair parts are available and can be dispatched to the required location quickly. The service module can also track usage and repair records to anticipate potential problems with preventative maintenance or equipment adjustment.

Human Resource Applications

The human resource module tracks employee records, assignments, and performance. This information is used to support payroll, tax, and work history documentation. In addition to the typical human resource applications, this module aids in costing supply chain activities by tracking time individuals spend on an order, an activity, or a process. Detailed activity tracking allows supply chain managers to determine the relative expense associated with customized or specialized cost of manufacturing and service.

Reporting Applications

The reporting module generates the standard and customized management reports for monitoring, performance measurement, and decision support. Using the central data warehouse, these report applications provide management with the capability to monitor activity levels and identify performance deficiencies and issues.

Common ERP Systems

Just as in manufacturing, the software industry, particularly for ERP software, is experiencing substantial consolidation. The result is that there are fewer and larger providers of ERP software. While a limited number of providers focus their efforts on

FIGURE 8-2

Enterprise application market 2000

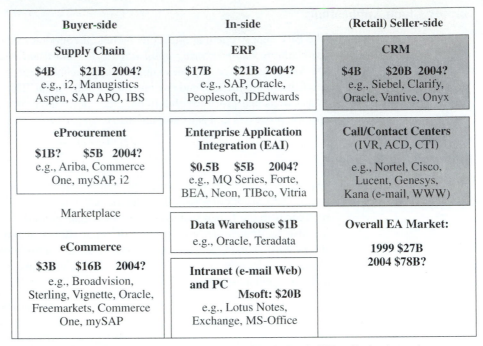

Buyer-side	In-side	(Retail) Seller-side
Supply Chain **$4B $21B 2004?** e.g., i2, Manugistics Aspen, SAP APO, IBS	**ERP** **$17B $21B 2004?** e.g., SAP, Oracle, Peoplesoft, JDEdwards	**CRM** **$4B $20B 2004?** e.g., Siebel, Clarify, Oracle. Vantive. Onyx
eProcurement **$1B? $5B 2004?** e.g., Ariba, Commerce One, mySAP, i2	**Enterprise Application Integration (EAI)** **$0.5B $5B 2004?** e.g., MQ Series, Forte, BEA, Neon, TIBco, Vitria	**Call/Contact Centers** (IVR, ACD, CTI) e.g., Nortel, Cisco, Lucent, Genesys, Kana (e-mail, WWW)
Marketplace	**Data Warehouse $1B** e.g., Oracle, Teradata	**Overall EA Market:** **1999 $27B** **2004 $78B?**
eCommerce **$3B $16B 2004?** e.g., Broadvision, Sterling, Vignette, Oracle, Freemarkets, Commerce One, mySAP	**Intranet (e-mail Web) and PC** **Msoft: $20B** e.g., Lotus Notes, Exchange, MS-Office	

Source: Peter Stedden at **http://www.dis.unimeld.edu.au/ staff/peter/enterprise%20 applications/enterprise application market summary 2000. ppt.**

specialized industries, most of the major systems incorporate a broad range of functions and features and market to a broad range of industries. Figure 8-2 summarizes the key components of enterprise software applications.[4] (The figure includes all major modules described in Figure 7-3.) For each enterprise application module, Figure 8-2 lists the current and estimated market size for 2004 along with the major software providers. The projections indicate the major growth modules to be CRM, supply chain, and e-commerce. This suggests that firms want to enhance their supply chain analysis, collaboration, and coordination capability over the next few years. The evaluation, selection, and implementation of an ERP package for a firm is a demanding, time-consuming, and usually expensive process. The evaluation must consider the fit of ERP to the firm's strategy, the functions and features, ongoing support, and, of course, the cost. Industry Insight 8-1 discusses some of the checks and balances that must be made before adopting an ERP system. A comprehensive evaluation of alternative ERP systems is beyond the scope of this text; however, software evaluation firms, such as AMR and Gardner Group, provide comprehensive assessments for their customers.

Supply Chain System Design

The supply chain information system is the backbone of modern logistics operations. In the past, this infrastructure focused on initiating and controlling activities required

---

[4]For a more detailed discussion of the relative capabilities of ERP software, see Eryn Brown, "The Best Software Business That Bill Gates Doesn't Own," *Fortune,* 136, no. 12 (December 1997), pp. 242–50.

INDUSTRY INSIGHT 8-1   THE CHALLENGES OF IMPLEMENTING AN ERP SYSTEM

Enterprise systems seem to be a dream come true. These commercial software packages promise the seamless integration of all the information flowing through a company—financial and accounting information, human resource information, supply chain information, customer information. For managers who have struggled with incompatible information systems and inconsistent operating practices, the promise of an off-the-shelf solution to the problem of business integration is enticing.

However, the growing number of horror stories about failed or out of control projects should certainly give managers pause. FoxMeyer Drug argues that its system helped drive it into bankruptcy. Dow Chemical spent 7 years and almost half a billion dollars implementing a mainframe system, only to start over again.

Some of the blame for such debacles lies in the enormous technical challenges; these systems are profoundly complex pieces of software, and installing them requires large investments of money, time, and expertise. But the technical challenges are not the main reason these systems fail. The biggest problems are business problems. Companies fail to reconcile the technological imperatives of the enterprise system with the business needs of the enterprise itself.

An enterprise system imposes its own logic on a company's strategy, organization, and culture. It pushes a company toward full integration even when a certain degree of business-unit segregation may be in its best interests. And it pushes a company to generic processes even when customized processes may be a source of competitive advantage. An enterprise system is, after all, a generic solution and reflects a series of assumptions about the way companies operate in general.

Imagine, for example, an industrial products manufacturer that has built its strategy around its ability to provide extraordinary customer service in filling orders for spare parts. Because it is able to consistently delivery parts 25 percent faster than competitors, it has gained a loyal clientele willing to pay a premium price. If, after installing an ERP, the company has to follow a more rational but less flexible process for filling orders, its core source of advantage is at risk. This danger becomes all the more pressing as it is now common for a single ERP package to be used by virtually every company in an industry. Such convergence around a single package should raise sobering questions in the minds of chief executives: How similar can our information flows be to those of our competitors before we begin to undermine our own sources of differentiation in the market?

Enterprise systems also have a direct, and often paradoxical, impact on a company's organization and culture. On the one hand, by providing universal real time access to data, the systems allow companies to streamline management structures, creating flatter, more flexible, and more democratic organizations. On the other hand, they also involve centralization of control over information and standardization of processes, which are characteristics of hierarchical organizations with uniform cultures.

For multinational corporations there is another important question: How much uniformity should exist in the way it does business in different regions or different countries? This is perhaps the most difficult challenge for a manager implementing an ERP: Corporate and business unit managers must sit down together, well before system implementation begins, to think through each major type of information and each major process in the company. Difficult questions need to be raised: How important is it for us to process orders in a consistent manner worldwide? Do we need to extend the system across all our functions, or should we implement only certain modules? Would it be better to roll the system out globally or restrict it to certain regional units? Does the term "customer" mean the same thing in every business unit? Answering such questions is essential to making an ERP successful.

Source: Thomas H. Davenport, "Putting the Enterprise into the Enterprise System," *Harvard Business Review,* July/August 1998, pp. 121–31.

FIGURE 8-3

Supply chain system
architecture

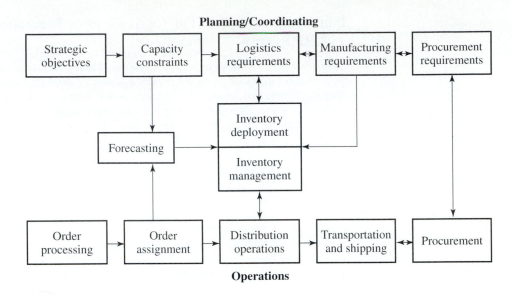

to take, process, and ship customer orders. For today's enterprises to remain competitive, the role of information infrastructure must be extended to include requirements planning, management control, decision analysis, and integration with other members of the supply chain.

While Figure 8-1 illustrates the supply chain modules relative to the other ERP modules, it does not describe the detailed flow of supply chain information and product through the process modules. Figure 8-3 repeats Figure 2-3 to illustrate the information flow and the relationship between key process modules. The key processes initiate, monitor, and measure activities required to fulfill customer and replenishment orders. These processes take two forms. The first are the planning and coordination processes to produce and deploy inventory. The second are the operating processes to receive, process, ship, and invoice customer orders.

Planning and coordination include the processes necessary to schedule and coordinate procurement, production, and logistics resource allocation throughout the enterprise. Specific components include definition of strategic objectives, rationalization of capacity constraints, and determination of market/distribution, manufacturing, and procurement requirements.

Operations include the processes necessary to manage customer order fulfillment, including order processing, inventory assignment, distribution operations, transportation operations, and procurement coordination. These processes are completed for both customer and replenishment orders. Customer orders reflect demands placed by enterprise customers. Replenishment orders initiate finished goods movement between manufacturing and distribution facilities.

Inventory deployment and management is the interface between planning/coordination and operations that controls the cycle and safety inventory stock whenever a Make-to-Order (MTO) or Assemble-to-Order (ATO) strategy is not possible. When an enterprise is able to utilize an MTO manufacturing strategy, the planning/coordination and operations processes essentially mirror each other. For example, when an MTO strategy is possible, it may not be necessary to schedule anticipatory raw materials and production or maintain buffer inventory.

Planning/Coordination

Supply chain system **planning/coordination components** form the information system foundation for manufacturers and merchandisers. These components define core activities that guide enterprise resource allocation and performance from procurement to product delivery.

As illustrated in Figure 8-2, planning/coordination includes materials planning processes both within the enterprise and between supply chain partners. The specific components are (1) strategic objectives; (2) capacity constraints; (3) logistics requirements; (4) manufacturing requirements; and (5) procurement requirements.

Strategic Objectives

Primary information drivers for many enterprises are strategic objectives that define marketing and financial goals. These strategic objectives are typically developed for a multiyear planning horizon that often includes quarterly updates. Marketing's strategic objectives define target markets, product development, marketing mix plans, and the role of logistics value-added activities such as service levels or capabilities. The objectives include customer scope, breadth of products and services, planned promotions, and desired performance levels. Marketing goals are the customer service policies and objectives that define logistics and supply chain activity and performance targets. The performance targets include service availability, capability, and quality elements discussed earlier. Financial strategic objectives define revenue, financial and activity levels and corresponding expenses, as well as capital and human resource constraints.

The combination of marketing and financial objectives defines the scope of markets, products, services, and activity levels that logistics and supply chain managers must accommodate during the planning horizon. Specific goals include projected annual or quarterly activity levels such as revenue, shipments, and case volume. Events that must be considered include product promotions, new product introductions, market rollouts, and acquisitions. Ideally, the marketing and financial plans should be integrated and consistent as inconsistencies result in poor service, excess inventory, or failure to meet financial goals.

The combination of marketing and financial objectives provides direction for other enterprise plans. While the process of establishing strategic objectives is, by nature, unstructured and wide ranging, it must develop and communicate a plan detailed enough to be operationalized.

Capacity Constraints

Logistics and manufacturing capacity limitations are imposed by internal and external manufacturing, warehousing, and transportation resource constraints. Based on the activity levels defined by the strategic objectives, these constraints determine material bottlenecks and guide resource allocation to meet market demands. For each product, capacity constraints influence the where, when, and how much for production, storage, and movement. The constraints consider aggregate limitations such as periodic production, movement, and storage capacities.

Capacity problems can be resolved by resource acquisition or speculation/postponement of production or delivery. Capacity adjustments can be made by acquisition or alliances such as contract manufacturing or facility leasing. Speculation reduces bottlenecks by anticipating production capacity requirements through prior scheduling or contract manufacturing. Postponement delays production and shipment until specific requirements are known and capacity can be allocated. It may be necessary to offer customer incentives such as discounts or allowances to postpone customer delivery. The capacity limitations time phase the enterprise's strategic objectives by considering facility, financial, and human resource limitations. These constraints have a major influence on logistics, manufacturing, and procurement schedules.

Capacity limitations decompose the enterprise's aggregate operating plan to weekly or daily logistics requirements and determine the level of monthly or weekly production for each manufacturing location. Capacity flexibility depends on the nature of the product and lead time. For the long term, there is usually substantial flexibility since a full range of postponement, speculation, and acquisition strategies may be used. But in the short term, such as within the current week, there is limited flexibility since resources are generally committed. The ability to jointly consider the enterprise requirements and constraints is critical to effective supply chain planning and coordination. The best enterprises typically demonstrate a high level of integration across all planning/coordination components. The APS systems, discussed in detail in Chapter 9, offer the information support to effectively consider these capacity constraints.

Logistics Requirements

Logistics requirements include time phased facility, equipment, labor, and inventory resources necessary to accomplish the logistics mission. For example, the logistics requirement component schedules shipments of finished product from manufacturing plants to distribution centers and retailers. The shipment quantity is calculated as the difference between customer requirements and inventory level. Logistics requirements are often implemented using Distribution Requirements Planning (DRP) as an inventory management and process control tool. Future requirements are based on forecasts, customer orders, and promotions. Forecasts are based on sales and marketing input in conjunction with historical activity levels. Customer orders include current orders, future committed orders, and contracts. Promotional activity is particularly important when planning logistics requirements since it often represents a large percentage of variation in volume and has a large impact on capacity. Current inventory status is product available to ship. Figure 8-4 illustrates the computation for determining periodic logistics requirements.

Specifically, for each planning period, day, week, or month, the sum of forecast plus future customer orders plus promotional volume represents period demand. It is not easy to determine the percentage of the forecasted volume that is accounted for by known customer orders, so some judgment must be made. Typically, period demand is actually a combination of the three since current forecasts may incorporate some future orders and promotional volume. When determining period demand, it is important that the overlap between forecast, future customer orders, and promotions be considered. Period logistics requirements are then determined as the period demand less inventory-on-hand plus planned receipts. Using this form, each period would ideally

FIGURE 8-4
Logistics requirements

+ Forecasts (sales, marketing, input, histories, accounts)

+ Customer orders (current orders, future committed orders, contracts)

+ Promotions (promotion, advertising plans)

= Period demand

− Inventory-on-hand

− Planned receipts

Period logistics requirements

end with zero inventory available, so planned receipts would exactly equal period demand. While perfect coordination of demand and supply is ideal from an inventory management perspective, it may not be possible or the best strategy for the firm.

Logistics requirements must be synchronized within both capacity constraints and manufacturing capabilities to achieve optimal system performance; otherwise finished goods inventory accumulates at the end of the production line.

Manufacturing Requirements

Manufacturing requirements schedule production resources and attempt to resolve day-to-day capacity bottlenecks within the materials management system. Primary bottlenecks result from raw material shortages or daily capacity limitations. Manufacturing requirements determine the Master Production Schedule (MPS) and Manufacturing Requirements Plan (MRP). The MPS defines weekly or daily production and machine schedules. Given the MPS, MRP time phases the purchase and arrival of materials and components to support the desired manufacturing plan. Although this discussion presents logistics requirements and manufacturing requirements serially, they actually must operate in parallel. This is particularly true for enterprises utilizing demand flow or market-paced manufacturing strategies. These strategies coordinate production schedules directly with market demands or orders and reduce the need to forecast or plan. In a sense, demand flow or market-paced manufacturing strategies design all production as make to order and thus totally integrate logistics and manufacturing requirements.

Within limits, the *Dell model* of MTO computers illustrates a process that matches manufacturing with demand. However, even the Dell model must operate within capacity constraints within a limited time horizon. Figure 8-5 illustrates how the MRP relates to the DRP for a firm.

Procurement Requirements

Procurement requirements schedule material purchase order releases, shipments, and receipts. Procurement requirements build on capacity constraints, logistics requirements, and manufacturing requirements to determine long-term material requirements and release schedules. The requirement and release schedule is then used for purchasing negotiation, contracting, coordination of transportation equipment, and arrival scheduling.

Planning/Coordination Integration

While each planning/coordination component can and frequently has operated independently, such independence often leads to inconsistencies that create excess manufacturing and logistics inventory as well as operating inefficiencies. It was not uncommon for enterprises to have different forecasts for each functional module since each was controlled by a separate organizational function. For example, the strategic objectives may develop high forecasts to motivate the sales force while logistics may plan on more conservative forecasts. Similarly, differences between logistics, manufacturing, and procurement forecasts resulted in inconsistencies between product acquisition, production scheduling, and logistics deployment which in turn gave rise to unnecessary safety stocks to buffer independent operations. This is a characteristic of the *great divide* discussed in Chapter 6.

Historically, the individual planning/coordination processes had limited ability to plan within capacity constraints. Each planning process was essentially *uncapacitated* as though there were infinite capacity. In essence, the initial planning process did not

FIGURE 8-5

Requirements planning system overview

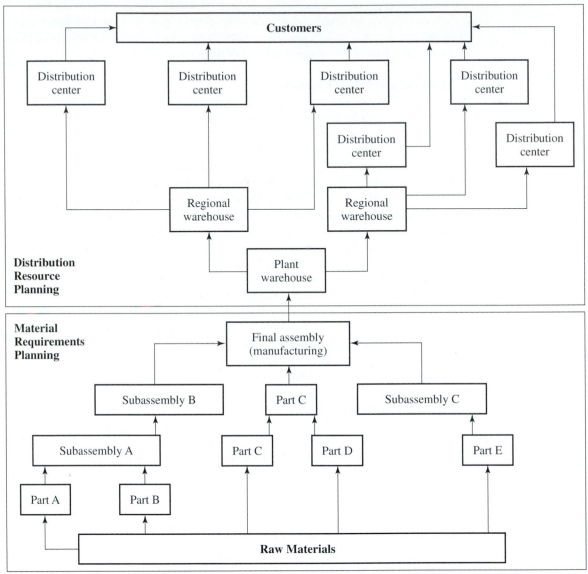

Source: Anonymous, "How DRP Helps Warehouses Smooth Distribution," *Modern Materials Handling* 39, no. 6 (April 1984), p. 53.

hold requirements, production, distribution, and transportation resources to any capacity constraints. Once the uncapacitated process was complete, heuristic processes were used to attempt to fit the demands within existing supply chain constraints. Eventually, more sophisticated planning tools were developed for each of the planning/coordination processes, resulting in a more direct treatment of resource capacity. However, capacity consideration seldom extended beyond the individual functional processes. For example, manufacturing developed a plan that was generally within its resource constraints and logistics did the same. But the resulting integrated plan seldom reflected the appropriate trade-offs between the two functional areas.

Enterprises are improving requirements and capacity coordination by enhancing forecast consistency and more integrated capacity consideration, resulting in lower inventories and better resource utilization. Increased coordination can be achieved through the use of common databases and forecasts, more frequent information exchange, and more sophisticated analysis tools. High-achieving logistics enterprises use planning/coordination integration as a major source of improved effectiveness.

Operations

Coordinated, integrated **operations information systems** are also essential for supply chain competitiveness. Coordination and integration facilitate smooth and consistent customer and replenishment order information flow throughout the enterprise and offer current order status visibility. Integrated information sharing reduces delays, errors, and resource requirements. The operations processes required for customer order fulfillment and to coordinate the receipt of purchase orders are (1) order processing, (2) order assignment, (3) distribution operations, (4) transportation, and (5) procurement.

Order Processing

Order processing is the entry point for customer orders and inquiries. It allows entry and maintenance of customer orders by using communication technologies such as mail, phone, fax, EDI, and the Internet. As orders or inquiries are received, order processing enters and retrieves required information, edits for appropriate values, and retains acceptable orders for assignment. Order processing can also offer information regarding inventory availability and delivery dates to establish and confirm customer expectations. Order processing, in conjunction with customer service representatives, forms the primary interface between the customer and the ERP or legacy system.

Table 8-2 lists primary order processing functionality. It includes entry for blanket, electronic, and manual orders. Blanket orders are large orders that reflect demand over an extended time period such as a quarter or year. Future shipments against blanket orders are triggered by individual order releases. Order processing creates and maintains the customer and replenishment order base that initiates remaining operations components.

Order Assignment

Order assignment allocates available inventory to open customer and replenishment orders. Assignment may take place in real time, as orders are received, or in a *batch mode*. Batch mode means that orders are grouped for periodic processing such as by day or shift. While real time allocation is more responsive, a batch process provides the firm with more control over situations when inventory is low. For example, in a batch process, order assignment can be designed to allocate stock from current inventory only or from scheduled production capacity. The operational system is more responsive if it allows inventory assignment from scheduled production quantities or capacity. Assignment of production quantities is referred to as using *available to promise* inventory, while assignment of production capacity refers to *capable to promise* inventory. However, there is a trade-off since assigning scheduled production capacity reduces the firm's ability to reschedule production. The best order assignment applications operate interactively in conjunction with order processing to generate an order solution that satisfies customer requirements within enterprise resource constraints. In this type of operational environment, the customer service representative and the customer interact to determine the combination of products, quantities, and

TABLE 8-2   Operations System Functionality

Order Processing	Order Assignment	Inventory Management	Distribution Operations	Transportation and Shipping	Procurement
Order entry (manual, electronic, blanket)	Create blanket order	Forecast analysis and modeling	Assign and track storage locations	Carrier selection	Match and pay
Credit check	Generate invoice	Forecast data maintenance and updates	Inventory cycle counting	Carrier scheduling	Open order review
Inventory availability	Generate order selection documents	Forecast parameter selection	Labor scheduling	Dispatching	Purchase order entry
Order acknowledgement	Inventory allocation	Forecast technique selection	Equipment scheduling	Document preparation	Purchase order maintenance
Order modification	Process blanket order	Inventory parameter selection	Lot control	Freight payment	Purchase order receipt
Order pricing	Release reserved inventory	Inventory simulation and testing	Order selection, location, replenishment	Performance measurement	Purchase order status
Order status inquiry	Reassign order source	Inventory requirements planning	Receiving	Shipment consolidation and routing	Quote request
Price and discount extension	Release blanket order	Promotion data integration	Putaway	Shipment rating	Requirements communication
Promotion check	Verify shipment	Replenishment order build, release, and scheduling	Storage	Shipment scheduling	Schedule receipt appointment
Returns processing		Define service objectives	Performance measurement	Shipment tracing and expediting	Supplier history
Service management				Vehicle loading	

performance cycle length that is acceptable for both parties. Possible solutions when there is conflict in order assignment include delivery date adjustments, product substitutions, or shipment from an alternative source.

Table 8-2 lists typical order assignment functionality, which includes inventory allocation, back-order creation and processing, order selection document generation, and order verification. Order selection documents, in paper or electronic form, direct distribution operations to select an order from the distribution center or warehouse and pack it for shipment. The customer or replenishment order, with its allocated inventory and corresponding order selection material, links order assignment with distribution center physical operations.

Distribution Operations

Distribution operations incorporate processes to guide distribution center physical activities, including product receipt, material movement and storage, and order selection. For this reason, they are often termed *inventory control* or *warehouse management systems* and sometimes *warehouse locator systems,* referring to the capability to track inventory storage locations in warehouses. Distribution operations direct all activities within distribution centers using a combination of batch and real time assignments. In a batch environment, the distribution operations system develops a "to do" list of instructions or tasks to guide each material handler in the warehouse. Material handlers are the individuals who operate equipment such as forklifts and pallet jacks. In a real time environment, information-directed technologies such as bar coding, radio frequency communication, and automated handling equipment operate interactively with the distribution operations process to reduce the elapsed time between decision and action. The real time information directed materials handling technologies, discussed in detail in Chapter 14, also must interface directly with the distribution operations process to provide operational flexibility and reduce internal performance cycle time requirements.

Table 8-2 lists typical distribution operations functionality. In addition to directing warehouse operations and activities, distribution operations must now also plan operating requirements and measure performance. Operations planning includes personnel and resource scheduling, including staff, equipment, and facility. Performance measurement includes developing personnel and equipment productivity reports.

Transportation and Shipping

Transportation and shipping processes, often referred to as the *Transportation Management System* (TMS), plan, execute, and manage transport and movement functions. The TMS includes shipment planning and scheduling, shipment consolidation, shipment notification, transport documentation generation, and carrier management. These processes facilitate efficient transport resource utilization as well as effective carrier management.

A unique characteristic of the TMS is that it often involves three parties—shipper, carrier, and consignee (recipient). To effectively manage the process, a basic level of information integration must exist. Information sharing requires standardized data formats for transport documents. In the United States, the Transportation Data Coordinating Committee (TDCC) and VICS have initiated and refined the standardization of transport document formats. These efforts to integrate transport documents with other commercial documents such as orders, invoices, and shipment notifications were discussed in Chapter 7.

Table 8-2 lists transportation and shipping functionality. The TMS generates the documentation to release the order for shipment and measures the enterprise's ability to satisfactorily deliver the order. Historically, the TMS focused on document generation and rate tracking. Transport documents include manifests and bills of lading, specifically discussed in Chapter 12; rates are the carrier charges incurred for product movement. The large numbers of shipments made by most enterprises require an automated and exception-driven TMS that can reduce errors and report performance. With the increased opportunity to enhance performance through better transport management, contemporary TMS functionality emphasizes performance monitoring, rate auditing, routing and scheduling, invoicing, reporting, and decision analyses. Advanced TMS applications incorporate increased planning and performance measurement capability and are being termed *enterprise execution systems,* which are discussed in the following section.

Procurement

Procurement manages PO preparation, modification, and release as well as tracks vendor performance and compliance. Although procurement systems have not traditionally been considered part of logistics systems, the importance of integrating procurement with logistics schedules is critical to facilitate the coordination of material receipt, facility capacity, and transportation backhaul.

For integrated supply chain management, procurement must track and coordinate receiving and shipping activities to optimize facility, transport, and personnel scheduling. For example, since loading and unloading docks are often a critical facility resource, an effective procurement system should coordinate the use of the same carrier for both deliveries and shipments. This capability requires the enterprise system to have both receipt and shipment visibility. Supply chain system integration can be further enhanced through electronic integration with suppliers. Table 8-2 lists procurement functionality. A state-of-the-art procurement system provides plans, directs activities, and measures performance, coordinating inbound and outbound activity movement.

Operational systems are typically well integrated, but it is necessary to continuously review systems to remove bottlenecks and enhance flexibility. An effective and efficient operations ERP system is essential for high-level firm performance, yet it alone will not move the firm into the high-performance category.

Inventory Deployment and Management

Inventory deployment and management serve as the primary interface between planning/coordination and operations by planning requirements and managing finished inventory from production until customer shipment. Specifically, where should finished inventory be moved through the supply chain? When should replenishment orders be placed? How much should be ordered? Firms with MTO materials systems have essentially integrated their planning/coordination and operations so there is minimal need for inventory deployment and management.

The first component of the inventory deployment and management system is the forecast process. The forecast process predicts product requirements by customer and distribution center to support enterprise planning.

The second module of inventory deployment and management is inventory allocation decision support ranging from simple reactive models to complex planning tools. The decision aids are necessary to guide inventory planners in deciding when and how much to order. Reactive models respond to current demand and inventory situations using reorder point and order quantity parameters. In other words, they make replenishment decisions by reacting to current inventory levels. Planning tools anticipate future requirements based on forecasts and cycle time projections. The planning tools allow managers to identify potential problems while they can still be resolved using proactive management.

Inventory deployment and management systems also differ in the amount of human interaction required. Some applications require inventory planners to manually place or approve all replenishment orders. Such systems are not exception-based since all replenishment orders require explicit planner approval. Manual approval-based systems require substantially more human resources but may incorporate better judgment. More sophisticated applications automatically place replenishment orders and monitor their progress through the replenishment cycle. The sophisticated applications illustrate a more exception-based philosophy since planners are required to intervene only for exceptional replenishment orders.

Primary drivers of inventory deployment and management are customer service objectives established by management. Service objectives define target fill rates for customers and products. The combination of service objectives, demand characteristics, replenishment characteristics, and operating policies determines the where, when, and how discussed above. Effective inventory deployment and management can significantly reduce the level of inventory assets required to meet specific service objectives.

In addition to initiating basic inventory decisions, inventory deployment and management must measure inventory performance by monitoring inventory level, turns, and productivity. Table 8-2 lists inventory deployment and management functionality for a relatively sophisticated logistics application. Note that the functionality includes a number of forecasting-related activities. Inventory deployment and management requires estimates of future demand in the form of implicit or explicit forecasts. Implicit, or default, forecasts assume that next month's sales will be the same as last month's sales. Explicit forecasts are developed more scientifically by using information about enterprise, customer, and competitor actions. The basic proposition is that more integrated forecast information facilitates inventory deployment and management and results in lower inventory requirements.

Since information technology is evolving much faster than most other logistics capabilities such as transportation and materials handling, new technologies must be constantly reviewed to determine potential logistics applications. It is impossible for a textbook to offer timely information regarding the status of all information technologies that may have logistics applications; however, there are several technologies that have demonstrated widespread logistics applications, such as those discussed next.

Enterprise Execution Systems

ERP systems are substantially enhancing process and information consistency and integration of supply chain operations. Yet the focus on integrated processes has generally reduced the system functionality and features, particularly for very operational elements such as warehouse and transportation management. While many ERP systems incorporate some warehouse and transportation management capability, they are often quite rudimentary or not *feature rich*. The result is that ERP modules are not capable of performing some of the major activities, particularly those focused on enhancing value, required to support supply chain operations. Enterprise execution systems, including CRM, TMS, and WMS, are evolving to meet these specific requirements.

Customer Relationship Management

CRM is designed to extend the functionality of the ERP sales and delivery applications as illustrated in Figure 8-6.[5] Firms are using CRM to transition from treating customers as income sources to be exploited to treating customers as assets to be nurtured. While the traditional sales and delivery application was designed to accept customer orders in a wide range of formats and allow those orders to be managed throughout the fulfillment process, a broader range of capabilities is necessary to manage the customer relationship. Beyond this basic functionality, CRM today requires sales tracking, sales history analysis, pricing management, promotion management, product mix management, and category management. In some cases, customers expect their supplier's

---

[5]For a more detailed discussion, see Charles Trepper, "Customer Care Goes End-to-End," *Information Week.com,* May 15, 2000, pp. 55–73.

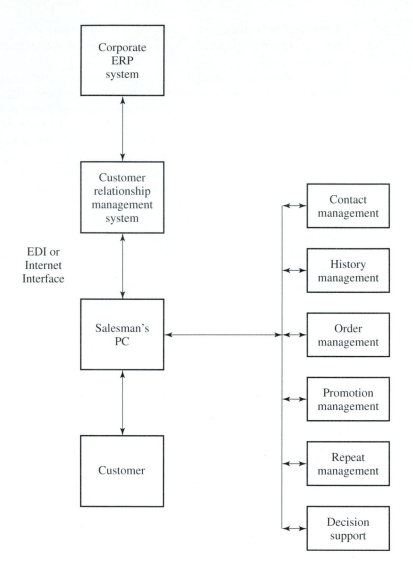

FIGURE 8-6

Typical customer relationship management extension system

sales force to manage the entire category of products at the customer's facility. For example, it is becoming more common for grocers to expect their suppliers to manage both the product mix and the shelf quantities for major product categories such as beverages and specialty products. This practice, termed *category management,* requires substantial information support from the manufacturer but also facilitates information sharing.

Transportation Management System

In general, the advanced TMS must proactively identify and evaluate alternative transportation strategies and tactics to determine the best methods to move product within the existing constraints. As shown in Table 8-3, this includes capabilities to select modes, plan loads, consolidate loads with other shippers, take advantage of current unbalances in traffic movement, route vehicles, and optimize use of transportation equip-

TABLE 8-3   Typical Transportation Management Execution System Functions

- Order consolidation
- Route optimization
- Carrier rate management
- EDI links with carriers
- Internet-based shipment tracking
- Integrated claims management
- Identify most economical mode: parcel, less-than-truckload, truckload, pool distribution, stops in transit
- Calculate best route
- Carrier selection based on cost and service including performance

ment. The principal deliverables of TMS are cost savings and increased functionality to provide credible ATP and CTP dates. Industry Insight 8-2 describes how a TMS was applied at Meldisco to drive down transportation cost.

Warehouse Management System

Historical warehouse system functionality focused on receiving replenishment shipments, stock putaway, and order picking. Figure 8-7 illustrates other traditionally standard activities under the category labeled *core WMS functionality.* (Chapter 13 discusses these specific activities in detail.) Warehouses today must offer a broader range of services as they are frequently performing some light manufacturing. They are also required to manage more inventory on a just-in-time basis. Figure 8-7 illustrates some of these activities as indicated by *advanced WMS functionality.* Yard management refers to the process of managing the vehicles and the inventory within vehicles while in the warehouse yard. Faster inventory turnover requires better visibility of inventory, even when in transportation vehicles. Labor management refers to maximizing the use of warehouse labor. Historically, warehouse labor has been quite specialized, allowing for relatively easy planning. Today, however, warehouse labor is expected to perform a wider range of activities to minimize the number of employees necessary at any given point in time. Warehouse optimization refers to selection of the best location within the warehouse for the storage and retrieval of product to minimize time and movement. *Value-Added Services* (VAS) refer to the coordination of warehouse activities to customize product, such as packaging, labeling, kitting, and setting up displays. Planned cross-docking and merging is the integration of two parts of a customer order that have been supplied from a different source without maintaining inventory. This strategy is sometimes used in the personal computer industry to merge a processing unit and the display monitor in a warehouse just prior to delivery to the ultimate customer. Since there is no inventory of either part in the warehouse, the merging activity requires precise timing and coordination. A final execution function is the capability to manage reverse logistics activities such as returns, repair, and recycling. Both customers and environmental interests are increasing their demands that supply chains can accommodate reverse logistics. Industry Insight 8-3 describes the use and benefits of a WMS for Moen.

INDUSTRY INSIGHT 8-2 MELDISCO: SOFTWARE DRIVES DOWN TRANSPORTATION COSTS

Meldisco is the lone supplier of shoes to Kmart stores worldwide. It acquired transportation management software in an effort to overhaul its supply chain management process to more effectively distribute product to stores.

In 1996, the company replaced four regional distribution centers (DCs), each of which received product from overseas and delivered direct to stores, with two new DCs. Now all shoes from overseas consolidators come to the Mira Loma, CA, facility, where they are cross-docked for shipment direct to stores, pools, or Meldisco's other DC in Gaffney, SC. The Mira Loma DC services about 25 percent of the chain, while Gaffney ships to the remainder.

Meldisco initially set out to find a system for automating freight claims. It soon saw the value of implementing a more robust transportation program that would manage inbound and outbound freight and interface with its WMS. Joe Bongiovanni, director of operations, states, "We wanted to be able to track our freight, not only within the four walls of the DC, but also outside."

The company began implementing the Metasys Enterprise Transportation Management system in February 1996. "About 80% of our product is coming from overseas, and one of our problems was that our receipts were heavily skewed to the first week of the month," says Bongiovanni. "Metasys provided the capability for leveling that inbound scheduling."

Metasys' MetaFreight module tracks inbound freight from the port at Mira Loma until its arrival at the DC, then hands off the information to Meldisco's WMS. Once product is loaded on the trailer, the WMS again interfaces with Metasys to track outbound freight.

Meldisco installed the Metasys software at its 45 third-party pool points across the country to alert when a truck is on the way. When it arrives, the pool scans the freight into the system. "There's a closed loop," says Bongiovanni. "What we ship and what they receive should be the same, and the system verifies that." Meldisco downloads the demand information to Metasys, which produces pick lists and sub-bills of lading at the pool points, telling when to ship product to specific stores. The system uploads this information to Medisco's WMS, which forwards it to the company's store information network to notify store managers of what's on the way.

Meldisco has seen a big increase in accuracy since it started testing Metasys' MetaPool module in June 1998. The company expects to raise the accuracy of its over, short, and damage forms from around 80 percent to approximately 98 percent. With more than 130 million pairs of shoes moving through Meldisco's pipeline annually, that translates into significant savings.

Anticipating fewer freight claim headaches, the pools provide Meldisco with a 1.5 percent reduction in carriers' rates. The company receives an additional 1 percent reduction from the pools by making invoiceless payments through the Metasys system. Another benefit directly attributed to having an automated in-transit tracking system is the ability to do postbilling to stores. "Prior to Metasys, when the product left the DC, it was billed immediately to the store," Bongiovanni explains. "It might be four or five days in transit, but it would already be showing on their books." Straightening out claims or shortages after the fact could be difficult, and often the shrinkage was eaten by the store.

Meldisco has dramatically improved the effectiveness and efficiency of its supply chain by implementing a TMS.

Source: Leslie Hansen Harps, "Warehouse Management Systems: What's Up with That?" *Inbound Logistics,* May 1999.

FIGURE 8-7

Typical warehouse management extension system

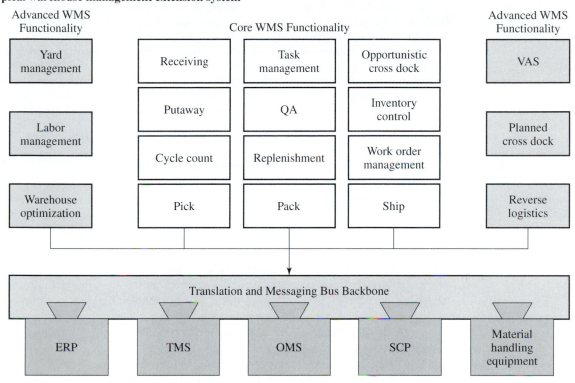

INDUSTRY INSIGHT 8-3 MOEN'S METHODS FOR SUPPLY CHAIN EXPANSION

"You can't do supply chain manually any longer," stated the vice president of logistics for Moen, a well-known manufacturer of kitchen faucets. As supply chain complexity increases through more unique customer requests, flexible and responsive systems are required to simultaneously meet specific customer requirements within the supply chain system constraints. When Moen's top management envisioned their customers' logistics requirements for the next 5 years, they anticipated the need for faster delivery, better fill rates, advanced shipping notices (ASN) via EDI, and a formal labeling system using UCC 128 transmissions. The company objective was to process one order, one shipment, and one invoice within 24 hours and have the product manufactured and arrive at the customer's location within 5 days.

To meet these service requirements, Moen investigated the use of a WMS to initiate and track warehouse activities, thereby enabling customers to scan the bar code on received goods, apply that data against the purchase order, and automatically update their inventories. The WMS was integrated with Moen's Order Management System (OMS) on its centralized computer. Moen sought to reduce safety stock to support production even as its product line was continuing to expand. The WMS helped achieve this reduction by facilitating make-to-order, which required supplying just the right parts on time to the in-house manufacturing sites.

Implementation of WMS taught Moen a number of lessons regarding information flow and accuracy. During the integration of the WMS with the OMS there were some unexpected data streams where the OMS had communicated with the previous warehouse system. Moen had to modify the legacy OMS to redirect or refine these communication streams to meet the expectations of WMS. Moen also quickly realized that accurate dimensional data on inventory is critical since picks, storage algorithms, and shipping software apply the product dimensions stored in the data files. Moen recalculated cube and weight for its products, resulting in improved data and better handling, shipping, and storage. Recently, a cube/weight device was added to automate this process.

Moen identified four major benefits resulting from the WMS implementation. First, the WMS in conjunction with the RFDC equipment made the entire process "paperless," which substantially increased timeliness, productivity, and accuracy. Second, the increased data accuracy resulting from the improved dimensional data enhanced the credibility of the planning process and provided better asset utilization for facilities and vehicles. Third, the WMS system increased product profiling accuracy, enhancing Moen's ability to make sure the right product mix is within the picking area to reflect customer changes over time. Lastly, the WMS reduced inventory levels by increasing certainty regarding product availability and status.

Source: Christopher Trunk, "How Moen Handles Supply Chain Expansion," *Supply Chain Flow Supplement,* June 1998, pp. 11–12.

Summary

The foundation of any firm's supply chain information system is the ERP and execution systems that provide the database and transaction systems to initiate and track supply chain activities. Firms continue to place a strong emphasis on ERP system implementation to achieve information consistency, economies of scale, and integration. These characteristics are becoming basic requirements for global commerce. A broad-based ERP system design includes an integrated database along with modules to support supply chain, service, and financial operations, and for human resource management.

Supply chain system design includes components for planning/coordination, operations, and inventory deployment. Based on the firm's strategic and marketing plans, the planning/coordination component manages the firm's production, storage, and movement capacities. The operations component provides the information transactions to initiate orders, assign inventory, select orders in the warehouse, transport, and invoice customer and replenishment orders. Based on sales and forecast levels, the inventory deployment component manages supply chain inventory to meet required service levels while minimizing inventory.

Enterprise execution systems interface the ERP system to the customer service, transportation, and warehouse functions. CRM provides detailed customer history and in-process activity information to sales and customer service personnel to reduce customers' uncertainty and enhance their success. A TMS tracks material movements and guides transportation resource utilization. A WMS initiates and controls warehouse activities and materials handling technology. Enterprise execution system capabilities are increasingly the differentiator in supply chain performance because they allow the firm to meet specific customer requirements.

While ERP systems provide the communications, process, and data infrastructure to conduct supply chain operations, insight and intelligence are needed to guide supply chain decisions. In Chapter 9, we will see how decision support is becoming more critical with the increasing scope and complexity of supply chain decisions.

Challenge Questions

1. Discuss the rationalization for ERP implementation by firms involved in supply chain management.

2. Discuss the major challenges a firm should expect when implementing an integrated ERP system, including financial, supply chain, service, and human resource applications.

3. Discuss how the planning/coordination and operation flow differs for MTO and MTS firms.

4. Compare and contrast the role of planning/coordination and operations in improving firm competitiveness.

5. Compare and contrast the drivers and the role of the MRP and the DRP systems.

6. Discuss why it is important to coordinate the arrival of procurement shipments with the dispatching of customer shipments.

7. Discuss the driver and role of the inventory deployment and management system.

8. Discuss the rationale and risks associated with using a common forecast to drive the firm's planning/coordination flow.

9. Discuss the role of the CRM system in enhancing the firm's competitiveness.

10. Discuss how advanced WMS functionality will change the role of the distribution center in the supply chain.

9 ADVANCED PLANNING AND SCHEDULING

Decision support is becoming more critical with the increasing scope and complexity of supply chain decisions. Decision Support Systems (DSS) guide managers and planners in the understanding and evaluation of complex supply chain alternatives. Specialized DSS, characterized as Advanced Planning and Scheduling (APS) systems, are necessary to help managers efficiently and effectively utilize key supply chain resources, including material, production, labor, facility, and transportation.

Rationale for Advanced Planning and Scheduling

Historically, logistics and supply chain planning processes were completed sequentially and independently. Each supply chain process developed both short- and long-term plans based on independent assumptions and constraints. The result was inconsistent sourcing, production, inventory, warehousing, and transportation plans. The planning differences resulted in excess inventories, redundant capacity, and poor resource utilization. Capacity and inventory buffers were necessary to allow for the requirement inconsistencies resulting from independent plans. While this ineffective use of resources was once viewed as a part of business, such resource waste is not acceptable today. Enhanced performance requires increased planning integration across logistics and eventually all supply chain processes.

APS systems seek to integrate information and coordinate overall logistics and supply chain decisions while recognizing the dynamics between functions and processes. The four factors driving APS development and implementation are (1) planning horizon recognition, (2) supply chain visibility, (3) simultaneous resource consideration, and (4) resource utilization.

Planning Horizon Recognition

The first consideration is the movement to a shorter and shorter **planning horizon** for operations decisions. In the past, supply chain activities were planned months in advance with limited flexibility for change within the current month and typically no flexibility for change within the current week. This lock-in time was often termed the *freeze period* for production and supply chain planning decisions. The reduced flexibility caused by extended freeze periods resulted in poor customer service because production and shipping could not respond quickly or failure to respond to required changes would result in excessive inventory.

Managerial focus on reduced inventory and increased attention to JIT processes have decreased or in some cases even removed freeze periods. The ability to accommodate change means shorter planning cycles that must be reevaluated weekly or even daily. The need for shorter planning cycles and requirement to accommodate complex dynamics between supply chain processes has driven the need for more comprehensive and effective planning tools.

Supply Chain Visibility

The second consideration in APS development is the need for **visibility** regarding location and status of supply chain inventory and resources. Visibility implies not only being able to track supply chain inventory and resources but also that information regarding available resources can be effectively evaluated and managed. For example, at any given point in time, manufacturers may have thousands of shipments in-transit and inventory stored in hundreds of locations around the globe. Simply being able to identify shipments and inventory is not sufficient; supply chain visibility requires exception management to highlight the need for resource or activity plans to minimize or prevent potential problems.

While the United States and its allies demonstrated the benefits of effective military planning and technology during the Persian Gulf War during the early 1990s, the Defense Department learned that its logistics and supply chain systems did not perform to the same standard. A major reason cited for poor logistical performance was lack of supply chain visibility. For security and other reasons, the Defense Department and its service suppliers did not have integrated information systems capable of documenting or identifying inventory status or location. There was minimal integration between each military service (Army, Navy, and Air Force) and the logistics service providers, such as the Defense Logistics Agency. Such logistics integration had not historically received a major focus. This lack of integration coupled with the fear that potential foes could gain an advantage by breaking into the tracking system or monitoring movements, resulted in performance that was not reflective of what should have been possible in 1991.

Since there was limited visibility regarding inventory in-transit and expected arrival times, there was significant uncertainty regarding product availability. The lack of certainty in a situation where product availability is critical resulted in additional inventory and requisitions to reduce the chance of stockouts. While it is clear that no military force can tolerate short supply, excessive inventories both are expensive and may be wasteful of critical resources. Numerous comments from Gulf War logisticians have suggested that effective supply chain visibility would have substantially reduced inventory commitments and transportation requirements.[1]

While ERP systems can provide resource visibility within the firm, external visibility and effective management capability require more sophistication. An effective APS system integrates with information provided by other supply chain partners to provide such visibility.

Simultaneous Resource Consideration

Once the planning system determines resource status and availability through visibility, the third APS consideration is the need to develop a plan that incorporates combined supply chain demand, capacity, material requirements, and constraints. Supply chain requirements reflect the customer demand for product quantity, delivery timing, and location. While some of these customer requirements may be negotiable, logistics must execute to the agreed-to requirements and standards.

The constraints to meeting customer requirements are materials, production, storage, and transportation capacity. These requirements represent the physical limitations of processes and facilities. Prior planning methods have typically considered these capacity constraints in a sequential manner. For example, an initial plan is made that operates within production constraints. The initial plan is then adjusted to reflect material and sourcing constraints. The second plan is then revised again to consider storage and transportation constraints. While the steps may be different, sequential decision making is characteristic of most planning systems but results in suboptimal and inferior planning and capacity utilization.

Achieving integrated supply chain performance requires simultaneous consideration of relevant supply chain capacity constraints to identify trade-offs where increased functional costs, such as in manufacturing or storage, might lead to lower

---

[1]Lt. General William G. Pagonis and Jeffrey L. Cruikshank, *Moving Mountains: Lessons of Leadership and Logistics from the Gulf War* (Boston, MA: Harvard Business School Press, 1994).

overall system costs. The APS system needs to quantitatively evaluate the trade-offs and suggest plans that can optimize overall performance.

Resource Utilization

Logistics and supply chain management decisions have major influences on many enterprise resources, including production, distribution facilities and equipment, transportation equipment, and inventories. These resources consume a substantial proportion of a typical firm's fixed and working assets. Just as was the case with planning systems, prior management focus stressed resource utilization for individual functions. For example, production management focused on minimizing plant and equipment required for manufacturing. The typical result was long production runs and minimum setups and changeovers. However, longer production runs invariably result in more finished inventory, as substantial quantities are manufactured in anticipation of projected demand. More inventory increases working capital requirements while the additional space requirements increase. This trend toward more inventory is further aggravated by the increased uncertainty resulting from the need to forecast longer into the future.

With functional resource trade-offs in mind, the final consideration driving APS system development and implementation is the need to implement an integrated planning approach that minimizes combined supply chain resources. This is a critical capability when supply chain and firm performance place a strong emphasis on overall asset utilization.

Supply Chain APS Applications

There are a growing number of APS applications. New applications are evolving by the need to consider a broader range of activities and resources within the scope of supply chain planning. There are, however, some applications that are typical for many supply chain planning environments. These include demand planning, production planning, inventory and requirements planning, and transportation planning.

Demand Planning

The increasing complexity of product offerings and marketing tactics in conjunction with shorter product life cycles requires more accuracy, flexibility, and consistency in determining inventory requirements. **Demand planning APS systems** attempt to provide such capabilities.

Demand planning develops the forecast that drives anticipatory supply chain processes. The forecasts are the projections of monthly, weekly, or daily demand that determine production and inventory requirements. Each projected quantity might include some portion of future orders placed in anticipation of customer demand along with some portion of forecasted demand based on history. Essentially, the demand planning process integrates historically based forecasts with other information regarding events that could influence future sales activity (e.g., promotional plans, pricing changes, and new product introductions) to obtain the best possible integrated statement of requirements.

Another aspect of the demand planning process focuses on creating forecast consistency across multiple products and distribution facilities. Effective integrated management requires a single accurate forecast for each item and distribution facility. The aggregate and combined requirements must reflect a plan that is consistent with divisional and overall firm sales and financial projections. For example, the sum of individual distribution facility sales should be consistent with national sales projections. Similarly, item level requirements need to be adjusted to reflect the activity level for related items. For instance, requirements for existing products may have to be reduced to reflect the market's reaction to a new product introduction or one item's requirements may need to be adjusted during the promotion of a substitutable item.

Production Planning

Production planning uses the statement of requirements obtained from demand planning in conjunction with manufacturing resources and constraints to develop a workable manufacturing plan. The statement of requirements defines the items that need to be produced and the time they will be needed. Although there has been a definite trend toward MTO and ATO manufacturing, such response-based practices are not always possible due to production capacity or resource constraints. The limitations occur in the form of facility equipment and labor availability.

Production planning APS matches the requirements plan with the production constraints. The objective is to satisfy the necessary requirements at the minimum total production cost while not violating any constraints. Effective production planning results in a time-sequenced plan to manufacture the correct items in a timely manner while operating within facility, equipment, and labor constraints. The production planning process identifies the requirements that should be produced early to remain within production constraints and yet minimize inventory. Production planning also identifies which customer orders might have to be delayed due to lack of availability.

Requirements Planning

Requirements planning APS extends the planning process beyond the plant walls. While it is important to achieve economical plant performance, effective supply chain management requires consideration of the impact production decisions have on downstream performance. For example, production plans may suggest a long run of a single item. This will build up finished inventory requiring storage and transport capacity. While such long manufacturing runs might minimize manufacturing cost, overall system performance might be better served with shorter runs resulting in less storage and transport requirements. The requirements planning process uses evaluative techniques to trade-off the costs of production, storage, and transportation. The analysis attempts to satisfy customer demand, minimize overall cost, and remain within the supply chain's physical constraints.

Transportation Planning

Another APS application focuses on **transportation planning.** This system's objective is to plan transportation requirements throughout the supply chain. Historically, purchasing and finished goods transportation both attempted to minimize their freight cost individually. Procurement minimized the expense of raw material movements by working with suppliers and inbound carriers. Logistics focused on minimizing outbound freight expense by working with customers and their transportation carriers. There was also often a third managerial focus on international and expedited shipments. The individual perspectives of transportation often resulted in limited economies of scale, limited information sharing, and excessive transportation expenses.

Transportation APS integrates transportation requirements, transportation resources, and relevant costs into a common tactical decision support system that seeks to minimize overall freight expense. The analysis suggests ways that freight can be shifted among carriers or consolidated to achieve scale economies. It also facilitates information sharing with carriers and other service providers to enable better asset utilization.

As we've seen, logistics and supply chain planning are essential for effective resource utilization. Lack of accurate and comprehensive logistics and supply chain planning tools historically resulted in poor utilization of production, storage, and transportation capacity. The increasingly strong focus on improved asset utilization in conjunction with improved information management and decision analysis capabilities and techniques has brought comprehensive APS to reality. The following section describes the major components of an APS system.

APS System Design Overview

To correspond with the planning and execution of effective logistics and supply chain strategies, APS incorporates both spatial and temporal considerations. The spatial considerations include movement between raw material providers, manufacturing plants, distribution centers, distributors, retailers, and the end customer. The temporal considerations include the timing and scheduling of the movements.

The APS system in Figure 9-1 is a simplified network including plants, distribution centers, and customers as well as transportation flows. This network, a simplified version of that illustrated in Chapter 1, reflects the resource status and allocation at a point in time, for example, on the first day of the month. Effective planning requires a process that can time phase and coordinate resource requirements and constraints over

FIGURE 9-1

Advanced planning and scheduling overview

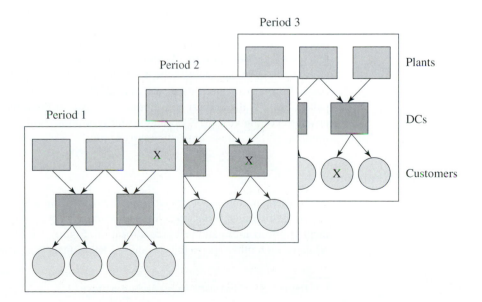

TABLE 9-1   Sample APS Planning Situation

	Time Period				
	1	2	3	4	5
Requirement	200	200	200	600	200
Production Capacity	300	300	300	300	300
Alternative 1 (overtime):					
Production	200	200	200	600	200
Inventory Carryover	—	—	—	—	—
Alternative 2 (build ahead):					
Production	300	300	300	300	200
Inventory Carryover	100	200	300	—	—

time. For example, if product X is needed by the customer in period 3, its movement through the supply chain must be time phased for arrival by period 3. Assuming a one-period performance cycle between each stage in the supply chain, this means that the APS must plan for the shipment of X from the plant during period 1 and shipment from the distribution center during period 2.

More specifically, suppose a firm is facing the situation summarized in Table 9-1. Customers require 200 units of product during each of the next five periods with the exception of period 4, when a special promotion will spike demand to 600 units. The firm's production capacity is 300 units per week. On the extremes, the firm can select between two approaches to satisfy customer requirements given the production constraints. Alternative 1 is to wait until the fourth time period and then run production overtime to meet customer requirements. This alternative results in higher production cost but no cost to carry or warehouse inventory. Alternative 2 is to build ahead using the extra 100-unit capacity in the time prior to period 4. With this alternative, an extra 100 units is built and added to inventory each period until it is required during period 4. This alternative will not require overtime production but will require increased inventory carrying and storage costs. There are, of course, intermediate alternatives to these two extremes. The ideal option is to select the combination resulting in the lowest combined cost of manufacturing and storage.[2] Using linear optimization techniques, APS can identify the most cost-effective trade-offs considering all relevant costs. While firms have attempted to evaluate these trade-offs in the past, analysis capabilities only allowed for considerations of two or three major trade-offs to minimize problem complexity. APS offers the ability to thoroughly evaluate complex trade-offs involving a large number of alternatives.

APS System Components

While there are many conceptual approaches to designing APS, the major components are fundamentally the same: demand management, resource management, requirements optimization, and resource allocation. Figure 9-2 illustrates how these modules relate to each other and to the corporate ERP or legacy system.

---

[2]The total cost of manufacturing was defined in Chapter 2.

FIGURE 9-2

APS system modules

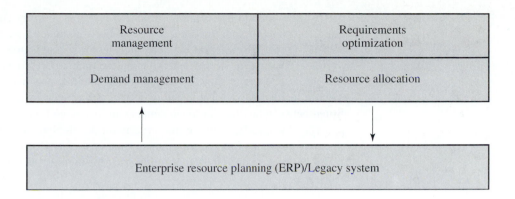

Resource management	Requirements optimization
Demand management	Resource allocation

Enterprise resource planning (ERP)/Legacy system

Demand Management

The **demand management** module develops the requirement projections for the planning horizon. In effect, it generates the sales forecasts based on sales history, currently scheduled orders, scheduled marketing activities, and customer information. Ideally, demand management works collaboratively and interactively both internally across the firm's functional components and externally with supply chain partners to develop a common and consistent forecast for each time period, location, and item. The forecast must also incorporate feedback from customers to integrate the influence of combined demand generation activities such as advertising and promotion. Since demand management and forecasting are so closely related and forecasting is an extensive topic in itself, forecasting details are discussed later in this chapter.

Resource Management

The **resource management** module coordinates and records supply chain system resources and constraints. Because APS systems use the resource and constraint information to evaluate the trade-offs associated with supply chain decisions, information accuracy and integrity are critical to provide optimal decisions and enhance planning system credibility. Obviously incorrect planning decisions not only suboptimize supply chain performance but also severely reduce management credibility in the planning system itself.

In addition to the requirements definition developed by the demand management module, APS requires four other types of information. These include product and customer definitions, resource definitions and costs, system constraints, and planning objective function.

The product and customer definitions provide the constants regarding the firm's products and customers to support the planning process. The product definitions provide the product descriptions and physical characteristics, such as weight and cube, standard costs, and bill of material. The customer definitions provide the ship-to location and distribution assignments, along with special service requirements. The combination of both defines what is being manufactured, distributed, where it is being delivered, and the performance cycles involved in distribution.

The resource definitions specify the physical resources used to accomplish supply chain activities such as manufacturing, storage, and movement. The resources include manufacturing equipment and process rates, storage facilities, and transportation equipment and availability. In addition to defining the existence of specific resources, the database must include the cost and performance characteristics and costs associated with resource usage.

System limitations define the major constraints limiting supply chain activities. The constraints include the capacity limitations associated with production, storage, and movement. Production capacity defines how much product can be produced within a specific time period and what are the trade-offs associated with making various products. Storage capacity defines the amount of product that can be stored in a specific facility. Movement capacity defines the volume of product that can be transported between facilities or to customers within a given time frame.

The objective function defines criteria for developing a planning solution. Typical objective functions include minimizing total cost or any of its subcomponents, meeting all customer requirements, or minimizing the number of instances when capacity is exceeded.

This combination of information provides the basis for the APS analysis. The module includes the databases to store the definitions, resources, constraints, and objectives as well as the processes to validate and maintain it. Users are finding that one of the major challenges to effective APS is the ability to develop and maintain accurate and consistent data.

Resource Optimization

The **resource optimization** module is the computational engine or "black box" of the APS system. Using the requirements from the demand management module and the definitions, resources, limitations, and objectives from the resource management module, resource optimization uses a combination of mathematical programming and heuristics to determine how to best meet customer requirements while utilizing resources most effectively. Mathematical programming is a combination of linear programming and mixed-integer programming, which is used to minimize the specified objective function; heuristics are computational rules of thumb or shortcuts that reduce the time or computational resources required to develop the integrated plan. In effect, the resource optimization module evaluates multiple planning alternatives and systematically completes the trade-offs to identify the best alternatives until a near-optimal result is achieved. The resource optimization module also determines when requirements cannot be met and which resources are the most limiting on supply chain performance. The resource optimization module output is a supply chain plan projected into future time periods that minimizes overall costs while attempting to operate within major resource constraints. The plan specifies which products should be produced when and determines movement and storage requirements across the supply chain.

The resource optimization module can also be used to conduct sensitivity or what-if analysis to determine the impact of changes in market requirements or assumptions. These analyses allow the supply chain planner to isolate the impact of demand and performance uncertainty on supply chain capabilities and operations. Using the insight regarding the trade-offs and the impact of uncertainty, the APS resource optimization module guides the planner in establishing the most effective sourcing, production, movement, and storage strategy.

Resource Allocation

Following planner review and judgement regarding the results of the resource optimization module, the **resource allocation** module refines the resource assignments and communicates them to the ERP system to initiate appropriate transactions. The results include requirements for procurement, production, storage, and transport. The specific requests can be communicated to the ERP system in the form of transactions or instructions to complete a specific activity. Each transaction includes detailed instructions regarding type of supply chain activity, suppliers, customer, products involved, and required timing, along with a list of relevant products and quantities. The resource allocation module also provides information regarding when product is available to promise (ATP) or capable to promise (CTP). ATP is used to designate that even though actual inventory is not currently available, it will be available for shipment (or promise) at a specific date in the future. In effect, the ATP designation allows firms to commit scheduled production to customers. CTP is used to designate when requested product can be promised for future delivery. CTP requires a much broader analysis as it determines whether there is future specific capacity or capability, given current and projected supply chain demands. ATP and CTP can dramatically enhance supply chain performance and effectiveness by allowing commitments against future production and capacity. The result is more rapid commitments to customers, fewer customer surprises, and enhanced resource utilization.

Forecasting

Whenever logistics involves any aspect of make-to-plan or make-to-stock, a forecast is required to drive the process. The forecast is a specific definition of what will be sold, when, and where. The forecast defines the requirements that the supply chain must schedule the inventory and resources to fulfill. Since there are still many logistics and supply chain activities that must be completed in anticipation of a sale, forecasting remains as a critical capability for planning.

Forecast Components

The forecast is generally a monthly or weekly figure for each Stock Keeping Unit (SKU) and distribution location. While the forecasted quantity is generally a single figure, the value is actually made up of six components: (1) base demand, (2) seasonal, (3) trend, (4) cyclic, (5) promotion, and (6) irregular. Assuming the base demand as the average sales level, the other components, except for irregular, are indices or factors that are multiplied by the base level to make a positive or negative adjustment. The resulting forecast model is

$$F_t = (B_t \times S_t \times T \times C_t \times P_t) + I,$$

where

F_t = Forecast quantity for period t;

B_t = Base level demand for period t;

S_t = Seasonality factor for period t;

T = Trend component—index reflecting increase or decrease per time period;

C_t = Cyclical factor for period t;

P_t = Promotional factor for period t; and

I = Irregular or random quantity.

While some forecasts may not include all components, it is useful to understand the behavior of each so that each component can be tracked and incorporated appropriately.

The **base demand** is the quantity that remains after the remaining components have been removed. A good estimate of base demand is the average over an extended time. The base demand is the appropriate forecast for items that have no seasonality, trend, cyclic, or promotional components.

The **seasonal** component is a generally recurring upward and downward movement in the demand pattern, usually on an annual basis. An example is the annual demand for toys, which peaks just prior to Christmas and then declines during the first three quarters of the year. It can be said that the demand pattern of toys exhibits low seasonality during the first three quarters with peak seasonality for the last quarter. It should be noted that the seasonality discussed above refers to consumer retail seasonality. Seasonality at the wholesale level precedes consumer demand by approximately one quarter. The seasonality factor or index has an average value of 1.0 for all periods (e.g., months), but individual monthly seasonality factors can range from 0 to 12. An individual seasonality factor of 1.2 indicates that sales for the forecasted period are projected at 20 percent above average for all periods.

The **trend** component is defined as the long-range general movement in periodic sales over an extended period of time. This trend may be positive, negative, or neutral in direction. A positive trend means that sales are increasing across time. For example, the trend for personal computer sales during the decade of the 1990s was increasing. Over the product life cycle, the trend direction may change a number of times. For example, due to a change in people's drinking habits, beer consumption changed from an increasing trend to a neutral trend during the early 1980s. Increases or decreases in trend are dependent on changes in overall population or consumption patterns. A knowledge of which factor impacts sales is significant when making such projections. For example, a reduction in the birth rate implies that a reduction in the demand for disposable diapers will follow. However, a trend toward usage of disposable as contrasted to cloth diapers may cause an increased demand of a specific product category while overall market size is decreasing. The above are obvious examples of forecast trend. While the impact of trend on short-range logistics forecasts is subtle, it still must be considered when developing the forecast. Unlike the other forecast components, the trend component influences base demand in the succeeding time periods. The specific relationship is:

$$B_{t+1} = B_t \times T,$$

where

B_{t+1} = Base demand in period $t + 1$;

B_t = Base demand in period t; and

T = Periodic trend index.

The trend index with a value greater than 1.0 indicates that periodic demand is increasing while a value less than 1.0 indicates a declining trend.

The **cyclic** component is characterized by swings in the demand pattern lasting more than a year. These cycles may be either upward or downward. An example is the business cycle in which the economy typically swings from recessionary to expansionary cycles every 3 to 5 years. The demand for housing, as well as the resulting demand for major appliances, is typically tied to this business cycle.

The **promotional** component characterizes demand swings initiated by the firm's marketing activities, such as advertising, deals, or promotions. These swings can often be characterized by sales increases during the promotion followed by sales declines as customers work off inventory purchased to take advantage of the promotion. Promotions can be deals offered to the consumer or deals offered only to wholesalers and retailers (*trade promotions*). The promotion can be regular and thus take place at the same time each year. From a forecasting perspective, a regular promotion component resembles a seasonal component. An irregular promotion component does not necessarily occur during the same time period, so it must be tracked and incorporated separately. The promotional component is particularly important to track, especially for consumer industries, since it has a major influence on sales variation. In some industries, promotional sales account for 50 to 80 percent of the periodic volume variations. This does not suggest that sales would only be 20 percent of current levels if there were no promotions. It does imply that promotions result in demand that is more "lumpy" than would otherwise be the case if actual consumption were tracked. The promotional component is different from the other forecasting components in that its timing and magnitude are controlled, to a large extent, by the firm. Thus, it should be possible to find information within the firm such as from sales or marketing regarding the timing and likely impact of scheduled promotional plans. Such internal information sharing can substantially enhance forecast accuracy.

The **irregular** component includes the random or unpredictable quantities that do not fit within the other categories. Due to its random nature, this component is impossible to predict. When developing a forecast process, the objective is to minimize the magnitude of the random component by tracking and predicting the other components.

It is beyond the scope of this text to provide a detailed discussion of how to formulate each forecast. There are a number of texts that provide detailed discussions of the process and examples of forecasting methods.[3] The important point is that the forecaster must recognize the potential impact of different components and treat them appropriately. For example, the treatment of a seasonal component as a trend component reduces forecast accuracy over time. The components significant to a particular item situation must be identified, analyzed, and incorporated with appropriate forecast techniques.

Forecast Management Approaches

Figure 9-3 illustrates that forecasts can be developed from two perspectives. The **bottom-up** or **aggregation** method develops SKU forecasts for each location and then builds them to an aggregate demand projection. Specifically, a SKU forecast for each distribution center is developed independently and then summed to calculate the national level SKU forecast. This decentralized approach is appropriate when demand for each SKU/location is independent of other SKUs or locations.

FIGURE 9-3

Top-down forecast example

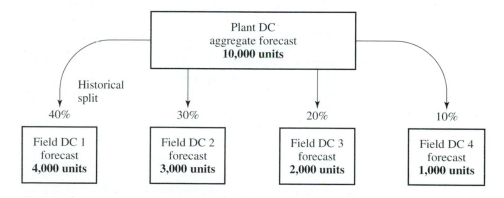

---

[3]John T. Mentzer and Carol C. Bienstock, *Sales Forecasting Management* (Thousand Oaks, CA: Sage Publications, 1998).

The **top-down** or **decomposition** approach, as illustrated in Figure 9-3, develops a national level SKU forecast and then spreads the volume across locations based on historical sales patterns. As an example, suppose the aggregate monthly forecast for the entire country is 10,000 units. Assuming the firm uses four distribution centers to service the demand with a historical demand split of 40, 30, 20, and 10 percent, respectively, then forecasts for individual distribution centers are projected to be 4000, 3000, 2000, and 1000.

Forecast management must select the best approach for each particular situation. The top-down approach is centralized and appropriate for stable demand situations or when the demand levels change uniformly throughout the market. For example, when demand levels are increasing 10 percent uniformly across all markets or when the firm uses national promotions, the use of the top-down approach facilitates development of new detailed forecasts since all changes are relative.

On the other hand, the bottom-up approach is decentralized since each distribution center forecast is developed independently. As a result, each forecast can more accurately track and consider demand fluctuations within specific markets. However, the bottom-up approach requires more detailed record keeping and makes it more difficult to incorporate systematic demand factors, such as the impact of major promotions or new product introductions.

While forecast management does not have to accept one alternative at the expense of the other, an acceptable combination must be selected. The correct combination must trade off the detail tracking of the bottom-up approach with the data manipulation ease of the top-down approach. When a combination is used, the challenge is to blend the individual estimates into a single representative forecast.

Forecast Management Process

Logistics planning and coordination require the best possible estimate of SKU/location demand. Although forecasting is far from an exact science, the demand management process should incorporate input from multiple sources, appropriate mathematical and statistical techniques, elaborate decision support capability, and trained and motivated individuals.

The time horizon for supply chain operational forecasts is normally 1 year or less. Depending upon the plan's intended use, forecasts may be required on a daily, weekly, monthly, quarterly, semiannual, or annual basis. The most common supply chain forecast period is monthly, although many firms are moving toward weekly forecasts. The important requirement is that the basic planning horizon be selected to accommodate supply chain operations.

An effective forecast management process requires a number of components as illustrated in Figure 9-4. The foundation of the process is the order history and forecast database that includes information such as orders, order history, and the tactics resulting in those orders, such as promotions, special deals, or strikes. This database includes past sales and forecast history as well as a record of activities such as price changes or promotions that occurred concurrently with the sales activity. The forecast database is ideally part of the ERP central data warehouse although some firms maintain independent forecast databases. Other environmental data, such as the state of the economy and competitive actions, could also be included in this database. To support effective forecasting, this database must include timely historical and planning information in a manner facilitating its manipulation, summarization, analysis, and report-

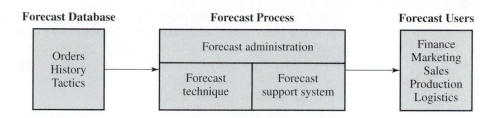

FIGURE 9-4

Forecast management process

ing. The specific database requirements include flexibility, accuracy, maintainability, and timeliness.

Next, an effective demand management process must develop an integrated, consistent forecast that supports the needs of users such as finance, marketing, sales, procurement, production, and logistics. In particular, users require accurate, consistent, detailed, and timely forecasts.

Finally, the development of an effective forecast requires a process that integrates three components: forecast technique, forecast support system, and forecast administration. The box on the right side of Figure 9-4 illustrates that it would be ideal if a firm could use a common and consistent forecast for all firm planning functions.

Forecast Technique

The forecast technique is the mathematical or statistical computation used to translate numerical parameters, including history, into a forecast quantity. Techniques include time series modeling, in which sales history is a major factor, and correlation modeling, in which relationships with other independent variables are the major factor. Techniques alone cannot deal with the complexities that are experienced in modern business forecasting: While techniques can easily connect historical patterns into future forecasts, they do not do as well at incorporating the input of anticipated future events. As a result, it is increasingly apparent that accurate demand management requires integration of the forecast techniques with appropriate support and administrative systems.

Forecast Support System

The forecast support system includes the data manipulation capability to gather and analyze data, develop the forecast, and communicate the forecast to relevant personnel and planning systems. This component supports the maintenance and manipulation of the data and allows consideration of external factors such as the impact of promotions, strikes, price changes, product line changes, competitive activity, and economic conditions. The system must be designed not only to allow the consideration of these factors but also to encourage them. For example, the marketing manager may know that the promotion scheduled for next month is likely to increase sales by 15 percent. However, if it is difficult to change the forecast figures for next month, the marketing manager may not bother making the change or may be reluctant to provide the data to a planner. Similarly, when a package size change is announced, it is obvious that the future forecast or the forecast history should be changed to reflect the new package size. If this is difficult to accomplish within the systems capabilities, the individual completing the forecast will probably not make the adjustments. It is thus very important that an effective demand management process include a support system to facilitate the maintenance, update, and manipulation of the historical database and the forecast. While it is easy to understand why this ability to make adjustments is necessary, it is often difficult to operationalize for thousands of SKUs at multiple locations. This combination of SKUs and locations means that many thousands of data points must be maintained on a regular basis. To complete this maintenance effectively, the forecast support system must include significant automation and exception procedures.

Forecast Administration

Forecast administration includes the organizational, procedural, motivational, and personnel aspects of the forecast management function and its integration into the other firm functions. The organizational aspect concerns individual roles and responsibilities. Specific issues include: (1) Who is responsible for developing the forecast? (2) How is forecast accuracy and performance measured? and (3) How does forecast performance impact job performance evaluation and rewards? Procedural aspects concern individual understanding of the relative impact of forecast activities, information systems, and techniques. Specific issues include: (1) Do forecast analysts understand how their actions impact logistics and supply chain coordination requirements? (2) Are analysts knowledgeable regarding the capabilities of the forecast system, and are capabilities used effectively? and (3) Are forecast analysts knowledgeable about the differences between techniques?

It is important that these questions be answered in detail when defining the forecast administration function. If these questions are not addressed, forecast responsibility and measurement often lose definition and accountability. For example, if marketing, sales, production, and logistics each develop a forecast independently, there is no integrated forecast and no overall accountability. If an integrated forecast is desirable, it is necessary to specifically define each organization's demand management responsibility and then hold it accountable with specific measurements. Effective forecast administration requires that organizational and procedural considerations be well defined. Without them, even though the forecast technique and the forecast support system are adequate, the overall forecast management process yields less than optimal performance.

Dynamic simulation illustrates the impact of forecast inconsistency across multiple members of the supply chain. From initial stimulant to feedback, the cost of direct communication of sales or forecasts is overshadowed by the cost of a faulty message. Since a great deal of supply chain action is initiated in anticipation of future transactions, communications containing overly optimistic predictions or projections may stimulate a fever of ultimately useless work. Analysis of communications between channel members suggests that anticipation has a tendency to amplify as it proceeds between supply chain participants, particularly as the information gets further from the ultimate consumer. Each error in the interpretation of transaction requirements creates a disturbance for the total logistical channel. In a classic work, Forrester simulated channel interrelationships to demonstrate how the total channel may enter into an oscillating corrective pattern, resulting in a series of over-and-under adjustments to real market requirements.[4] Figure 9-5 illustrates the channel inventory oscillations that are stimulated when the retailer increases demand by 10 percent but does not directly inform the other members of the channel.

The figure illustrates that an increase of retail demand by 10 percent without clear communication back to other members of the supply chain results in inventory swings

---

[4]Jay W. Forrester, *Industrial Dynamics* (Cambridge, MA: The MIT Press, 1961); and "Industrial Dynamics," *Harvard Business Review* 36 (July/August 1958), p. 43.

FIGURE 9-5

Response of a simulated production/distribution system to a sudden 10 percent increase in sales at the retail level

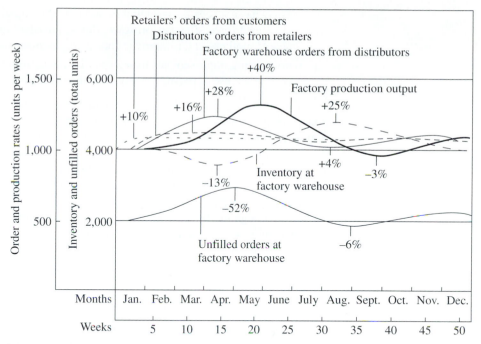

Source: Jay W. Forrester, *Industrial Dynamics* (Cambridge, MA: The MIT Press, 1961); and "Industrial Dynamics," *Harvard Business Review* 36 (July/August 1958), p. 43.

of 16 percent for the distributor, 28 percent for the factory warehouse, and 40 percent for factory production. These swings obviously increase supply chain variance, which increases costs and diminishes asset utilization.

By the very nature of its mission, a distribution channel must respond to transaction requirements. The system must stand ready to initiate logistical action upon receipt of a message. Extreme care must be taken to structure the communication function with a high degree of reliability while retaining the flexibility required for change and adaptation.

As Figure 9-4 illustrated, it is important to realize that a meaningful forecast process requires an integrated and consistent combination of components. Historically, it was thought that intensive effort in one of the individual components such as technique could overcome problems in the other components. For example, it was thought that a "perfect" forecast technique could be identified that would overcome the need for systems support and a consistent process. There is increasing realization that all three components must work together. The design process must adequately consider the strengths and weaknesses of each individual component and design for the optimal performance of the integrated system.

Mentzer and Bienstock have made the following observations regarding the status of forecasting at U.S. firms:[5]

- Firms are generally employing more sophisticated processes and incorporating input from a wider range of firm functions.

---

[5]John T. Mentzer and Carol C. Bienstock, op.cit.

- There has not been a substantial improvement in the evaluation of firm and individual forecasting performance; this has resulted in little enthusiasm and lack of motivation for improved forecasting performance.

- Forecasting improvements have primarily come from technology advancements such as the use of personal computers and related software.

They cite two major challenges for the future. First, firms need to encourage shared responsibility for the forecasting process. This means that cross-functional teams need to work together to develop common and consistent forecasts. Second, sales forecasting system access for marketing, sales, planning, product management, and logistics needs to be increased. The systems must include aspects of forecast systems support and forecast administration as well as collaborative involvement by suppliers and customers.

Even though the forecast technique is only one component of the overall demand management process, it is useful to understand the breadth of techniques available and the measures to evaluate them.

Forecast Techniques

Demand management requires the selection of appropriate techniques to generate periodic forecasts. Effective technique use requires matching the characteristics of the situation with the abilities of the technique. In their text, Makridakis et al. suggest the following criteria for evaluating the applicability of a technique: (1) accuracy, (2) forecast time horizon, (3) the value of forecasting, (4) data availability, (5) type of data pattern, and (6) experience of the forecaster.[6] Each alternative forecast technique must be evaluated both qualitatively and quantitatively with respect to these six criteria.

There are literally hundreds of articles describing approaches to and effectiveness of forecasting alternatives. During the last four decades, forecasting techniques have become increasingly complex with advanced statistical and analytical capabilities. The general development assumes that greater complexity and sophistication result in improved forecast accuracy. While this is often true, considerable research has indicated that simpler is sometimes better. The more sophisticated techniques do not always provide significantly better results than the simpler techniques, particularly when one considers the resource requirements, both in terms of information and expertise, that the more complex techniques require.[7]

While it would be advantageous to be able to identify a specific forecast technique, simple or complex, that is appropriate for each application, the development and evaluation of forecast techniques are not that exact. The selection of the appropriate forecast technique is much more art than science. Simply stated, supply chain management should choose the technique or techniques that provide the best results. The concept of **composite forecasting** illustrates one approach that is results-driven.[8] Composite forecasting incorporates a number of techniques ranging from very simple to reasonably complex. For each time period, a forecast is generated for each SKU using each technique. Composite forecasting then combines the results as an average

---

[6]Spyros Makridakis, Steven Wheelwright, and Robert Hyndman, *Forecasting, Methods and Applications,* 3rd. ed. (New York: John Wiley and Sons, 1997).

[7]For a detailed analysis of the results, see J. Scott Armstrong, "Forecasting by Extrapolation: Conclusions from 25 Years of Research," *Interfaces,* November/December 1984, pp. 52–66.

[8]Charles W. Chase, Jr., "Composite Forecasting: Combining Forecasts for Improved Accuracy," *Journal of Business Forecasting Methods & Systems,* 19, no. 2 (Summer 2000), pp. 2–6.

or weighted value based on the combination that would have yielded the best results for recent time periods. For example, suppose that it is necessary to create a forecast for June. At the end of May, composite forecasting would create a forecast for May using all the data available from the end of April and a number of techniques. The May forecast for each technique would be compared with May's actual sales to determine which combination of techniques *would* have been most accurate for May. The assumption is that the best combination for June is the one that would have been best for May. **Focus forecasting** provides another example of a combined technique.[9]

With the continued interest in improved forecasting and advanced information technology, there are an increasing number of forecast packages available on personal computers as well as other platforms. In general, the packages incorporate a number of techniques as well as demand management support systems to facilitate data manipulation and analysis. Yurkiewicz offers a listing of these packages along with a summary of the major features.[10]

Forecast Technique Categories

There are three categories of forecast techniques: (1) qualitative, (2) time series, and (3) causal. The **qualitative techniques** use data such as expert opinion and special information to forecast the future. A qualitative technique may or may not consider the past. **Time series techniques** focus entirely on historical patterns and pattern changes to generate forecasts. **Causal techniques,** such as regression, use refined and specific information regarding variables to develop a relationship between a lead event and forecasted activity.

Qualitative   Qualitative techniques rely heavily on expertise and are quite costly and time-consuming. They are ideal for situations where little historical data and much managerial judgement are required. Using input from the sales force as the basis of the forecast for a new region or a new product is an example of a supply chain application of a qualitative forecast technique. However, qualitative methods are generally not appropriate for supply chain forecasting because of the time required to generate the detailed SKU forecasts necessary. Qualitative forecasts are developed using surveys, panels, and consensus meetings.

Time Series   Time series techniques are statistical methods utilized when historical sales data containing relatively clear and stable relationships and trends are available. Using historical sales data, time series analysis is used to identify seasonality, cyclical patterns, and trends. Once individual forecast components are identified, time series techniques assume the future will reflect the past. This implies that past demand patterns will continue into the future. This assumption is often reasonably correct in the short term, so these techniques are most appropriate for short-range forecasting.

When the rate of growth or trend changes significantly, the demand pattern experiences a turning point. Since time series techniques use historical demand patterns and weighted averages of data points, they are typically not sensitive to turning points. As a result, other approaches must be integrated with time series techniques to determine when turning points will likely occur.

---

[9]Everette Gardner and Elizabeth Anderson, "Focus Forecasting Reconsidered," *International Journal of Forecasting* 13, no. 4 (December 1997), pp. 501–8.

[10]Jack Yurkiewicz, "Forecasting 2000," *OR/MS Today,* February 2000, pp. 58–65.

Time series techniques include a variety of methods that analyze the pattern and movement of historical data to establish recurring characteristics. Based upon specific characteristics, techniques of varying sophistication can be used to develop time series forecasts. Four time series techniques in order of increasing complexity are (1) moving averages, (2) exponential smoothing, (3) extended smoothing, and (4) adaptive smoothing.

Moving average forecasting uses an average of the most recent period's sales. The average may use any number of previous time periods although 1, 3, 4, and 12 period averages are common. A 1-period moving average results in next period's forecast being projected by last period's sales. A 12-period moving average, such as monthly, uses the average of the last 12 periods. Each time a new period of actual data becomes available, it replaces the oldest time period's data; thus, the number of time periods included in the average is held constant.

Although moving averages are easy to calculate, there are several limitations. Most significantly, they are unresponsive or sluggish to change and a great amount of historical data must be maintained and updated to calculate forecasts. If the historical sales variations are large, average or mean value cannot be relied upon to render useful forecasts. Other than the base component, moving averages do not consider the forecast components discussed earlier.

Mathematically, moving average is expressed as

$$F_t = \frac{\sum_{i=1}^{n} S_{t-i}}{n},$$

where

F_t = Moving average forecast for time period *t;*

S_{t-i} = Sales for time period *i;* and

n = Total number of time periods.

For example, an April moving forecast based on sales of 120, 150, and 90 for the previous 3 months is calculated as follows

$$F_{April} = \frac{120 + 150 + 90}{3}$$

$$= 120$$

To partially overcome these deficiencies, *weighted moving averages* have been introduced as refinements. The weight places more emphasis on recent observations. **Exponential smoothing** is a form of weighted moving average. Exponential smoothing bases the estimate of future sales on the weighted average of the previous demand and forecast levels. The new forecast is a function of the old forecast incremented by some fraction of the differential between the old forecast and actual sales realized. The increment of adjustment is called the *alpha factor.* The basic format of the model is

$$F_t = \alpha D_{t-1} + (1 - \alpha) F_{t-1}$$

where

F_t = Forecasted sales for a time period *t;*

F_{t-1} = Forecast for time period $t - 1$;

D_{t-1} = Actual demand for time period $t - 1$; and

α = Alpha factor or smoothing constant $(0 \leq \alpha \leq 1.0)$.

To illustrate, assume that the forecasts for the most recent time period were 100 and actual sales experience was 110 units. Further, assume that the alpha factor being employed is 0.2. Then, by substitution,

$$F_t = \alpha D_{t-1} + (1 - \alpha) F_{t-1}$$

$$= (0.2)(110) + (1 - 0.2)(100)$$

$$= 22 + 80$$

$$= 102$$

So the forecast for period *t* is for product sales of 102 units.

The prime advantage of exponential smoothing is that it permits a rapid calculation of a new forecast without substantial historical records and updating. Thus, exponential smoothing is highly adaptable to computerized forecasting. Depending on the value of the smoothing constant, it is also possible to monitor and change technique sensitivity.

The major decision when using exponential smoothing is selecting the alpha factor. If a factor of 1 is employed, the net effect is to use the most recent period's sales as the forecast for next period. A very low value, such as .01, has the net effect of reducing the forecast to almost a simple moving average. Large alpha factors make the forecast very sensitive to change and therefore highly reactive. Low alpha factors tend to react slowly to change and therefore minimize response to random fluctuations. However, the technique cannot tell the difference between seasonality and random fluctuation. Thus, exponential smoothing does not eliminate the need for judgment. In selecting the value of the alpha factor, the forecaster is faced with a trade-off between eliminating random fluctuations or having the forecast fully respond to demand changes.

Extended exponential smoothing incorporates the influence of trend and seasonality when specific values for these components can be identified. The extended smoothing calculation is similar to that of the basic smoothing model except that there are three components and three smoothing constants to represent the base, trend, and seasonal components.

Similar to basic exponential smoothing, **extended smoothing** allows rapid calculation of new forecasts with minimal data. The technique's ability to respond depends on the smoothing constant values. Higher smoothing constant values provide quick responsiveness but may lead to overreaction and forecast accuracy problems.

Adaptive smoothing provides a regular review of alpha factor validity. The alpha value is reviewed at the conclusion of each forecast period to determine the exact value that would have resulted in a perfect forecast for the previous period. Once determined, the alpha factor used to generate the subsequent forecast is adjusted to a value that would have produced a perfect forecast. Thus, managerial judgment is partially replaced by a systematic and consistent method of updating alpha. Most forecast software packages include the capability to systematically evaluate alternative smoothing constants to identify the one that would have given the best performance in the most recent time periods.

More sophisticated forms of adaptive smoothing include an automatic tracking signal to monitor error. When the signal is tripped due to excessive error, the constant is automatically increased to make the forecast more responsive to smoothing recent periods. If the recent period sales demonstrate substantial change, increase responsiveness should decrease forecast error. As the forecast error is reduced, the tracking signal automatically returns the smoothing constant to its original value. While adaptive techniques are designed to systematically adjust for error, their weakness is that they sometimes overreact by interpreting random error as trend or seasonality. This misinterpretation leads to increased errors in the future.

Causal   Forecasting by regression estimates sales for a SKU based on values of other independent factors. If a good relationship can be identified, such as between expected price and consumption, the information can be used to effectively predict requirements. Causal or regression forecasting works well when a leading variable such as price can be identified. However, such situations are not particularly common for supply chain applications. If the SKU forecast is based upon a single factor, it is referred to as *simple regression analysis.* The use of more than one forecast factor is *multiple regression.* Regression forecasts use the correlation between a leading or predictable event and the dependent demand SKU's sales. No cause/effect relationship need exist between the product's sale and the independent event if a high degree of correlation is consistently present. A correlation assumes that the forecasted sales are proceeded by some leading independent factor such as the sale of a related product. However, the most reliable use of regression forecasting of sales is based on a cause/effect relationship. Since regression can effectively consider external factors and events, causal techniques are more appropriate for long-term or aggregate forecasting. For example, causal techniques are commonly used to generate annual or national sales forecasts.

Forecast Error

Forecast accuracy refers to the difference between forecasts and corresponding actual sales. Forecast accuracy improvement requires error measurement and analysis. There are three steps for reducing forecast error. First, appropriate measures must be defined. Second, measurement level must be identified. Finally, feedback loops must be defined to improve forecast efforts.

Error Measurement

Forecast error can be measured on either an absolute or a relative basis by using a number of methods. While forecast error can be defined generally as the difference between actual demand and forecast, a more precise definition is needed for calculation and comparison. Table 9-2 provides monthly unit demand and forecast for a specific personal computer model at a regional distribution center. This example illustrates alternative forecast error measures.

One approach for error measurement is to sum up the errors over time such as illustrated in column 4. With this approach, errors are summed over the year and a simple average is calculated. As illustrated, the average error is very near zero even though there are some months with significant error. The concern with this approach is that the positive errors cancel negative errors, masking a significant forecasting problem. To avoid this problem, an alternative approach is to ignore the "sign" and evaluate absolute error.

Column 5 illustrates the computation of the absolute error and the resulting Mean Absolute Deviation (MAD). While the MAD approach is often used to measure forecast error, MAD places equal weight on small and large deviations. Another alternative is to square the error and then use the Mean Squared Error (MSE) for comparing forecast alternatives. Column 6 illustrates the squared error approach. The advantage of the MSE approach is that it penalizes a system more for a few large errors than for a

TABLE 9-2   Monthly Personal Computer Demand and Forecast

(1) Month	(2) Demand	(3) Forecast	(4) Error	(5) Absolute Error	(6) Squared Error
January	100	110	−10	10	100
February	110	90	20	20	400
March	90	90	0	0	0
April	130	120	10	10	100
May	70	90	−20	20	400
June	110	120	−10	10	100
July	120	120	0	0	0
August	90	110	−20	20	400
September	120	70	50	50	2500
October	90	130	−40	40	1600
November	80	90	−10	10	100
December	90	100	−10	10	100
Sum	1200	1240	−40	200	5800
Mean	100	103.3	−3.3	16.7[a]	483.3[b]
Percent (Error/Mean)		3.3%[c]		16.7%[d]	22.0%[e]

a = Mean absolute deviation (MAD).
b = Mean squared error (MSE).
c = Mean error/mean demand.
d = Absolute value of mean forecast error/mean demand.
e = Square root of sum of errors squared/mean demand.

large number of smaller ones. For example, the MAD approach penalizes a forecast deviation of 2 only twice as much as a deviation of 1. The MSE approach penalizes a forecast measurement deviation of 2 four times more than a forecast deviation of 1.

Although the mean, absolute, and squared errors are good measures for evaluating individual SKUs and locations, they are not good measures when evaluating aggregate forecast performance. These absolute measures treat a mean error of 40 the same for SKUs with monthly demand of 40 or 4000.

The first case illustrates a 100 percent error, which demonstrates relatively poor forecasting. For the second case, however, the relative forecast error is 1 percent, which demonstrates very accurate forecasting. To compare forecasts across SKUs and locations with different mean demands, error percentages are usually calculated. Percentage error is calculated by dividing a mean error measure by mean demand. The mean error measure can be the absolute measure illustrated in column 5 of Table 9-2 or the squared error measure illustrated in column 6. Table 9-2 illustrates the two measures and their relative magnitude. While either relative error measure is appropriate for comparison purposes, the relative forecast error using squared error facilitates identification of *problem* SKUs.

Measurement Level

The second step considers measurement level or aggregation. Assuming that individual SKU detail is recorded, forecast error can be calculated for individual SKU location combinations, groups of SKUs or locations, and nationally. Generally, more aggregation results in lower relative forecast errors. For example, Figure 9-6 illustrates comparative forecast errors at the national, brand for groups of SKUs, and SKU

FIGURE 9-6

Comparative forecast
errors

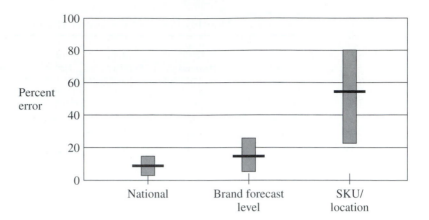

location level. In this example, relative error is calculated by using the squared errors. The figure illustrates the minimum, maximum, and mean relative forecast error for a sample of firms marketing consumer products. As Figure 9-6 illustrates, while a relative error of 40 percent is average for a SKU/location level of aggregation, it would reflect very poor forecasting if measured at the national level.

There are two considerations when determining level of forecast aggregation. First, less aggregation facilitates problem identification and focuses efforts to improve forecast performance. Second, less aggregation requires more computation and storage resources due to the number of SKU location combinations for the typical firm. However, this is a minor consideration with the availability of low-cost computing and exception-based processing.

As noted in the discussion of current forecast techniques, a major concern is identification and tracking of forecast error. To provide long-term consistency, it is necessary that measurement level be defined and then error tracked regularly. Relative forecast error both for individual items and aggregates can be plotted over time to indicate changes in forecast effectiveness.

Feedback

The third step is establishment of appropriate forecast feedback loops so the demand management process is motivated to improve. Demand management improvement results from a process and individuals motivated to identify problems and improvement opportunities. The motivation follows from having forecaster performance measures dependent on demand management accuracy. For example, demand management accuracy often improves when forecasters are recognized with bonuses or competitive rewards. With appropriate motivation, demand managers can identify major sources of error and develop techniques and information sources that can reduce error. In some cases, more sophisticated forecasting techniques, such as composite forecasting, have led to dramatic improvements. In other cases, it is possible to significantly reduce forecast error through other demand management activities, for example, improved communication regarding marketing activities such as price changes, promotions, or package changes. When evaluating demand management performance, it is important to recognize that a perfect forecast is not likely and expectations should not be set too high.

Collaborative Planning, Forecasting, and Replenishment

The forecasting processes and techniques described above have achieved significant benefits in providing superior logistical performance in distribution channels; how-

FIGURE 9-7

CPFR in the retail information technology environment

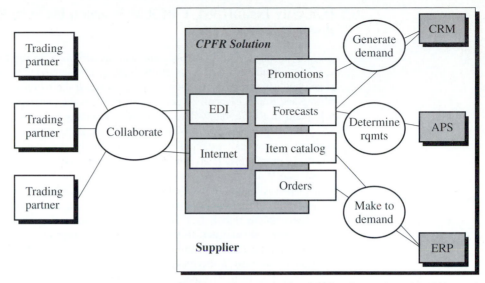

Source: Matt Johnson, "Collaboration Data Modeling: CPFR Implementation Guidelines," *Proceedings of the 1999 Annual Conference of the Council of Logistics Management* (Chicago, IL: Council of Logistics Management), p. 17.

ever, there can still be costly unplanned and uncoordinated events that distort smooth flow of product through the supply chain. These distortions occur because channel participants frequently fail to coordinate their individual forecasts of final consumer demand and marketing events designed to stimulate demand. Imagine, for example, that at the beginning of the month, the manufacturer forecasts sales of 100,000 cases to a particular retail customer with planned advertising and sales promotions to support that level of sales. Meanwhile, that same retailer forecasts sales of 150,000 and plans specific promotional events to achieve that forecast. Clearly, joint planning and information sharing concerning such events would increase the likelihood of a successful relationship.

Collaborative Planning, Forecasting, and Replenishment (CPFR) is a process initiated by the consumer products industry to achieve such coordination. It does not replace automatic replenishment strategies but supplements them by a cooperative process.[11] In essence, CPFR coordinates the requirements plan for the demand creation and demand fulfillment activities. Figure 9-7 illustrates the base CPFR relationships. The CPFR solution shares information involving promotions, forecasts, item data, and orders with trading partners using either EDI or the Internet. The collaboratively developed information is then used jointly and iteratively by planners to generate demand, determine replenishment requirements, and match production to demands.

The first step in the CPFR process is joint business planning wherein a retailer and supplier share, discuss, coordinate, and rationalize their own individual strategies to create a partnership strategy. The joint plan offers a common and consistent vision of what is expected to be sold, how it will be merchandised and promoted, in which marketplace, and over what time period. A joint calendar is created to share information determining product flow. A common sales forecast is created and shared between retailer and supplier based on shared knowledge of each trading partner's plan. CPFR includes an iterative process where the forecast and requirements plan is exchanged and refined between the partners until a consensus is developed. Using this consensus

---

[11]For more detailed and timely information, see the CPFR website at **www.cpfr.org.**

INDUSTRY INSIGHT 9-1 CPFR AT NABISCO INC. AND WEGMANS FOOD MARKETS

Category management and supply chain management have proven to provide a competitive advantage to firms that can successfully implement them. Trading partners can gain an even greater advantage by linking these activities through the CPFR (Collaborative Planning Forecasting and Replenishment) process. CPFR provides the opportunity to link the output of business plans that were jointly developed between trading partners into the supply chain process. The business plans and forecasts are monitored and kept current by both trading partners. This is accomplished by the creation of a two-way interactive communication process that enables the transfer of promotional plans and forecasts among manufacturers and distributors.

Nabisco, a major international manufacturer of biscuits, snacks, and premium grocery products, markets products in the United States, Canada, and more than 85 other countries around the world. Wegmans Food Markets, Inc., a 58-store supermarket chain in New York and Pennsylvania (with one store in New Jersey), is a family-owned company that is recognized as an industry leader and innovator. In 1998 these firms engaged in a CPFR pilot to validate the VICS (Voluntary Interindustry Commerce Standards) business model. The pilot was limited to 22 Planters nut items. It was conducted without increasing resources in the area of headcount or technology. For the first 6 months, transfer of information was accomplished using spreadsheets and e-mail.

Actual results from the CPFR pilot from July 1998 through January 1999 included an increase in category sales by 13 percent versus an 8 percent decline for other retailers in the market. Sales increase for the Planters brand was especially dramatic at 53 percent as measured by IRI for 30 weeks ending January 17, 1999. The majority of the increases in retail sales can be attributed to jointly developed business plans that leveraged enhanced category management strategy and increased category focus.

These results were achieved with minimal stress on the supply chain due to CPFR. On the operations side, service level to stores increased from 93 percent to 97 percent, and days of inventory declined 2.5 days (18 percent). These positive results led both Nabisco and Wegmans to decide to extend the timeline for this pilot and to expand its scope to include Milk-Bone pet snack products. In addition, commercially available collaboration software will be tested as potential technology solutions. Both companies are also establishing pilots with other trading partners.

Source: "Nabisco Inc. and Wegmans Food Markets," *1999 Voluntary Interindustry Commerce Standards Association*, pp. 33–44.

---

forecast, production, replenishment, and shipment plans are developed. Ideally, the forecast becomes a commitment by the two trading partners—for sales by the retailer and for replenishment by the manufacturer. The benefits of CPFR extend beyond automatic replenishment. See Industry Insight 9-1 to learn how Nabisco Brands' collaborative planning efforts with major customers have returned significant benefits for all involved.

Relational distribution channels hold great promise for superior logistical performance. Traditional conventional channels are primarily adversarial in nature, fail to acknowledge dependency, and are driven by information hoarding rather than sharing so they cannot achieve the sophisticated logistical interfaces required by CPFR. Alliances and partnerships create long-term relationships between supply chain partnerships. When problems occur, as they inevitably will, they can be quickly resolved. Ultimately, the close-working arrangements reduce the cost of doing business for all channel members.

APS Benefits and Considerations

There are substantial benefits that may be achieved through the application of APS to integrated supply chain planning. However, this potential does not come without significant challenges.

Benefits

While specific APS benefits were discussed earlier, there are three broad benefits that accrue from APS utilization. These include responsiveness to changes, comprehensive perspective, and resource utilization.

Historically, logistics and supply chain managers have used extended lead times and schedule freezes to plan for future supply chain activity. For example, production would be scheduled 3 to 4 weeks into the future and then frozen to minimize uncertainty. The long lead times and freeze periods were necessary since the planning process was complex and required substantial analyses. The plans had to be defined early and then frozen to allow the firm time to execute them. While this approach reduced uncertainty, it also substantially reduced flexibility and responsiveness.

Today's customer requires more responsiveness to market needs, and demand for lower inventory levels rules out long cycle times. Marketplace and firm changes can be quickly made in the demand management and resource management modules, allowing for the planning process to use the most current and accurate information. The requirements optimization module then solves the allocation, allowing daily and single week planning cycles rather than multiple weeks or months. APS thus results in a planning process that can be much more responsive to marketplace or firm changes.

Second, effective supply chain management requires planning and coordination across the firm and between firms. The process must consider the trade-offs associated with shifting activities and resources across functions and organizations. Such a comprehensive perspective increases planning process complexity substantially. The complexity follows from the number of organizations, facilities, products, and assets that must be considered when coordinating activities and resources across an entire supply chain. APS offers the capability to consider a comprehensive perspective and make the appropriate trade-offs to achieve optimal supply chain performance.

Third, APS typically results in substantial supply chain performance improvements. While more comprehensive planning and reduced uncertainty usually result in improved customer service, the major APS benefit is enhanced resource utilization. More effective and responsive planning allows a more even assignment of requirements to existing sourcing, production, storage, and transportation capacity. The result is that existing capacity is used more effectively. Firms also report that APS has significantly reduced asset requirements by smoothing resource demands. The decreases include estimates of 20 to 25 percent reductions in plant, equipment, facilities, and inventory. Industry Insight 9-2 describes the performance improvements observed by Heineken USA following the implementation of APS.

While comprehensive APS is a relatively new capability, the future outlook is bright as the technology and capacity to effectively evaluate and manage integrated supply chains are developed. APS can take a comprehensive and dynamic perspective of the entire supply chain and focus on reducing the supply chain asset requirements as demanded by financial markets.

INDUSTRY INSIGHT 9-2 WHEN GROUPTHINK IS GOOD

The Internet and intranet phenomenon that has revolutionized the way people communicate, shop, and read the news is also reshaping the way companies manage the supply chain process. Savvy, progressive companies are tying together their suppliers, distributors, and customers via the Internet or intranets so that all the players can share information and build supply and production plans collaboratively.

Heineken USA has reaped great benefits from collaborative planning. As competition intensified from regional and local microbreweries in the late 1980s and the early 1990s, the then-family-owned Heineken USA was slow to react. As a result, Heineken USA's market share eroded and Heineken NV, the parent company in The Netherlands, decided to take over its American distribution and marketing operations. Heineken USA in its current form began operation in 1995 and set about overhauling its demand and production forecasting process.

Heineken's old forecast and ordering mechanisms involved face-to-face meetings with distributors and several steps of faxing orders among Heineken USA district offices, its headquarters, and the world headquarters in Amsterdam. Consequently, it took an average of 10 to 12 weeks for distributors to receive shipments.

To resolve the problem, Heineken USA implemented a private network connecting the company to its suppliers, distributors, and customers through Internet technology. Distributors log onto customized Heineken USA Web pages using a standard Internet browser and connection. By simply entering their ID and password, they can view their sales forecast and modify and submit their orders.

Heineken USA reassessed the company's entire strategy of getting product from the factory to the distributors. The company assembled a cross-functional team including representatives from the marketing, sales, finance, ordering, and shipping departments of the company. For collaborative planning to work and enhance the efficiency of the supply chain, each department had to embrace the process and make it work in its sector. The new collaborative planning program has reduced order cycle times from 3 months to 4 weeks and simplified planning for Heineken USA's distributor customers. The results are reduced inventory levels and fresher product to consumers.

Eastman Chemical Company, a $5 billion-a-year maker of chemicals, fibers, and plastics, has also revamped its forecasting and supply chain management through online collaborative planning. Eastman needed a way to align annual demand and production forecasts with long-term financial plans. Synchronizing short- and longer-term forecasts would help reduce inventories, improve customer satisfaction, and cut costs.

The company turned to its intranet, which was already in place but rarely used. Since real time input from Eastman's 300 salespeople was crucial to support the forecasting process, the company provided a broad range of employees with standardized hardware and software to access the intranet. The now broadly accessible intranet provided a basis for implementing collaborative planning applications software. Eastman's new system allows everyone involved in the forecasting process to view the current and planned forecast and make changes as market conditions change. Using its intranet for collaborative planning, Eastman expects to reduce costs by 2 to 4 percent—a substantial sum in such a large company.

A company which implements collaborative supply chain planning via the Internet or an intranet must thoroughly integrate the new process into its existing operations, processes, and culture. Collaborative planning via the Internet or intranets can be a vital element in tightening the links in the supply chain, matching production with the overall flow of orders through the chain.

Source: Andrew White, "When Groupthink Is Good: Collaborative Planning via Internet and Intranets Reduces Costs, Enhances Supply Chain Management," *Enterprise Systems Journal,* September 1999.

Considerations

Prior to the actual implementation, there are many considerations regarding APS application. Managers cite their major concerns as (1) integrated versus bolt-on application, (2) data integrity, and (3) application education.

Integrated versus Bolt-on Applications

Technically, there are four approaches for acquiring and implementing APS applications. The first is development using internal firm resources. This is not very common as APS development requires substantial expertise and it isn't likely that a firm that is not focused on APS systems as its core competency would be able to develop the software, experience, or maintain the support capabilities. In addition, the planning process of individual industries or firms is not usually different enough to be able to achieve any significant competitive advantage.

Options two and three are to use an APS application that is integrated with the firm's ERP system or one from a third-party that bolts-on to the firm's ERP system. Some ERP providers, such as SAP, offer an APS that is designed to be closely integrated with their ERP system. The obvious benefits of such integration include data consistency and integrity, as well as reduced need to transfer data between applications, which results in delays and potential errors. The alternative is to use a *bolt-on* or *Best-of-breed approach* that seeks to identify the best APS system for the firm based on features and functionality and then bolt it on to the firm's ERP system. The result is an APS system that better meets the firm's specific requirements or offers improved performance but at a probable cost of reduced integration. While providers of both integrated and bolt-on APS applications are attempting to enhance their integration with ERP system providers, operational integration between execution and planning systems remains a challenge. A fourth option, discussed in Chapter 7, of using an application service provider is beginning to develop more interest.

Data Integrity

Data integrity is the second major consideration cited as an issue for APS implementation. APS systems rely on absolute data integrity for effective decision making. While data integrity has always been important, APS makes it more critical as missing and inaccurate data can dramatically impact decision reliability and stability.

One often-cited data integrity problem concerns product level detail such as cube and weight. While this is pretty basic data, it is not easy to maintain accuracy when there are a large number of products with constant changes and introductions. Managers cite that in the process of implementing APS, it is not uncommon to find a few hundred products with incorrect or missing physical characteristics. While it may not be a large percentage of products in number, the inaccuracy can substantially impact APS decision making. For example, missing or inaccurate cube can result in a transportation APS making a recommendation to load a transportation vehicle with so much product that it exceeds the physical capacity. Specifically, the APS will think that a large amount of product can be loaded into a truck when the product data contains an incorrect or zero cube.

While the decision errors resulting from data integrity problems can be significant, the larger problem is that such errors substantially reduce the credibility of APS systems in general. A few highly visible errors such as overloading transportation vehicles or storage facilities cause management and planners to question the integrity of the entire APS system. The result is that they don't trust the results and they prefer to return to the old tried and true methods of planning and scheduling. Thus, the potential for improved planning is reduced until the trust can be redeveloped. A strong focus on developing and maintaining data integrity is critical to effective APS implementation.

Application Education

Education regarding APS application is the third major consideration for APS implementation. User training for supply chain execution and planning systems has usually focused on the mechanics to initiate the transactions. So, the user would be trained in data or parameter entry where the system would provide quick feedback regarding the acceptability of the entry. Supply chain planning systems are relatively more complex as the feedback is not immediate and the impact may be extensive. For example, changing the requirements or forecast for one item in a time period may shift production schedules for related items on the other side of the world. Understanding APS system dynamics is critical to successful application. Such understanding requires thorough knowledge of APS system mechanics and system dynamics. Although such knowledge can be initiated through training, it must be refined and extended through APS education and experience. The APS education will focus on the characteristics and relationships between supply chain management activities and processes both internal and external to the firm. The education process must be much broader than existing training approaches. APS experience can be developed using job shadowing experience and simulations. The shadowing environment provides actual on-the-job experience in a real time environment. The simulated environment provides a laboratory where inexperienced planners can see or observe the results of their planning environment at low risk to the firm. The combination of these two educational experiences provides a solid foundation for implementing APS. This foundation is critical for successful APS.

Industry Insight 9-3 shows how a division of IBM employed and expanded upon APS to achieve world-class performance.

INDUSTRY INSIGHT 9-3 IBM MICROELECTRONICS DIVISION: TRANSFORMING THE SUPPLY CHAIN

IBM Microelectronics Division (MD) develops, manufacturers, and markets semiconductors, related electronic packaging, and subassemblies for internal IBM divisions and external customers. The semiconductors are developed, fabricated, packaged, and tested at 12 sites around the world. The primary products are microprocessors, memory, application specific integrated circuits, input/output logic chips, and communication processes for applications in data processing, communications, and select consumer segments.

Historically, the planning process was completed independently on a monthly basis for each site. The individual plans were aggregated into a combined plan. The long planning cycles and data inconsistencies resulted in extended customer commitment times and often conflicts resulting in significant customer dissatisfaction.

MD began a transformation to reengineer the total management process, focusing on the fundamental business requirements. The MD objectives were to achieve world-class performance by providing instantaneous customer response through real time ATP, on-time shipment consistent across all sites, enhanced inventory turnover, and e-business initiatives.

The change management process incorporated four stages. The first stage assessed the current business processes and compared them to the best practices as identified for the semiconductor industry. This stage identified the required changes and provided a framework regarding reengineering objectives, principles, and guidelines. The second stage used cross-functional and cross-geographic teams, with executive sponsorship, to develop and refine a comprehensive business process model for Total Order Management (TOM). The refined business model included an APS system that was integrated throughout the division. MD made the choice to acquire the basic APS capability from an outside vendor with substantial internal customization. The third stage implemented process changes and planning tools which were supported by weekly meetings, a staged rollout, and significant training and education. The fourth stage evaluated the results in terms of customer responsiveness, on-time shipment, and inventory turnover.

MD experienced substantial improvements following the implementation of the reengineered process and the TOM system in 1999. The demand/supply rationalization process allows weekly planning based upon integrated division level requirements and capacity constraints for all product levels. The demand allocation process provides divisional capability for instantaneous order commitment and timely communication with the SAP ERP application. Specific operating improvements resulting from TOM and the advanced planning capabilities are:

- Single divisionwide weekly planning process;
- 97 percent of high-volume parts committed through ATP;
- Order response time reduced from 4 days to 1 day with over 65 percent of ATP order committed in less than 1 day;
- On-time delivery to promised commit date increased from 93 percent to 97 percent;
- Delivery performance to customer request improved from 45 to 70 percent;
- 20 percent improvement in surveyed customer satisfaction;
- Reduction in required assets of $80 million;
- Reduction in average inventory of $20 million; and
- The ability to facilitate e-business through Web-enablement.

With the reengineered process and additional APS experience, MD is planning to increase its revenue above industry average, further improve asset utilization, increase customer satisfaction levels, and become the role model for the e-enabled semiconductor company.

Source: David J. Closs, with information provided by Stuart Reed, vice president, Integrated Supply Chain, International Business Machines, 2000.

Summary

There is increasing interest in APS systems due to their ability to enhance supply chain resource utilization. Typical supply chain APS applications include demand planning, production planning, requirements planning, and transportation planning. Given supply chain service objectives and the corresponding resource constraints, APS systems attempt to develop a management decision that meets the service objectives within the constraints at the lowest total cost. The major modules of APS systems are demand management, resource management, resource optimization, and resource allocation. Demand management develops a forecast of product and service requirements based on history and market intelligence. Resource management facilitates the maintenance of the information documenting system resources, costs, compatibility, and constraints. Resource optimization is the engine that solves the management decision problem, typically using a combination of linear programming and heuristics. The optimization component attempts to find the solution that achieves the designated service requirements while minimizing cost and remaining within resource constraints. The resource allocation module operationalizes the plan by assigning resources to serve a specific customer or order.

Unless a supply chain is totally MTO, there are logistics and supply chain activities that must be anticipated by using forecasts. Forecasts include a number of components with the major ones being level, trend, and seasonality. While these external components are significant, significant demand variation also results from firm-controlled factors such as promotions, price changes, and new product introductions. Bottom-up forecasts are more appropriate for markets that respond independently, while top-down forecasts are more useful for situations where there are more centralized actions such as promotions and product introductions. The forecasting process must incorporate a combination of techniques, support systems, and administrative support. The techniques provide a quantitative starting point, the support system refines the data to consider changes in the market, and forecast administration provides a management process to guide and monitor the efforts of forecasters. There are qualitative and causal forecasting techniques, but most logistics and supply chain forecasts are developed using time series methods. While there have been some advancements in forecasting techniques and methods, substantial forecast improvements have been achieved through the use of collaborative techniques such as CPFR involving multiple supply chain partners.

Applications of APS will become more common and extensive as firms and supply chain partners continue to focus on enhancing overall supply chain performance, particularly from an asset management perspective.

Challenge Questions

1. Discuss the major supply chain APS applications with particular focus on the role and anticipated benefits for each application.
2. Discuss overall information flow and the major role of each APS system component.
3. Describe the major rationale and anticipated benefits for implementing advanced planning and scheduling.
4. Discuss the major considerations that a firm must address when implementing APS.
5. Discuss the primary differences between top-down and bottom-up forecasting process.
6. Identify and discuss the major forecast components. Why is it important to decompose demand into these components when developing new forecasts?
7. Compare and contrast the role of the forecast support system, forecast technique, and forecast process.
8. Compare and contrast the basic logic differentiator of time series and causal forecast techniques. Under what conditions would each be appropriate?
9. Discuss how error accountability can be a major factor in improving forecast performance.
10. Discuss how a minor change in demand at the retail level can significantly impact supply chain variation at distributors, manufacturers, and suppliers.

PROBLEM SET 1   INFORMATION AND FORECASTING

1. Mike McNeely, logistics manager for the Illumination Light Company, has considered replacing the firm's manual customer order management system with electronic ordering, an EDI application. He estimates the current system, including labor, costs $2.50/order for transmission and processing when annual order volume is under 25,000. Should the order volume equal or exceed 25,000 in any given year, Mr. McNeely will have to hire an additional customer service representative to assist order reception in the manual process. This would raise the variable cost to $3.00/order. He has also estimated the rate of errors in order placement and transfer to be 12/1000 orders.

   EDI would cost $100,000 upfront to implement and variable costs are determined to be $.50/order regardless of volume. EDI could acquire and maintain order information with an error rate of 3/1000 orders. An EDI specialist would be required to maintain the system at all times as well. Her salary is $38,000 in the first year and increases 3 percent each year thereafter.

   Order errors cost $5.00 per occurrence on average to correct in the manual system. EDI errors cost $8.00 on average to correct since the specialist inspects the system for flaws on most occasions.

   a. If the firm expects order volume over the next 5 years to be 20,000, 22,000, 25,000, 30,000, and 36,000 annually, would EDI pay for itself within the first 5 years?

   b. What effects aside from cost might Mr. McNeely consider when implementing EDI?

2. Mr. McNeely currently batches orders for processing under the manual order management system. The orders are batched for daily processing. If Mr. McNeely opts to implement EDI, might this affect his current means of order processing? If so, how?

3. Quality Marketing Technologies, Inc., has hired you as a sales representative. You have been asked to call on Quikee Stop, a small convenience store chain with five locations in your region. What benefits of UPC and bar coding applications might you illustrate to encourage Quikee Stop to utilize these technologies to track sales at its retail outlets?

4. Comfortwear Hosiery, Inc., produces men's socks at its manufacturing facility in Topeka, Kansas. The socks are stored in a warehouse near the factory prior to distribution to DC locations in Los Angeles, Memphis, and Dayton. The warehouse uses a top-down forecasting approach when determining the expected quantities demanded at each DC.

   The aggregate monthly forecast for June is 12,000 pairs of socks. Historically, the Los Angeles DC has demanded 25 percent of the warehouse's stock. Memphis and Dayton have demanded 30 percent and 35 percent, respectively. The remaining 10 percent is shipped directly from the warehouse.

   a. Based on the aggregate forecast, how many pairs of socks should you expect each DC to demand in June?

   b. Suppose the aggregate forecast for July results in a 6 percent increase over June's forecast. How many pairs of socks would each DC anticipate in July?

5. Ms. Kathleen Boyd, director of logistics for the Scenic Calendar Company, wishes to evaluate two methods of time series forecasting. She has collected quarterly calendar sales data from the years 1993 and 1994.

1993		1994	
Qtr.	**Actual Sales**	**Qtr.**	**Actual Sales**
1	1200	1	1300
2	800	2	800
3	200	3	250
4	1000	4	1200

   a. Use the moving averages technique to find forecasted sales for the third quarter of 1994 based on actual sales from the previous 3 quarters.
   b. Use simple exponential smoothing to forecast each quarter's sales in 1994, given that Ms. Boyd qualitatively forecasted 900 calendars for quarter 4, 1993. Ms. Boyd has assigned an alpha factor of .1 for time series sensitivity.
   c. Repeat the simple exponential smoothing problem above (part 5b) with Ms. Boyd employing an alpha factor of .2.
   d. How well do the moving averages and simple exponential smoothing techniques seem to work in Ms. Boyd's situation? In what ways do the techniques appear to fail?

6. Michael Gregory, logistics manager of Muscle Man Fitness Equipment, has determined that his current forecast system for national sales has historically shown a 20 percent error rate. Due to this level of error, Muscle Man's DC managers maintain inventory at their locations costing the company, on average, $3000 per month.

   By improving his forecast methodology and shortening forecast horizons, Mr. Gregory anticipates cutting the error level down to 12 percent. With improved forecasting, Muscle Man's DC managers have indicated that they feel comfortable with lower inventory levels. Mr. Gregory anticipates monthly inventory carrying cost reductions of 40 percent.

   a. If the forecast system improvement will cost $1000 more per month than the old system, should Mr. Gregory implement the change?
   b. Why might Muscle Man's customers encourage the firm to improve its forecasting capabilities?

III   OPERATIONS

Part III consists of five chapters that describe detailed logistics activities and functions. Chapter 10 focuses on inventory management, including the rationale for inventory, costs associated with carrying inventory, procedures for setting and monitoring appropriate inventory levels, and a framework for managing overall inventory resources. Chapter 11 describes the transportation infrastructure, including role, functionality, and principles. The chapter continues with a description of the transportation regulatory environment, characteristics of transportation modes, and the range of services provided. Chapter 12 focuses on the more managerial aspects of transportation, considering economics, pricing, and functional administration. Together, costs related to inventory and transportation are a significant majority of total logistics expense. Chapter 13 discusses the rationale for warehousing and the activities required for facility design and operations. Chapter 14 focuses inside the warehouse by reviewing packaging and materials handling technologies. The chapter discusses requirements for packaging materials and efficiency followed by a discussion of materials handling equipment capabilities and trade-offs. These chapters focus on specific detail essential to creating logistical excellence. Issues regarding interrelationships and cross-functional trade-offs are reserved for Part IV.

10 INVENTORY MANAGEMENT AND STRATEGY

Inventory decisions are high risk and high impact for supply chain management. Inventory committed to support future sales drives a number of anticipatory supply chain activities. Without a proper inventory assortment lost sales and customer dissatisfaction may occur. Likewise, inventory planning is critical to manufacturing. Material or component shortages can shut down a manufacturing line or force modification of a production schedule, which creates added cost and potential finished goods shortages. Just as shortages can disrupt planned marketing and manufacturing operations, inventory overstocks also create operating problems. Overstocks increase cost and reduce profitability as a result of added warehousing, working capital, insurance, taxes, and obsolescence. Management of inventory resources requires an understanding of the principles, cost, impact, and dynamics.

Inventory Functionality and Principles

Inventory policy formation requires understanding the role of inventory in a manufacturing and logistics environment. To understand the importance of inventory decisions, consider the magnitude of assets committed by a typical enterprise. Table 10-1 presents sales, net profit, and inventory investment for select consumer and industrial goods manufacturers and merchandisers. The table illustrates the significant percentage of assets that are inventory related. Because inventory is a significant cost center, the reduction of a firm's inventory commitment by a few percentage points can result in dramatic profit improvement.

Attention to inventory management has significantly decreased inventory required to support Gross Domestic Product (GDP). These reductions have been achieved during a period when new product proliferation has been widespread. Figure 10-1 illustrates overall performance in inventory to sales ratio.

Inventory Types and Characteristics

Inventory management is risky, and risk varies depending upon a firm's position in the distribution channel. The typical measures of inventory commitment are time duration, depth, and width of commitment.

For a manufacturer, inventory risk is long term. The manufacturer's inventory commitment starts with raw material and component parts, includes work-in-process, and ends with finished goods. In addition, finished goods are often positioned in

TABLE 10-1   Selected Data for Consumer and Industrial Goods Manufacturers and Merchandisers ($ Millions)

Company	Sales	Net Income	Net Income as a Percent of Sales	Total Assets	Inventory Investment	Inventory as a Percent of Assets
Albertson's	$37,478	$10,314	27.52	$15,701	$3,249	20.69
Kroger	28,200	12,200	43.26	17,966	3,938	21.92
Safeway	28,859	8,511	29.49	14,900	2,445	16.41
Fleming	14,646	1,437	9.81	3,573	998	27.93
Spartan Stores	3,050	407	13.34	571	82	14.36
Supervalu	20,339	2,128	10.46	6,495	1,491	22.96
Hershey	3,971	1,616	40.70	3,347	602	17.99
Kellogg	6,984	3,659	52.39	4,809	503	10.46
Nabisco	8,268	3,766	45.55	11,961	898	7.51

Source: 1999 Annual Reports.

FIGURE 10-1

Inventories to sales ratio

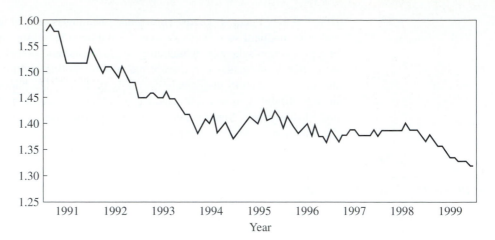

Source: Robert V. Delaney, "Logistics and the Internet: In the Frantic Search for Space, It Is Still About Relationships," *Eleventh Annual State of Logistics Report,* ProLogis and Cass Logistics, Inc., National Press Club, Washington, D.C., June 5, 2000.

warehouses in anticipation of customer demand. In some situations, manufacturers are required to consign inventory to customer facilities. In effect, this practice shifts all inventory risk to the manufacturer. Although a manufacturer typically has a narrower product line than a retailer or wholesaler, the manufacturer's inventory commitment is deep and of long duration.

A wholesaler purchases large quantities from manufacturers and sells smaller quantities to retailers. The economic justification of a wholesaler is the capability to provide retail customers with assorted merchandise from different manufacturers in specific quantities. When products are seasonal, the wholesaler may be required to take an inventory position far in advance of the selling season, thus increasing depth and duration of risk. One of the greatest challenges of wholesaling is product-line expansion to the point where the width of inventory risk approaches that of the retailer while depth and duration of risk remain characteristic of traditional wholesaling. In recent years, retail clientele have also forced a substantial increase in depth and duration by shifting inventory responsibility back to wholesalers.

For a retailer, inventory management is about buying and selling velocity. The retailer purchases a wide variety of products and assumes a substantial risk in the marketing process. Retailer inventory risk can be viewed as wide but not deep. Due to the high cost of store location, retailers place prime emphasis on inventory turnover and direct product profitability. Inventory turnover is a measure of inventory velocity and is calculated as the ratio of annual sales divided by average inventory.

Although retailers assume a position of risk on a variety of products, their position on any one product is not deep. Risk is spread across more than 30,000 stockkeeping units (SKUs) in a typical supermarket. A discount store offering general merchandise and food often exceeds 25,000 SKUs. A full-line department store may have as many as 50,000 SKUs. Faced with this width of inventory, retailers attempt to reduce risk by pressing manufacturers and wholesalers to assume greater and greater inventory responsibility. Pushing inventory *back up* the channel has resulted in retailer demand for fast delivery of mixed-product shipments from wholesalers and manufacturers. Specialty retailers, in contrast to mass merchandisers, normally experience less width of inventory risk as a result of handling narrower assortments; however, they must assume greater risk with respect to depth and duration of inventory holding.

TABLE 10-2   Inventory Functionality

Geographical Specialization   Allows geographical positioning across multiple manufacturing and distributive units of an enterprise. Inventory maintained at different locations and stages of the value-creation process allows specialization.

Decoupling   Allows economy of scale within a single facility and permits each process to operate at maximum efficiency rather than having the speed of the entire process constrained by the slowest.

Supply/Demand Balancing   Accommodates elapsed time between inventory availability (manufacturing, growing, or extraction) and consumption.

Buffering Uncertainty   Accommodates uncertainty related to demand in excess of forecast or unexpected delays in order receipt and order processing on delivery and is typically referred to as safety stock.

If a business plans to operate at more than one level of the distribution channel, it must be prepared to assume related inventory risk. For example, the food chain that operates a regional warehouse assumes risk related to the wholesaler operation over and above the normal retail operations. To the extent that an enterprise becomes vertically integrated, inventory must be managed at all levels of the supply chain.

Inventory Functionality

From an inventory perspective, the ideal situation would be a response capability to manufacture products to customer specification. At various points in early chapters, the practicality of becoming fully response-based has been discussed in terms of the total costs and timeliness of customer support. While a zero-inventory manufacturing/distribution system is typically not attainable, it is important to remember that each dollar invested in inventory is a trade-off with an alternative use of assets that may provide a better return.

Inventory is a major asset that should provide return for the capital invested. The return on inventory investments is the marginal profit on sales that would not occur without inventory. Accounting experts have long recognized that measuring the true cost and benefits of inventory on the corporate profit-and-loss is difficult.[1] Lack of measurement sophistication makes it difficult to evaluate the trade-offs among service levels, operating efficiencies, and inventory levels. While aggregate inventory levels have decreased, many enterprises still carry an average inventory that exceeds their basic requirements. This generalization can be understood better through a review of the four prime functions of inventory. Table 10-2 summarizes inventory functionality.

These four functions—geographical specialization, decoupling, balancing supply and demand, and buffering uncertainty—require inventory investment to achieve managerial operating objectives. While lean logistics, as discussed in Chapter 2, has made significant progress in reducing overall supply chain inventory, inventory properly deployed can create value and reduce total cost. Given a specific manufacturing/marketing strategy, inventories planned and committed to operations can only be reduced

---

[1]Douglas M. Lambert, *The Development of an Inventory Costing Methodology* (Chicago, IL: National Council of Physical Distribution Management, 1976), p. 3; and *Inventory Carrying Cost, Memorandum 611* (Chicago, IL: Drake Sheahan/Stewart Dougall, Inc., 1974).

to a level consistent with performing the four inventory functions. All inventories exceeding the minimum level are excess commitments.

At the minimum level, inventory invested to achieve geographical specialization and decoupling can only be modified by changes in facility location and operational processes of the enterprise. The minimum level of inventory required to balance supply and demand depends on the difficult task of estimating seasonal requirements. With accumulated experience over a number of seasonal periods, the inventory required to achieve marginal sales during periods of high demand can be projected fairly well. A seasonal inventory plan can be formulated based upon this experience.

Inventories committed to safety stocks represent the greatest potential for improved logistical performance. These commitments are operational in nature and can be adjusted rapidly in the event of an error or policy change. A variety of techniques are available to assist management in planning safety stock commitments. The focus in the balance of this chapter is on a thorough analysis of safety stock relationships and policy formulation.

Inventory-Related Definitions

When formulating inventory management policy, specific inventory relationships must be considered. A firm must use these relationships to determine the optimum inventory policy with respect to when and how much to order. The inventory policy essentially determines inventory performance. The two key indicators of inventory performance are *service level* and *average inventory*.

Inventory Policy

Inventory policy consists of guidelines concerning what to purchase or manufacture, when to take action, and in what quantity. It also includes decisions regarding geographical inventory positioning. For example, some firms may decide to postpone inventory positioning by maintaining stock at the plant. Other firms may use a more speculative policy by electing to position more product in local markets or regional warehouses to have product closer to the market. The development of sound inventory policy is the most difficult issue within overall inventory management.

A second aspect of policy concerns inventory management practice. One approach is to independently manage inventory at each stocking facility. At the other extreme is central inventory management of all stocking locations. Centralized inventory management requires effective communication and coordination. The increased availability of affordable information technology and integrated planning systems are allowing more firms to move toward centralized inventory planning.

Service Level

The **service level** is the performance target specified by management. It defines inventory performance objectives. Service level is often measured in terms of an order cycle time, case fill rate, line fill rate, order fill rate, or any combination of these. The *performance cycle* is the elapsed time between the release of a purchase order by a buyer and the receipt of the corresponding shipment. A *case fill rate* defines the percent of cases or units ordered that are shipped as requested. For example, a 95 percent case fill rate indicates that, on average, 95 cases out of 100 are filled from available stock. The remaining 5 cases are backordered or deleted. The *line fill rate* is the percent of order lines filled completely. *Order fill* is the percent of customer orders filled completely.

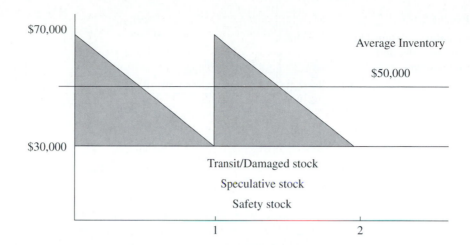

FIGURE 10-2

Inventory cycle for typical product

Inventory management is a major element of logistical strategy that must be integrated to meet service objectives. While one strategy to achieve a high service level is to increase inventory, other alternative approaches are the use of fast transportation and collaboration with customers and service providers to reduce uncertainty.

Average Inventory

Average inventory consists of the materials, components, work-in-process, and finished product typically stocked in the logistical system. From a policy viewpoint target inventory levels must be planned for each facility. Figure 10-2 illustrates the performance cycles for one item at one warehouse location. At the maximum, the facility has in stock and during the normal performance cycle $70,000 and a minimum of $30,000. The difference between these two levels, $40,000 ($70,000 – $30,000), is the order quantity resulting in a cycle inventory of $20,000. Cycle inventory or base stock (also called *lot size stock*) is the portion of average inventory that results from replenishment. At the beginning of a performance cycle, stock level is at a maximum. Customers deplete inventory until the stock level reaches its minimum. Prior to the stock level reaching the minimum, a replenishment order is initiated so that inventory will arrive before an out-of-stock occurs. The replenishment order must be initiated when the available inventory is less than or equal to forecasted demand during the performance cycle time. The amount ordered for replenishment is termed the order quantity. *Given this basic order formulation, average cycle inventory or base stock equals one-half order quantity.* The majority of inventory in the typical logistics system is typically **safety stock.** Safety stock is maintained in a logistical system to protect against demand and performance cycle uncertainty. Safety stock inventory is used only at the end of replenishment cycles when uncertainty has caused higher than expected demand or longer than expected performance cycle times. Thus, the average inventory focus of logistical management is *one-half order quantity plus safety stock.*

Average Inventory Over Multiple Performance Cycles

In initial policy formulation, it is necessary to determine how much inventory to order at a specified time. For purposes of illustration, assume the replenishment performance cycle is a constant 10 days and daily sales rate is 10 units per day. Also assume the replenishment order quantity is 200 units.

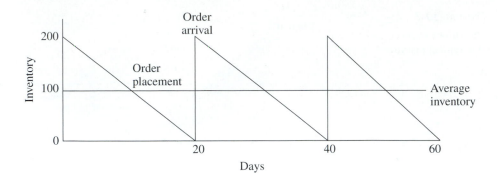

Figure 10-3 illustrates these relationships. This type of chart is referred to as a *sawtooth diagram* because of the series of right triangles. Since complete certainty exists with respect to usage and performance cycle, orders are scheduled to arrive just as the last unit is sold. Thus, no safety stock is necessary. Since the rate of sale in the example is 10 units per day and it takes 10 days to complete inventory replenishment, a sound reorder policy might be to order 200 units every 20 days. Given these conditions, terminology related to policy formulation can be identified.

First, the **reorder point** is specified as 100 units on hand. The reorder point defines when a replenishment order is initiated. In this example, whenever the quantity on hand drops below 100, an additional order for 200 units is placed. The result of this policy is that daily inventory level ranges from a maximum of 200 to a minimum of zero over the performance cycle.

Second, average inventory is 100 units, since stock on hand exceeds 100 units one-half of the time, or for 10 days, and is less than 100 units one-half of the time. In fact, average inventory is equal to one-half the 200-unit order quantity.

Third, assuming a work year of 240 days, 12 purchases will be required during the year. Therefore, over a period of 1 year, 200 units will be purchased 12 times for a total of 2400 units. Sales are expected to equal 10 units per/day over 240 days for a total of 2400 units. As discussed above, average inventory is 100 units. Thus, inventory turns will be 24 (2400 total sales/100 units of average inventory).

In time, the sheer boredom of such routine operations would lead management to ask some questions concerning the arrangement. What would happen if orders were placed more frequently than once every 20 days? Why not order 100 units every 10 days? Why order as frequently as every 20 days? Why not reorder 600 units once every 60 days? Assuming that the inventory performance cycle remains a constant 10 days, what would be the impact of each of these alternative ordering policies on reorder point, average base inventory, and inventory turnover?

The policy of ordering a smaller volume of 100 units every 10 days means that two orders would always be outstanding. Thus, the reorder point would remain 100 units on hand or on order to service average daily sales of 10 units over the 20-day inventory cycle. However, average inventory on hand would drop to 50 units, and inventory turnover would increase to 48 times per year. The policy of ordering 600 units every 60 days would result in an average base inventory of 300 units and a turnover of approximately eight times per year. These alternative ordering policies are illustrated in Figure 10-4.

The figure illustrates that average inventory is a function of the reorder quantity. Smaller replenishment order quantities do result in lower average inventory, but there

FIGURE 10-4

Alternative order quantity and average inventory

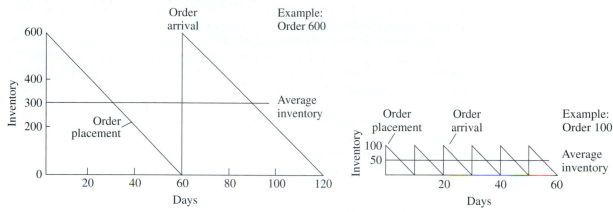

are other factors such as performance cycle uncertainty, purchasing discounts, and transportation economies that are important when determining order quantity.

An exact order quantity policy can be determined by balancing the cost of ordering and the cost of maintaining average inventory. The **Economic Order Quantity** (EOQ) model provides a specific quantity balancing of these two critical cost components. By determining the EOQ and dividing it into annual demand, the frequency and size of replenishment orders minimizing the total cost of cycle inventory is identified. Prior to reviewing EOQ, it is necessary to identify costs typically associated with ordering and maintaining inventory.

Inventory Carrying Cost

Inventory carrying cost is the expense associated with maintaining inventory. Inventory expense is calculated by multiplying annual inventory carrying cost percent by average inventory value. Standard accounting practice is to value inventory at purchase or standard manufacturing cost rather than at selling price.

Assuming an annual inventory carrying cost percentage of 20 percent, the annual inventory expense for an enterprise with $1 million in average inventory would be $200,000 (20% × $1,000,000). While the calculation of inventory carrying expense is basic, determining the appropriate carrying cost percent is less obvious.

Determining carrying cost percent requires assignment of inventory-related costs. Financial accounts relevant to inventory carrying cost percent are capital, insurance, obsolescence, storage, and taxes. While cost of capital is typically a standard assessment, expense related to insurance, obsolescence, storage, and taxes varies depending on the specific attributes of individual products.

Capital Cost

The appropriate charge to place on capital invested in inventory varies widely. Review of a variety of enterprises indicates that assessments range from the prime interest rate to as high as 25 percent.[2] The logic for using the prime interest rate or a specified rate pegged to the prime rate is that cash to replace capital invested in inventory can be obtained in the money markets at that rate. Higher managerially specified capital costs are based on expected or target return on investment for all funds available to an enterprise. This target rate is often termed a *hurdle* rate. Any funds invested in inventory lose their earning power, restrict capital availability, and limit other investment. For example, if a firm expects a 20 percent before-tax return on invested capital, similar logic suggests that capital tied up in inventory should be assessed or charged the same 20 percent.

Confusion often results from the fact that senior management frequently does not establish a clear-cut capital cost policy. For logistical planning, the cost of capital must be thought out clearly since the final rate of assessment will have a significant impact on system design and performance.

Taxes

Taxing authorities typically assess inventory held in warehouses. The tax rate and means of assessment vary by location. The tax expense is usually a direct levy based on inventory level on a specific day of the year or average inventory level over a period of time.

Insurance

Insurance cost is an expense based upon estimated risk or loss over time. Loss risk depends on the product and the facility storing the product. For example, high-value products that are easily stolen and hazardous products result in high insurance cost. Insurance cost is also impacted by facility characteristics such as security cameras and sprinkler systems that might help reduce risk.

Obsolescence

Obsolescence cost results from deterioration of product during storage. A prime example of obsolescence is product that ages beyond recommended sale date, such as food and pharmaceuticals. Obsolescence also includes financial loss when a product becomes obsolete in terms of fashion or model design. Obsolescence costs are typically estimated based on past experience concerning markdowns, donations, or quantity destroyed. This expense is the percent of average inventory value declared obsolete each year.

Storage

Storage cost is facility expense related to product holding rather than product handling. Storage cost must be allocated on the requirements of specific products since it is not related directly to inventory value. In public or contract warehouses, storage

---

[2]For a list of 13 different approaches to arrive at this figure, see Douglas M. Lambert, *The Development of an Inventory Costing Methodology* (Chicago, IL: National Council of Physical Distribution Management, 1976), pp. 24–25.

TABLE 10-3   **Inventory Carrying Cost Components**

Element	Average Percent	Percent Ranges
Cost of Money	15.00%	8–40%
Taxes	1.00	.5–2
Insurance	.05	0–2
Obsolescence	1.20	.5–2
Storage	2.00	0–4
Totals	19.25%	9–50%

charges are billed on an individual basis. With privately owned facilities, the total annual depreciated expense of the warehouse must be calculated in terms of a standard measure such as cost per day per square or cubic foot. The cost of total annual occupancy for a given product can then be assigned by multiplying the average daily physical space occupied by the standard cost factor for the year. This figure can then be divided by the total number of units of merchandise processed through the facility to determine average storage cost per merchandise unit.

Table 10-3 illustrates the components of annual inventory carrying cost and typical range of component costs. It should be clear that the final carrying cost percent used by a firm is determined by managerial policy. Decisions regarding inventory carrying cost level are important because carrying cost is traded off against other logistics cost components in system design and operating decisions.

Planning Inventory

Key parameters and procedures, namely, when to order, how much to order, and inventory control, guide inventory planning. The when to order is determined by the demand and performance average and variation. The how much to order is determined by the order quantity. Inventory control determines the process for monitoring inventory status.

Determining When to Order

As discussed earlier, the reorder point defines when a replenishment shipment should be initiated. A reorder point can be specified in terms of units or days' supply. This discussion focuses on determining reorder points under conditions of demand and performance cycle certainty.

The basic reorder point formula is:

$$R = D \times T,$$

where

R = Reorder point in units;

D = Average daily demand in units; and

T = Average performance cycle length in days.

To illustrate this calculation, assume demand of 20 units/day and a 10-day performance cycle. In this case,

$$R = D \times T$$

$$= 20 \text{ units/day} \times 10 \text{ days}$$

$$= 200 \text{ units.}$$

An alternative form is to define reorder point in terms of days of supply. For the above example, the days of supply reorder point is 10 days.

The use of reorder point formulations implies that the replenishment shipment will arrive as scheduled. When uncertainty exists in either demand or performance cycle length, safety stock is required. When safety stock is necessary to accommodate uncertainty, the reorder point formula is:

$$R = D \times T + \text{SS},$$

where

R = Reorder point in units;

D = Average daily demand in units;

T = Average performance cycle length in days; and

SS = Safety stock in units.

Computation of safety stock under conditions of uncertainty is discussed later in this chapter.

Determining How Much to Order

Lot sizing balances inventory carrying cost with the cost of ordering. The key to understanding the relationship is to remember that average inventory is equal to one-half the order quantity. Therefore, the greater the order quantity, the larger the average inventory and, consequently, the greater the annual carrying cost. However, the larger the order quantity, the fewer orders required per planning period and, consequently, the lower the total ordering cost. Lot quantity formulations identify the precise quantities at which the annual combined total inventory carrying and ordering cost is lowest for a given sales volume. Figure 10-5 illustrates the basic relationships. The point at which the sum of ordering and carrying cost is minimized represents the lowest total cost. Simply stated, the objectives are to identify the ordering quantity that minimizes the total inventory carrying and ordering cost.

Economic Order Quantity

The EOQ is the replenishment practice that minimizes the combined inventory carrying and ordering cost. Identification of such a quantity assumes that demand and costs are relatively stable throughout the year. Since EOQ is calculated on an individual product basis, the basic formulation does not consider the impact of joint ordering of products.

The most efficient method for calculating EOQ is mathematical. Earlier in this chapter a policy dilemma regarding whether to order 100, 200, or 600 units was discussed. The answer can be found by calculating the applicable EOQ for the situation. Table 10-4 contains the necessary information.

FIGURE 10-5

Economic order quantity

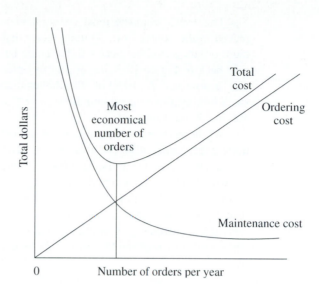

TABLE 10-4   Factors for Determining EOQ

Annual demand volume	2400 units
Unit value at cost	$5.00
Inventory carrying cost percent	20% annually
Ordering cost	$19.00 per order

To make the appropriate calculations, the standard formulation for EOQ is:

$$EOQ = \sqrt{\frac{2C_o D}{C_i U}}$$

where

EOQ = Economic order quantity;

C_o = Cost per order;

C_i = Annual inventory carrying cost;

D = Annual sales volume, units; and

U = Cost per unit.

Substituting from Table 10-4,

$$EOQ = \sqrt{\frac{2 \times 19 \times 2400}{0.20 \times 5.00}}$$

$$= 91,200$$

$$= 302 \text{ (round to 30\{)}$$

Total ordering cost would amount to $152 (2400/300 × $19.00), and inventory carrying cost to $150 [300/2 × (5 × .20)]. Thus, after rounding to allow ordering in multiples of 100 units, annual reordering and inventory carrying cost have been equated.

To benefit from the most economical purchase arrangement, orders should be placed in the quantity of 300 units rather than 100, 200, or 600. Thus, over the year, eight orders would be placed and average base inventory would be 150 units. Referring back to Figure 10-5, the impact of ordering in quantities of 300 rather than 200 can be observed. An EOQ of 300 implies that additional inventory in the form of base stock has been introduced into the system. Average inventory has been increased from 100 to 150 units on hand.

While the EOQ model determines the optimal replenishment quantity, it does require some rather stringent assumptions. The major assumptions of the simple EOQ model are: (1) all demand is satisfied; (2) rate of demand is continuous, constant, and known; (3) replenishment performance cycle time is constant and known; (4) there is a constant price of product that is independent of order quantity or time; (5) there is an infinite planning horizon; (6) there is no interaction between multiple items of inventory; (7) no inventory is in transit; and (8) no limit is placed on capital availability. The constraints imposed by some of these assumptions can be overcome through computational extensions; however, the EOQ concept illustrates the importance of the trade-offs associated with inventory carrying and replenishment ordering cost.

Relationships involving the inventory performance cycle, inventory cost, and economic order formulations are useful for guiding inventory planning. First, the EOQ is found at the point where annualized order cost and inventory carrying cost are equal. Second, average base inventory equals one-half order quantity. Third, the value of the inventory unit, all other things being equal, will have a direct relationship with replenishment order frequency. In effect, the higher the product value, the more frequently it will be ordered.

EOQ Extensions

While the EOQ formulation is relatively straightforward, there are other factors that must be considered in actual application. These factors refer to various adjustments necessary to take advantage of special purchase situations and unitization characteristics. Three typical adjustments are volume transportation rates, quantity discounts, and other EOQ adjustments.

Volume Transportation Rates.   In the EOQ formulation discussed previously, no consideration was given to the impact of transportation cost upon order quantity. When products are purchased on a delivered basis and the seller pays transportation cost from origin to the inventory destination, such neglect may be justified. However, when product ownership is transferred at origin, the impact of transportation rates upon total cost must be considered when determining order quantity.

As a general rule, the greater the weight of an order, the lower the cost per pound of transportation from any origin to destination. A freight-rate discount for larger shipments is common for both truck and rail. Thus, all other things being equal, a firm naturally wants to purchase in quantities that offer maximum transportation economies. Such quantities may be larger than the purchase quantity determined using the EOQ method. Increasing order size has a twofold impact upon inventory cost. Assume for purposes of illustration that the most desirable transportation rate is obtained when a quantity of 480 is ordered as compared to the EOQ-recommended order of 300 calculated earlier.[3] The first impact of the larger order is to increase the average base inven-

---

[3]To determine transportation rates, the unit quantity must be converted to weight.

TABLE 10-5   EOQ Data Requirements for Consideration of Transportation Economies

Annual demand volume	2400 units
Unit value at cost	$5.00
Inventory carrying cost percentage	20% annually
Ordering cost	$19.00 per order
Small shipment rate	$1.00 per unit
Large shipment rate	$0.75 per unit

TABLE 10-6   Volume Transportation Rate Modified EOQ

	Alternative 1: $EOQ_1 = 300$	Alternative 2: $EOQ_2 = 480$
Inventory Carrying Cost	$150	$240
Ordering Cost	$152	$95
Transportation Cost	<u>$2,400</u>	<u>$1,800</u>
Total Cost	$2,702	$2,135

---

tory from 150 to 240 units. Thus, ordering in larger quantities increases inventory carrying cost.

The second impact is a decrease in the number of orders required to satisfy annual requirements. Decreased number of orders increases the shipment size that offers better transportation economies.

To complete the analysis it is necessary to formulate the total cost with and without transportation savings. While this calculation can be directly made by modification of the EOQ formulation, direct comparison provides a more insightful answer. The only additional data required are the applicable freight rate for ordering in quantities of 300 and 480. Table 10-5 provides the data necessary to complete the analysis.

Table 10-6 shows the analysis of total cost. Taking into consideration the potential transportation savings by purchasing in larger lot sizes, total annual cost by purchasing 480 units five times per year rather than the EOQ solution of 300 units eight times per year results in approximately a $570 savings.

The impact of volume transportation rates upon total cost of procurement cannot be neglected. In the example above, the equivalent rate per unit dropped from $1 to $0.75, or by 25 percent. The cost-per-hundredweight range from a minimum truck rate to a carload maximum weight may significantly exceed this 25 percent figure. Thus, any EOQ must be tested for transportation cost sensitivity across a range of weight breaks if transportation expenses are the buyer's responsibility.

A second point illustrated in the data in Table 10-6 is the fact that rather substantial changes in the size of an order and the number of orders placed per year result in only a modest change in the total ordering and inventory carrying cost. The EOQ quantity of 300 had a total annual cost of $302, whereas the revised order quantity had a comparative cost of $335.

EOQ formulations are much more sensitive to significant changes in order cycle or frequency. Likewise, substantial changes in cost factors are necessary to significantly change the economic order quantity.

TABLE 10-7   Example of Quantity Discounts

Cost	Quantity Purchased
$5.00	1–99
4.50	100–200
4.00	201–300
3.50	301–400
3.00	401–500

Finally, two factors regarding inventory cost under conditions of origin purchase are noteworthy. FOB (Free On Board) origin purchase means that the buyer is responsible for freight cost and product risk when the product is in transit. First, purchase at origin means that the buyer assumes full risk on inventory at time of shipment. Depending upon time of required payment, this could mean that transit inventory is part of the firm's average inventory and therefore subjected to an appropriate charge.[4] It follows that any change in weight break leading to a shipment method with a different transit time should be considered, using the added cost or savings as appropriate in a total cost analysis.

Second, the transportation cost must be added to the purchase price to obtain an accurate assessment of the value of goods tied up in inventory. Once the inventory has been received, the amount invested in the product must be increased to reflect the transportation expenses required to move the inventory to its current location. Inventory carrying cost should then be assessed on the combined cost of the item plus transportation.

Quantity Discounts.   Purchase quantity discounts represent an EOQ extension analogous to volume transportation rates. Table 10-7 illustrates a sample schedule of discounts. Quantity discounts can be handled directly with the basic EOQ formulation by calculating total cost at any given volume-related purchase price to determine associated EOQs. If the discount at any associated quantity is sufficient to offset the added inventory carrying cost less the reduced cost of ordering, then the quantity discount offers a viable alternative. It should be noted that quantity discounts and volume transportation rates each affect larger purchase quantities. This does not necessarily mean that the lowest total cost purchase will always be a larger quantity than would otherwise be the case under basic EOQ.

Other EOQ Adjustments.   A variety of special situations may occur that will require adjustments to the basic EOQ. Examples are (1) production lot size, (2) multiple-item purchase, (3) limited capital, and (4) private trucking. Production lot size refers to the most economical quantities from a manufacturing perspective. Multiple-item purchase refers to situations when more than one product is bought concurrently, so quantity and transportation discounts must consider the impact of product combinations. Limited capital describes situations with budget limitations for total inventory investment. Since the multiple product order must be made within the budget limitations, order quantities must recognize the need to allocate the inventory investment across

---

[4]In such situations, the cost of money invested in inventory should be appropriately charged, provided that it is paid for at origin.

the product line. Private trucking influences order quantity since it represents a fixed cost once the decision is made to replenish product. Once it is decided to use a private fleet to transport replenishment product, the enterprise should fill the truck regardless of the EOQ. It does not make sense to transport a half-empty truck simply so that a single item order quantity represents the EOQ.

Another consideration when determining replenishment order quantity is unitization. Many products are stored and moved in standard units such as cases or pallets. Since these standardized units are often designed to fit transportation or handling vehicles, there may be significant diseconomies when the EOQ is not a standard unit. As an example, suppose that a full pallet quantity is 200 units of a specified product. Using an EOQ of 300 units would require shipments of 1.5 pallets. From a handling or transportation utilization perspective, it is probably more effective to order either one or two pallets alternatively or permanently. Chapter 14 presents a more comprehensive discussion of unitization characteristics and their strategic impact.

While standard unit EOQ consolidations are important, their importance is declining as shippers' ability and willingness to provide mixed units or mixed pallets increases. Mixed units or pallets contain product combinations and are designed to provide a product assortment while maintaining transportation and handling economies.

Managing Uncertainty

Although it is useful to understand inventory relationships under conditions of certainty, formulation of inventory policy must realistically consider uncertainty. One of the main functions of inventory management is to plan safety stock to protect against out-of-stocks.

Two types of uncertainty have a direct impact upon inventory policy. **Demand uncertainty** is rate of sales during inventory replenishment. **Performance cycle uncertainty** concerns inventory replenishment time variations.

Demand Uncertainty

Sales forecasting estimates unit demand during the inventory replenishment cycle. Even with good forecasting, demand during replenishment cycle often exceeds or falls short of what is anticipated. To protect against a stockout when demand exceeds forecast, safety stock is added to base inventory. Under conditions of demand uncertainty, average inventory represents one-half order quantity plus safety stock. Figure 10-6 illustrates the inventory performance cycle under conditions of demand uncertainty. The dashed line represents the forecast. The solid line illustrates inventory on hand from one performance cycle to the next. The task of planning safety stock requires three steps. First, the likelihood of stockout must be gauged. Second, demand potential during a stockout period must be estimated. Finally, a policy decision is required concerning the desired level of stockout protection.

Assume for purposes of illustration that the inventory performance cycle is 10 days. Historical experience indicates that daily sales range from 0 to 10 units with average daily sales of 5 units. The economic order is assumed to be 50, the reorder point is 50, the planned average inventory is 25, and sales during the performance cycle are forecasted to be 50 units.

During the first cycle, although daily demand experienced variation, the average of 5 units per day was maintained. Total demand during cycle 1 was 50 units, as

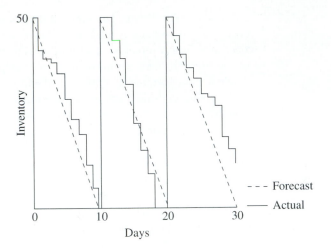

TABLE 10-8 **Typical Demand Experience During Three Replenishment Cycles**

	Forecast Cycle 1		Stockout Cycle 2		Overstock Cycle 3	
Day	Demand	Accumulated	Demand	Accumulated	Demand	Accumulated
1	9	9	0	0	5	5
2	2	11	6	6	5	10
3	1	12	5	11	4	14
4	3	15	7	18	3	17
5	7	22	10	28	4	21
6	5	27	7	35	1	22
7	4	31	6	41	2	24
8	8	39	9	50	8	32
9	6	45	Stockout	50	3	35
10	5	50	Stockout	50	4	39

expected. During cycle 2, demand totaled 50 units in the first 8 days, resulting in a stockout; thus, no sales were possible on days 9 and 10. During cycle 3, demand reached a total of 39 units. The third performance cycle ended with 11 units remaining in stock. Over the 30-day period total sales were 139 units, for average daily sale of 4.6 units.

From the history recorded in Table 10-8, it is observed that stockouts occurred on 2 of 30 total days. Since sales never exceed 10 units per day, no possibility of stockout exists on the first 5 days of the replenishment cycle. Stockouts were possible on days 6 through 10 based on the remote possibility that demand during the first 5 days of the cycle averaged 10 units per day and no inventory was carried over from the previous period. Since during the three performance cycles 10 units were sold on only one occasion, it is apparent that the real risk of stockout occurs only during the last few days of the performance cycle, and then only when sales exceed the average by a substantial margin.[5] Some approximation is possible concerning sales potential for days 9 and

---

[5]In this example, daily statistics are used. An alternative, which is technically more correct from a statistical viewpoint, is to utilize demand over performance cycles. The major limitation of order cycles is the length of time and difficulty required to collect the necessary data.

TABLE 10-9   Frequency of Demand

Daily Demand (in units)	Frequency (Days)
Stockout	2
0	1
1	2
2	2
3	3
4	4
5	5
6	3
7	3
8	2
9	2
10	1

FIGURE 10-7

Historical analysis of demand history

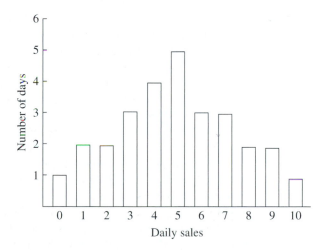

10 of cycle 2. A maximum of 20 units might have been sold if inventory had been available. On the other hand, it is remotely possible that even if stock had been available, no demand would have occurred on days 9 and 10. Based on average demand of 4 to 5 units per day, a reasonable appraisal of lost sales is 8 to 10 units.

It should be apparent that the risk of stockouts created by variations in sales is limited to a short time and includes a small percentage of total sales. Although the sales analysis presented in Table 10-8 helps achieve an understanding of the opportunity, the appropriate course of action is still not clear. Statistical probability can be used to assist management in planning safety stock. The following discussion applies statistical techniques to the demand uncertainty problem.

The sales history over the 30-day period has been arranged in Table 10-9 in terms of a frequency distribution. The main purpose of a frequency distribution is to observe variations around the average daily demand. Given an expected average of 5 units per day, demand exceeded average on 11 days and was less than average on 12 days. An alternative way of illustrating a frequency distribution is by a bar chart, as in Figure 10-7.

Figure 10-8

Normal distribution

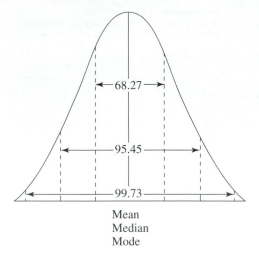

Mean
Median
Mode

Given the historical frequency of demand, it is possible to calculate the safety stock necessary to provide a specified degree of stockout protection. Probability theory is based on the random chance of a specific occurrence within a large number of occurrences. The situation illustrated uses 28 days. In actual application, a larger sample size would be desirable.

The probability of occurrences assumes a pattern around a measure of central tendency, which is the average value of all occurrences. While a number of frequency distributions can be used in inventory control, the most basic is the **normal distribution.**

A normal distribution is characterized by a symmetrical bell-shaped curve, illustrated in Figure 10-8. The essential characteristic of a normal distribution is that the three measures of central tendency have equal value. The *mean* (average) value, the *median* (middle) observation, and the *mode* (most frequently observed) value are all the same. When these three measures are nearly identical, the frequency distribution is normal.

The basis for predicting demand during a performance cycle using a normal distribution is the standard deviation of observations around the measures of central tendency. The **standard deviation** is a measure of dispersion of events within specified areas under the normal curve. For the inventory management application, the event is unit sales per day and the dispersion is the variation in daily sales levels. Within ± 1 standard deviation, 68.27 percent of all events occur. This means that 68.27 percent of the days during a performance cycle will experience daily sales within ± 1 standard deviation of the average daily sales. Within ± 2 standard deviations, 95.45 percent of all events occur. At ± 3 standard deviations, 99.73 percent of all events are included. In terms of inventory policy, the standard deviation provides a method of estimating the safety stock required to offer a specified degree of protection above average demand.

The first step in setting safety stocks is to calculate the standard deviation. Most calculators and spreadsheets calculate standard deviation, but if one of these aids is not available, another method to compute the standard deviation is:

$$\sigma = \sqrt{\frac{\Sigma F_i D_i^2}{n}}$$

TABLE 10-10   **Calculation of Standard Deviation of Daily Demand**

Units	Frequency (F_i)	Deviation from Mean (D_i)	Deviation Squared (D_i^2)	$F_iD_i^2$
0	1	−5	25	25
1	2	−4	16	32
2	2	−3	9	18
3	3	−2	4	12
4	4	−1	1	4
5	5	0	0	0
6	3	+1	1	3
7	3	+2	4	12
8	2	+3	9	18
9	2	+4	16	32
10	1	+5	25	25
$n = 28$	$\bar{s} = 5$			$\Sigma F_iD_i^2 = 181$

where

σ = Standard deviation;

F_i = Frequency of event i;

D_i = Deviation of event from mean for event i; and

n = Total observations available.

The necessary data to determine standard deviation are contained in Table 10-10.

The standard deviation of the data in Table 10-9 is rounded to 3 units. When setting safety stocks, 2 standard deviations of protection, or 6 units, would protect against 95.45 percent of all events included in the frequency distribution. However, the only situations of concern are the probabilities of events that exceed the mean value. No problem exists concerning inventory to satisfy demand equal to or below the average. Thus, on 50 percent of the days, no safety stock will be required. Safety stock protection at the 95 percent level will, in fact, protect against 97.72 percent of all possible events. The 95 percent coverage will cover all situations when daily demand is ± 2 standard deviations of the average plus the 2.72 percent of the time when demand is more than 2 standard deviations below the mean. This added benefit results from what is typically called a *one-tail* statistical application.

The above example illustrates how statistical probability can assist with the quantification of demand uncertainty, but demand conditions are not the only source of uncertainty. Performance cycles can also vary.

Performance Cycle Uncertainty

Performance cycle uncertainty means that inventory policy cannot assume consistent delivery. The planner should expect that actual performance cycle experience will cluster near the average and be skewed in excess of the planned duration. If performance cycle uncertainty is not evaluated statistically, the most common practice is to

TABLE 10-11   **Calculation of Standard Deviation of Replenishment
                Cycle Duration**

Performance Cycle (days)	Frequency (F_i)	Deviation from Mean (D_i)	Deviation Squared (D_i^2)	$F_iD_i^2$
6	2	−4	16	32
7	4	−3	9	36
8	6	−2	4	24
9	8	−1	1	8
10	10	0	0	0
11	8	+1	1	8
12	6	+2	4	24
13	4	+3	9	36
14	2	+4	16	32
				$\Sigma F_iD_i^2 = 200$

$$N = 50 \qquad t = 10$$

$$\sigma = \sqrt{\frac{F_iD_i^2}{N}} = \sqrt{\frac{200}{50}} = \sqrt{4} = 2 \text{ days}$$

base safety stock requirements on the planned replenishment time. However, if there is substantial variation in the performance cycle, a formal evaluation is desirable.

Table 10-11 presents a sample frequency distribution of performance cycles. Although 10 days is the most frequent, replenishment experience ranges from 6 to 14 days. If the performance cycle follows a normal bell-shaped distribution, an individual performance cycle would be expected to fall between 8 and 12 days 68.27 percent of the time.

From a practical viewpoint, when cycle days drop below 10, no immediate problem exists with safety stock. If the performance cycle were consistently below the planned performance cycle over a period of time, then adjustment of expected duration would be in order. The situation of most immediate concern occurs when the duration of the performance cycle consistently exceeds 10 days.

From the viewpoint of the probability of exceeding 10 days, the frequency of such occurrences from the data in Table 10-11 can be restated in terms of performance cycles greater than 10 days and equal to or less than 10 days. In the example data, the standard deviation would not change because the distribution is normal. However, if the actual experience has been skewed in excess of the expected cycle duration, then a *Poisson distribution* may have been more appropriate.[6] In Poisson frequency distributions, the standard deviation is equal to the square root of the mean. As a general rule, the smaller the mean, the greater the degree of skewness.

[6]Edward Silver, David Pyke, and Rein Peterson, *Inventory Management and Production Planning and Scheduling,* 3rd ed. (New York: John Wiley & Sons, 1998).

FIGURE 10-9

Combined demand and performance cycle uncertainty

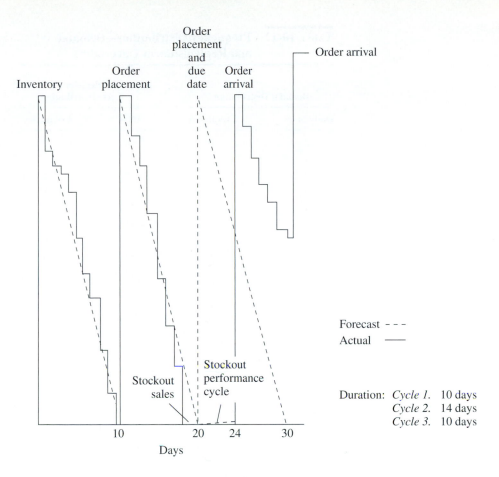

Duration: *Cycle 1.* 10 days
             Cycle 2. 14 days
             Cycle 3. 10 days

Determining Safety Stock with Uncertainty

The typical situation confronting the inventory planner is illustrated in Figure 10-9, where both demand and performance cycle uncertainties exist. Treating both demand and performance cycle uncertainty requires combining two independent variables. The duration of the cycle is, at least in the short run, independent of the daily demand. However, in setting safety stocks, the joint impact of the probability of both demand and performance cycle variation must be determined. Table 10-12 presents a summary of sales and replenishment cycle performance. The key to understanding the potential relationships of the data in Table 10-12 is the 10-day performance cycle. Total demand during the 10 days potentially ranges from 0 to 100 units. On each day of the cycle, the demand probability is independent of the previous day for the entire 10-day duration. Assuming the full range of potential situations illustrated in Table 10-12, total sales during a performance cycle could range from 0 to 140 units. With this basic relationship between the two types of uncertainty in mind, safety stock requirements can be determined by either numerical or simulation procedures.

Numerical Compounding

The exact compounding of two independent variables involves multinominal expansion. This type of procedure requires extensive calculation. A direct method is to

TABLE 10-12   Frequency Distribution—Demand and Replenishment Uncertainty

Demand Distribution		Replenishment Cycle Distribution	
Daily Sales	Frequency	Days	Frequency
0	1	6	2
1	2	7	4
2	2	8	6
3	3	9	8
4	4	10	10
5	5	11	8
6	3	12	6
7	3	13	4
8	2	14	2
9	2		
10	1		
	$n = 28$	$n = 50$	
	$T = 5$	$T = 10$	
	$S_s = 2.54$	$S_t = 2$	

determine the standard deviations of demand and performance cycle uncertainty and then to approximate the combined standard deviation using the convolution formula:

$$\sigma_c = \sqrt{TS_s^2 + D^2 S_t^2},$$

where

σ_c = Standard deviation of combined probabilities;

T = Average performance cycle time;

S_t = Standard deviation of the performance cycle;

D = Average daily sales; and

S_s = Standard deviation of daily sales.

Substituting from Table 10-12,

$$\sigma_c = \sqrt{10.00(2.54)^2 + (5.00)^2(2)^2}$$

$$= \sqrt{64.52 + 100} = \sqrt{164.52}$$

$$= 12.83 \text{ (round to 13)}.$$

This formulation estimates the convoluted or combined standard deviation of T days with an average demand of D per day when the individual standard deviations are S_t and S_s, respectively. The average for the combined distribution is the product of T and D, or 50.00 (10.00 × 5.00).

Thus, given a frequency distribution of daily sales from 0 to 10 units per day and a range in replenishment cycle duration of 6 to 14 days, 13 units (1 standard deviation multiplied by 13 units) of safety stock is required to protect 84.14 percent of all performance cycles. To protect at the 97.72 percent level, a 26-unit safety stock is neces-

TABLE 10-13   Average Inventory Impact Resulting from Changes in EOQ

	Order Quantity	Safety Stock	Average Inventory
Assume constant S sales and constant T performance cycle	50	0	25
Assume demand protection $+2\sigma$ and constant T performance cycle	50	6	31
Assume constant S demand and $+2\sigma$ performance cycle protection	50	20	45
Assume joint $+2\sigma$ for demand and performance cycle	50	26	51

sary. These levels assume a one-tail distribution since it is not necessary to protect against lead time demand below average.

It is important to note that the specific event being protected against is a stockout during the performance cycle. The 68.27 and 97.72 percent levels are *not* product availability levels. These percentages reflect the probability of a stockout during a given order cycle. For example, with a 13-unit safety stock, stockouts would be expected to occur during 31.73 (100 − 68.27) percent of the performance cycles. Although this percentage provides the probability of a stockout, it does not estimate magnitude. The relative stockout magnitude indicates the percentage of units stocked out relative to demand.

Average inventory requirements would be 25 units if no safety stock were desired. The average inventory with 2 standard deviations of safety stock is 51 units [25 + (2 × 13)]. This inventory level would protect against a stockout during 97.72 percent of the performance cycles. Table 10-13 summarizes the alternatives confronting the planner in terms of assumptions and corresponding impact on average inventory.

Estimating Fill Rate

The fill rate represents the magnitude of a stockout rather than the probability. The case fill rate is the percentage of units that can be filled when requested from available inventory. Figure 10-10 graphically illustrates the difference between stockout probability and stockout magnitude. Both illustrations in Figure 10-10 have a safety stock of 1 standard deviation or 13 units. For both situations, given any performance cycle, the probability of a stockout is 31.73 percent. However, during a 20-day period, the figure illustrates two instances where the stock may be depleted. These instances are at the ends of the cycle. If the order quantity is doubled, the system has the possibility of stocking out only once during the 20-day cycle. So, while both situations face the same demand pattern, the first one has more stockout opportunities and potential. In general, for a given safety stock level, increasing the order quantity decreases the relative magnitude of potential stockouts and conversely increases customer service availability.

The mathematical formulation of the relationship is:

$$SL = 1 - \frac{f(k)\sigma_c}{Q},$$

where

   SL = The stockout magnitude (the product availability level);

   $f(k)$ = A function of the normal loss curve which provides the area in a right tail of a normal distribution;

FIGURE 10-10

Impact of order quantity on stockout magnitude

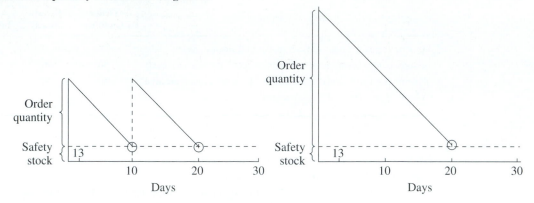

TABLE 10-14   Information for Determining
                        Required Safety Stock

Desired Service Level	99%
σ_c	13
Q	300

> σ_c = The combined standard deviation considering both demand and replenishment cycle uncertainty; and
>
> Q = The replenishment order quantity.

To complete the example, suppose a firm desired 99 percent product availability or case fill rate. Assume the Q was calculated to be 300 units. Table 10-14 summarizes the required information.

Since $f(k)$ is the item used to calculate safety stock requirements, the above equation must be solved for $f(k)$ using algebraic manipulation. The result is:

$$f(k) = (1 - \text{SL}) \times (Q/\sigma_c).$$

Substituting from Table 10-14,

$$f(k) = (1 - 0.99) \times (300/13)$$

$$= 0.01 \times 23.08 = .2308.$$

The calculated value of $f(k)$ is then compared against the values in Table 10-15 to find the one that most closely approximates the calculated value. For this example, the value of k that fits the condition is 0.4. The required safety stock level is:

$$\text{SS} = k \times \sigma_c,$$

where

> SS = Safety stock in units;
>
> k = The k factor that corresponds with $f(k)$;
>
> σ_c = The combined standard deviation.

TABLE 10-15   Table of Loss Integral for Standardized Normal Distribution

k	f(k)	k	f(k)
0.0	.3989	1.6	.0232
0.1	.3509	1.7	.0182
0.2	.3068	1.8	.0143
0.3	.2667	1.9	.0111
0.4	.2304	2.0	.0085
0.5	.1977	2.1	.0065
0.6	.1686	2.2	.0049
0.7	.1428	2.3	.0037
0.8	.1202	2.4	.0027
0.9	.1004	2.5	.0020
1.0	.0833	2.6	.0015
1.1	.0686	2.7	.0011
1.2	.0561	2.8	.0008
1.3	.0455	2.9	.0005
1.4	.0366	3.0	.0004
1.5	.0293	3.1	.0003

Source: Edward Silver, David Pyke, and Rein Peterson, *Inventory Management and Production Planning and Scheduling,* 3rd ed. (New York: John Wiley & Sons, 1998), pp. 724–34.

TABLE 10-16   Impact of Order Quantity on Safety Stock

Order Quantity (Q)	k	Safety Stock	Average Inventory
300	0.40	5	155
200	0.70	8	108
100	1.05	14	64
50	1.40	18	43
25	1.70	22	34

So, substituting in for the example,

$$SS = k \times \sigma_c$$

$$= .04 \times 13 = 5.2 \text{ units.}$$

The safety stock required to provide a 99 percent product fill rate when the order quantity is 300 units is approximately 5 units. Table 10-16 shows how the calculated safety stock and average inventory levels vary for other order quantities. An increased order size can be used to compensate for decreasing the safety stock levels, or vice versa. The existence of such a trade-off implies that there is a combination of replenishment order quantities that will result in desired customer service at the minimum cost.

Dependent Demand Replenishment

The planning aspect of dependent demand is understanding that dependent inventory requirements are a function of known events and are generally not random. Therefore, dependent demand does not require forecasting since uncertainty is eliminated. It follows that no specific safety stock is necessary to support a time-phased procurement program such as MRP. The basic notion of time phasing is that parts and subassemblies need not be carried in inventory as long as they arrive when needed.

The case for carrying no safety stocks under conditions of dependent demand rests on two assumptions. First, procurement replenishment is predictable and constant. Second, vendors and suppliers maintain adequate inventories to satisfy 100 percent of purchase requirements. The second assumption may be operationally attained by use of volume-oriented purchase contracts that assure vendors and suppliers of eventual purchase. In such cases the safety stock requirement still exists for the overall channel, although the primary responsibility has been shifted to the supplier.

The assumption of performance cycle certainty is more difficult to achieve. Even in situations where private transportation is used, an element of uncertainty is always present. The practical result is that safety stocks do exist in most dependent demand situations.

Three basic approaches have been used to introduce safety stocks into a system coping with dependent demand. First, a common practice is to put *safety time* into the requirements plan. Thus, a component is ordered 1 week earlier than needed to assure timely arrival. A second approach is to increase the requisition by a quantity specified by some estimate of expected forecast error. As an example, assume that forecast error will not exceed 5 percent. This procedure is referred to as *overforecasting top-level demand.* The net result is to increase procurement of all components in a ratio to their expected usage plus a cushion to cover forecast error. Components common to different end products or subassemblies covered by the overforecasting technique will naturally experience greater quantity buildups than single-purpose components and parts. To accommodate the unlikely event that all common assemblies will simultaneously require safety stock protection, a widely used procedure is to set a total safety stock for an item at a level less than the sum of 5 percent protection for each potential usage. The third method is to utilize the previously discussed statistical techniques for setting safety stocks directly to the component rather than to the item of top-level demand.

Inventory Management Policies

Inventory management is the process that implements inventory policy. The reactive or pull inventory approach uses customer demand to pull product through the distribution channel. An alternative philosophy is a planning approach that proactively allocates inventory based on forecasted demand and product availability. A third, or hybrid, logic uses a combination of push and pull.

Inventory Control

Inventory control is the managerial procedure for implementing an inventory policy. The accountability aspect of control measures units on hand at a specific location and tracks additions and deletions. Accountability and tracking can be performed on a manual or computerized basis.

TABLE 10-17   Sample Demand, Performance Cycle, and Order Quantity Characteristics

Average daily demand	20 units
Performance cycle	10 days
Order quantity	200 units

Inventory control defines how often inventory levels are reviewed to determine when and how much to order. It is performed on either a perpetual or a periodic basis.

Perpetual Review

A perpetual inventory control process reviews inventory status daily to determine inventory replenishment needs. To utilize perpetual review, accurate tracking of all SKUs is necessary. Perpetual review is implemented through a reorder point and order quantity.

As discussed earlier,

$$ROP = D \times T + SS,$$

where

ROP = Reorder point in units;

D = Average daily demand in units;

T = Average performance cycle length in days; and

SS = Safety or buffer stock in units.

The order quantity is determined using the EOQ.

For purposes of illustration, assume no uncertainty so no safety stock is necessary. Table 10-17 summarizes demand, performance cycle, and order quantity characteristics. For this example,

$$ROP = D \times T + SS$$

$$= 20 \text{ units/day} \times 10 \text{ days} + 0 = 200 \text{ units.}$$

The perpetual review compares on-hand and on-order inventory to the item's reorder point. If the on-hand plus on-order quantity is less than the established reorder point, a replenishment order is required.

Mathematically, the process is:

$$\text{If } I + Q_O \leq ROP, \text{ then order } Q,$$

where

I = Inventory on hand;

Q_O = Inventory on order from suppliers;

ROP = Reorder point in units; and

Q = Order quantity in units.

For the previous example, a replenishment order of 200 is placed whenever the sum of on-hand and on-order inventory is less than or equal to 200 units. Since the reorder point equals the order quantity, the previous replenishment shipment would arrive just as the next replenishment is initiated. The average inventory level for a perpetual review system is:

$$I_{avg} = Q/2 + SS,$$

where

I_{avg} = Average inventory in units;

Q = Order quantity units; and

SS = Safety stock units.

Average inventory for the previous example is calculated as:

$$I_{avg} = Q/2 + SS$$
$$= 300/2 + 0 = 150 \text{ units.}$$

Most illustrations throughout this text are based on a perpetual review system with a fixed reorder point. The reorder formulation is derived from two assumptions: purchase orders for the item under control will be placed when the reorder point is reached, and the method of control provides a continuous monitoring of inventory status. If these two assumptions are not satisfied, the control parameters (ROP and Q) determining the perpetual review must be refined.

Periodic Review

Periodic inventory control reviews the inventory status of an item at regular time intervals such as weekly or monthly. For periodic review, the basic reorder point must be adjusted to consider the extended intervals between reviews. The formula for calculating the periodic review reorder point is:

$$ROP = D(T + P/2) + SS,$$

where

ROP = Reorder point;

D = Average daily demand;

T = Average performance cycle length;

P = Review period in days; and

SS = Safety stock.

Since inventory counts occur periodically, any item could fall below the desired reorder point prior to the review period. Therefore, the assumption is made that the inventory will fall below ideal reorder status prior to the periodic count approximately one-half of the review times. Assuming a review period of 7 days and using conditions similar to those of the perpetual example, the ROP then would be as follows:

$$ROP = D(T + P/2) + SS$$
$$= 20(10 + 7/2) + 0 = 20(10 + 3.5) = 270 \text{ units.}$$

The average inventory formulation for the case of periodic review is:

$$I_{avg} = Q/2 + (P \times D)/2 + SS,$$

where

I_{avg} = Average inventory in units;

Q = Order quantity in units;

P = Review period in days;

D = Average daily demand in units;

SS = Safety stock in units.

For the preceding example, the average inventory is calculated as:

$$I_{avg} = Q/2 + (P \times D)/2 + SS$$

$$= 300/2 + (7 \times 10)/2 + 0 = 150 + 35 = 185 \text{ units.}$$

Because of the time interval introduced by periodic review, periodic control systems generally require larger average inventories than perpetual systems.

Reactive Methods

The **reactive** or **pull inventory system,** as the name implies, responds to a channel member's inventory needs by drawing the product through the distribution channel. Replenishment shipments are initiated when available warehouse stock levels fall below a predetermined minimum or order point. The amount ordered is usually based on some lot-sizing formulation, although it may be some variable quantity that is a function of current stock levels and a predetermined maximum level.

The basic perpetual or periodic review process discussed earlier exemplifies a typical reactive system. Figure 10-11 illustrates a reactive inventory environment for a warehouse serving two wholesalers. The figure shows the current inventory (I), reorder point (ROP), order quantity (Q), and average daily demand (D) for each wholesaler. A review of the wholesaler inventory indicates that a resupply order for 200 units should be placed by wholesaler A from the warehouse. Since current inventory is above ROP for wholesaler B, no resupply action is necessary at this time. However, more thorough analysis illustrates that the independent actions by wholesaler A will likely cause a stockout at wholesaler B within a few days. Wholesaler B will likely stock out because inventory level is close to the reorder point and the supplying warehouse center will not have enough inventory to replenish wholesaler B.

Classical reactive inventory logic is rooted in the following assumptions. First, the system is founded on the basic assumption that all customers, market areas, and products contribute equally to profits.

Second, a reactive system assumes infinite capacity at the source. This assumption implies that product can be produced as desired and stored at the production facility until required throughout the supply chain.

FIGURE 10-11

A reactive inventory environment

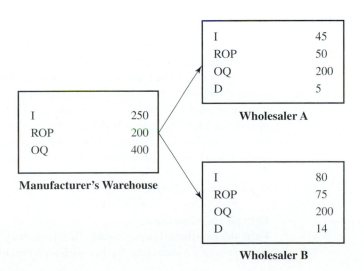

Third, reactive inventory logic assumes infinite inventory availability at the supply location. The combination of assumptions two and three implies relative replenishment certainty. The reactive inventory logic provides for no backorders or stockouts when processing replenishment orders.

Fourth, reactive decision rules assume that performance cycle time can be predicted and that cycle lengths are independent. This means that each performance cycle is a random event and that extended cycles don't generally occur for subsequent replenishment orders. Although reactive logic assumes no control over cycle times, many managers are, in fact, able to influence performance cycle length through expediting and alternative sourcing strategies.

Fifth, reactive inventory logic operates best when customer demand patterns are relatively stable and consistent. Ideally, demand patterns should be stable over the relevant planning cycle for statistically developed inventory parameters to operate correctly. Most reactive system decision rules assume demand patterns based on standard normal, gamma, or Poisson distributions. When the actual demand function does not resemble one of the above functions, the statistical inventory decision rules based on these assumptions will not operate correctly.

Sixth, reactive inventory systems determine each distribution center's timing and quantity of replenishment orders independently of all other sites, including the supply source. Thus, there is little potential to effectively coordinate inventory requirements across multiple distribution centers. The ability to take advantage of inventory information is not utilized—a serious defect when information and its communication are among the few resources that are decreasing in cost in the distribution channel.

The final assumption characteristic of reactive inventory systems is that performance cycle length cannot be correlated with demand. The assumption is necessary to develop an accurate approximation of the variance of the demand over the performance cycle. For many situations higher demand levels create longer replenishment performance cycles since they also increase the demands on inventory and transportation resources. This implies that periods of high demand should not necessarily correspond to extended performance cycles caused by stockouts or limited product availability.

Operationally, most inventory managers limit the impact of such limitations through the skillful use of manual overrides. However, these overrides often lead to ineffective inventory decisions since the resulting plan is based on inconsistent rules and managerial policy.

Planning Methods

Inventory planning methods use a common information base to coordinate inventory requirements across multiple locations or stages in the supply chain. Planning activities may occur at the plant warehouse level to coordinate inventory allocation and delivery to multiple destinations. Planning may also occur to coordinate inventory requirements across multiple channel partners such as manufacturers and retailers. The Advanced Planning and Scheduling (APS) systems discussed in Chapter 9 represent planning method applications. While APS systems computerize the process, it is important for logistics managers to understand the underlying logic and assumptions. Two inventory planning methods are Fair Share Allocation and Distribution Requirements Planning (DRP).

Fair Share Allocation

Fair share allocation is a simplified inventory management planning method that provides each distribution facility with an equitable or "fair share" of available inven-

FIGURE 10-12

Fair share allocation example

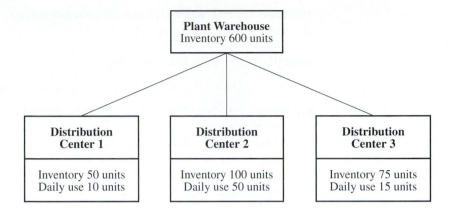

tory from a common source such as a plant warehouse. Figure 10-12 illustrates the network structure, current inventory level, and daily requirements for three warehouses served by a common plant warehouse.

Using fair share allocation, the inventory planner determines the amount of inventory that can be allocated to each warehouse from the available inventory at the plant. For this example, assume that it is desirable to retain 100 units at the plant warehouse; therefore, 500 units are available for allocation. The calculation to determine the common days supply is:

$$DS = \frac{AQ + \sum_{j=1}^{n} I_j}{\sum_{j=1}^{n} D_j},$$

where

    DS = Common days supply for warehouse inventories;

    AQ = Inventory units to be allocated from plant warehouse;

    I_j = Inventory in units for warehouse j; and

    D_j = Daily demand for warehouse j.

In this example,

$$DS = \frac{500 + (50 + 100 + 75)}{10 + 50 + 15}$$

$$= \frac{500 + 225}{75} = 9.67 \text{ days.}$$

The fair share allocation dictates that each warehouse should be stocked to 9.67 days of inventory. The amount to be allocated to each warehouse is determined by:

$$A_j = (DS - I_j/D_j) \times D_j$$

where

    A_j = Amount allocated to warehouse j;

    DS = Days supply that each warehouse is brought up to;

    I_j = Inventory in units for warehouse j; and

    D_j = Daily demand for warehouse j.

The amount allocated to warehouse 1 for this example is:

$$A_1 = (9.67 - 50/10) \times 10$$

$$= (9.67 - 5) \times 10$$

$$= 4.67 \times 10 = 46.7 \text{ (round to 47 units)}.$$

The allocation for warehouses 2 and 3 can be determined similarly and is 383 and 70 units, respectively.

While fair share allocation coordinates inventory levels across multiple sites, it does not consider specific factors such as differences in performance cycle time, EOQ, or safety stock requirements. Fair share allocation methods are therefore limited in their ability to manage multistage inventories.

Distribution Requirements Planning

DRP is a more sophisticated planning approach that considers multiple distribution stages and their unique characteristics. DRP is the logical extension of Manufacturing Requirements Planning (MRP), although there is one fundamental difference between the two techniques. MRP is driven by a production schedule that is defined and controlled by management policy. On the other hand, DRP is driven by customer demand. So, while MRP generally operates in a dependent demand situation, DRP operates in an independent demand environment where uncertain customer demand drives inventory requirements. MRP coordinates scheduling and integration of materials into finished goods, and so controls inventory until manufacturing or assembly is completed. DRP takes coordination responsibility once finished goods are received in the plant warehouse.

DRP Process.   Figure 10-13 illustrates the conceptual design of a combined DRP/MRP system that integrates finished goods, work-in-process, and materials planning. The bottom half of the figure illustrates an MRP system that time phases raw material arrivals to support the production schedule. The result of MRP execution is finished goods inventory at the manufacturing site. The top half of the figure illustrates the DRP system that moves the finished inventory from the manufacturing site to distribution centers and ultimately to customers. DRP time phases the movements to coordinate inventory arrivals to meet customer requirements and commitments. The MRP and DRP systems interface with each other via the finished goods inventory located at the manufacturing site. Close coordination between the two systems results in minimal need for safety stock. DRP coordinates inventory levels, schedules, and when necessary, reschedules inventory movement between levels.

The fundamental DRP planning tool is the schedule, which coordinates requirements across the planning horizon. There is a schedule for each SKU at each warehouse. Schedules for the same SKU are integrated to determine the overall requirements for replenishment facilities such as a plant warehouse.

Figure 10-14 illustrates DRP planning schedules for three warehouses and a central supply facility. The schedules are developed using weekly time increments known as *time buckets*. Each bucket projects one period of activity. Although weekly increments are most common, daily or monthly increments can be used. For each site and SKU, the schedule reports current on-hand balance, safety stock, performance cycle length, and order quantity. In addition, for each planning period, the schedule reports gross requirements, scheduled receipts, and projected inventory on hand. Using the combination of requirements and projected availability, DRP determines the planned

FIGURE 10-13

Conceptual design of integrated DRP/MRP system

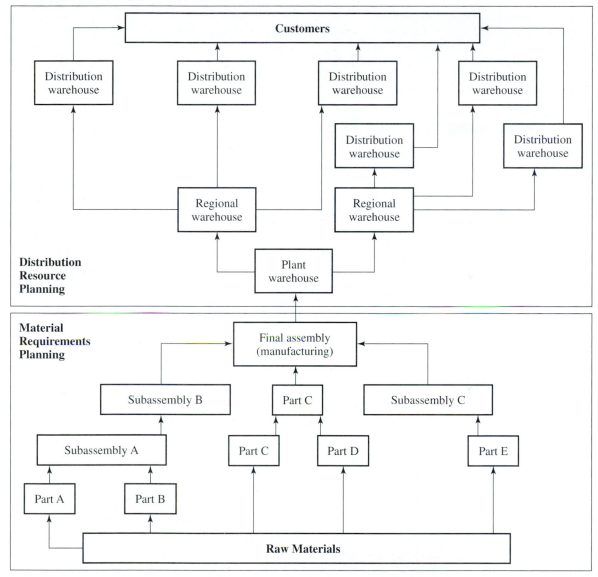

orders necessary to meet anticipated requirements. Gross requirements reflect customer demand and other distribution facilities supplied by the site under review. For Figure 10-14, the gross requirements of the central supply facility reflect the cascading demands of the Boston, Chicago, and San Diego warehouses. Scheduled receipts are the replenishment shipments planned for arrival at the distribution warehouse. Projected on-hand inventory refers to the anticipated week-ending level. It is equal to the prior week's on-hand inventory level less the current week's gross requirements plus any scheduled receipts. While planning approaches to inventory management offer significant benefits, there are some constraints to their effectiveness.

FIGURE 10-14

DRP planning process

Boston Distribution Warehouse

On-hand balance: 352   Lead time: 2 weeks
Safety stock: 55   Order quantity: 500

	Past due	Week							
		1	2	3	4	5	6	7	8
Gross requirements		50	50	60	70	80	70	60	50
Scheduled receipts						500			
Projected on-hand	352	302	252	192	122	542	472	412	362
Planned orders				500					

San Diego Distribution Warehouse

On-hand balance: 140   Lead time: 2 weeks
Safety stock: 2 weeks   Order quantity: 150

	Past due	Week							
		1	2	3	4	5	6	7	8
Gross requirements		20	25	15	20	30	25	15	30
Scheduled receipts						150			
Projected on-hand	140	120	95	80	60	180	155	145	110
Planned orders				150					

Chicago Distribution Warehouse

On-hand balance: 220   Lead time: 2 weeks
Safety stock: 115   Order quantity: 800

	Past due	Week							
		1	2	3	4	5	6	7	8
Gross requirements		115	115	120	120	125	125	125	120
Scheduled receipts		800							
Projected on-hand	220	905	790	670	550	425	300	175	855
Planned orders							800		

Central Supply Facility

On-hand balance: 1,250
Safety stock: 287
Lead time: 3 weeks
Order quantity: 2,200

	Past due	Week							
		1	2	3	4	5	6	7	8
Gross requirements	0	0	0	650	0	0	800	0	0
Scheduled receipts									
Projected on-hand	1250	1250	1250	600	600	600	2000	2000	2000
Master sched-rept							2200		
Master sched-start				2200					

⎣———→ To Material Requirements Planning Schedule ———→

Source: Adapted from original illustration presented in Anonymous, "How DRP Helps Warehouses Smooth Distribution," *Modern Materials Handling* 39, no. 6 (April 1984), p. 57.

First, inventory planning systems require accurate and coordinated forecasts for each warehouse. The forecast is necessary to direct the flow of goods through the supply chain. Ideally, the system does not maintain excess inventory at any location, so little room for error exists in a lean inventory system. To the extent this level of forecast accuracy is possible, inventory planning systems operate well.

Second, inventory planning requires consistent and reliable product for movement between warehouse facilities. While variable performance cycles can be accommodated through safety lead times, such uncertainty reduces planning system effectiveness.

Third, integrated planning systems are subject to system nervousness, or frequent rescheduling, because of production breakdowns or delivery delays. System nervousness leads to fluctuation in capacity utilization, rescheduling cost, and confusion in deliveries. This is intensified by the volatile operating environment characteristic of logistics. Uncertainties such as transportation and vendor delivery reliability can cause an extreme DRP nervousness. While DRP is not the universal solution for inventory management, many firms have reported substantial performance improvements with its use. As illustrated in Industry Insight 10-1, Johnson & Johnson is one such firm.

INDUSTRY INSIGHT 10-1 DRP AT JOHNSON & JOHNSON

Demand planning, or distribution requirements planning (DRP), focuses on the customer, placing inventory requirements within the larger context of supply chain planning. Although the idea behind DRP has been around since the 1970s, the technology to support it has only recently been adopted on a large scale. DRP software facilitates better forecasting of purchases. Since the early 1990s, a growing number of Canadian companies have embraced DRP—often as a component of an enterprise requirements planning system.

Like earlier methods, DRP analyzes forecast and demand data. In addition, they examine the activities in each warehouse within an organization and incorporate all the inventory levels into the decision-making process.

Planners at Johnson & Johnson Medical Products in Peterborough, Ontario, selected a DRP system from J.D. Edwards to increase productivity and streamline activities. The company has been using DRP since mid-1992 to manage product flow across Canada—at one time linking six warehouses for tighter control over distribution. Today, the company manages inventory from two warehouses.

"Using a reorder point system, we had no way of linking our sites to see total demand for our products," notes Darrell Clark, the marketing logistics manager at Johnson & Johnson. "With DRP, we get the overall picture without having to go through the guesswork."

Johnson & Johnson Medical products stocks about 12,000 products, roughly 500 of which are in its DRP system. Good candidates for DRP are medium- to high-volume products with volatile sales fluctuations. Products with relatively low and stable sales volumes are best handled using reorder point formulas.

"Every year there's more pressure to reduce inventories, have better control, and better forecasts," says Clark. "The only way you can succeed is to have a forward vision, and that's where DRP comes in."

Since Johnson & Johnson deals with time-sensitive medical products scheduled around surgeries, a goal of zero inventory is impractical. Instead, a minimum/maximum logic ensures that correct product levels are maintained. But, according to Clark, Johnson & Johnson has reduced inventory levels by 10 to 20 percent and is now in a stronger position to meet customer demands for its products.

Three components are fed into the planning department's DRP system: forecasts, optimum stock levels, and lead times for each product. When an order is placed that causes inventory levels to drop below the safety threshold, the DRP system triggers a reorder, timed so that stock will arrive at the warehouse before critical shortages occur.

The process isn't automatic. Rather, it's suggestion-based, meaning a planner will be notified about the proposed activity and still have a chance to override it. In instances where a suggestion seems unrealistic, planners simply change the parameters in the DRP system to prevent a similar scenario from occurring in the future. The idea is to reach a point where merely pushing a button will confirm suggested activities. For example, a DRP message may tell the buyer to expedite a purchase order because demand is unusually high, at which point the buyer can investigate what's causing the demand and whether the circumstances are likely to continue.

"DRP is a future-looking process," says Clark. "It looks at both yesterday's and today's activities, allowing us to accurately predict tomorrow's requirements."

Source: Peter Weiler, "Too Big for Your Warehouse?" *CA Magazine,* September 1998, pp. 41–42.

Collaborative Inventory Planning

Replenishment programs are designed to streamline the flow of goods within the distribution channel. There are several specific techniques for collaborative replenishment, all of which build on the common denominator of rapidly replenishing inventory according to actual sales experience. The intent is to reduce reliance on forecasting when and where inventory will need to be positioned to meet consumer or end-user demand and instead allow suppliers to respond to demand on a just-in-time basis. Effective collaborative replenishment programs require extensive cooperation and information sharing among distribution channel participants. Specific techniques for automatic replenishment include quick response, continuous replenishment, vendor-managed inventory, and profile replenishment.

Quick Response (QR) is a cooperative effort between retailers and suppliers to improve inventory velocity while providing merchandise supply closely matched to consumer buying patterns. QR is implemented by monitoring retail sales for specific products and sharing information across the supply chain to guarantee that the right product assortment will be available when and where it is required. For example, instead of operating on 15- to 30-day order cycles, a QR arrangement can replenish retail inventories in 6 or fewer days. Continuous information exchange regarding availability and delivery reduces uncertainty for the total supply chain and creates the opportunity for maximum flexibility. With fast, dependable order response, inventory can be committed as required, resulting in increased turnover and improved availability.

Continuous Replenishment (CR) and **Vendor-Managed Inventory (VMI)** are modifications of QR that eliminate the need for replenishment orders. The goal is to establish a supply chain arrangement so flexible and efficient that retail inventory is continuously replenished. Industry Insight 10-2 illustrates how Procter & Gamble's continuous replenishment efforts with major customers have returned significant benefits for all parties. The distinguishing factor between CR and VMI is who takes responsibility for setting target inventory levels and making restocking decisions. In CR, the retailer makes the decisions. In VMI, the supplier assumes more responsibility and actually manages inventory for the retailer. By receiving daily transmission of retail sales or warehouse shipments, the supplier assumes responsibility for replenishing retail inventory in the required quantities, colors, sizes, and styles. The supplier commits to keeping the retailer in stock and to maintaining inventory velocity. In some situations, replenishment involves cross-docking or Direct Store Delivery (DSD) designed to eliminate the need for warehousing between the factory and retail store.

Some manufacturers, wholesalers, and retailers are experimenting with an even more sophisticated collaboration known as **Profile Replenishment (PR).** The PR strategy extends QR and VMI by giving suppliers the right to anticipate future requirements according to their overall knowledge of a merchandise category. A category profile details the combination of sizes, colors, and associated products that usually sell in a particular type of retail outlet. Given PR responsibility, the supplier can simplify retailer involvement by eliminating the need to track unit sales and inventory level for fast-moving products.

Many firms, particularly manufacturers, are using DRP and even APS logic to coordinate inventory planning with major customers. The manufacturers are extending their planning framework to include customer warehouses and, in some cases, their retail stores. Such integrated planning capabilities facilitate manufacturer coordination and management of customer inventories.

Collaborative planning effectively shares inventory requirements and availability between supply chain partners, thus reducing uncertainty. Table 10-18 illustrates the service and inventory impact in a simulated environment under conditions of low and high uncertainty.[7] Industry results also suggest that collaborative inventory management

---

[7]David J. Closs, et al., "An Empirical Comparison of Anticipatory and Response-Based Supply Chain Strategies," *The International Journal of Logistics Management* 9, no. 2 (1998), pp. 21–34.

INDUSTRY INSIGHT 10-2 CRP BENEFITS

Companies trying to develop efficient consumer response initiatives traditionally begin with replenishment. Continuous Replenishment Programs (CRP) have been most widely implemented. Proctor & Gamble (P&G) was among the first companies to test CRP initiative.

Forty percent of P&G's case volume is handled by CRP. Due to the task's complexity, P&G has contracted with IBM as its solution provider. IBM uses a program called Continuous Replenishment Service, a total service offering that includes all necessary EDI connections, continuous replenishment software, training, a help desk, and complete processing of the data which includes automated replenishment ordering. P&G has found the outsourcing of CRP to be highly effective and more cost-efficient. According to Ralph Drayer, vice president of ECR for P&G Worldwide, IBM's continuous replenishment service "has allowed many manufacturers new to CRP to go from zero to 30 percent of their volume on CRP in a matter of months."

P&G is managing inventories for most large food, drug, and mass merchandise retailers. P&G's customer service representatives use CRP to monitor the movement of goods at the retailer's distribution center, basing everyday or basic goods replenishments on movement, inventory, and the short-term forecast. The everyday replenishment process is handled by the software without the need for human intervention unless there are exceptions that fall outside the established parameters. These customer service reps maintain a close collaborative relationship with their retail partners to forecast promotional replenishments more accurately. The P&G rep and the retailer's category manager make a decision on how much promotional product to order; this is manually fed into the IBM CRP database. The program then predicts the retailer's total replenishment needs.

Retailers experienced the following benefits from participating in a CRP relationship with P&G:

- Inventory turns increased 107%.
- Inventory levels were reduced by 12.5 days, translating into a cash flow improvement of 12.5 days.
- Store service levels increased by 2%.
- Store service levels average 99% or 99.5% for most chain drug CRP customers.
- Total retail sales for P&G products managed via CRP were up 2%.
- Retail savings from reductions in storage and handling costs were 20 cents a case.

P&G also received numerous benefits:

- Shipments of perfect orders (complete, on-time, invoiced correctly, and delivered without damage) increased by 5%.
- Damage rates for CRP accounts decreased by 19%.
- Returns were reduced by 36%.
- Plant surge savings (surges generated because of the variability of shipments; CRP has leveled the peaks and valley of demand) were 10 cents a case at the plant level.
- Delivery expenses declined by 20 cents a case due to the more productive use of cube space in transit.

CRP programs are viable for drug chains and grocery stores. "As unlikely as it seems," Drayer states, "CRP programs are as beneficial to drug chains as they are to food chains. Food chains handle more high-volume, high-cube products, but chain drug stores handle more higher-value products. CRP is ideally suited for drug chains because of the combination of high dollar value and total number of SKUs they carry. A case of health and beauty aids has triple the dollar value of a case of paper products."

Source: Liz Parks, "CRP Investment Pay Off in Many Ways," *Drug Store News,* February 1, 1999, p. 26.

TABLE 10-18   **Comparative Service and Inventory Characteristics for Anticipatory versus Responsive Inventory Systems**

	Low Uncertainty Anticipatory	Low Uncertainty Responsive	High Uncertainty Anticipatory	High Uncertainty Responsive
Customer Service				
Fill rate percent	97.69	99.66	96.44	99.29
Inventories				
Supplier inventory	12.88	13.24	14.82	13.61
Manufacturer inventory	6.05	6.12	7.03	6.09
Distributor inventory	5.38	5.86	5.04	5.63
Retailer inventory	30.84	15.79	32.86	20.30
System inventory	55.15	41.01	59.76	45.83

Source: Adapted from David J. Closs et al., "An Empirical Comparison of Anticipatory and Response-Based Supply Chain Strategies," *The International Journal of Logistics Management 9,* no. 2 (1998), pp. 21–34. Used with permission.

yields service improvements of 10 percent in terms of case fill rate and channel inventory reductions of 25 percent.[8] For a more detailed discussion regarding the relative benefits and performance of inventory control techniques, see deLeeuw, van Goor, and vanAmstel.[9]

Adaptive Logic

A combined inventory management system may be used to overcome some of the problems inherent in using either a reactive or a planning method. The factors that might make a reactive system better in one situation may change over time to favor the use of an inventory planning system. Thus, the ideal approach is an **adaptive inventory management system** that incorporates elements of both types of logic and allows different strategies to be used with specific customer or product segments.

The rationale for an adaptive system is that customer demand must usually be treated as independent; however, there are some supply chain collaborations where demand can be treated as dependent. Thus, at some locations and time within the supply chain, an interface exists between independent and dependent demand. The closer that interface is to the final customer, the lower the amount of overall system inventory since dependent demand environments reduce system demand uncertainty. For example, a major consumer promotion might cause demand even at the consumer level to behave like dependent demand since a major demand spike can be anticipated through knowledge of the promotion schedule.

The uniqueness of adaptive inventory management logic is that it adjusts to change. For example, during some parts of the year it may be most efficient to push products to field warehouses, while at other times the best alternative may be to hold the stock at the manufacturing location and wait for customers to pull it through the supply chain. An example of different inventory management requirements is the rela-

---

[8]Newton Birkheard and Robert Schirmer, "Add Value to Your Supply Chain," *Transportation & Distribution,* September 1999, p. 59.

[9]Sander deLeeuw, Ad R. vanGoor, and Rien Ploos vanAmstel, "The Selection of Distribution Control Techniques," *The International Journal of Logistics Management* 10, no. 1 (1999), pp. 97–112.

INDUSTRY INSIGHT 10-3 KIMBERLY-CLARK KEEPS COSTCO IN DIAPERS

One morning, a Costco store in Los Angeles began running low on size 1 and size 2 Huggies. Crisis loomed. So what did Costco managers do? Nothing. They didn't have to thanks to a special arrangement with Kimberly-Clark Corp., the company that makes the diapers.

Under this deal, responsibility for replenishing stock falls on the manufacturer, not Costco. In return, the big retailer shares detailed information about individual stores' sales. So, long before babies in Los Angeles would ever notice it, a diaper dearth was avoided by a Kimberly-Clark data analyst working at a computer hundreds of miles away in Neenah, Wisconsin. A special computer link allows the analyst to make snap decisions about where to ship more Huggies and other Kimberly-Clark products.

Just a few years ago, the sharing of such data between a major retailer and a key supplier would have been unthinkable. But the arrangement between Costco and Kimberly-Clark underscores a sweeping change in American retailing. Across the country, powerful retailers are pressuring their suppliers to take a more active role in shepherding products from the factory to store shelves.

In the case of Costco and Kimberly-Clark, per the VMI arrangement Kimberly-Clark oversees and pays for everything involved with managing Costco's inventory except the actual shelf-stockers in the aisles. Whatever the arrangement, the major focus is the same: cutting costs along the so-called supply chain which comprises every step from lumber mill to store shelf. The assumption is that suppliers are in the best position to spot inefficiencies and fix them.

By several accounts, the close collaboration between Kimberly-Clark and Costco serves as a model for other merchandisers and also helps explain strong recent sales gains by both companies. In the past 2 years, Kimberly-Clark gradually expanded the program and now manages inventory for 44 retailers of its products. The company says it wrung $200 million in costs from its supply chain during that period and vows to squeeze out another $75 million this year.

For Costco, the benefits are equally clear. Costco saves money on staffing and on storage. What's more, Costco says its shelves are less likely to go empty under the new system. That's important for both retailer and supplier.

The importance of the supply chain hasn't been lost on Kimberly-Clark itself, which is trying to apply the same principles to its own suppliers. These days, it keeps less than a month's supply of diapers in its own warehouses, down nearly 50 percent over the past 2 years.

For now, raw material shipments are the weak link. Advances are small, focusing on such details as how the company stocks Velcro tabs for its diapers. Two years ago, the company began sharing its production plans with Velcro USA Inc. via weekly e-mails. That cut Velcro inventory 60 percent, saving several million dollars.

Source: Emily Nelson and Ann Zimmerman, "Minding the Store: Kimberly-Clark Keeps Costco in Diapers, Absorbing Costs Itself," *The Wall Street Journal*, September 7, 2000, pp. A1, A12.

---

tionship between manufacturers and retailers. Usually, retailers generate replenishment orders as required, and manufacturers react to them, but in some situations, the manufacturer assumes the responsibility of managing retailer distribution center inventory. As a result, the manufacturer has visibility of multiple levels of channel demand, which reduces uncertainty and safety stock. The VMI arrangement between Costco and Kimberly-Clark discussed in Industry Insight 10-3 underscores the benefits of such a relationship. While such arrangements are appropriate for some relationships, they are not appropriate for all customers or products because they are labor- and information-intensive.

An adaptive inventory management system adjusts to location and time. In other words, the appropriate inventory management system may change for different

TABLE 10-19   Suggested Inventory Management Logic

Use Planning Logic Under Conditions of	Use Reactive Logic Under Conditions of
Highly profitable segments	Cycle time uncertainty
Dependent demand	Demand uncertainty
Economies of scale	Destination capacity limitations
Supply uncertainty	
Source capacity limitations	
Seasonal supply buildup	

locations and also at different times during the year. This adjustment capability requires that the information base for such a system be totally integrated. The primary difficulty in implementing such a system is determining the adjustment decision rules. Table 10-19 illustrates managerial considerations that may drive adaptations of control logic.

Inventory Management Practices

An integrated inventory management strategy defines the policies and process used to determine where to place inventory, when to initiate replenishment shipments, and how much to allocate. The strategy development process employs three steps to classify products and markets, define segment strategies, and operationalize policies and parameters.

Product/Market Classification

The objective of product/market classification is to focus and refine inventory management efforts. Product/market classification, which is also called **fine-line** or **ABC classification,** groups products, markets, or customers with similar characteristics to facilitate inventory management. The classification process recognizes that not all products and markets have the same characteristics or degree of importance. Sound inventory management requires that classification be consistent with enterprise strategy and service objectives.

Classification can be based on a variety of measures. The most common are sales, profit contribution, inventory value, usage rate, and nature of the item. The typical classification process sequences products or markets so that entries with similar characteristics are grouped together. Table 10-20 illustrates product classification using sales. The products are classified in descending order by sales volume so that the high-volume products are listed first, followed by slower movers. Classification by sales volume is one of the oldest methods used to establish selective policies or strategies. For most marketing or logistics applications, a small percentage of the entities account for a large percentage of the volume. This operationalization is often called the *80/20 rule* or *Pareto's law*. The 80/20 rule, which is based on widespread observations, states that for a typical enterprise 80 percent of the sales volume is typically accounted for by 20 percent of the products. A corollary to the rule is that 80 percent of enterprise sales are accounted for by 20 percent of the customers. The reverse perspective

TABLE 10-20   Product Market Classification (Sales)

Product Identification	Annual Sales (in 000s)	Percent Total Sales	Accumulated Sales (%)	Products (%)	Classification Category
1	$ 45,000	30.0%	30.0%	5%	A
2	35,000	23.3	53.3	10	A
3	25,000	16.7	70.0	15	A
4	15,000	10.0	80.0	20	A
5	8,000	5.3	85.3	25	B
6	5,000	3.3	88.6	30	B
7	4,000	2.7	91.3	35	B
8	3,000	2.0	93.3	40	B
9	2,000	1.3	94.6	45	B
10	1,000	0.7	95.3	50	B
11	1,000	0.7	96.0	55	C
12	1,000	0.7	96.7	60	C
13	1,000	0.7	97.4	65	C
14	750	0.5	97.9	70	C
15	750	0.5	98.4	75	C
16	750	0.5	98.9	80	C
17	500	0.3	99.2	85	C
18	500	0.3	99.5	90	C
19	500	0.3	99.8	95	C
20	250	0.2	100.0	100	C
	$150,000				

of the rule would state that the remaining 20 percent of sales are obtained from 80 percent of the products, customers, etc. In general terms, the 80/20 rule implies that a majority of sales results from a relatively few products or customers.

Once items are classified or grouped, it is common to label each category with a character or description. High-volume, fast-moving products are often described as "A" items. The moderate volume items are termed the "B" items, and the low-volume or slow movers are known as "Cs." These character labels indicate why this process is often termed ABC analysis. While fine-line classification often uses three categories, some firms use four or five categories to further refine classifications. Grouping of similar products facilitates management efforts to establish focused inventory strategies for specific product segments. For example, high-volume or fast-moving products are typically targeted for higher service levels. This often requires that fast-moving items have relatively more safety stock. Conversely, to reduce overall inventory levels, slower-moving items may be allowed relatively less safety stock, resulting in lower service levels.

In special situations, classification systems may be based on multiple factors. For example, item gross margin and importance to customers can be weighted to develop a combined index instead of simply using sales volume. The weighted rank would then group items that have similar profitability and importance characteristics. The inventory policy, including safety stock levels, is then established using the weighted rank.

The classification array defines product or market groups to be assigned similar inventory strategies. The use of item groups facilitates the identification and specification of inventory strategies without requiring tedious development of individual item strategies. It is much easier to track and manage 3 to 10 groups instead of hundreds of individual items.

Segment Strategy Definition

The second step is to define the integrated inventory strategy for each product/market group or segment. The integrated strategy includes specification for all aspects of the inventory management process including service objectives, forecasting method, management technique, and review cycle.

The key to establishing selective management strategies is the realization that product segments have different degrees of importance with respect to achieving the enterprise mission. Important differences in inventory responsiveness should be designed into the policies and procedures used for inventory management.

Table 10-21 illustrates a sample integrated strategy for four item categories. In this case, the items are grouped by ABC sales volume and as a promotional or basic stock item. Promotional items are those commonly sold in special marketing efforts that result in considerable demand lumpiness. Lumpy demand patterns are characteristic of promotional periods with high volume followed by postpromotion periods with relatively low demand.

Table 10-21 illustrates a management segmentation scheme based on service objectives, forecasting process, review period, inventory management approach, and replenishment monitoring frequency. Additional or fewer characteristics of the inventory management process may be appropriate for some enterprises. Although this table is not presented as a comprehensive inventory strategy framework, it illustrates the issues that must be considered. The rationale behind each element is presented based on the full-line classification.

The first consideration is the service objective. The A items are assigned a high service objective since there are typically few items (as per the 80/20 rule), and they significantly impact overall customer service performance because of their high volume. Conversely, a lower service objective is appropriate for slow-moving items because they involve low-volume items and, thus, have relatively small impact on customer service performance.

The second consideration has to do with forecast procedure. Since promotional item sales are influenced by the promotional calendar, their forecast should be developed using a top-down explosion of the total promotion volume. The high-volume products would benefit most from CPFR activities. Since the demand for the remain-

---

TABLE 10-21   Integrated Strategy

Fine-Line Classification	Service Objective	Forecasting Procedure	Review Period	Inventory Management	Replenishment Monitoring
A (Promotional)	99%	CPFR	Perpetual	Planning—DRP	Daily
A (Regular)	98	Sales history	Perpetual	Planning—DRP	Daily
B	95	Sales history	Weekly	Planning—DRP	Weekly
C	90	Sales history	Biweekly	Reorder point	Biweekly

ing product categories is less lumpy, forecasts should be developed using sales history, time series methods, and bottom-up forecasting.

The third consideration involves the replenishment review period. While minimizing the number of inventory reviews may not be as important as it was in the past because of today's advanced information technology, it is still vital for manual elements of the review process. For example, when replenishment or purchase orders must be reviewed or consolidated manually, personnel time constraints may limit the inventory management process to weekly reviews. However, fast-moving items may require more frequent reviews to avoid stockouts. Assuming different review periods are appropriate, high-volume items should use perpetual review while B and C items should be reviewed on a periodic basis, such as weekly or biweekly, respectively.

The fourth consideration is the specific inventory management logic for each group. The continuum of options ranges from a pure reactive system to a planning method as discussed earlier. It is likely that higher-volume product can be forecast with relatively greater accuracy because demand is more stable or because additional effort is possible to develop better forecasts since there are fewer A items. Low-volume items are often difficult to forecast because they typically have relatively greater demand uncertainty. Assuming that better forecasts are possible for A items and that substantial scale benefits exist for planned product movements to distribution facilities and customers, a planning (DRP or APS) approach should be used for high-volume products. Conversely, reactive inventory management is more appropriate for low-volume items so that speculative movement downstream in the channel can be minimized. The reactive logic also minimizes the data collection and manipulation required to support inventory planning system application for the large number of low-volume items.

The final consideration is replenishment monitoring frequency. This refers to the review and expediting efforts to ensure that replenishment orders arrive on time. The monitoring process may include inquiries to the supplier and the carrier to identify shipment status and determine its arrival time. If the monitoring determines that the replenishment order will not arrive on time, replenishment should be expedited or an alternative source identified. Table 10-21 reflects daily monitoring for high-volume items and weekly monitoring of low-volume items. Daily monitoring is appropriate for high-volume products because even a 1- or 2-day stockout would negatively impact service. On the other hand, low-volume items can be monitored weekly since the inventory position does not change as rapidly and stockouts should not substantially impact service performance.

Integrating the above characteristics defines a process that focuses management efforts on providing high service performance for the bulk of the sales or unit volume A items and establishing low inventory and personnel requirements for a large percentage of products. While an initial strategy may be designed for three or four groups, experience and the desire to refine service performance and reduce inventory motivate additional strategies. These can be implemented by increasing the number of groups and refining the policies and procedures for each.

Operationalize Policies and Parameters

The final step in implementing a focused inventory management strategy is to define detailed procedures and parameters. The procedures define data requirements, software applications, performance objectives, and decision guidelines. The parameters delineate values such as review period length, service objectives, inventory carrying cost percentage, order quantities, and reorder points. The combination of parameters either determines or can be used to calculate the precise quantities necessary to make inventory management decisions.

Once the procedures and parameters have been implemented, the environment and performance characteristics must be monitored on a regular basis. Ongoing monitoring is necessary to ensure that the inventory management system is meeting desired objectives and that the customer and product environment does not change substantially. For example, as demand increases for a specific product, inventory process monitoring should recognize the need and perhaps suggest a shift from a reactive to an inventory planning system.

Summary

Inventory typically represents the second largest component of logistics cost next to transportation. The risks associated with holding inventory increase as products move down the supply chain closer to the customer because the potential of having the product in the wrong place or form increases and costs have been incurred to move the product down the channel. In addition to the risk of lost sales due to stockouts because adequate inventory is not available, other risks include obsolescence, pilferage, and damage. Further, the cost of carrying inventory is significantly influenced by the cost of the capital tied up in the inventory. Geographic specialization, decoupling, supply/demand balancing, and buffering uncertainty provide the basic rationale for maintaining inventory. While there is substantial interest in reducing overall supply chain inventory, inventory does add value and can result in lower overall supply chain costs with appropriate trade-offs.

From a logistics perspective, the major controllable inventory elements relate to replenishment cycle stock, safety stock, and in-transit stock. The appropriate replenishment cycle stock is determined using an EOQ formula to reflect the trade-off between storage and ordering cost. Safety stock depends on the mean and variance of daily demand and replenishment performance cycle. In-transit stock depends on the transport mode and time waiting at terminals.

Inventory management uses a combination of reactive and planning logics. Reactive logic is most appropriate for items with low volume, high demand, and high performance cycle uncertainty because it postpones the risk of inventory speculation. Inventory planning logic is appropriate for high-volume items with relatively stable demand. Inventory planning methods offer the potential for effective inventory management because they take advantage of improved information and economies of scale. Adaptive logic combines the two alternatives depending on product and market conditions. Collaboration offers a way for parties in the supply chain to jointly gain inventory efficiency and effectiveness.

Challenge Questions

1. How does the cost of carrying inventory impact the traditional earnings statement of the enterprise?
2. Discuss the relationship between service level, uncertainty, safety stock, and order quantity. How can trade-offs between these elements be made?

3. Discuss the disproportionate risk of holding inventory by retailers, wholesalers, and manufacturers. Why has there been a trend to push inventory back up the channel of distribution?

4. What is the difference between the probability of a stockout and the magnitude of a stockout?

5. Data suggest that while overall average inventory levels are declining, the relative percentage being held by manufacturers is increasing. Explain why you think this observation is either true or false. Describe how such a shift could benefit the operations of the entire channel and how manufacturers could take advantage of the shift.

6. Discuss the differences between reactive and planning inventory logics. What are the advantages of each? What are the major implications of each?

7. Illustrate how fine-line inventory classification can be used with product and market segments. What are the benefits and considerations when classifying inventory by product, market, and product/market?

8. What advantage does DRP have over a fair share method of inventory deployment?

9. Discuss the importance of collaboration in the developing of supply chain inventory strategies. Provide an example.

10. Customer-based inventory management strategies allow the use of different availability levels for specific customers. Discuss the rationale for such a strategy. Are such strategies discriminatory? Justify your position.

11 TRANSPORTATION INFRASTRUCTURE AND REGULATION

The role of transportation in logistics operations has changed dramatically over the last three decades. Prior to transportation deregulation, the purchase of transportation could be likened to buying a commodity such as coal or grain. There was very little difference between transportation suppliers in terms of product, service, or price. Transportation deregulation in 1980 introduced pricing flexibility and significantly increased the range of services transportation companies could provide customers.

Today a wide range of transportation alternatives are available to support product or raw material logistics. For example, logistics managers may integrate private with for-hire transportation to reduce total logistics costs. Many for-hire carriers offer a wide variety of value-added services such as product sortation, sequencing, and customized freight delivery and presentation. Technology has enhanced real time visibility of where freight is throughout the supply chain and when it will be delivered. Precise product delivery reduces inventory, storage, and materials handling. As such, the value of transportation has become greater than simply moving product from one location to another. This chapter provides an overview of the transportation infrastructure and its current regulatory framework to establish a broad understanding of the important role transportation plays in successful logistics.

Transport Functionality, Principles, and Participants

Transportation is a very visible element of logistics. Consumers are accustomed to seeing trucks and trains transporting product or parked at business facilities. Few consumers fully understand just how dependent our economic system is upon economical and dependable transportation. This section provides a foundation by reviewing transportation functionality and the underlying principles of transport operation.

Transport Functionality

Transportation enterprises provide two major services: product movement and product storage.

Product Movement

Whether in the form of materials, components, work-in-process, or finished goods, the basic value provided by transportation is to move inventory to the next stage of the business process. The primary transportation value proposition is product movement up and down the supply chain. The performance of transportation is vital to procurement, manufacturing, and market distribution. Transportation also plays a key role in the performance of reverse logistics. Without reliable transportation, most commercial activity could not function. Transportation consumes time, financial, and environmental resources.

Transportation uses time resources because product is generally inaccessible during the transportation process. Product captive to the transport system is referred to as *in-transit inventory.* Naturally, when designing logistical systems, managers strive to reduce in-transit inventory to a minimum.

Transportation also uses financial resources. In the United States approximately 59 percent of total logistics cost consists of transportation services.[1] Transportation cost results from driver labor, vehicle operation, capital invested in equipment, and administration. In addition, cost results from product loss and damage.

Transportation uses environmental resources both directly and indirectly. In direct terms, transportation represents one of the largest consumers of fuel and oil in the U.S. economy. Although the level of fuel and oil consumption has improved as a result of more fuel-efficient vehicles, total consumption remains high. Indirectly, transportation impacts the environment through congestion, air pollution, and noise pollution.

Product Storage

A less visible aspect of transportation is product storage. While a product is in a transportation vehicle, it is being stored. Transport vehicles can also be used for product storage at shipment origin or destination, but they are comparatively expensive storage

---

[1]For an overview of total logistics cost see Chapter 2, pp. 32–34.

facilities. Since the main value proposition of transportation is movement, a vehicle committed to storage is not otherwise available for transport. A trade-off exists between using a transportation vehicle versus temporarily placing products in a warehouse. If the inventory involved is scheduled to move within a few days to a different location, the cost of unloading, warehousing, and reloading the product may exceed the temporary charge of using the transportation vehicle for storage.[2]

Another form of temporary product storage is *diversion*. Diversion occurs when a shipment destination is changed while product is in transit. For example, the destination of a product initially shipped from Chicago to Los Angeles may be changed to San Francisco while in transit. Traditionally, the telephone was used to implement diversion strategies. Today, satellite communication between enterprise headquarters and vehicles allows more efficient diversion. While diversion is primarily used to improve logistical responsiveness, it also impacts transit storage.

So although costly, product storage in transportation vehicles may be justified from a total cost or performance perspective when loading or unloading costs, capacity constraints, and ability to extend lead times are considered.

Transport Principles

There are two fundamental economic principles that impact transportation efficiency: economy of scale and economy of distance.

Economy of scale in transportation is the cost per unit of weight decrease as the size of a shipment increases. For example, truckload shipments that utilize an entire vehicle's capacity have lower cost per pound than smaller shipments that utilize a limited portion of vehicle capacity. It is also generally true that larger capacity transportation vehicles such as rail and water are less costly per unit of weight than smaller capacity vehicles such as trucks and air. Transportation economies of scale exist because fixed cost associated with moving a load is allocated over the increased weight. Fixed costs include administration related to scheduling, cost of equipment, time to position vehicles for loading or unloading, and invoicing. Such costs are considered fixed because they do not vary with shipment size. In other words, it costs as much to administer a 100 pound shipment as one weighing 1000 pounds.

Economy of distance refers to decreased transportation cost per unit of weight as distance increases. For example, a shipment of 800 miles will cost less to perform than two shipments of the same weight each moving 400 miles. Transportation economy of distance is often referred to as the *tapering principle*. The rationale for distance economies is similar to economies of scale. Specifically, longer distances allow fixed cost to be spread over more miles, resulting in lower per mile charges.

These scaling principles are important when evaluating transportation alternatives. The goal from a transportation perspective is to maximize the size of the load and the distance being shipped while still meeting customer service expectations.

Transport Participants

The transportation environment impacts the range of decisions that can be implemented in a logistical system. Unlike most commercial transactions, transportation decisions are influenced by six parties: (1) shipper; (2) destination party, traditionally

---

[2]The technical terms for using transportation vehicles for storage are *demurrage* for rail cars and *detention* for trucks. See Chapter 12.

FIGURE 11-1

Relationship among transportation participants

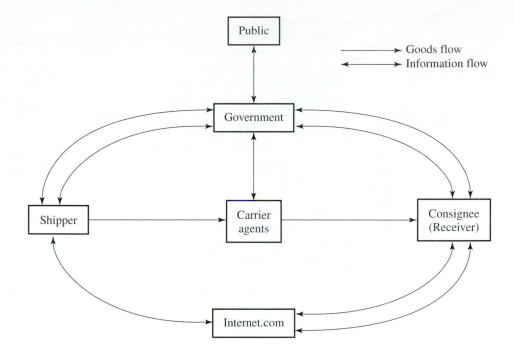

FIGURE 11-1

Relationship among transportation participants

called the *consignee;* (3) carriers and agents; (4) government; (5) Internet; and (6) the public. Figure 11-1 illustrates the relationship among the involved parties. To understand the complexity of the transportation environment it is useful to review the role and perspective of each party.

Shipper and Consignee

The shipper and consignee have a common interest in moving goods from origin to destination within a given time at the lowest cost. Services related to transportation include specified pickup and delivery times, predictable transit time, and zero loss and damage as well as accurate and timely exchange of information and invoicing.

Carrier Agents

The carrier, a business that performs a transportation service, desires to maximize its revenue for movement while minimizing associated costs. As a service business, carriers want to charge their customers the highest rate possible while minimizing labor, fuel, and vehicle costs required to complete the movement. To achieve this objective, the carrier seeks to coordinate pickup and delivery times in an effort to group or consolidate many different shippers' freight into movements that achieve economy of scale and distance. Brokers and freight forwarders are transport agents that facilitate carrier and customer matching.

Government

The government has a vested interest in transportation because of the critical importance of reliable service to economic and social well-being. Government desires a stable and efficient transportation environment to support economic growth.

A stable and efficient transportation environment requires that carriers provide essential services at reasonable cost. Because of the direct impact of transportation on economic success, governments have traditionally been more involved in the practices of carriers than in most other commercial enterprises. In some situations, such as the United States Postal Service, government is directly involved in providing the transportation service. Government traditionally regulated carriers by restricting markets they could service and regulating prices they could charge. Governments also promote carrier development by supporting research and providing right-of-way such as roadways and airports. In some countries government maintains absolute control over markets, services, and rates. Such control allows government to have a major influence on the economic success of regions, industries, or firms.

The overall nature of transportation regulation has changed significantly over the past three decades. A later section of this chapter provides an overview of this regulatory change.

Internet

A recent development in the transportation industry is a wide assortment of Internet-based services. The primary advantage of Internet-based communication is the ability of carriers to share real time information with customers and suppliers. In addition to direct Internet communication between businesses engaged in logistical operations, a wide variety of Web-based enterprises have been launched in recent years. Such Web-based enterprises typically provide two types of marketplaces. The first is a marketplace to exchange information for matching carrier freight capacity with available shipments. These Web-based services may also provide a marketplace to facilitate transactions.

Beyond freight matching a second form of Internet-based information exchange relates to the purchase of fuel, equipment, parts, and supplies. Information exchange operating over the Internet provides carriers the opportunity to aggregate their purchasing and identify opportunities across a wide range of potential vendors.

The primary reason that B2B Internet usage has grown rapidly in motor carrier transport is because the U.S. freight market is highly fragmented. While in excess of 450,000 truckload carriers are in business, 70 percent operate six or fewer trucks.[3] The use of Internet services to aggregate information is attractive for both carriers and shippers.

Finally, the use of the Internet as a communications backbone is rapidly changing the nature of transportation operations. The availability of real time information is improving shipment visibility to the point where tracing and tracking are no longer a challenge. In addition to real time visibility, the Internet can be used to share information concerning scheduling and capacity planning.

Public

The final transportation system participant, the public, is concerned with transportation accessibility, expense, and effectiveness as well as environmental and safety standards. The public indirectly creates transportation demand by purchasing goods. While minimizing transportation cost is important to consumers, concerns also involve environmental impact and safety. The effect of air pollution and oil spillage is a significant transportation-related social issue. The cost of environmental impact and safety is ultimately paid by consumers.

The formation of transportation policy is complex due to interaction between these six parties. Such complexity results in frequent conflict between shippers, con-

---

[3]American Trucking Association, *American Trucking Trends* (Alexandra, VA: American Trucking Association Inc., 1996), p. 1.

signees, and carriers. The concern to protect public interest served as the historical justification for government involvement in economic and social regulation. The next section provides a brief review of how government regulation has changed over the years.

Transportation Regulation

Since transportation has a major impact on both domestic and international commerce, government has historically taken special interest in both controlling and promoting transportation. Control takes the form of federal and state government regulation as well as a wide range of administration and judicial administration. With the passage of the Act to Regulate Interstate Commerce on February 4, 1887, the federal government became active in protecting the public interest with respect to performance and provision of transportation services.

Types of Regulation

Government transportation regulation can be grouped into two categories: economic regulation and safety and social regulation. Regulatory initiatives have historically focused on economic issues; however, recent regulatory initiatives have increasingly been directed toward safety and social issues.

Economic Regulation

Regulation of business practices is the oldest form of government control. To provide dependable transportation service and to foster economic development, both federal and state governments have actively engaged in economic regulation. For over 100 years, government regulation sought to make transportation equally accessible and economical to all without any discrimination. Regulatory policy has attempted to foster competition among privately owned transportation companies. To encourage economical and widespread transportation supply, government invested in public infrastructure such as highways, airports, waterways, and deep water ports. However, to actually provide transportation service, the government supported and regulated a system of privately owned for-hire carriers.

Due to transportation's importance to economic growth, governments believed that carriers needed to be regulated to ensure service availability and stability. Availability meaning that carrier services would be accessible to all business enterprises. Stability meaning that carriers would be guaranteed sufficient profits to ensure viable long-term operation. Economic regulation generally sought to achieve its goals by controlling entry, rates, and services. In addition, economic regulatory practice treated each method of transport independently. This practice limited carrier ability to develop intermodal relationships and offerings. By 1970, federal economic regulation had reached the point where it affected 100 percent of rail and air ton-miles, 80 percent of pipeline, 43.1 percent of trucking, and 6.7 percent of domestic water carriers.[4] The degree of direct government economic regulation began to decline during the 1970s and took a dramatic turn in 1980 with the passage of major deregulatory legislation. The

---

[4]Derived from Department of Transportation, *1972 National Transportation Report* (Washington, DC: U.S. Government Printing Office, 1972), pp. 2–44.

contemporary economic regulatory environment is dominated by free market competition more or less regulated by antitrust laws.

Safety and Social Regulation

In direct contrast to reduced transportation regulation, another trend in the 1970s and 1980s was expanded safety and social regulation. Since its inception in 1966, the federal Department of Transportation (DOT) has taken an active role in controlling the transport and handling of hazardous material and rules related to maximum driver hours and safety. The form of regulation was institutionalized by the passage of the Transportation Safety Act of 1974, which formally established safety and social regulation as a governmental initiative. Substantial legislation impacting logistical performance was passed during the next three decades. The Hazardous Materials Transportation Uniform Safety Act of 1990, which provided federal government control over equipment design, hazardous material classification, packaging, and handling, took precedence over state and local environmental regulations. Additional emphasis on transportation safety has increased due to environmental and related liability lawsuits.

History of Regulation

The following discussion is divided into time periods reflecting dominant regulatory posture. The early period regulation discussion serves to provide future logistics managers insight into the legislative, administrative, and judicial foundations of today's transportation market.

Pre-1920: Establishing Government Control

The original purpose of interstate regulation was to scrutinize the activities of for-hire carriers for the public interest. Since railroads dominated early transportation, they enjoyed a near monopoly. Individual states maintained the legal right to regulate discriminatory practices within their borders, but no federal regulation existed to provide consistent interstate controls. In 1887, the Act to Regulate Commerce was passed by Congress and became the foundation of U.S. transportation regulation.[5] The act also created the Interstate Commerce Commission (ICC).

The refinement of federal regulatory power over carriers evolved from legislation and judicial decisions from 1900 through 1920. At the turn of the century, destructive competitive practices resulted from independent pricing by carriers. Although the ICC had the authority to review groups of rates with respect to their just and reasonable nature once published by individual carriers, no regulation existed over proposed rate making. Attempts at joint rate making by railroads had been declared illegal. In 1903, the railroads supported the passage of the Elkins Act. This legislation eliminated secret rebates and special concessions while increasing the penalty for departures from published rates. It did not, however, eliminate the cause of discriminatory practices— independent and nonregulated pricing.

The passage of the Hepburn Act of 1906 began to establish federal regulatory power over pricing. The just-and-reasonable-review authorization of the 1887 act was expanded to include examination of maximum rates. However, the regulatory posture remained *expost,* or after the fact, until passage of the Mann-Elkins Act in 1910. This

---

[5]For an early history of legislative attempts prior to 1887, see L. H. Hanley, *A Congressional History of Railroads in the United States, 1850–1887,* Bulletin 342 (Madison: University of Wisconsin, 1910).

act permitted the ICC to rule on the reasonableness of proposed rates *prior* to their effective date and to suspend rates when they appeared discriminatory.

The posture of modern rate regulation was completed with the passage of the Transportation Act of 1920. The review power of the ICC was expanded to prescribe reasonableness of minimum as well as maximum rates. The ICC was instructed to assume a more aggressive nature concerning proposed rates. The original Act to Regulate Commerce was modified to instruct the commission to initiate, modify, and adjust rates as necessary in the public interest. The 1920 act also changed the name of the 1887 act to the Interstate Commerce Act.

1920–1940: Regulatory Formalization

Several additional transportation laws were enacted during these two decades. With some exceptions, their primary objective was to clarify issues related to the basic acts of 1887 and 1920. In 1935 the Emergency Transportation Act further instructed the ICC to set standards with respect to reasonable rate levels. By the 1930s motor carriers had become an important transportation factor. In 1935 the Motor-Carrier Act placed regulation of common carrier highway transportation under the jurisdiction of the ICC. This act, which became Part II of the Interstate Commerce Act, defined the basic nature of the legal forms of for-hire and motor carriers.

In 1938 the Civil Aeronautics Act established the Civil Aeronautics Authority (CAA) as the ICC's counterpart for regulating air transport. The powers and charges of the CAA were somewhat different from those of the ICC, in that the act specified that the CAA would promote and actively develop the growth and safety of the airline industry. In 1940 the functions of the original CAA were reorganized into the Civil Aeronautics Board (CAB) and the Civil Aeronautics Administration, later known as the Federal Aeronautics Administration (FAA). In addition, the National Advisory Committee on Aeronautics was formed in the mid-1930s and in 1951 became known as the National Aeronautics and Space Administration (NASA). Starting in the 1960s, NASA concentrated attention on exploration of outer space. However, NASA was specifically charged with the responsibility for increasing aviation safety, utility, and basic knowledge through the deployment of science and technology. Thus, in the regulatory structure that resulted, the CAB regulated rate making; the FAA administered the airway system; and NASA was concerned with scientific development of aerospace, commercial, and private aviation.

The regulation of pipelines was not as clear-cut as that of railroads, motor carriers, and air transport. In 1906 the Hepburn Act declared that oil pipelines were common carriers. The need for regulation developed from the early market dominance that the Standard Oil Company gained by developing crude oil pipelines to compete with rail transport. In 1912 the ICC ruled, subsequently upheld by the Supreme Court, that private pipelines could be regulated as common carriers. While there are substantial differences between pipeline and other forms of regulation, for all effective purposes the ICC fully regulated pipeline traffic. Interestingly, a significant difference regarding pipeline regulation is that this type of common carrier was allowed to transport goods owned by the carrier.

1940–1970: Status Quo

Regulation of water transport prior to 1940 was extremely fragmented. Some standards existed under both the ICC and the Federal Maritime Commission (FMC). In addition, a series of acts placed regulation of various aspects of the domestic water transport under specific agencies. For example, the Transportation Act of 1940 put domestic water transport under ICC jurisdiction and gave the FMC authority over water transport in foreign commerce and between Alaska and Hawaii and other U.S. ports.

It is important to understand that the ICC did not actually set or establish carrier prices. Rather, the ICC reviewed and either approved or disapproved rates. Carriers under federal regulation were allowed to jointly set prices because they were exempt from the antitrust provisions of the Sherman, Clayton, and Robinson-Patman acts. This exemption was provided by the Reed-Bulwinkle Act of 1948, which permitted carriers to collaborate in ratemaking bureaus. Collaborative pricing was a common feature among for-hire carriers. In particular, for-hire transportation carriers in motor and rail organized freight bureaus that standardized prices and published price lists, called tariffs, for specific geographic areas.

From 1970 until 1973 several acts were passed to aid the then rapidly deteriorating rail industry of the United States. In 1970 the Rail Passenger Service Act established the National Railroad Passenger Cooperation (AMTRAK). The Regional Rail Reorganization Act of 1973 (3-R) was passed to provide economic aid to seven major northeastern railroads facing bankruptcy. As a result of 3-R Act provisions, the Consolidated Rail Corporation (CONRAIL) began to operate portions of the seven lines on April 1, 1976.

The establishment of AMTRAK and CONRAIL represented the first modern attempt of the federal government to own and operate transportation. While the subsequent passage of the Railroad Revitalization and Regulatory Reform Act of 1976 (4-R) and the Rail Transportation Improvement Act of 1976 provided financial support for AMTRAK and CONRAIL, these acts also began to reverse the trend of regulatory expansion that had prevailed for nine decades.

1970–1980: Prelude to Deregulation

In the early 1970s, a movement was gaining momentum to review and modify economic regulation to better meet the requirements of contemporary society. A Presidential Advisory Committee recommended that increased transportation competition would be in the general public's interest. The committee's recommendations were published in a 1960 report issued by the Commerce Department.[6] A Senate Committee in 1961 produced a revised National Transportation Policy. Among other recommendations the 1961 report advocated formation of a Department of Transportation (DOT).[7] After its formation in 1966, DOT became a dominant force seeking regulatory modification. From 1972 to 1980 DOT introduced or significantly influenced legislation at 2-year intervals to modify the regulatory scope of for-hire carriers.

The initial success in regulatory reform was administrative in nature. From 1977 to 1978 CAB Chairman Alfred Kahn forced de facto deregulation of the Civil Aeronautics Board by virtue of administrative rulings that encouraged air carrier price competition and eased the establishment of new airlines. In 1977, the Federal Aviation Act was amended to deregulate domestic cargo airlines, freight forwarders, and shippers' associations with respect to pricing and entry. The standard for entry into the air cargo

---

[6]Department of Commerce, *Federal Transportation Policy and Program* (Washington, D.C.: U.S. Government Printing Office, 1960).

[7]Senate Committee on Commerce, 87th Congress, *National Transportation Policy* (Washington, DC: U.S. Government Printing Office, 1961). The Department of Transportation was established by Public Law 86-670 in 1966 and initiated operation on April 1, 1967.

industry was modified to require that a new competitor be judged *fit, willing,* and *able* to carry out the proposed service. The traditional regulatory criteria of judging entry applications on the basis of *public convenience* and *necessity* were eliminated. On October 24, 1978, the Airline Deregulation Act was passed, extending free market competition to all forms of passenger air transport. The CAB was closed November 30, 1984.

1980–Present: Deregulation

The drive for economic regulatory change in trucking and the railroads became official with the passage of the Motor Carrier Act of 1980 (MC 80) and the Staggers Rail Act (Staggers Act).[8]

MC 80 was a formal effort to stimulate competition and promote efficiency in trucking. Entry restrictions or right to conduct operations were relaxed, allowing firms to offer trucking services if they were judged fit, willing, and able. Restrictions relating to the types of freight carriers could legally haul and the range of services carriers could provide were abolished. While the ICC retained the right to protect the public against discriminatory practices and predatory pricing, individual carriers were given the right to price their services. The trucking industry's collective rate-making practices were restricted and soon would be abolished. The structural impact of MC 80 on the for-hire motor carrier industry was dramatic. Overnight the industry was transformed from a highly regulated to a highly competitive structure.

On October 14, 1980, President Carter deregulated the railroad industry by signing the Staggers Rail Act. This act was a continuation of a trend initiated in the 3-R and 4-R acts and supplemented the Rail Transportation Improvement Act of 1976. The dominant philosophy of the Staggers Act was to provide railroad management with the freedom necessary to revitalize the industry. As such, the most significant provision of the Staggers Act was increased pricing freedom. Railroads were authorized to selectively reduce rates to meet competition while increasing other rates to cover operating cost. Carriers were also given increased flexibility with respect to surcharges. Contract rate agreements between individual shippers and carriers were specifically legalized. In addition to price flexibility, railroad management was given liberalized authority to proceed with abandonment of poorly performing rail service. The act also provided the framework for a liberalized attitude toward mergers and increased the ability of railroads to be involved in motor carrier service.

Since the passage of the landmark legislation of 1980, several major legislative acts have further defined railroad practice and structure. The trend toward a competitive transportation marketplace was reinforced by key administrative and judicial rulings. The Negotiated Rates Act of 1993 provided a framework for motor carriers to settle undercharge claims. The undercharge issue resulted from failure of some firms to file discounted rates with the ICC. Several legal claims were filed against carriers for failure to comply with ICC filing regulations.[9]

The authority of the ICC to regulate transportation was generally weakened following passage of the Trucking Industry Reform Act of 1994.[10] This act eliminated the need for motor carriers to file rates with the ICC. Effective January 1, 1966, the ICC was abolished by passage of the ICC Termination Act of 1995. This act further

---

[8]Motor Carrier Act of 1980 (Public Law 96-296) and the Staggers Rail Act of 1980 (Public Law 96-488).
[9]Negotiated Rates Act of 1993 (Public Law).
[10]Trucking Industry Reform Act of 1994 (Public Law S.B. 2275).

deregulated transportation and established a three-person Surface Transportation Board (STB) within the DOT to administer remaining economic regulation issues across the industry.[11] The authority of the STB includes all transportation modes and incorporates freight forwarders and brokers.

Over the decades, considerable conflict existed between the federal government and state governments concerning legal right to regulate interstate commerce. Both levels of government claimed inherent rights to regulate. State government clearly had the right to regulate interstate shipments in terms of vehicle size, entry, rates, and routes. At the height of the regulatory era, 42 states were actively engaged in some form of regulation.[12] The issues of state right to regulate were not as clear-cut with respect to freight moving in interstate commerce.

In an effort to increase intrastate regulatory consistency across states, the ICC attempted to clarify and expand interstate transportation. Interstate commerce was traditionally defined as product movement across state lines. In a 1993 ruling, the ICC concluded that shipments from warehouses to markets in the same state could be deemed interstate movements if the commodity had originally been shipped from out of state. The ICC argued that such shipments are part of a *continuing movement* and that interstate regulation should apply. In an effort to gain more direct control over intrastate regulation, the Federal Aviation Administration Authorization Act and the Reauthorization Act of 1996 essentially preempted economic regulations of intrastate transportation.[13] The preemption was placed in the act because Congress found that the states' regulation of intrastate transport had (1) imposed an unreasonable cost on interstate commerce; (2) impeded the free flow of trade, traffic, and transportation of interstate commerce; and (3) placed unreasonable cost on American consumers.

This provision preempted state regulation of prices, routes, and services for direct air carriers and related motor carriers. The purpose was to level the playing field between air and motor carriers with respect to intrastate economic trucking regulation. The net effect was to remove intrastate regulation of transportation. In 1998 the Ocean Shipping Reform Act revised and updated a previous act passed in 1984. This act served to greatly reduce the regulatory authority of the Federal Maritime Commission. While the FMC continues to regulate ocean liner shipping, carriers no longer are required to file tariffs with the FMC. The act gave carriers substantially more freedom to negotiate rates and contracts with shippers.

A final act of significance to transportation was passed in 2000. The Electronic Signatures in Global and National Commerce Act gave electronic documents signed by digital signature the same legal status as paper documents. Industry Insight 11-1 illustrates the range of legal complexities that accompanies such major change.

In today's market regulation is primarily limited to safety and social issues. Matters related to competition are enforceable under the general antitrust laws that govern fair business practice. Thus, while a logistics executive is free from the historical burden of explicit transportation regulation, executive actions remain accountable to the Federal Trade Commission and the Justice Department.

---

[11]ICC Termination Act of 1995 (Public Law).

[12]Cassandra Chrones Moore, "Interstate Trucking: Stronghold of the Regulations," *Policy Analysis 204,* February 16, 1994, p. 6.

[13]Federal Aviation Administration Authorization Act of 1994 (H.R. 103-2739) and Federal Aviation Reauthorization Act of 1996 (USCS 40101).

INDUSTRY INSIGHT 11-1 SIGN ON THE WWW._____

In August 2000, President Clinton ushered in a new era of contract law when he signed—with pen and keyboard—the Electronic Signatures in Global and National Commerce Act. The law gives electronic documents signed by digital signature the same legal weight that any paper with a dotted line has long enjoyed.

Now, the difficult part begins. Uncertainties surrounding the legality and implementation of digital signatures remain—not everyone is exactly sure what a digital signature is. The bill drawn up in the U.S. Congress was designed to be nondescript when it comes to methods used in making digital signatures and authenticating electronic documents. U.S. lawmakers didn't want to stifle the creation of new technology. Trade and transportation interests are trying to figure out precisely what effect the law will have on existing practices, such as the transmission of electronic bills of lading, air waybills, and letters of credit.

The law supports the transmission of electronic non-negotiable bills of lading and airway bills, which could facilitate using the Internet to verify delivery and change of ownership and to make payments on letters of credit. More importantly, it opens up the opportunity for replacing paper sales contracts, letters of credit, and negotiable bills of lading. The law could spur the option of new Internet-based procurement practices.

Developers of online B2B marketplaces in the automotive, retail, and steel industries, to name a few, have been pitching a concept called "dynamic sourcing" as a prime benefit of the online exchange. Enterprise buyers, such as Ford Motor Co., Sears, and Bethlehem Steel, will be able to go online and source goods from myriad suppliers all over the globe.

Some analysts argue that companies, particularly smaller enterprises, would benefit from more choice. Setting up overseas supplier relationships or supplier/carrier contracts can be a very costly and time-consuming exercise. B2B marketplace proponents say the Internet can instantly bring together buyers and sellers, thus creating greater competition and efficiencies in international trade.

Digital signatures make it possible for the entire procurement process to be managed without paper.

In 1998 U.S. Bank introduced PowerTrack, an electronic freight payment system, to shippers and carriers. The system is designed to eliminate paper from the freight payment process by automatically paying carriers and electronically billing shippers. PowerTrack provides U.S. Bank with electronic proof of deliveries so that it can release payments directly into carriers' accounts. To date, the company has been verifying the identity of users via passwords and membership agreements.

Digital signatures could allow U.S. Bank to offer its electronic services to anyone using electronic bills of lading and letters of credit. All U.S. Bank needs is verifiable proof of delivery and change of ownership. "The acknowledgment of delivery can happen electronically, freeing the bank to pay off the funds immediately, creating a much clearer and more auditable path of documentation," says Langer, general manager of PowerTrack.

Internet companies involved in moving funds and documentation welcomed the law as further support of their visions for future commerce.

Source: Gordon Forsyth, "Sign on the **www.**_____," *American Shipper,* August 2000, pp. 22–24.

Transportation Structure

The freight transportation structure consists of the rights-of-way, vehicles, and carriers that operate within five basic transportation modes. A *mode* identifies a basic transportation method or form. The five basic transportation modes are rail, highway, water, pipeline, and air.

TABLE 11-1 The Nation's Freight Bill ($ Billions)

	1960	1970	1980	1990	2000
Truck	32.3	62.5	155.3	270.1	481.0
Railroad	9.0	11.9	27.9	30.0	36.0
Water	3.4	5.3	15.3	20.1	26.0
Pipeline	.9	1.4	7.6	8.3	9.0
Air	.4	1.2	4.0	13.7	27.0
Other Carriers	.4	.4	1.1	4.0	6.0
Other Shipper Costs	1.3	1.4	2.4	3.7	5.0
Grand Total	47.8	83.9	213.7	350.8	590
GNP (Trillions)	.5	1,046	2,831	5,832	9,960
Grand Total % of GNP	9.00%	8.03%	7.55%	6.02%	5.92%

Source: Robert V. Delaney, Twelfth Annual "State Of Logistics Report," presented to the National Press Club, Washington, DC, June 4, 2001.

TABLE 11-2   Domestic Shipments by Mode and Volume

	Freight Volume (millions of tons)		Mode Share Percent		1996–2006 Percent Change
	1996	**2006**	**1996**	**2006**	
Truck	6,549	8,242	60.3%	62.9%	25.9%
Rail	1,682	1,979	15.5	15.0	17.7
Rail Intermodal	135	211	1.2	1.6	56.3
Air	11	24	0.1	0.2	118.2
Water	1,044	1,137	9.6	8.6	8.9
Pipeline	1,443	1,600	13.3	12.1	10.9

Source: ATA Foundation 3rd Annual United States Freight Forecast to 2006.

The relative importance of each transportation mode in the United States is measured in terms of system mileage, traffic volume, revenue, and nature of freight transported. Table 11-1 provides a summary of transportation expenditure by mode from 1960 to 2000. Tables 11-2 and 11-3 provide tonnage and revenue share by mode in 1996 as projected to 2006. These data confirm that the truck share of the domestic freight market far exceeds that of all other modes combined. The 1996 tonnage share was 60.3 percent, and revenue share of truck transport was 82.3 percent. While all transport modes are vital to a sound national transportation structure, it is clear that the U.S. economy, current and projected, depends on trucks. The following discussion provides a brief overview of the essential operating characteristics of each mode.

Rail

Historically, railroads have handled the largest number of ton-miles within the continental United States. A ton-mile is a standard measure of freight activity that combines weight and distance. As a result of early development of a comprehensive rail

---

TABLE 11-3   Domestic Shipments by Mode and Revenue

	Freight Revenue ($ billions)		Mode Share Percent		1996–2006 Percent Change
	1996	**2006**	**1996**	**2006**	
Truck	346.0	446.0	82.3%	81.5%	29.0%
Rail	29.6	35.1	7.0	6.4	18.6
Rail Intermodal	5.6	8.7	1.3	1.6	55.4
Air	13.3	29.4	3.2	5.4	121.1
Water	7.4	8.1	1.8	1.5	9.5
Pipeline	18.3	20.2	4.4	3.7	10.4

Source: ATA Foundation 3rd Annual United States Freight Forecast to 2006.

---

network connecting almost all cities and towns, railroads dominated intercity freight tonnage until after World War II. This early superiority resulted from the capability to transport large shipments economically and to offer frequent service, which gave railroads a somewhat monopolistic position. However, with the advent of serious motor carrier competition following World War II, the railroads' share of revenues and ton-miles declined.

Railroads once ranked first among all modes in terms of the number of miles in service. The extensive development of roads and highways to support the growth of automobiles and trucks after World War II altered this ranking. In 1970 there were 206,265 miles of rail track in the United States. By 1998, track mileage had declined to 128,730 miles due to significant abandonment.[14] Over the last few years, track mileage has stabilized.

The capability to efficiently transport large tonnage over long distances is the main reason railroads continue to handle significant intercity tonnage. Railroad operations have high fixed costs because of expensive equipment, right-of-way and tracks, switching yards, and terminals. However, rail enjoys relatively low variable operating costs. The development of diesel power reduced the railroads' variable cost per ton-mile, and electrification is providing further reductions. Modified labor agreements have reduced human resource requirements, resulting in variable cost reductions.

As a result of deregulation and focused business development, rail traffic has shifted from transporting a broad range of commodities to specific freight. Core railroad tonnage comes from raw material-extractive industries located a considerable distance from improved waterways and items such as automobiles, farm equipment, and machinery. The rail fixed-variable cost structure offers competitive advantages for long-haul moves. Starting in the mid-1970s, railroads began to segment the transportation market by focusing on carload, intermodal, and container traffic. Marketing emphasis became even more segmented following passage of the Staggers Rail Act. Railroads became more responsive to specific customer needs by emphasizing bulk industries and heavy manufacturing, as contrasted to standardized boxcar service. Intermodal operations were expanded by forming alliances and motor carrier ownership. For example, United Parcel Service, primarily a multifaceted motor carrier, is the largest user of rail service to transport trailers in the United States.

---

[14]ENO Transportation Foundation, Inc., *Transportation in America*, 1999, p. 64.

To provide improved service to major customers, progressive railroads have concentrated on the development of specialized equipment, such as enclosed trilevel automobile railcars, cushioned appliance railcars, unit trains, articulated cars, and double stack container flatcars. These technologies are being applied by the railroads to reduce weight, increase carrying capacity, and facilitate interchange. The last three innovations are explained in greater detail.

On unit trains all car capacity is committed to transporting a single product. Typically, the product is a bulk commodity such as coal or grain. Unit trains have also been used to support assembly operations for the automobile industry. The unit train is faster and less expensive to operate than traditional trains since it can be routed direct and nonstop from origin to destination.

Articulated cars have an extended rail chassis that can haul up to 10 containers on a single flexible unit. The concept is to reduce weight and time required for interchanging railcars.

Double stack railcars, as the name implies, are built to transport two levels of containers on a single flatcar, thereby doubling the capacity of each railcar. The containers, discussed later in this chapter, are essentially truck bodies without wheels.

The above examples are by no means a comprehensive review of recent railroad innovations. They are representative of attempts to retain and grow railroad market share. It is clear that significant change is occurring in traditional concepts of railroading. The 1970s challenges of survival and potential nationalization have been replaced by a revitalized rail network. Railroads currently perform a highly focused and important role in the transportation structure as the intermodal leaders of the 21st century.

Motor

Highway transportation has expanded rapidly since the end of World War II. To a significant degree the rapid growth of the motor carrier industry has resulted from speed and ability to operate door-to-door.

Motor carriers have flexibility because they are able to operate on all types of roadways. Nearly one million miles of highway are available to motor carriers, which is more mileage than all other modes combined. The fleet of over-the-road trucks exceeds 1.5 million tractors and 4.4 million trailers.[15]

In comparison to railroads, motor carriers have relatively small fixed investment in terminal facilities and operate using publicly financed and maintained roads. Although the cost of license fees, user fees, and tolls is considerable, these expenses are directly related to the number of trucks and miles operated. The variable cost per mile for motor carriers is high because a separate power unit and driver are required for each trailer or combination of tandem trailers. Labor requirements are also high due to driver safety restrictions and need for substantial dock labor. Motor carrier operations are characterized by low fixed and high variable costs. In comparison to railroads, motor carriers more efficiently handle small shipments moving short distances.

Motor carrier characteristics favor manufacturing and distributive trades, at distances up to 500 miles for high-value products. Motor carriers have made significant inroads into rail traffic for medium and light manufacturing. Due to delivery flexibility, motor carriers dominate freight moving from wholesalers or warehouses to retail stores. The prospect for maintaining stable market share in highway transport remains

---

[15]ENO Transportation Foundation, Inc, op. cit.

bright. Today, with the exception of small package goods moving in premium service, almost all less-than-15,000-pound intercity shipments are transported by truck.

The motor carrier industry is not without problems. The primary difficulties relate to increasing cost to replace equipment, maintenance, safety, driver shortages, and platform and dock wages. Although accelerating labor rates influence all modes of transport, motor carriers are labor-intensive, causing high wages to be a major concern. To counteract this trend, carriers have placed a great deal of attention on improved line-haul scheduling, computerized billing systems, mechanized terminals, tandem operations that haul two or three trailers with a single power unit, and participation in coordinated intermodal transport systems.

One threat to the for-hire motor carrier industry is over-the-road transportation by shipper-owned trucks or trucks operated by integrated logistics service providers (ISPs) who are under contract to perform transport services for shippers. Approximately 55 percent of all intercity truck tonnage is hauled by shipper-owned or shipper-controlled trucks. Following deregulation, this ratio reached a high of 66 percent by 1987.[16] The decline to 55 percent resulted from shippers realizing the numerous complexities and problems of operating a private fleet. The growth of ISP-operated trucking offers a service that combines the flexibility of private with the consolidation potential of for-hire operators. An ISP may perform services for multiple shippers and thus gain both economies of scale and distance.[17] Current projections are that for-hire carriers will enjoy 54.7 percent of primary freight tonnage and 57.6 percent of revenue by 2006.[18]

Since 1980, deregulation has dramatically changed the nature of the for-hire motor carrier industry. The industry segments, which have become more defined since deregulation, include truckload (TL), less-than-truckload (LTL), and specialty. The dramatic change is related to the type of carriers operating in each category.

The TL segment includes loads over 15,000 pounds that generally do not require intermediate stops between origin and destination. Although large firms such as Schneider National and J. B. Hunt provide nationwide TL service, the segment is characterized by a large number of relatively small carriers and is generally very price competitive.

The LTL segment involves shipments less than 15,000 pounds that generally must be consolidated to achieve trailer capacity. Due to origin and destination terminal costs and relatively higher marketing expenses, LTL experiences a higher percentage of fixed costs than TL. The operating characteristics of LTL freight segment have caused extensive industry consolidation, resulting in a few relatively large national carriers and a strong regional network of smaller carriers. Some major nationwide LTL carriers are Yellow Freight, Consolidated Freightways, Roadway, and TNT Freightways.

Specialty carriers include bulk and package haulers such as Waste Management, United Parcel Service, and Federal Express. Specialty firms focus on specific transport requirements of a market or product. Specialty carriers are not generally direct competitors with the other two segments.

Based on the sheer size of the trucking industry and the services provided, it is quite apparent that highway transportation will continue to function as the backbone of logistical operations for the foreseeable future.

[16]Bernard Campbell, "Strategy: Economic Forecast: Good News, Bad News for Trucking," *Fleet Owner* 84, no. 1, (January 1987) p. 103.

[17] Helen L. Richardson, "Who's Driving Your Truck," *Transportation and Distribution,* September 1998, p. 59, or "Pooling with Competitors," *Transportation and Distribution,* November 1988, p. 105.

[18]ATA Foundation 3rd Annual United States Freight Forecast to 2006.

Water

Water is the oldest mode of transport. The original sailing vessels were replaced by steam-powered boats in the early 1800s and by diesel in the 1920s. A distinction is generally made between deepwater and navigable inland water transport.

Domestic water transport, which involves the Great Lakes, canals, and navigable rivers, has maintained a relatively constant annual ton-mile share of 13 percent over the past three decades.[19] While the share has remained relatively constant, the mix has changed dramatically. The percentage of river and canal ton-miles has increased from 4.9 to 10.8 percent over the past 30 years while the Great Lakes ton-miles have decreased from 10.5 to 2.6 percent. These figures reflect a shift of bulk product transportation from rail and highway to lower-cost water movements on rivers and canals.

In 1998, 25,777 miles of inland waterways were available, not including the Great Lakes or coastal shipping.[20] This network size has been stable over the past decade and is expected to remain for the foreseeable future. Fewer system miles exist for inland water than for any other transportation mode.

The main advantage of water transport is the capacity to transport extremely large shipments. Water transport employs two types of vessels for movement: Deepwater vessels are generally designed for coastal, ocean, and Great Lakes transport; diesel-towed barges generally operate on rivers and canals and have considerably more flexibility.

Water transport ranks between rail and motor carrier in terms of fixed cost. Although water carriers must develop and operate their own terminals, the right-of-way is developed and maintained by the government and results in moderate fixed costs compared to rail. The main disadvantages of water transport are the limited range of operation and transport speed. Unless the origin and destination of the movement are adjacent to a waterway, supplemental haul by rail or truck is required. The capability of water to transport large tonnage at low variable cost places this mode of transport in demand when low freight rates are desired and speed of transit is a secondary consideration.

Water transport will continue to be a viable transportation option in future logistical systems. The slow transit time of river transport provides a form of product storage in transit that can benefit integrated logistics system design. In addition, the North American Free Trade Agreement continues to offer the potential for increased utilization of the St. Lawrence Seaway to link new producer and consumer markets in Mexico, the Midwest, and the Canadian port cities. Finally, ocean transport remains the primary form of global logistics.

Pipeline

Pipelines are a significant part of the U.S. transportation system. Pipelines accounted for approximately 56.8 percent of all crude and petroleum ton-mile movements. In 1998, 178,648 miles of pipeline were operational in the United States.[21]

In addition to petroleum products, the other important product transported by pipeline is natural gas. Similar to petroleum, natural gas pipelines in the United States are privately owned and operated, and many gas companies act as both gas distribution and contract transportation providers.

---

[19]ENO Transportation Foundation, Inc., op. cit., p. 44.
[20]ENO Transportation Foundation, Inc., op. cit. p. 64.
[21]ENO Transportation Foundation, Inc., op. cit. p. 64.

The basic nature of a pipeline is unique in comparison to any other mode of transport. Pipelines operate on a 24-hour basis, 7 days per week and are limited only by commodity changeover and maintenance. Unlike other modes, there is no empty container or vehicle that must be returned. Pipelines have the highest fixed cost and lowest variable cost among transport modes. High fixed costs result from the right-of-way for pipeline, construction and requirements for control stations, and pumping capacity. Since pipelines are not labor-intensive, the variable operating cost is extremely low once the pipeline has been constructed. An obvious disadvantage is that pipelines are not flexible and are limited with respect to commodities that can be transported as only products in the forms of gas, liquid, or slurry can be handled.

Experiments regarding potential movement of solid products in the form of slurry or hydraulic suspension continue to be conducted. Coal slurry pipelines have proven to be an efficient and economical mode of transporting coal over long distances. Coal slurry lines require massive quantities of water, which is a significant concern of environmentalists. Currently, only one coal slurry line, the Black Mesa, is operational in the United States. Noncoal slurry lines are somewhat more common in foreign countries.

Air

The newest but least utilized mode of transportation is airfreight. The significant advantage of airfreight lies in the speed with which a shipment can be transported. A coast-to-coast shipment via air requires only a few hours contrasted to days with other modes of transport. While costly, the speed of air transport allows other aspects of logistics such as field warehousing and inventory to be reduced or eliminated.

Air transport, despite its high profile, still remains more of a potential than a reality. Although air routes exceed 394,000 miles, airfreight accounts for less than one-half of 1 percent of intercity ton-miles. Air transport capability is limited by load size, weight lift capacity, and aircraft availability. Traditionally, intercity airfreight was transported on scheduled passenger flights. While the practice was economically justified, it resulted in a limited capacity and flexibility of freight operations. The high cost of jet aircraft, coupled with the erratic nature of freight demand, served to limit the economic commitment of dedicated aircraft to all-freight operations.

However, the advent of premium air carriers such as Federal Express, United Parcel Air, DHL, and Airborne Express introduced dedicated global airfreight service. While such premium service was originally targeted at high-priority documents, it has expanded to include package freight. For example, premium carriers have integrated their service to include overnight parts delivery from centralized distribution centers located at their air hub. Overnight air delivery from a centralized warehouse is attractive to firms with a large number of high-value products and time-sensitive service requirements.

The fixed cost of air transport is low compared to rail, water, and pipeline. In fact, air transport ranks second only to highway with respect to low fixed cost. Airways and airports are generally developed and maintained by government. The fixed costs of airfreight are associated with aircraft purchase and the requirement for specialized handling systems and cargo containers. On the other hand, air freight variable cost is extremely high as a result of fuel, user fees, maintenance, and the labor intensity of both in-flight and ground crews.

Since airports require significant real estate, they are generally limited with respect to integration with other transport modes. However, there is substantial interest in integrating air transport with other modes and developing all-freight airports to eliminate conflict with passenger service. For example, Alliance Airport, located in Fort Worth, was designed to integrate air, rail, and truck distribution from a single location.

No particular commodity dominates the traffic carried by airfreight operations. Perhaps the best distinction is that most freight is handled on a high-priority basis. Businesses tend to utilize scheduled or nonscheduled air cargo movements when the service proposition justifies high cost. Products with the greatest potential for regular air movement are those having high value or extreme perishability. When the marketing period for a product is extremely limited, such as Christmas, high-fashion clothing, fresh fish, or cut flowers, air may be the only practical transportation method to support national operations. Routine logistics of products such as computers, repair parts, and consumer catalogs also utilize airfreight.

Modal Classification

Table 11-4 compares the fixed-variable cost structure of each mode. Table 11-5 ranks modal operating characteristics with respect to speed, availability, dependability, capability, and frequency.

Speed refers to elapsed movement time. Airfreight is the fastest of all modes. *Availability* refers to the ability of a mode to service any given pair of locations. Highway carriers have the greatest availability since they can drive directly to origin and destination points. *Dependability* refers to potential variance from expected or pub-

TABLE 11-4   Cost Structure for Each Mode

- *Rail.* High fixed cost in equipment, terminals, tracks, etc. Low variable cost.
- *Highway.* Low fixed cost (highways in place and provided by public support). Medium variable cost (fuel, maintenance, etc.).
- *Water.* Medium fixed cost (ships and equipment). Low variable cost (capability to transport large amount of tonnage).
- *Pipeline.* Highest fixed cost (rights-of-way, construction, requirements for control stations, and pumping capacity). Lowest variable cost (no labor cost of any significance).
- *Air.* Low fixed cost (aircraft and handling and cargo systems). High variable cost (fuel, labor, maintenance, etc.).

TABLE 11-5   Relative Operating Characteristics by Mode*

Operating Characteristics	Rail	Truck	Water	Pipeline	Air
Speed	3	2	4	5	1
Availability	2	1	4	5	3
Dependability	3	2	4	1	5
Capability	2	3	1	5	4
Frequency	4	2	5	1	3
Composite Score	14	10	18	17	16

*Lowest rank is best.

lished delivery schedules. Pipelines, because of their continuous service and limited interference due to weather and congestion, rank highest in dependability. *Capability* is the ability of a mode to handle any transport requirement, such as load size. Water transport is the most capable. The final classification is *frequency,* which relates to the quantity of scheduled movements. Pipelines, again because of their continuous service between two points, lead all modes in frequency.

As Table 11-5 illustrates, the appeal of highway transport is in part explained by its high relative ranking across the five operating characteristics. Operating on a world-class highway system, motor carriers rank first or second in all categories except capability. Although substantial improvements in motor capability resulted from relaxed size and weight limitations on interstate highways and approval to use tandem trailers, it is not realistic to assume motor transport will surpass rail or water capability.

Transportation Service

Transportation service is achieved by combining the capabilities of modes. Prior to deregulation government policy limited carriers to operating in a single mode. Such restrictive ownership sought to promote competition between modes and limit the potential for monopoly practices. Following deregulation carriers were free to develop integrated modal services in efforts to more efficiently and effectively meet the needs of customers. The following section reviews the current range of services offered by different carriers. The description also includes examples of carriers representative of each category.

Traditional Carriers

The most basic carrier type is a transportation firm that provides service utilizing only one of the five basic transport modes. Focus on a single operational mode permits a carrier to become highly specialized.

Although single-mode operators are able to offer extremely efficient transport, such specialization creates difficulties for a shipper who desires intermodal transport solutions because it requires negotiation and business planning with multiple carriers. Airlines are an example of a single-mode carrier for both freight and passenger service that traditionally limit service from airport to airport. Since deregulation most carriers are developing services that facilitate multimodal integration.

Package Service

Over the past several decades a serious problem existed in the availability of small-shipment transportation. It was difficult for common carriers to provide reasonably priced small-shipment service due to overhead cost associated with terminal and line-haul operations. This overhead forced motor carriers to charge a *minimum charge.* The minimum was generally in the range of $100, regardless of shipment size or distance. Due to the minimum charge and lack of alternatives, an opportunity existed for companies offering specialized service to enter the small-shipment or package-service market.

Package services represent an important part of logistics, and the influence of carriers in this segment is increasing due to their size and intermodal capabilities. The advent of e-commerce and the need for consumer-direct fulfillment have significantly increased demand for package delivery. While package services are expanding, the services required do not fall neatly into the traditional modal classification scheme. Packages are regularly transported using the line-haul services of rail, motor, and air. Package service provides both regular and premium services.

Ground Package Service

Numerous carriers offer delivery services within metropolitan areas. Other carriers offer package delivery service on an interstate and intrastate basis. The most recognizable carriers are United Parcel Service (UPS), the United States Postal Service, and Federal Express Ground.

The original service offered by UPS was contract delivery of local shipments for department stores. Today, UPS offers a diverse range of intercity package services. In fact, UPS has expanded its scope of overall operating authority by shipping packages that conform to specialized size and weight restrictions nationwide and globally for consumers and business enterprises. While UPS provides logistical services related to all types of products, specialization in small packages enabled a cost-effective overnight service between most cities within 300 miles. For shippers located at key commercial centers, UPS 2-day service covers approximately 55 percent of the continental U.S. population.

UPS has various capabilities and offers a range of services, including ground and premium air. Table 11-6 summarizes the integrated services offered by package carriers such as UPS. It is interesting to note that ground service frequently involves intermodal movement by using a combination of truck and train capacity.

The United States Postal Service operates ground and air parcel service. Charges for parcel post are based on weight and distance. Generally, parcels must be delivered to a post office for shipment origination. However, in the case of large users and when it is convenient for the Postal Service, pickup is provided at the shipper's location. Intercity transport is accomplished by purchasing air, highway, rail, and even water service from for-hire carriers. Delivery is provided to the destination by the Postal Service.

The importance of parcel service to the logistical system cannot be overemphasized. One of the expanding forms of marketing in the United States is nonstore retailing, in which orders are placed via the Internet, telephone, or mail for subsequent home delivery. Firms that specialize in consumer fulfillment are one of the fastest growing forms of logistics service providers.

Air Package Service

Several carriers, such as Federal Express, UPS, Emery Worldwide Logistics, and DHL, have entered the package or premium transportation market over the past two decades. Most organizations that provide routine package service also offer premium service. UPS, for example, offers next-day and second-day service, while the United States Postal Service provides a variety of priority services.

The first widely recognized premium package service was initiated by Federal Express (FedEx) in 1973. FedEx provides nationwide overnight service utilizing a fleet of dedicated cargo aircraft. The original FedEx service attracted attention because of the innovative line-haul plan in which all packages were flown overnight to a terminal hub located in Memphis, Tennessee, for sorting and redistribution. FedEx's original service has been considerably expanded by offering larger package size and weight restrictions and adding global connectivity.

The demand for parcel delivery service has attracted many competitors into overnight premium package service. In addition to specialized firms like FedEx, UPS,

---
TABLE 11-6   Example of Integrated Parcel Carrier Services

Freight Services

- *Next-day air.* Guaranteed overnight air delivery for letters and packages.
- *Second-day air.* Air delivery at substantial savings compared to overnight.
- *Ground delivery service.* Routine 2-day delivery within 800 miles from origin.
- *Hundredweight service.* Contract service for multipackage shipments over 200 pounds sent to single consignee at one location on a single day.
- *Ground saver.* High-volume B2B package delivery between designated metropolitan areas.
- *International air.* Automatic daily pickup and expedited delivery to more than 180 countries.
- *Air cargo service.* Oversized/heavy domestic and international freight.
- *Service to Canada.* Ground and air delivery with computer linkup between both countries' Customs offices.
- *Worldwide expedited package service.* Multipackage alternative to air freight.
- *Worldwide document service.* Document delivery requiring minimal Customs clearance.
- *Truck leasing.* Full-service vehicle leasing and rental.

Value-Added Services

- *Electronic tracking.* Monitors shipments from pickup to delivery.
- *Advanced Label Imaging System* (ALIS). Bar code package tracking labels for customer inquiry.
- *Delivery confirmation service.* Automatic proof of delivery via bar coding.
- *Customs clearance service.* Expedited service for UPS International Air.
- *MaxiShip package processing system.* Software program to assist customer management of shipping operations.
- *MaxiTrac customer access software.* Direct customer linkup to the UPS tracking and tracing systems for online delivery information.
- *Consignee billing.* Management and direct payment of inbound customer transportation charges.
- *Inventory express.* Logistical support (inventory control, distribution, and reporting) for time-sensitive products requiring fast, reliable distribution.
- *On-call air pickup.* Same-day pickup for all UPS air services via customer phone call.
- *UPS properties.* Facility development for site leasing close to UPS operations.

Source: United Parcel Service promotional materials.

Airborne Freight, and Emery Worldwide, major motor carriers and airlines have begun to offer competitive service. Many services appeal to commercial business because they satisfy demand for rapid delivery.

Intermodal Transportation

Intermodal transportation combines two or more modes to take advantage of the inherent economies of each and thus provide an integrated service at lower total cost. Many efforts have been made over the years to integrate different transportation modes. Initial attempts at modal coordination trace back to the early 1920s, but during that early period, cooperation was restrained by regulatory restrictions designed to limit monopoly practices. Intermodal offerings began to develop more successfully during the 1950s with the advent of integrated rail and motor service commonly termed *piggyback service.* This common intermodal arrangement combines the flexibility of motor for short distances with the low line-haul cost associated with rail for longer distances.

The popularity of such offerings has increased significantly as a means to achieve more efficient and effective transportation.[22]

Technically, coordinated or intermodal transportation could be arranged among all basic modes. Descriptive jargon—piggyback, fishyback, trainship, and airtruck—have become standard transportation terms. Industry Insight 11-2 illustrates the far-reaching implications of multimodal integration for Deutsche Post.

Piggyback/TOFC/COFC

The best known and most widely used intermodal system is the trailer (TOFC) or container (COFC) on a flatcar. Containers are the boxes utilized for intermodal product storage and movement between motor freight, railroads, and water transportation. Containers are typically 8 feet wide, 8 feet high, 20 or 40 feet long, and do not have highway wheels. Trailers, on the other hand, are of similar width and height but can be as long as 53 feet and have highway wheels. As the name implies, a trailer or container is placed on a railroad flatcar for some portion of the intercity line-haul and pulled by a truck at origin and destination. Line-haul cost is the expense to move railcars or trucks between cities. Since the original development of TOFC, various combinations of trailer or container on flatcar, double stack, for instance, have increased significantly.

A variety of coordinated rail–truck service plans have been developed. Each plan defines the railroad or motor carrier responsibility. Table 11-7 illustrates the most common operating plans. The plans differ by responsibility for equipment, pickup, and delivery.

While the TOFC concept facilitates direct transfer between rail and motor carriage, it also presents several technical limitations. The placement of a trailer with highway wheels attached, transferred to a railcar, can lead to wind resistance, damage, and weight problems. The use of containers reduces these potential problems, as they can be double stacked and are easily transferred to water carriers. However, they require special equipment for over-the-road delivery or pickup.

Containerships

Fishyback, trainship, and containerships are examples of the oldest form of intermodal transport. They utilize waterways, which are one of the least expensive modes for line-haul movement. The fishyback, trainship and containership concept loads a truck trailer, railcar, or container onto a barge or ship for the line-haul move. Such services are provided in coastal waters between Atlantic and Gulf ports, from the Great Lakes to coastal points, and along inland navigable waterways.

A variant of this intermodal option is the *land bridge* concept that moves containers in a combination of sea and rail transport. The land bridge is commonly used for containers moving between Europe and the Pacific Rim to reduce the time and expense of all-water transport. For example, containers are shipped to the West Coast of North America from the Pacific Rim, loaded onto railcars for movement to the East Coast, and then reloaded onto ships for movement to Europe. The land bridge concept is based on the benefit of ocean and rail combinations that utilize a single tariff, which is lower than the combined total cost of two separate rates.

---

[22]For a comprehensive discussion of contemporary intermodal operations, see John C. Taylor and George C. Jackson, "Conflict, Power and Evolution in the Intermodal Transportation Industry's Channel of Distribution," *Transportation Journal,* Spring 2000, pp. 5–17.

INDUSTRY INSIGHT 11-2 ONE-STOP SHOP REALITY

Deutsche Post has integrated traditional air and ocean forwarding, express parcel delivery, and mail services in a 2-year buying spree. Germany will eliminate Deutsche Post's monopoly on mail delivery in 2003, which will inevitably lead to a loss of significant revenue. It hopes to replace lost sales with international transport business.

Customer demand, more than postal deregulation, is driving Deutsche Post's vision. "More and more customers are seeing the advantage of directly working with their suppliers," says Klaus Zumwinkel, CEO of Deutsche Post. "They will not use only one supplier, but they will choose from a few suppliers. To be one of those suppliers, one has to be global. One cannot say, 'Well, in Africa business is so complicated. Please, mister customer, we would love to have United States and Europe, but in Africa we do not have any facilities.'" To some extent, Deutsche Post is creating a consolidation trend more than following one.

More than just reacting to competition, the largest transport firms want to position themselves as premium providers of global logistics services to multinational clients.

Deutsche Post and Lufthansa have merged their respective 25 percent voting stakes in DHL International into a joint venture called Aerologic, which will seek out areas of cooperation for the three partners. Deutsche Post will take management control over Aerologic because DHL sits closer to the German post office's core interest—pickup and delivery. DHL is a key part of Deutsche Post's international expansion plans. DHL offers a world mail delivery product of which Deutsche Post is a heavy supporter. Deutsche Post's Global Mail division has been expanding aggressively, particularly in South America. DHL provides cross-border express transport services, but also offers Deutsche Post a valuable global pickup and delivery network.

"All of the global shippers—and also more and more of the local and smaller ones—are demanding transparency," said Jean-Peter Jansen, the new chairman of Lufthansa Cargo. "They want to have a continuous flow of information and a continuous flow of the goods themselves."

Lufthansa's core deliverable product will always be international air freight capacity. Lufthansa wants to strengthen its leading position through alliances with other freight carriers. Lufthansa describes its alliance strategy geometrically. It will partner with airlines in horizontal alliances and with forwarders in vertical industry partnerships. Through its deal with Deutsche Post, the airline added a diagonal line to its chart, representing new initiatives in electronic commerce.

Deutsche Post and Lufthansa have formed a joint venture called e-logic to pursue mutual interests in e-commerce logistics. The new company will make investments in new technology and startup ventures and also work to develop joint fulfillment solutions for e-commerce shippers.

Jansen states, "We believe that putting us more closely together, not in a way that we integrate, but in a way that we support each other, will make a lot of difference for the future. What we are looking for really is growth and stabilization of our market position."

Source: Gordan Forsyth, "The New Integrators," *American Shipper,* July 2000, pp. 28–35.

Coordinated Air–Truck

Another form of intermodal transport combines air and truck. Local cartage is a vital part of every air movement because airfreight must eventually move from the airport to the final delivery destination. Air–truck movements usually provide service and flexibility comparable to straight motor freight.

Air–truck is commonly used to provide premium package services, such as those offered by UPS and FedEx, but can also be used for more standard freight applications for several reasons. First, there is a lack of airfreight service to smaller cities in the United States. Smaller cities are often served by narrow-body aircraft and commuter planes that are not equipped to handle freight. Thus, motor carriage into small cities

TABLE 11-7   **Summary of Basic Rail–Truck Coordination Plans**

- *Plan 250.* Rail transportation of a shipment loaded in a carrier vehicle from terminal at origin to terminal at destination. Shipper is responsible for pickup and delivery services beyond the terminal.
- *Plan 300.* Rail transportation of a shipment loaded in a shipper vehicle from terminal at origin to terminal at destination. Shipper is responsible for pickup and delivery beyond the terminal.
- *Plan 310.* Rail transportation of an empty shipper vehicle having an immediate prior or subsequent loaded domestic movement via mail. Shipper is responsible for pickup and delivery beyond the terminal.
- *Plans 400 to 470.* These services apply only to domestic container shipments involving carrier containers or the repositioning of international containers owned or controlled by steamship companies. They include, where indicated, truck pickup at origin and/or delivery at destination.

    Plan 400: Door at origin, door at destination.

    Plan 420: Door at origin, ramp at destination.

    Plan 450: Ramp at origin, ramp at destination.

    Plan 470: Ramp at origin, door at destination.

- *Plans 600 to 625 or Service Code 20 to 67.* Their services apply to shipments involving carrier vehicles and shipper vehicles. They include truck pickup at origin and/or delivery at destination.

    Plan 600: Door at origin, door at destination (carrier vehicle).

    Plan 605: Door at origin, door at destination (shipper vehicle).

    Plan 610: Door at origin, ramp at destination (carrier vehicle).

    Plan 615: Door at origin, ramp at destination (shipper vehicle).

    Plan 620: Ramp at origin, door at destination (carrier vehicle).

    Plan 625: Ramp at origin, door at destination (shipper vehicle).

- *Plan 800.* Rail transportation of a loaded shipper vehicle from the terminal at origin to the terminal at destination where the shipment has had/will have an immediate prior or subsequent movement via water transport in international commerce without transfer of cargo. Shipper is responsible for pickup and delivery beyond the terminal.
- *Plan 810.* Rail transportation of an empty shipper vehicle from the terminal at origin to the terminal at destination having an immediate prior or subsequent loaded movement via rail in conjunction with water transport in international commerce. Shipper is responsible for pickup and delivery beyond the terminal.

from metropolitan airports provides a needed service at a competitive cost. Second, package carriers, while suited to serve small cities, have limited ability to handle heavy freight. Package carriers that are focused on smaller parcels and materials handling systems are limited in ability to handle heavy freight. As a result, many air carriers have extended their motor freight range to provide service to expanded geographical areas.

The concept of intermodalism appeals to both shippers and carriers due to the economic leverage of linking two modes. In fact, many authorities believe the only way to maintain a strong national transportation network is to encourage and foster increased intermodalism. Efforts to increase intermodalism are of prime interest to logistical planners because such development expands options available in logistical system design. It should be noted, however, that intermodal growth is primarily due to increased container use rather than truck trailers.

Nonoperating Intermediaries

The overall transportation industry also includes several business types that do not own or operate equipment. These nonoperating intermediaries broker the services of other firms. A transportation broker is somewhat analogous to a wholesaler in a market channel.

Nonoperating intermediaries economically justify their function by offering shippers lower rates for movement between two locations than would be possible by direct shipment via common carrier. Because of peculiarities in the common-carrier rate structure, such as minimum freight charges, surcharges, and less-than-volume rates, conditions exist whereby nonoperating intermediaries can facilitate savings for shippers. Interestingly, there are cases where nonoperating intermediaries charge higher rates than offered by carriers. The justification for the higher charges is based on ability to arrange faster delivery and/or more complete service. The primary intermediaries are freight forwarders, shipper associations, and brokers.

Freight Forwarders

Freight forwarders are for-profit businesses that consolidate small shipments from various customers into bulk shipment and then utilize a common surface or air carrier for transport. At destination, the freight forwarder splits the bulk shipment into the original smaller shipments. Local delivery may or may not be arranged by the forwarder. The main advantage of the forwarder is a lower rate per hundredweight obtained from large shipment and, in most cases, faster transport of small shipments than would be experienced if the individual customer dealt directly with the common carrier. Freight forwarders accept full responsibility for shipment performance.

Shipper Association/Cooperatives and Agents

Shipper associations are operationally similar to freight forwarders in that they consolidate small shipments into large movements to gain cost economies. Shipper associations are voluntary nonprofit entities where members, operating in a specific industry, collaborate to gain economies related to small-shipment purchases. Typically, members purchase product from common sources or from sources of supply located in one area. A common practice is to order small quantities at frequent intervals to minimize retail inventory. Participation in a shipper association typically means improved speed of delivery since a large number of different products may be purchased at one location, such as the garment district in New York City.

The association requires a group of shippers to establish an administrative office or arrange an agent at the location of frequent merchandise purchase. The agent arranges for individual purchases to be delivered to a local facility. When sufficient volume is accumulated, a consolidated shipment is arranged to the association's destination for local delivery. Some associations operate their own intercity transportation. Each member is billed a proportionate share for transportation plus a prorated share of the association's fixed costs.

Brokers

Brokers are intermediaries who coordinate transportation arrangements for shippers, consignees, and carriers. They also arrange shipments for exempt carriers and owner operators. Brokers typically operate on a commission basis. Prior to deregulation, brokers played a minor role in logistics due to service restrictions. Today, brokers provide more extensive services such as shipment matching, rate negotiation, billing, and tracing. The entire area of brokerage operations is highly adaptable to Internet-based transactions.

Summary

Transportation is a key activity in logistics because it moves product through the various stages of production and ultimately to the consumer. This chapter introduced major principles of transportation economies and provided a brief introduction to the history of government regulation. It is important that logistics managers have appreciation and understanding of the history of regulation to fully appreciate the logic underlying today's transportation system.

The transportation system has five modes of operation—rail, motor, water, pipeline, and air. Each mode has specific attributes that render it the transportation choice appropriate for a specific movement. Traditional transport supply consisted of a large number of specialized carriers, each limiting operations to one specific mode. The original lack of coordinated transportation resulted in inefficiencies and high cost. Deregulation introduced competitive pricing and carrier flexibility. It became common for carriers to combine multimodal services and offer specialized services to individual customers. As a result, a wide range of specialized transport service is now available to satisfy specific customer requirements. Attention in Chapter 12 is focused on transportation management, followed by a discussion of carrier economics, pricing, and documentation.

Challenge Questions

1. Compare and contrast the transport principles of economy of scale and economy of distance. Illustrate how they combine to create efficient transportation.
2. Describe the five modes of transportation, identifying the most significant characteristic of each.
3. Why is motor carrier freight transportation the most preferred method of product shipment?
4. What is the economic justification for the recent rapid growth of premium package services?
5. Why is it important for a logistics manager to have a degree of understanding of transportation regulatory history?
6. Why have railroad miles declined during a period of national growth?
7. Railroads have the largest percentage of intercity freight ton-miles, but motor carriers have the largest revenue. How do you explain this relationship?
8. Discuss the fundamental difference between TOFC and COFC. Why was double stacking considered a major innovation in multimodal transportation?
9. Explain the value proposition offered by freight forwarding. Provide an example that illustrates why shippers would be attracted to using the services of a freight forwarder as contrasted to arranging their own transportation.
10. The five basic modes of transportation have been available for well over 50 years. Is this the way it will always be or can you identify a sixth mode that may become economically feasible in the foreseeable future?

12 TRANSPORTATION MANAGEMENT

Transportation is critical to logistical performance. The historical view of traffic departments being staffed with individuals wearing green eyeshades and sitting amidst bookcases filled with tariffs and rate tables is a scenario far from reality in today's competitive environment. Traffic departments commit and manage nearly 60 percent of a typical firm's logistics expenditures. Transportation managers are responsible for arranging for inventory to be moved in a timely and economical manner. A fundamental responsibility is to determine whether transportation services should be performed using private capacity or for-hire specialists. Decisions related to internal versus outsourcing are not totally different from those faced in many other operational areas. What is different about transportation is the critical impact that operations have on logistical performance. As operational expectations become more precise, performance cycles more compact, and margins for error reduced to zero, successful firms have come to realize that *there is no such thing as cheap transportation*. Unless transportation is managed in an effective and efficient manner, procurement, manufacturing, and market distribution performance will fail to meet expectations. This chapter provides an overview of how transportation is managed within the logistical process.

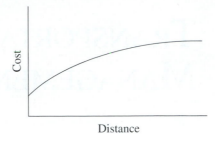

Distance

Transportation Economics and Pricing

Transportation economics and pricing are concerned with factors and characteristics that drive cost. To develop effective logistics strategy, it is necessary to understand such factors and characteristics. Successful negotiation requires a full understanding of transportation economics. An overview of transportation economics and pricing builds upon four topics: (1) the factors that drive transport costs, (2) the cost structures or classifications, (3) carrier pricing strategy, and (4) transportation rates and ratings.

Economic Drivers

Transportation costs are driven by seven factors. While not direct components of transport tariffs, each factor influences rates. The factors are: (1) distance, (2) volume, (3) density, (4) stowability, (5) handling, (6) liability, and (7) market. In general, the discussion sequence reflects the relative importance of each factor from the shipper's perspective. Keep in mind that the precise impact of each factor varies based on specific product characteristics.

Distance

Distance is a major influence on transportation cost since it directly contributes to variable expense, such as labor, fuel, and maintenance. Figure 12-1 illustrates the general relationship between distance and transportation cost. Two important points are illustrated in this figure. First, the cost curve does not begin at the origin because there are fixed costs associated with shipment pickup and delivery regardless of distance. Second, the cost curve increases at a decreasing rate as a function of distance. This characteristic is known as the tapering principle.[1]

Volume

The second factor is load volume. Like many other logistics activities, transportation scale economies exist for most transportation movements. This relationship, illustrated in Figure 12-2, indicates that transport cost per unit of weight decreases as load volume increases. This occurs because the fixed costs of pickup, delivery, and administration can be spread over incremental volume. This relationship is limited by the size of the transportation vehicle. Once the vehicle is full, the relationship begins again for each additional vehicle. The management implication is that small loads should be consolidated into larger loads to maximize scale economies.

---

[1]The principles of economy of scale and economy of distance were introduced in Chapter 11, p. 330.

FIGURE 12-2

Generalized relationship between weight and transporation cost/pound

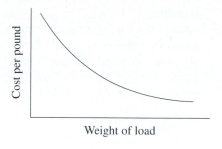

FIGURE 12-3

Generalized relationship between density and transportation cost/pound

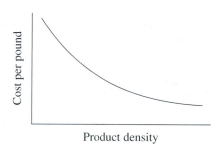

Density

A third factor is product density. Density is a combination of weight and volume. Weight and volume are important since transportation cost for any movement is usually quoted in dollars per unit of weight. Transport charges are commonly quoted as amount per hundredweight (CWT). In terms of weight and volume, vehicles are constrained more by cubic capacity than by weight. Since actual vehicle, labor, and fuel expenses are not dramatically influenced by weight, higher-density products allow relatively fixed transport costs to be spread across more weight. As a result, higher density products are typically assessed lower transport costs per unit of weight. Figure 12-3 illustrates the relationship of declining transportation cost per unit of weight as product density increases.

In general, traffic managers seek to improve product density so that trailer cubic capacity can be fully utilized. For example, Kimberly-Clark was able to reduce transportation expense by reducing air contained in paper products. Such compression increased product density.

Stowability

Stowability refers to how product case dimensions fit into transportation equipment. Odd package sizes and shapes, as well as excessive weight or length, may not fit well in transportation equipment; this results in wasted cubic capacity. Although density and stowability are similar, it is possible to have items with similar densities that stow very differently. Items having rectangular shapes are much easier to stow than odd-shaped items. For example, while steel blocks and rods may have the same physical density, rods are more difficult to stow than blocks due to their length and shape. Stowability is also influenced by other aspects of size, since large numbers of items may be *nested* in shipments whereas they may be difficult to stow in small quantities. For example, it is possible to accomplish significant nesting for a truckload of trashcans while a single can is difficult to stow.

Handling

Special handling equipment may be required to load and unload trucks, railcars, or ships. In addition to special handling equipment, the manner in which products are physically grouped together in boxes or on pallets for transport and storage will impact handling cost. Chapters 13 and 14 specifically address handling issues related to packaging and storage.

Liability

Liability includes product characteristics that can result in damage and potential claims. Carriers must either have insurance to protect against possible claims or accept financial responsibility for damage. Shippers can reduce their risk, and ultimately transportation cost, by improved packaging or reducing susceptibility to loss or damage.

Market

Finally, market factors such as lane volume and balance influence transportation cost. A *transport lane* refers to movements between origin and destination points. Since transportation vehicles and drivers must return to their origin, either they must find a *back-haul* load or the vehicle is returned or *deadheaded* empty. When empty return movements occur, labor, fuel and maintenance costs must be charged against the original front-haul movement. Thus, the ideal situation is to achieve two-way or balanced movement where volume is equal in both directions. However, this is rarely the case due to demand imbalances in manufacturing and consumption locations. For example, many goods are manufactured and processed on the East Coast of the United States and then shipped to consumer markets in the western portion of the country; this results in more volume moving west than east. This imbalance causes rates to be generally lower for eastbound moves. Movement balance is also influenced by seasonality, such as the movement of fruits and vegetables to coincide with growing seasons. Demand location and seasonality result in transport rates that change with direction and season. Logistics system design must take such factors into account to achieved back-haul movement whenever possible.

Cost Structure

The second dimension of transport economic and pricing concerns the criteria used to allocate cost. Cost allocation is primarily the carrier's concern, but since cost structure influences negotiating ability, the shipper's perspective is important as well. Transportation costs are classified into a number of categories.

Variable

Variable costs change in a predictable, direct manner in relation to some level of activity. Variable costs can only be avoided by not operating the vehicle. Aside from exceptional circumstances, transport rates must at least cover variable cost. The variable category includes direct carrier cost associated with movement of each load. These expenses are generally measured as a cost per mile or per unit of weight. Typical variable cost components include labor, fuel, and maintenance. On a per mile basis, the carrier variable costs range from $.75 to $1.50 per vehicle mile. The variable cost of operations represents the minimum amount a carrier must charge to pay its day-to-day bills. It is not possible for any carrier to charge below its variable cost and expect to remain in business long. In fact, rates should fully cover all costs.

Fixed

Fixed costs are expenses that do not change in the short run and must be serviced even when a company is not operating, such as during a holiday or a strike. The fixed category includes costs not directly influenced by shipment volume. For transportation firms, fixed components include vehicles, terminals, rights-of-way, information systems, and support equipment. In the short term, expenses associated with fixed assets must be covered by contribution above variable costs on a per shipment basis.

Joint

Joint costs are expenses unavoidably created by the decision to provide a particular service. For example, when a carrier elects to haul a truckload from point A to point B, there is an implicit decision to incur a *joint* cost for the back-haul from point B to point A. Either the joint cost must be covered by the original shipper from A to B or a back-haul shipper must be found. Joint costs have significant impact on transportation charges because carrier quotations must include implied joint costs based on considerations regarding an appropriate back-haul shipper and/or back-haul charges against the original shipper.

Common

seems like these costs should be fixed costs of doing business.

This category includes carrier costs that are incurred on behalf of all or selected shippers. **Common costs,** such as terminal or management expenses, are characterized as overhead. These are often allocated to a shipper according to a level of activity like the number of shipments or delivery appointments handled. However, allocating overhead in this manner may incorrectly assign costs. For example, a shipper may be charged for delivery appointments when it doesn't actually use the service.

Carrier Pricing Strategies

When setting rates to charge shippers, carriers typically follow one or a combination of two strategies. Although it is possible to employ a single strategy, the combination approach considers trade-offs between cost of service incurred by the carrier and value of service to the shipper.

Cost-of-Service

The **cost-of-service** strategy is a build up approach where the carrier establishes a rate based on the cost of providing the service plus a profit margin. For example, if the cost of providing a transportation service is $200 and the profit markup is 10 percent, the carrier would charge the shipper $220. The cost-of-service approach, which represents the base or minimum for transportation charges, is most commonly used as a pricing approach for low-value goods or in highly competitive situations.

Value-of-Service

Value-of-service is an alternative strategy that charges a price based on value as perceived by the shipper rather than the carrier's cost of actually providing the service. For example, a shipper perceives transporting 1000 pounds of electronics equipment as more critical or valuable than 1000 pounds of coal since electronics are worth substantially more than the coal. As such, a shipper is probably willing to pay more for transportation. Carriers tend to utilize value-of-service pricing for high-value goods or when limited competition exists.

Value-of-service pricing is illustrated in the premium overnight freight market. When FedEx first introduced overnight delivery, there were few competitors that could provide comparable service, so it was perceived by shippers as a high-value alternative. They were willing to pay $22.50 for overnight delivery of a single package. Once competitors such as UPS and the United States Postal Service entered the market, rates dropped to current discounted levels of $5 to $10 per package. This rate decrease more accurately reflects the value and cost of this service.

Combination Pricing

The **combination pricing** strategy establishes the transport price at an intermediate level between the cost-of-service minimum and the value-of-service maximum. In practice, most transportation firms use such a middle value. Logistics managers must understand the range of prices and the alternative strategies so they can negotiate appropriately.

Net-Rate Prices

By taking advantage of regulatory freedom generated by the Trucking Industry Regulatory Reform Act (TIRRA) of 1994 and the reduced applicability of the filed rate doctrine, a number of common carriers are experimenting with a simplified pricing format termed **net-rate pricing.** Because TIRRA eliminated tariff filing requirements for motor carriers that set rates individually with customers, carriers are now, in effect, able to simplify pricing to fit an individual customer's circumstances and needs. Specifically, carriers can replace individual discount sheets and class tariffs with a simplified price sheet. The net-rate pricing approach does away with the complex and administratively burdensome discount pricing structure that has become common practice since deregulation.

Established discounts and accessorial charges are built into the net rates. In other words, the net rate is an all-inclusive price. The goal is to drastically reduce carriers' administrative cost and directly respond to customer demand to simplify the rate-making process. Shippers are attracted to such simplification because it promotes billing accuracy and provides a clear understanding of how to generate savings in transportation.

Rates and Rating

The previous discussion reviewed key strategies used by carriers to set prices. Building on this foundation, this section presents the pricing mechanics used by carriers. This discussion applies specifically to common carriers, although contract carriers utilize a similar approach.

Class Rates

In transportation terminology, the price in dollars and cents per hundredweight to move a specific product between two locations is referred to as the **rate.** The rate is listed on pricing sheets or on computer files known as **tariffs.** The term *class rate* evolved from the fact that all products transported by common carriers are classified for pricing purposes. All product legally transported in interstate commerce can be shipped via class rates.

Determination of common carrier class rates is a two-step process. The first step is the classification or grouping of the product being transported. The second step is the determination of the precise rate or price based on the classification of the product and the origin/destination points of the shipment.

Classification

All products transported are typically grouped together into uniform classifications. The classification takes into consideration the characteristics of a product or commodity that will influence the cost of handling or transport. Products with similar density, stowability, handling, liability, and value characteristics are grouped together into a class, thereby reducing the need to deal with each product on an individual basis. The particular class that a given product or commodity receives is its *rating,* which is used to determine the freight rate. It is important to understand that the classification does not identify the price charged for movement of a product. It refers to a product's transportation characteristics in comparison to other commodities.

Motor carriers and rail carriers each have independent classification systems. The motor carrier system uses the *National Motor Freight Classification,* while rail classifications are published in the *Uniform Freight Classification.* The motor classification system has 23 classes of freight, and the rail system has 31. In local or regional areas, individual groups of carriers may publish additional classification lists. Since deregulation, considerable attention has been directed to overall simplification of the traditional classification scheme.

Classification of individual products is based on a relative index of 100. Class 100 is considered the class of an average product, while other classes run as high as 500 and as low as 35. Each product is assigned an item number for listing purposes and then given a classification rating. As a general rule, the higher a class rating, the higher the transportation cost for the product. Historically, a product classified as 400 would be approximately four times more expensive to transport than a product rated 100. While the actual current multiple may not be four, a class 400 rating will still result in substantially higher freight costs than a class 100 rating. Products are also assigned classifications on the basis of the quantity shipped. Less-than-truckload (LTL) shipments of identical products will have higher ratings than carload (CL) or truckload (TL) shipments.

Table 12-1 illustrates a page from the *National Motor Freight Classification.* It contains general product grouping 86750, which is *glass, leaded.* Notice that the leaded glass category is further subdivided into specific types of glass such as "glass, microscopical slide or cover, in boxes" (item 86770). For LTL shipments, item 86770 is assigned a 70 rating. TL shipments of leaded glass are assigned a class 40 rating, provided a minimum of 360 hundredweight is shipped.

Products are also assigned different ratings on the basis of packaging. Glass may be rated differently when shipped loose, in crates, or in boxes than when shipped in wrapped protective packing. It should be noted that packaging differences influence product density, stowability, and damage, illustrating that cost factors discussed earlier enter into the rate-determined process. Thus, a number of different classifications may apply to the same product depending on where it is being shipped, shipment size, transport mode, and product packaging.

One of the major responsibilities of transportation managers is to obtain the best possible rating for all goods shipped, so it is useful for members of a traffic department to have a thorough understanding of the classification systems. Although there are differences in rail and motor classifications, each system is guided by similar rules; however, rail rules are more comprehensive and detailed than those for motor freight.

It is possible to have a product reclassified by written application to the appropriate classification board. The classification board reviews proposals for change or additions with respect to minimum weights, commodity descriptions, packaging requirements, and general rules and regulations. An alert traffic department will take an

TABLE 12-1   National Motor Freight Classification 100-S

Item	Articles	Classes		
		LTL	TL	MW
86737	*Note:* TL provisions will also apply when glass is shipped on its flat surface in wooden boxes on pallets.			
86750	Glass, leaded, see Note, item 86752:			
Sub 1	With landscape, pictorial, or religious designs, packed in boxes.	200.	70.	24.
Sub 2	With curved, angled, or straight-line patterns, or with designs other than landscape, pictorial, or religious, in boxes.	100.	70.	24.
86752	*Note:* The term "leaded glass" means glass either colored or clear, set in lead or in other metal.			
86770	Glass, microscopical slide or cover, in boxes.	70.	40.	36.
86830	Glass, rolled, overlaid with aluminum strips with metal terminals attached, in boxes, crates, or Package 1339.	77.5	45.	30.
86840	Glass, rolled, overlaid with aluminum strips, NOI, in boxes, crates, or Package 1339.	70.	37.5	36.
86900	Glass, silvered for mirrors, not framed, backed, or equipped with hangers or fastening devices:			
Sub 1	Shock (window glass, silvered), in boxes, see Note, item 86902; also TL, in Packages 227 or 300.	86.	40.	30.
Sub 2	Other than shock glass; also TL, in Packages 227 or 300:			
	Bent:			
Sub 3	Not exceeding 15 feet in length or 9 feet in breadth, in boxes.	100.	70.	24.
Sub 4	Exceeding 15 feet in length or 9 feet in breadth, in boxes.	250.	70.	24.
Sub 5	Not bent, see Package 785:			
Sub 6	120 united inches or less, in boxes, crates, or Packages 198,	70.	40.	30.
Sub 7	235, or 1339.			
Sub 8	Exceeding 120 united inches but not exceeding 15 feet in length or 9 feet in breadth, in boxes or crates.	100.	40.	40.
Sub 9	Exceeding 15 feet in length or 9 feet in breadth, in boxes or crates.	200.	45.	40.
86902	*Note:* Glass, silvered for mirrors, which has been framed or backed, or equipped with large hangers or fastening devices, is subject to the classes for mirrors, NOI.			
85940	Glass, window, other than plate, with metal edging other than sash or frames, in boxes.	77.5	45.	30.
86960	Glazing units, glass, not in sash, see Note, item 86966, in boxes, crates, or Packages 2133, 2149, or 2281.	70.	45.	30.
86966	*Note:* Applies on units consisting of sheets of glass separated by air or vacuum, sealed at all edges with same or other materials.			
87040	Skylight, roofing, or sidewall construction material consisting of rough rolled glass, wired or not wired, and installation accessories, see Note, item 87042, in boxes or crates.	65.	35.	40.

Source: *National Motor Freight Classification* (Alaxandria, VA: American Trucking Association, 1992).

active role in classification. Significant savings may be realized by finding the correct classification for a product or by recommending a change in packaging or shipment quantity that will reduce a product's rating.

Rate Administration

Once a classification rating is obtained for a product, rate must be determined. The rate per hundredweight is usually based on the shipment origin and destination, although the actual price charged for a particular shipment is normally subject to a minimum charge and may also be subject to surcharge assessments. Historically, the origin

TABLE 12-2   Example of Rates from Atlanta, Georgia (zip 303), to Lansing, Michigan (zip 489)

Origin 303: Destination 489: MC: 81.00: RBNO 00775E

Rate Class	L5C	M5C	M1M	M2M	M5M	M10M	M20M	M30M	M40M
500	233.58	193.89	147.14	119.10	84.05	65.37	40.32	32.25	28.24
400	188.24	156.25	118.58	95.98	67.73	52.69	32.55	26.03	22.79
300	144.11	119.63	90.78	73.48	51.86	40.34	24.94	19.95	17.45
250	126.30	104.84	79.56	64.40	45.45	35.34	21.86	17.48	15.31
200	98.37	81.66	61.97	50.16	35.40	27.53	17.00	13.60	11.91
175	88.65	73.58	55.84	45.20	31.90	24.81	15.30	12.24	10.72
150	76.11	63.18	47.94	38.81	27.38	21.30	13.20	10.56	9.24
125	64.76	53.76	40.80	33.03	23.31	18.12	11.25	9.00	7.88
110	56.27	46.71	35.43	28.69	20.25	15.75	9.88	7.90	6.92
100	52.62	43.68	33.15	26.83	18.94	14.73	9.22	7.38	6.46
92	49.79	41.33	31.37	25.39	17.92	13.94	8.91	7.12	6.24
85	46.15	38.31	29.07	23.53	16.61	12.92	8.58	6.86	6.01
77	42.91	35.62	27.03	21.88	15.44	12.01	8.34	6.67	5.84
70	40.48	33.59	25.50	20.64	14.57	11.33	8.10	6.48	5.67
65	38.46	31.92	24.22	19.61	13.84	10.76	8.02	6.41	5.61
60	36.84	30.58	23.21	18.78	13.26	10.31	7.94	6.35	5.56
55	34.81	28.90	21.93	17.75	12.53	9.74	7.85	6.28	5.50
50	32.79	27.22	20.66	16.71	11.80	9.18	7.77	6.22	5.44
Weight Limits (lb)	Under 500	500— 1000	1000— 2000	2000— 5000	5000— 10,000	10,000— 20,000	20,000— 30,000	30,000— 40,000	Over 40,000

and destination rates were manually maintained in notebooks that had to be updated and revised regularly. Today, rates are provided in diskette form by carriers and the administration process is typically computerized.

Origin and destination rates are organized by three- or five-digit zip codes. Table 12-2 illustrates rates for all freight classes from Atlanta, Georgia (zip 303), to Lansing, Michigan (zip 489). The table lists rates for shipments ranging in size from the smallest LTL (less than 500 pounds; listed as L5C) to the largest TL (greater than 40,000 pounds; listed as M40M). The rate is quoted in cents per hundredweight. Assuming a shipment of 10,000 pounds, the rate for class 85 between Atlanta and Lansing is $12.92 per hundredweight.

Historically, the published rate had to be charged for all shipments of a specific class and origin/destination combination. This required frequent reviews and maintenance to keep rates current. Following deregulation, carriers offered more flexibility through rate discounts. Now instead of developing an individual rate table to meet the needs of customer segments, carriers apply a discount from class rates for specific customers. The discount, generally in the range of 30 to 50 percent, depends on the shipper's volume and market competition.

An alternative to the per hundredweight charge is a per mile charge, which is common in TL shipments. As discussed previously, TL shipments are designed to reduce handling and transfer costs. Since the entire vehicle is used in a TL movement and there is no requirement to transfer the shipment at a terminal, a per mile basis offers a more appropriate pricing approach. For a one-way move, charges may range from $1.25 to $3.00 per mile, depending on the market. Although it is negotiable, this charge typically includes LTL services such as loading, unloading, and liability.

In addition to the variable shipment charge applied on either a per hundredweight or per mile basis, two additional charges are common for transportation: **minimum charges** and **surcharges.** The minimum charge represents the amount a shipper must pay to make a shipment, regardless of weight. To illustrate, assume that the applicable class rate is $15/CWT and the shipper wants to transport 100 pounds to a specific location. If no minimum charge exists, the shipper would pay $15. However, if the minimum charge were $150 per shipment, the shipper would be required to pay the minimum. Minimum charges cover fixed costs associated with a shipment.

A surcharge represents an additional charge designed to cover specific carrier costs. Surcharges are used to protect carriers from situations not anticipated when publishing a general rate. The surcharge may be assessed as a flat charge, a percentage, or a sliding scale based on shipment size. A common use of surcharges is to compensate carriers for dramatic changes in fuel cost. For example, in the fall of 2000, when fuel prices experienced steep increases, it was common to see transportation rates with 10 to 20 percent surcharges. The surcharge approach provides a means of immediate relief for the carrier to recover unexpected costs while not including such cost in the long-term rate structure.

Class rates, minimum charges, arbitrary charges, and surcharges form a pricing structure that, in various combinations, is applicable within the continental United States. The tariff indicates the class rate for any rating group between specified origins and destinations. In combination, the classification scheme and class rate structure form a generalized pricing mechanism for rail and motor carriers. Each mode has specific characteristics applicable to its tariffs. In water, specific tariff provisions are made for cargo location within the ship or on the deck. In addition, provisions are made to charter entire vessels. Similar specialized provisions are found in air cargo and pipeline tariffs. Nonoperating intermediaries and package services also publish tariffs specialized to their service.

Commodity Rates

When a large quantity of a product moves between two locations on a regular basis, it is common practice for carriers to publish a **commodity rate.** Commodity rates are special or specific rates published without regard to classification. The terms and conditions of a commodity rate are usually indicated in a contract between the carrier and shipper. Commodity rates are usually published on a point-to-point basis and apply only on specified products. Today, most rail freight moves under commodity rates. They are less prevalent in motor carriage. Whenever a commodity rate exists, it supersedes the corresponding class or exception rate.

Exception Rates

Exception rates, or exceptions to the classification, are special rates published to provide shippers lower rates than the prevailing class rate. The original purpose of the exception rate was to provide a special rate for a specific area, origin/destination, or commodity when either competitive or high-volume movements justified it. Rather than publish a new tariff, an exception to the classification or class rate was established.

Just as the name implies, when an exception rate is published, the classification that normally applies to the product is changed. Such changes may involve assignment of a new class or may be based on a percentage of the original class. Technically, exceptions may be higher or lower, although most are less than original class rates. Unless otherwise noted, all services provided under the class rate remain under an exception rate.

Since deregulation, several new types of exception rates have gained popularity. For example, an **aggregate tender** rate is utilized when a shipper agrees to provide multiple shipments to a carrier in exchange for a discount or exception from the prevailing class rate. The primary objective is to reduce carrier cost by permitting multiple shipment pickup during one stop at a shipper's facility or to reduce the rate for the shipper because of the carrier's decreased operations or marketing expenses. To illustrate, UPS offers customers that require multiple small package shipments a discount based on aggregate weight and/or cubic volume. Since 1980, numerous pricing innovations have been introduced by common carriers based on various aggregation principles.

A **limited service** rate is utilized when a shipper agrees to perform selected services typically performed by the carrier, such as trailer loading, in exchange for a discount. A common example is a *shipper load and count* rate, where the shipper takes responsibility for loading and counting the cases. Not only does this remove the responsibility for loading the shipment from the carrier, but it also implies that the carrier is not responsible for guaranteeing case count. Another example of limited service is a *released value* rate, which limits carrier liability in case of loss or damage. Normally, the carrier is responsible for full product value if loss or damage occurs in transit. The quoted rate must include adequate insurance to cover the risk. Often it is more effective for manufacturers of high-value product to self-insure to realize the lowest possible rate. Limited service is used when shippers have confidence in the carrier's capability. Cost can be reduced by eliminating duplication of effort or responsibility.

Under aggregate tender and limited service rates, as well as other innovative exception rates, the basic economic justification is the reduction of carrier cost and subsequent sharing of benefits based on shipper/carrier cooperation.

Special Rates and Services

A number of special rates and services provided by for-hire carriers are available for logistical operations. Several important examples are discussed.

Freight-All-Kind Rates.   As indicated earlier, **Freight-All-Kind (FAK) rates** are important to logistics operations. Under FAK rates, a mixture of different products is transported under a generic rating. Rather than determine the classification and applicable rate of each product, an average rate is applied for the total shipment. In essence, FAK rates are line-haul rates since they replace class, exception, or commodity rates. Their purpose is to simplify the paperwork associated with the movement of mixed commodities to lower the costs, so they are of particular importance in physical distribution.

Local, Joint, Proportional, and Combination Rates.   Numerous special rates exist that may offer transportation savings on specific freight movements. When a commodity moves under the tariff of a single carrier, it is referred to as a **local rate** or single-line rate. If more than one carrier is involved in the freight movement, a **joint rate** may be applicable even though multiple carriers are involved in the actual transportation process. Because some motor and rail carriers operate in restricted territory, it may be necessary to utilize the services of more than one carrier to complete a shipment. Utilization of a joint rate can offer substantial savings over the use of two or more local rates.

Proportional rates offer special price incentives to utilize a published tariff that applies to only part of the desired route. Proportional provisions of a tariff are most often applicable to origin or destination points outside the normal geographical area of a single-line tariff. If a joint rate does not exist and proportional provisions do, the strategy of moving a shipment under proportional rates provides a discount on the single-line part of the movement, thereby resulting in a lower overall freight charge.

Combination rates are similar to proportional rates in that a shopper may combine two or more rates when no single-line or joint rate exists between an origin and a destination. The rates may be any combination of class, exception, and commodity rates. The utilization of combination rates often involves several technicalities that are beyond the scope of this discussion. Their use substantially reduces the cost of an individual shipment. In situations involving regular freight movement, the need to utilize combination rates is eliminated by publication of a **through rate.** A through rate is a standardized rate that applies from origin to destination for a shipment.

Transit Services.   **Transit services** permit a shipment to be stopped at an intermediate point between initial origin and destination for unloading, storage, and/or processing. The shipment is then reloaded for delivery to the destination. Typical examples of transit services are milling for grain products and processing for sugar beets. When transit privileges exist, the shipment is charged a through rate from origin to destination plus a transit privilege charge. Transit services are most typical in rail tariffs. From the viewpoint of the shipper, the use of this specialized service is restricted to routings and destinations. Therefore, a degree of flexibility is lost when the product is placed in transit because the final destination can be altered only at significant added expense or, at the least, with loss of the through rate privilege. The added cost of administration must be carefully weighed in evaluating the true benefits gained from utilizing a transit privilege. During the last decade railroads have generally reduced the availability of such transit services.

Diversion and Reconsignment.   For a variety of reasons, a shipper or consignee may desire to change routing, destination, or even the consignee after a shipment is in transit. This flexibility can be extremely important, particularly with regard to the transportation of food and other perishable products where market demand quickly changes. It is a normal practice among certain types of marketing intermediaries to purchase commodities with the full intention of selling them while they are in transit. **Diversion** consists of changing the destination of a shipment prior to its arrival at the original destination. **Reconsignment** is a change in consignee prior to delivery. Both services are provided by railroads and motor carriers for a specified charge.

Split Delivery.   A **split delivery** is desired when portions of a shipment need to be delivered to different facilities. Under specified tariff conditions, delivery can be extended to multiple destinations. The payment is typically structured to reflect a rate as if the shipment were going to the most distant destination. In addition, there typically is a charge for each delivery stop-off.

Demurrage and Detention.   Demurrage and detention are charges assessed for retaining freight cars or truck trailers beyond specified loading or unloading time. The term **demurrage** is used by railroads for holding a railcar beyond 48 hours before unloading the shipment. Motor carriers use the term **detention** to cover similar delays. In the case of motor carriers, the permitted time is specified in the tariff and is normally limited to a few hours.

Accessorial Services.   In addition to basic transportation, motor and rail carriers offer a wide variety of special or ancillary services that can aid in planning logistical operations. Table 12-3 provides a list of the most frequently utilized ancillary services.

TABLE 12-3   Typical Carrier Ancillary Services

- *COD.* Collect payment on delivery.
- *Change COD.* Change COD recipient.
- *Inside delivery.* Deliver product inside the building.
- *Marking or tagging.* Mark or tag product as it is transported.
- *Notify before delivery.* Make appointment prior to delivery.
- *Reconsignment of delivery.* Redirect shipment to a new destination while in transit.
- *Redeliver.* Attempt second delivery.
- *Residential delivery.* Deliver at a residence without a truck dock.
- *Sorting and segregating.* Sort commodity prior to delivery.
- *Storage.* Store commodity prior to delivery.

Carriers may also offer environmental services and special equipment. **Environmental services** refer to special control of freight while in transit, such as refrigeration, ventilation, and heating. For example, in the summer, Hershey's typically transports its chocolate confectionery products in refrigerated trailers to protect them from high temperature levels. **Special equipment charges** refer to the use of equipment that the carrier has purchased for the shipper's economy and convenience. For example, specialized sanitation equipment is necessary to clean and prepare trailers for food storage and transit if the trailer has been previously utilized for nonfood products or commodities.

Although the brief coverage of special services is not all-inclusive, it does offer several examples of the range and type of services carriers offer. A carrier's role in a logistical system is most often far greater than providing line-haul transportation.

Traffic Department Administration

While traffic managers administer many different activities, they are fundamentally responsible for: (1) operations management, (2) freight consolidation, (3) rate negotiation, (4) freight control, (5) auditing and claims, and (6) logistical integration.

Operations Management

The fundamental responsibility of a traffic department is to oversee day-to-day shipping. In large-scale organizations, traffic operations management involves a wide variety of administrative responsibilities. Firms are increasingly implementing Transportation Management Systems (TMS) as integral parts of their integration information technology strategies.[2] From an operational perspective, key elements of transportation management are equipment scheduling, load planning, routing, and carrier administration.

Equipment Scheduling

One major responsibility of the traffic department is equipment scheduling. Scheduling is an important process in both common carrier and private transportation. A

---

[2]The functionality of TMS was discussed in Chapter 8. See pp. 242–243.

serious and costly operational bottleneck can result from transportation equipment waiting to be loaded or unloaded. Proper scheduling requires careful load planning, equipment utilization, and driver scheduling. Additionally, equipment preventative maintenance must be planned, coordinated, and monitored. Finally, any specialized equipment requirements must be planned and implemented.

Closely related to equipment scheduling is the arrangement of delivery and pickup appointments. To avoid extensive waiting time and improve equipment utilization, it is important to preschedule dock positions or slots. It is becoming common practice to establish regular or standing appointments to facilitate loading and unloading. Some firms are implementing the practice of establishing appointments at the time of purchase or sale commitment. Increasingly, the effective scheduling of equipment is key to implementing time-based logistical arrangements. For example, cross-dock arrangements are totally dependent on precise scheduling of equipment arrival and departure.

Load Planning

How loads are planned directly impacts transportation efficiency. In the case of motor carriers, capacity is limited in terms of weight and cube. Planning the load sequence of a trailer must consider product physical characteristics, the size of individual shipments, and delivery sequence if multiple shipments are loaded on a single trailer. As noted earlier, TMS software is available to help facilitate load planning.

How effectively load planning is performed will directly impact overall logistical efficiency. For example, the load plan drives timing of product selection and the work sequence at warehouses. Transportation equipment must be available to maintain an orderly flow of product and material from warehouse or factory to shipment destination.

Routing

An important part of achieving transportation efficiency is shipment routing. Routing plans the geographical path a vehicle will travel to complete transportation requirements. Once again, routing software is an integral part of TMS.

From an administrative viewpoint, the traffic department is responsible for assuring that routing is performed in an efficient manner while meeting key customer service requirements. How routes are implemented must take into consideration special requirements of customers in terms of delivery time, location, and special unloading services.

Carrier Administration

Traffic managers have the basic responsibility of administering the performance of for-hire and private transportation. Effective administration requires continuous carrier performance measurement and evaluation. Until recently, efforts to measure actual carrier service were sporadic and unreliable. A typical procedure was to include postcards with shipments requesting consignees to record time and condition of arrival. The development of information technology has significantly improved shipment information reliability. The fact that most shippers have reduced their carrier base has greatly simplified administration. Effective administration requires carrier selection, integration, and evaluation.

Carrier Selection.   A basic responsibility of the traffic department is to select carriers to perform for-hire transport. To some degree all firms use the services of for-hire carriers. Even those with commitment to private fleets regularly require the supplemented services of common, contract, and specialized carriers to complete transportation requirements. Most firms that use for-hire transportation have implemented what is commonly called a **core carrier strategy.**

The concept of a core carrier is to build a working relationship with a small number of transportation providers. Historically, shippers followed the practice of spreading their transportation requirements across a wide variety of carriers to assure equipment supply. During the regulated era, few differences in price existed between carriers. As a result, shippers often conducted business with hundreds of different carriers. Examples exist where shippers have reduced carriers from 400 to 500 down to 20 or even as few as 10.[3] The concentration of volume in a few core carriers seeks to establish a business relationship that standardizes operational and administrative processes. Mutual planning and acknowledged dependency between a shipper and carrier result in dependable equipment supply, customized services, improved scheduling, and more efficient overall administration.

In a number of situations, the core carrier relationships are directly between the shipper and the transportation provider. A recent development is the use of integrated service providers (ISPs) to establish and maintain business relationships with core carriers. In such situations, the ISP facilitates administration and consolidates freight across a wide variety of shippers. Industry Insight 12-1 describes the development of a new technology implemented at Meijer, Inc., to manage its inbound transportation activity. In other situations, core carriers serve as coordinators by arranging the services of several, even competitive, carriers to satisfy the shipment requirements of key customers.

The range of relationship models is ever-changing as service providers devise new and better methods of identifying and integrating transportation requirements. However, at the end of the day, it remains a fundamental responsibility of transportation management to assure a firm is supported by reliable and economical transportation. This fundamental responsibility cannot be delegated.

Carrier Integration.   Carrier integration is similar to introducing new product and service capabilities into logistics operations. The two challenges of carrier integration are long-term trends and carrier services. These two types of integration are critical for shippers to achieve their functional and strategic performance in the marketplace.

Monitoring long-term market trends requires assessment of trailer or railcar capacity that will be needed to meet shipping requirements on a seasonal or yearly basis. Related is planning the supply of equipment type to satisfy operational requirements. An example is to determine whether container or trailer supply will be sufficient to meet industry demand across a planning horizon. Such awareness of supply and demand is essential for effective negotiation.

Monitoring demand for carrier services is also important. For successful integration, carriers must plan equipment and provide services essential to a customer's logistical requirements. Unless carriers are available to perform essential services, operational discontinuity can be expected.

Carrier Evaluation.   Prior to deregulation, purchasers of transportation services had a relatively easy task. Shippers selected a carrier for a specific shipment from a long

---

[3]Peter Buxbaum, "Core Carrier Programs: Poetry in Motion," *Inbound Logistics,* September 1997, pp. 32–39.

INDUSTRY INSIGHT 12-1 LEANLOGISTICS MANAGES INBOUND TRANSPORTATION

Officials at LeanLogistics announced that Meijer, Inc., has begun using the LeanLogistics Internet-based private transportation exchange for online tendering, executing, and managing all of its inbound transportation. Meijer is using LeanLogistics proprietary technology to communicate critical data for all inbound transportation within its distribution network. The system is processing Meijer inbound transactions for TL, LTL, and consolidated LTL orders.

According to Ed Nieuwenhuis, Meijer vice president of logistics, "With the increasing complexity in distribution as a result of shorter lead times, lower inventory levels, smaller and more frequent shipments, and a need for greater visibility, the opportunity to utilize this type of new technology never existed until now. The LeanLogistics technology in the private exchange environment allows Meijer to build upon existing carrier relationships while achieving efficiencies inherent in a seamless, highly visible replenishment system. We are able to take logistics to the next level without disrupting any valuable relationships."

LeanLogistics is an Internet-based solution that provides a highly secure, scalable environment for transportation e-commerce. Based on the philosophies of lean manufacturing, LeanLogistics technology utilizes the Internet to efficiently transact business between shippers and carriers and reduce the overall cost of freight movement. LeanLogistics technology allows shippers and carriers to manage the entire transportation transaction from customer order to delivery, including payment and settlement, via the Internet.

For example, one of the greatest benefits of LeanLogistics technology is that it allows the shipper to streamline the tendering process with core carriers. The shipper can efficiently tender loads to the core carrier audience, using a contract rate. The technology automatically retenders loads to the next available carrier group if the first carrier group does not accept it.

As another example, LeanLogistics automatically captures all rate and service charge data as part of the load tendering process—loads are automatically preaudited before execution. It eliminates auditing and time-consuming reconciliation between shippers and carriers.

LeanLogistics technology allows end-to-end, 24/7 visibility on all load and purchase order status to Meijer logistics and purchasing staff, as well as participating core carriers and vendors. If an exception occurs, such as a missed appointment, the system automatically alerts concerned parties for proactive management of inbound load issues, thereby reducing stockouts and assuring a higher degree of on-time order fulfillment.

For carriers, load information is received electronically, eliminating rekeying into the carriers' systems. Carriers also have the ability to make online delivery appointments at the Meijer distribution centers.

Source: Materials provided by LeanLogistics, Holland, MI.

---

list, knowing that each offered essentially standardized service for the same price. Due to economic regulation, there wasn't much room to negotiate price or service.

Since deregulation, however, carrier evaluation has become far more complex and important because a number of factors must be measured. Carrier evaluation should focus on criteria judged important by the consignee rather than the shipper. Such considerations typically include cost, transit time, reliability, capability, accessibility, and security.

Transportation *cost* is the most basic consideration. The freight rate is only part of the total cost. Overall cost must consider transit time and consistency impact on inventory, ease of system interface, equipment, and related activities such a loading and counting. Carriers offering faster and more reliable *transit times* offer attributes that are important to overall logistical performance. Regardless of how fast a supplier is

TABLE 12-4   Sample Carrier Evaluation

Evaluation Factor	Relative Importance	×	Carrier Performance	=	Carrier Rating
1 Cost	1	×	1	=	1
2 Transit Time Length	3	×	2	=	6
3 Transit Time Reliability	1	×	2	=	2
4 Capability	2	×	2	=	4
5 Accessibility	2	×	2	=	4
6 Security	2	×	3	=	6
			Total Carrier Rating		23

Relative importance measure: 1 = high importance; 2 = moderate importance; 3 = low importance.

Carrier performance measure: 1 = good performance; 2 = fair performance; 3 = poor performance.

able to ship, it must provide a high degree of *reliability.* If the transportation carrier provides inconsistent delivery, problems will result. Sales will be lost and production lines shut down if carriers do not meet delivery obligation. Some carriers are superior to others, and those offering advantage change rapidly. The task is to maintain an up-to-date evaluation of carrier consistency.

The typical assessment of reliability is statistical evaluation of shipment release and arrival time. Technology is making such data increasingly available to shippers. The variation between actual and expected performance can be measured and maintained in a carrier reliability report. *Capability* refers to a carrier's capacity to provide power and specialized equipment such as temperature control, bulk products, and side unloading. Overall capabilities include EDI, Internet, scheduling and invoicing, online shipment tracking, and storage and consolidation.

Accessibility is generally not a problem for motor carriers; however, it can be a consideration for other modes. The specific concern is initial product movement to and from airport, railhead, and port or pipeline access points. While physical accessibility has become less of an issue due to expansion of intermodal services, accessibility to carriers with through or joint operating agreements has increased. These agreements generally increase service speed while reducing the necessity to negotiate multiple rates, prepare multiple copies of shipping documentation, or require multiple calls to trace shipments.

A final consideration is a carrier's *security.* Security is a carrier's ability to protect a load from loss, damage, or theft. Related is the carrier's ability to quickly resolve a loss or damage claim.

Using the above considerations, a two-step process can be used to comparatively evaluate carriers. The first step determines the relative importance of service elements to the shipper. The approach then assigns an importance weight factor to each element. For example, a very important item may be rated 1 while a less important element is rated 3. Table 12-4 illustrates such an approach.

The second step is to assess carrier performance concerning each element. Table 12-4 illustrates a three-point rating scale ranging from good to poor performance. The carrier performance evaluation should include both quantitative and qualitative elements. A combined carrier rating can be established by multiplying relative importance and carrier performance. In Table 12-4, a carrier evaluation of 23 is the sum of individual factor ratings and relative importance. In this evaluation, the best carrier within a group would be the one with the lowest point total.

Freight Consolidation

At several different points throughout this text the importance of freight consolidation is discussed. The fact that freight costs are directly related to size of shipment and length of haul places a premium upon freight consolidation. In terms made famous by the late President Truman, *the buck stops here,* meaning traffic management is the business function responsible for achieving freight consolidation.

The traditional approach to freight consolidation was to combine LTL or parcel shipment moving to a general location. The objective of outbound consolidation was straightforward. The transportation savings in moving a single consolidated shipment versus multiple individual, small shipments were typically sufficient to pay for handling and local delivery while achieving total cost reduction.

The shift to response-based logistics has introduced new challenges regarding consolidation. Time-based logistics tends to transpose the impact of unpredictable demand from inventory safety stock to creation of small shipments. All members of the supply chain are seeking to reduce inventory dwell time by more closely synchronizing replenishment with demand. The result is more frequent, small orders. Not only does the increase in small shipment result in higher transportation cost, it also translates to more handling and dock congestion. Industry Insight 12-2 discusses this shift to similar order sizes and some of the strategies implemented by companies to deal with it.

To control transportation cost when using a time-based strategy, managerial attention must be directed to the development of ingenious ways to realize benefits of transportation consolidation. To plan freight consolidation, it is necessary to have reliable information concerning both current and planned inventory status. It is also desirable to be able to reserve or promise scheduled production to complete planned consolidations. To the extent practical, consolidations should be planned prior to order processing and warehouse order selection to avoid delays. All aspects of consolidation require timely and relevant information concerning planned activity.

From an operational viewpoint, freight consolidation techniques can be grouped as *reactive* and *proactive.* Each type of consolidation is important to achieving transportation efficiency.

Reactive Consolidation

A reactive approach to consolidation does not attempt to influence the composition and timing of transportation movements. The consolidation effort takes shipments as they come and seeks to combine freight into larger shipments for line-haul movement. Perhaps the most visible example of effective reactive line-haul is United Parcel Service's nightly sortation and consolidation of package freight for intercity movement.

From an operational viewpoint, there are three ways to achieve effective reactive freight consolidation: (1) market area, (2) scheduled delivery, and (3) pooled delivery.

Market Area.   The most basic method of consolidation is to combine small shipments going to different customers within a geographical market area. This procedure does not interrupt the natural freight flow by changing the timing of shipments. Rather, the overall quantity of shipments to a market area provides the consolidation basis.

The difficulty of developing either inbound or outbound market area consolidations is the variation in daily volume. To offset the volume deficiency, three operating arrangements are commonly used. First, consolidated shipments may be sent to an intermediate break-bulk point for purposes of line-haul transportation savings. There,

INDUSTRY INSIGHT 12-2 MARKET CHANGES REQUIRE NEW SUPPLY CHAIN THINKING

In an effort to reduce their inventory levels and improve their return on assets, companies are pushing inventory back to their suppliers and expecting smaller, more frequent service to quickly replenish their reduced stock level. This allows the manufacturer to cut inventory to a few days' supply, but cost has not really been taken out of the supply chain.

The impact of smaller order quantities is measurable and material. It is a reasonable assumption that shrinking orders are a primary factor in driving up overall transportation expenditures. Research indicates transportation represents not only the largest component of total logistics costs but also the fastest growing component, up from 44 percent of the total in 1980 to 57 percent in 1995.

As a result of the shift to smaller, more frequent orders, many companies have seen a shift in modal mix toward parcel freight from TL and LTL shipments. Freight costs can rise rapidly when orders must be shipped using smaller LTL or parcel freight modes. Freight costs can increase by two to three times in cases of drastic shifts in order profile and mode mix. This could mean outbound freight going from 1 percent to 2 percent or 3 percent of sales. On a company with a 10 percent profit margin, this represents a 10 percent to 20 percent reduction in margin.

Cost-Cutting Strategies

Direct store delivery (DSD) or drop shipping is how some trading partners avoid the cost of handling smaller orders in a retailer's or a distributor's distribution center. By letting the supplier ship the order directly to the store or end customer, a whole step is removed from the supply chain and the retailers (or buyers) achieve their objective of pushing inventory upstream to the suppliers. DSD is a valid approach for addressing smaller, more frequent orders as long as the supplier can respond quickly and cost-effectively. Whether or not DSD actually provides a cost or service advantage in a given situation requires careful assessment. Since transportation costs and receiving costs typically increase, the benefits can easily be offset.

In addition to DSD, there are other options for dealing with smaller, more frequent shipments: Freight consolidation is an effective way to recoup some of the rising transportation costs associated with smaller shipment sizes. Consolidation can be used for either inbound or outbound freight but requires a concentration of volume in a given transportation lane to be cost-effective. Inbound consolidation may make sense if a number of suppliers are shipping LTL from the same geographic region. To make it work, suppliers ship LTL orders to a regional consolidation point where they can be combined into full TLs for shipment to the buyer. Consolidation becomes more attractive over longer distances due to the opportunity to eliminate a high-cost, long-haul LTL shipment. Likewise, if there is a concentration of outbound LTL shipments to a region, those orders can be combined into a TL shipment to a deconsolidation point. Delivery to the end customer can be accomplished with short-haul LTL or contract delivery.

Zone skipping is a consolidation technique used to reduce outbound parcel freight. By combining packages into a truckload and shipping directly to the parcel carrier's hub near the final delivery point, the parcels can be rated for a lower cost zone.

Third-party logistics providers offer another savings alternative by leveraging the combined volume of their customer base to realize economies of scale not available to one shipper. These service offerings could involve warehousing, consolidation, inventory management, zone skipping, or milk-run opportunities.

Logistics managers have been dealing with shrinking order profiles for some time. Looking at supply chain trends that are driving smaller, more frequent ordering, we can be fairly certain shrinking orders will continue to be an issue. We can also be certain the pressure to reduce distribution expense will not subside. Logistics managers must be creative in applying innovative ideas and technologies as well as proven approaches that now make sense.

Source: Paul Huppertz, "Market Changes Require New Supply Chain Thinking," *Transportation and Distribution,* 40, no. 3 (March 1999), pp. 70–74.

individual shipments are separated and forwarded to their destination. Second, firms may elect to hold consolidated shipments for scheduled delivery on specific days to given destination markets. Third, firms may achieve consolidation of small shipments by utilizing the services of a third-party logistics firm to pool delivery. The last two methods require special arrangements, which are discussed in greater detail below.

Scheduled Delivery.   Scheduled delivery consists of limiting shipments to specific markets to selected days each week. The scheduled delivery plan is normally communicated to customers in a way that highlights the mutual benefits of consolidation. The shipping firm commits to the customer that all orders received prior to a specified cut-off time will be guaranteed for delivery on the scheduled day.

Scheduled delivery may conflict with the trend toward customer-specified delivery appointments. Specified delivery time means that an order is expected to be delivered within a narrow time window. In today's world, a requirement to provide ± 1-hour delivery of a component or part may be written into the purchase contract. Pushed to the limit, customer-specified delivery requires the capability to deliver any size shipment at any time specified by a customer. The objective of scheduled delivery is to offer a solution that the customer can depend upon while also achieving consolidation benefits.

Pooled Delivery.   Participation in a pooled delivery plan typically means that a freight forwarder, public warehouse, or transportation company arranges consolidation for multiple shippers serving the same geographical market area. Integrated source providers that arrange pooled consolidation services typically have standing delivery appointments at high-volume delivery destinations. It is common, under such arrangements, for the consolidation company to perform value-added service such as sorting, sequencing, or segregation of inbound freight to accommodate customer requirements.

Proactive Consolidation

While reactive efforts to develop transportation consolidations have been successful, firms are becoming more innovative concerning pretransaction planning. Two forces are driving a more proactive approach to consolidation. First, the impact of time-based responsive logistical systems is creating a larger number of small shipments. This trend towards increased smaller shipments has been intensified by increased e-commerce fulfillment. Second, proactive consolidation has increased the desire for shippers, carriers, and consignees to participate in consolidation savings. Traditional consolidation programs typically favored one of the three to the exclusion of one or both of the others. A willingness to share benefits can provide incentive for all members of the supply chain to achieve freight consolidation.

Preorder Planning.   An important step toward achieving proactive consolidation is preorder planning of order quantities and timing to facilitate consolidated freight movement. Simply stated, the creation of orders should not be restricted to standard buying times or inventory replenishment rules. Buyer participation in order creation can greatly facilitate freight consolidation.[4]

Multifirm Consolidation.   Significant freight consolidation opportunities also may exist if non-related firms can be coordinated. Commonly referred to as *multivendor*

---

[4]Carol Casper, "Multi-Vendor Consolidation," *Food Logistics,* January/February 1999, pp. 37–48.

consolidation, the general idea of grouping different shippers' freight has always been integral to line-haul operations of LTL carriers. The new initiative is jointly planning warehousing and order processing across different companies to facilitate such consolidation. Creating such multivendor consolidation is a value-added service offered by a growing number of ISPs.[5] Likewise, firms are increasingly endorsing pooling arrangements with competitors to achieve logistical efficiency.[6]

Rate Negotiation

In Chapter 11, a description of basic transportation rates and associated rate regulation was discussed. For any given shipment it is the responsibility of the traffic department to obtain the lowest possible rate consistent with service requirements. The prevailing price for each transport alternative—rail, air, motor, pipeline, water, and so on—is found by reference to tariffs.

Since 1980 the prevailing tariff represents the starting point in transportation negotiation. The key to effective negotiation is to seek win–win agreements wherein both carriers and shippers share productivity gains. As indicated several times throughout this text, the lowest possible cost for transportation may not be the lowest total cost of logistics. The traffic department must seek the lowest rate consistent with service standards. For example, if 2-day delivery is required, the traffic department seeks to select the method of transport that will meet this standard at the lowest possible cost. Given the special considerations of transportation, several factors discussed throughout this section must guide rate negotiation. However, in the context of building solid carrier relationships, traffic managers must seek fair and equitable rates.

Freight Control

Other important responsibilities of transportation management are tracing and expediting. **Tracing** is a procedure to locate lost or late shipments. Shipments committed across a transportation network are bound to be misplaced or delayed from time to time. Most large carriers maintain online tracing to aid shippers in locating a shipment. The tracing action must be initiated by the shipper's traffic department, but once initiated, it is the carrier's responsibility to provide the desired information. **Expediting** involves the shipper notifying a carrier that it needs to have a specific shipment move through the carrier's system as quickly as possible and with no delays.

Traditional problems related to tracing and expediting have been significantly reduced through the use of information technologies such as bar coding, online freight information systems, satellite, and Internet-based communications. Bar coding provides quick and error-free transfer of shipment information that facilitates shipment tracking at intermediate points. Online freight information systems allow shippers and consignees to directly access a carrier's computer to determine shipment status. Schneider National utilizes satellite tracking to provide location and projected movement across its truck fleet to identify potential problems and work proactively with customers to implement acceptable solutions.

---

[5]Katherine Doherty, "The Faster Freight Moves the Better Off We Are," *Food Logistics,* October 1998, pp. 54–58.

[6]Helen L. Richardson, "Pooling with Competitors," *Transportation and Distribution,* November 1998, pp. 105–10.

Auditing and Claim Administration

When transportation service or charges are not performed as promised, shippers can make claims for restitution. Claims are typically classified as loss and damage or overcharge/undercharge. Loss and damage claims occur when a shipper demands the carrier pay for partial or total financial loss resulting from poor performance. As the name implies, loss and damage claims usually occur when product is lost or damaged while in transit. Overcharge/undercharge claims result when the amount billed is different from that expected and are typically resolved through freight bill audit procedures described below.

Agreements stipulate the proper procedure for filing claims and help define which parties are responsible. Two factors regarding claim administration are of primary importance. First, detailed attention should be given to claim administration because recoveries are only achieved by aggressive audit programs. Second, large volumes of claims are indicative of carriers who are not performing their service obligations. Regardless of the dollars recovered by claim administration, the breakdown in customer service performance resulting from loss and damage claims impacts a shipper's reputation with its customers.

Auditing freight bills is an important function of the traffic department. The purpose of auditing is to ensure billing accuracy. Transport rate complexity results in higher error probabilities than in most other purchasing decisions. There are two types of freight audits. A *preaudit* determines proper charges prior to payment of a freight bill. A *postaudit* makes the same determination after payment has been made. Auditing may be either external or internal. If external, specialized freight-auditing companies are employed utilizing personnel who are experts in specific commodity groupings. This is generally more efficient than the use of internal personnel who may not have the same level of expertise. Payment for external audit is usually based on a percentage of recovered overcharges. It is crucial that a highly ethical firm be employed for this purpose, because valuable marketing and customer information is contained in the freight bill and corporate activities may be adversely affected if sensitive information is not held in confidence.

A combination of internal and external auditing is frequently employed based on the value of the freight bill. For example, a bill of $600 with a 10 percent error results in a $60 recovery, but a $50 bill with a 10 percent error results in only a $5 recovery. As such, bills with larger recovery potential may be audited internally.

External versus internal auditing may also be affected by the size of the firm and degree of rate computerization. For instance, large traffic departments are in a position to have specialized clerks for auditing purposes. Also, firms utilizing computerized systems of freight payment can build in rates on a majority of origin/destination points and weights. Such computer capability allows automatic check of proper payment.

Logistical Integration

For any given operating period, traffic management is expected to provide the required transportation services at budgeted cost. It is also traffic management's responsibility to search for alternative ways to deploy transportation to reduce total logistics cost. For example, a slight change in packaging may create an opportunity for negotiation of a lower freight classification rating for a product. Although packaging costs may increase, this added expense may be offset by a substantial reduction in transportation cost. Unless such proposals originate from the traffic department, they will likely go undetected in the average firm. As indicated earlier, transportation is the highest single cost area in most logistical systems. This expenditure level combined with the dependence of logistical operations on effective transportation means that the traffic departments must play an active role in strategic planning.

Documentation

Well-defined documentation is required to perform a transportation service. With the exception of private transfer within the confines of a single firm, products are typically being sold between the shipper and the consignee. Thus, legal title to ownership is occurring at the time the transport service is performed. When for-hire carriers are engaged to perform the transportation, the transaction must establish clear legal responsibility for all parties involved. The primary purpose of transportation documentation is to protect the interest of all parties involved in the performance of the transaction. Three primary types of transport documentation are bills of lading, freight bills, and shipment manifests.

Bill of Lading

The **bill of lading** is the basic document utilized in purchasing transport services. It serves as a receipt and documents products and quantities shipped. For this reason, accurate product description and count are essential. In case of loss, damage, or delay, the bill of lading is the basis for damage claims. The designated individual or buyer on a bill of lading is the only bona fide recipient of goods. A carrier is responsible for proper delivery according to instructions contained in the document. In effect, title is transferred with completion of delivery.

The bill of lading specifies terms and conditions of carrier liability and documents responsibilities for all possible causes of loss or damage except those defined as acts of God. It is important that terms and conditions be clearly understood so that appropriate actions can be taken in the event of substandard performance. Government rules permit uniform bills of lading to be computerized and electronically transmitted between shippers and carriers.

In addition to the *uniform* bill of lading, other commonly used types are *order-notified, export,* and *government.* It is important to select the correct bill of lading for a specific shipment.

An order-notified or negotiable bill of lading is a credit instrument. It provides that delivery not be made unless the original bill of lading is surrendered to the carrier. The usual procedure is for the seller to send the order-notified bill of lading to a third party, usually a bank or credit institution. Upon customer payment for the product the credit institution releases the bill of lading. The buyer then presents it to the common carrier, which in turn releases the goods. This facilitates international transport where cross-border payment for goods may be a major consideration. An export bill of lading permits a shipper to use export rates, which may be lower than domestic rates. Export rates may reduce total cost when applied to domestic origin or destination line-haul transport. Government bills of lading may be used when the product is owned by the U.S. government.

Freight Bill

The **freight bill** represents a carrier's method of charging for transportation services performed. It is developed using information contained in the bill of lading. The freight bill may be either *prepaid* or *collect*. A prepaid bill means that transport cost must be paid prior to performance, whereas a collect shipment shifts payment responsibility to the consignee.

Considerable administration is involved in preparing bills of lading and freight bills. There has been significant effort to automate freight bills and bills of lading through EDI transactions. Some firms now elect to pay their freight bills at the time the bill of lading is created, thereby combining the two documents. Such arrangements are based upon the financial benefits of reduced paperwork cost. Many attempts are underway to produce all transport documents simultaneously.

Shipment Manifest

The **shipment manifest** lists individual stops or consignees when multiple shipments are placed on a single vehicle. Each shipment requires a bill of lading. The manifest lists the stop, bill of lading, weight, and case count for each shipment. The objective of the manifest is to provide a single document that defines the overall contents of the load without requiring review of individual bills of lading. For single-stop shipments, the manifest is the same as the bill of lading.

Summary

Transportation is usually *the* largest single cost expenditure in most logistics operations. Prior to deregulation, transportation services were standardized and inflexible, resulting in limited ability to develop a competitive advantage. As a result of deregulation service offerings have been expanded and restrictions relaxed, allowing transportation resources to be effectively integrated into the overall supply chain.

Knowledge of transportation economics and pricing is essential to effective logistics management. The primary drivers of transportation costs are distance, volume, density, stowability, handling, liability, and market factors. These drivers determine transportation prices that are presented to buyers as rates related to specific services. Logistics managers need to have a working familiarity with the basic rate structure for line-haul and specialized transport-related services.

The fundamental responsibilities of traffic administration are operations management, freight consolidation, rate negotiation, freight control, auditing and claims, and logistical integration. All aspects of administration are essential for effective transportation management. The extent to which the administrative responsibilities discussed are performed by an internal traffic department or are provided by an integrated service provider is a matter of managerial preference.

Challenge Questions

1. Seven economic drivers that influence transportation cost were presented. Select a specific product and discuss how each factor will impact determination of a freight rate.

2. Compare and contrast variable, fixed, and joint costs.

3. Compare and contrast cost-of-service with value-of-service as alternative rate-making strategies.

4. Discuss the concept of net pricing. What advantage does net pricing provide to carriers and shippers?

5. What is the purpose of freight classification? Does the concept of classification have relevancy given deregulation of transportation?

6. Describe the difference between a rate and a rating. How do they relate to classification?

7. What is the role of the freight bill and the bill of lading in a transportation transaction?

8. What is the basic concept of multivendor consolidation? How do ISPs help achieve such consolidation?

9. Compare and contrast reactive and proactive consolidation. Provide an example of each.

10. Four aspects of transportation operations management were identified as: (1) equipment scheduling, (2) load planning, (3) routing, and (4) carrier administration. Identify a commercial transportation movement you are aware of and discuss how each managerial aspect was involved.

13   WAREHOUSING

Warehousing incorporates many different aspects of logistics operations. Due to the interaction, warehousing does not fit the neat classification schemes used when discussing order management, inventory, or transportation. A warehouse is typically viewed as a place to hold or store inventory. However, in contemporary logistical systems, warehouse functionality can be more properly viewed as inventory mixing. This chapter provides a foundation for understanding the value warehousing contributes to logistics. The discussion is relevant for all types of warehouses ranging from distribution centers, consolidation terminals, break-bulk facilities, and cross-docks. The objective is to introduce general managerial responsibilities related to warehousing.

Warehouse Strategy and Functionality

While effective logistics systems should not be designed to hold inventory for extended times, there are occasions when inventory storage is justified on the basis of cost and service.

Strategic Warehousing

Storage has always been an important aspect of economic development. In the pre-industrial era, storage was performed by individual households forced to function as self-sufficient economic units. Consumers performed warehousing and accepted the attendant risks.

As transportation capability developed, it became possible to engage in specialization. Product storage shifted from households to retailers, wholesalers, and manufacturers. Warehouses stored inventory in the logistics pipeline, serving to coordinate product supply and consumer demand.[1] Because the value of strategic storage was not well understood, warehouses were often considered "necessary evils" that added cost to the distribution process. The concept that middlemen simply increase cost follows from that belief. The need to deliver product assortments was limited. Labor productivity, materials handling efficiency, and inventory turnover were not major concerns during this early era. Because labor was relatively inexpensive, human resources were used freely. Little consideration was given to efficiency in space utilization, work methods, or materials handling. Despite such shortcomings, these initial warehouses provided a necessary bridge between production and marketing.

Following World War II, managerial attention shifted toward strategic storage. Management began to question the need for vast warehouse networks. In the distributive industries such as wholesaling and retailing, it was traditionally considered best practice to dedicate a warehouse containing a full assortment of inventory to every sales territory. As forecasting and production scheduling techniques improved, management questioned such risky inventory deployment. Production planning became more dependable as disruptions and time delays during manufacturing decreased. Seasonal production and consumption still required warehousing, but overall need for storage to support stable manufacturing and consumption patterns was reduced.

Changing requirements in retailing more than offset any reduction in warehousing obtained as a result of these manufacturing improvements. Retail stores, faced with the challenge of providing consumers an increasing assortment of products, found it more difficult to maintain purchasing and transportation economics when buying from suppliers. The cost of transporting small shipments made direct ordering prohibitive. This created an opportunity to establish strategically located warehouses to provide timely and economical inventory replenishment for retailers. Progressive wholesalers and

---

[1]Chapter 4 discussed the contribution of logistics to the development of economic specialization. See p. 96.

integrated retailers developed state-of-the-art warehouse systems to logistically support retail replenishment. Thus, the focus on warehousing shifted from passive storage to strategic assortment.

Improvements in retail warehousing efficiency soon were adopted by manufacturing. For manufacturers, strategic warehousing offered a way to reduce holding or dwell time of materials and parts. Warehousing became integral to Just-in-Time (JIT) and stockless production strategies. While the basic notion of JIT is to reduce work-in-process inventory, such manufacturing strategies need dependable logistics. Achieving such logistical support across the U.S. geography requires strategically located warehouses. Utilizing centralized parts inventory at a central warehouse reduces the need for inventory at each assembly plant. Products can be purchased and shipped to the strategically located central warehouse, taking advantage of consolidated transportation. At the warehouse, products are sorted, sequenced, and shipped to specific manufacturing plants as needed. Where fully integrated, sortation and sequencing facilities become a vital extension of manufacturing.

On the outbound side of manufacturing, warehouses can be used to create product assortments for customer shipment. The capability to receive mixed product shipments offers customers two specific advantages. First, logistical cost is reduced because an assortment of products can be delivered while taking advantage of consolidated transportation. Second, inventory of slow-moving products can be reduced because of the capability to receive smaller quantities as part of a consolidated shipment. Manufacturers that provide assorted product shipments can achieve a competitive advantage.

An important charge in warehousing is maximum flexibility. Such flexibility can often be achieved through information technology. Technology-based applications have influenced almost every area of warehouse operations and created new and better ways to perform storage and handling. Flexibility is also an essential part of being able to respond to expanding customer demand in terms of product assortments and the way shipments are delivered and presented. Information technology facilitates this flexibility by allowing warehouse operators to quickly react to changing customer requirements.[2]

Warehouse Functionality

Benefits realized from strategic warehousing are classified on the basis of cost and service. No warehouse functionality should be included in a logistical system unless it is fully justified on some combination of cost and service basis. Ideally a warehouse will simultaneously provide economic and service benefits.

Economic Benefits

Economic benefits of warehousing occur when overall logistics costs are reduced. For example, if adding a warehouse in a logistical system reduces overall transportation cost by an amount greater than required investment and operational cost, then total cost will be reduced. When total cost reductions are achievable, the warehouse is economically justified. Five basic economic benefits are: (1) consolidation and break-bulk, (2) assortment, (3) postponement, (4) stockpiling, and (5) reverse logistics.

---

[2]Kenneth B. Ackerman, "The Changing Role of Warehousing," *Warehousing Forum* 8, no. 12 (November 1993), p. 1.

FIGURE 13-1

Consolidation and break-bulk arrangements

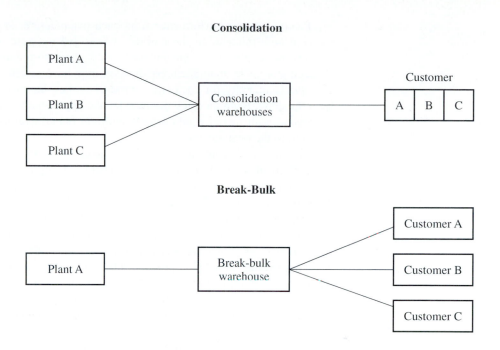

Consolidation

Break-Bulk

Consolidation and Break-Bulk.   The economic benefits of consolidation and break-bulk are to reduce transportation cost by using warehouse capability to increase shipment economies of scale.

In consolidation, the warehouse receives materials from a number of sources, which are combined into a large single shipment to a specific destination, such as a customer. The benefits are the realization of the lowest possible freight rate, timely and controlled delivery, and reduced congestion at a customer's receiving dock. The warehouse enables both the inbound movement from origin and the outbound movement to destination to be consolidated into a larger shipment, which generally incurs lower transportation charges and often quicker delivery.

A break-bulk operator receives a single large shipment and arranges for delivery to multiple destinations. Economy of scale is achieved by transporting the larger consolidated shipment. The break-bulk warehouse or terminal sorts or splits out individual orders and arranges local delivery.

Both consolidation and break-bulk arrangements use warehouse capacity to improve transportation efficiency. Many logistical arrangements involve both consolidation and break-bulk. Figure 13-1 illustrates each activity.

Assortment.   The basic benefit of assortment is to reconfigure freight as it flows from origin to destination. Three types of assortments—cross-docking, mixing, and assembly—are widely used in logistical systems.

The objective of cross-docking is to combine inventory from multiple origins into an assortment for a specific customer. Retailers make extensive use of cross-dock operations to replenish fast-moving store inventories.[3]

---

[3]For an expanded discussion, see "The Nuts and Bolts of Cross-Docking," *Grocery Distribution,* April 1997, pp. 18–20; and Arnold Maltz, *The Changing Role of Warehousing* (Oak Brook, IL: Warehousing Education and Research Council, 1998) or "Warehousing After 2000," *Warehousing Forum,* February 1998, pp. 1–2.

Precise on-time performance from each manufacturer is required. As product is received and unloaded at the facility, it is sorted by store destination. In most instances, the retailer has communicated precise volume requirements of each product for each store. The manufacturers, in turn, may have sorted, loaded, and labeled the appropriate quantity for each store. Product is then literally moved across the dock from the delivery into a truck destined for the appropriate store location. Once trucks are loaded with mixed product from multiple manufacturers, they are released for transport to the retail destination.

Mixing achieves an end result similar to cross-docking. However, mixing is usually performed at an intermediate location between shipment origin and destination. In a typical mixing operation, carloads or truckloads of products are shipped from origin to mixing warehouses. The shipments are planned to minimize inbound transportation cost. Upon arrival at the mixing warehouse, shipments are unloaded and sorted into the combination desired by each customer. In-transit mixing has been traditionally supported by special transportation rates that provide incentives to facilitate the process.[4] During the mixing process, inbound products can be combined with those regularly stored at the warehouse. Warehouses that perform in-transit mixing have the net effect of reducing overall product storage in a logistical system while achieving customer-specific assortments and minimizing transportation cost.

The objective of assembly is to support manufacturing operations. Products and components are assembled from a variety of second-tier suppliers by a warehouse located in close proximity to the manufacturing plant. While manufacturing organizations have traditionally performed assembly, it is becoming common to utilize value-added services of lead or tier one suppliers to sort, sequence, and deliver components when needed in manufacturing. Vector Supply Chain Management provides such an integrating and coordination service for General Motors' inbound and outbound logistics.[5] Similar to cross-docking and mixing, assembly serves to achieve a process grouping of inventory at a precise time and location. Figure 13-2 illustrates these three assortment applications.

Processing/Postponement.   Warehouses can also postpone commitment to final product configuration by completing final packaging, labeling, and light manufacturing. For example, vegetables can be processed and canned in *brights* at the processing plants. Brights are cans without labels. Holding inventory as brights means that product is not committed to specific customers or carton configuration during processing. Once a specific customer order is received, the warehouse can complete labeling and finalize packaging.

Postponement provides two economic benefits. First, risk is minimized because customized packaging is not performed in anticipation of customer orders or to accommodate a forecast. Second, total inventory can be reduced by using inventory of the base product to support multiple customers' labeling and package requirements. The combination of reduced risk and lower inventory can result in reduced total cost to service even if packaging performed at the warehouse is more expensive per unit than if it were completed during manufacturing. Industry Insight 13-1 reveals several ways in which such value-added services are provided at warehouses.

---

[4]See Chapter 12, p. 366.
[5]See **www.vectorscm.com** for more information regarding this joint venture between CNF and General Motors.

FIGURE 13-2

Assortment arrangements

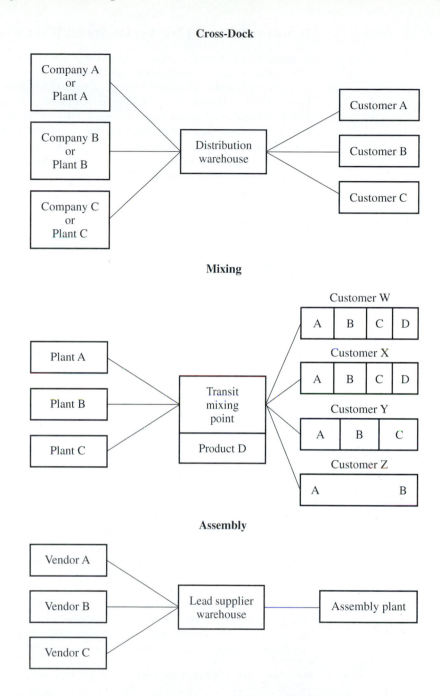

Stockpiling.   The direct economic benefit of stockpiling is to accommodate seasonal production or demand. For example, lawn furniture and toys are typically produced year-round but are sold only during a very short marketing period. In contrast, agricultural products are harvested at specific times, with subsequent consumption occurring throughout the year. Both situations require inventory stockpiling to support marketing efforts. Stockpiling provides an inventory buffer, which allows production efficiencies within the constraints imposed by material sources and consumers.

INDUSTRY INSIGHT 13-1   VALUE-ADDED WAREHOUSING

In addition to traditional economic and service benefits, warehouse operators must offer other value-added services to remain competitive today.

The most common value-added services relate to packaging. Product is shipped to the warehouse in bulk or unlabeled form, so inventory is undifferentiated. Once a customer order is received, the warehouse operator customizes and releases the product. An example of this service is an automotive battery manufacturer that ships unmarked product to the warehouse. The warehouse is supplied with decals for the brand names the batteries are sold under. Once an order for a specific private label is received, the warehouse operator places the decals on the batteries and packages the product in a customized box. The customer receives customized product and packaging. The battery manufacturer reduces its inventory because less safety stock is required to support individual customer demand. A corresponding reduction in forecasting and production planning complexity is also achieved.

Warehousing can increase the value-added by refining product packaging to better meet the needs of customers down the channel. For example, the warehouse may add value by stretch-wrapping or changing pallets. This allows the manufacturer to deal with only one type of unitization while postponing commitment to specialized packaging requirements. Another example of warehousing value-added is the removal of protective packaging prior to product delivery to consumers. This is a valuable service offering in the case with large appliances, since it is sometimes difficult for consumers to dispose of large amounts of packaging.

Warehouse operators can also add value by changing packaging characteristics such as for an antifreeze supplier that ships in bulk quantities to the warehouse. The warehouse operator bottles the product to meet brand and package size requirements. This type of postponement minimizes inventory risk, reduces transportation cost, and can reduce damage (i.e., for product packaged in glass).

Warehousing can also complete production activities to postpone product specialization and refine product characteristics. At times, reassembly at a warehouse may be done to correct a production problem. For example, automobile engines might be shipped to the warehouse. If a quality problem arises with the carburetors, they might be changed at the warehouse without returning each unit to the engine plant. In this case, the warehouse is operating as the last stage of production.

Another value-added service is climatizing products such as fruits and vegetables. Warehouse operators can promote or delay the ripening process of bananas depending on storage temperature. The product can be ripened as required by market conditions.

Value-added warehousing services can also provide market confidentiality. One importer relabels a product for private brand customers. The relabeling is done after the product has entered the United States to prevent the supplier from identifying the ultimate customers of the importer.

Providing value-added warehousing services places a special responsibility on the warehouse operator or the distribution center manager overseeing the contract operations. While outsourcing activities and operations may increase inventory effectiveness and operating efficiency, it also takes key responsibilities outside the control of the firm.

Source: Kenneth B. Ackerman, "Value-Added Warehousing Cuts Inventory Costs," *Transportation & Distribution,* July 1989, pp. 32–35.

Reverse Logistics.   Warehousing plays a key role in performing reverse logistics. Most of the physical work related to product recall, reclamation, and disposal of overstock and damaged inventory is performed at warehouses.[6] Many firms are generating significant cash flow from refurbishment, recycling, and disposal of damaged and defective product. Reverse logistics is concerned with controlled and regular inventory.

Controlled inventory consists of hazardous materials and product recalls that have potential consumer health or environmental considerations. The reclamation of controlled inventory must be performed under strict operating scrutiny that prevents possible redistribution or improper disposal. As one might expect, varied governmental agencies, such as the Consumer Product Safety Commission, Department of Transportation (DOT), the Environmental Protection Agency (EPA), Food and Drug Administration (FDA), and the Occupational Safety and Health Administration (OSHA), are directly involved in disposal of controlled inventory.[7]

Less attention has traditionally focused on reclamation of **regular inventory.** In 1997 the disposition of unsaleable product was estimated to cost companies $4 billion.[8] The food industry alone was estimated to have unsaleable inventory approaching $2.6 billion and growing at a rate approaching 20 percent per year.[9] The product involved in such reclamation is typically damaged or aged beyond the recommended sell-by date. While some unsaleable product results from warehouse damage, most is returned from retail or even from the consumer.

While reclamation is difficult for regular inventory, it is far more challenging for controlled inventory. In both return situations, product flow lacks the orderly process characteristic of outbound movement. Reverse movement typically consists of nonuniform individual packages and cartons as contrasted to outbound movement of cases and pallet loads. Packages are often broken, and product is not packaged correctly. Return products typically require significant manual sortation and inspection to determine appropriate disposal.[10] However, the opportunity to recover cost by reimbursement and recycling is significant.[11] Industry Insight 13-2 illustrates some challenges of reverse logistics.

Service Benefits

Warehouse service can provide benefits through enhanced revenue generation. When a warehouse is primarily justified on service, the supporting rationale is that sales can be increased, in part, by such logistical performance. It is typically difficult to quantify service return-on-investment because it's difficult to measure. For example, establishing a warehouse to service a specific market may increase cost but should also increase

[6]For a comprehensive discussion of reverse logistics and related challenges, see James R. Stock, *Development and Implementation of Reverse Logistics Programs* (Oak Brook, IL: Council of Logistics Management, 1998); and Dale S. Rogers and Ronald S. Tibben-Lembke, "Going Backwards: Reverse Logistics Trends and Practices," Pittsburgh, PA: Reverse Logistics Executive Council, 1999.

[7]Toby B. Gooley, "Many Happy Returns," *Logistics Management,* May 1997, pp. 53–55.

[8]"The ABC's of OSD," *WERC Sheet,* October 1998, pp. 1–3.

[9]"Fixing the Cracks in the System," *Food Logistics,* October 1998, pp. 29–35.

[10]Tom Andel, "Reverse Logistics: A Second Chance to Profit," *Transportation and Distribution,* July 1997, pp. 61–66; and Deborah Catalano Ruriani, "Return Reverse Recycle," *Inbound Logistics,* August 1997, pp. 42–44.

[11]"Bringing It Back," *WERC Sheet,* March 1999, pp. 1–3.

INDUSTRY INSIGHT 13-2 MANAGING WASTE FROM OLD PAINT

The paint industry has been active in minimizing the impact of its products on the environment. But where do those empty containers and unused residues go when the customer's done with them? Presently, the majority end up in landfills. What responsibilities do paint and container manufacturers and their channel members have for them?

Many states and local communities developed regulations and services to deal with latex paint containers and residues. They allow do-it-yourself and professional paint markets to trash their cans and plastic pails (which, incidentally, are not of the right class to be economically recycled) in landfills. But the empty and partially filled containers must be opened and dried first.

The responsibility for disposition, recovery strategies, and operations is now shifting to paint manufacturers, retailers, and users. Reverse logistics strategies include the flow of paint containers and residues to a material recovery facility with component materials going to several different market segments:

- Brokers for scrap metal and plastic markets,
- Waste-to-energy or waste-to-elements recyclers,
- Reprocessing centers for leftover paints to be blended into so-called "green" paints and sold to users for limited applications.

Leftover paints and containers, because of landfill restrictions and/or required can deposits, could also be taken back to retail point-of-sale establishments, such as is the case with automobile batteries. For paint and containers, channel members use a reverse logistics process similar to that presently used for pallet returns. Many paint manufacturers have private or dedicated fleets handling their deliveries.

A University of Wisconsin–Madison research team also identified a segmented approach dealing with the returned goods. Since professional painters account for approximately 70 percent of paint sales, they would be more apt to return containers to stores or designated disposition centers that paint manufacturers jointly sponsored.

The paint industry has tremendous opportunities to control its destiny concerning wastes. Rather than be regulated into positions that may not be advantageous to channel members, paint manufacturers and their customers can reconfigure channel flows to better serve paint users while reducing costs. As consumers continue to be more environmentally conscious both domestically and globally, this can be a competitive advantage to any manufacturer.

Source: Ed Marien and Fred Ristow, "Managing Waste from Old Paint," *Transportation & Distribution,* July 1997, p. 62.

---

market sales, revenue, and potentially gross margin. Warehouses can provide service as a result of spot stocking, full line stocking, product support, and market presence.

Spot Stocking. Spot stocking is typically used to support market distribution. Manufacturers of highly seasonal products often spot stock. Rather than maintaining inventory in a warehouse year-round, or shipping to customers direct from manufacturing plants, responsiveness in peak selling periods can be enhanced through temporary inventory positioning in strategic markets. Under this concept, select inventory is positioned or *spot stocked* in a local market warehouse in anticipation of responding to customer need during the critical sales period. Utilizing warehouse facilities for spot stocking allows inventories to be placed in a variety of markets adjacent to key customers just prior to a maximum period of seasonal sales.[12] For example, agricultural

---

[12]For an expanded discussion, see Tom Andel, "Temporary Warehousing to the Rescue," *Transportation and Distribution,* November 1997, pp. 88–90.

fertilizer companies sometimes spot stock near farmers in anticipation of the growing season. After the growing season, such spot stocking would likely be reduced.

Full Line Stocking.   The traditional use of warehouses by manufacturers, wholesalers, and retailers is to stock product inventory combinations in anticipation of customer orders. Typical retailers and wholesalers provide assortments representing multiple products from different manufacturers. In effect, these warehouses can provide one-stop shopping capability for goods from multiple manufacturers.

The difference between stock spotting and full line stocking is the degree and duration of warehouse utilization. A firm following a spot stocking strategy would temporarily warehouse a narrow product assortment in a large number of warehouses for a limited time period. The full line stocking warehouse is more often restricted to a few strategic locations and operates year-round. Full line stocking warehouses improve service by reducing the number of suppliers that a customer must deal with. The combined assortments also make economical larger shipments possible.

Production Support.   The economics of manufacturing may justify warehousing an inventory of specific parts and components. Production support warehouses stock inventory to support manufacturing operations. Safety stocks on items purchased from outside vendors may be justified because of long lead times, potential supply discontinuity, and significant variations in usage rates. In such situations the most effective supply practice may be the establishment of a production support warehouse containing an inventory of processed materials, components, and subassemblies. This service benefit of warehousing is closely related to assembly assortment discussed under economic benefits. The primary difference between production support warehousing and assortment assembly is the size and purpose of the warehouse. In production support warehousing, average inventory is higher and turnover is lower.

Market Presence.   While benefits of market presence may not be as obvious as other service benefits, it is often cited by executives as a major advantage of local warehouses. The underlying belief is that a local warehouse can respond faster to customer needs than can a more distant warehouse. It is anticipated that local warehouse presence will increase market share and potentially profitability. While the market presence factor is a frequently discussed strategy, little solid research exists to confirm or refute its existence. In addition, more reliable transportation and technology-based order processing are closing the response time gap regardless of distance. Unless a warehouse is economically or service justified it is unlikely that local market presence will favorably influence operational results.

Warehouse Operations

Once a warehouse mission is determined, managerial attention focuses on establishing the operation. A typical warehouse contains materials, parts, and finished goods on the move. Warehouse operations consist of break-bulk, storage, and assembly procedures. The objective is to efficiently receive inventory, possibly store it until required by the market, assemble it into complete orders, and initiate movement to customer. This emphasis on product flow renders a modern warehouse as a mixing facility. As such, a great deal of managerial attention concerns how to perform storage to facilitate efficient materials handling.

Handling

The first consideration focuses on movement continuity and scale economies throughout the warehouse. Movement continuity means that it is better for a material handler with a piece of handling equipment to perform longer moves than to undertake a number of short handlings to accomplish the same overall move. Exchanging the product between handlers or moving it from one piece of equipment to another wastes time and increases the potential for product damage. Thus, as a general rule, longer warehouse movements are preferred. Goods, once in motion, should be continuously moved until arrival at their final destination.

Scale economies justify moving the largest quantities or loads possible. Instead of moving individual cases, handling procedures should be designed to move cases grouped on pallets, slipsheets, or containers.[13] The overall objective of materials handling is to eventually sort inbound shipments into unique customer assortments. The three primary handling activities are receiving, in-storage handling, and shipping.

Receiving

Merchandise and materials typically arrive at warehouses in large quantity shipments. The first handling activity is unloading. At most warehouses, unloading is performed mechanically, using a combination of a lift truck and manual processes. When freight is floor stacked on the transport vehicle, the typical procedure is to manually place products on pallets or to use a conveyor. When inbound product has been unitized on pallets or containers, lift trucks can be used to facilitate receiving. A primary benefit of receiving unitized loads is the ability to turn inbound transportation equipment more rapidly. Receiving is usually the unloading of a relatively high volume of similar product.

In-Storage Handling

In-storage handling consists of movements within the warehouse. Following receipt and movement to a staging location, product must be moved within the facility for storage or order selection. Finally, when an order is processed it is necessary to select the required products and move them to a shipping area. These two types of in-storage handling are typically referred to as *transfer* and *selection.*

There are at least two and sometimes three transfer movements in a typical warehouse. The merchandise is initially moved from the receiving area to a storage location. This movement is typically handled by a lift truck when pallets or slipsheets are used or by other mechanical means for other types of unit loads. A second internal movement may be required prior to order assembly depending upon warehouse operating procedures. When unit loads have to be broken down for order selection, they are usually transferred from storage to an order selection or picking area. When products are large or bulky, such as appliances, this intermediate movement to a picking area may not be necessary. Such product is often selected from the storage area and moved directly to the shipping staging area. The shipping staging area is the area adjacent to the shipping dock. In order selection warehouses, the assembled customer order is transferred from the selection area to the shipping staging area. Characteristically, in-storage handling involves lower volume movements than receiving but still relatively similar products.

Order selection is one of the major activities within warehouses. The selection process requires that materials, parts, and products be grouped to facilitate order as-

---

[13]Specific types of handling equipment, pallets, and unitization are discussed in Chapter 14.

sembly. It is typical for one area of a warehouse to be designated as a selection or picking area to assemble orders. For each order, the combination of products must be selected and packaged to meet specific customer order requirements. The typical selection process is coordinated by a warehouse management system.

Shipping

Shipping consists of order verification and transportation equipment loading. Similar to receiving, firms may use conveyors or unit load materials handling equipment such as lift trucks to move products from the staging area into the transportation vehicle. Relative to receiving, warehouse shipping must accommodate relatively low-volume movements of a mixture of product, thus reducing the potential for economies of sale. Shipping unit loads is becoming increasingly popular because considerable time can be saved in vehicle loading. A unit load consists of unitized or palletized product. To facilitate this loading and subsequent unloading upon delivery, many customers are requesting that suppliers provide mixed combinations of product within a unit. The alternative is to floor stack cases in the transportation vehicle. Shipment content verification is typically required when product changes ownership. Verification may be limited to a simple carton count or a piece-by-piece check for proper brand, size, and in some cases serial number to assure shipment accuracy.

Storage

The second consideration is that warehouse utilization should position products based upon individual characteristics. The most important product variables to consider in a storage plan are product volume, weight, and storage requirements.

Product volume or velocity is the major factor driving warehouse layout. High-volume product should be positioned in the warehouse to minimize movement distance. For example, high-velocity products should be positioned near doors, primary aisles, and at lower levels in storage racks. Such positioning minimizes warehouse handling and reduces the need for frequent lifting. Conversely, products with low volume should be assigned locations more distant from primary aisles or higher up in storage racks. Figure 13-3 illustrates a storage plan based on product movement.

FIGURE 13-3

Storage plan based on product movement

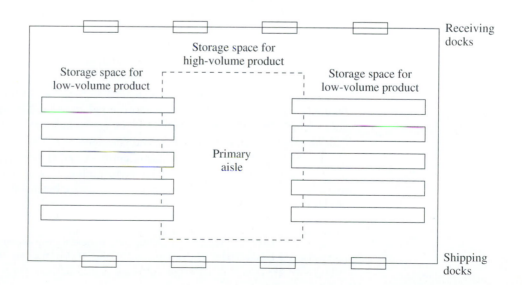

Similarly, the storage plan should take into consideration product weight and special characteristics. Relatively heavy items should be assigned storage locations low to the ground to minimize lifting. Bulky or low-density product requires cubic space. Floor space along outside walls is ideal for such items. On the other hand, smaller items may require storage shelves, bins, or drawers. The integrated storage plan must consider individual product characteristics.

A typical warehouse is engaged in a combination of *active* and *extended* product storage alternatives. Warehouses that directly serve customers typically focus on active short-term storage. In contrast, warehouses use extended storage for speculative, seasonal, or obsolete inventory. When controlling and measuring warehouse operations, it is important to differentiate the relative requirements and performance capabilities of active and extended storage.

Active Storage

Regardless of inventory velocity, most goods must be stored for at least a short time. Storage for basic inventory replenishment is referred to as active storage. Active storage must provide sufficient inventory to meet the periodic demands of the service area. The need for active storage is usually related to the capability to achieve transportation or handling economies of scale. For active storage, materials handling processes and technologies need to focus on quick movement and flexibility with relatively minimal consideration for extended and dense storage.

The active storage concept includes **flow-through distribution,** which uses warehouses for consolidation and assortment while maintaining minimal or no inventory in storage. The resulting need for reduced inventory favors flow-through and cross-docking techniques that emphasize movement and de-emphasize storage. Flow-through distribution is most appropriate for high-volume, fast-moving products where quantities are reasonably predictable. While flow-through distribution places minimal demands on storage requirements, it does require that product be quickly unloaded, de-unitized, grouped and sequenced into customer assortments, and reloaded into transportation equipment. As a result, the materials handling emphasis is or accurate information-directed quick movement.[14]

Extended Storage

Extended storage, a somewhat misleading term, refers to inventory in excess of that required for normal replenishment of customer stocks. In some special situations, storage may be required for several months prior to customer shipment. Extended storage uses materials handling processes and technologies that focus on maximum space utilization with minimal need for quick access.

A warehouse may be used for extended storage for several other reasons. Some products, such as seasonal items, require storage to await demand or to spread supply across time. Other reasons for extended storage include erratic demand items, product conditioning, speculative purchases, and discounts.

Product conditioning sometimes requires extended storage, such as to ripen bananas. Food warehouses typically have ripening rooms to hold products until they reach peak quality. Storage may also be necessary for extended quality checks.

---

[14]For a more comprehensive discussion of the materials handling requirements of flow-through distribution, see Thomas Feare, "Storage Less, Stage More," *Modern Materials Handling* 55, no. 5 (May 2000), pp. 80–83.

Warehouses may also store goods on an extended basis when goods are purchased on a speculative basis. The magnitude of speculative buying depends upon the specific materials and industries involved, but it is very common in marketing of commodities and seasonal items. For example, if a price increase for an item is expected, it is not uncommon for a firm to buy ahead at the current price and warehouse the product for later use. In this case, the discount or savings has to be traded off against extended storage and inventory carrying cost. Commodities such as grains, oil, and cardboard are often stored for speculative reasons.

The warehouse may also be used to realize special discounts. Early purchase discounts may justify extended storage. The purchasing manager may be able to realize a substantial price reduction during a specific period of the year. Under such conditions the warehouse is expected to hold inventory in excess of active storage. Manufacturers of fertilizer, toys, and lawn furniture often attempt to shift the warehousing burden to customers by offering off-season warehouse storage allowances.

Warehouse Ownership Classification

Warehouses are typically classified based on ownership. A private warehouse is operated by the enterprise that owns the merchandise handled and stored in the facility. A public warehouse, in contrast, is operated as an independent business offering a range of for-hire services, such as storage, handling, and transportation. Public warehouse operators generally offer a menu of relatively standardized services to customers. **Contract warehousing,** which is a customized extension of public warehousing, combines the benefits of private and for-hire warehousing. Contract warehousing is a *long-term* business arrangement that provides unique or tailored logistics services for a limited number of customers. The client and the integrated service supplier typically share the risks associated with the operation.[15] The important differences between contract and public warehouse operators are the anticipated length of the relationship, degree of exclusive or tailored services, and shared incorporation of benefits and risks.

Private

A private warehouse is typically operated by the firm owning the product. The building, however, may be owned or leased. The decision concerning ownership or lease is essentially financial. Sometimes it is not possible to find a warehouse for lease that fits specialized logistical requirements; for example, the physical nature of an available building may not be conducive for efficient materials handling, such as buildings with inappropriate storage racks or with dock well or pillar constraints. The only suitable course of action may then be to design and arrange for construction.

The major benefits of private warehousing are control, flexibility, cost, and a range of intangibles. Private warehouses offer substantial control since management has authority to prioritize activities. Such control should facilitate integration of warehouse operations with the balance of a firm's logistics operations.

Private warehouses generally offer more flexibility since operating policies and procedures can be adjusted to meet specific customer and product requirements. Firms

---

[15]*Contract Warehousing: How It Works and How to Make It Work Effectively* (Oak Brook, IL: Warehousing Education and Research Council, 1993), p. 7.

with very specialized customers or products are often motivated to own and operate warehouses.

Private warehousing is usually considered less costly than public warehousing because private facilities are not operated for a profit even though they may be required to make some contribution to the firm to ensure competitiveness. As a result, both the fixed and variable cost components of a private warehouse may be lower than for-hire counterparts.

Finally private warehousing may offer intangible benefits. A private warehouse, with the firm's name on its sign, may stimulate customer perceptions of responsiveness and stability. This perception may provide marketing advantage over competitors.

Nonetheless, the use of private warehousing is declining due to an increasing interest in reducing logistics assets since warehouse facilities account for a substantial portion of those assets. Also, the perceived cost benefit of private warehousing is potentially offset by a public warehouse's ability to gain economies of scale based on leveraging the combined throughput of multiple clients.

Public

Public warehouses are used extensively in logistical systems. Almost any combination of services can be arranged on a for-hire basis for either short or long term. Public warehouses have traditionally been classified based on operational specialization such as (1) general merchandise, (2) refrigerated, (3) special commodity, (4) bonded, and (5) household goods and furniture.

General merchandise warehouses are designed to handle package products such as electronics, paper, food, small appliances, and household supplies. Refrigerated warehouses typically offer frozen or chilled capacity designed to protect food, medical, photographic, and chemical products requiring special temperatures. Special commodity warehouses are designed to handle bulk material or items requiring special handling considerations, such as tires or clothing. Bonded warehouses are licensed by the government to store goods prior to payment of taxes or import/export duties. They exert tight control over movements in and out of the facility since documents must accompany each move. Finally, household goods or furniture warehouses specialize in handling and storing large, bulky items such as appliances and furniture. Of course, many public warehouses offer a combination of services. Public warehouses provide flexibility and shared services benefits. They have the potential to offer operating and management expertise since warehousing is their core business.

From a financial perspective, public warehousing may be able to achieved lower operating cost than private facilities. Such variable cost differential may result from lower pay scales, better productivity, shared resources, and economy of scale. Public warehouses typically do not require capital investment on the part of customers. When management performance is judged according to return on investment, the use of public warehousing can be an attractive alternative. Public warehousing offers flexibility concerning size and number of warehouses, thus allowing users to respond to supplier, customer, and seasonal demands. In comparison, private warehouses are relatively fixed and difficult to change because buildings have to be constructed, expanded, or sold.

Public warehousing can also have the potential to share scale economies since the combined requirements of users can be leveraged. Such leverage spreads fixed costs and may justify investment in state-of-the-art handling equipment. A public warehouse may also leverage transportation by providing combined customer delivery consolida-

TABLE 13-1   Warehouse/Value-Added Services

- Cross dock/transloading
- Customer returns
- Customization/postponement
- Home or catalog delivery
- In-transit merge
- Inventory control
- Kan Ban
- Kitting
- Labeling/pre-ticketing
- Lot control
- Manufacturing support
- Order fulfillment
- Pick/pack
- Pool distribution
- Repair/refurbish
- Returnable container management
- Reverse logistics
- Sequencing/metering
- Specialty packaging
- Store support/direct store delivery (DSD)

tion. For example, rather than requiring both supplier A and supplier B to deliver to a retail store from its own warehouse, a public warehouse serving both clients could arrange combined delivery, thus providing reduced transportation cost for the customer. Table 13-1 summarizes the types of services and capabilities characteristic of many public warehouse operators.

A great many firms utilize public warehouses for market distribution because of the variable cost, scalability, range of services, and flexibility. Industry Insight 13-3 illustrates a creative use of public warehousing for distribution of presold products. In a variety of situations, public warehouse facilities and services can be designed and performed to meet exact operational requirements.

A public warehouse charges clients a basic fee for handling and storage. In the case of handling, the charge is assessed on the cases or pounds moved. For storage, the charge is assessed on the cases or weight in storage over a designated time period. Special or value-added services are typically priced on a negotiated basis.

Contract

Contract warehousing combines characteristics of private and public operations. A long-term contractual relationship will typically result in lower total cost than a public warehouse. At the same time, contract warehouse operations can provide benefits of expertise, flexibility, scalability, and economies of scale by sharing management, labor, equipment, and information resources with multiple clients.

Contract warehouses typically offer a range of logistical services such as transportation management, inventory control, order processing, customer service, and

INDUSTRY INSIGHT 13-3 HARLEY-DAVIDSON GOES PUBLIC

Planning, building, and operating a new distribution center represent a substantial investment for any organization. Many companies consider public warehousing as a viable option to obtain management expertise and increase operating efficiency. Public warehouses may offer a competitive edge by (1) reducing overhead and thus freeing up corporate capital for investment in other areas, (2) allowing companies to concentrate on their specific strengths, (3) allowing start-up companies and foreign manufacturers to enter the U.S. market effortlessly, and (4) enabling companies to strengthen their bottom lines and obtain optimum logistics efficiency.

For example, in the early 1980s, Harley-Davidson desired to increase the productivity of its existing facilities when it considered public warehousing as a logistical option.

Streamlined operations, reduced production times, and JIT inventory control have improved Harley-Davidson's competitive position. Today, the company controls 60 percent of the market for heavyweight (850 or more cubic centimeters) motorcycles—a significant increase from its 20 percent share in 1982. The increase in sales forced the company to consider alternative ways of moving presold inventory at its York, Pennsylvania, plant to increase its production capacity. In Harley-Davidson's case, presold inventory (e.g., product that has been sold to consumers or dealers but not yet delivered or desired by the customer) may be in storage for up to several months. This inventory typically involves 500 to 1000 motorcycles.

Each of the motorcycles is designated for a specific customer and requires a detailed identification tag defining customer and delivery requirements. The public warehouse has the responsibility to make sure the right motorcycle is shipped to the right customer. This means that each motorcycle must be stored so that it and the identification tag are easily accessible.

"By turning our presold inventory over to a public warehouse, we have the extra capacity we need and, most importantly, we have the specialized inventory management we require," says the general manager, Tom Sowarz. The move to public warehousing has also helped Harley-Davidson maintain tighter control over labor cost. Sowarz further commented that "even during a market slowdown, the staff of a private warehouse must be maintained to cover the workload when sales accelerate again. The advantages of public warehousing are inherent; you're only paying for the space you need, when your company needs it."

Source: M. L. Jenkins, "Utilizing Public Warehouse," *Plants, Sites & Parks,* November/December 1992, p. 88.

---

return merchandise processing. There are contract warehouse operators, typically called ISPs, who are capable of assuming total logistics responsibility for an enterprise.[16]

For example, Kraft Foods has increasingly utilized contract warehousing as a replacement for private and public frozen and dry grocery facilities. Since the late 1990s, Kraft has used AmeriCold Logistics, an integrated warehousing and distribution services company, to perform storage, handling, and distribution services. The arrangement has multiple benefits for both parties. The long-term contractual arrangement allows Kraft to expand its distribution network without incurring the time or cost of building expansion. Kraft is assured that there will always be space for new products, so its distribution network is protected. AmeriCold doesn't have to be concerned with selling space for the Kraft warehouses—it can focus on providing service. Moreover, the longer Kraft utilizes AmeriCold's services, the better the contract warehousing firm's capability to understand business needs and provide customized services.

---

[16]For a more comprehensive discussion of contract warehouse services, see the Warehousing Research Council, *Contract Warehousing: How It Works and How to Make It Work Effectively* (Oak Brook, IL: Warehousing Education and Research Council, 1993).

FIGURE 13-4

Combined private and public warehouse facilities

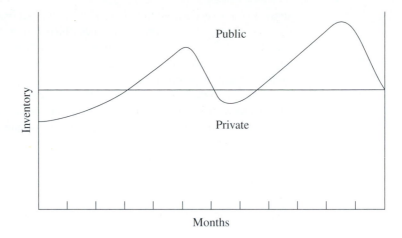

Deployment Strategy

As would be expected, many firms utilize a combination of private, public, and contract facilities.[17] Full warehouse utilization throughout a year is rare. As a managerial guideline, a typical warehouse will be fully utilized between 75 and 85 percent of the time; so from 15 to 25 percent of the time, space needed to satisfy peak requirements will not be used. In such situations an attractive strategy may be the use of private or contract warehouses to cover the 75 percent requirement while using public facilities to accommodate peak demand. Figure 13-4 illustrates this concept.

Developing a warehouse strategy requires answers to two questions. The first is how many warehouses should be established. (Chapter 16 provides a framework for answering this strategic network question.) The second question focuses on which warehouse ownership types should be used in specific markets. For many firms, the answer is a combination of warehouse alternatives, differentiated by customer and product. Specifically, some customer groups may be served best from a private warehouse, while public or contract warehouses may be appropriate for others. This warehouse segmentation is increasingly popular as key customers are requiring more customized and focused services and capabilities.

Warehouse Planning

Initial decisions related to warehousing are planning based. The basic concept that warehouses provide as an enclosure for material storage and handling requires detailed analysis before the size, type, and shape of the facility can be determined. This section reviews planning issues that establish the character of the warehouse, which in turn determines attainable handling efficiency.

Site Selection

The first task is to identify both the general and then the specific warehouse location. The general area concerns the broad geography where an active warehouse makes

---

[17]For a comprehensive discussion of the strategic use of warehousing, see Ken Ackerman, *Warehousing Profitability: A Manager's Guide* (Columbus, OH: Ackerman Publications, 1994).

sense from a service, economic, and strategic perspective. The general question focuses on the broader geographic area as illustrated by the need to place a warehouse in the Midwest, which generally implies having a facility in Illinois, Indiana, or Wisconsin. There are a number of techniques that can assist in determining the best combination of general warehouse areas.[18]

Once the combinations of broad areas are determined, a specific building site must be identified. Typical areas in a community for locating warehouses are the commercial zone, outlying areas served primarily by motor truck only, and the central or downtown area.

Drivers in site selection are service availability and cost. Land cost is the most important factor. A warehouse need not be located in a major industrial area. In many cities, warehouses are among industrial plants and in areas zoned for light or heavy industry. Most warehouses can operate legally under the restrictions placed upon general commercial property.

Beyond procurement cost, setup and operating expenses such as rail sidings, utility hookups, taxes, insurance rates, and highway access require evaluation. The cost of such services typically varies extensively between sites. For example, a food-distribution firm recently rejected what otherwise appeared to be a totally satisfactory warehouse site because of projected insurance rates. The site was located near the end of a water main. During most of the day, adequate water pressure was available to handle operational and emergency requirements. However, a water problem was possible during two short periods each day. From 6:30 A.M. to 8:30 A.M. and from 5:00 P.M. to 7:00 P.M. the overall demand for water along the line was so great that a sufficient pressure was not available to handle emergencies. Because of this deficiency, abnormally high insurance rates were required and the site was rejected.

Several other requirements must be satisfied before a site is purchased. The site must offer adequate room for expansion. Necessary utilities must be available. The soil must be capable of supporting the structure. The site must be sufficiently high to afford proper water drainage. Additional requirements may be situationally necessary, depending upon the structure to be constructed. For these reasons and others, the final selection of the sight must be preceded by extensive analysis.[19]

Design

Warehouse design must consider product movement characteristics. Three factors to be determined during the design process are the number of floors to include in the facility, a cube utilization plan, and product flow.

The ideal warehouse design is a one-floor building that eliminates the need to move product vertically. The use of vertical handling devices, such as elevators and conveyors, to move product from one floor to the next requires time, energy, and typically creates handling bottlenecks. So, while it is not always possible, particularly in central business districts where land is restricted or expensive, as a general rule warehouses should be designed as one-floor operations to facilitate materials handling.

---

[18]The general process is discussed further in Chapter 16, and the specific tools are described in Ronald Ballou and James Masters, "Facility Location Commercial Software Study," *Journal of Business Logistics* 20, no. 1 (1999), pp. 215–32.

[19]Steven Gold, "A New Approach to Site Selection," *Distribution* 90, no. 13 (December 1991), pp. 29–33; "A Guide to Site Selection in the 90's," *Traffic Management,* September 1991, pp. 205–235; and David Luton, "Selecting a New Warehouse Site," *Modern Materials Handling* 55, no. 4 (April 2000), p. 37.

FIGURE 13-5

Basic warehouse design

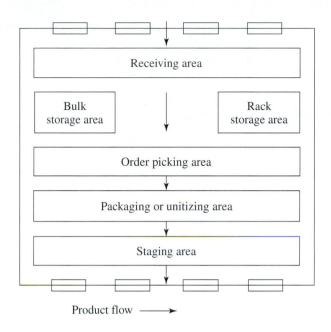

Product flow ⟶

Warehouse design should maximize cubic utilization. Most warehouses are designed with 20- to 30-foot clear ceilings, although modern automated and high-rise facilities effectively use heights over 100 feet. Maximum effective warehouse height is limited by the safe lifting capabilities of materials handling equipment, such as lift trucks, rack design, and fire safety regulations imposed by sprinkler systems.

Warehouse design should facilitate continuous straight product flow through the building. This is true whether the product is moving into storage or is being cross-docked. In general, this means that product should be received at one end of a building, stored as necessary in the middle, and shipped from the other end. Figure 13-5 illustrates straight line product flow that facilitates velocity while minimizing congestion and redundant handling.

Product-Mix Analysis

Another independent area of quantitative analysis is detailed study of products to be distributed through the warehouse. The design and operation of a warehouse are related directly to the product mix. Each product should be analyzed in terms of annual sales, demand, weight, cube, and packaging. It is also desirable to determine the total size, cube, and weight of the average order to be processed through the warehouse. These data provide necessary information for determining warehouse space, design and layout, materials handling equipment, operating procedures, and controls.

Future Expansion

Because warehouses are increasingly important in contemporary logistical networks, their future expansion should be considered during the initial planning phase. Well-managed organizations often establish 5- to 10-year expansion plans. Potential expansion may justify purchase or option of a site three to five times larger than required to support initial construction.

Building design should accommodate future expansion without seriously affecting ongoing operations. Some walls may be constructed of semipermanent materials to allow quick removal. Floor areas, designed to support heavy movements, can be extended during initial construction to facilitate expansion.

Materials Handling Considerations

A materials handling system is the basic driver of warehouse design. As noted previously, product movement and assortment are the main functions of a warehouse. Consequently, the warehouse is viewed as a structure designed to facilitate efficient product flow. It is important to stress that the materials handling system must be selected early in the warehouse development process. Material handling technology is discussed in Chapter 14.

Layout

The layout or storage plan of a warehouse should be planned to facilitate product flow.[20] The layout and the material handling system are integral. In addition, special attention must be given to location, number, and design of receiving and loading docks.[21]

It is difficult to generalize warehouse layouts since they are usually customized to accommodate specific handling requirements. If pallets are utilized, an early step is to determine the appropriate size. A pallet of nonstandard size may be desirable for specialized products. However, whenever possible, a standard size pallet should be used throughout a warehouse. The most common pallet sizes are 40 × 48 inches and 32 × 40 inches. In general, the larger the pallet load, the lower the movement cost per pound or package over a given distance. One lift truck operator can move a large load in the same time and with the same effort required to move a smaller load. Analysis of product cases and stacking patterns will determine the size of pallet best suited to the operation. Regardless of the size finally selected, management should adopt one pallet size for the overall warehouse.

The second step in planning warehouse layout involves pallet positioning. The most common practice in positioning pallets is 90 degree, or square, placement. Square positioning is widely used because of layout ease. Square placement means that the pallet is positioned perpendicular to the aisle. Figure 13-6 illustrates this method of positioning.

FIGURE 13-6

Basic method of pallet placement

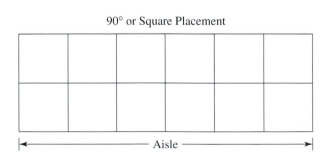

90° or Square Placement

← Aisle →

[20]"Loading Dock 2000," *Grocery Distribution,* October 1998, pp. 28–31.
[21]"The Importance of Proper Sequence," *Warehousing Forum,* June 1997, pp. 1–2.

Finally, the handling equipment must be integrated to finalize layout. The path and tempo of product flow depend upon the materials handling system. To illustrate the relationship between materials handling and layout, two systems and their respective layouts are illustrated. These examples represent two of many possible layouts.

Layout A, illustrated in Figure 13-7, illustrates a materials handling system and layout utilizing lift trucks for inbound and inventory transfer movements and tow tractors with trailer for order selection. This scenario assumes that products can be palletized. This layout is greatly simplified because offices, special areas, and other details are omitted.

The floor plan of layout A is approximately square. The advocates of square design feel that it provides the best framework for overall operating efficiency. As indicated earlier in this chapter, products should be positioned in a specific area of the warehouse for order selection. Such is the case in layout A. This area is labeled the *selection,* or *picking, area.* Its primary purpose is to minimize the distance order pickers must travel when assembling an order.

The selection area is supported by a *storage area.* When products are received they are palletized and moved to the storage area. The selection area is replenished from storage as required. Within the selection area, products are positioned according to weight, bulk, and replenishment velocity to minimize outbound movement. Customer orders are assembled by an order selector using a tow tractor pulling trailers through the selection area. The arrows in layout A indicate product selection flow.

FIGURE 13-7

Layouts A and B

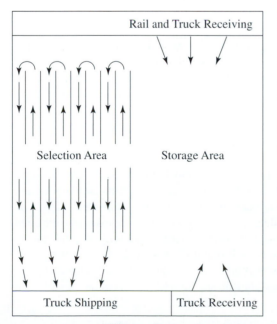

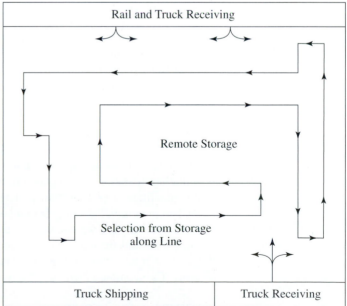

Layout A.   Layout B.

Layout B illustrates a materials handling system utilizing lift trucks to move product inbound and for transfer movements. A continuous towline is used for order selection. The floor plan in layout B is rectangular. In a system using a continuous-movement towline, the compact selection area is replaced by order selection directly from storage. Products are moved from receiving areas into storage positions adjacent to the towline. The orders are then selected directly from storage and loaded onto carts, which are propelled around the warehouse by the towline. Merchandise is stored or positioned to minimize inbound movement. The weakness of the fixed towline is that it facilitates selection of all products at an equal speed and frequency and does not consider special needs of high-velocity products. The arrows in layout B indicate major product movements. The line in the center of the layout illustrates the path of the towline.

As indicated, both layouts A and B are greatly simplified. The purpose is to illustrate the extremely different approaches managers have developed to reconcile the relationship between materials handling and warehouse layout.

Sizing

Several techniques are available to help estimate warehouse size. Each method begins with a projection of the total volume expected to move through the warehouse during a given period. The projection is used to estimate base and safety stocks for each product to be stocked in the warehouse. Some techniques consider both normal and peak utilization rates. Failure to consider utilization rates can result in overbuilding, with corresponding increase in cost. It is important to note, however, that a major complaint of warehouse managers is underestimation of warehouse size requirements. A good rule of thumb is to allow 10 percent additional space to account for increased volume, new products, and new business opportunities.

Initiating Warehouse Operations

To initiate warehouse operations, management must plan and perform initial stocking, personnel staffing, and work procedures, as well as implement a Warehouse Management System (WMS) and outbound distribution operations.[22] Although this focuses on the warehouse start-up process, many of these activities are relevant for ongoing warehouse operations as well.

Stocking

The ideal initial stocking procedure is to receive and stock all inventory items prior to initiating operations. Individual products to be distributed through the warehouse and the quantities of each inventory SKU are determined during warehouse planning. The challenge in initial stocking is to schedule and sequence product arrival. Time required to initially stock a warehouse depends upon the number and quantity of products. In most situations the initial stocking process will require 2 to 4 weeks for completion.

In a storage area, full pallet loads of product are assigned to predetermined positions. Two common methods of slot assignment are *variable* and *fixed*. A variable-slot

---

[22]For a discussion of using project teams to facilitate warehouse start-ups, see Marille Tatalias, "Warehouse Start-Ups," *Warehousing Forum,* April 1998, pp. 1–2.

placement system, also called *dynamic slotting,* allows the warehouse location to be changed each time a new shipment arrives. The goal of variable slotting is efficient utilization of warehouse space. A fixed-slot system assigns product to a permanent location in the warehouse. The product is stocked at this location as long as it sustains volume. As volume increases or decreases, the product location may be reassigned. The advantage of fixed slotting is that warehouse operations personnel become familiar with the location of specific product, making them more efficient. However, newer WMS and RF capabilities have substantially increased location recording accuracy. Regardless of which slotting system is employed, each inbound product must be assigned an initial location.

Training

A major concern in logistical operations over the past several decades has been labor productivity. The basic nature of raw materials, parts, and finished goods flowing through and between a vast network of facilities makes logistics labor-intensive. In fact, warehousing is the single largest consumer of logistics labor.

Hiring and training qualified personnel to operate a warehouse is a challenge. Regardless of how efficient the proposed warehouse system is in theory, in practice it will only be as good as its operating personnel. Part of the challenge is to attract competent, productive workers to a warehouse environment. Because warehousing is demanding physical work completed at times and in locations that are less than ideal, it becomes particularly difficult to attract workers in periods of relatively full employment. Compounding this challenge in warehouse start-up as well as ongoing operations is the need to find operating personnel who can pass necessary aptitude and drug tests. Newer materials handling equipment requires the ability to interface with computers and the discipline to follow specific directions. The drug tests are required to reduce the liability for personal injury or damage while operating materials handling equipment.

Once hired, personnel then must be properly trained to ensure desired system results. The full workforce should be available for test operations prior to the arrival of merchandise. Personnel hired for specific assignments should be fully trained to perform job requirements and to understand the role of their contribution to total system performance. After orientation, all employees should be given specific training. Personnel hired to operate a warehouse may be grouped in the following categories: administrators, supervisors, selectors, equipment operators, laborers, material handlers, and support workers such as maintenance.

Prior to actual operations it is desirable to simulate the work that each group performs. Such simulation provides hands-on experience doing work without the risk of creating operational problems. When initial warehouse stocking begins, the workforce receives actual experience in merchandise handling. Normally, the manufacturer supplying the basic materials handling system and equipment provides instruction regarding operations under both simulated and initial stocking conditions. Once the initial inventory is on hand, it is good practice to simulate fulfilling customer orders. Simulated orders can be selected and loaded into delivery trucks, and the merchandise may then be treated as a new arrival and transferred back into stock.

Warehouse Management Systems

The development of work procedures goes hard in hand with training warehouse personnel. Most firms implement a WMS to standardize work procedure and encourage best practice. It is management's responsibility to see that all personnel understand and use these procedures.

In a mechanized warehouse, approximately 65 percent of personnel are employed in some facet of order selection. The two basic methods of order picking are individual and area selection, also known as batch selection. Using individual selection, one employee completes a customer's total order. This system is not widely used. Its primary application occurs when a large number of small orders is selected for repack or consolidated shipment, such as e-commerce fulfillment. Under the more commonly used area selection system each employee is assigned responsibility for a specific portion of the warehouse. To complete a customer's order, several different selectors are required. Because each employee has a thorough knowledge of a specific selection area, less time is required to locate items.

Work procedures are also important for receiving and shipping. Established procedures for receiving and ensuring product entry into inventory records are critical. If pallets are used, the merchandise must be stacked in appropriate patterns to ensure maximum load stability and consistent case counts. Personnel working in shipping must have knowledge of trailer loading practices. In specific types of operations, particularly when merchandise changes ownership, items must be checked during loading.

Work procedures are not restricted to floor personnel. Procedures must be established for administration and maintenance. Replenishment of warehouse inventory can cause operational problems if proper ordering procedures are lacking. Normally, there is limited interaction between buyers and warehouse personnel although such communication is improving with integrated supply chain management organizations. Buyers tend to purchase in quantities that afford the best price, and little attention is given to pallet compatible quantities or available warehouse space.

Ideally buyers should coordinate with warehouse personnel before commissioning large orders or introducing new products. The experience of some companies has forced management to require buyers to predetermine warehouse space assignment prior to ordering. Another potential problem is the quantity of cases ordered. The goal is to purchase in pallet-multiple quantities. For example, if a product is ideally stacked on pallets in a 50-case pattern, the buyer should order in multiples of 50. If an order is placed for 120 cases, upon arrival the cases will fill two pallets plus 20 on a third pallet. The extra 20 cases will require the warehouse cubic space typically used for a pallet of 50 and will require the same amount of materials handling capacity to move.

Security

In a broad sense, security in a warehouse involves protection against merchandise pilferage and deterioration. Each form of security requires management attention.

Pilferage Protection

In warehouse operations it is necessary to protect against theft by employees and thieves as well as from riots and civil disturbances. Typical security procedures used throughout a business should be strictly enforced at each warehouse. Security begins at the fence. As standard procedure, only authorized personnel should be permitted into the facility and surrounding grounds. Entry to the warehouse yard should be controlled through a single gate. Without exception, no private automobile, regardless of management rank or customer status, should be allowed to enter the yard or park adjacent to the warehouse.

To illustrate the importance of security guidelines, the following experience may be helpful. A firm adopted the rule that no private vehicles would be permitted in the warehouse yard. Exceptions were made for two office employees with special needs. One night after work, one of these employees discovered a bundle taped under one fender of his car. Subsequent checking revealed that the car was literally a loaded delivery truck. The matter was promptly reported to security, who informed the employee not to alter any packages taped to the car and to continue parking inside the yard. Over the next several days, the situation was fully uncovered, with the ultimate arrest and conviction of seven warehouse employees who confessed to stealing thousands of dollars worth of company merchandise. The firm would have been far better off had it provided transportation for the two special-needs employees from the regular parking lots to their work locations.

Shortages are always a major concern in warehouse operations. Many are honest mistakes that occur during order selection and shipment, but the purpose of security is to restrict theft from all angles. The majority of thefts occur during normal working hours.

Inventory control and order processing systems help protect merchandise from being carried out of the warehouse unless accompanied by a computer release document. If samples are authorized for salesperson use, such merchandise should be maintained in a separate inventory. Not all pilferage occurs on an individual basis. Organized efforts between warehouse personnel and carrier truck drivers can result in deliberate overpicking, or high-for-low-value product substitution occurring in order to move unauthorized merchandise out of the warehouse. Employee work assignment rotation, total case counts, and occasional complete line-item checks can reduce vulnerability to such collaboration.

A final concern is the increased incidence of hijacking over-the-road trailer loads from yards or while in transit. Hijacking is a major logistical concern. Over-the-road hijack prevention is primarily a law-enforcement matter, but in-yard theft can be eliminated by tight security provisions. Such over-the-road theft is a significant problem in developing countries. One beverage company manager reported that he budgeted to lose one truck a week due to theft for his South American operation. He instructed his drivers to simply turn over the keys and walk away rather than risk their life.

Product Deterioration

Within the warehouse, a number of factors can reduce a product or material to nonsaleable status. The most obvious form of product deterioration is damage from careless materials handling. For example, when pallets of merchandise are stacked in great heights, a marked change in humidity or temperature can cause packages supporting the stack to collapse. The warehouse environment must be carefully controlled and measured to provide proper product protection. Of major concern is warehouse employee carelessness. In this respect, the lift truck may well be management's worst enemy. Regardless of how often lift truck operators are warned against carrying overloads, some still attempt such shortcuts when not properly supervised. In one situation, a stack of four pallets was dropped off a lift truck at the receiving dock of a food warehouse. Standard procedure was to move two pallets per load. The dollar cost of the damaged merchandise exceeded the average daily profit of two retail supermarkets. Product deterioration from careless handling within the warehouse is a form of loss that cannot be insured against or offset with compensating revenue.

Another major form of deterioration is incompatibility of products stored or transported together. For example, care must be taken when storing or shipping chocolate to make sure that it doesn't absorb odors from products it is being transported with, such as household chemicals.

Delivery

Most shipments from distribution warehouses to customers are completed by truck. When private trucking is utilized, a managerial concern is to schedule shipments to achieve efficient transportation. Computer-assisted load planning and equipment routing techniques are very useful for organizing transportation requirements.

Safety and Maintenance

Accident prevention is a concern of warehouse management. A comprehensive safety program requires constant examination of work procedures and equipment to locate and take corrective action to eliminate unsafe conditions before accidents result. Accidents occur when workers become careless or are exposed to mechanical or physical hazards. The floors of a warehouse may cause accidents if not properly cleaned. During normal operation, rubber and glass deposits collect on aisles and, from time to time, broken cases will result in product seepage onto the floor. Proper cleaning procedures can reduce the accident risk of such hazards. Environmental safety has become a major concern of government, such as OSHA, and cannot be neglected by management.

A preventive maintenance program is necessary for materials handling equipment. Unlike production machines, movement equipment is not stationary, so it is more difficult to properly maintain. A preventive maintenance program scheduling periodic checks of all handling equipment should be applied in every warehouse.

Summary

Warehousing can contribute to manufacturing and retailing efficiency. While the role of the warehouse has traditionally been to stock inventory, contemporary warehousing provides a broader value proposition in terms of economic and service benefits. Economic benefits include consolidation and break-bulk, assortment, postponement, stockpiling, and reverse logistics. Service benefits include spot stocking, full line stocking, production support, and market presence. The perspective of warehousing is changing from a storage mission to one characterized by velocity and movement.

Distribution centers and warehouses are designed to accommodate the two primary activities of handling and storage. Handling activities include receiving inbound shipments, in-storage handling to move between different types of storage such as long-term, bulk, and picking, and packing and staging shipments to customers. Active storage activities facilitate cross-docking, consolidation, break-bulk, production support, and postponement. Extended storage activities facilitate balancing supply and demand, speculation, and decoupling.

Warehouses are usually classified based on ownership. A private warehouse is operated by the enterprise that owns the merchandise in the facility. A public warehouse is operated independently and offers various for-hire value-added services. A contract warehouse is a long-term business arrangement that provides tailored services for a limited number of customers. An integrated warehousing strategy incorporates a combination of warehouse ownership options.

There are numerous managerial considerations in planning and initiating warehouse operations, including design, stocking, staffing, training, security, safety, maintenance, and WMS implementation. Each of these requires considerable managerial effort to ensure facilities start up and run smoothly on a day-to-day basis and can accommodate change rapidly and successfully, as necessary to meet current business demands.

Challenge Questions

1. Provide a definition and an example of strategic storage from a logistical system you are familiar with.
2. Discuss and illustrate the economic justification for establishing a warehouse.
3. Why would a warehouse be described as a "necessary evil"?
4. How do warehouses perform assortment?
5. Under what conditions could it make sense to combine private and public warehouses in a logistical system?
6. What role can a warehouse play in postponement strategies?
7. What is the concept of market presence, and how does it relate to the functionality of warehousing?
8. Discuss and illustrate the role warehouses play in reverse logistics.
9. Illustrate the relationship between the size and shape of a distribution warehouse and the materials handling system. Why do some warehouses have square design while others are rectangular?
10. Explain the following statement: "A warehouse should merely consist of walls enclosing an efficient handling system."

14 PACKAGING AND MATERIALS HANDLING

Packaging Perspectives
    Packaging for Materials Handling Efficiency
    Packaging Materials
Materials Handling
    Basic Handling Considerations
    Mechanized Systems
    Semiautomated Systems
    Automated Systems
    Information-Directed Systems
    Special Handling Considerations
Summary

Within a warehouse and while being transported throughout a logistics system, the package serves to identify and protect product. The package, containing a product, is the entity that must be moved by a firm's materials handling system. For this reason we will jointly discuss packaging and materials handling as integral parts of warehousing and a firm's logistical system.

Packaging Perspectives

Packaging is typically viewed as being either *consumer,* focused primarily on marketing, or *industrial,* focused on logistics. The primary concern of logistics operations is industrial package design. Individual products or parts are typically grouped into cartons, bags, bins, or barrels for handling efficiency. Containers used to group individual products are called master cartons. When master cartons are grouped into larger units for handling, the combination is referred to as *containerization* or *unitization.*

    The master carton and the unitized load become basic handing units for logistical operations. The weight, cube, and damage potential of the master carton determines transportation and materials handling requirements. If the package is not designed for efficient logistical processing, overall system performance suffers.

    Retail sale quantity or presentation should not be the prime determinant of master carton size. For example, beer, often sold at retail in units of 6, is normally packed in master cartons containing 24 units. The master carton should be large enough to provide handling economies of scale but light enough to facilitate handling by an individual without mechanical assistance. A prime objective in logistics is to design operations to handle a limited assortment of standardized master cartons. Master carton standardization facilitates materials handling and transportation. The importance of standardization can be illustrated by an example adapted from a shoe retailer.

The initial logistical system employed by the retailer to ship shoes from the warehouse to retail stores consisted of reusing vendor cartons. Individual pairs of shoes were grouped as best as possible into available repack cartons. The result was a variety of carton sizes going to each retail store. The method of order selection used to assemble a retail store's order was to work from warehouse-sequenced picking lists that grouped shoes by style and quantity. Shoes were selected in the warehouse, packed into cartons, and then manually stacked on a four-wheel truck for transfer to the shipping dock. The cartons were then loaded into trucks for delivery to stores. While the order picking list provided a summary of all shoes in the total shipment, it was impossible for the retail stores to determine the contents of any given carton.

Viewing materials handling delivery and store operations as an integrated system resulted in a decision to discontinue reusing vendor cartons. The new procedure used a standardized master carton that facilitated order picking and materials handling. The new logistics practice was designed around two concepts. First, standardized master cartons were adopted to permit continuous conveyor movement from point of warehouse order selection to truck loading. Second, the integrated system used a computer process to assure that each standardized master carton was packed to maximum practical cube utilization. Under the new system a picking list was generated for each carton. After the individual pairs of shoes were placed into the carton, the pick list was attached to the carton, providing a summary of contents for retail store personnel.

The advantages of a standardized master carton extended to the retail store's backroom. Because the contents of each master carton were easily determined, it was not necessary to search through cartons to find a specific style or size of shoe. Standard master cartons could be more efficiently stacked, resulting in less backroom congestion. Finally, complete identification of master carton contents facilitated retail inventory management and replenishment.

The new integrated system required purchase of master cartons, since each could be reused only about three times. However, this added cost was more than justified by reduced order picking labor, continuous movement of cartons into over-the-road trailers, and more efficient utilization of transportation trailer capacity. Since each master carton was cubed out to near capacity, *dead* or unusable space in cartons was reduced. The standardized master carton size was selected to achieve maximum conformity with a high-cube over-the-road trailer, thereby eliminating dead space in stacking. The end result of standardized master carton usage was a substantial reduction in total cost combined with a far more effective materials handling system at both the warehouse and the retail shoe store.

This packaging example illustrates the importance of integrated logistical planning and the principle of lowest total cost. However, the most important point is that master carton standardization facilitated supply chain integration.

Naturally, few organizations can reduce their master carton requirements to a one size fits all. When master cartons of more than one size are required, extreme care should be taken to arrive at an assortment of compatible units. Figure 14-1 illustrates one such concept utilizing four standard master carton sizes that achieves modular compatibility.

FIGURE 14-1

Example and benefits of the modular system of packing

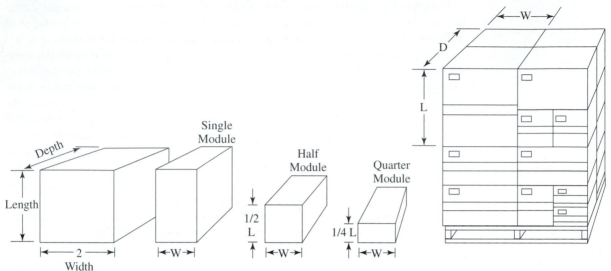

Source: Adapted from the work of Walter Frederick Friedman and Company, New York.

Of course, logistical considerations cannot fully dominate packaging design. The ideal package for materials handling and transportation would be a perfect cube having equal length, depth, and width while achieving maximum possible density. Seldom will such a package exist. The important point is that logistical requirements should be evaluated along with manufacturing, marketing, and product design considerations when finalizing master carton selection.

Another logistical packaging concern is the degree of protection required to cope with the anticipated environments. Package design and material must combine to achieve the desired level of protection without incurring the expense of overprotection. It is possible to design a package that has the correct material content but does not provide the necessary protection. Arriving at a satisfactory packaging solution involves defining the degree of allowable damage in terms of expected overall conditions and then isolating a combination of design and materials capable of meeting those specifications. For package design, there are two key principles. First, the cost of absolute protection will, in most cases, be prohibitive. Second, package construction is properly a blend of design and material.

A final logistics packaging concern is the relationship between the master carton size, retail replenishment quantity, and retail display quantity. From a materials handling perspective, master cartons should be standardized and reasonably large to minimize the number of units handled in the warehouse. For ease of warehouse handling, it is desirable to have retailers purchase in master carton quantities. However, for a slow-moving product, a master carton could contain a substantial overstock for an item that sells only one unit per week but is packed in a case containing 48. Finally, in order to minimize labor, retailers often place trays from master cartons on the retail shelf so that each unit does not have to be unloaded and placed individually. Master cartons or trays meeting retail requirements for shelf space are preferred.

The determination of final package design requires a great deal of testing to assure that both marketing and logistics concerns are satisfied. Such tests can be conducted in a laboratory or on an experimental basis. While the marketing aspects are generally the focus of consumer research, logistics packaging research has not been as formalized. During the past decade the process of package design and material selection has become far more scientific. Laboratory analysis offers a reliable way to evaluate package design as a result of advancements in testing equipment and measurement techniques. Instrumented recording equipment is available to measure shock severity and characteristics while a package is in transit. To a large degree, care in design has been further encouraged by increased federal regulation regarding hazardous materials.

The four most common causes of product damage in a logistical system are vibration, impact, puncture, and compression. Combinations of damage can be experienced whenever a package is being transported or handled. Test shipment monitoring is expensive and difficult to conduct on a scientific basis. To obtain increased accuracy, computerized environmental simulations can be used to replicate typical conditions that a package will experience in the logistical system. Laboratory test equipment is available to evaluate the impact of shock upon the interaction of product fragility and packaging materials and design.

Packaging for Materials Handling Efficiency

Packaging utility reflects how packaging impacts logistical productivity and efficiency. All logistical operations are affected by packaging utility—from truck loading and warehouse picking productivity to transportation and storage cube utilization. Materials handling efficiency in all of these cases is significantly influenced by package design, unitization, and communication characteristics.

Package Design

Product packaging in standard configurations and order quantities facilitates logistical efficiency. For example, cube utilization can be improved through reduced package size by concentrating products such as orange juice or fabric softener, by eliminating air inside packages, and by shipping items unassembled, nested, and with minimal dunnage. In most cases, dunnage materials, like polystyrene foam peanuts, can be minimized simply by reducing box size. IKEA, the Swedish retailer of unassembled furniture, emphasizes cube minimization to the point that it ships pillows vacuum-packed. IKEA uses a cube minimization packaging strategy to successfully compete in the United States even though the company ships furniture from Sweden. Some experts believe that improving cube utilization is packaging's greatest opportunity and predict that, in general, packaging cube can be reduced by as much as 50 percent, which essentially doubles transportation efficiency.[1] Hewlett-Packard ships computer printers from the United States to Europe using airfreight and minimal packaging.[2] They shrink-wrap unit loads of printers to provide stability and reduce damage. In addition to lowering transportation cost, the overall practice reduces import duties since substantial value-added is postponed until the product is finally assembled and sold in Europe.

Cube minimization is most important for lightweight products such as assembled lawn furniture that *cubes out* a transport vehicle before weight limits are reached. On

[1]James Goff, "Packaging-Distribution Relationships: A Look to the Future," *Logistical Packaging Innovation Proceedings* (Oakbrook, IL: Council of Logistics Management, 1991).

[2]Edward Feitzinger and Han L. Lee, "Mass Customization at Hewlett-Packard: The Power of Postponement," *Harvard Business Review,* January/February 1999, pp. 116–20.

the other hand, heavy products like steel ball bearings or liquid in glass bottles *weigh out* a transport vehicle before its cube is filled. When a vehicle or container weighs out, the firm ends up shipping air in any space that can't be filled with product, which results in reduced transportation effectiveness. Total weight can sometimes be reduced by product or package changes. For example, substituting plastic bottles for glass significantly increases the number of bottles that can be loaded in a trailer. The recent move by Gerber Baby Food toward plastic bottles is partially designed to reduce transportation expenses.[3] Even when package design is not changed, products that weight out before cubing out may offer special opportunities as lightweight product can be top loaded to take advantage of the empty cube without substantially changing total weight or transportation cost.

Cube and weight minimization are a special challenge for mail order and e-commerce operations. These operations tend to use standardized packaging for both purchasing and operating efficiencies. This results in oversized packages that require excessive dunnage and increased shipping cost. The nature of the products and the breadth of e-commerce product lines often require multiple packages to be combined in a single order. This is of great public concern for consumers who are becoming more aware of the cost of shipping and handling direct shipments as well as for environmental movements concerned about packaging disposal.

Unitization

Unitization is the process of grouping master cartons into one physical unit for materials handling or transport. The concept of containerization includes all forms of unitization, from taping two master cartons together to the use of specialized transportation equipment. All types of containerization have the basic objective of increasing handling and transport efficiency. Unit loads provide many benefits over handling individual master cartons. First, unloading time and congestion at destination are minimized. Second, product shipped in unit load quantities facilitates materials handling. Unit loads utilize approximately one-fifth the time required for manual loading or unloading. Inbound shipment verification is also simplified as more unitized inbound shipments are bar coded. Inventory can be positioned rapidly for order selection. Finally, in-transit damage is reduced by unit load shipping and specialized transportation equipment. All these factors reduce logistical cost. The following discussion is limited to unitization methods up to transportation vehicles.

Rigid Containers.   Rigid containers provide a device within which master cartons or loose products are unitized. The premise is that placing merchandise within a container will both protect it and facilitate handling. The prospects for extensive domestic containerization have been the subject of a great deal of attention since the early 1950s. The potential to increase productivity by containerization is obvious. Approximately one-half the total cost of transporting domestic goods is spent shuffling products between vehicles, handling across docks and platforms, packaging, and filing loss and damage claims for pilferage and for insurance. The airlines use rigid containerization both for freight and for passenger baggage. The containers, which are designed to fit in the cargo area of aircraft, facilitate loading and unloading while reducing product damage and pilferage. Table 14-1 summarizes the benefits of rigid containerization.

---

[3]Anonymous, "Gerber Serves Convenience in Plastic Packaging," *Packaging Digest,* August 2001, p. 2.

TABLE 14-1   Benefits of Rigid Containerization

- Improves overall material movement efficiency.
- Reduces damage in handling and transit.
- Reduces pilferage.
- Reduces protective packaging requirements.
- Provides greater protection from element environment.
- Provides a shipment unit that can be reused a substantial number of times, thereby reducing waste and the need to dispose of the container.

FIGURE 14-2

Example of a hardwood pallet

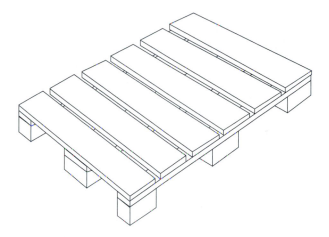

Flexible Containers.   As the name implies, flexible containers do not protect a product by complete enclosure. The most common type of nonrigid containerization is stacked master cartons on pallets or slipsheets. A hardwood pallet is illustrated in Figure 14-2. A slipsheet, which is similar to a pallet in size and purpose, is generally made of corrugated cardboard or plastic film. Because the slipsheet lays flat on the floor, special lift trucks are required to handle slipsheet unit loads. The primary advantage of slipsheets is cost. Slipsheets permit one-way utilization and are insignificant from a weight and cube perspective. Flexible containers are typically used to provide the foundation for unit loads.

Most industry associations recommend that a standardized pallet or slipsheet size be used as a unit load platform. The Grocery Manufacturers of America have adopted the 40 × 48-inch pallet with four-way entry and similar size slipsheets for food distribution. The beverage industry, on the other hand, has standardized on 32 × 36-inch pallets. Throughout industry, the sizes most frequently used are 40 × 48, 32 × 40, and 32 × 36. It is common practice to first identify the dimension of most frequent entry by handling equipment.

Generally, the larger a platform, the more economical for materials handling. For instance, the 40 × 48-inch pallet provides 768 more square inches per stacking tier than the 32 × 36-inch size. Assuming that master cartons can be stacked as high as 10 tiers, the total added unitization space of the 40 × 48-inch pallet is 7680 square inches. This is 60 percent larger than the 32 × 36-inch size. The final determination of size should be based upon load, compatibility with the handling and transport equipment used

FIGURE 14-3

Basic pallet master carton stacking patterns

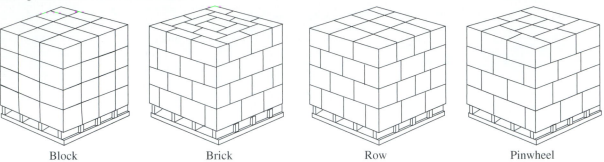

| Block | Brick | Row | Pinwheel |

Source: Adapted from palletization guides of the National Wooden Pallet & Container Association, Arlington, VA.

throughout the logistical system, and standardized industry practice. With modern handling equipment, few restrictions are encountered in weight limitations.

While a variety of different approaches can be used to tier master cartons on slip-sheets and pallets, the four most common are block, brick, row, and pinwheel. The block method is used with cartons of equal width and length. With differential widths and lengths, the brick, row, or pinwheel pattern is employed. Figure 14-3 illustrates these four basic patterns. Except for the block method, cartons are placed in the unit load arranged in an interlocking pattern with adjoining tiers placed at 90-degree angles to each other. Load stability is enhanced with interlocking. The block pattern does not have this benefit. While these patterns provide a good starting point when there are limited master carton sizes, most pallet patterns are determined using computer programs.

The use of flexible unitization can increase damage potential if it is not properly restrained during handling or transport. In most situations, the stability of stacking is insufficient to secure a unit load. Standard methods of improving stability include rope tie, corner posts, steel strapping, taping and antiskid treatment, breakaway adhesives, and wrapping. These methods essentially tie the master cartons to the pallet. Increasingly popular methods for securing unit loads are shrink-wrap and stretch-wrap. Both wraps use film similar to that used in a kitchen for food preservation. (Stretch-wrapping and shrink-wrapping are discussed in more detail later in this chapter.)

Communication

The third important logistical packaging function is communication or information transfer. This function is becoming increasingly critical to provide content identification, tracking, and handling instructions.

Content Identification.   The most obvious communications role is identifying package contents for all channel members. Typical information includes manufacturer, product, container type, count, and Universal Product Code (UPC) number.

The carton information is used to identify product for receiving, order selection, and shipment verification. Visibility is the major content identification consideration as material handlers should be able to see the label from reasonable distances in all directions. The exception for high-visibility packaging are high-value products that often have small or minimal labels to minimize the potential for pilferage.

Tracking.   Ease of package tracking is also important. Effective internal operation and increasingly customers require that product be tracked as it moves through the supply chain. Positive control of all movement reduces product loss and pilferage. Such detailed tracking would be prohibitively expensive if performed manually. However, extensive availability of portable bar code scanners and Radio Frequency Identification (RFID) allows detailed tracking. RFID uses a computer chip embedded in the package, container, or vehicle to allow the container and contents to be scanned and verified as it passes checkpoints in the distribution facility and transportation gateways. Low-cost scanning equipment and increased coding standardization improve tracking capabilities and effectiveness.

Handling Instructions.   The final role of logistics packaging is to provide handling and damage instruction to material handlers. The information should note any special product handling considerations such as glass containers, temperature restrictions, stacking considerations, or potential environmental concerns. If the product is potentially dangerous, such as some chemicals, the packaging or accompanying material should provide instructions for dealing with spills and container damage.

Packaging Materials

Numerous material types are used for logistics packaging, ranging from traditional corrugated cardboard to more exotic plastics. Traditional alternatives are reviewed first, followed by a discussion of emerging material alternatives.

Traditional Materials

Since the early 1900s, common carriers in the United States have attempted to regulate the nature of the packages they transport. The American Trucking Association, the American Association of Railroads, and United Parcel Service publish packaging material requirements in their freight classifications. These standards, which have primarily been developed in conjunction with the Fiber Box Association, generally require more corrugated material than may be necessary to achieve desired protection.

Historical use for these standards is directly related to carrier damage responsibility. One of a carrier's common law defenses against paying damage claims is that packaging was not in compliance with the classification standards. In effect, common practice forced shippers to overpackage their products. Carrier enforcement of the standards resulted in many firms ignoring packaging as an area of productivity improvement. In fact, packaging requirements have traditionally been a barrier to packaging innovation. In recent years, however, barriers to packaging innovation have been greatly reduced for two reasons. First, large integrated channel members in today's competitive environment have considerable stake in preventing damage and controlling packaging-related costs. Second, transportation deregulation has reduced the amount of freight subject to common carrier packaging rules and increased the amount of freight moving under truckload, negotiated contracts with released value rates. As a result, cardboard content rules today apply only to LTL common carrier freight. Many LTL carriers now accept packaging containers that differ from traditional standards provided the containers pass designated performance tests.

In addition to corrugated cardboard boxes, other traditional packaging materials include burlap bags, blankets, steel cans, pails, drums and straps, cages, and multiwall paper bags and drums. New options include low-density plastic film, shrink-wrap, stretch-wrap, bags and barriers, high-density plastic boxes and totes, plastic strapping, and plastic foam cushioning and dunnage for fragile and irregular shapes.

Shrink-wrapping consists of placing a prestretched plastic sheet or bag over the unitizing platform and master cartons. The material is then heat-shrunk to lock the cartons to the platform. Stretch-wrap consists of wrapping the unit load with a tightly drawn external plastic material. The unit load is rotated on a turntable to place the wrap under tension so that it binds the stack together. The platform is wrapped directly into the unit load. With shrink- and stretch-wrapping the unit load assumes many of the characteristics of a rigid container. However, shrink- and stretch-wrap often provide greater physical protection than a rigid container because of exact fit and weight support. Other benefits of wrapping are reduced exposure of master cartons to logistical environment, low cost, adaptability to various shipment sizes, insignificant added weight, and ability to identify contents and damage. The major problem of shrink-wrap is waste material disposal.

Bags and barriers are paper or plastic containers that provide protection by wrapping bulk or loose product. Bags and barriers are flexible and relatively easy to dispose of. The weakness of such packaging is a failure to provide product protection against damage and an inability to be used for a wide variety of products.

High-density plastic boxes or totes are lidded plastic storage containers similar to those purchased for home storage applications. They are rigid and sturdy, offering substantial product protection. Totes work well for selecting and shipping product assortments to retail stores. The weakness of totes is that they are inflexible, reasonably heavy, and must be reused to justify the economics.

Plastic strapping is used to contain or unitize a load so that multiple smaller containers can be handled as a single larger container. The strapping is usually about 1/2 to 1 inch wide and is banded tightly around the containers.

Plastic foam dunnage is the familiar peanut-shaped material used to pack irregular shaped products into standard shaped boxes. The peanuts are light and do not increase transportation cost while providing substantial protection. Disposal is a major issue associated with foam dunnage.

New Emerging Packaging Alternatives

Loosening of traditional cardboard standards, competitive industry conditions driving an integrated solution, technological innovation, and OSHA (Occupational Safety and Health Administration) requirements have triggered a logistical packaging renaissance. Shippers are increasingly questioning traditional and alternative packaging materials and forms and encouraging experimentation with new, less costly, and creative packaging systems.

Emerging packaging alternatives include film-based packaging, blanket-wrapping, returnable containers, intermediate bulk containers, pallet pools, plastic pallets, and alternatives that require special materials handling equipment. Although several of these are adaptations of traditional packaging concepts, they are differentiated from traditional methods in two critical respects. First, they are customized for specific logistical systems and products; and second, they are designed to minimize the costs of packaging and solid waste disposal.

Film-Based Packaging.   Film-based packaging utilizes flexible packaging materials rather than rigid packaging such as corrugated fiberboard boxes. Traditionally, film-based shrink-wrap and stretch-wrap systems have been used to stabilize unit loads. In today's emerging applications, they are used to form actual shipping packages for consumer goods such as cans and bottles, furniture, appliances, and small vehicles. The new packages generally are combined with rigid materials. For example, cans are shrink-wrapped into a corrugated fiberboard tray, plastic bottle trays have corner support for stacking, filing cabinets have corrugated corner protection from nicks, and appliances have panel protection on two sides to facilitate clamp-handling.

Film-based flexible packaging offers several advantages over traditional rigid packaging methods. Film-based systems operate automatically, reducing the labor costs of manually boxing products. Packaging standardization is achieved since a roll of film fits most product configurations equally well and thus eliminates the need to maintain inventories of various sized boxes. A related benefit is that film-based systems minimize shipment weight and cube because the package is essentially the same size and weight as its contents. Film-based systems provide reductions in inventory storage space because a roll of film is smaller than pallets of empty or flattened boxes; additionally, less trash remains after the product is unpacked. A final advantage, and the one that may seem contrary, is that damage is reduced with film-based packaging compared to traditional rigid packaging methods. Research shows that freight is generally handled more carefully when it is clearly visible rather than concealed in a box. Additionally, concealed product damage is reduced, allowing for immediate identification of damage and reduced complexity for freight claims and administrative haggling.

Film-based packaging applications work best for strong products that are able to bear a topload, since the package does not provide compression strength for stacking. Suitable product types include square products such as filing cabinets, cans or bottles, appliances, or round products like insulation rolls. In comparison, irregular-shaped products such as chairs do not lend themselves very well to film-based packaging.

Blanket-Wrapping.   Blanket-wrapping is a traditional form of packaging provided by household goods movers. Packaging of this nature is ideally suited for nesting irregular products like tables or chairs that otherwise would have to be individually packed in corrugated boxes. Support decking is erected with plywood and bars that lock into trailer walls; products are stacked into the decking and the product surfaces are protected with blankets.

The blanket-wrap concept has been extended into premium uncartoned transportation service. Carriers own, supply, and manage the package system materials, load and unload the trailers, and are directly accountable for any damage incurred in the process.

Uncartoned transportation service is best suited for truckload quantities of large, rugged products like sofas, office furniture, laboratory equipment, mainframe computers and minicomputers, restaurant furnishings, or store fixtures. Advantages include elimination of package material and waste, minimization of transportation cube, and easier unpacking of products.

Returnable Containers.   Returnable containers have traditionally been used for some products. Most reusable packages are steel or plastic, although some firms reuse corrugated fiberboard boxes. Automobile manufacturers use returnable racks for interplant shipment of body parts, and chemical companies reuse steel drums. There is an increasing trend, however, to reusable packaging applications for many small items and parts such as ingredients, grocery perishables, interplant shipments, and retail warehouse-to-store totes.

Returnable containers are particularly appropriate for integrated environments where there is reasonable container control between shippers and customers. The automobile industry uses returnable racking and packaging extensively between component suppliers and assembly plants. In a returnable package system, the parties must explicitly cooperate to maximize container usage; otherwise, containers may be lost, misplaced, or forgotten. Alternatively, deposit systems may be necessary in more free-flow supply chains, where members are linked by occasional or nonrepetitive transactions. Deposit systems are frequently used for beverage bottles, kegs, pallets, and steel drums.

The decision to invest in a returnable package system involves explicit consideration of the number of shipment cycles and return transportation costs versus the purchase and disposal cost of expendable containers. Benefits of improved handling and reduced damage should be taken into account, as well as the future costs of sorting, tracking, and cleaning the reusable containers. Financial analysis of returnable systems should be made based upon net present value calculations rather than the payback period method to accurately assess operational and strategic potential.[4]

Intermediate Bulk Containers.   Intermediate Bulk Containers (IBC) are used for granular and liquid product shipment quantities that are smaller than tank cars but larger than bags or drums. Typical products include resin pellets, food ingredients, and adhesives. The most frequently used intermediate bulk containers are bulk bags and boxes. Bulk bags are made from woven plastic with a liner barrier and have a 1- to 2-ton capacity. Bulk boxes are usually pallet size and lined with a plastic bag. IBCs for wet products require the use of a rigid box or cage.

Pallet Pools.   Pallet pools have been implemented as a way to overcome traditional problems of disposal and exchange. High-quality pallets are expensive and are difficult to retrieve once they leave the owner's control. When transfer to an external organization occurs, warehouses routinely exchange poor quality pallets and keep the higher quality ones.

Pallet pools are third-party suppliers that maintain and lease high-quality pallets throughout the country for a variable fee for a single cycle. A cycle might be defined as loading of pallets at a manufacturer and transporting to a retailer's warehouse. Pallet pool firms such as CHEP, which is one of the largest, assume responsibility for developing, purchasing, and maintaining pallets as well as providing control and management systems.[5] Pallet pools are common in Europe and Asia and are increasingly becoming the standard for the North American grocery industry.

Plastic Pallets.   Plastic pallets have been an issue of research and examination for many years, particularly within the grocery industry.[6] Plastic pallets attempt to ad-

---

[4]For a detailed financial analysis of the cost elements involved in returnable packaging and the relative sensitivity, see Sangjin Lee, *An Analysis of Factors Affecting the Cost of Returnable Logistical Packaging Systems,* unpublished Master's Thesis, Michigan State University, 1999.

[5]For information regarding the products and services offered by a pallet pool organization like CHEP, see **www.chep.com.**

[6]To review the results of some of these tests, see Anonymous, "The Problems with Pallets," *Modern Materials Handling,* June 1, 1996; Anonymous, "In Search of Pallet Solutions," *Modern Materials Handling,* July 1, 2000; and David Maloney, "What Buyers Say about Pallets," *Modern Materials Handling,* May 1, 2000. All of the above articles can be found at the *Modern Materials Handling* website at **www.manufacturing.net/magazine/mmh.**

TABLE 14-2 **Pallet Type Comparison**

Unit-Load Base	Cost[a]	Base weight (lb)[b]	Durability[c]	Repairability	Typical Applications
Wood pallet	$3.50–25.00	55–112	Medium	High	Wide general use, including grocery, automotive, durable goods, hardware
Pressed wood fiber pallet	4.75–6.65	30–42	Medium	Low	Bulk bags, order picking, printing, building materials
Solid molded plastic pallet	30–80	35–75	High	Medium	Captive or closed-loop systems, FDA and USDA applications, AS/RS, automotive
Metal pallet	30–350	32–100	High	Medium	Captive or closed-loop systems, FDA and USDA applications, AS/RS, military, heavy equipment, aerospace
Corrugated fiberboard pallet	3.00–8.00	8–12	Low	Low	Export shipping, one-way shipping applications in grocery, lightweight paper products, industrial parts
Corrugated fiberboard slipsheet	1.00–4.00	2–6	Low	Low	One-way export shipping applications, slip-sheet one-way shipping applications requiring a cushioned base, grocery, lightweight paper products

[a]Numbers in this table represent a range of values. Prices may be higher or lower, depending on the specific requirements of the applications, dimensions, load capacity, quantity ordered, and manufacturer.

[b]Weight of the unit-load base may be higher or lower, depending on the specific requirements of the application. Check with individual manufacturer for load capacities.

[c]Durability is defined as the expected number of trips to first repair.

Source: Karen Auguston, "Selection Guidelines for Pallets and Slipsheets," *Modern Materials Handling,* 48, no. 13 (November 1993), p. 43.

dress the shortcomings of wooden pallets. They are sanitary, lightweight, and recyclable, and their life cycle costs are comparable to traditional wooden pallets. However, they do require greater initial investment, and because of that expense, the only way they can be utilized on an industrywide basis is through tightly controlled networks.

The grocery industry is testing alternative plastic pallet designs for durability and operational performance.[7] Pallet manufacturers can submit designs to independent laboratories for testing to assess whether specifications have been met. Table 14-2 compares the cost, durability, reparability, environmental impact, and typical applications of alternate pallet types.

Refrigerated Containers. Refrigerated pallets are introducing a new technology that integrates the environmental and unitization demands of specialty products. They are self-contained refrigerated shipping units comparable in size to a loaded shipping pallet. The self-contained refrigerated units can be loaded inside a regular dry van, which eliminates dependency on trucks with refrigerated power units and makes JIT delivery of perishable products more flexible. Refrigerated pallets can facilitate the efficient and effective flow of a full range of products that depend on controlled temperatures to extend shelf life and marketability, including fresh foods, flowers, chemicals, pharmaceuticals, confections, and frozen foods.

---

[7]Alison Paddock, "Making a Case for Plastic," *Grocery Distribution,* July/August 2000, p. 43.

TABLE 14-3   Principles of Materials Handling

- Equipment for handling and storage should be as standardized as possible.
- When in motion, the system should be designed to provide maximum continuous product flow.
- Investment should be in handling rather than stationary equipment.
- Handling equipment should be utilized to the maximum extent possible.
- In handling equipment selection the ratio of dead weight to payload should be minimized.
- Whenever practical, gravity flow should be incorporated in system design.

Materials Handling

Investments in materials handling technology and equipment offer the potential for substantially improved logistics productivity. Materials handling processes and technologies impact productivity by influencing personnel, space, and capital equipment requirements. Material handling is a key logistics activity that can't be overlooked. While the technical details of materials handling technology are extensive and beyond the scope of this text, the following section discusses basic handling considerations and alternative systems.

Basic Handling Considerations

Logistical materials handling is concentrated in and around the warehouse. A basic difference exists in the handling of bulk materials and master cartons. Bulk handling is a situation where protective packaging at the master carton level is unnecessary. However, specialized handling equipment is required for bulk unloading, such as for solids, fluids, pellets, or gaseous materials. Bulk handling of such material is generally completed using pipelines or conveyors. The following discussion focuses on the nonbulk handling using master cartons.

There are several basic principles to guide the selection of materials handling processes and technologies. The principles summarized in Table 14-3 offer an initial foundation for evaluating materials handling alternatives.

Handling systems can be classified as *mechanized, semiautomated, automated,* and *information-directed.* A combination of labor and handling equipment is utilized in mechanized systems to facilitate receiving, processing, and/or shipping. Generally, labor constitutes a high percentage of overall cost in mechanized handling. Automated systems, in contrast, attempt to minimize labor as much as possible by substituting equipment capital investment. When a combination of mechanical and automated systems is used to handle material, the system is referred to as semiautomated. An information-directed system applies computerization to sequence mechanized handling equipment and direct work effort. Mechanized handling systems are most common, but the use of semiautomated and automated systems is increasing. The main drawback to automated handling is lack of flexibility. One factor contributing to low logistical productivity is that information-directed handling has yet to achieve its full potential. This situation is predicted to dramatically change during the first decade of the 21st century.

Mechanized Systems

Mechanized systems employ a wide range of handling equipment. The types of equipment most commonly used are lift trucks, walkie-rider pallet trucks, towlines, tractor-trailer devices, conveyors, and carousels. Figure 14-4 provides examples of a variety of mechanized handling equipment.[8]

Lift Trucks

Lift trucks—also called forklifts—can move loads of master cartons both horizontally and vertically but are not limited to unit load handling. Skids or boxes may also be transported depending upon the nature of the product.

Many types of lift trucks are available. High-stacking trucks are capable of up to 40 feet of vertical movement. Palletless side-clamp versions are available for handling bulky product without pallets or slipsheets. Other lift truck variations are available for narrow aisle and side-loading operations. Particular attention to narrow-aisle lift trucks has increased in recent years, as warehouses seek to increase rack density and overall storage capacity. The lift truck is not economical for long-distance horizontal movement because of the high ratio of labor per unit of transfer; it is most effectively utilized in shipping and receiving and to place merchandise in high cube storage. The two most common power sources for lift trucks are propane gas and electricity.

Walkie-Rider Pallet Trucks

Walkie-rider pallet trucks provide a low-cost, effective method of general materials handling utility. Typical applications include loading and unloading of transportation equipment, order selection and accumulation, and shuttling loads over longer transportation distances throughout the warehouse. Walkie pallet trucks are widely used in grocery warehouses.

Towlines

Towlines consist of either in-floor or overhead-mounted cable or drag devices. They are utilized to provide continuous power to four-wheel trailers. The main advantage of a towline is continuous movement. However, such handling devices have far less flexibility than lift trucks. The most common application of towlines is for order selection. Order selectors place merchandise on four-wheel trailers that are then towed to the shipping dock. A number of automated decoupling devices are available to route trailers from the main towline to the shipping docks.

A point of debate is the relative merit of in-floor versus overhead towline installation. In-floor installation is costly to modify and difficult to maintain from a housekeeping viewpoint. Overhead installation is more flexible, but unless the warehouse floor is absolutely level, the line may jerk the front wheels of the trailers off the ground and risk product damage. The overhead line also represents a potential danger to fork truck operations.

Tow Tractor with Trailers

A tow tractor with trailer consists of a driver-guided power unit towing a number of individual four-wheel trailers that hold several unitized loads. The typical size of the trailers is 4×8 feet. The tow tractor with trailer, like the towline, is used to facilitate order selection. The main advantage of a tow tractor with trailers is flexibility. It is not as economical as the towline because it requires more labor.

---

[8]For a more detailed and timely summary of materials handling equipment alternatives, characteristics, and providers, see **www.manufacturingmarketplace/magazine/mmh/glossary/egtruck.htm.**

FIGURE 14-4

Mechanized handling equipment examples

Two-wheeled hand trucks come in three constructions: hardwood/steel, all steel, or aluminum/magnesium. Load capacities range up to 2000 lb. Special designs are available.

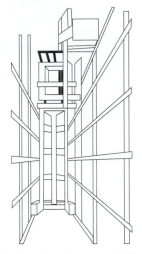

Outrigger rising-cab turret trucks lift the operator to the same height as the pallet. These trucks are for stacking pallets on both sides of very narrow aisles to 40-ft heights.

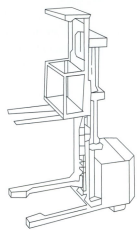

Orderpicker trucks place the operator on an elevating platform along with the forks. The operator picks items or cases from racks onto a pallet or shelf-type structure.

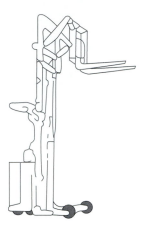

Reach trucks operate in narrow aisles, storing and retrieving pallets in racks. Some are equipped with a pantograph mechanism and can shelve pallets two-deep.

Balance-tilt floor trucks are highly maneuverable, even with long or bulky loads because the truck balances on the center wheels and on one or two smaller swivel casters.

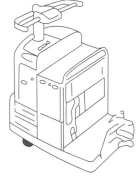

Tow tractors are straight-forward, operator-aboard, self-powered tractors for towing wagons or carts over long distances. Some can operate outdoors.

Shelf-type truck superstructures customize a nontilt platform truck to carry loose items and packages and make the truck useful for orderpicking.

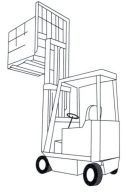

Counterbalanced lift trucks can be battery-powered or powered by LP, gas, or diesel engines. Three- or four-wheel models are available, with pneumatic or cushion tires.

Walkie pallet trucks are highly versatile low-lift pallet and/or skid handlers with load capacities from 3000 to 8000 lb. These trucks are very popular in grocery warehouses.

Pallet trucks or "pallet jacks" remain one of the basic unit-load handlers. Load capacities now reach 10,000 lb. Trucks can be customized with options such as skid adapters.

Burden carriers have large heavy-duty cargo platforms and a driver's compartment. They are excellent for long hauls, and most can be used indoors or outdoors.

Source: *Modern Materials Handling*, 47, no. 11, September 1992, pp. 21–22.

Conveyors

Conveyors are used widely in shipping and receiving operations and form the basic handling device for a number of order selection systems. Conveyors are classified according to power, gravity, and roller or belt movement.[9] In power systems, the conveyor is powered by a drive chain from either above or below. Considerable conveyor flexibility is sacrificed in such power configuration installations. Gravity and roller or belt systems permit the basic installation to be rearranged with minimum difficulty. Portable gravity-style roller conveyors are often used for loading and unloading and, in some cases, are transported on over-the-road trailers to assist in unloading vehicles. Conveyors are effective in that only the product is moved, eliminating the need for a movement unit to return.

Carousels

A carousel operates on a different concept than most other mechanized handling equipment. Rather than requiring the order selector to go to the inventory storage location, the carousel moves inventory to the order selector. A carousel consists of a series of bins mounted on an oval track or rack. There may be multiple track levels, allowing for very high-density carousel storage. The entire carousel rotates, moving the selection bin to a stationary operator. The typical carousel application is the selection of packages in pack, repack, and service parts. The rationale behind carousel systems is to shrink order selection labor requirements by reducing walking length and time. Carousels, particularly modern stackable or multitiered systems, also significantly reduce storage space requirements. Figure 14-5 provides examples of horizontal and vertical carousel storage and order picking systems. Some carousel systems also utilize computer-generated pick lists and computer-directed carousel rotation to further increase selection productivity. These systems are referred to as *paperless picking* because no paperwork exists to slow down employee efforts. A variation of the carousel system is movable racks. Such racks move horizontally to eliminate the permanent aisle between the racks. This system, often used in libraries, provides more storage density but reduces picking efficiency since the racks must be moved to access specific products.

The mechanized materials handling equipment discussed is representative of a wide range of alternatives. Most systems combine different handling devices. For example, lift trucks may be used for vertical movements while tow tractor with trailers and walkie-rider pallet trucks are the primary methods of horizontal transfer.

Semiautomated Systems

Mechanized handling is often supplemented by semiautomatic equipment. Typical equipment utilized in semiautomated handling includes automated guided vehicle systems, computerized sortation, robotics, and various forms of live racks.

Automated Guided Vehicle System

An AGVS can be used to replace mechanized tow tractors and trailers. The essential difference is that AGVSs are automatically routed and positioned without a driver.

AGVS equipment typically relies on an optical or magnetic guidance system. In the optical application directional lines are placed on the warehouse floor. The AGVS

---

[9]For a more detailed discussion of conveyor alternatives and characteristics, see David Maloney, "e-Conveyors," *Modern Materials Handling,* 55, no. 1 January 2000, pp. 49–53.

FIGURE 14-5

Examples of carousel materials handling systems

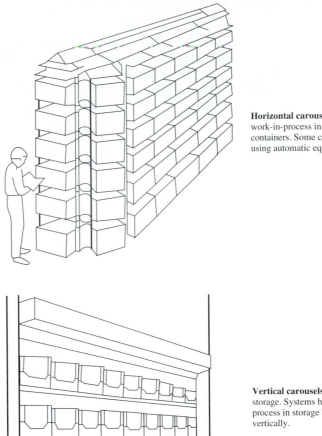

Horizontal carousels store small parts or work-in-process in tote boxes or other containers. Some carousels are self-loading, using automatic equipment for high efficiency.

Vertical carousels provide high-density storage. Systems hold small parts or work-in-process in storage bins on shelves that rotate vertically.

Source: **www.manufacturing.net/magazine/mmg/glossary/egstore.htm.**

is then guided by a light beam focused on the guidepath. Magnetic AGVSs follow an energized wire installed within the floor. The primary advantage of an AGVS is direct labor reduction and predetermined warehouse flow. Newer AGVSs use video and information technology to follow paths without the need for fixed tracks. Lower cost and particularly increased flexibility have enhanced the applicability of AGVSs for warehouse movements that are repetitive and frequent or are in very congested areas, as is illustrated in Industry Insight 14-1.

Sortation

Automated sortation devices are typically used in combination with conveyors. As products are selected in the warehouse and placed on a conveyor for movement to the shipping dock, they must be sorted to specific shipment loads. For example, inventory to satisfy multiple orders may be selected in batches, creating the need for sortation into individual shipments. In order for automated sortation systems to operate, the

INDUSTRY INSIGHT 14-1 AGVS EASES TRAFFIC AT THE HOME DEPOT

The home improvement business at The Home Depot (HD) Imports Distribution Center in Savannah, Georgia, has grown to an estimated $365 billion business. Estimates take into account total purchases of do-it-yourselfers and professional business customers, including construction tradespeople and building maintenance professionals.

Don Harrison, HD's public relations director, says, "We stock upward of 50,000 different kinds of building material, home improvement supplies, and home and garden products. The 1.4-million square foot distribution center services approximately 500 stores located in the eastern half of the U.S. Imported products range from ceiling fans and window blinds, to table saws and park benches. Containerized shipments from many countries in Europe and the Far East arrive by sea, at either the Port of Charleston or Savannah Harbor. Some items arrive by air freight."

Marc Schumacher, maintenance manager at the distribution center, says, "Material receiving, incoming product storage, and order picking activities are handled smoothly using conventional distribution strategy and techniques. It's at the shipping end of the supply chain where advanced automation tools are considered imperative to expedite the final distribution step—maintaining a steady stream of merchandise out the door and on its way to HD retail stores."

A seven-vehicle AGVS has simplified traffic patterns and coordinated individual AGV moves to remove potential for shipping floor gridlock. Each AGV can handle two full pallets at a time.

The "main street" for AGV travel is 1/3 mile long. Located on one side are six pallet pickup zones, each having room for two pallets. On the other side, 100 shipping lanes await delivery of full pallet loads.

HD's TRACE (Traffic Routing AGV Command Executive) system assigns an available AGV to a request for pallet movement, commands the AGV to perform proper sequences of movement to carry out the request, monitors the status of the AGV throughout the process, and prevents vehicles from colliding.

The materials handling area is compartmentalized: compartment A is for full pallets, compartment B is for floor stack of items too big for palletizing, and compartment C is for partial mixed load pallets.

As pallets exit a main conveyor, they are scanned by a stationary bar code scanner, then advance to the AGV pickup zone. A vehicle is assigned to pick up the pallets, pickup is confirmed, and the vehicle is sent to either the shipping lane or the partial pallet drop-off location.

Schumacher says, "The AGV system is designed to shuttle full pallets from pick conveyor to shipping lanes. Other physical moves—sending partial pallets to staging zones for manual handling later, and diverting problematical palletloads out of the handling system—are important to the operation.

"The TRACE system performs secondary tasks such as logging for historical and reporting purposes, diagnostic functions, and reporting system and AGV malfunctions if they occur. All system maintenance and programming alterations can be performed by our staff. The time and expense saved by HD personnel is obvious."

Source: Anonymous, "AGVS Ease Traffic at Home Depot," *Material Handling Management,* April 2000, p. 97.

---

master cartons must have distinguishing identification.[10] Frequently, bar codes are read by optical scanning devices, which in turn automatically route product to the desired location. Most sortation controllers can be programmed to permit customized flow and decision logic to meet changing requirements.

---

[10]For a detailed discussion of bar coding technologies and their capabilities typically used in the warehouse, see Norm Weiland, "On-Demand Printing of Barcode Symbols," *Parcel Shipping & Distribution,* September 1999, pp. 12–15.

Automated sortation provides two primary benefits. The first is an obvious reduction in labor. The second is a significant increase in speed and accuracy. High-speed sortation systems, such as those used by United Parcel Service, can sort and align packages at rates exceeding one per second.

Robotics

The robot is a humanlike machine that can be programmed to perform one or a series of functions. The appeal of robotics lies in the ability to program functionality based on expert systems using decision logic to direct the handling process. The popularity of robotics resulted from their widespread adoption in the automotive industry during the early 1980s in an effort to automate select manual tasks. However, a warehouse provides a far different challenge to robotics than found in a typical manufacturing plant. In warehousing, the goal is to efficiently accumulate the unique inventory requirements of a customer's order. Thus, requirements can vary extensively from one order to the next, resulting in far less routine than is typical of manufacturing.

The primary use of robotics in warehousing is to build and break down unit loads. In the breakdown process, the robot is programmed to recognize stacking patterns on unitized loads and place products in the desired position on a conveyor belt. The use of robots to build unit loads is essentially the reverse of breakdown. Another use of robotics in warehousing occurs in environments where it is difficult for humans to function. Examples include materials handling in high noise areas, hazardous materials, and extreme temperature operations, such as frozen foods.

Significant potential exists to use robots in a mechanized warehouse to perform select functions. The capability to incorporate artificial intelligence, in addition to their speed, dependability, and accuracy, makes robotics an attractive alternative to traditional manual handling in situations that are highly repetitive or very unfriendly to humans.

Live Racks

A device commonly used to reduce manual labor in warehouses is storage rack design in which product automatically flows to the desired selection position. The typical live rack contains roller conveyors and is constructed for rear loading. The rear of the rack is elevated higher than the front, causing a gravity flow forward. When cartons or unit loads are removed from the front, all other cartons or loads in that specific rack flow forward.

The use of the live rack reduces the need to use lift trucks to transfer unit loads. A significant advantage of live rack storage is the automatic rotation of product that results from rear loading. Rear loading facilitates **first-in, first-out (FIFO)** inventory management. Applications of gravity flow racks are varied. For example, live racks are utilized to sequence fresh bread on pallets for shipping for bakery manufacturers. Flow-rack staging is also used for sequencing automotive seats in JIT systems.

Automated Systems

For several decades the concept of automated handling has offered great potential and limited accomplishment. Initial automated handling efforts focused on master carton order selection systems. Recently, emphasis has shifted to automated high-rise storage and retrieval systems.

Potential to Automate

The appeal of automation is that it substitutes capital equipment for labor. In addition to requiring less direct labor, an automated system operates faster and more accurately than its mechanized counterpart. Its shortcomings are the high capital investment, development complexity, and inflexibility.

To date, most automated systems have been designed and constructed for specific applications. The six guidelines previously noted for selection of mechanized handling systems are not applicable to automated systems. For example, storage equipment in an automated system is an integral part of the handling capability and can represent as much as 50 percent of the total investment. The ratio of dead weight to payload has little relevance when handling is automated.

Although computers play an important part in all handling systems, they are essential in automated systems. The computer controls the automated selection equipment and interfaces with the WMS. A major disadvantage of automation is its dependency on computer and communication networks. To reduce such dependency, newer automated systems are being linked to the Internet and using standard browsers as the network for controlling warehouse operations. Automated warehouses require tight integration between the WMS and the material handling operating systems.

Order Selection Systems

Initially, automation was applied to master carton selection or order assembly in the warehouse. Because of high labor intensity in order selection, the basic objective was to integrate mechanized and automated handling into a total system that offered both high productivity and accuracy using minimal labor.

The general process begins with an automated selection device preloaded with product. The device itself consists of a series of flow racks stacked vertically. Merchandise is loaded from the rear and permitted to flow forward in the live rack on gravity conveyors until stopped by a rack door. Between or down the middle of the racks, power conveyors create a merchandise flow line, with several flow lines positioned above each other, one to service each level of rack doors.

Upon receipt of an order, the warehouse control system generates sequenced instructions to trip the rack doors and allow merchandise, as required, to flow forward onto the powered conveyors. The conveyors in turn transport merchandise to an order packing area for placement in shipment containers and transfer to the staging area. Product is often selected and loaded sequentially so it can be unloaded in the sequence desired by the customer.

When compared to modern automation, these initial attempts at automated package handling are highly inefficient. A great deal of labor is required to perform merchandise loading into the racks, and the automated selection equipment is expensive. Applications are limited to merchandise of extremely high value, with common or standardized master carton size, or situations where working conditions justify such investment. For example, these initial systems were widely tested for frozen food order selection.

Substantial advancements have been made in automated selection of case goods. The handling of fast-moving products in master cartons can be fully automated from the point of merchandise receipt to placement in over-the-road trailers. Such systems use an integrated network of power and gravity conveyors linking power-motivated live storage. The entire process is computer controlled coupled with the order and warehouse management system. Upon arrival, merchandise is automatically routed to the live storage position and inventory records are updated. When orders are received, merchandise is precubed to package or vehicle size and scheduled for selection. At the appropriate time, all merchandise is selected in loading sequence and automatically transported by conveyor to the loading dock. In some situations, the first manual handling of the merchandise within the warehouse occurs when it is stacked into the outbound transport vehicle.

The solution of the input/output interface problem and the development of sophisticated control systems continues to have the potential to achieve highly effective and efficient package handling. The major problems associated with order selection system automation remain reliability and flexibility. While the information systems and the necessary power systems are generally reliable, failures in either will result in complete operational shutdowns, at one or multiple sites. Highly automated systems are generally not flexible due to required hardware/control system integration, so it is difficult to be responsive to changes in product or market requirements.

Automated Storage/Retrieval Systems

An automated unit-load handling system, or **Automated Storage and Retrieval System (AS/RS),** that uses high-rise storage is a popular form of automation. Figure 14-6 illustrates the concept of a high-rise AS/RS. AS/RSs are particularly appropriate for nonergonomic items such as heavy boxes or those products in freezer environments. The high-rise concept of handling is typically automated from receiving to shipping. The four primary AS/RS components include storage racks, storage and retrieval equipment, input/output system, and control system.

The name high-rise derives from the physical appearance of the storage rack. The rack is structured steel vertical storage, which can be as high as 120 feet. The typical stacking height of palletized cartons in a mechanized handling system is 20 feet, so the potential of high-rise storage is clear.

The typical high-rise facility consists of rows of storage racks. The rows of racks are separated by aisles ranging from 120 to over 800 feet in length. Primary storage and retrieval activities occur within these aisles. A storage and retrieval crane travels up and down the aisle alternatively storing and selecting product. A variety of storage and retrieval equipment is available. Most machines require guidance at the top and bottom to provide the vertical stability necessary for high-speed horizontal movement and vertical hoisting. Horizontal speeds range from 300 to 400 feet per minute (fpm) with hoisting speeds of up to 100 fpm or more.

The initial function of the storage and retrieval equipment is to reach the desired storage location rapidly. A second function is to deposit or retract merchandise. For the most part, load deposit and retraction are achieved by shuttle tables, which can enter and exit from the rack at speeds up to 100 fpm. Since the shuttle table moves only a few feet, it must accelerate and stop rapidly.

The storage and retrieval machine is essentially a combined lift truck and pallet holder built into a movable crane. The machine moves up and down the aisle to insert or remove a unit load from a storage bin. When the AS/RS operates with unit loads, the process is typically automated. However, the AS/RS often incorporates manual picking when the system selects cases or master cartons. In some installations, the storage and retrieval machine is positioned to service different aisles by transfer cars. Numerous transfer arrangements and layouts are available. Transfer units may be *dedicated* or *nondedicated.* The dedicated transfer car is always stationed at the end of the aisle in which the storage and retrieval equipment is working. The nondedicated transfer car works a number of aisles and retrieval machines on a scheduled basis to achieve maximum equipment utilization. The decision as to whether to include aisle-to-aisle transfer in a high-rise storage system rests with the economics of throughput rate and number of aisles included in the overall system.

FIGURE 14-6

High-rise warehouse facility with AS/RS. The size of Canadian Tire's new AS/RS is, to put it simply, hard to comprehend. To begin with, the rack-supported section of the center that houses it measures 234 feet × 657 feet and reaches an incredible 108 feet into the air. The rack structure itself contains 78,400 pallet storage positions, with each palletized load weighing up to 2500 lb. That translates into roughly 3.3 million cubic feet of product storage. The structure features an unusual double-deep, three-post design with 39,200 load openings. The structure is intersected by 10 aisles; vertically, it is divided into 14 levels.

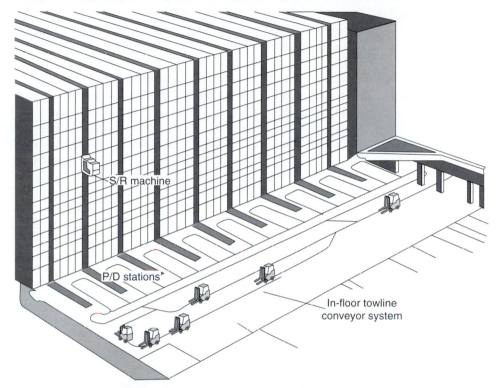

Source: Les Gould, "Canadian Tire's 1.1 Million-Sq-Ft Formula for Success," *Modern Materials Handling* 47, no. 8 (July 1992), p. 37.

The input/output system in high-rise storage is concerned with moving loads to and from the rack area. Two types of movement are involved. First, loads must be transported from receiving docks or production lines to the storage area. Second, within the immediate peripheral area of the racks, loads must be positioned for entry or exit. The greatest potential handling problem is in the peripheral area. A common practice assigns separate stations for pickup and removal capable of staging an adequate supply of loads to each aisle to fully utilize the storage and retrieval equipment. For maximum input/output performance, the normal procedure requires different stations for transfer of inbound and outbound loads assigned to the same aisle. The pickup and discharge (P/D) stations are linked to the handling systems that transfer merchandise to and from the high-rise storage area. The control system in high-rise storage is similar to the automated order selection systems described earlier. In addition to scheduling arrivals and location assignments, the control system handles inventory control and stock rotation. The control system also tracks product location within the AS/RS, storage bin utilization, and crane operations. In the case of high-rise storage, system reliability and integrity are critical to achieving productivity and maximum equipment utilization.

In manufacturing application, product flowing from production is automatically formed into unit loads. The unit load is then transported to the high-rise storage area by power conveyor. When the load arrives, it is assigned to a storage bin and transferred by power conveyor to the appropriate pickup station. At this point, the storage and retrieval equipment takes over and moves the unit load to its planned storage location. When orders are received, the control system directs the retrieval of specified unit loads. From the outbound delivery station, the unit load flows by power and gravity conveyor to the appropriate shipping dock. While retrieval and outbound delivery are being accomplished, all paperwork necessary to initiate product shipment is completed. One firm replaced 13 distribution centers across the United States with a single centralized DC located next to its plant. The new DC employed AS/RS along with a refined inventory management strategy to provide the higher service levels that more sophisticated customers are demanding. The inventory management strategy stocked only the fast-moving items while the slow-moving items were supplied on an MTO basis. The consolidation reduced facility cost while substantially improving inventory turns and increased line fill rate from 74 to 97 percent. Thus, the AS/RS and new inventory management strategy had immediate impact on firm performance and the service provided to other supply chain members.[11]

Another innovative application of AS/RS technology is found in the automotive industry. In Toledo, Ohio, Chrysler manufactures vehicle bodies for both pickup trucks and jeeps at one plant. As manufacturing is completed, two SR machines pick up each body in sequence for loading canvas-sided over-the-road trailers to transport the vehicle bodies to a final assembly plant 4 miles away. At the second plant, two SR machines are used to coordinate JIT staging and delivery of the vehicle bodies to the appropriate assembly lines. As another example, Industry Insight 14-2 shows how IBM upgraded its 15-year-old AS/RS system to meet current requirements.

These examples illustrate AS/RS applications in a variety of industries. The systems all seek to increase materials handling productivity by providing maximum storage density per square foot of floor space and to minimize direct labor required in handling. The highly controlled nature of an AS/RS achieves reliable pilferage-free and damage-free handling with extremely accurate control. However, high-rise AS/RS are generally better as storage than as handling devices, thus reducing their appeal in situations where fast inventory turns are more important than inexpensive storage.

Information-Directed Systems

The concept of information-directed handling is relatively new and the subject of a great deal of research and development. The concept is appealing because it combines the control typical of automated handling with the flexibility of mechanized systems. Information-directed systems use mechanized handling controlled by information technology. Two common examples of information-directed materials handling systems are RF-controlled equipment and light-directed operations.

RF-Controlled Handling Equipment
Radio Frequency Data Communications (RFDC)-controlled handling equipment is standard mechanized materials handling equipment coordinated by information technology to provide operator directions and control in real time. Typical RF systems uti-

[11]Anonymous, "How Aeroquip Slashed Inventory 90% Yet Fills, Ships Order in Hours," *Modern Materials Handling* 53, no. 10 (November 1998), p. A6–7.

INDUSTRY INSIGHT 14-2 AS/RS UPGRADE PUTS BIG BLUE IN THE BLACK

After more than 16 years of continuous service, the AS/RS at IBM's Charlotte, North Carolina, manufacturing facility was showing extensive wear and tear. Much of the existing control system was quickly becoming obsolete. Parts were either proprietary or very difficult to find. Plus, there were Y2K problems. Safety was also an issue, as cracks had appeared in the rails used to guide the system's Storage and Retrieval Machines (S/RMs).

IBM faced either the purchase of a new system or a total upgrade to its existing AS/RS, which serves as the primary warehousing system for raw materials used in production of PCs and point-of-sale terminals. About one-fifth of the AS/RS capacity is also used for finished goods. After investigating the alternatives, it was determined that a true systems upgrade would provide substantial savings—about one-tenth the estimated cost of a new system.

Since completing the upgrade, the AS/RS' operating costs have been greatly reduced. Productivity has increased, storage density is higher, and better tracking systems have been implemented. The system can now handle 50 percent more throughput at 220 moves an hour, and up-time is now 98 percent.

Today, the AS/RS houses more than 28,000 SKUs in its 10 80-foot high, 500-foot long aisles. An S/RM is dedicated to each aisle, handling both receiving and picking functions.

The entire AS/RS system is controlled by a series of PCs networked to an RS/6000 computer. The mainframe decides which products are needed for the day's manufacturing and builds a list of materials. An S/RM is instructed to travel to an individual location where parts are stored. Photo eyes direct the S/RM to the exact location of the desired SKU, and an extractor removes the load. The SR/M then delivers the part to a pickup/deposit station at the front of the aisle, placing the pallet on a slipsheet. A conveyor delivers the unit to the manufacturing workstation.

Previously, controllers for the conveyor that replenishes the front of the AS/RS and the conveyor that outputs to production worked independently and required separate control rooms. After the upgrade, both operate from the same PLCs, eliminating one control room and the need for operators in two locations. Monitoring and reporting functions have also been greatly improved.

Installing the new AS/RS system was not an easy task. As an essential component of the plant's production process, the AS/RS needed to continue to store and retrieve inventory throughout the entire retrofit process. The crew had to meet a tight schedule to perform that day's installation work, do required testing and verification, and then be ready to switch it all back over for full production the next day.

The upgrade on the S/RM was performed aisle by aisle, with the first aisle taking 7 days for its upgrade and 3 days each for the remaining nine aisles.

All 4800 feet of floor rails that guide the S/RMs were also replaced with new thermite-welded epoxy-grouted rails designed to prevent deterioration.

The original safety concerns have now vanished. Gone too are obsolete and proprietary parts, as all components are state-of-the-art and Y2K compliant and readily available from a variety of suppliers.

Source: David Maloney, "AS/RS Upgrade Puts Big Blue in the Black," *Modern Materials Handling,* 54, no. 4 (April 1999), pp. 40–41.

---

lize lift trucks. However, the basic use of RFDC to instruct movement of lift trucks is expanded in an information-directed application to become a highly integrated materials handling system. In the layout and design, the warehouse facility is essentially the same as any mechanized facility. The difference is that all lift truck movements are directed and monitored by some combination of computer mounted on the lift truck, handheld computer, or voice-activated communication. The real time information interchange is designed to achieve flexibility and better utilization.

The main advantage of RF is to improve speed and flexibility of lift truck operations. Instead of following handwritten instructions or computer listings generated in batches, drivers receive work assignments through either handheld or vehicle-mounted RF terminals. Use of RF technology provides real time communication to central data processing systems. In operation, the WMS in conjunction with the operations control computer plans and initiates all movements, communicates the requirements to the material handlers, and tracks the completion of all tasks. Decision support systems analyze all movement requirements to assign equipment in such a way that direct movement is maximized and deadhead movement is minimized. Less exotic applications use computer-generated movement printouts picked up at printer locations throughout the warehouse. Information-directed handling offers great potential because selected benefits of automation can be achieved without substantial capital investment. Information-directed systems can also substantially increase productivity by tracking lift truck performance, thereby allowing compensation to be based on achievement level. The main drawback of information-directed handling is flexibility of work assignment. As a specific lift truck proceeds during a work period, it may be involved in loading or unloading several different vehicles, selecting items for many orders, and completing several nonrelated handling assignments. The wide variety of work assignments increases the complexity of work direction and can decrease performance accountability. This complexity increases the demands placed on driver capabilities.

Industry Insight 14-3 illustrates how the Pioneer Hi-Bred International Company uses technology to direct lift truck operations. Voice-over-IP (Internet Protocol) systems use RF networks to allow individuals on a shop or warehouse floor to talk directly with others in the distribution center about the status of a shipment or the need to supplement workers to complete an assignment. The voice-over-IP technology can allow the material handler to interface with the WMS, the Internet, and even with a phone.[12]

Pick-to-Light Systems

Pick to light, a technology using a variation of a carousel system, is also becoming increasingly common. In these systems, order selectors pick designated items directly into cartons or onto conveyors from *lighted* carousel locations or storage bins. A series of lights or a *light tree* in front of each pick location indicates the number of items to pick from each location. The light system may also be used to facilitate a carton progression. In systems where an item is picked to fill multiple orders, *sortbars* show the order selector how many of the selected items are needed in each carton to meet fulfillment needs of individual orders. A variation of the pick-to-light system is **put-to-light,** where order selectors place product in the *lighted* containers. Each container or tote is assigned to a specific order or customer, so the light is telling which customers are to receive a specific product.

Table 14-4 provides general guidelines and managerial considerations across a range of storage and handling alternatives. The primary contrast is between the installation and operational costs related to automated and mechanized alternatives.

Special Handling Considerations

The primary mission of materials handling is to facilitate merchandise flow in an orderly and efficient manner from manufacturer to point of sale. This section identifies and discusses special considerations important to selection and operation of materials handling equipment.

---

[12]Robert Preston, "Value-Oriented Companies Place Bets on Supply Chain," *Internetweek,* February 19, 2001. Issue 849.

INDUSTRY INSIGHT 14-3 HANDS-FREE DATA COLLECTION

Pioneer Hi-Bred International, located in Durant, Iowa, is the world's largest seed company. It produces 600 genetic products that represent thousands of SKUs.

As well as being a leader in agricultural genetics and seed production, Pioneer has a reputation for experimenting with warehouse technologies to support its operations. In recent years, as the number of specialized products increased, the company decided to explore some of the newer warehouse technologies to increase efficiency. Several years ago, Pioneer replaced its manual inventory tracking methods with a customized WMS that allowed personnel to collect data with handheld terminals. However, warehouse personnel were not comfortable with the need to key in data. Management initially considered bar codes and RF identification tags to eliminate the need for a keyboard, but ultimately it determined that either option would require too many major systems changes.

In late 1993, Pioneer began testing a "handsfree" mobile terminal-data collection system that utilized voice recognition technology at one of its seed production locations. "We were looking for a system we could work into an existing warehouse, and we felt that our way into keyless data collection might be with voice recognition systems," explains Mike Doty, Pioneer's information systems manager. How does the system work? It consists of a headset equipped with a microphone, speaker, and a miniature head-mounted display terminal that measures 1.2×1.3 inches. Although the display terminal is very tiny, to the mind it looks like a full-screen computer monitor. Voice is used to collect data and send the information via RF link to a host computer. The system directs a warehouse order selector to each picking location by displaying one line item at a time. As the order selector retrieves an item, he/she reads aloud the storage location. The system verifies that the right pallet of merchandise has been selected by repeating the information back to the operator and flashing it on the display terminal.

The rationale for the system was to give the warehouse forklift operators the ability to collect inventory data in real time while simultaneously providing the mobility to perform routine warehouse activities, such as storing and selecting product, building mixed pallet loads for shipping, and processing returns. As these productivity objectives have been achieved while maintaining warehouse safety standards, the major savings have been derived from the improved inventory tracking capability. Specifically, the tracking allows random storage of pallets in bulk stacking areas, improving storage efficiency by over 20 percent. "We've streamlined shipping, and are moving a lot more material with a lot less people," says Joe Kaufman, plant manager. Considering that part of the warehouse is refrigerated, the savings have produced an impressive 200 percent return on investment.

Pioneer is so satisfied with the experimental technology that it is preparing to test out the system at some of its more complex warehouses.

Source: Nancy Hitchcock, "Hands-Free Data Collection Blazes New Trail at Pioneer," *Modern Material Handling,* 48, no. 12, October 1993, pp. 46–48.

E-Fulfillment

Satisfaction of Internet fulfillment places some special demands on a firm's warehousing and materials handling. Both e-tailers and brick-and-mortar retailers moving into the e-tail environment have been forced to adapt their processes to meet the specific needs of this marketplace. Four specific considerations that influence warehousing and materials handling in an e-fulfillment environment are order volume, products, people, and tracking.[13] First, to serve end consumers, an e-fulfillment facility typically must process a large number of very small orders. This means that it is difficult to achieve any substantial economies of scale for picking operations. Second, e-fulfillment facilities must

---

[13]Amy Hardgrove, "e-Fulfillment: The Last Step in the e-tail Process," *Grocery Distribution,* July/August 2000, pp. 27–30.

TABLE 14-4   **Storage Guidelines for the Warehouse**

Equipment	Type of Materials	Benefits	Other Considerations
Manual			
Racking:			
Conventional pallet rack	Pallet loads	Good storage density, good product security	Storage density increased further by storing loads two deep
Drive-in racks	Pallet loads	Fork trucks can access loads, good storage density	Fork truck access is from one direction only
Drive-through racks	Pallet loads	Same as above	Fork truck access is from two directions
High-rise racks	Pallet loads	Very high storage density	Often used in AS/RS and may offer tax advantages when used in rack-supported building
Cantilever racks	Long loads or rolls	Designed to store difficult shapes	Each different SKU can be stored on a separate shelf
Pallet stacking frames	Odd-shaped or crushable parts	Allow otherwise unstackable loads to be stacked, saving floor space	Can be disassembled when not in use
Stacking racks	Odd-shaped or crushable parts	Same as above	Can be stacked flat when not in use
Gravity-flow racks	Unit loads	High density storage, gravity moves loads	FIFO or LIFO flow of loads
Shelving	Small, loose loads and cases	Inexpensive	Can be combined with drawers for flexibility
Drawers	Small parts and tools	All parts are easily accessed, good security	Can be compartmentalized for many SKUs
Mobile Racking or Shelving	Pallet loads, loose materials, and cases	Can reduce required floor space by half	Come equipped with safety devices
Automated			
Unit-Load AS/RS	Pallet loads and a wide variety of sizes and shapes	Very high storage density, computer-controlled	May offer tax advantages when rack-supported
Car-in-Lane	Pallet loads, other unit loads	High storage density	Best used where there are large quantities of only a few SKUs
Miniload AS/RS	Small parts	High storage density, computer-controlled	For flexibility, can be installed in several different configurations
Horizontal Carousels	Small parts	Easy access to parts, relatively inexpensive	Can be stacked on top of each other
Vertical Carousels	Small parts and tools	High storage density	Can serve dual role as storage and delivery system in multifloor facilities
Man-Ride Machines	Small parts	Very flexible	Can be used with high-rise shelving or modular drawers

Source: "Storage Equipment for the Warehouse," *Modern Materials Handling: 1985 Warehousing Guidebook 40,* Vol. 4 (Spring 1985), p. 53.

generally deal with a wide range of product, which translates to large inventories and the use of flow-through practices to consolidate orders for shipment. Firms electing to consolidate orders must have the capability to effectively receive and merge a large number of very small orders rapidly. Third, an e-fulfillment facility is people-intensive because the required flexibility in picking reduces order selection to manual or limited application of pick-to-light technology. In many cases, e-fulfillment operations are seasonal, increasing the need for ongoing training for new and seasonal employees. Fourth, increased consumer expectations regarding tracking require that many activities within the warehouse and interfacing with the carrier be electronically scanned and tracked. Despite rapid growth in e-tailing, many firms are still trying to resolve the warehousing and materials handling processes most appropriate to support this activity. In many cases, these e-tailers are outsourcing fulfillment to third-party logistics firms. In any case, the e-tailing environment will continue to place increasing demands on a more timely, responsive, and integrated warehouse and materials handling operation.

Environmental Concerns

There is increased concern regarding environment impact of warehouse operations. In particular, attention has been directed to the impact of materials handling equipment such as lift trucks. Pollution controls on new spark-ignited motors for lift trucks are similar to automobile engines, making them more efficient, but more complicated to maintain.[14] There is also increasing interest regarding the handling and disposal of hazardous materials used or stored in warehouse operations. Firms have to ensure that such materials are disposed of properly to avoid pollution liability.

Regulatory Environment

The distribution warehouse is one of the most labor-intensive operations for most firms. It is also one of the most dangerous as approximately 100 deaths and 95,000 injuries occur annually.[15] To reduce these numbers OSHA is extending its regulatory influence over warehouse operations and technology. In March 1999, OSHA established the Powered Industrial Truck Operator Training (PITOT) regulation requiring the training and reevaluation of all lift truck drivers. Drivers failing evaluation and those involved in accidents must undergo refresher training. Another evolving regulation focuses on lift and angle weight. Many of the injuries identified above are back and spinal injuries caused by improper lifting of master cartons or of unitizing equipment. OSHA now places limits on the weight an individual can lift, the angle of lift, and the number of repetitive actions. The recommended weight is calculated starting at 51 pounds and subtracting for factors relating to how far, how much, and how many. For most repetitive materials handling jobs, the approved weight limits range from 20 to 30 pounds. A third OSHA focus is warehouse cleanliness, particularly for facilities dealing with food and pharmaceuticals. Floors and work areas must be clean to inhibit rodents and to guarantee worker safety from slippage or tripping. Designing warehouse operations to consider these limits is critical since fines can be substantial and legal liability can result in excessive judgments.

Returns Processing

For a variety of reasons, merchandise may be recalled by or returned to a manufacturer. This is particularly true in an e-tailing environment where up to 30 percent of orders are returned. Normally such reverse logistics is not of sufficient quantity or regularity to justify unitized movement, so the only convenient method for processing reverse flows of merchandise is manual handling. To the degree practical, materials handling design should consider the cost and service impact of reverse logistics. Such

---

[14]Tom Feare, "It's Not Easy Being Green," *Modern Materials Handling* 55, no. 4 (April 1, 2000), pp. 45–49.

[15]Alison Paddock, "Operator Training: Setting the Goals," *Grocery Distribution,* July/August 2000, p. 34.

flows often involve pallets, cartons, and packaging materials in addition to damaged, dated, or excess merchandise. Handling and overall logistical systems design in many industries will require the ability to handle two-way movement efficiently.[16] Many firms are choosing to have returns processed by a third-party service provider to separate flows and reduce the chance for error or contamination.

Summary

Packaging has a significant impact on the cost and productivity of logistics. Purchasing of packaging materials, packaging operations, and the subsequent need for material disposal represent the most obvious costs of packaging. Packaging affects the cost of every logistical activity. Inventory control depends upon the accuracy of manual or automatic identification systems keyed by product packaging. Order selection speed, accuracy, and efficiency are influenced by package identification, configuration, and handling ease. Handling cost depends upon unitization capability and techniques. Transportation and storage costs are driven by package size and density. Customer service depends upon packaging to achieve quality control during distribution, to provide customer education and convenience, and to comply with environmental regulations. The concept of packaging postponement to achieve strategic flexibility is particularly important given the increasing length and complexity of global supply chains and the costs of locating new facilities.

High-performance materials handling is a key to warehouse productivity for several important reasons. First, a significant number of labor hours are devoted to materials handling. Second, materials handling capabilities limit the direct benefits that can be gained by improved information technology. While computerization has introduced new technologies and capabilities, the preponderance of materials handling involves labor. Third, until recently, materials handling has not been managed on an integrated basis with other logistical activities, nor has it received a great deal of senior management attention. Finally, automation technology capable of reducing materials handling labor is only now beginning to reach full potential. However, early indications are that the downside of such automation is reduced operating flexibility.

Although discussed separately, packaging, containerization, and materials handling represent integral parts of the logistical operating system. All three must be considered when designing an integrated supply chain.

A number of integrated shipping programs between manufacturing concerns and customers have been successfully implemented. The impetus for such programs is to integrate material handling capability, transportation, warehousing, inventory policy, and communications into the logistics systems of as many supply chain partners as possible to minimize handling and communication confusion during the exchange of merchandise. To the degree that duplication and misunderstanding can be reduced, cost savings are possible for both the manufacturer and the customer.

Standardization of unit load platforms, bar coding, and instruction formats can significantly enhance supply chain integration. While there is agreement regarding the goal, the process is not without pitfalls as all participants must agree to and implement common technologies with common interpretations.

---

[16]For a more detailed discussion of returns processing, see Anonymous, "Return to Sender," *Modern Materials Handling* 55, no. 6 (May 15, 2000), pp. 64–65.

Challenge Questions

1. Provide an illustration that highlights the differences between consumer and industrial packaging.
2. What is the primary purpose of bar coding in packaging? Is the role of bar coding different in materials handling?
3. Discuss the differences between rigid and nonrigid containers. Discuss the role of load securing in unitization.
4. What benefits do flexible unit-load materials have in contrast to rigid containers? How do return or reverse logistics considerations impact the two approaches?
5. What trade-offs are involved in the use of returnable racks?
6. In terms of basic materials handling, what is the role of a unit load?
7. Until recently, why have automated handling systems failed to meet their expected potential? What changed to encourage automation in the 1980s?
8. Compare and contrast order selection and unit load automation.
9. What is the logic of a "live rack"?
10. What type of products and logistics applications are most suitable to AS/RS handling?

PROBLEM SET 2 OPERATIONS

1. Mr. Stan Busfield, distribution center manager for Hogan Kitchenwares, must determine when to resupply his stock of spatulas. The DC experiences a daily demand of 400 spatulas. The average length of the performance cycle for spatulas is 14 days. Mr. Busfield requires that 500 spatulas be retained as safety stock to deal with demand uncertainty.
   a. Use simple reorder point logic to determine the order quantity for spatulas.
   b. Based on your answer to part (a), find Mr. Busfield's average inventory level of spatulas.

2. Mr. Busfield recently completed a course in logistics management and now realizes that there are significant costs associated with ordering and maintaining inventory at his distribution center. Mr. Busfield has learned that the EOQ is the replenishment logic that minimizes these costs. In an effort to find the EOQ for measuring cups, Mr. Busfield has gathered relevant data. Mr. Busfield expects to sell 44,000 measuring cups this year. Hogan acquires the measuring cups for 75 cents each from Shatter Industries. Shatter charges $8 for processing each order. In addition, Mr. Busfield estimates his company's inventory carrying cost to be 12 percent annually.
   a. Find Mr. Busfield's EOQ for measuring cups. Assume that Mr. Busfield accepts ownership of products upon arrival at his DC.
   b. Now assume Mr. Busfield must arrange for inbound transportation of the measuring cups since Hogan accepts ownership of products at the supplier's shipping point. Quantities of fewer than 4000 measuring cups cost 5 cents per unit to ship. Quantities of 4000 and above cost 4 cents per unit to ship. Determine the difference in total costs associated with an EOQ of 4000 units and the EOQ level found in part (a) when transportation costs must be considered.
   c. Given the information above and the low cost EOQ alternative determined in part (b), use period-order-quantity logic to determine the number of orders Hogan would place each year for measuring cups and the time interval between orders.

3. Mr. Dave Jones manages the warehouse inventory for Athleticks, a distributor of sports watches. From his experience, Mr. Jones knows that the PR-5 jogging watch has an average daily demand of 100 units and a performance cycle of 8 days. Mr. Jones requires no buffer stock at this time.

a. Assume Mr. Jones perpetually reviews inventory levels. Find the reorder point for the PR-5 jogging watch.

b. Find the average inventory level of the PR-5 watch.

c. How might the reorder point change if Mr. Jones reviews inventory once each week? Find the reorder point under these conditions.

d. Find the average inventory level of the PR-5 watch under this periodic review.

4. Mr. John Estes oversees the distribution of Tastee Snacks products from the plant warehouse to its two distribution centers in the United States. The plant warehouse currently has 42,000 units of the company's most popular product, Chocolate Chewies. Mr. Estes retains 7000 units of the product at the warehouse as a buffer. The Cincinnati DC has an inventory of 12,500 units and daily requirements of 2500 units. The Phoenix DC has an inventory of 6000 units and daily requirements of 2000 units.

a. Determine the common days' supply of Chocolate Chewies at each DC.

b. Given the above information and your answer to part (a), use fair share allocation logic to determine the number of Chocolate Chewies to be allocated to each DC.

5. Stay Safe International manufactures industrial safety equipment at its plant in Evansville, Indiana. The company has initiated DRP to coordinate finished goods distribution from the plant to DCs in Dallas, Texas, and Lexington, Virginia.

a. Given the accompanying information regarding hardhats, complete the DRP schedule for the warehouse and each DC.

Dallas Distribution Center

On-hand balance: 220   *Performance cycle:* 1 week
Safety stock: 80   *Order quantity:* 200

	Past due	Week					
		1	2	3	4	5	6
Gross requirements		60	70	80	85	90	80
Scheduled receipts							
Projected on-hand							
Planned orders							

DC1

Lexington Distribution Center

On-hand balance: 420   *Performance cycle:* 2 weeks
Safety stock: 100   *Order quantity:* 400

	Past due	Week					
		1	2	3	4	5	6
Gross requirements		100	115	120	125	140	125
Scheduled receipts							
Projected on-hand							
Planned orders							

DC2

Evansville Warehouse

On-hand balance: 900   *Lead time:* 2 weeks
Safety stock: 250   *Order quantity:* 650

	Past due	Week					
		1	2	3	4	5	6
Gross requirements	0						
Scheduled receipts							
Projected on-hand							
Planned orders							
Master sched.-rept.							
Master sched.-start							

b. Suppose that, without warning, no more than 500 units can be distributed from the warehouse to the DCs on a given week due to a manufacturing breakdown. Hardhats sell for $12 each out of the Dallas DC and $14 from Lexington. Discuss whether the warehouse should delay shipments until both DC requirements can be satisfied or allocate based on need.

6. Scorekeeper, Inc., manufactures stadium scoreboards. Table 1 illustrates the demand for Scorekeeper's scoreboards over the past 25 days. The mean of daily demand is 6 units.

TABLE 1

Day	Demand	Day	Demand
1	4	14	6
2	3	15	4
3	4	16	2
4	6	17	5
5	7	18	6
6	8	19	7
7	6	20	6
8	5	21	6
9	6	22	5
10	10	23	7
11	8	24	8
12	7	25	9
13	5		

a. Is the demand distribution normal? How do you know?
b. Calculate the standard deviation for daily demand. Assume in this case that the performance cycle is constant.

Table 2 summarizes Scorekeeper's performance cycles over the past 40 replenishments. The expected cycle duration is 12 days.

TABLE 2

Performance Cycle (in days)	Frequency (f)
10	4
11	8
12	16
13	8
14	4

c. Is the performance cycle distribution normal? How do you know?
d. Calculate the standard deviation for the performance cycle.
e. Given your answers to parts (b) and (d), find the safety stock required at 1 combined standard deviation under conditions of demand and performance cycle uncertainties.
f. If the typical order quantity is 36 units, find the average inventory at 3 standard deviations under demand and performance cycle uncertainty.

g. Scorekeeper is striving for a 99 percent product availability level. Given the above information as well as your answer to (e), find the function value of the normal loss curve, $f(k)$.

h. Use Table 10-15 to find the value for k, given your answer to part (g), and calculate the required safety stock for the desired 99 percent availability level.

i. What would be the required safety stock for 99 percent availability should the order quantity change to 30 units?

7. The XYZ Chemical Company must ship 9500 gallons of pesticides from its plant in Cincinnati, Ohio, to a customer in Columbia, Missouri. XYZ has a contract in place with Henderson Bulk Trucking Company as well as with the Central States Railroad. Both carriers are available for the move. Henderson will charge $600 per tank truck, and Central States' rate is $1000 per tankcar. Henderson tanks can hold a maximum quantity of 7000 gallons. XYZ has a fleet of 23,500-gallon tankcars available in Cincinnati.

   a. Given the above information, evaluate the cost of each alternative.

   b. What other qualitative factors should be considered in this decision?

8. Shatter Industries, Inc., manufactures household and commercial glass products that serve a variety of purposes.

   a. Refer to the National Motor Freight Classification 100-S (Table 12-1) to determine the LTL and TL product classifications for the following Shatter items:

      i.   Item 86960, glazed glass, boxed.

      ii. Glass slides for microscopes.

      iii. Bent mirror glass, dimensions 7 feet × 5 feet.

   b. Shatter ships many of its products from a warehouse in Atlanta, Georgia, to a distribution center in Lansing, Michigan. Refer to the rate tariff in Table 12-2 to find applicable charges for the following shipments over the route:

      i.   5200 lb. of mirrored shock glass (Item 86900, Sub 1—class 85).

      ii. 32,000 lb. of class 65 product.

      iii. 200 lb. of class 60 product.

      iv. 19,000 lb. of class 150 product.

      v. 2500 lb. of class 200 product with a 5 percent temporary fuel surcharge added to the line-haul charge.

9. Gigoflop Electronics has three shipments of class 100 product to be transported from Atlanta, Georgia, to Lansing, Michigan. The shipments weigh 5000 lb., 10,000 lb., and 7000 lb., respectively. Gigoflop can ship each quantity individually or consolidate them as a multiple-stop shipment. Each shipment is to be delivered to a different location in Lansing. The carrier, Eckgold Trucking, charges $50 for each stop-off (not including the final destination). Refer to Table 12-2 and evaluate the costs of shipping individually versus consolidation. Which option should be used by Gigoflop?

10. Stanley Harris, traffic manager of This n' That Manufacturers, is considering the negotiation of a freight-all-kinds (FAK) rate for shipments between Atlanta and Lansing. The company ships 200 (class 65) shipments of 5000 lb., 40 (class 400) shipments of 1200 lb., 30 (class 100) shipments of 10,000 lb., and receives a 45 percent discount on published rates.

   a. Refer to Table 12-2 to determine the current freight bill for the above shipments. *Note:* Take the discount from the published rate and round *up* for the applicable hundredweight rate.

   b. Should Mr. Harris accept an FAK rate of $10 per hundredweight?

   c. What factors aside from price should Mr. Harris consider with an FAK rate?

11. Carole Wilson, Transportation Manager of Applied Technologies, has a shipment of 150 computer monitors originating at the company's plant in Santa Fe Springs, California. The shipment, valued at $29,250, is destined for a DC in St. Louis, Missouri. John Miller, receiving manager at the St. Louis DC, has established a standardized transit time for the shipment to be 2.5 days. Mr. Miller assesses an opportunity cost of

$6.00 per monitor for each day beyond the standard. Ms. Wilson has three transportation options available.

   a. Cross Country Haulers, a long-haul trucking company, can ship the monitors at a contracted rate of $1.65/mile. The distance from Santa Fe Springs to St. Louis is 1940 miles. Cross Country estimates that it can deliver the shipment in 3 days. A truck can carry 192 monitors.

   b. The Sea-to-Shining Sea (STSS) Railway can pick up the shipment at the plant's dock and deliver the monitors directly to the St. Louis DC. STSS can ship the railcar of monitors for a flat charge of $1500. Ms. Wilson has recently experienced delays with the switching of its railcars and expects delivery to take 5 days.

   c. Ms. Wilson has also negotiated an agreement with Lightning Quick Intermodal, Inc. (LQI), a third-party carrier that utilizes both motor and rail transportation. LQI can pick up the shipment by truck at the plant and deliver it to an intermodal railyard in Bakersfield, California, where the trailer is placed onto a flat railcar. The servicing railway, the Rocky Mountain Railway (RMR), then delivers the trailer to another intermodal yard near St. Louis, where the trailer is unloaded and transported by truck to the DC. Lightning Quick offers the origin-to-destination transportation for $2500. Transit time is anticipated at 2.5 days. From past experience, Mr. Miller has discovered that the additional handling inherent with Lightning Quick's service results in 3 percent product loss and damage. Recovery of these losses is difficult and typically results in only 33.3 percent immediate reimbursement of the losses.

     Evaluate the cost of each transportation alternative.

12. Moving Hands, Inc., ships alarm clocks from Atlanta to Lansing. The company has begun packaging the clocks in a stronger corrugated box to reduce the likelihood of damage in storage and transit. As a result of the improved packaging, the clocks' product classification has dropped from 100 to 85 without significantly adding weight to the package.

   a. What effect does the new packaging have on the transportation cost of a single 1000 lb. shipment? Refer to Table 12-2.

   b. Suppose Moving Hands ships 300 loads of the 1000 lb. quantity each year and the new packaging costs $10,000 to develop and produce. Will Moving Hands realize a full payback of the packaging investment in its first year?

13. **a.** Bill Berry, transportation sales manager of Speedy Trucking Company, has considered serving a new customer, El Conquistador, Inc., an importer of Venezuelan goods, by hauling 12 truckloads of product each month from the receiving port in Bayonne, New Jersey, to a distributor in Pittsburgh, Pennsylvania, for $850 per truckload. Each serving truck must depart from the Speedy terminal in Seacaucus, New Jersey, 12 miles from the seaport. The distance from Bayonne to Pittsburgh is 376 miles. Upon unloading at Pittsburgh, trucks return empty (deadhead) to the Seacaucus terminal 380 miles from the distributor. If it costs Speedy an average of $1.20 per mile to operate a truck, should Mr. Berry accept the business at the negotiated rate? Why or why not?

   b. Mr. Berry has coordinated back-haul moves for the Conquistador shipments above with a new customer in Youngstown, Ohio. The new customer, Super Tread, Inc., ships tires from its plant in Youngstown to the port in Bayonne for exporting. Each Conquistador shipment will be accompanied with a return shipment from Super Tread (12 truckloads/month). Speedy will charge Super Tread $1.30 per mile. Bayonne is 430 miles from Youngstown. The distance from Pittsburgh to Youngstown is 65 miles. Trucks must return to the terminal in Seacaucus upon delivering product from the back-haul (before picking up again at Bayonne). The terms of the Conquistador agreement outlined in part (a) remain intact. How much can Mr. Berry expect Speedy to profit (lose) per trip from the new arrangement?

   c. How much can Mr. Berry expect Speedy to profit (lose) per month from the new arrangement should the company accept the business?

   d. Is it worthwhile for Mr. Berry to arrange for the back-haul? Why or why not?

14. Super Performance Parts (SPP) produces braking devices exclusively for the Ace Motor company, an automotive manufacturer. SPP has been leasing warehouse space at a public facility 20 miles from the company's plant. SPP has been approached by a group of four other Ace suppliers with the idea of building a consolidated warehouse to gain transportation and materials handling economies. An investment of $200,000 would be required by each of the five companies to acquire the warehouse. Payment of the initial investment secures 10 years of participation in the agreement. Annual operating expenses are anticipated to be $48,000 for each party. SPP is currently charged $6000 per month for use of the public warehouse facilities.

    SPP's outbound transportation from the public warehouse often consists of LTL quantities. Its annual outbound transportation bill is currently $300,000. SPP expects consolidated warehousing to more fully utilize truckload quantities with transportation expenses shared among the supplier pool. SPP's annual outbound bill would be reduced by 25 percent in the consolidated plan. Differences in inbound transportation costs are assumed negligible in this case.

    a. Compare the storage and shipping costs associated with consolidated warehousing as opposed to SPP's current, direct shipping plan. Are any efficiencies apparent through consolidation?

    b. Aside from potentially reducing costs, how else might SPP benefit by participating in the consolidated warehouse?

    c. What disadvantages might exist in a consolidated warehouse as opposed to a direct-shipping situation?

15. Essen Beer Company has a brewery in Michigan's Upper Peninsula and is setting up distribution at Jackson, Michigan, in the state's Lower Peninsula. Essen packages its beverages in barrels and in 24-can cases. Barrels must be maintained at temperatures below 60 degrees Fahrenheit until retail delivery. The company's logistics department must determine whether to operate individual private warehouses for barrels and cases or to utilize a single warehouse with barrels placed in a carefully controlled environment separate from cases. Assume that cases are not to be stored or transported in refrigerated environments.

    Essen experiences a weekly demand of 300 barrels and 5000 cases. The company has arranged truckload transportation with Stipe Trucking Service. Stipe operates refrigerated and nonrefrigerated trailers, as well as multicompartmented trailers that are half refrigerated and half not. A refrigerated truckload can hold 72 barrels, while a nonrefrigerated truckload holds 400 cases. The multicompartmented trailer can hold 36 barrels and 200 cases. The costs for these services and other related expenses are detailed below:

Truckload costs

Refrigerated	$550
Nonrefrigerated	$400
Multicompartmented	$500

Warehouse expenses

Individual warehouses

For case storage only:

Capital	$1,250/week
Labor	$2,500/week

For barrel storage:

Capital	$2,500/week
Labor	$1,600/week

Single, consolidated warehouse

Capital	$3,500/week
Labor	$3,200/week

    a. Considering demand and all costs depicted above, does the single, consolidated warehouse or the two individual warehouses represent the least-total-cost alternative?

    b. Now assume that Stipe Trucking Service will provide *only* the multicompartmented trailers to serve the proposed consolidated warehouse. Which plan is the least-cost alternative in this scenario?

16. Comfy Mattresses, Inc., is opening a new plant in Orlando, Florida. Ron Lane, distribution manager, has been asked to find the lowest cost outbound logistics system. Given an annual sales volume of 24,000 mattresses, determine the costs associated with each option below.

    a. Build a private warehouse near the plant for $300,000. The variable cost, including warehouse maintenance and labor, is estimated at $5 per unit. Contract carrier transportation costs $12.50 per unit on average. No external transportation services are necessary for shipment of mattresses from the plant to the warehouse in this scenario. The fixed warehouse investment can be depreciated evenly over 10 years.

    b. Rent space in a public warehouse 10 miles from the plant. The public warehouse requires no fixed investment but has variable costs of $8 per unit. Outbound contract carrier transportation would cost $12.50 per unit on average. The carrier also charges $5 per unit to deliver the mattresses to the warehouse from the plant.

    c. Contract the warehousing and transportation services to the Freeflow Logistics Company, an integrated logistics firm with a warehouse location 25 miles from the plan. Freeflow requires a fixed investment of $150,000 and charges $20 per unit for all services originating at the plant. The fixed investment covers a 10-year agreement with Freeflow.

    d. Name a few advantages aside from cost that the low-cost alternative above may have over the other alternatives.

17. Ms. Sara Ritter is the distribution manager for the Fiesta Soft Drink Company. She is considering full automation of the plant's warehouse. At present, the warehouse utilizes a mechanized system of materials handling. The current system employs 20 laborers at an average wage rate of $13/hour. Laborers work an average of 2000 hours per year. The mechanization costs $18,000 annually to maintain. The equipment was purchased 2 years ago with uniform payments of $25,000 made annually. In year 9 the mechanical equipment will be replaced by new machinery with fixed annual costs of $35,000. In addition, it will cost Fiesta $12,000 per year to maintain the new equipment with the same 20 laborers.

    The automated equipment would cost $1.2 million upfront for implementation. Only eight laborers and an automation specialist would be required to maintain operations in the new system. The laborers would earn $16/hour over 2000 hours each year. The automation specialist would earn a salary of $56,000 per year, increasing 2 percent annually after the first year. Much of the old mechanized equipment could be sold immediately for a total of $125,000. Maintenance of the automated system is estimated at $60,000 each year with this cost growing by 3 percent annually after the first year. The automated system is expected to serve Fiesta for 15 years.

    a. Examine the cash flow under each system. What is the payback period for automation?

    b. What advantages aside from long-term cost savings might an automated warehouse have over more labor-intensive systems?

18. Dandy Collectibles is opening a new warehouse. Bob Lee, the warehouse manager, is trying to determine the labor compensation package that most productively utilizes resources. The typical compensation plan offers an hourly wage rate of $13. Mr. Lee is also considering an incentive plan. The incentive plan rewards solely on performance with order pickers earning $0.40/unit prepared for shipping. A typical week shows the number of ordered units that must be prepared for shipping.

    Errors sometimes happen in Dandy's order picking. Product mishandling occurs in 1 percent of the orders under the incentive plan and in 0.5 percent of the orders under the hourly wage plan. Errored orders are scrapped and result in lost revenue of $60 per occurrence. Hourly workers pick 20 units per hour. Incentive workers pick 28 units per hour. Regardless of the plan designation, employees work 40-hour weeks. Union restrictions prevent Dandy from operating on Saturday and Sunday. The labor union also restricts Dandy from hiring part-time workers. Orders need not be filled daily, but all orders must be shipped by week's end (Friday). Assume that hiring and training costs are negligible.

  a. How many workers are needed under each plan for the typical week's demand?

  b. Which plan meets the typical week's demand at the lowest cost, including lost sales resulting from errors?

19. Mitchell Beverage Company produces Cactus Juice, a popular alcoholic beverage. Recently the firm has experienced problems of product pilferage at the warehouse. In one month, 3200 bottles of Cactus Juice, representing 0.4 percent of the month's volume, could not be located for shipping. Should the problem go unresolved, it is anticipated that it will continue at this rate. The forecasted annual sales volume for Cactus Juice is 9.6 million bottles. Each bottle sells for $4.50.

   Steve Davis, vice president of distribution, has asked you to look into the following security options to reduce the pilferage problem.

   a. Hire four security guards to patrol the warehouse floor all hours of the day, 7 days a week. The firm would offer a wage of $14.50/hour to the guards as well as a benefits package expected to be worth $2000 per employee per year. The presence of security guards should lower pilferage to 0.2 percent of volume. Only one guard would be on duty at any one time.

   b. Implement an electronic detection system based on bar code technology. This would require purchasing bar code equipment for the packaging facility and warehouse. Electronic scanning devices must also be purchased and placed at warehouse entrances. Alarms sound whenever a bar-coded item passes through a warehouse entrance without clearance. The electronic detection package, including bar code printers and readers, will cost $120,000. In addition, employees at the plant and warehouse will be trained to use the new equipment at a one-time cost of $8000. Monthly maintenance of the system is expected to cost $800. Also, a bar code specialist must be hired. The specialist would earn a salary of $49,000 per year. Product pilferage is expected to be lowered to 0.1 percent of volume with the electronic security system. The system has an estimated life of 8 years. Accrue all costs evenly over the life of the equipment.

   c. Install security cameras in key locations throughout the warehouse. It has been determined that six cameras could adequately record warehouse operations. Each camera costs $1200. The support devices and installation will cost $36,000. Four security guards would be hired for the purpose of viewing the security monitors for suspicious activity. One guard would be on duty at all times. The guards each earn $12/hour, in a 42-hour workweek, and receive a benefits package worth $1000 per year. Pilferage under this system would be 0.05 percent of volume. The monitoring equipment is expected to have a life of 12 years. Accrue all fixed costs evenly over the life of the equipment.

   Should the firm implement any of the options above, or make no investment and allow the pilferage to continue at the rate of 0.4 percent of volume? Compare the costs and benefits of each option on an annual basis.

20. Chronotronics produces two models of clock radios, the X-100 and the X-250 deluxe. Both products are currently packaged in a single-wall corrugation. Through close observation, the firm has discovered that 0.5 percent of both X-100s and X-250s are damaged between packaging and customer delivery. Chronotronics can package either model, or both, in double-wall corrugated fiberboard, which would reduce product damage by half. The current single-wall packaging costs $0.80 per unit. Double-wall packaging costs 20 percent more. The X-100 and X-250 have market values of $40 and

$70, respectively. Damaged units are a total loss. Chronotronics sold 12,000 X-100s and 7000 X-250s last year. Forecasts indicate consistent sales for the X-100 and a 5 percent increase in X-250 sales over the next year. *Note:* Round up for whole units lost.

    a. From a least-cost perspective, should Chronotronics utilize double-wall corrugation with the X-100 next year?

    b. From a least-cost perspective, should Chronotronics utilize double-wall corrugation with the X-250 next year?

    c. From discussion earlier in the text, how might packaging improvements affect transportation costs?

21. Your firm is planning to introduce a new product line. Your task is to determine the inventory implications of the new product. The typical product will ship an average of 20 units per day from the firm's central DC. Historical sales patterns indicate that the standard deviation of daily sales should be approximately 3. The typical performance cycle for comparable products has been a mean of 7 days and a standard deviation of 2.

    a. Assuming a replenishment quantity from the plant of 200 units, what are the safety stock and resulting average inventory for a 95 percent case fill rate?

    b. What are the inventory implications (safety stock and average inventory) of increasing the case fill rate objective to 99 percent?

    c. What would be the inventory implications for daily replenishment with a 99 percent fill rate objective, assuming that the same level of demand and performance cycle uncertainty is maintained?

22. As the logistics representative on a manufacturer's sales team, you have been asked to quantify the benefits that can be sold to a customer using more consistent service and transportation. The customer wants 99 percent case availability from its distribution centers that are resupplied from the manufacturer. The average daily demand in cases from the customer's DC is 1000 units with a standard deviation of 250. Historically, the replenishment performance cycle has been 10 days with a standard deviation of 4 days. The customer has traditionally used a 20 percent inventory carrying cost, and the average value of each case is $25. The customer orders weekly an order quantity of 7000 units.

    a. What is the average inventory and annual carrying cost for the current situation?

    b. What is the average inventory and carrying cost impact of reducing the manufacturer's performance cycle variation by 2 days?

    c. How does reducing the performance cycle variation by 2 days compare with reducing the average performance cycle length by 2 days in terms of average inventory and inventory carrying cost?

23. Spartan Plastics provides components to assembly plants in the automobile industry. Currently, they ship directly from their plant in St. Louis, Missouri, to plants in Lansing, Michigan; Toledo, Ohio; and eight assembly plants surrounding Detroit, Michigan. In total, there are 10 assembly plants that each receive approximately 3000 pounds per day in shipments. Currently, the company ships LTL from its plant to each assembly plant for a cost of $0.0013 per pound per mile. The company is considering two transportation alternatives to reduce cost. The first alternative is using a milk-run approach where a truckload begins in St. Louis, stops in Lansing, then the Detroit plants, and finally Toledo. The transportation cost for the milk-run approach would be $1.30 per truck mile plus $100/stop, not including the final stop in Toledo. The second alternative is to consolidate a truckload to Ypsilanti, Michigan, and then cross-dock the components for delivery to the assembly plant by the logistics provider. The truckload cost is still $1.30 per mile, and the cost per delivery to each assembly plant from Ypsilanti is $200.

    a. What are the cost characteristics of each delivery option?

    b. What are the qualitative and service characteristics of each delivery option?

24. Presswick Industries supplies plastics used for medical applications such as pharmaceutical injections and collecting laboratory samples. Presswick produces the containers and tubes and then ships them to customers who incorporate the plastics into kits that are used in hospitals and labs. Currently, Presswick simply loads the containers and tubes into corrugated boxes and ships them to customers who are then responsible for disposing of the corrugated. Presswick is considering the possibility of using returnable packaging with some of its key customers to be more environmentally friendly and perhaps reduce cost as well. The current corrugated cost per unit (container or tube) is $.05 with an additional $.02 per unit for disposal. The cost of the recyclable container is $.25 per unit of capacity that can be used multiple times. The recyclable container does not have to be disposed of, but it must be transported back to Presswick at a cost of $.02 per unit of capacity. Assume that the recyclable containers can only be used for 1 year because the plastic in the containers begins to break down.

a. At what annual volume level does it make sense to use the recyclable containers versus the corrugated containers?

b. What other qualitative factors should be considered in the decision?

25. Forest Green Products provides private label vegetables for grocery chains throughout the Midwest. They currently have distribution centers in Columbus, Ohio; St. Louis, Missouri; and Minneapolis, Minnesota. The typical annual capacity requirements for Forest Green are 5 million cases with a case split of 35 percent, 40 percent, and 25 percent for Columbus, St. Louis, and Minneapolis, respectively. The company is reassessing its materials handling and storage capability in each facility. The technology alternatives being considered are mechanized, semiautomated, and information-directed systems. Table 3 summarizes the acquisition, annual fixed cost, per case variable cost, and life span of each system alternative. The acquisition and annual fixed cost are quoted in terms of dollars per million units of capacity. In other words, a DC requiring two million units of capacity would double the specified cost. The annual fixed cost does not include depreciation for the acquisition cost. Assume that the total square footage of the 3 DCs is the same.

TABLE 3

Materials Handling Alternative	One-Time Acquisition Cost	Annual Fixed Cost	Per Case Variable Cost	Usage Life Span (Years)
Mechanized	$1,000,000	$50,000	$0.30	10
Semiautomated	$3,000,000	$200,000	$0.08	5
Information-directed	$1,500,000	$150,000	$0.15	7

a. What system alternative should be used for each DC based on annual cost? How does this decision change if Net Present Value (NPV) is considered over the life of the system? Assume a 10 percent discount rate.

b. Assume that for simplicity's sake, Forest Green wants to use only one system alternative for all three DCs. What is the system with the lowest NPV for the life of the system for the combination of DCs?

c. What other qualitative factors should be considered?

IV　NETWORK DESIGN

One of the two primary responsibilities of a firm's logistical management, as established in Chapters 1 and 2, is to participate in supply chain design. Part IV consists of two chapters devoted to the design responsibility. The focus of Chapter 15 is network integration theory. An integrative model is developed and illustrated that relates the temporal and spatial dimensions of logistics to a single theoretical structure. The integration structure provides the basis for process development, trade-off quantification, and holistic measurement. In Chapter 16 the theoretical structure is operationalized in terms of strategic choices to support specific marketing and manufacturing initiatives. This chapter also develops methodology and technique to guide logistical system design. This step-by-step design process provides a guide to deal with complex channel structure and strategy design and implementation. Part IV is supported by five cases that illustrate various facets of network design.

15 NETWORK INTEGRATION

For the most part, managers confront a new and challenging assignment when they are asked to participate in a logistical system reengineering. Because of the rapid rate of change in almost every facet of logistical operations, managers can expect considerable discontinuity when they try to use previous experience to guide the creation and integration of new logistical competencies. Therefore, success or failure may depend on how well the planning team is able to quantify the forces at work and rationalize them into a logical and believable action plan. Having a comprehensive understanding of the theoretical constructs that serve as the foundation of logistical integration provides an important step toward conceptualizing an integrated strategy.

In earlier chapters, the essence of logistical strategy was identified as achieving least total cost operations while simultaneously maintaining flexibility. Flexibility is the key to providing high-level basic customer service while maintaining sufficient operating capacity to meet and exceed key customer expectations. To exploit flexibility, an enterprise needs to achieve a high level of logistical process integration. Integration is required at two operating levels. First, the operating areas of logistics must be integrated across a network of facilities supportive of market distribution, manufacturing, and procurement requirements. Such network integration is essential if a firm is using logistical competency to gain competitive advantage. Second, integration must extend beyond a single firm by supporting relationships across the supply chain. This chapter presents a framework to assist managers in achieving such integration.[1]

Enterprise Facility Network

Prior to the availability of low-cost dependable surface transportation, most of the world's commerce relied on movement by water. During this early period, commercial activity concentrated around port cities. Overland transport of goods was costly and slow. For example, the lead time to order custom clothing from across the continental United States could exceed 9 months. Although the need for fast and efficient transport existed, it was not until the invention of the steam locomotive in 1829 that the transportation technology revolution began in the United States. Today, the transportation system in this country is a highly developed network of rail, water, air, highway, and pipeline services. Each transport alternative provides a different type of service for use within a logistical system. This availability of economical transportation creates the opportunity to establish a competitively superior facility network to service customers.

The importance of location network analysis has been recognized since the middle of the 19th century, when the German economist Joachim von Thünen wrote *The Isolated State.*[2] For von Thünen, the primary determinant of economic development was the price of land and the cost to transport products from farm to market. The value of land was viewed as being directly related to the cost of transportation and the ability of a product to command an adequate price to cover all cost and result in profitable operation. Von Thünen's basic principle was that the value of specific produce at the growing location decreases with distance from the primary selling market.

Following von Thünen, Alfred Weber generalized location theory from an agrarian to an industrial society.[3] Weber's theoretical system consisted of numerous consuming locations spread over a geographical area and linked together by linear weight-distance transportation costs. Weber developed a scheme to classify major materials as either *ubiquitous* or *localized*. Ubiquitous materials were those available at all locations. Localized raw materials consisted of mineral deposits found only at selected areas. On the basis of his analysis, Weber developed a **material index.** This was the ratio of the localized raw material in the weight of the finished product. Various types of industry were assigned a **locational weight** based on the material index. Utilizing these two measures, Weber generalized that industries would locate facilities at the point of consumption when the manufacturing process was weight-gaining and near

---

[1]The reader is cautioned that this chapter stresses theoretical constructs that determine logistical system design. The material offers a framework to guide trade-off analysis. While theoretical discussions tend to be abstract, the principles presented are logically consistent regardless of the competitive or cultural setting within which logistical reengineering is performed.

[2]Joachim von Thünen, *The Isolated State,* Beziehung auf Landwirtschaft und Nationalökonomie. Hamburg, 1862.

[3]Alfred Weber, *Theory of the Location of Industries,* translated by Carl J. Friedrich (Chicago, IL: University of Chicago Press, 1928).

the point of raw material deposit when the manufacturing process was weight-losing. Finally, if the manufacturing process were neither weight-gaining nor weight-losing, firms would select plant locations at an intermediate point of convenience.

Several location theorists followed von Thünen and Weber. The most notable contributions toward a general theory of location were developed by August Lösch, Edgar Hoover, Melvin Greenhut, Walter Isard, and Michael Webber.[4] In their writings, these five authors highlighted the importance of geographical specialization in industrial location, including quantification of the importance of transportation.

Spectrum of Location Decisions

In terms of logistical planning, transportation offers the potential to link geographically dispersed manufacturing, warehousing, and market locations into an integrated system. Logistical system facilities include all locations at which materials, work-in-process, or finished inventories are handled or stored. Thus, all retail stores, finished goods warehouses, manufacturing plants, and material storage warehouses are logistical network locations. It follows that selection of individual locations, as well as the overall locational network, represents important competitive and cost-related logistical decisions.

A manufacturing plant location may require several years to fully implement. For example, General Motors' decision to build a new Cadillac assembly plant in Lansing, Michigan, spanned over 5 years from concept to reality. In contrast, some warehouse arrangements are sufficiently flexible to be used only at specified times during a year. The selection of retail locations is a specialized decision influenced by marketing and competitive conditions. The discussion that follows concentrates on warehouse location. Among all the location decisions faced by logistical managers, those involving warehouse networks are most frequently reviewed.

Local Presence: An Obsolete Paradigm

A long-standing belief in business is that a firm must have facilities in local markets to successfully conduct business. During economic development of North America, erratic transportation services created serious doubt about a firm's ability to promise delivery in a timely and consistent manner. In short, customers felt that unless a supplier maintained inventory in local market areas it would be difficult, if not impossible, to provide consistent delivery. This perception, commonly referred to as the **local presence paradigm,** resulted in logistical strategies committed to forward deployment of inventory. As recently as the early 1960s it was not uncommon for manufacturers to operate 20 or more distribution warehouses to service mainland United States. Some firms went so far as to have full line inventory warehouses located near all major sales offices.

---

[4]August Lösch, *Die Räumliche Ordnung der Wirtschaft* (Jena: Gustav Fischer Verlag, 1940); Edgar M. Hoover, *The Location of Economic Activity* (New York: McGraw-Hill Book Company, 1938); Melvin L. Greenhut, *Plant Location in Theory and Practice* (Chapel Hill, NC: University of North Carolina Press, 1956); Walter Isard et al., *Methods of Regional Analysis: An Introduction to Regional Science* (New York: John Wiley & Sons, Inc. 1960); Walter Isard, *Location and Space Economy* (Cambridge, MA: The MIT Press, 1968); and Michael J. Webber, *Impact of Uncertainty on Location* (Cambridge, MA: The MIT Press, 1972).

When a tradition is part of a successful strategy, it is difficult to change. However, for the past several decades inventory cost and risk associated with local presence have driven reexamination. Transportation services have dramatically expanded, and reliability has increased to the point where arrival times are dependable and predictable. Rapid advances in information technology have reduced the time required to identify and communicate customer requirements. Technology is available to track transportation vehicles, thereby providing accurate delivery information.[5] Next-day delivery from a warehouse facility located as far away as 800 to 1000 miles is common practice.

Transportation, information technology, and inventory economics all favor the use of fewer rather than greater numbers of distribution warehouses to service customers within a geographical area. In many situations, customer perceptions concerning local presence continue to influence decentralization of inventory. The answer to the question, How much local presence is desirable? is best understood by carefully examining the relationships that drive logistical system design.

Warehouse Requirements

Warehouses are established in a logistical system to lower total cost or to improve customer service. In some situations, the benefits of lower cost and improved service can be achieved simultaneously.

Warehouses create value for the processes they support. Manufacturing requires warehouses to store, sort, and sequence materials and components. Facilities used for inbound materials and components are often referred to as **supply facing warehouses.** Warehouses are also used to store, sequence, and combine inventory for consolidated shipment to next level customers in the supply chain. Warehouses used support market distribution are often referred to as **demand facing warehouses.** Demand facing warehouse requirements are directly related to manufacturing and market distribution strategies.

Because of specialized materials handling and inventory process requirements, warehouses typically specialize in performing either supply or demand facing services. Warehouses committed to supporting manufacturing are typically located close to the factories they support; in contrast, warehouses dedicated to marketing distribution are typically strategically located throughout the geographical market area serviced.

The combinations of information technology, e-procurement fulfillment, and response-based business strategies have combined to radically alter how and why warehouses are used. The economic justification and desired functionality of a warehouse can be distinctly different for facilities dedicated to procurement, manufacturing, or market distribution.

---

[5]Transportation vehicles can be tracked through wireless data systems. The main form of tracking is through various mobile communication systems that are common among truckload carriers. For more information, see Jim Mele, "Guide to Mobile Communications," *Fleet Owner,* December 1992, pp. 45–52. Another form of wireless data systems is satellite-based tracking. These systems require a more significant investment but allow complete national tracking coverage. As such, satellite systems are more relevant for national truckload markets, not local LTL deliveries. Satellite systems may be increasing due to the FCC's plan to develop a national satellite system in an effort to reduce costs so more operators could utilize satellite technology. For more information, see Jim Mele, "Wireless Data Communications," *Fleet Owner,* February 1993, pp. 44–50). Today's technology has been available for almost a decade.

Procurement Drivers

Procurement drivers center on using warehouses to help purchase materials and components at the lowest total cost. Sophisticated purchasing executives have long realized that the combination of purchase price, quantity discount, payment terms, and logistical performance is required to achieve lowest delivered cost. In an effort to develop and support improved working relationships, most firms have reduced the number of suppliers they do business with. The logic is to develop a limited number of relationships with suppliers who can be operationally integrated into a firm's supply chain. The goals of relationship buying are to eliminate waste, duplication, and unplanned redundancy.

In an effort to improve overall operating efficiency, life cycle considerations have become prominent in purchase decisions. This relational dynamic of working with limited suppliers is based on a cradle-to-grave philosophy. The relationship is positioned to focus on all aspects of life cycle spanning from new product development to reclamation and disposal of unused materials and unsold product inventory. Such a life cycle focus is the result of distinct buying practices that directly impact the nature and functionality of supply faced warehousing. Value-added services related to procurement are increasingly being debundled from the purchase price. Such debundling facilitates functional absorption and spin-off between manufacturers and their suppliers. There is also a trend toward more response-based business strategies which is redefining expectations concerning supplier support and participation in the value-added process. The result is new structural relationships, such as tier one suppliers and lead facilitators. Finally, the seasonality of selected supplies, opportunities to purchase at reduced prices, and the need to rapidly accommodate manufacturing spikes continue to make selected warehousing of materials a sound business decision.

As a result of the above-noted trends, the role of supply facing warehouses continues to change. Warehouses were traditionally used to stockpile raw materials and component parts. Today such facilities place greater emphasis on sorting and sequencing materials as they flow into manufacturing. In many organizations the unbundling of services from the price of materials has facilitated outsourcing of warehouse requirements. Warehouse services required to most efficiently support manufacturing are increasingly being provided by lead suppliers or integrated logistics service providers. The goal is to streamline the flow of materials and components by eliminating duplicate handling and storage of identical inventories at multiple locations throughout the material supply network.

Manufacturing Drivers

Warehouses that support manufacturing are used to combine finished product for customer shipment. The capability to consolidate contrasts to individual order shipment. A primary advantage of a manufacturing demand facing warehouse is the ability to offer customers full line product assortment on a single invoice at truckload transportation rates. In fact, a manufacturer's capability to provide such consolidation may be the primary reason for its selection as a preferred supplier.

Leading examples of demand facing warehouses are the networks used by such firms as General Mills, Johnson & Johnson, Kraft, Kimberly-Clark, and Nabisco Foods. At Johnson & Johnson, warehouses are used to support hospital and consumer business sectors by serving as consolidators for a variety of different business units. As a result, customers are afforded full assortments of products from different business units on a single invoice for shipment in one transportation vehicle. Kimberly-Clark produces a wide variety of individual products on specific manufacturing lines at specialized plants. Such products as Kleenex®, Scott Tissue®, and Huggies® disposable diapers are manufactured at economy-of-scale volume, then temporarily are positioned in demand facing warehouses. Customer-specific truckloads of assorted products are assembled at the warehouse. At Nabisco, branch warehouses are located adjacent to individual bakeries. Inventories of all major products are maintained at each branch to facilitate full-service shipments to customers.

The primary determinant of the warehousing required to support manufacturing is the specific production strategy being implemented. In Chapter 5, three basic manufacturing strategies—make to plan (MTP), make to order (MTO), and assemble to order (ATO)—were discussed.[6] The extent of demand faced warehousing can be directly linked to the support requirements of each manufacturing strategy. In a general sense, MTO manufacturing strategies require supply facing warehousing support but little, if any, demand facing storage. Conversely, MTP manufacturing strategies, which focus resources to achieve maximum manufacturing economy of scale, require substantial demand facing warehouse capacity.

Market Distribution Drivers

Market support warehouses create value by providing inventory assortments to wholesalers and retailers. A warehouse located geographically close to customers seeks to minimize inbound transportation cost by maximizing consolidation and length of haul from manufacturing plants followed by relatively short outbound movement to final destination customers. The geographic size of a market area served from a support warehouse depends on the desired service speed, size of average order, and cost per unit of local delivery. A large number of market distribution warehouses are operated as public or contract facilities by third-party logistics service providers. Regardless of who operates the warehouse, the facility exists to provide inventory assortment and replenishment to customers. A warehouse is justified if it offers a way to achieve a competitive service or cost advantage.

Rapid Replenishment

Market distribution warehouses have traditionally provided assortment of products from varied manufacturers and various suppliers for retailers. A retail store typically does not have sufficient demand to order inventory in large quantities directly from wholesalers or manufacturers. A typical retail replenishment order is placed with a wholesaler who sells a variety of different manufacturer products.

Market support warehouses are common in the food and mass merchandise industries. The modern food distribution warehouse usually is located geographically near the retail stores it services. From this central warehouse, consolidated product assortments can rapidly replenish retail inventories because of the close geographical proximity. Large retail stores may receive multiple truckloads from the warehouse on a daily basis. Location of the warehouse within the market served is justified as the least cost way to rapidly replenish an assortment of inventory to either an end customer or a retailer.

---

[6]See Chapter 5, pp. 153–156.

Market-Based ATO

The design of a market distribution warehouse network is directly related to inventory deployment strategy. The establishment of market distribution warehouses is a result of forward inventory deployment in anticipation of future market requirements. This assumption means that a manufacturing firm utilizing such a distributive network is to some degree depending upon anticipatory inventory deployment to offset response time to meet customer requirements. Based on the preceding discussion, inventories deployed forward after manufacturing are typical in situations where firms are manufacturing to plan and when they are engaged in decentralized assembly to order. In ATO situations, common or undifferentiated components are stocked in warehouse inventory in anticipation of performing customized manufacturing or assembly at the warehouse upon receipt of customer orders.

An increasing amount of ATO operations are performed in market-positioned warehouses as contrasted to centralized manufacturing locations. Assembly in close proximity to major markets allows the benefits of postponement while avoiding the high cost and time related to long-distance direct shipment.

Warehouse Justification

Warehouses are justified in a logistical system when a service or cost advantage results from their positioning between suppliers, manufacturers, and customers. Competitive advantage generated by establishing a warehouse network can result from lower total cost or faster to-destination service. From the viewpoint of transportation economies, cost advantage results from using the warehouse to achieve freight consolidation. However, freight consolidation typically requires inventory to support assembly of customized orders. Alternatively, consolidation or assortment may be achieved by establishing flow-through facilities or cross-dock sortation that operates without preestablished inventories. Such continuous movement effectively converts warehouses from inventory storage to mixing facilities. Of course some business situations will justify a combination of inventory storage and continuous flow-through to effectively and economically service customers. From the perspective of integrative management, the key logistics system design questions become: How many and what kinds of warehouses should a firm establish? Where should they be located? What services should they provide? What inventories should they stock? and Which customers should they service? This sequence of interrelated questions represents the classical logistics network design challenge. For manufacturing firms, network design begins with marketing strategy and continues into manufacturing and procurement planning. In retailing and wholesaling enterprises the framework spans from purchasing to market distribution strategies.

Total Cost Integration

Economic forces such as transportation and inventory determine a firm's most appropriate network of warehouse facilities. This discussion identifies cost trade-offs related to transportation and inventory followed by integration to identify the least total cost facility network.

Transportation Economics

The key to achieving economical transportation is summarized in two basic principles. The first, often called the **quantity principle,** is that individual shipments should be as large as the involved carrier can legally transport in the equipment being used. The second, often called the **tapering principle,** is that large shipments should be transported distances as long as possible. Both of these principles serve to spread the fixed cost related to transportation over as many pounds and as many miles as possible. Economies of transportation consolidation may justify establishment of a single warehouse or may be achieved across a network of warehouses.

Cost-Based Warehouse Justification

The basic economic principle justifying establishment of a warehouse is transportation consolidation. Manufacturers typically sell products over a broad geographical market area. If customer orders tend to be small, then the potential cost savings of consolidated transportation may provide economic justification for establishing a warehouse.

To illustrate, assume a manufacturer's average shipment size is 500 pounds and the applicable freight rate to a customer is $7.28 per hundredweight. Each shipment made direct from the manufacturing location to the market would have a transportation cost of $36.40. The quantity or volume transportation rate for shipments 20,000 pounds or greater is $2.40 per hundredweight. Finally, local delivery within the market area is $1.35 per hundredweight. Under these conditions, products shipped to the market via quantity rates and distributed locally would cost $3.75 per hundredweight, or $18.75 per 500-pound shipment. If a warehouse could be established, stocked with inventory, and operated for a total cost of less than $17.65 per 500-pound shipment ($36.40 − $18.75) or $3.53 per hundredweight, the overall cost of distributing to the market using a warehouse would be lower. Given these economic relationships, establishment of a warehouse offers the potential to reduce total logistics cost.

Figure 15-1 illustrates the basic economic principle of warehouse justification. PL is identified as the manufacturing location, and WL is the warehouse location within a given market area. The vertical line at point PL labeled P_c reflects the handling and shipping cost associated with preparation of a 500-pound LTL shipment (C) and a 20,000-pound truckload shipment (A). The slope of line *AB* reflects the truckload freight rate from the plant to WL, the warehouse, which is assumed for this example to be linear with distance. The vertical line labeled *WC* at point WL represents the cost of

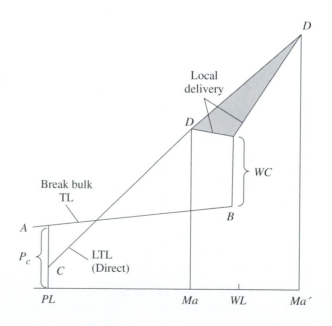

operating the warehouse and maintaining inventory. The lines labeled *D* reflect delivery cost from the warehouse to customers within the market area Ma to Ma′. The slope of line *CD* reflects the LTL rate from the plant to customers located between the plant and the boundary Ma′. The shaded area represents the locations to which the total cost of a 500-pound customer shipment using a consolidation warehouse would be lower than direct shipment from the manufacturing plant.

From the perspective of cost alone, it would make no difference whether customers located exactly at points Ma and Ma′ were serviced from the manufacturing plant or the warehouse.

Network Transportation Cost Minimization

As a general rule, warehouses would be added to the network in situations where

$$\sum \frac{P_{\overline{v}} + T_{\overline{v}}}{N_{\overline{x}}} + W_{\overline{x}} + L_{\overline{x}} \leq \sum P_{\overline{x}} + T_{\overline{x}},$$

where $P_{\overline{v}}$ = Processing cost of volume shipment;

$T_{\overline{v}}$ = Transportation cost of volume shipment;

$W_{\overline{x}}$ = Warehousing cost of average shipment;

$L_{\overline{x}}$ = Local delivery of average shipment;

$N_{\overline{x}}$ = Number of average shipments per volume shipment;

$P_{\overline{x}}$ = Processing cost of average shipment; and

$T_{\overline{x}}$ = Direct freight cost of average shipment.

The only limitation to this generalization is that sufficient shipment volume be available to cover the fixed cost of each warehouse facility. As long as the combined cost of warehousing and local delivery is equal to or less than the combined cost of shipping direct to customers, the establishment and operation of additional warehouse facilities would be economically justified.

The generalized relationship of transportation cost and number of warehouses in a network is illustrated in Figure 15-2. Total transportation cost will initially decline as warehouses are added to the logistical network. In actual operations, a consolidation

FIGURE 15-2

Transportation cost as a function of the number of warehouse locations

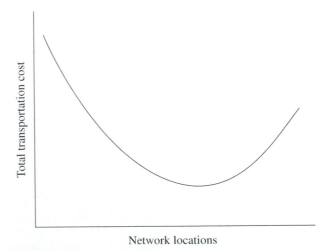

location can be a warehouse or a cross-dock facility offering transportation break-bulk. It is not necessary to stock inventory in a warehouse to achieve the lowest transportation cost. The reduction in transport cost results from consolidated volume shipments to the break-bulk location, coupled with short-haul small shipments to final destination. The cost of shipping small orders direct from manufacturing to customers is at the extreme upper left of the cost curve illustrated in Figure 15-2. At the low point near the middle of the transportation cost curve, the number of facilities required to achieve maximum freight consolidation is indicated. Transportation cost is minimized at the point of maximum freight consolidation.

If facilities are expanded beyond the maximum consolidation point, total cost will increase, because the inbound volume capable of being consolidated to each facility decreases. The increased frequency of smaller inbound shipments results in a higher cost per hundredweight for shipments into the facility. In other words, as the frequency of small inbound shipments increases, total transportation cost increases.

Inventory Economics

Inventory level in a logistical system directly relates to the location network. The framework for planning inventory deployment is the performance cycle. Although one element of the performance cycle is transportation, which provides spatial closure, the key driver of inventory economics is time. The forward deployment of inventory in a logistical system potentially improves service response time. Such deployment also increases overall system inventory, resulting in greater cost and risk.

Service-Based Warehouse Justification

The use of warehouses can be a vital part of the logistics strategy of a firm engaged in national distribution. The inventory related to a warehouse network consists of *base, transit,* and *safety stock.* For the total logistical network, average inventory commitment is

$$\bar{I} = \sum_{i=1}^{n} \frac{Q_s}{2} + SS_i,$$

where $\bar{I}$ = Average inventory in the total network;

   n = Number of performance cycles in the network;

   Q_s = Order quantity for a given performance cycle identified by the appropriate subscript; and

   SS_s = safety stock, for a given performance cycle identified by the appropriate subscript.

As warehouses are added to a logistics system, the number of performance cycles increases. This added complexity directly relates to the quantity of inventory required across the network.

Base Inventory.   The impact on base stock by adding inventory is not significant. The base stock level within a logistical system is determined by manufacturing and transportation lot sizes, which do not change as a function of the number of warehouses. The combination of maintenance and ordering cost, adjusted to take into consideration volume transportation rates and purchase discounts, determines the replenishment EOQ and the resultant base stock. In just-in-time procurement situations, base stock is determined by the discrete order quantity required to support the planned manufacturing run or assembly. In either situation, the base stock determination is independent of the number of warehouses included in the logistical system.

Transit Inventory.   Transit stock is inventory captive in transportation vehicles. While in transit, this inventory is available to promise but it cannot be physically accessed. Available to promise means it can be committed to customers by use of a reservation or inventory mortgaging capability in the order management system. As more performance cycles are added to a logistical network, the anticipated impact is that existing cycles will experience a reduction in transit inventory. This reduction occurs because the total network transit days are reduced. To illustrate, assume a single product is being sold in markets A and B and is currently being supplied from warehouse X, as presented in Figure 15-3. Assume the forecasted average daily sales are 6 units for market A and 7 for market B. The performance cycle duration is 6 days to market A and 10 days to market B.

FIGURE 15-3

Logistical network: Two markets, one warehouse

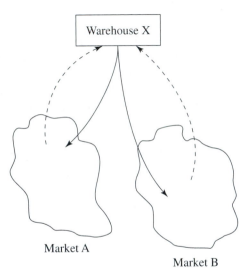

FIGURE 15-4

Logistical network: Two markets, two warehouses

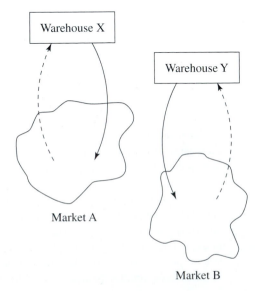

With all things held constant, what will happen to transit inventory if a second warehouse is added, as in Figure 15-4? Table 15-1 provides a summary of results. The main change is that the performance cycle to market B has been reduced from 10 to 4 days. Thus, the second warehouse reduced average transit inventory for the network from 53 to 32 units. It should be noted that the second warehouse did not create additional performance cycles on the market distribution side of the logistics flow. However, on the inbound side, each product stocked in the new warehouse requires a replenishment source. Assuming a full product line at each warehouse, the number of performance cycles required to replenish the network will increase each time a new warehouse is added.

Despite the increased need for inventory replenishment, the average in-transit inventory for the total network drops as new warehouses are added because of a reduction in days required to service customers. Assume that warehouse X is supplied by four manufacturing plants whose individual performance cycles and forecasted average usage are illustrated in Table 15-2.

For purposes of comparison, assume a unit value of $5 for all warehouse products. Utilizing only warehouse X, the average transit inventory would be 2835 units at $5 each, or $14,175.

TABLE 15-1   Transit Inventory under Different Logistical Networks

Forecasted Average Daily Sales	Market Area	Warehouse X Only	Two-Warehouse Facilities		
			Warehouse X	Warehouse Y	Combined
6	A	36	36	—	36
7	B	70	—	28	28
	$\Sigma A + B$	106			64
	$\bar{I}_a$	18			18
	$\bar{I}_b$	35			14
	$\Sigma \bar{I}$	53			32

TABLE 15-2   Logistical Structure: One Warehouse, Four Plants

	Warehouse X			
Manufacturing Plant	Performance Cycle Duration	Forecasted Average Sales	Transit Inventory	$\bar{I}$
A	10	35	350	175
B	15	200	3,000	1,500
C	12	60	720	360
D	20	80	1,600	800
	57	375	5,670	2,835

TABLE 15-3   Logistical Structure: Two Warehouses, Four Plants

Manufacturing Plant	Performance Cycle Duration	Forecasted Average Sales	Transit Inventory	$\bar{I}$
Warehouse X				
A	10	20	200	100
B	15	100	1,500	750
C	12	35	420	210
D	20	30	600	300
	57	185	2,720	1,360
Warehouse Y				
A	5	15	75	38
B	8	100	800	400
C	6	25	150	75
D	15	50	750	375
	34	190	1,775	888
	$\Sigma xy = 91$	$\Sigma xy = 375$	$\Sigma xy = 4{,}495$	$\Sigma \bar{x}xy = 2{,}248$

Table 15-3 illustrates the addition of warehouse Y. Average transit inventory under the two-warehouse logistical network dropped to 2248 units or, at $5 each, $11,240. Thus, even though four new plant-to-warehouse replenishment cycles were added to the logistical network, the average transit time was reduced because of the reduction in total replenishment days.

The addition of warehouses typically will reduce total in-transit days and, thus, in-transit inventory level. This result will vary in accordance with the particulars of each situation. Each network of locations must be carefully analyzed to determine average transit inventory impact. The key to understanding the general nature of such is to remember that total transit days are reduced even though the number of required performance cycles increases. A qualification is that while an increase in the number of performance cycles typically reduces transit days, it may also increase overall lead time uncertainty. As the number of performance cycles is increased, the possibility of breakdowns leading to potential service failures also increases. This potential impact is treated under safety stock.

Safety Stock Inventory.   Safety stock is added to base and transit stock to provide protection against sales and performance cycle uncertainty. Both aspects of uncertainty are time-related. Sales uncertainty is concerned with customer demand that exceeds forecasted sales during the replenishment time. Performance cycle uncertainty is concerned with variation in the total days required to replenish the inventory of a warehouse. From the viewpoint of safety stock, the expected result of adding warehouses will be an increase in average system inventory. The purpose of safety stock is to protect against unplanned stockouts during inventory replenishment. Thus, *if safety stock increases as a function of adding warehouses, then the overall network uncertainty must also be increasing.*

The addition of warehouses to the logistical network impacts uncertainty in two ways. First, as performance cycle days are reduced, the variability in sales during re-

TABLE 15-4   Summary of Sales in One Combined and Three Separate Markets

Month	Combined Sales, All Markets	Unit Sales per Market		
		A	B	C
1	18	9	0	9
2	22	6	3	13
3	24	7	5	12
4	20	8	4	8
5	17	2	4	11
6	29	10	5	14
7	21	7	6	8
8	26	7	7	12
9	18	5	6	7
10	24	9	5	10
11	23	8	4	11
12	23	12	2	9
Total Sales	265	90	51	124
Average Monthly Sales	21.1	7.5	4.3	10.3
Value Greater Than Average	7	4	3	4

plenishment as well as cycle variability are both reduced. Therefore, reducing the length of the performance cycle relieves, to some degree, the need for safety stock to protect against variability.

Adding locations also has a significant impact on average inventory. Each new performance cycle added to the system creates the need for an additional safety stock. The introduction of an additional warehouse to service a specific market area reduces the size of the statistical distribution used to determine safety stock requirements. In effect, the size of the market area being serviced by any given facility is reduced without a corresponding reduction in uncertainty. For example, when the demand of several markets is aggregated using a single warehouse, the variability of demand is averaged across markets. This allows peaks in demand in one market to be offset by low demand in another. In essence, the idle stock of one market can be used to meet safety stock requirements of other markets.

To illustrate, Table 15-4 provides a summary of monthly sales in three markets on a combined and separate basis. Average sales for the three markets combined is 22 units per month, with the greatest variation above the average in month 6, when sales reached 29 units, or 7 units over the average. If the goal is to provide 100 percent protection against stockout and total sales of 29 units have an equal probability of occurring in any month, a safety stock of 7 units would be required.

The average monthly sales for markets A, B, and C are 8, 4, and 10 units (rounded), respectively. The maximum demand in excess of forecast is in market A, with 5 units in month 12; for market B, 3 units in month 8; and for market C, 4 units in month 6. The total of each of these three extreme months equals 11 units. If safety stocks are planned for each market on a separate basis, 11 units of safety stock would be required for the total network while only 7 units of safety stock would be required to service all markets from a single warehouse. An increase in total system safety stock of 4 units is required as a result of using three warehouses.

FIGURE 15-5

Average inventory as a function of number of warehouse locations

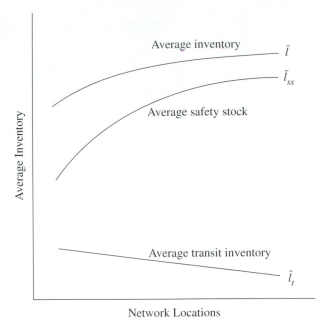

This simplified example illustrates the general safety stock impact of adding warehouses to a logistical network. The important point to understand is that increased safety stock results from an inability to aggregate uncertainty across market areas. As a consequence, unique safety stocks are required to accommodate local demand variation.

Network Inventory Cost Minimization

The overall impact upon average inventory of increasing the number of warehouses in a logistical network is generalized in Figure 15-5. A reduction in average transit inventory is assumed as illustrated by the line $\bar{I}_t$. The assumption is that a linear relationship exists between average transit inventory and the number of warehouses in the network.

The curve labeled $\bar{I}_{ss}$ (average safety stock) increases as warehouses are added to the network. Inventory increases at a decreasing rate, since the net increase required for each new facility declines. The incremental safety stock is the sum of added inventory to accommodate uncertainty of demand minus the inventory reduction required to accommodate for less lead time uncertainty. Thus, the incremental inventory required to maintain customer service performance diminishes for each new warehouse location added to the system. The average inventory curve, $\bar{I}$, represents the combined impact of safety stock and transit inventory. The significant observation is that the safety stock dominates the impact of transit inventory. For the overall network, the average inventory is the safety stock plus half of the order quantity and transit inventory. Thus, given the same demand and customer service goals, total inventory increases at a decreasing rate as the number of warehouses in a logistical network increases.

Total Cost Network

As noted earlier, the identification of the least total cost network design is the goal of logistical integration. The basic concept of total cost for the overall logistical system is illustrated in Figure 15-6. The low point on the total transportation cost curve is eight facilities. Total cost related to average inventory commitment increases with each ad-

FIGURE 15-6

Least total cost network

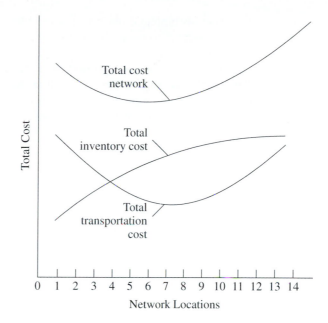

Network Locations

ditional warehouse. For the overall system, the lowest total cost network is 6 locations. The point of lowest inventory cost would be a single warehouse.

Trade-off Relationships

The identification of the least total cost network of six warehouses in Figure 15-6 illustrates the trade-off relationships. The minimal total cost point for the system is not at the point of least cost for either transportation or inventory. This is the hallmark of integrated logistical analysis.

In actual practice, it is difficult to identify and measure all aspects of total logistical cost. Many assumptions are required to operationalize logistical network analysis. An additional concern is the fact that a two-dimensional analysis, such as illustrated in Figure 15-6, does not encompass the complexity of total cost integration.

Critical Assumptions and Limitations

The two-dimensional display in Figure 15-6 represents a projected level of sales volume across a single planning period. Transportation requirements are represented by a single average size shipment. In actual operations, it is likely that neither of these simplifying assumptions will be valid. First, the nature of logistical network design is not a short-term planning problem. When facility decisions are involved, the planning horizon extends across several years and must accommodate a range of different annual sales projections. Second, actual shipment and order sizes will vary substantially around an average. A realistic approach to planning must incorporate a range of shipment sizes supported by alternative logistical methods to satisfy customer service requirements. In actual operation, alternative modes of transportation are employed, as necessary, to upgrade the speed of delivery.

Significant cost trade-offs exist between inventory and transportation. Inventory cost as a function of the number of warehouses is directly related to the desired level of inventory availability. If no safety stock is maintained in the system, total inventory requirement is limited to base and transit stock. Under a no safety stock situation, the total least cost for the system would be at or near the point of lowest transportation cost. Thus, assumptions made with respect to the desired inventory availability and fill rate are essential to trade-off analysis and have a significant impact on the least total cost design solution.

The locational selection aspect of logistical network planning is far more complex than simply deciding how many facilities to choose from a single array of locations such as illustrated in Figure 15-6. A firm engaged in nationwide logistics has a wide latitude in choice of where to locate warehouses. Within the United States there are 50 states within which one or more distribution warehouses could be located. Assume that the total allowable warehouses for a logistical system cannot exceed 50 and locations are limited to a maximum of one in each state. Given this range of options, there are 1.1259×10^{15} combinations of warehouses to be evaluated in the selection of a least total cost network.

To overcome some of these limitations, variations in shipment size and transportation alternatives need to be introduced to the two-dimensional analysis illustrated in Figure 15-6. Extending the analysis to a more complete treatment of variables typically requires the use of planning models and techniques discussed in Chapter 16. Three critical variables are shipment size, transportation mode, and location alternatives. The constants are level of inventory availability, performance cycle duration, and the specific warehouse locations being evaluated.

In constructing a more comprehensive analysis, shipment size can be grouped in terms of frequency of occurrence and transportation mode economically justified to handle each shipment size within the specified performance cycle time constraints. For each shipment size, a total cost relationship can be identified. The result is a two-dimensional analysis for each shipment size and appropriate transportation mode. Next, the individual two-dimensional profiles can be linked by joining the points of least cost by a planning curve. In a technical sense, this is an **envelope curve** that joins the low total-cost points of individual shipment size/transport mode relationships. Fig-

FIGURE 15-7

**Three-dimensional
total-cost curve**

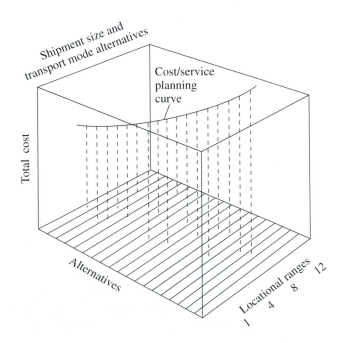

ure 15-7 offers a three-dimensional pictorial of integrated shipment size, transportation mode, and location.

The planning curve joins the point of total least cost for each shipment size. It does not join locational points. For example, the number of locations to support least cost for one size of shipment may be more or less than for another. Further analysis is required to identify the specific locations that offer the least cost alternative for each shipment size and transport combination. Assume that the locations under consideration consist of a network ranging from 1 to 12 warehouses. Within this range, the planning curve will identify a smaller number of acceptable locations for detailed evaluation. In Figure 15-7, the points of least cost, shipment size, and transportation combinations fall within a range of four to eight locations.

Analysis is required to select the final warehouse network. Initially, the time duration of the performance cycle and inventory availability assumptions should be held constant. The service availability and performance cycle duration serve as parameters to help isolate an initial least cost approximation. At a later point in strategy formulation, these parameters can be relaxed and subjected to sensitivity analysis. The fit of the least cost planning curve requires marginal cost analysis for each shipment size/transportation mode combination for networks of four, five, six, seven, and eight warehouse locations. Provided customer service objectives are achieved within the four-to-eight warehouse range, a first-cut least total cost network of potential warehouses is identified.

A final refinement involves the evaluation of specific warehouse sites or facilities. In the case of Figure 15-7, which is also the situation in most complex modeling approaches, the best-fit location network is limited to an array of warehouse locations selected for analysis. The results may be managerially satisfactory but not cost superior to a different group of locations. Each warehouse assortment selected for analysis will have a least cost combination. The final policy may require that the analysis be completed with several different network combinations to identify those most suitable for a given business situation. The final warehouse selection using such a trial and error methodology will never identify the mathematical optimal solution to minimize total logistical cost. It will, however, help management identify a superior network to the existing operation that may better service customers at lower total logistics cost.

To evaluate the wide range of variables in designing a logistical system, complex models have been developed. The assumptions required to support integrated system design are important from the viewpoint of their impact upon strategy formulation. The integrated total cost curve must take into consideration all relevant variables that are critical to logistical system design.

Formulating Logistical Strategy

To finalize logistical strategy, it is necessary to evaluate the relationships between alternative customer service levels and associated cost. While substantial difficulties exist in the measurement of revenue, the comparative evaluation of marginal service performance and related cost offers a way to approximate an ideal logistical system design. The general approach consists of (1) determining a least total cost network, (2) measuring threshold service availability and capability associated with the least total cost system design, (3) conducting sensitivity analysis related to incremental service and cost directly with revenue generation, and (4) finalizing the plan.

Cost Minimization

Just as a physical replication of a geographical area illustrates elevations, depressions, and contours of land surface, an economic map can highlight logistical cost differentials. Generally, peak costs for labor and essential services occur in large metropolitan areas. However, because of demand concentration, least total logistics cost resulting from transportation and inventory consolidation benefits is often minimized in metropolitan areas.

A strategy of least total cost seeks a logistical system network with the lowest fixed and variable costs. A system design to achieve least total cost is driven purely by cost-to-cost trade-offs. In terms of basic relationships, a total least cost design was illustrated in Figure 15-6. The level of customer service that is associated with a least cost logistical design results from safety stock policies and the locational proximity of warehouses to customers. The overall level of customer service associated with any given least total cost system design is referred to as the **threshold service level.**

Threshold Service

To establish a threshold service level it is necessary to initiate network reengineering with policies regarding desired inventory *availability* and *capability.* It is common practice to have the customer service capability based on the existing order entry and processing system, warehouse operations based on standard order fulfillment time at existing facilities, and transportation delivery time-based on capabilities of least cost transportation methods. Given these assumptions, existing performance is the starting point for evaluating potential service improvement.

The typical starting point for customer service availability analysis is to assume performance at a generally acceptable fill rate. Often the prevailing industry standard is used as a first approximation. For example, if the safety stock availability goal were established at a 97.75 percent performance for combined probability of demand and lead time uncertainty, it would be anticipated that approximately 98 out of 100 items ordered would be delivered to specification.

Given the initial assumptions, each customer is assigned a shipment location on the basis of least total cost. In multiproduct situations, selection of service territories for each facility will depend on the products stocked at each warehouse and the degree of consolidation required by customers. Because costs have significant geographical differentials, the service area for any given facility will vary in size and configuration. Figure 15-8 provides an illustration of the assignment of warehouse service areas based upon equalized total delivered cost. The irregularity of service territories results from outbound transportation cost differentials from the three warehouses.

In Figure 15-8 the warehouses are identified by the letters X, Y, and Z. The hypothetical cost associated with each facility represents all logistical cost for an average order except transportation. The differential of average order cost between facilities reflects local differentials.

Around each facility total cost lines are displayed at intervals of $1.50, $2.50, and $3.50. The cost represented by the line is the total cost of logistics, including transportation to points connected along the line. Customers located within a given area can be serviced at a cost less than displayed on the line. The overall service area of each warehouse is determined by lowest total cost assignment. The territory boundary line represents the point of equal total cost between two warehouses. Along this line, total

FIGURE 15-8

Determination of service territories: Three-point, least cost system

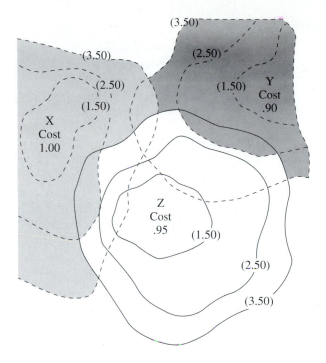

cost to service a customer is equal. However, a substantial difference could exist in delivery time.

Two conditions are assumed in Figure 15-8. First, the illustration is based on distribution of an average order. Thus, outbound logistics costs are equated on the average. To the degree that order size varies from the average, alternative territory boundaries would vary based on shipment size. Second, delivery time is estimated on distance. Transit inventory also is estimated based on delivery time. In accordance with this initial analysis of threshold service, it cannot be concluded that delivery times will be consistent within territories or that equal total logistics cost will be experienced within a service area.

The fact that the initial network is designed to achieve logistical least cost does not mean that threshold customer service will be low. The elapsed time from the customer's order placement to product delivery in a least cost system is expected to be longer on average than would be experienced in alternative networks that have been modified to improve overall service performance. However, customers located near a warehouse facility in all networks have potential to receive rapid delivery. Because the least cost location tends to favor areas of high demand concentration, a substantial number of customers will have rapid delivery potential.

Given an estimate of expected order cycle time, management is in a position to make basic customer delivery commitments. A service statement policy may be as follows:

> Order performance for area A will be 5 days from receipt of orders at the warehouse facility. It is our policy to be able to fill 90 percent of all orders within the 5-day period.

The actual performance of a logistical system is measured by the degree to which such service standards are consistently achieved. Given quantification of the variables involved, the threshold service related to the least total cost system offers the starting point of developing a firm's basic service platform. The next step in policy formulation is to test the customer suitability of the threshold service level.

Service Sensitivity Analysis

The threshold service resulting from the least total cost logistical design provides a basis for sensitivity analysis. The basic service capabilities of a network can be increased or decreased by variation in number of warehouses, change in one or more performance cycles to increase speed or consistency of operations, and/or change in safety stock policy.

Locational Modification

The warehouse structure of the logistical system establishes the service that can be realized without changing the performance cycle or safety stock policy. To illustrate the relationship between number of warehouses and resultant service time, assume an important measure is the percentage of demand fulfilled within a specified time interval. The general impact of adding warehouses to the system is presented in Table 15-5. Several points of interest are illustrated.

First, incremental service is a diminishing function. For example, the first five warehouse locations provided 24-hour performance to 42 percent of all customers. To double the percentage of 24-hour service from 42 to 84 percent, 9 additional warehouses, or a total of 14, are required.

Second, high degrees of service are achieved much faster for longer performance intervals than for the shorter intervals. For example, four warehouse locations provide 85 percent performance within the 96-hour performance cycle. Increasing the total locations from 4 to 14 improved the 96-hour performance by only 9 percent. In contrast, a total of 14 warehouses cannot achieve 85 percent given a 24-hour performance cycle.

TABLE 15-5   Service Capabilities within Time Intervals as a Function of Number of Locations

Network Locations	Percentage Demand by Performance Cycle Duration (hours)			
	24	48	72	96
1	15	31	53	70
2	23	44	61	76
3	32	49	64	81
4	37	55	70	85
5	42	60	75	87
6	48	65	79	89
7	54	70	83	90
8	60	76	84	90
9	65	80	85	91
10	70	82	86	92
11	74	84	87	92
12	78	84	88	93
13	82	85	88	93
14	84	86	89	94

Finally, the total cost associated with each location added to the logistical network increases dramatically. Thus, while the incremental service resulting from additional locations diminishes, the incremental cost associated with each new location increases: the service payoff for each new facility is incrementally less.

Logistics managers are often asked to estimate the inventory impact of adding or deleting warehouses. This relationship between uncertainty and required inventory is called the **portfolio effect.**[7] The portfolio effect can be estimated using the *square root rule*. The square root rule, originally proposed by Maister, suggests that the safety stock increase as a result of adding a warehouse is equal to the ratio of the square root of the number of locations in the newly prepared network divided by the square root of the number of existing locations.[8]

For example, assume that a manager wants to estimate the inventory impact of shifting from a one- to a two-warehouse network. In effect, the network is being doubled. For reasons discussed earlier demand variability will be increased. Using the square root rule, the firm's aggregate safety stock (SS_2) for a two-warehouse system can be estimated as:

$$SS_2 = \frac{\sqrt{N_2}}{\sqrt{N_1}} \times SS_1$$

$$= \frac{1.41}{1.0} \times SS_1$$

$$= 1.41 \times SS_1$$

where

SS_2 = Aggregate safety stock for N_2 warehouses or product variations;

N_2 = Number of warehouse locations or product variations for the new configuration;

N_1 = Number of warehouse locations or product variations for the existing configuration; and

SS_1 = Aggregate safety stock for N_1 warehouses or product variations.

The projected inventory increase resulting from adding a second warehouse is estimated as a 141 percent increase in safety stock. Table 15-6 illustrates the impact of the change for a range of warehouses or product variations. Although the square root rule works reasonably well for inventory projections, it does require some assumptions regarding demand to improve precision. The first assumption is that the stocking locations or product variations must have approximately the same level of demand. Specifically, if there are currently two stocking locations, they must have approximately the same demand levels for the square root rule to work accurately. Second, the demand levels at each warehouse or for each product variation must not be correlated. This means that demand deviation for each location must be independent. Finally, the square root rule requires that demand for each warehouse approximate a normal distri-

---

[7] For a more detailed discussion of the portfolio effect, see Walter Zinn, Michael Levy, and Donald J. Bowersox, "Measuring the Effect of Inventory Centralization/Decentralization on Aggregate Safety Stock: The Square Root Law Revisited," *Journal of Business Logistics* 10, no. 1 (1989), pp. 1–14; and Philip T. Evers, "Expanding the Square Root Law: An Analysis of Both Safety and Cycle Stocks," *Logistics and Transportation Review* 31, no. 1 (1995), pp. 1–20.

[8] D. H. Maister, "Centralization of Inventories and the 'Square Root Law,'" *International Journal of Physical Distribution* 6, no. 3 (1976), pp. 124–134.

TABLE 15-6   **Inventory Impact of Modified Warehouse Network**

Network Locations	Safety Stock Level
1	97
2	141
3	175
4	203
5	229

bution. While the appropriateness of these assumptions must be reviewed, the square root rule is a useful way to estimate the inventory impact of adding or deleting warehouses to a logistical network.

Performance Cycle Modification

Speed and consistency of service can be varied to a specific market or customer by a modification of some aspect of the performance cycle. To improve service, electronic ordering and premium transportation can be used. Therefore, geographical proximity and the number of warehouses do not equate directly to fast or consistent delivery. The decision to increase service by adopting a faster performance cycle arrangement will typically increase variable cost. In contrast, service improvement, by virtue of added warehouses, involves a high degree of fixed cost and could result in less overall system flexibility.

No generalizations can be offered regarding the cost/service improvement ratio attainable from performance cycle modification. The typical relationship of premium to lowest cost transportation results in a significant incentive in favor of large shipments. Thus, if order volume is substantial, the economics of logistics can be expected to favor use of a warehouse or consolidation point to service a market area.

The impact of using premium transportation will increase total cost. Adjustments from the least total cost logistical system can typically be justified if the improved service results in increased revenue. Industry Insight 15-1 illustrates how Timberland Company adjusted its threshold service level after realizing its customer profile was changing.

Safety Stock Modification

A direct way to change service is to increase or decrease the amount of safety stock held at one or more warehouses. The impact of increasing the safety stock across a total system will shift the average inventory cost curve upward. A goal of increasing customer service availability will result in increased safety stocks at each warehouse. As availability is increased, the safety stocks required to achieve each equal increment of availability increase at an increasing rate.

Finalizing Strategy

Management often falls into the trap of being overly optimistic in terms of service commitments to customers. The result may be excessively high customer expectations followed by erratic performance. In part, such overcommitment results from lack of understanding of the total cost required to support high, zero-defect service.

The final step in establishing a strategy is to evaluate the cost of incremental service in terms of generating offsetting revenue. To illustrate, assume that the current

INDUSTRY INSIGHT 15-1 PUTTING A SHINE ON SHOE OPERATIONS

At Timberland Co. reengineering has unraveled some old assumptions. The Hampton, New Hampshire, shoemaker had always measured productivity by the size of each delivery, so priority was given to department store orders rather than those from the small boutiques that were a growing chunk of its business. Two years ago, Timberland set out to change its routine.

Timberland began by scheduling two or more shipments to each customer a week, instead of one big delivery. Scanners automatically track inventory and create shipping bills, so it's as efficient to handle small orders as big ones.

Reengineering is hitting other operations, too. Instead of having one department take orders and another verify credit, the two were merged. Now, orders are sent to manufacturing via a network, faster and with fewer errors.

Timberland is also taking to the electronic highway to reach customers. By letting stores transmit orders automatically to its computers, the company expects to double sales volume for every 25 percent increase in its sales force. At Timberland, staying a top shoemaker means not sticking to its last—or the past.

From Gary McWilliams, "The Technology Payoff: A Sweeping Reorganization of Work Itself Is Boosting Productivity," *Business Week,* June 14, 1993, p. 59.

---

system is geared to service at least 90 percent of all customers at a 95 percent inventory availability within 60 hours of order receipt. Furthermore, assume that the current logistical system is meeting these objectives at lowest total cost by utilizing a network of five warehouses. Marketing, however, is not satisfied and believes that service capability should be increased to the point where 90 percent of all customers would receive 97 percent inventory availability delivered within 24 hours. Logistical management needs to estimate the cost of this strategic commitment.

Figure 15-9 illustrates how the alternative strategies can be evaluated. Marketing is requesting a 2 percent improvement in inventory availability combined with a 36-hour improvement in delivery capability. Assume design analysis identifies that 12 warehouse facilities represent the lowest cost network capable of achieving the new service standards. The total cost of this expanded service capability is measured on the vertical axis of Figure 15-9 by the distance from points A and B. The total cost of achieving marketing's requested service will require approximately a $400,000 per year increase in logistical cost. Assuming an average before-tax profit margin of 10 percent of sales, it would be necessary to generate $4 million in incremental sales to break even on the cost of providing the added service.

Acceptance or rejection of marketing's proposal for increased service involves strategic positioning. Logistics can provide whichever performance the firm's overall customer service strategy requires. Policy changes, once adopted, will influence the logistical network design. To finalize logistical policy management typically requires considering a range of strategic alternatives. In addition to lowest total cost, at least four other strategic models are available: maximum service, profit maximization, maximum competitive advantage, and minimum asset deployment. Each strategy will drive a unique logistical network design.

Maximum Service

A maximum service strategy is rarely implemented. A system designed to provide maximum service shifts design emphasis from cost to availability and delivery performance. Maximum service areas can be developed similar to the least cost service areas illustrated in Figure 15-8; however, the cost lines are replaced by service time

FIGURE 15-9

Comparative total cost for 5- and 12-distribution point systems

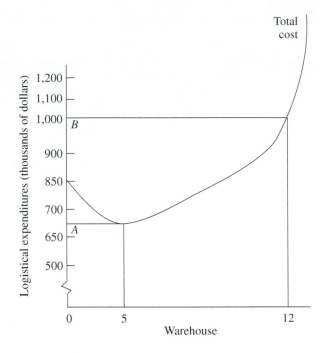

boundaries. The limits of each facility service area are determined by the capability to provide the required delivery. As with cost-oriented service areas, time-oriented areas will be irregular because of transport-route configurations. Total cost variation from a least cost to a maximum service system to service the same customers will be substantial. Servicing the total U.S. market on an overnight basis could require from 30 to 40 warehouses and the use of highly dependable transportation. The number of warehouses could be reduced by the use of premium transportation.

Maximum Profit

Most enterprises aspire to maximize profit in the design of logistical systems. Theoretically, the service area of each warehouse should be determined by establishing a minimum profit contribution for customers located at varying distances from the facility. Because warehouses are normally located near high-volume markets, the greater the distance a customer is located from the service area center, generally the higher the cost of logistics. This cost increase occurs not only because of distance but also because of lower customer density at the periphery of the warehouse service area. At the point where the cost of serving peripheral customers results in minimum allowable profit margins, further extensions of the service territory become unprofitable on a total-cost-delivered basis.

If the customer were provided improved service, it is possible that it would purchase more of the overall product assortment sold by a firm. In theory, additional service should be introduced to the point where marginally generated revenue equals marginal costs. At this point of equilibrium, no additional service would be justified. Additional service may or may not result from increasing the number of warehouses. The desired service might be provided best by a supplemental delivery system using direct or dual distribution. The theoretical profit maximization position is easier to state than to actually measure. Referring back to Figure 15-8, the point of equalization normally will be found along the total cost curve to the right of the least cost point but considerably short of the point where total costs rise rapidly. For the situation illustrated in Figure 15-8, the profit maximization system as a first approximation could be expected to fall between a network of 6 and 10 warehouses.

Table 15-5 presented a quantification of the service capabilities of 14 warehouses for a given customer configuration. The actual service gains that will result from adding warehouses can be expected to vary in each business situation. As a general rule, the service benefits of adding warehouses become progressively smaller. The dollar increase for adding each warehouse reflects the additional cost of achieving faster delivery. Such operating cost estimates allow an assessment of the marginal value of increased service. Given a range of cost/service relationships, management has considerable information to help in the establishment of a customer service strategy.

Maximum Competitive Advantage

Under special situations, the most desirable strategy to guide logistical system design may be to seek maximum competitive advantage. Although there are many ways in which systems can be modified to gain competitive advantage, two are presented to illustrate strategic considerations.

Segmental Service.   A common modification in least cost design consists of improving service to protect major customers from competitive inroads. Management needs to be concerned with how expectations of key customers are being satisfied. If the existing service policy is only capable of providing 42 percent of the customers with 24-hour delivery at 95 percent inventory availability, care must be taken to be sure that the most profitable customers are getting the best service possible.

To illustrate, assume that a firm is a typical mass marketer and that 20 percent of its customers purchased 80 percent of its products. Furthermore, assume that this group of critical customers is located at 75 different delivery destinations. The key to strategic positioning is to determine whether the 75 critical customer destinations are included in the 42 percent of all customers receiving 24-hour delivery. Under conditions of equal customer geographical dispersion, the probability is about 0.5 that the individual customer would be included in the 42 percent. In other words, the expectation would be that on the average only approximately 40 to 45 of the core customers would receive 24-hour service.

Table 15-7 presents the type of results generated from such an assessment process. The actual number of core customers receiving 24-hour delivery service in this example is 53. Thus, although 42 percent of *all* customers receive 24-hour service, 76 percent of the *core* customers receive this service. In addition, the iterative process identifies core customers who receive less than superior service. In this analysis, two key customers are getting 60-hour delivery.

TABLE 15-7   Core-Customer Interrogative Results

Total Core Customers	Number of Core Customers Serviced by Hour Intervals			
	24	36	48	60
75	53	16	4	2

This situation can be rectified by modifying capabilities to accommodate specific customers. The cost of a system providing 24-hour service to all core customers can be isolated to estimate the cost of implementing a segmental service policy. A logical alternative might be the use of premium transportation to service key customers that do not currently receive 24-hour delivery.

Several alternative systems modifications are also possible. Management may wish to examine service provided to the most profitable customers. Evaluations can be made regarding customers or noncustomers with the greatest growth potential. In addition, an enterprise may wish to evaluate the incremental cost of providing superior service to the best customers of major competitors. Although all such modifications may increase total cost and decrease short-range profits, the long-term gain may be a substantial improvement in competitive position.

Justified High-Cost Warehouse.   An additional application of design modification to capitalize on competitive situations is an economically justified high-cost warehouse. This situation is pertinent especially to smaller or niche businesses. Because of the rigidities inherent in large firms, pricing policies are likely to be inflexible. Antitrust legislation reinforces such rigidities. The result is that large firms selling in broad geographical markets tend to disregard unique cost and demand situations in localized markets or find it nearly impossible to adjust marketing and logistical systems to accommodate such unique opportunities. This inflexibility creates opportunities for smaller firms, enabling them to make significant investment in logistical capability to attract the localized market segment.

Location of a small-scale plant or warehouse facility in a minor market some distance from major competitors can establish a localized service capability more or less insulated from competition. The logic of this special situation was developed under the general discussion of factors influencing facility location. At this time it is sufficient to highlight that major firms typically follow one or two policies concerning these unique opportunities.

First, a large enterprise can elect to avoid such localized situations. This policy of concentrating on primary markets can be an opportunity for the higher-cost, smaller firm. Second, major producers may introduce smaller-scale facilities or institute direct logistical systems in an effort to service local demand. Following the first policy will result in a system approaching a least cost configuration. The second policy will require substantial logistical system modification, with higher costs and lower short-range profits.

Minimal Asset Deployment

A final logistical strategy may be motivated by a desire to minimize assets committed to the logistical system. A firm that desires to maintain maximum flexibility may use variable cost logistical components such as public warehouses and for-hire transportation. Such a strategy might result in higher total logistical costs than could be realized by asset commitment to obtain economies of scale. However, risk would be less and the strategy would increase overall flexibility.

Integration of logistical strategy to support overall enterprise operations requires precise customer service commitment. From the viewpoint of designing a logistical system, total least cost and associated threshold service offer an ideal platform for undertaking cost/service sensitivity analysis.

Summary

The primary determinants of logistics network design are requirements established by integrated procurement, manufacturing, and market distribution strategies. Within the framework of these interlocking strategies, logistics requirements are satisfied by blending transportation and inventory capabilities. These capabilities play out across a network of enterprise facilities. Important in the performance of logistics requirements are warehouse facilities. Such facilities are justified by logistical system design in terms of their contribution to cost reduction, service improvement, or a combination of both.

Transportation and inventory economics are critical network design considerations. When seeking least cost logistics, transportation deals with the spatial aspects of logistics. The ability to consolidate transportation is a primary justification for including warehouses in a network design. Inventory introduces the temporal dimension of logistics. Average inventory increases as the number of warehouses in a system increase given a constant demand situation. Total cost integration provides a framework for simultaneous integration of logistics, manufacturing, and procurement costs. Thus, total cost analysis provides the methodology for integration across the network.

Accurate total cost analysis is not without practical problems. Foremost is the fact that a great many important costs are not specifically measured or reported by standard accounting systems. A second problem involved in total cost analysis is the need to consider a wide variety of network design alternatives. To develop complete analysis of a planning situation, alternative shipment sizes, modes of shipment, and range of available warehouse locations must be considered.

These problems can be overcome if care is taken in network analysis. The cost format recommended for total cost analysis is to group all functional costs associated with inventory and transportation. The significant contribution of total cost integration is that it provides a simultaneous analysis of time-and space-related costs in logistical network design.

The formulation of a logistical strategy requires that total cost analysis be evaluated in terms of customer service performance. Logistical service is measured in terms of availability, capability, and quality of performance. The ultimate realization of each service attribute is directly related to logistical network design. To realize the highest level of logistical operational support within overall enterprise integration, customers should be provided service to the point where marginal cost equates to marginal revenue. Such marginal equalization is not practical to achieve; however, the relationship serves as a normative planning goal.

The formulation of a service policy starts from the identification and analysis of the least total cost system design. Given a managerially specified inventory availability target, service capability associated with the least cost design can be identified. This initial service level is referred to as the threshold service level. To evaluate potential modifications to the least cost design, sensitivity analysis is used. Service levels may be improved by modifying (1) variation in the number of facilities, (2) change in one or more aspects of the performance cycle, and/or (3) change in safety stock.

Beyond least cost design, four potential strategies are maximum service, maximum profit, maximum competitive advantage, and minimal asset deployment. From among this range of strategic options the end objective of logistical system design is to select a logistics strategy that supports overall business strategy.

Challenge Questions

1. Describe in your words the meaning of spatial/temporal integration in logistical system integration.

2. What justification of logic can be presented to support the placement of a warehouse in a logistical system?

3. Why do transportation costs decrease as the number of warehouses in a system increases? Why do inventory costs increase as the number of warehouses in a system increases?

4. In your words, what is the locational impact of inventory? How does it differ for transit inventories and safety stocks?

5. What is meant by the level of threshold service of a least cost system?

6. Why does customer service not increase proportionately to increases in total cost when a logistical system is being designed?

7. In Table 15-5, why does customer service speed of performance increase faster for customers located greater distances from a warehouse facility? What is the implication of this relationship for system design?

8. Discuss the differences between improving customer service through faster and more consistent transportation, higher inventory levels, and/or expanded numbers of warehouses.

9. What is the difference between minimum total cost and short-range profit maximization policies in system design?

10. In what ways can customer service performance be improved by incorporating flexible distribution operations into a logistical system design?

16   DESIGN PROCESS AND TECHNIQUES

The logistics environment is constantly evolving as a result of changes in markets, competitors, suppliers, and technology. To develop and focus the enterprise strategy to match this changing environment, a systematic planning and design methodology is required to effectively evaluate alternatives. This chapter describes a generalized methodology that includes an overview of techniques used for logistics planning.

Planning Methodology

Even for established industries, a firm's markets, demands, costs, and service requirements change rapidly in response to customer and competitor behavior. In response to these changes, firms often face questions such as: (1) How many distribution warehouses should be used and where should they be located? (2) What are the inventory/service trade-offs for each warehouse? (3) What types of transportation

Figure 16-1

Research process

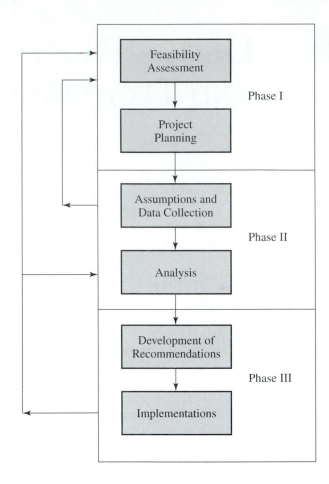

equipment should be used and how should vehicles be routed? and (4) Is investment in a new materials handling technology justified?

Such questions are usually characterized as complex and data-intensive. The complexity is due to the large number of factors influencing logistics total cost and the range of alternative solutions. The data-intensiveness is due to the large amount of information required to evaluate logistics alternatives. Typical information analyses must include possible service alternatives, cost characteristics, and operating technologies. These analyses require a structured process and effective analytical tools.

Just as no ideal logistical system is suitable for all enterprises, the method for identifying and evaluating alternative logistics strategies can vary extensively. However, there is a general process applicable to most logistics design and analysis situations. Figure 16-1 illustrates the generalized process flow.

The process is segmented into three phases: problem definition and planning, data collection and analysis, and recommendation and implementation.

Phase I: Problem Definition and Planning

Phase I of logistics system design and planning provides the foundation for the entire project. A thorough and well-documented problem definition and plan are essential to all that follows.

Feasibility Assessment

Logistics design and planning must begin with a comprehensive evaluation of the current logistics situation. The objective is to understand the environment, process, and performance characteristics of the current system and to determine what, if any, modifications might be necessary. The process of evaluating the need for change is referred to as **feasibility assessment,** and includes the activities of situational analysis, supporting logic development, and cost/benefit estimation.

Situational Analysis

Situational analysis is the collection of performance measures and characteristics that describe the current logistics environment. A typical appraisal requires an internal review, a market assessment, a competitive evaluation, and a technology assessment to determine improvement potential and opportunities.

The internal review is necessary to develop a clear understanding of existing logistics processes. It profiles historical performance, data availability, strategies, operations, and tactical policies and practices. The review usually covers the overall logistics process as well as each logistics function.

A complete self-appraisal for an internal review examines all major resources, such as workforce, equipment, facilities, relationships, and information. In particular, the internal review should focus on a comprehensive evaluation of the existing system's capabilities and deficiencies. Each element of the logistics system should be carefully examined with respect to its stated objectives and its capabilities to meet those objectives. For example, is the logistics management information system consistently providing and measuring the customer service objectives desired by the marketing department? Likewise, does the material management process adequately support manufacturing requirements? Does the current network of distribution centers effectively support customer service objectives? Finally, how do logistics performance capabilities and measures compare across business units and locations? These and many similar questions form the basis of the self-appraisal required for the internal analysis. The comprehensive review attempts to identify the opportunities that might motivate or justify logistics system redesign or refinement.

Table 16-1 lists some of the topics frequently covered during an internal review. The suggested format is not the only approach, but it does highlight the fact that the assessment must consider the processes, decisions, and key measures for each major logistics activity. Process considerations focus on physical and information flows through the value chain. Decision considerations focus on the logic and criteria currently used for value chain management. Measurement considerations focus on the key performance indicators and the firm's ability to measure them.

The specific review content depends on the scope of the analysis. It is unusual that the information desired is readily available. The purpose of the internal review is not detailed data collection but rather a diagnostic look at current logistics processes and procedures as well as a probe to determine data availability. Most significantly, the internal review is directed at the identification of areas where substantial opportunity for improvement exists. The external assessment is a review of the trends and service demands required by customers. The market assessment objective is to document and formalize customer perceptions and desires with regard to changes in the firm's logistics capabilities. The assessment might include interviews with select customers or more substantive customer surveys.[1]

---

[1] Francis J. Gonillart and Frederick D. Sturdivant, "Spend a Day in the Life of Your Customers," *Harvard Business Review* 72, no. 1 (January/February 1994), pp. 116–25.

TABLE 16-1   **Selected Internal Review Topics**

	Processes	Decisions	Measurements
Customer Service	What is the current information flow? What is the order profile and how is it changing? How are orders received?	How are order sourcing decisions made? What happens when inventory is not available to fill an order?	What are the key measures of customer service? How are they measured? What is the current performance level?
Materials Management	What is the current material flow through plants and distribution centers? What processes are performed at each manufacturing site and distribution center?	How are manufacturing and distribution center capacity allocation decisions made? How are production planning and scheduling decisions made?	What are the key manufacturing and distribution center capacity limitations? What are the key measures of materials management performance? How are they measured? What is the current performance level?
Transportation	What modes are currently used? What is the weight profile of orders and shipments and how are they different? What is the flow for requesting, paying, and exchanging information with carriers? What is the information flow for shipment documentation?	How are the mode and carrier choice decisions made for each shipment? How are carriers evaluated?	What are the key transportation performance measures? How are they measured? What is the current performance level? What are the relative economic performance characteristics of each mode and carrier?
Warehousing	What storage and handling facilities are currently used and what functions do they perform? What product lines are maintained in each facility? What are the storage, handling, and other value-added functions that are or may be performed at each facility?	How are shipment consolidation decisions made at each facility? What decisions are made by material handlers and how do they make those decisions? How is product stored in the facility and how are product selection decisions made?	What is the throughput and storage volume of each facility? What are the key warehouse performance measures? How are they measured? What is the current performance level? What are the relative economic performance characteristics of each facility?
Inventory	What value-added functions do current inventory stockpiles play?	How are inventory management decisions made? Who makes them and what information is used to support the decisions?	What is the corporate inventory carrying cost? What are the key inventory performance measures? How are they measured? What is the current performance level?

Table 16-2 illustrates typical market assessment topics. The assessment should focus on external relationships with suppliers, customers, and consumers. The assessment should consider trends in requirements and processes as well as enterprise and competitor capabilities.

TABLE 16-2   Sample External Assessment Topics

	Market Trends	Enterprise Capabilities	Competitive Capabilities
Suppliers	What value-added services are suppliers providing? What are the major bottlenecks with current suppliers?	What are the opportunities to internalize or outsource value-added services? How can processes be changed to reduce bottlenecks?	What actions are competitors taking to refine product and information flow with suppliers? What are competitive benchmarks in terms of number of suppliers, cost characteristics, and performance measures?
Customers	What are the major constraints and bottlenecks when servicing key customers? What are the cost impacts of these constraints and bottlenecks? How are customer ordering patterns changing? What are the primary customers' criteria?	What functions or activities can be shifted to or from customers to enhance logistics system performance? How do customers evaluate our performance on their key measurement criteria?	What services are competitors providing our customers? How do competitors perform on key performance measures as identified by customers?
Consumers	How are consumer purchasing patterns changing with respect to purchase locations, times, and selection criteria? What are the consumer trends with respect to logistics activities such as purchase quantities, packaging, home delivery, and product quality?	How are we able to respond to changes in consumer purchasing patterns and selection criteria?	How are our competitors responding to changes in consumer purchasing patterns and selection criteria?

Technology assessment focuses on the application and capabilities of key logistics technologies, including transportation, storage, materials handling, packaging, and information processing. The assessment considers the firm's capabilities in terms of current technologies and the potential for applying new technologies. For example, can advanced materials handling capabilities offered through third-party suppliers enhance logistics performance? What is the role of advanced information technology, communication, and decision support systems in guiding responsive logistics capabilities? Finally, what can satellite and scanning communications technologies contribute to logistics system capability? The objective of the technology assessment is to identify technology advancements that can provide effective trade-offs with other logistics resources such as transportation or inventory. Table 16-3 illustrates typical technology assessment topics for a number of logistics functions. Such an assessment should be completed with respect to each component of the logistics system as well as from the perspective of overall integration.

Supporting Logic Development

The second feasibility assessment task is development of a **supporting logic** to integrate the findings of the internal review, external assessment, and technology study. Supporting logic development often constitutes the most difficult part of the strategic planning process. The purpose of the situational analysis is to provide senior management with the best possible understanding of the strengths and weaknesses of existing

TABLE 16-3   **Typical Technology Assessment**

	Current Technology	State-of-the-Art Technology
Forecasting	What are the current technologies for collecting, maintaining, and developing forecasts?	How are the best firms developing forecasts?
Order Entry	What order entry technologies are used currently?	How are the best firms performing order entry?
	What order entry technology are customers requiring?	What new technologies are available to improve order entry effectiveness?
Order Processing	What is the process to allocate available inventory to customer orders?	How are the best firms performing order processing?
	What are the limitations of the current approach?	What new technologies (hardware and software) are available to improve order processing effectiveness?
Requirements Planning	What decision processes are used to determine production and distribution inventory requirements?	How are the best firms making production and inventory planning decisions?
	How are these processes supported with current information and decision aids?	What new technologies are available to improve requirements planning effectiveness?
Invoicing and EDI	How are invoices, inquiries, advanced shipment notifications, and payments currently transmitted?	How are the best firms using EDI?
		What new communications and data exchange technologies are available to improve invoicing and other forms of customer communication?
Warehouse Operations	How are warehouse personnel and scheduling decisions made?	How are the best firms using information and materials handling technologies in the warehouse?
	How are warehousing operating instructions provided to supervisors and material handlers?	What new information and materials handling technologies are available to improve warehouse operating effectiveness?
	How do warehouse supervisors and material handlers track activities and performance?	
Transportation	How are transportation consolidation, routing, and scheduling decisions made?	How are the best firms using information, packaging, and loading technologies with carriers?
	How is transportation documentation developed and communicated with carriers and customers?	What new information, packaging, loading, and communication technologies are available to improve transportation operating effectiveness?
	How are transportation costs determined, assessed, and monitored?	
	What packaging and loading technologies are used?	
Decision Support	How are logistics tactical and strategic planning decisions made?	How are the best companies making similar tactical or strategic decisions?
	What information is used and what analysis is completed?	What information and evaluation technologies are available to enhance decision effectiveness?

logistics capabilities for both current and future environments. Supporting logic development builds on this comprehensive review in three ways.

First, it must determine if there are sufficient logistics improvement opportunities to justify detailed research and analysis. In a sense, supporting logic development forces a critical review of potential opportunities and a determination of whether additional investigation is justified. Supporting logic development uses the logistics principles (e.g., tapering principle, principle of inventory aggregation) discussed in previous chapters to determine the feasibility of conducting detailed analysis and the potential benefits. While completing the remaining tasks in the managerial planning process does not commit a firm to implementation or even guarantee a new logistics system design, the potential benefits of change should be clearly identified when developing the supporting logic.

Second, supporting logic development critically evaluates current procedures and practices with a comprehensive factual analysis to remove perceptual biases. Identification of areas with improvement potential, as well as those where operations are satisfactory, provides a foundation to determine the need for strategic adjustment. For example, it may be apparent that excess inventory is a serious problem and significant potential exists to reduce cost and improve service. While the appraisal process frequently confirms that many aspects of the existing system are more right than wrong, the conclusion should be based on improvement. If supporting logic affirms the current number and location of distribution centers, subsequent analysis can focus on streamlining inventory levels without serious risk of suboptimization. The deliverables of this evaluation process include classification of planning and evaluation issues prioritized into primary and secondary categories across short- and long-range planning horizons.

Third, the process of developing supporting logic should include clear statements of potential redesign alternatives. The statement should include: (1) definition of current procedures and systems, (2) identification of the most likely system design alternatives based on leading industry and competitive practices, and (3) suggestion of innovative approaches based on new theory and technologies. The alternatives should challenge existing practices, but they must also be practical. The less frequently a redesign project is conducted to reevaluate current procedures and designs, the more important it is to identify a range of options for consideration. For example, evaluation of a total logistics management system or distribution network should consider a wider range of options if done every 5 years than if completed every 2 years.

At this point in the planning and design process, it is well worth the effort to construct flow diagrams and/or outlines illustrating the basic concepts associated with each alternative. The illustrations frame opportunities for flexible logistics practices, clearly outline value-added and information flow requirements, and provide a comprehensive overview of the options. Some refined or segmented logistics practices are difficult to illustrate in a single flow diagram. For example, regional variations, product-mix variations, and differential shipment policies are difficult to depict, although they do form the basis of design alternatives. When segmental strategies are proposed, it is easier to portray each option independently.

A recommended procedure requires the manager responsible for evaluating the logistical strategy to develop a logical statement and justification of potential benefits. Using the customer service concept (Chapter 3) and logistics integration logic and methodology (Chapter 15), the manager should document and rationalize the most attractive strategy alternatives.

Cost/Benefit Estimate

The final feasibility assessment task, the **cost/benefit estimate,** is an estimate of the potential benefits of performing a logistics analysis and implementing the recommendations. Benefits should be categorized in terms of service improvements, cost reduction, and cost prevention. The categories are not mutually exclusive given that an ideal logistics strategy might include some degree of all three benefits simultaneously.

Service improvement includes results that enhance availability, quality, or capability. Improved service increases loyalty of existing customers and may also attract new business.

Cost reduction benefits may be observed in two forms. First, benefits may occur as a result of a one-time reduction in financial or managerial resources required to operate the logistics system. For example, logistical redesign may allow the sale of distribution facilities, materials handling devices, or information technology equipment.

Reductions in capital deployed for inventory and other distribution-related assets can significantly enhance a firm's performance if ongoing costs are eliminated and capital is freed up for alternative development. Second, cost reductions may be found in the form of out-of-pocket or variable expenses. For example, new technologies for materials handling and information processing often reduce variable cost by allowing more efficient processing and operations.

Cost prevention reduces involvement in programs and operations experiencing cost increases. For example, many materials handling and information technology upgrades are at least partially justified through financial analysis of the implications of future labor availability and wage levels. Naturally, any cost-prevention justification is based on an estimate of future conditions and therefore is vulnerable to some error. While logistics system redesign may not be approved entirely on the basis of cost prevention because of such uncertainty, these preventative measures are still important to consider.

No rules exist to determine when a planning situation offers adequate cost/benefit potential to justify an in-depth effort. Ideally, some review should be completed on a continuous basis at regularly specified intervals to assure the viability of current and future logistics operations. In the final analysis, the decision to undertake in-depth planning will depend on how convincing the supporting logic is, how believable estimated benefits are, and whether estimated benefits offer sufficient return on investment to justify organizational and operational change. These potential benefits must be balanced against the out-of-pocket cost required to complete the process.

Although they are not always a goal of a planning and design project, immediate improvement opportunities are a frequent feasibility assessment result. Enhanced logistics performance achieved through immediate improvements can often increase revenue or decrease cost sufficiently to justify the remainder of an analysis. As the project team identifies these opportunities, a steering committee should evaluate each opportunity to determine the return and implementation requirements.

Project Planning

Project planning is the second Phase I activity. Logistics system complexity requires that any effort to identify and evaluate strategic or tactical alternatives must be planned thoroughly to provide a sound basis for change. Project planning involves five specific items: statement of objectives, statement of constraints, measurement standards, analysis procedures, and project work plan.

Statement of Objectives
The **statement of objectives** documents the cost and service expectations for the logistics system revisions. It is essential that they be stated specifically and in terms of measurable factors. The objectives define market or industry segments, the time frame for revisions, and specific performance requirements. These requirements typically define specific service levels that management is seeking to achieve. For example, the following suggest a combination of measurable objectives that might be used to guide a logistics analysis:

1. Inventory availability:
   - 99% for category A products,
   - 95% for category B products,
   - 90% for category C products;

2. Desired delivery of 98% of all orders within 48 hours of order placement;

3. Minimize customer shipments from secondary distribution centers;

4. Fill mixed commodity orders without back order on a minimum of 85 percent of all orders;

5. Hold back orders for a maximum of 5 days; and

6. Provide the 50 most profitable customers with perfect order performance on 98 percent of all orders.

Specific definition of these objectives directs system design efforts to achieve explicit customer service performance levels. Total system cost to meet the service objectives can then be determined using the appropriate analytical method. To the extent that logistics total cost does not fall within management expectations, alternative customer service performance levels can be evaluated using sensitivity analysis to determine the impact on overall logistics cost.

Alternatively, performance objectives can establish maximum total cost constraints, and then a system that achieves maximum customer service level within an acceptable logistics budget may be designed. Such cost-oriented objectives are practical since recommendations are guaranteed to function within acceptable budget ranges but lack sensitivity to service-oriented system design.

Statement of Constraints

The second project planning consideration concerns **design constraints.** On the basis of the situational analysis, it is expected that senior management will place restrictions on the scope of permissible system modifications. The nature of such restrictions will depend upon the specific circumstances of individual firms. However, two typical examples are provided to illustrate how constraints can affect the overall planning process.

One restriction common to distribution system design concerns the network of manufacturing facilities and their product-mix assortment. To simplify the study, management often holds existing manufacturing facilities and product mix constant for logistical system redesign. Such constraints may be justified on the basis of large financial investments in existing production facilities and the ability of the organization to absorb change.

A second example of constraints concerns marketing channels and physical distribution activities of separate divisions. In firms with a traditional pattern of decentralized profit responsibility, management may elect to include some divisions while omitting others from redesign consideration. Thus, some divisions are managerially identified as candidates for change while others are not.

All design constraints serve to limit the scope of the plan. However, as one executive stated, "Why study things we don't plan to do anything about?" Unless there is a reasonable chance that management will be inclined to accept recommendations to significantly change logistics strategy or operations, their limitations may best be treated as a study constraint.

The purpose of developing a statement of constraints is to have a well-defined starting point and overall perspective for the planning effort. If computerized analysis techniques are used, major constraints may be reconsidered later. In contrast to the situation assessment discussed earlier, the statement of constraints defines specific organizational elements, buildings, systems, procedures, and/or practices to be retained from the existing logistical system.

Measurement Standards

The feasibility assessment often highlights the need for development of **managerial performance standards.** Such standards direct the project by identifying cost structures and performance penalties and by providing a means to assess success. Management must stipulate measurement standards and objectives for each category as a prerequisite to plan formulation. It is important that the standards adequately reflect total system performance rather than a limited, suboptimal focus on logistics functions. Once formulated, such standards must be monitored and tracked throughout system development to allow benchmarking the result of the changes. Although considerable managerial discretion exists in the formulation of standards, care must be exercised not to dilute the validity of the analysis and subsequent results by setting impractical goals.

An important measurement requirement is to quantify a list of assumptions that underlie or provide the logic supporting the standards. These assumptions should receive top-management approval because they can significantly shape the results of the strategic plan. For example, a relatively small variation in the standard cost and procedure for evaluating inventory can create major variations in the strategic plan.[2]

Measurement standards should include definitions of how cost components such as transportation, inventory, and order processing are calculated, including detailed financial account references. The standards must also include specification of relevant customer service measures and methods for calculation.

Analysis Technique

Once the critical issues and alternatives are defined, the appropriate **analysis technique** should be determined. Analysis techniques range from simple manual analysis to elaborate computerized decision support tools. For example, models incorporating optimization or simulation algorithms are common when evaluating and comparing alternative logistics warehouse networks. However, many planning and design projects can be effectively completed using only manual or spreadsheet-based analyses. Once the project objectives and constraints are defined, project planning must identify alternative solution techniques and select the best approach. Accenture annually publishes information regarding software applications for logistics decision support.[3] Specific types of applications are discussed later in the chapter.

Selection of an analysis technique must consider the information necessary to evaluate the project issues and options. Specifically, critical performance measures and logistics system scope must be identified and evaluated. Technique selection must also consider the availability and format of required data.

Project Work Plan

On the basis of feasibility assessment, objectives, constraints, and analysis technique, a project work plan must be determined and the resources and time required for completion identified. The alternatives and opportunities specified during the feasibility assessment provide the basis for determining the scope of the study. In turn, the scope determines the completion time.

---

[2]For a detailed measurement discussion, see Patrick M. Byrne and William J. Markham, *Improving Quality and Productivity in the Logistics Process* (Oak Brook, IL: Council of Logistics Management, 1991), chap. 10.

[3]Accenture, *Logistics Software* (Oak Brook, IL: Council of Logistics Management, 2000).

Project management is responsible for the achievement of expected results within time and budget constraints. One of the most common errors in strategic planning is to underestimate the time required to complete a specific assignment. Overruns require greater financial expenditures and reduce project credibility. Fortunately, there are a number of PC-based software packages available to structure projects, guide resource allocation, and measure progress. Such methodologies identify deliverables and the interrelationship between tasks.[4]

Phase II: Data Collection and Analysis

Once the feasibility assessment and project plan are completed, Phase II focuses on data collection and analysis. This includes activities to define assumptions and collect data and to analyze alternatives.

Assumptions and Data Collection

This activity builds on the feasibility assessment and project plan to develop detailed planning assumptions and identify data collection requirements by (1) defining analysis approaches and techniques, (2) defining and reviewing assumptions, (3) identifying data sources, (4) collecting data, and (5) collecting validation data.

Defining Analysis Approaches and Techniques

Although it is not necessarily first, an early task is the determination of the appropriate analysis approach and the acquisition of necessary analysis techniques. While a wide number of options are available, the most common techniques are analytical, simulation, and optimization. The analytical approach uses standard numerical methods such as those available through spreadsheets to evaluate each logistics alternative. A typical example of an analytical approach is the determination of inventory/service trade-offs using the formulas discussed in Chapter 10. Spreadsheet availability and capability have increased the application of analytical tools for distribution applications.

A simulation approach can be likened to a laboratory for testing supply chain alternatives. Simulation is widely used, particularly when significant uncertainty is involved. The testing environment can be *physical,* such as a model materials handling system that physically illustrates product flow in a scaled-down environment, or *numerical,* such as a computer model of a materials handling environment that illustrates product flow on a computer screen. Current software makes simulation one of the most cost-effective approaches for evaluating dynamic logistics alternatives.[5] For example, a PC-based simulation can model the flows, activity levels, and performance characteristics. Many simulations can also illustrate system characteristics graphically. For example, supply chain dynamic simulation can be used to illustrate the trade-off between inventory allocation strategy and supply chain performance.[6]

---

[4]An example of such planning software is *Microsoft Project* (Redmond, WA).

[5]For a comprehensive discussion of simulation alternatives, see James J. Swain, "Flexible Tools for Modeling," *OR/MS Today,* December 1993, pp. 62–78; and John D. Sterman, *Business Dynamics: Systems Thinking and Modeling for a Complex World* (Burr Ridge, IL: McGraw-Hill, 2000).

[6]David J. Closs, et al., "An Empirical Comparison of Anticipatory and Response-Based Strategies," *The International Journal of Logistics Management* 9, no. 2 (1998), pp. 21–34.

Optimization uses linear or mathematical programming to evaluate alternatives and select the best one. While it has the benefit of being able to select the best option, optimization applications are often smaller in scope than typical simulation approaches. Because of its powerful capabilities, optimization is used extensively for evaluating logistics network alternatives such as the number and location of distribution centers.

Defining and Reviewing Assumptions

Assumption definition and review builds on the situation analysis, project objectives, constraints, and measurement standards. For planning purposes, the assumptions define the key operating characteristics, variables, and economics of current and alternative systems. While the format will differ by project, assumptions generally fall into three classes: (1) business assumptions, (2) management assumptions, and (3) analysis assumptions.

Business assumptions define the characteristics of the general business environment, including relevant market, consumer, and product trends and competitive actions. The assumptions define the broad environment within which an alternative logistics plan must operate. Business assumptions are generally outside the ability of the firm to change.

Management assumptions define the physical and economic characteristics of the current or alternative logistics environment and are generally within the firm's ability to change or refine. Typical management assumptions include a definition of alternative distribution facilities, transport modes, logistics processes, and fixed and variable cost.

Analysis assumptions define the constraints and limitations that must be included to fit the problem to the analysis technique. These assumptions frequently concern problem size, degree of analysis detail, and solution methodology. Table 16-4 offers detailed descriptions for each assumption category.

Identifying Data Sources

In actual practice, the process of data collection begins with a feasibility assessment. In addition, a fairly detailed specification of data is required to formulate or fit the analytical technique. However, at this point in the planning procedure, detailed data must be collected and organized to support the analysis. For situations when data is extremely difficult to collect or when the necessary level of accuracy is unknown, sensitivity analysis can be used to identify data collection requirements. For example, an initial analysis may be completed using transportation costs estimated with distance-based regressions. If analysis indicates that the best answer is very sensitive to the actual freight rates, there should be additional effort to obtain more precise transport rates from carrier quotes. Once operational, sensitivity analysis can be used to determine the major factors involved. When these factors, such as outbound transportation expense, are identified, more effort can be directed to increasing transportation accuracy; correspondingly, less effort can be directed toward other data requirements.

The majority of data required in a logistical study can be obtained from internal records. Although considerable searching may be needed, most information is generally available.

The first major data category is sales and customer orders. The annual sales forecast and percentage of sales by month, as well as seasonality patterns, are usually necessary to determine logistics volume and activity levels. Historical samples of customer invoices are also necessary to determine shipping patterns by market and

TABLE 16-4   Assumption Categories Elements

Assumption Classes/Categories	Description
Business Assumptions	
Scope	Definition of business units and product lines to be included.
Alternatives	Range of options that can be considered.
Market trends	Nature and magnitude of change in market preferences and buying patterns.
Product trends	Nature and magnitude of change in product buying patterns, particularly with respect to package size and packaging.
Competitive actions	Competitive logistics strengths, weaknesses, and strategies.
Management Assumptions	
Markets	Demand patterns by market area, product, and shipment size.
Distribution facilities	Locations, operating policies, economic characteristics, and performance history of current and potential distribution facilities.
Transportation	Transportation rates for movement between potential and existing distribution facilities and customers.
Inventory	Inventory levels and operating policies for each distribution facility.
Analysis Assumptions	
Product groups	Detailed product information aggregated to fit within scope of analysis technique.
Market areas	Customer demand grouped to aggregate market areas to fit the scope of analysis technique.

shipment size. The combination of aggregate measures of demand and shipment profiles characterizes the logistics requirements that must be met.

Specific customer data are also required to impart a spatial dimension to a logistics analysis. The spatial dimension reflects the fact that effective logistics must consider the cost and time associated with moving product across distance. Customers and markets are often aggregated by location, type, size, order frequency, growth rate, and special logistical services to reduce analysis complexity while not substantially reducing analysis accuracy.

For integrated channel analysis, it is necessary to identify and track the costs associated with manufacturing and purchasing. This often requires further classification using a bill of materials. While manufacturing plant locations may not be a variable component in a logistical system design, it is often necessary to consider the number and location of plants, product mix, production schedules, and seasonality. Policies and costs associated with inventory transfer, reordering, and warehouse processing must be identified. In particular, inventory control rules and product allocation procedures are often important elements. Finally, for each current and potential warehouse, it is necessary to establish operating costs, capacities, product mix and storage levels, and service capabilities.

Transportation data requirements include the number and type of modes utilized, modal selection criteria, rates and transit times, and shipping rules and policies. If private transportation is included in the analysis, then corresponding information is required for the private fleet.

The preceding discussion offers some perspective regarding the necessary data to evaluate logistics alternatives. The primary justification for placing the formal data collection process after the selection of analysis technique is to allow data collection to match specific analysis technique requirements. In other words, the design solution can be no better than the data it is based on.

For most logistics analysis applications, market data is useful for evaluating future scenarios. Management can normally provide an estimate of anticipated sales for future planning horizons. The difficulty lies in obtaining market-by-market projections.

One solution to the problem is to use demographic projections that correlate highly with sales. For example, assume that sales or usage correlates highly with population. Using such a correlation and government population projections, it is possible to estimate future demand levels and thus determine future logistics requirements. A variety of projections concerning demographic factors are regularly published by various government agencies and universities. A number of zip code sources exist which provide useful data for logistics planning.[7] Thus, a reasonable data bank of environmental information is readily available.

It is also useful to document competitive logistical system designs and flows to provide information regarding competitor strategies and capabilities. In most cases, this information is readily available from published material, annual reports, and general knowledge of company executives. The main purpose in collecting such data is to provide competitive benchmarks that compare customer service capabilities, distribution networks, and operating capabilities.

Collecting Data

Once alternative data sources have been identified, the data collection process can begin. The process includes assembly of required data and conversion to appropriate formats for the analysis tool. This is often a tedious and time-consuming task, so errors are likely. Potential errors include collecting data from a misrepresentative time period and overlooking data that do not reflect major components of logistics activity, such as customer pickup volume. For this reason, the data collection process should be carefully documented to assist in identifying errors that might reduce analysis accuracy and to determine any necessary changes to achieve acceptable accuracy.

Collecting Validation Data

In addition to collecting data to support alternative analyses, **base case** or **validation data** must also be collected to verify that the results accurately reflect reality. The specific question concerns whether the chosen analytical approach accurately replicates historical results when distribution practices and operating environments are evaluated. Comparison should focus on historical activity (e.g., sales and volume) and expense levels both in total and by facility, if possible.

The objective of validation is to increase management credibility regarding the analysis process. If the process does not yield credible results, management will have little confidence in the alternative analyses. It is critical that data collection efforts include investigations into why analytical results may not accurately reflect the past. For example, changes in distribution center operating practices or a one-time event such as a strike may make it impossible to exactly replicate the past. When such situations occur, the validation data collection process should include an assessment of the likely impact of such changes so that appropriate considerations can be made.

---

[7]American Map Corporation, *United States ZIP Code Atlas* (Maspeth, NY: published annually).

Analysis

The analysis activity uses the technique and data from the previous activity to evaluate strategic and tactical logistics alternatives. This four-stepped activity includes the following specific tasks: (1) defining analysis questions, (2) completing and validating a baseline analysis, (3) completing analyses of alternatives, and (4) completing sensitivity analysis.

Defining Analysis Questions

The first task defines specific analysis questions concerning alternatives and the range of acceptable uncertainty. The specific questions build on research objectives and constraints by identifying specific operating policies and parameters. For example, the questions for a distribution center site analysis must identify the specific location combinations to be evaluated. In the case of an inventory analysis, questions might focus on alternative service and uncertainty levels.

Suppose that a strategic planning effort is focusing on the identification of an optimal network of distribution facilities to serve the U.S. domestic market. Assume that the current network uses four distribution centers located in Newark, New Jersey; Atlanta, Georgia; Chicago, Illinois; and Los Angeles, California. Table 16-5 summarizes the shipment volume, cost, and service characteristics of the existing system. Shipment volume is defined in terms of weight shipped; cost, in terms of transportation and inventory carrying expenses; and service level, in terms of the percentage of sales volume within 2 days' transit of the distribution center. Likely questions for the sample analysis include: (1) What is the performance impact of removing the Chicago distribution center? (2) What is the performance impact of removing the Los Angeles distribution center? and (3) What is the performance impact of removing the Atlanta distribution center?

These questions represent a small subset of the potential alternatives for evaluation. Other alternatives could include fewer or more distribution centers or evaluation of different locations. It is important to recognize that care must be taken to define the analysis questions so that a wide range of possible options can be evaluated without requiring time-consuming analysis of options that have little likelihood of implementation.

Completing and Validating Baseline Analysis

The second task completes the baseline analysis of the current logistics environment using the appropriate method or tool. Results are compared with the validation data collected previously to determine the degree of fit between historical and analytical findings. The comparison should focus on identifying significant differences and

TABLE 16-5   Summary Distribution Performance

Distribution Center	Shipment Volume (000 lbs)	Inbound Transportation	Outbound Transportation	Inventory Carrying Cost ($)	Total Cost
Newark	693,000	317,000	264,000	476,000	1,750,000
Atlanta	136,400	62,000	62,000	92,000	216,000
Chicago	455,540	208,000	284,000	303,000	795,000
Los Angeles	10,020	5,000	5,000	6,000	16,000
Total	1,294,960	592,000	615,000	877,000	2,777,000

determining sources of possible error. Potential errors may result from incorrect or in-accurate input data, inappropriate or inaccurate analysis procedures, or unrepresentative validation data. As discrepancies are encountered, errors should be identified and corrected. In some cases the error cannot be corrected but can be explained and rationalized. Once discrepancies have been removed or explained to ± 2 percent, the application can be accepted as valid and the analysis can continue.

Completing Analyses of Alternatives

Once the approach has been validated, the next step is to complete an evaluation of supply chain alternatives. The analysis must be accomplished to determine the relevant performance characteristics of each alternative design or strategy. The options should consider possible changes in management policies and practices involving factors such as the number of distribution centers, inventory target levels, or the transportation shipment size profile.

Completing Sensitivity Analysis

Once this analysis is completed, the best performing alternatives can be targeted for further sensitivity evaluation. Here uncontrollable factors such as demand, factor costs, and competitive actions are varied to assess each alternative's ability to operate under a variety of conditions. For example, suppose that the alternative analysis indicates that five distribution centers provide the ideal cost/service trade-off for the firm's market area assuming the base demand level. Sensitivity analysis investigates the appropriateness of this ideal solution for different demand or cost levels. In other words, would five distribution centers still be the correct decision if demand increased or decreased by 10 percent? Sensitivity analysis in conjunction with an assessment of potential scenario probabilities is then used in a decision tree to select the best alternative.

Phase III: Recommendations and Implementation

Phase III operationalizes planning and design efforts by making specific management recommendations and developing implementation plans.

Develop Recommendations

Alternative and sensitivity analysis results are reviewed to determine recommendations for proposal to management. This review process includes four tasks: (1) identifying the best alternative, (2) evaluating costs and benefits, (3) developing a risk appraisal, and (4) developing a presentation.

Identifying Best Alternative

The alternatives and sensitivity analyses should identify the best options to consider for implementation. However, multiple alternatives often yield similar or comparable results. Performance characteristics and conditions for each alternative must be compared to identify the two or three best options. Although the concept of *best* may have different interpretations, it will generally be the alternative that meets desired service objectives at the minimum total cost.

Evaluating Costs and Benefits

In the earlier discussion of strategic planning, potential benefits were identified as service improvement, cost reduction, and cost prevention. It was noted that these benefits

FIGURE 16-2

Total cost

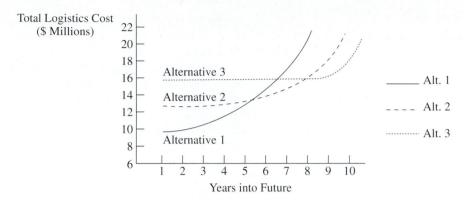

Alternative 1: Expand Existing Facilities
Alternative 2: Expand Existing Facilities and Add Two Distribution Centers
Alternative 3: Expand Existing Facilities and Add Three Distribution Centers

FIGURE 16-3

Performance cycle characteristics

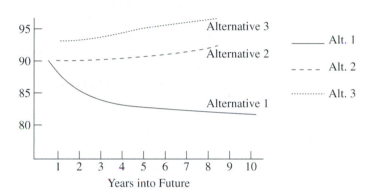

are not mutually exclusive and that a sound strategy might realize all benefits simultaneously. When evaluating the potential of a particular logistics strategy, an analysis comparing present cost and service capabilities with projected conditions must be completed for each alternative. The ideal cost/benefit analysis compares the alternatives for a base period and then projects comparative operations across some planning horizon. Benefits can thus be projected on the basis of both one-time savings that result from system redesign as well as recurring operating economies. The importance of viewing cost/benefit results across the planning horizon is illustrated by the following examples.

For the first example, suppose a heuristic analysis established three design alternatives that management wished to evaluate in detail: (1) expand existing facilities, (2) expand existing facilities and add two more, and (3) expand existing facilities and add three more. The cost/service results of the detailed simulation runs are graphically illustrated in Figures 16-2 and 16-3. These figures show dramatically different performance characteristics for each alternative. Alternative 1 offers low cost in the initial years, but the service level is low and declines further as demand grows in distant markets. Alternative 2 is the lowest cost during years 5 through 8, and service level actually increases as the demand grows in distribution centers. Alternative 3 offers substantially better service, although there are significant cost penalties early in the planning horizon.

All three alternatives can achieve the management objective of 90 percent volume within 5 days in the early years. While the lowest cost option is alternative 1 for the

FIGURE 16-4

Order cycle time

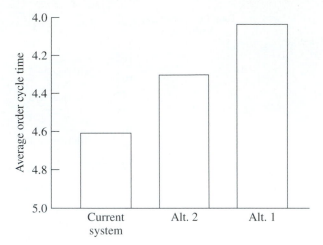

first year, alternative 2 is superior for years 5 through 8. From a strategic perspective, management has the option of enhancing the firm's competitive position by offering better than competitive service by using alternative 3, albeit at a higher cost. After year 8, management would select alternative 3 since it provides better service at relatively lower total cost.

Prior to the planning process, management believed that additional warehouses would be required to maintain desired service standards and that total system cost would increase substantially with increased distribution centers. The planning analysis identified the most effective long-term plan to maintain competitive or even enhanced service.

A second example concerns an inventory planning situation for a market area of eight states. In this situation, the marketing organization desires the addition of a second warehouse to improve service capability and reduce average order cycle. Expectations suggest that the total cost of serving the overall market will increase by adding a second facility. Another alternative to improve customer service is to increase safety stock at the existing warehouse. This is expected to improve average order cycle time by reducing back orders. Existing average order cycle time is 4.6 days with 75 percent of all orders filled within 5 days. The marketing department desires a 10 percent improvement at minimum total cost.

Addition of the warehouse (alternative 1) reduces average order cycle time to 4.1 days while increasing orders filled within 5 days from 75 to 92 percent. Increasing safety stock at the existing warehouse (alternative 2) reduces average order cycle to 4.3 days. This is equivalent to improving the percentage of orders filled within 5 days from 75 to 87 percent. Over the 10-year planning horizon, the addition of a second warehouse provides the lowest total cost alternative.

The cost/service relationship of the two alternatives is illustrated in Figures 16-4 and 16-5. In this situation, the warehouse addition results in the lowest total cost and provides the highest average customer service. It is interesting to note that the addition of a warehouse is the more costly alternative for approximately the first 3 years of simulated operations; however, it is the least costly over the 10-year planning horizon. In other words, marketing could realize a 12 percent increase in service capability for the initial 3 years at the lowest total cost by increasing safety stock at the existing warehouse. Establishment of a second warehouse to be operational by the fourth year

FIGURE 16-5

Example 2: Total cost

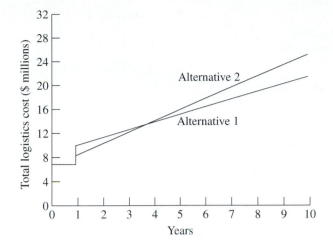

FIGURE 16-6

Relationship of distribution centers to total order time

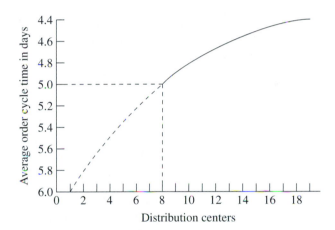

would realize an additional 5 percent improvement in service and a continuation of the least cost arrangement.

The third example, in Figure 16-6, illustrates the management trade-offs associated with increasing the number of distribution centers. The specific issue concerns increasing the number of distribution centers from six to eight. An analysis is conducted to determine the relationship of inventory carrying cost to average performance delays for the eight-warehouse configuration. In effect, the original constraint of 90 percent of all orders satisfied within a 5-day average order cycle is simulated to obtain the service improvement possible from increased levels of safety stock. Figure 16-7 shows that for the eight-DC alternative, an increase from $10 million to $14 million of annual inventory cost would be required to increase service from 90 to 100 percent of all orders filled within a 5-day average order cycle.

Developing Risk Appraisal

A second type of justification necessary to support strategic planning recommendations is an appraisal of the risk involved. Risk appraisal considers the probability that the planning environment will match the assumptions. Additionally, it considers the potential hazards related to system changeover.

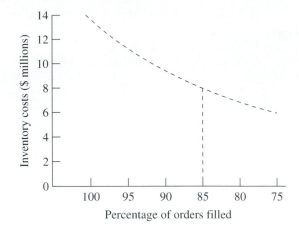

Risk related to adoption of a specific alternative can be quantified using sensitivity analyses. For example, assumptions can be varied and the resulting impact on system performance for each alternative can be determined. To illustrate, sensitivity analysis can be used to identify the system performance for different demand and cost assumptions. If the selected alternative is still best even though demand increases or decreases by 20 percent, management can conclude that there is little risk associated with moderate errors in the demand environment. The end result of a risk appraisal provides a financial evaluation of the downside risk if planning assumptions fail to materialize.

Risk related to system changeover can also be quantified. Implementation of a logistics strategic plan may require several years to execute. The typical procedure is to develop an implementation schedule to guide system changeover. To evaluate the risk associated with unanticipated delays, a series of contingency plans can be tested to determine their possible impact.

Typical sources of external risk include uncertainty associated with demand, performance cycle, cost, and competitive actions. Common sources of internal risk include labor and productivity considerations, changes in firm strategy, and changes in resource accessibility. These considerations must be assessed both quantitatively and qualitatively to provide management with direction and justification.

Developing a Presentation

The final task develops a presentation to management that identifies, rationalizes, and justifies suggested changes. The presentation and accompanying report must identify specific operating and strategic changes, provide a qualitative rationale as to why such change is appropriate, and then quantitatively justify the changes in terms of service, expense, asset utilization, and productivity improvements. The presentation should incorporate extensive use of graphs, maps, and flowcharts to illustrate changes in logistics operating practices, flows, and distribution network.

Implementation

The actual plan or design implementation is the final process activity. An adequate implementation plan is critical since putting the plan or design into action is the only means to obtain a return on the planning process. While actual implementation may require a number of events, there are four broad tasks: defining the implementation plan, scheduling implementation, defining acceptance criteria, and implementing the plan.

Defining the Implementation Plan

The first task defines the implementation plan in terms of the individual events, their sequence, and dependencies. While the initial plan may be macro level, it must ultimately be refined to provide individual assignment responsibility and accountability. Plan dependencies identify the interrelationships between events and, thus, define the completion sequence.

Scheduling Implementation

The second task schedules the implementation and time phases the assignments identified previously. The schedule must allow adequate time for acquiring facilities and equipment, negotiating agreements, developing procedure, and training. Implementation scheduling should employ one of the software scheduling aids discussed earlier.

Defining Acceptance Criteria

The third task defines the acceptance criteria for evaluating the success of the plan. Acceptance criteria should focus on service improvements, cost reduction, improved asset utilization, and enhanced quality. If the primary focus is service, acceptance criteria must identify detailed components such as improved product availability or reduced performance cycle time. If the primary focus is cost, the acceptance criteria must define the expected positive and negative changes in all affected cost categories. It is important that the acceptance criteria take a broad perspective so that motivation focuses on total logistics system performance rather than performance of an individual function. It is also important that the acceptance criteria incorporate broad organizational input.

Implementing the Plan

The final task is actual implementation of the plan or design. Implementation must include adequate controls to ensure that performance occurs on schedule and that acceptance criteria are carefully monitored.

It is critical that a formalized process be used to guide logistics system design and refinement projects to ensure that the objectives are documented and understood and the analyses are completed appropriately. While the preceding methodology supports logistics planning and design analysis, it can also be adapted to guide logistics information system design. For a system design application, the situation analysis focuses on the characteristics and capabilities of the current system, while the data collection and analysis activities focus on new system design, development, and validation.

Decision Analysis Methods and Techniques

High-performance logistics requires regular comprehensive analysis of supply chain tactics and strategies. Regular freight lane analysis is necessary to respond to rate changes and balance of freight flows; tactical inventory analyses, to identify items with excess inventory and to determine the appropriate inventory target levels; and location analysis, now often termed *supply chain planning,* to perform the strategic evaluation of supply chain alternatives such as sourcing, plant location, warehouse location, and market service areas, increasingly important to optimize flows for global supply chains. Dynamic simulation is used to investigate the dynamics of multiple-stage inventories such as among suppliers, plants, and distribution centers, and tactical transportation analysis assists in truck routing and scheduling. For each of these types of decisions, the following sections describe the specific questions, alternative analytical techniques, and typical data requirements.

Freight Lane Analysis

One common logistics analysis concerns transportation movements on specific *freight lanes.* A freight lane refers to the shipment activity between a pair of origin and destination points. The analysis can be completed on a very specific basis between facilities or on a broader regional basis. **Freight lane analysis** focuses on the balance of volume between origin and destination points. To maximize vehicle utilization, movements should be balanced, or roughly equal, in both directions. Lanes may include two or more points, as Figure 16-8 illustrates. Triangular freight lanes attempt to coordinate movement between three points by moving combinations of material and finished product between suppliers, manufacturers, and customers.

Freight lane analysis involves both movement volume and the number of shipments or trips between points. The objective is to identify imbalances that offer opportunities for enhanced logistics productivity. Once lane imbalances are identified, management attempts to identify volume that can be transported in the underutilized direction. This might be accomplished by switching carriers or modes, shifting volume to or from a private fleet, increasing back-haul of raw materials, or creating an alliance with another shipper. Conversely, volume in the overutilized direction might be diverted to other carriers or shippers or sourced from an alternative location.

Table 16-6 illustrates a lane analysis, which clearly identifies shipment imbalances. The transportation manager should attempt to balance the triangular move by developing additional volume between Cincinnati and Detroit. The volume could be developed either by moving product sources to the Cincinnati area or by creating an

FIGURE 16-8

Example of triangular freight lane

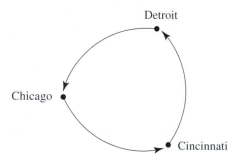

TABLE 16-6   Freight Lane Analysis of Monthly Movements

Origin	Destination	Weight (CWT)	Shipments
Detroit	Chicago	8740	23
Chicago	Cincinnati	5100	17
Cincinnati	Detroit	2000	8

alliance with a shipper that moves volume between Cincinnati and Detroit with no back-haul.

Inventory Analysis

The second common logistics ad-hoc analysis focuses on inventory performance and productivity. Typical inventory analysis considers relative product sales volume and inventory turnover and is performed on an ABC basis, as discussed in Chapter 10. For example, by listing the top 10 sales and inventory groupings in decreasing sequence, a logistics manager can quickly determine product groups that have a major influence on volume and inventory levels. As indicated in Chapter 10, 80 percent of sales are typically accounted for by 20 percent of the items. It is also typical that 80 percent of the inventory accounts for only 20 percent of the volume. Knowledge of these characteristics and the items that make up each product group is useful in targeting inventory management efforts. Items that demonstrate a large inventory commitment relative to sales can be selected for intensive management efforts to reduce inventory level and improve performance (e.g., turnover).

Table 16-7 illustrates a typical inventory analysis report. This example is sorted by item sales, although there is some logic to sequencing the report by decreasing inventory level or inventory turns. Items with relatively high inventories or low turns should be targeted for management attention.

Location Decisions

Plant and distribution center location is a common problem faced by logistics managers. Increased production economies of scale and reduced transportation cost have focused attention on warehouses.[8] In recent years, location analysis has been further extended to include logistics channel design as a result of global sourcing and marketing considerations. Because global operations increase logistics channel decision complexity, design alternatives, and related logistics cost, the importance of location analysis has increased substantially. Now described as *supply chain design,* location analysis frequently considers material suppliers, manufacturing sites, distribution centers, and service providers.

As the name implies, location decisions focus on selecting the number and location of warehouses. Typical management questions include: (1) How many warehouses should the firm use, and where should they be located? (2) What customers or market areas should be serviced from each warehouse? (3) Which product lines should be produced or stocked at each plant or warehouse? (4) What logistics channels should be used to source material and serve international markets? and (5) What combination of public and private warehouse facilities should be used? More refined logistics network problems increase issue complexity by requiring combinatorial analysis integrating the above questions.

---

[8]A number of authors have discussed the issues and process used to locate distribution centers. A representative sample includes: A.M. Geoffrion and G. W. Graves, "Multicommodity Distribution System Design by Bender's Decomposition," *Management Science* 20, no. 5 (January 1974), pp. 822–44; P. Bender, W. Northrup, and J. Shapiro, "Practical Modeling for Resource Management," *Harvard Business Review* 59, no. 2 (March/April 1981), pp. 163–73; and Jeffrey J. Karrenbauer and Glenn W. Graves, "Integrated Logistics Systems Design," in James M. Masters and Cynthia L. Coykendale, eds., "Logistics Education and Research: A Global Perspective," *Proceedings of the Eighteenth Annual Transportation and Logistics Educators Conference,* St. Louis, Missouri, October 22, 1989, pp. 142–71.

TABLE 16-7 Typical Inventory Analysis Report

Date 7/01/00
Total sales: $74,282

Product Rank Analysis Report
Total inventory: $22,470

Inrank list
Total items: 53

Part Number	Loc	Item Count	Pct Items	Unit Cost	Sales at Cost	Cum Sales at Cost	Cum pct Sales	Dollar Inventory	Cum Dollars Inventory	Cum pct Inventory	Inv Turns	Unit Sales	Class
SQDFAL36100 3P-600V 100A CDR BREAKER	1	1	1.9	141.780 E	14,462	14,462	19.5	2,836	2,836	12.6	5.1	102	A
SQDFAL36040 3P-600V 40A CDR BREAKER	1	2	3.8	115.420 E	14,428	28,890	38.9	4,040	6,876	30.6	3.6	125	A
SQDFAL36015 3P-600V 15A CDR BREAKER	1	3	5.7	115.420 E	11,311	40,201	54.1	2,539	9,415	41.9	4.5	98	A
SQDFAL36030 3P-600V 30A CDR BREAKER	1	4	7.5	115.420 E	7,156	47,357	63.8	2,424	11,839	52.7	2.9	62	A
SQDFAL36050 3P-600V 50A CDR BREAKER	1	5	9.4	.000 E	5,194	52,551	70.7	0	11,839	52.7	0.0	45	A
SQDFAL36060 3P-600V 60A CDR BREAKER	1	6	11.3	115.420 E	4,501	57,052	76.8	693	12,532	55.8	6.5	39	A
SQDFAL36020 3P-600V 20A CDR BREAKER	1	7	13.2	115.420 E	2,306	59,360	79.9	1,385	13,917	61.9	1.7	20	A
SQDQ0215 2P-120/240V 15A CDR BREAKER	1	8	15.1	9.500 E	1,796	61,156	82.3	437	14,354	63.9	4.1	189	B
SQDQ0220 2P-120/240V 20A CDR BREAKER	1	9	17.0	9.500 E	1,748	62,094	84.7	760	15,114	67.3	2.3	184	B
SQDQ0230 2P-120/240V 30A CDR BREAKER	1	10	18.9	9.500 E	1,748	64,652	87.0	817	15,931	70.9	2.1	184	B
SQDQ0120 3P-120/240V 20A CDR BREAKER	1	11	20.8	4.180 E	1,739	66,391	89.4	67	15,998	71.2	25.9	416	B
SQDQ0130 3P-120/240V 30A CDR BREAKER	1	12	22.6	4.180 E	1,267	67,658	91.1	109	16,107	71.7	11.6	303	C
SQDQ0240 2P-120/240V 40A CDR BREAKER	1	13	24.5	9.500 E	1,235	68,893	92.7	627	16,734	74.5	1.9	130	C
SQDQ0115 3P-120/240V 20A CDR BREAKER	1	14	26.4	4.180 E	1,124	70,017	94.3	422	17,156	76.4	2.7	269	C
SQDQ0140 3P-120/240V 40A CDR BREAKER	1	15	28.3	4.180 E	1,066	71,083	95.7	435	17,591	78.3	2.4	255	D

Source: Adapted from Eugene R. Roman, Inventory Management Seminar, Systems Design, Inc., South Holland, Illinois, 1993.

Typical location analysis problems can be characterized as very complex and data-intense. Complexity is created by the number of plant, distribution center, market, and product alternatives that can be considered; data intensity is created because the analysis requires detailed demand and transportation data. Sophisticated modeling and analysis techniques must be employed to effectively deal with such complexity and data intensity to identify the best alternatives. The tools used to support location analysis can generally be categorized as *mathematical programming* and *simulation*.

Mathematical Programming

Mathematical programming methods, which are classified as optimization techniques, are one of the most widely used strategic and tactical logistics planning tools. **Linear programming,** one of the most common techniques used for location analysis, selects the optimal supply chain design from a number of available options while considering specific constraints. House and Karrenbauer provided a long-standing definition of optimization relevant to logistics:

> An optimization model considers the aggregate set of requirements from the customers, the aggregate set of production possibilities for the producers, the potential intermediary points, the transportation alternatives and develops the optimal system. The model determines on an aggregate flow basis where the warehouses should be, where the stocking points should be, how big the warehouses should be and what kinds of transportation options should be implemented.[9]

To solve a problem using linear programming, several conditions must be satisfied. First, two or more activities or locations must be competing for limited resources. For example, shipments must be capable of being made to a customer from at least two locations. Second, all pertinent relationships in the problem structure must be deterministic and capable of linear approximation. Unless these enabling conditions are satisfied, a solution derived from linear programming, while mathematically optimal, may not be valid for logistical planning.

While linear programming is frequently used for strategic logistics planning, it is also applied to operating problems such as production assignment and inventory allocation. Within optimization, distribution analysts have used two different solution methodologies for logistics analysis.

One of the most widely used forms of linear programming for logistics problems is **network optimization.** Network optimization treats the distribution channel as a network consisting of nodes to identify production, warehouses, and markets and arcs reflecting transportation links. Costs are incurred for handling goods at nodes and moving goods across arcs. The network model objective is to minimize the total production, inbound, and outbound transportation costs subject to supply, demand, and capacity constraints.

Beyond the basic considerations for all analytical techniques, network optimization has specific advantages and disadvantages that both enhance and reduce its application for logistics analyses. Rapid solution times and ease of communication between specialists and nonspecialists are the primary advantages of network models. They may also be applied in monthly, rather than annual, time increments, which allows for longitudinal or across-time analysis of inventory level changes. Network formulations may also incorporate fixed costs to replicate facility ownership. The results of a

---

[9]Robert G. House and Jeffrey J. Karrenbauer, "Logistics System Modeling," *International Journal of Physical Distribution and Materials Management* 8, no. 4 (May 1978), pp. 189–99.

network model identify the optimum set of distribution facilities and material flows for the logistics design problems as it was specified for the analysis.[10]

The traditional disadvantages of network optimization have been the size of the problem that can be solved and the inclusion of fixed cost components. The problem size issue was of particular concern for multistage distribution systems such as those including suppliers, production locations, distribution centers, wholesalers, and customers. While problem size is still a concern, advancements in solution algorithms and hardware speed have significantly improved network optimization capabilities. The fixed cost limitation concerns the capability to optimize both fixed and variable costs for production and distribution facilities. There have been significant advancements in overcoming this problem through the use of a combination of network optimization and mixed-integer programming.

Mixed-integer programming is the other optimization solution technique successfully applied to logistics problems. The formulation offers considerable flexibility, which enables it to incorporate many of the complexities and idiosyncrasies found in logistics applications. The primary advantage of the mixed-integer format is that fixed as well as different levels of variable cost can be included in the analysis. For example, demand can be treated on a noninteger basis, thus allowing increments to system capacity in specific step increases. In other words, mixed-integer programming allows solutions to accurately reflect increased fixed costs and economies of scale as larger distribution centers are employed. The mixed-integer approach permits a high degree of practicality to accommodate restrictions found in day-to-day logistics operations.

Historically, the major limitation of optimization has been constraints on problem sizes. Along with other advances in mixed-integer programming, problem size constraints have been overcome, for a considerable period of time, through the application of *decomposition* to the solution techniques.[11] Decomposition permits multiple commodities to be incorporated into logistical system design. Most firms have a variety of products or commodities that are purchased by customers in varied assortments and quantities. While such products may be shipped and stored together, they are not interchangeable from the viewpoint of servicing customers.

The **decomposition technique** provides a procedure for dividing the multicommodity situation into a series of single-commodity problems. The procedure for arriving at commodity assignment follows an iterative process wherein costs associated with each commodity are tested for convergence until a minimum cost or optimal solution is isolated.

These optimization approaches provide effective tools for analysis of location-related issues such as facility location, optimum product flow, and capacity allocation. Mixed-integer approaches are typically more flexible in terms of capacity to accommodate operational nuances, while network approaches are more computationally efficient. Both types of linear programming optimization approaches are effective techniques for evaluating situations where significant facility capacity limitations exist.

---

[10]Examples of time-based linear programming applications are discussed in S. Kumer and S. Arora, "Customer Service Effect in Parts Distribution Design," *International Journal of Physical Distribution and Logistics Management* 20, no. 2 (1990), pp. 31–39; and M. Cohen, et al., "Optimizer: IBM's Multi-Echelon Inventory System for Managing Service Logistics," *Interfaces* 20, no. 1 (January/February 1990), pp. 65–82.

[11]For a discussion of the application of decomposition to logistical system design, see A. M. Geoffrion and G. W. Graves, "Multicommodity Distribution System Design by Bender's Decomposition," *Management Science* 20, no. 1 (January 1974), pp. 822–44; and Arthur M. Geoffrion, "Better Distribution Planning with Computer Models," *Harvard Business Review* 54, no. 4 (July/August 1976), pp. 92–99.

Figure 16-9

**Network cost
components**

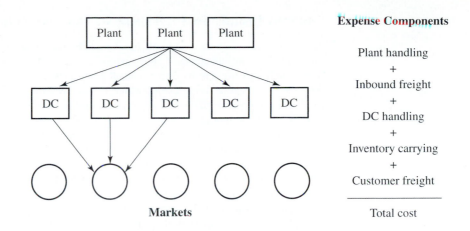

Expense Components

Plant handling
+
Inbound freight
+
DC handling
+
Inventory carrying
+
Customer freight
_____
Total cost

Notwithstanding the value of optimization, linear programming confronts some major problems when dealing with complex logistical system designs. First, to format a comprehensive design, it is necessary to develop explicit functional relationships for the full range of design options. The functional relationship must consider all possible combinations for suppliers, production locations, distribution locations, wholesalers, markets, and products. The sheer number of alternatives and the associated constraints result in a very large problem. Second, the optimality feature of the technique is relative; that is, it is only as valid as the design problem definition. Too many simplifying assumptions can render a solution mathematically optimal but useless in terms of business practice. Third, the capability of existing linear programming procedures is typically limited by the number of echelons or stages in the distribution system and by the problem size. For example, problems requiring the analysis of flows from production locations to distribution centers and then to markets (i.e., three echelons) can be solved easily by most optimizers. However, the size limitations may make it difficult to perform a complete supply chain analysis. Industry Insight 16-1 discusses the application of supply chain design and its impact on resource requirements.

Significant advancements have been made in both the speed and capability of optimization algorithms and software. While there are still some scope and complexity limitations, new capabilities are continuously being reported in the literature.[12]

Simulation

A second location analysis method is **static simulation.** The term *simulation* can be applied to almost any attempt to replicate a situation. Robert Shannon originally defined simulation as "the process of designing a model of a real system and conducting experiments with this model for the purpose of either understanding system behavior or of evaluating various strategies within the limits imposed by a criterion or set of criteria for the operation of the system."[13]

Static simulation replicates the product flows and related expenses of existing or potential logistics channel networks. Figure 16-9 illustrates a typical network and the major cost components. The network includes plants, distribution centers, and markets. The major expense components include raw material sourcing, manufacturing,

[12]For an overview of the facility location process, see Paul S. Bender, "How to Design an Optimum Worldwide Supply Chain," *Supply Chain Management Review* 1, no. 1 (Spring 1997), pp. 70–81.

[13]Robert E. Shannon, *Systems Simulation: The Art and Science* (Englewood Cliffs, NJ: Prentice-Hall, Inc., 1975), p. 1.

INDUSTRY INSIGHT 16-1 OPTIMIZING TRANSPORTATION

JELD-WEN Inc. is a perfect example of a vertically integrated company. From its own timberlands, this large manufacturer of doors, windows, millwork, and specialty wood products cuts lumber and ships it off to its own cut-stock plants. There, the lumber is prepared and sent to JELD-WEN's manufacturing plants, which in turn feed the company's distribution business. The latter sells products to the end user, thus completing a full chain of vertical integration.

Bob Smith, transportation manager in JELD-WEN's corporate office in Winnipeg, Canada, oversees 18 Canadian locations. The company has 150-plus divisions, more than 20,000 employees worldwide, and is well diversified. Manufacturing and distribution activities take place in both the U.S. and Canada, making the need for a streamlined, productive supply chain on both sides of the border critical for the company's growth. "Basically, we always want to make sure that our transportation system is as efficient as our plants are when it comes to production," says Smith. "To do that, we focus on trying to reduce both time and waste from our supply chain."

With that in mind, JELD-WEN embarked on an effort to overhaul its Canadian locations. In reviewing the company's geographically dispersed facilities north of the border, JELD-WEN realized that some had become unnecessary over the years. "We decided that we could provide the same type of services from larger locations," says Smith, "and realize a lot of improvements in our operations at the same time." The end result was a consolidation of five locations.

This consolidation also released a transportation fleet and an assortment of excess equipment that needed to be disposed of efficiently. "We went in and conducted physical inspections of all the units while also doing a detailed review of the maintenance records," says Smith. "We reviewed the equipment usage, the mileage, and other important aspects of unit use over the last few years." Smith sold a good portion of the equipment at fair market value. "We also tapped into some other options," he says, "such as what early return penalties we might expect with regard to leased equipment. We also discussed swapping those over-specified units for vehicles that would be more suitable for us." In addition, before disposing of any equipment or vehicle, Smith's team first consulted with other facilities within the JELD-WEN family to see if they could use it. "We also did careful checks of new vehicle orders to see if they could be filled with some of these existing units and we sought out opportunities to upgrade some of our existing vehicles at other locations with a unit that might have had lower mileage, or that was in better condition," says Smith. After exhausting those options, any units left over were sold.

The consolidation process yielded positive results for JELD-WEN by reducing transportation-related costs by more than $1 million and reducing its overall warehousing costs. "As a company, we want to be known for providing world-class customer service all the time," says Smith. "Though we reduced our number of warehouses, we know we'll be able to meet our service objectives. In fact, without the reduction and the sell-off of the equipment, we probably wouldn't have been able to realize the level of transportation, inventory, and warehousing cost savings that we did in the last year."

Source: Bridget McCrea, "Optimizing Transportation," *Warehousing Management,* March 2001, pp. T2–T3.

---

inbound freight, fixed and variable distribution center cost, outbound customer freight, and inventory carrying cost.

Static simulation evaluates product flow as if it all occurred at a single point during the year. In this sense, the primary difference between static and dynamic simulation is the manner in which time-related events are treated. Whereas dynamic simulation evaluates system performance across time, static simulation makes no attempt to consider the dynamics between time periods. Static simulation treats each operating period within the overall planning horizon as a finite interval. Final results represent an assumption of operating performance for each period in the planning horizon. For example, in the formulation of a 5-year plan, each year is simulated as an independent event.

Figure 16-10

Heuristic simulation methodology

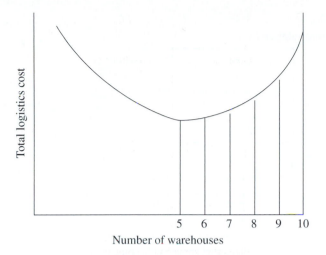

Static simulation seeks to project the outcome of a specified plan or course of future action. If the potential system design is identified, simulation can be used to quantify customer service levels and total cost characteristics. Used in this sense, a static simulator provides a tool to rapidly measure the capabilities and costs related to system design and sensitivity analyses.[14]

An expanded use of static simulation involves a heuristic computation procedure to assist in the selection of warehouses. In this capacity, the static simulator can be programmed to evaluate and quantify various combinations of warehouses from a potential list of locations provided during problem specification.

When utilized to help identify the best logistics network, the typical heuristic procedure includes all possible warehouse locations in the initial simulation. Customer destinations are assigned to the best warehouse based on the lowest total logistics cost. A major benefit of static simulation is the flexibility in the distribution channel alternatives that can be evaluated. Static simulation heuristics can be designed to consider lowest total cost, maximum service, or a combination of the two in the algorithm that assigns markets to distribution centers.

Given the design objective, the simulation deletes warehouse locations one at a time from the maximum number of potential locations to a managerially specified minimum or until only one facility remains in the system. The typical deletion procedure eliminates the most costly warehouse from the remaining *in-system* facilities on a marginal cost basis. The demand previously serviced by the *eliminated* warehouse is then reassigned to the next-lowest-cost supply point, and the quantification procedure is repeated. If a full system deletion process is desired, the static simulation will require as many iterations as there are potential warehouse locations under consideration.

For example, as Figure 16-10 illustrates, the first simulation might consider a logistics network with 10 warehouses. The simulation heuristic would then evaluate the relative value of each facility by weighing the fixed cost reductions and variable cost increments that would occur if that facility were closed. If the heuristic determines that the total cost declines, as illustrated in Figure 16-10, the simulator would *close* the

[14]Examples of software to complete static simulation analyses can be found in R. Ballou and J. Masters, "Facility Location Commercial Software Survey," *Journal of Business Logistics* 20, no. 1 (1999), pp. 215–32.

FIGURE 16-11

Static simulation solution flow

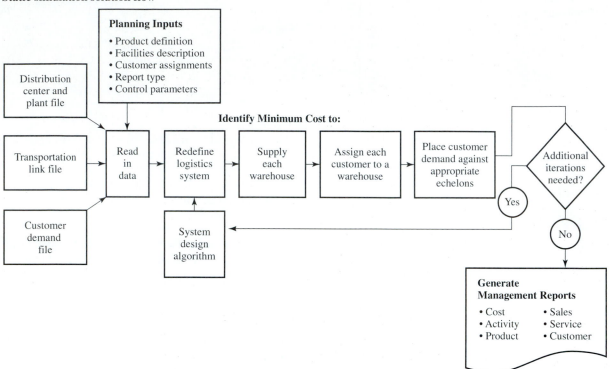

specified facility and recompute the cost and service characteristics of a nine-warehouse network. The iterative process continues until the minimal cost distribution network is identified. For this example, the minimum cost network employs six warehouse locations.

Static simulation identifies the *best* solution by comparison of the total cost and threshold service capabilities among the distribution facility combinations resulting from the deletion procedure. This analysis is performed by direct comparison of cost and service characteristics of the alternative networks. There is no guarantee that the combination of facilities selected as a result of the deletion procedure will be the optimum or even the near-optimum facility configuration. The fact that a warehouse location, once it is deleted, is no longer available for consideration in subsequent replications is one of the major shortcomings of static simulation procedures. Figure 16-11 illustrates the solution flow for a typical static simulation model. The system design algorithm represents the facility deletion procedure discussed above.

The main advantage of static simulation is that it is simpler, less expensive to operate, and more flexible than most optimization techniques. The replication capabilities of a multiechelon static simulator create almost unlimited design possibilities. Unlike mathematical programming approaches, simulation does not guarantee an optimum solution. However, static simulation offers a very flexible tool that may be used to evaluate a wide range of complex channel structures. As a result of the process of numerical computation, static simulation does not require explicit functional relationships. The capabilities and operating range of a comprehensive static simulator can often incorporate significantly more detail in terms of markets, products, distribution facilities, and shipment sizes than optimization techniques can.

While site analysis, particularly for a single location, can be done manually or with a spreadsheet, more complex problems often require the use of specialized computer applications.[15] There are number of commercial software applications specifically designed to address the location analysis problem. Ballou and Masters have identified available software; specified characteristics such as price, nature of the problem that can be handled, solution methodology, and distinguishing features; assessed the state of the art in program development; and asked users about their satisfaction with location programs and factors they consider important in selecting such programs.[16]

Location Analysis Data Requirements

The primary location analysis data requirements are definitions of markets, products, network, customer demand, transportation rates, and variable and fixed costs.

Market Definition. Location analysis requires that demand be classified or assigned to a geographic area. The combination of geographic areas constitutes a logistics service area. Such an area may be a country or global region. The demand for each customer is assigned to one of the market areas. The selection of a market definition method is an extremely important element of the system design procedure.

A number of market definition structures have been developed. The most useful structures for logistics modeling are (1) county, (2) standard metropolitan statistical area (SMSA), and (3) zip or postal codes. (Postal codes are the international equivalent of zip codes.) The most common structure uses zip or postal codes since company records usually include such information. In addition, extensive government and transportation data is available by zip codes. The major issues for selecting a market definition approach concern the number of areas required to provide accurate results. While more market detail increases accuracy, it also increases analysis efforts. Research indicates that approximately 200 markets offer an effective trade-off between accuracy and analysis effort.[17]

Product Definition. Although individual product flows can be considered when performing location analysis, it is usually not necessary to use such detail. Individual items, especially those with similar distribution characteristics, production sites, and channel arrangements, are grouped or aggregated to simplify the analysis. Typical supply chain analyses are completed at the product family level.

Network Definition. The network definition specifies the channel members, institutions, and possible locations to be included in the analysis. Specific issues concern the combinations of suppliers, production locations, distribution centers, wholesalers, and retailers that are to be included. Network definition also includes consideration of

---

[15]For small-scale logistics problems, spreadsheets such as Excel can be used to solve optimization problems. The specific solution approach is discussed in the "Solver" documentation of the appropriate user manual.

[16]Ronald H. Ballou and James M. Masters, op. cit. A listing of specific software applications is available in the *Annual Guide to Logistics Software* provided by the Council of Logistics Management at **www.clm1.org.**

[17]For original research regarding the number of market areas, see Robert G. House and Kenneth D. Jaime, "Measuring the Impact of an Alternative Method Classification System in Distribution Planning," *Journal of Business Logistics,* 2, no. 2 (1981), pp. 1–31; and Ronald H. Ballou, "Information Considerations for Logistics Network Planning," *International Journal of Physical Distribution and Materials Management,* 17, no. 7 (1987), pp. 3–14.

Figure 16-12

Channel network example

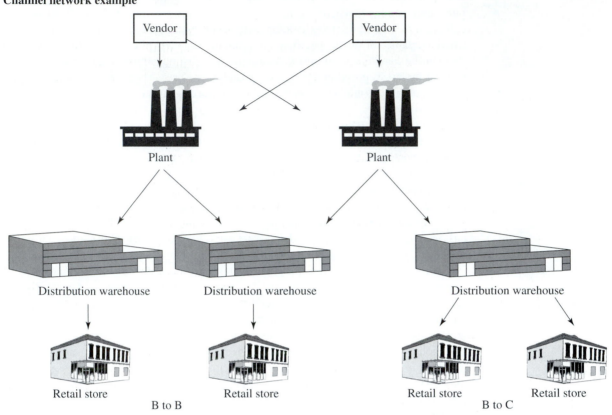

new distribution centers or channel member alternatives. Figure 16-12 illustrates a channel. While using a more comprehensive definition reduces the chance of suboptimizing system performance, total channel location analysis increases analysis complexity. Supply chain analysts must evaluate the trade-offs between increasing analysis complexity and improved potential for total supply chain optimization.

Market Demand.   Market demand defines shipment volume to each geographic area identified as a market. Specifically, supply chain analysis is based on the relative product volume shipped to each market area. While the volume may pertain to the number of units or cases shipped to each market, most location analyses are based on weight since transportation cost is strongly influenced by weight moved. Market demand utilized in the analysis may also be based on historical shipments or anticipated volume if substantial changes are expected. The market demand must be profiled into different shipment sizes since transportation cost is significantly influenced by shipment size.

Transportation Rates.   Inbound and outbound transportation rates are a major data requirement for location analyses. Rates must be provided for shipments between existing and potential distribution channel members and markets. In addition, rates must be developed for each shipment size and for each transportation link between distribution centers and markets. It is common for supply chain analysis to require in excess of a million individual rates. Because of the large number, rates are commonly developed using regressions or are retrieved from diskettes provided by most carriers.

Variable and Fixed Costs.   The final location analysis data requirements are the variable and fixed costs associated with operating distribution facilities. Variable cost includes expenses related to labor, energy, utilities, and materials. In general, variable expenses are a function of throughput. Fixed costs include expenses related to facilities, equipment, and supervisory management. Within a relevant distribution facility operating range, fixed costs remain relatively constant. While variable and fixed cost differences by geography are typically not substantial, there are minor locational considerations, which should be included to ensure analysis accuracy. The major differences result from locational peculiarities in wage rates, energy cost, land values, and taxes.

Substantial logistics planning emphasis is placed on location analysis. In the past, distribution networks were relatively stable, so it was unnecessary for firms to complete logistics system analyses regularly; however, the dynamics of alternative supply chain options, changing cost levels, and availability of third-party services requires that supply chain networks be evaluated and refined more frequently today. It is common for firms to perform evaluations annually or even monthly.

Inventory Decisions

Inventory analysis decisions focus on determining the optimum inventory management parameters which meet desired service levels with minimum investment. Inventory parameters refer to safety stock, reorder point, order quantity, and review cycles for a specific facility and product combination. This analysis can be designed to refine inventory parameters on a periodic or daily basis. Daily refinements make parameters more sensitive to environmental changes such as demand levels or performance cycle length; however, they also result in *nervous* inventory management systems. System nervousness causes frequent expediting and deexpediting of numerous small shipments.

Inventory analysis focuses on the decisions discussed in Chapter 10. Specific questions include: (1) How much product should be produced during the next production cycle? (2) Which distribution centers should maintain inventories of each item (e.g., should slow-moving items be centralized)? (3) What is the optimum size of replenishment orders (the order quantity decision)? and (4) What is the necessary reorder point for replenishment orders (the safety stock decision)?

There are two types of methods to evaluate and select from inventory management options: *analytic* and *simulation.*

Analytic Inventory Techniques

Analytic inventory methods utilize functional relationships such as those discussed in Chapter 10 to determine ideal inventory stocking parameters and the desired service level. Figure 16-13 illustrates the analytic inventory concept. The technique uses service objectives, demand characteristics, performance cycle characteristics, and the logistics system characteristics as input to calculate optimum inventory parameters. From an inventory management perspective, service objectives are typically defined in terms of case or order fill rates. Demand characteristics describe the periodic average and standard deviation of customer demand; performance cycle characteristics, the average and standard deviations for replenishment performance cycles; and logistics system characteristics, the number of distribution stages or echelons requiring inventory

FIGURE 16-13

Analytic inventory overview

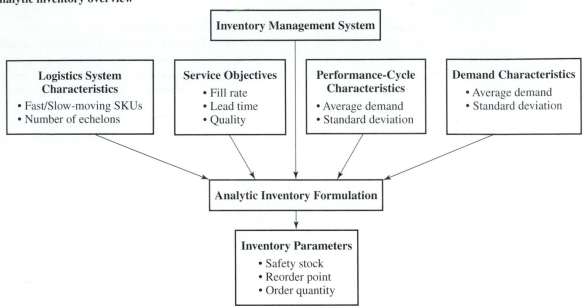

management decisions. The analytical inventory technique is based on assumptions describing the logistics system characteristics (stocking echelons) and the probabilities relating demand and performance cycle characteristics. The probability relationships, along with the service level objectives, determine the optimal inventory management parameters in terms of replenishment order quantities and reorder points. Numerous examples of software applications exist that utilize analytic techniques to determine optimum inventory management parameters.[18]

The advantage of analytic inventory techniques is the ability to directly determine optimum inventory parameters given certain assumptions regarding operating environment. On the other hand, analytic inventory techniques are limited in terms of accuracy when assumptions are not met. For example, since most analytic inventory techniques assume normally distributed demand and performance cycles, the techniques lose accuracy when the shape of actual demand or performance cycles deviates from the normality assumption.[19] Nevertheless, analytical inventory techniques are often a good place to start when attempting to determine optimum inventory parameters.

---

[18]Examples of such inventory management systems include: *Linx* from Numetrix Software, Toronto, Ontario, Canada; *Optimal Planner* from CSC Consulting, Cleveland, OH; and *Inventory Analyst* from Intex Solutions, Inc., Needham, MA. The first two applications include inventory management applications within a much larger enterprise modeling application. The final application is an example of a spreadsheet-based model that primarily computes the inventory parameters. Most APS applications, such as i2's *Rhythm,* SAP's *Advanced Planning Optimizer,* and *Manugistics* incorporate analytic techniques into their planning software.

[19]These assumptions regarding normal demand and lead times can be overcome with numerical methods such as those discussed in J. Masters, "Determination of Near Optimal Stock Levels for Multi-Echelon Distribution Inventories," *Journal of Business Logistics* 14, no. 2 (1993), pp. 165–96.

FIGURE 16-14

Inventory simulation
overview

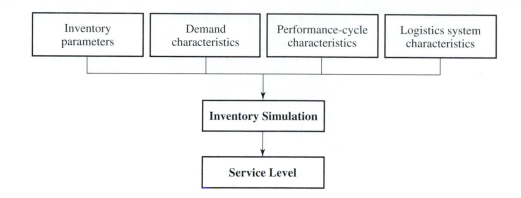

Simulation Inventory Techniques

The inventory simulation approach creates a mathematical and probabilistic model of the logistics operating environment as it actually exists. As Figure 16-14 illustrates, the simulation approach is similar to creating a laboratory testing environment for the logistics network and operating policies. Simulation is similar to the analytic approach except the roles of the inventory parameters and service levels are reversed.

In simulation, inventory parameters such as the order quantities and the reorder points that are to be tested become the simulation inputs. These inputs define the environment to be tested. The major simulation outputs are the service level and inventory performance characteristics of the testing environment. The simulation, in effect, evaluates the performance of a specific situation. If the reported performance does not achieve desired objectives, the inventory parameters must be changed and a new environment is simulated. It is sometimes necessary to complete a number of simulations to identify the combination of inventory parameters that yields optimum performance.

The major benefit of inventory simulation techniques is the ability to model a wide range of logistics environments without requiring simplifying assumptions. It is possible to accurately simulate virtually any logistics environment by incorporating characteristics and operating policies. The major shortfall of simulation techniques is their limited ability to search for and identify optimum solutions. While there are inventory simulation examples that incorporate search algorithms, they are limited in capability and scope. There are indications that simulation is becoming more popular as firms attempt to understand inventory dynamics in the logistics channel.[20]

Inventory decision support applications are increasing in importance because of the emphasis on streamlining inventory levels to reduce the logistics asset base. The demand for more refined inventory parameters has increased the need for more sophisticated inventory analysis techniques. Software firms have responded by developing both stand-alone and integrated applications.[21] Industry Insight 16-2 describes an application of simulation for inventory analysis.

---

[20]Process simulation is broadly discussed in K. Mabrouk, "Mentorship: A Stepping Stone to Simulation Success," *Industrial Engineering,* February 1994, pp. 41–43. Simulation package capabilities are described in J. Swain, "Flexible Tools for Modeling," *OR/MS Today,* December 1993, pp. 62–78.

[21]Examples include: James Aaron Cooke, "Simulate Before You Act," *Logistics Management and Distribution Report* 38, no. 9 (September 1999), pp. 77–80; and Anonymous, "IBM Product Analyzes Your Supply Chain," *Industrial Distribution* 88, no. 8 (August 1999), p. 44.

INDUSTRY INSIGHT 16-2 SIMULATE BEFORE YOU RESTRUCTURE

Before launching a supply chain restructuring, Tesco Ltd., Great Britain's leading food retailer, used a state-of-the-art simulation tool to determine whether to revamp its frozen foods distribution network. This computer simulation validated corporate plans to restructure the network and build a separate facility specifically for frozen foods storage.

Eight of Tesco's British distribution centers carry a mixture of ambient (general grocery and nonfood items), chilled, and frozen products.

Two years ago, Tesco executives began weighing the idea of creating a stand-alone warehouse strictly for frozen food items, which account for about 10 percent of the company's grocery store sales. The rationale was that a separate facility would allow the retailer to expand its range of frozen food products and gain operational efficiencies. Before they approached the company's board of directors with the plan, Tesco's distribution executives decided to simulate the plan's impact on distribution with a computer model. They selected IBM's software simulation tool, *The Supply Chain Analyzer.* Because it can depict different hypothetical situations, the software gives companies a way to see the physical, financial, and informational impact of supply chain restructuring on a distribution network.

It took IBM consultants 6 weeks to set up and run the computer model with Tesco's help. Joe Galloway, Tesco's divisional director of supply chain information technology, reports that much of that time was spent gathering a year's worth of detail-laden data about its distribution center operations to input into the model. "We were looking for data on the actual orders that went through our supply chain by (product) line and by store," he says. Once the data were fed into the application, it corroborated the soundness of the model.

When Tesco executives ran the same data through the computer model to simulate a restructured supply chain with a dedicated frozen food facility, the results supported their assumptions. The model indicated that the food retailer could achieve distribution savings in the range of 2 to 5 percent, depending on the actual mix of frozen food products stored in the dedicated facility.

Transportation costs would drop because Tesco could eliminate trips between distribution centers and make more direct store deliveries. In addition to consolidating outbound trips, Tesco also determined that it could realize some savings on the inbound haul because it would only have to move products from suppliers to a single point rather than to two or three warehouses.

Inventory carrying costs would decline. If all of the frozen food supplies were stored in a dedicated facility, the model showed Tesco could actually reduce its stock holdings or even expand its mix of frozen food products and increase store sales in this category. Tesco also would eliminate the need to construct more facilities in the future. Moving frozen foods out of the distribution centers would free up warehousing space for the expansion of chilled products, says Galloway.

The computer modeling demonstrated that using a single-point facility would not impair service to Tesco's stores. The simulation also indicated that the company might benefit by trying some alternative approaches. "We could see an advantage to not servicing all of the products through one central point, but having some kind of cross-docking through the other four [distribution centers] for stores not close to the central facility," Galloway recalls.

Finally, the simulation gave Tesco some insights into its current operation that allowed it to make an immediate, money-saving change. The company discovered that it could cut back deliveries of certain slow-moving items to once a week and still maintain adequate stock for its stores.

Although computer simulation helped persuade the board to approve the restructuring plan, it had another benefit as well. The simulation gave Tesco's logistics managers a deeper insight into their own supply chain's operation. "By the end of the exercise," says Galloway, "they had a better understanding of that area of the business. It got them thinking about costs and efficiencies of the supply chain."

Source: James Aaron Cooke, "Simulate Before You Act," *Logistics Management and Distribution Report,* September 1999, pp. 77–80.

FIGURE 16-15

Typical routing or delivery problem

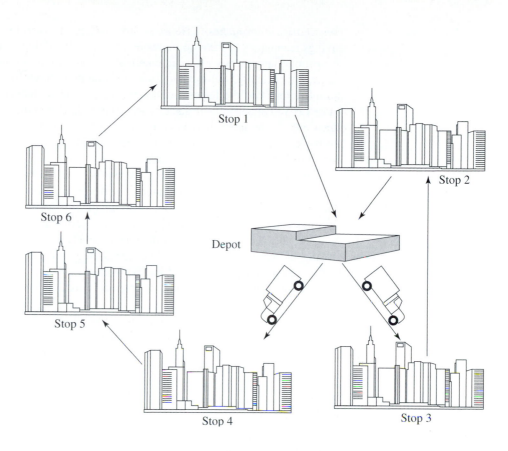

Transportation Decisions

Transportation analyses focus on routing and scheduling of transportation equipment to optimize vehicle and driver utilization while meeting customer service requirements. Transportation decisions can be characterized as *strategic* or *tactical.* Strategic transportation decisions concern long-term resource allocation, such as for extended time periods. Thus, strategic routing decisions identify fixed transport routes that may be used for months or years. Tactical transportation decisions concern short-term resource allocations such as daily or weekly routes. The objective of transportation analysis is to minimize the combination of vehicles, hours, or miles required to deliver product. Typical transportation analysis questions include: (1) How should deliveries be grouped to form routes? (2) What is the best delivery sequence for servicing customers? (3) Which routes should be assigned to which vehicle types? (4) What is the best type of vehicle for servicing different customer types? and (5) How will delivery time restrictions be imposed by customers? Figure 16-15 illustrates a typical routing or delivery problem. The distribution center represents the central departure site for all delivery vehicles, and each stop represents a customer location, such as a retailer.

Transportation Analysis Techniques

Routing and scheduling analyses have been well researched for logistics design and planning. They are particularly important for firms completing partial load delivery activities such as package or beverage distribution. The techniques can generally be classified as *heuristic approaches, exact approaches, interactive approaches,* and *combination approaches.*[22] Heuristic approaches utilize rule-of-thumb clustering or savings techniques to develop routes by sequentially adding and deleting stops. Exact, or optimal, approaches use mathematical (linear) programming to identify the best routes. Historically, optimization solution methods have been too computationally complex for even the fastest computers, but recent mathematical programming advances have enhanced their capabilities. The main difficulties with most exact procedures are (1) the large number of constraints and variables needed to represent even the basic routing and scheduling problem and (2) the impact of this size on computation time and computer storage space.

Interactive approaches utilize a combination of simulation, cost calculator, or graphics capability to support an interactive decision process. The decisionmaker identifies the alternatives for evaluation. The interactive decision support system then determines and plots the routes and calculates the performance characteristics in terms of time and cost. The decisionmaker then interactively evaluates the performance characteristics of each alternative and refines the strategy until no additional improvement is likely. The obvious drawback of interactive approaches is the dependence on the skill and ability of the decisionmaker, particularly as the problem size and complexity increase.

Combinations of the three approaches have proven very effective. Two criteria are important when evaluating alternative solution approaches: generalizability and accuracy. Generalizability is the ability to efficiently incorporate extensions for special situations, such as pickups and deliveries, multiple depots, time windows, vehicle capacities, and legal driving times, in an actual setting. Accuracy refers to the ability to closely approximate performance characteristics and the results' proximity to an optimal solution. Accuracy determines the level of and credibility in the possible savings as a result of decreased vehicle operating expense, better customer service, and improved fleet productivity.[23] Industry Insight 16-3 describes an application of transportation routing analysis.

Transportation Analysis Data Requirements

Transportation analysis requires three types of data: network, pickup or delivery demand, and operating characteristics. The network defines all possible routes and is the backbone of any transportation system analysis. In some cases, a network is defined using street maps of the delivery area. Each intersection is a node, and the streets become links. The network contains the links between each node, the road distance, the transit time, and any special constraints such as weight limits or tolls. A street-level network is very accurate and precise, particularly when there are constraints such as rivers and mountains. The deficiency of a street-level network is the high cost of development and maintenance. The other approach involves plotting customers on a grid and then computing the possible links between customers using the straight line distance. Latitude and longitude coordinates are often used. While a grid system is less costly to develop and maintain than a street-level network, it is less accurate and does not consider constraints as well.

---

[22]For a further discussion of each of these approaches, see Kevin Bott and Ronald H. Ballou, "Research Perspectives in Vehicle Routing and Scheduling," *Transportation Research* 20A, no. 3 (1986), pp. 239–43.

[23]For an expanded discussion of alternative analysis approaches, see Kevin Bott and Ronald Ballou, op. cit.; Ronald H. Ballou and Yogesh K. Agerwal, "A Performance Comparison of Several Popular Algorithms for Vehicle Routing and Scheduling," *Journal of Business Logistics* 9, no. 1 (1988), pp. 51–64; and Ronald H. Ballou, "A Continued Comparison of Several Popular Algorithms for Vehicle Routing and Scheduling," *Journal of Business Logistics* 11, no. 2 (1990), pp. 111–26.

INDUSTRY INSIGHT 16-3 ROUTE YOUR WAY TO COST SAVINGS

Aspen Distribution, a public warehousing and transportation company in Salt Lake City, has approximately 100 customers for which it provides distribution throughout 11 western states. Chuck Mullinex, director of transportation and strategic planning, says, "One of the things that pushed us toward a [Prophesy's Shipper TPL] system was we just couldn't keep up anymore. Doing it manually, you couldn't throw enough bodies at it to take care of the situation."

Buffalo Rock Distribution, the largest private distributor of Pepsi products in the U.S., handled its operations a little differently before implementing a planning system. "We didn't plan. That was the problem," says Rick Dodd, an operations manager at Buffalo Rock. "We would load the trucks with whatever the driver thought he could sell the next day. He would work a specific territory and sell whatever he could." That was before they installed Descartes Systems' *Roadshow* system.

Even Emery Worldwide operated the old-fashioned way—a real challenge when you consider it serves more than 200,000 customers in 206 countries through a network of 590 service centers. Cynthia Stoddard, VP of information systems at Emery, says, "Pickup and delivery supervisors would look at all the different customers we had in service and actually plot them on a map, then manually figure out what the most effective route was and divide it up between the different drivers."

Company goals may include speed, mileage optimization, service, and load capabilities. Mullinex says, "You want to make sure loads are profitable. I know I still have to ship tomorrow. It becomes a balancing act." Companies want a package that can optimize their distribution and is easy to work with.

Cost savings are a prime motivating factor for implementing routing software. Companies expect a significant return on investment. Routing software can shave expenses from a wide range of areas. Some of the more common savings include: increased utilization and fleet reduction, increased productivity, reduction of internal personnel, decreased fuel use, and increased customer service.

Buffalo Rock expected part of its savings to appear in fleet utilization. "I expected my actual fleet cost to go down, but figured we would still have to use the same amount of trucks," says Dodd. "By using *Roadshow* we cut our fleet by 50%."

Reduction in personnel can be another cost-saving result, but moving people around might be a touchy subject. "What surprised us the most was, with the reduction in people, we could still operate and run the department," reported Mullinex. "That saved us two people initially."

Emery saves the most in its pickup and delivery area. "The savings are really there," says Stoddard. "We're seeing, conservatively, about 10% savings."

Some companies are looking for basic future need fulfillment and others, like Emery, are looking to go more global. Emery Worldwide is already deriving benefits from real time information capabilities. Drivers are currently downloading shipment information for their information system called EMCON—showing all of the shipments destined for their own location. The new application creates optimal routes even while they're in transit. These are loaded onto each driver's mobile data terminal. During the day, on a real time basis as pickups are necessary or as conditions change, the data terminals are updated for rapid response. Emery is looking toward implementing this service at all its service centers and key international sites. Stoddard says, "An example of that might be international routings needed to move freight through different countries."

Automating your transportation functions is a huge project, but it doesn't have to be intimidating. If you want to cash in on potential savings, make sure you invest in a system that will handle your needs. The vast capabilities incorporated in the system may be impressive, but you might not need them. Take a package through a test run with your data. Only then will its transportation management potential for your operations make sense.

Source: J. Michael McGovern, "Route Your Way to Cost Savings," *Transportation and Distribution,* April 1998, pp. 42–46.

Demand data defines periodic customer pickup and delivery requirements. For strategic or long-term analysis, demand is specified in terms of average periodic pickups or deliveries per customer. Routes are then created based on the average demand with a capacity allowance for extremely high demand periods. For tactical routing analysis, demand typically represents customer orders scheduled for delivery during the period being planned, such as daily. Tactical analysis allows the routes to be precisely designed for delivery requirements with no allowance for uncertainty.

Operating characteristics define the number of vehicles, vehicle limitations, driver constraints, and operating costs. Vehicle limitations include capacity and weight restrictions as well as unloading constraints such as dock requirements. Driver constraints include driving time and unloading restrictions. Operating costs include fixed and variable expenses associated with vehicles and drivers.

Transportation analysis for vehicle routing and scheduling is receiving increased interest because of the effectiveness and availability of low-cost software. Many firms involved in day-to-day transportation operations have reduced transportation expenses by 10 to 15 percent through the use of tactical or strategic transportation analysis. As customers continue to demand smaller orders, transportation analysis will become increasingly important to make effective routing, scheduling, and consolidation decisions.

Summary

This chapter provides a comprehensive review of the logistics planning process, decisions, and techniques. It is designed to guide the logistics manager through the overall process of situation analysis, alternative identification, data collection, quantitative evaluation, and development of viable recommendations.

The methodology, which is generic enough for most logistics problem solving, includes three phases: problem definition and planning, data collection and analysis, and recommendations and implementation. The problem definition and planning phase is concerned with the feasibility assessment and project planning. Feasibility assessment includes situation analysis, supporting logic development, and cost/benefit estimation. Project planning requires statements of objectives and contraints, measurement standard definition, analysis technique specification, and project work plan development.

The data collection and analysis phase develops assumptions, collects data, and completes the quantitative and qualitative analyses. Assumptions development and data collection include tasks to define the analysis approach, formalize assumptions, identify data sources, and collect data. The analysis step involves definition of analysis questions, completion of validation and baseline analyses, and completion of alternative and sensitivity analyses.

The recommendations and implementation phase develops the final plan. The recommendation development step includes identification and evaluation of the best alternatives. The implementation step defines a recommended course of action, schedules development, defines acceptance criteria, and schedules final implementation.

Ad hoc tactical analyses such as freight lane balancing and ABC inventory analysis must be completed regularly to respond to changes in transportation rates, flows, and product demands. Regular supply chain planning and location analysis is becoming increasingly critical to respond to changes in global material availability, market demands, and production resource availability. More tactical tools such as dynamic simulation and routing and scheduling algorithms can be used to investigate and evaluate inventory and transportation alternatives. The importance of such comprehensive planning and analysis methods and tools is growing due to the possible alternatives to and complexity of global supply chains.

Challenge Questions

1. What is the basic objective in a logistics design and analysis study? Is it normally a one-time activity?

2. What is sensitivity analysis, and what is its role in systems design and analysis?

3. Why is it important to develop supporting logic to guide the logistical planning process?

4. Both internal and external review assessments must consider a number of measures. What are they and why are they important?

5. Why is a cost/benefit evaluation important to logistical systems design efforts?

6. What is the key objective in freight lane analysis?

7. In a general sense, what are the essential differences between analytic and simulation techniques?

8. What is the main advantage of the typical optimization technique in comparison to simulation?

9. At what point in the typical analysis does the technique give way to the managerial review and evaluation process?

10. Compare and contrast strategic and tactical transportation decisions.

V   ADMINISTRATION

The final part deals with the second primary responsibility of a firm's logistical management—administration. Chapter 17 develops principles of organization and relationship management that are essential for realizing integrated operations. Alternative collaborative models are developed and illustrated as a means to facilitate cooperation among customers, material suppliers, service suppliers, and the enterprise orchestrating the supply chain arrangement. Attention is also directed to cross-organizational change management and concepts of human resource organization. The ubiquitous nature of logistical operations creates a unique organizational structure challenge. The dispersion of logistical operations across vast geographical areas serves to place special attention on developing effective management. Chapter 18 shifts focus to performance assessment and the development of cost measurement to support activity-based management. Particular attention is directed to the development of logistics and supply chain performance metrics. The text concludes with Chapter 19, which discusses the major challenges facing 21st century logistics. Part V is supported by four cases that illustrate issues related to administration.

17 ORGANIZATION AND RELATIONSHIP MANAGEMENT

Among the topics of logistics, few hold more managerial interest than organization. The vast change taking place in logistical organization practice makes it one of the most difficult topics to accurately describe. The information revolution and the focus on supply chain integration are forcing logistics managers to rethink nearly every aspect of traditional organization logic. Guided by continuous redesign and reengineering of basic work, hierarchical organizations are being modified to accommodate information networking and self-directed work teams. The vertical bureaucratic structure that prevailed for centuries is giving way to horizontal approaches that focus on managing key processes.

Because of the geographically dispersed nature of logistics work and the fact that operations typically span more than one business, no absolutely right or wrong organization structure exists. Two firms competing for the same customers may choose to organize their operations in substantially different ways. Each will seek to match its unique capabilities to satisfy what it perceives as critical customer requirements. The old-fashioned notion of stamping out organization charts using "cookie cutter" principles of management doesn't work in today's dynamic world and is not likely to work in the future.

Logistical Organization Development

Prior to the 1950s, functions now accepted as logistics were generally viewed as facilitating or support work. Organization responsibility for logistics was typically dispersed throughout the firm. This fragmentation often meant that aspects of logistical work were performed without cross-functional coordination, often resulting in duplication and waste. Information was frequently distorted or delayed, and lines of authority and responsibility were typically blurred. Managers, recognizing the need for total cost control, began to reorganize and combine logistics functions into a single managerial group. Structuring logistics as an integrated organization first appeared in the 1950s.[1]

The motivation driving functional aggregation was a growing belief that grouping logistics functions into a single organization would increase the likelihood of integration and facilitate improved understanding of how decisions and procedures in one operational area impact performance in other areas. The belief was that eventually all functions would begin to work as a single group focused on total system performance. This integration paradigm, based on organizational proximity, prevailed throughout a 35 year period. However, by the mid-1980s, it became increasingly clear that the paradigm of functional aggregation might not, in the final analysis, offer the best approach to achieve integrated logistics. For many firms, the ink had barely dried on what appeared to be the perfect logistics organization when new and far more pervasive rethinking of what constituted the ideal structure emerged.

Almost overnight, the emphasis shifted from function to process. Firms began to examine the role logistical competency could play in the overall process of creating customer value. This ushered in new thinking regarding how to best achieve integrated logistical performance. To a significant degree, the focus on process reduced the pressure to aggregate functions into all-encompassing organizational units. The critical question became not how to organize individual functions, but rather how to best manage the overall logistical process. The challenges and opportunities of functional disaggregation and information-driven integration began to emerge.

The mission of logistics work is to position inventory when and where it is required to facilitate profitable sales. This supportive work must be performed around the clock and typically throughout the world, which means that logistics needs to be an integral part of all processes. The ideal structure for logistics would be an organization that performs essential work as part of the processes it supports while achieving the synergism of cross-functional integration.

Information technology introduced the potential of virtual integration as contrasted to physically combining logistics functions. Using information technology to coordinate or orchestrate integrated performance allows the responsibility for performing work itself to be distributed throughout the overall organization. Integration requires that logistics combine with other areas such as marketing and manufacturing. For example, rather than focusing on how to relate transportation and inventory, the real challenge is to integrate transportation, inventory, new product development, flexible manufacturing, and customer success. To achieve overall organization integration,

---

[1]For early articles discussing this initial integration of logistics activities, see Donald J. Bowersox, "Emerging Patterns of Physical Distribution Organization," *Transportation and Distribution Management,* May 1968, pp. 53–59; John F. Stolle, "How to Manage Physical Distribution," *Harvard Business Review,* July/August 1967, pp. 93–100; and Robert E. Weigand, "The Management of Physical Distribution: A Dilemma," *Michigan State University Business Topics,* Summer 1962, pp. 67–72.

FIGURE 17-1

Logistical organizational development cycle

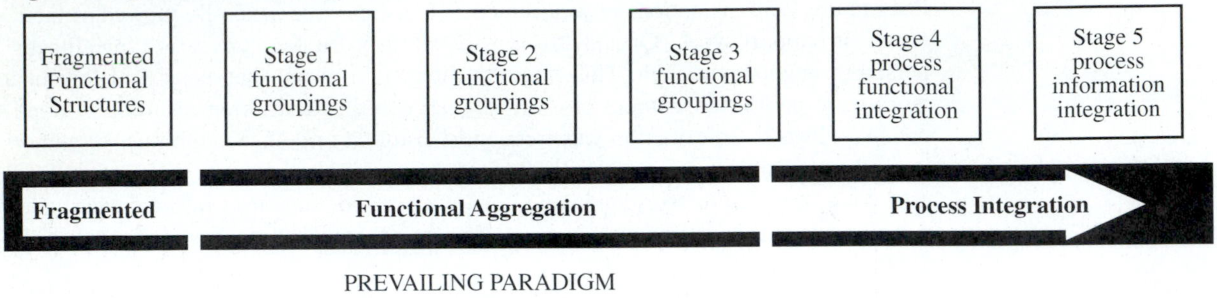

Fragmented Functional Structures	Stage 1 functional groupings	Stage 2 functional groupings	Stage 3 functional groupings	Stage 4 process functional integration	Stage 5 process information integration

Fragmented — **Functional Aggregation** — **Process Integration** →

PREVAILING PARADIGM

a firm must combine a wide variety of capabilities into new organization units. This means that traditional single-function departments must be assimilated into a process. Such assimilation often requires that traditional organizations be disaggregated and then recombined in new and unique ways. In one sense, such functional disaggregation may appear to come back full circle to the early days of fragmented single-function departments. However, the critical difference in the emerging organization model is the widespread availability of information. The new organization format is characterized by an extremely different culture concerning how information and knowledge are managed and shared.

Logistics managers can benefit from understanding the organization development process. Such understanding permits managers to evaluate their firm's current state of organization and plan changes that can be accommodated. To fully understand and manage change, it is useful to understand how traditional bureaucratic organizations evolved. Research suggests that managers initially stabilized logistics through functional aggregation. Such aggregation was essential to embarking upon the use of information networking to facilitate process integration. Figure 17-1 illustrates five stages of organization development based on relative balance of functional aggregation and information integration.

At any given time, the array of observable logistics organizations runs the full gamut of development stages. Some firms are just embracing the challenge of stage 1, while others are pushing the frontiers of stage 5. While the organization evolution can be accelerated, research suggests it cannot be jump-started.[2] The challenge for logis-

---

[2]For a review of empirical research related to logistics organization evolution, see: A. T. Kearney, *Measuring Productivity in Physical Distribution: The $40 Billion Gold Mine* (Oak Brook, IL: Council of Logistics Management, 1978); A. T. Kearney, "Organizing Physical Distribution to Improve Bottom Line Results," *Annual Proceedings of the Council of Logistics Management,* 1981, pp. 1–14; A. T. Kearney, *Measuring and Improving Productivity in the Logistics Process: Achieving Customer Satisfaction Breakthroughs* (Oak Brook, IL: Council of Logistics Management, 1991). A. T. Kearney completed and published studies in Europe, Asia, and North America in 1993. These studies were distributed by Kearney in captive publications. For a review of Michigan State University research on logistics organization and best practice, see: Donald J. Bowersox et al., *Leading Edge Logistics: Competitive Positioning for the 1990s* (Oak Brook, IL: Council of Logistics Management, 1989); Donald J. Bowersox et al., *Logistical Excellence: It's Not Business as Usual* (Burlington, MA: Digital Press, 1992); The Global Logistics Research Team at Michigan State University, *World Class Logistics: The Challenge of Managing Continuous Change* (Oak Brook, IL.: Council of Logistics Management, 1995); Donald J. Bowersox, David J. Closs, and Theodore P. Stank, *21st Century Logistics: Making Supply Chain Integration a Reality* (Oak Brook, IL: Council of Logistics Management, 1999).

FIGURE 17-2

Traditional organization of logistically related functions

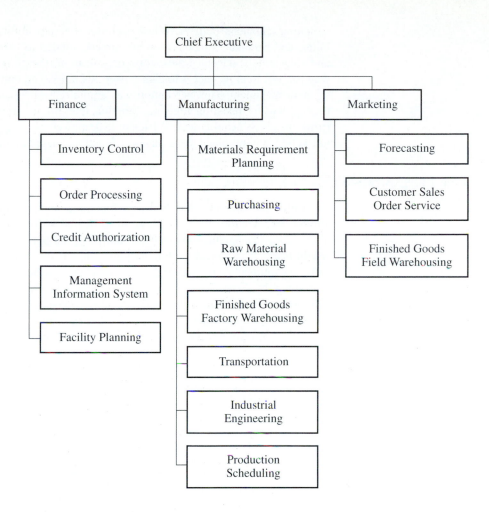

tics managers is to be able to assess how their particular organization should be structured to best exploit logistics competency.

Stages of Functional Aggregation

Figure 17-2 illustrates a traditional organization structure with dispersed logistical functions. (Only functions typically involved in logistical operations are shown in the hypothetical organization charts.) The initial belief was that integrated performance would be facilitated by grouping logistical functions normally spread throughout the traditional organization into a single command and control structure. It was felt that logistical functions would be better managed, trade-offs better analyzed, and least total cost solutions better identified if all logistics work was integrated into one organization.

While the idea of functional integration is logical and appeals to common sense, it is not always supported by other unit managers. It is natural that any attempt to reposition managerial authority and responsibility will meet resistance. Many logistics executives can provide examples of how attempts to reorganize were met with rivalry and mistrust—not to mention accusations of empire building. Traditionally, in organization structures, financial budgets follow operational responsibility. Likewise, power, visibility, and personal compensation are directly related to managing large head counts and substantial budgets. Logistical reorganization, therefore, was often viewed as a way for logistical managers to gain power, visibility, and compensation at the expense of other managers. This perception was ample reason for other managers to protect their power by resisting logistics function integration. In an increasing number of firms, however, benefits were sufficient to empower reorganization. The resulting evolution typically involved three stages of functional aggregation.

Stage 1 Organization

The initial attempts to group logistical functions emerged during the 1950s and early 1960s. Organizations with even a minimal degree of formal unification only emerged after senior management became committed to the belief that improved performance would result. The typical evolutionary pattern was for two or more logistics functions to be operationally grouped without significant modification of the overall organization hierarchy. Seldom were organization units engaged in purchasing and market distribution integrated during this initial development stage.

Figure 17-3 illustrates a typical stage 1 organization. For the most part, stage 1 organization change involved grouping functions within the traditional domains of mar-

FIGURE 17-3

Stage 1 logistical organization

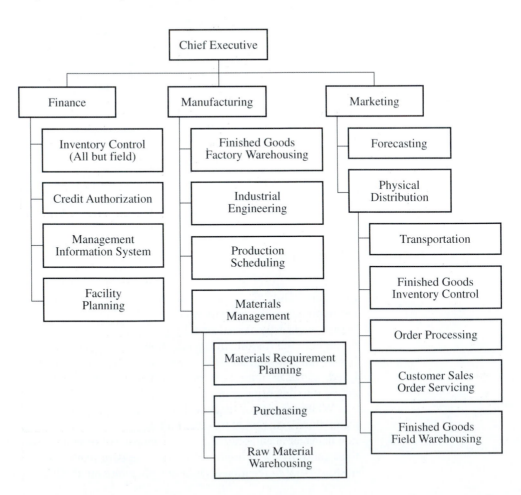

keting and manufacturing. In the marketing area, the grouping typically centered around customer service; in the manufacturing area, on inbound materials or parts procurement. With few exceptions, most traditional departments were not changed and the organization hierarchy was not altered significantly. The notable deficiency of a stage 1 organization was a failure to focus direct responsibility for inventory. For example, initial physical distribution organizations typically controlled warehousing, transportation, and order processing. Few stage 1 organizations had direct responsibility to manage trade-offs between transportation and finished inventory deployment.

Stage 2 Organization

As the overall enterprise gained operational experience with unified logistics and cost-benefits, a second stage of organization began to evolve. Figure 17-4 illustrates stage 2, which began to emerge in the late 1960s and early 1970s.

FIGURE 17-4

Stage 2 logistical organization

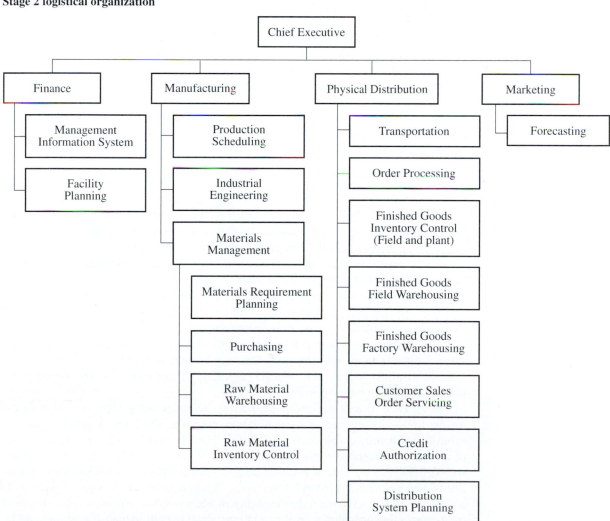

The significant feature of a stage 2 organization was that logistics was singled out and positioned as an area of organizational authority and responsibility, usually focusing on physical distribution or materials management. The motivation was simple: positioning logistics at a higher and more visible organization level increased the likelihood of strategic impact. Independent status allowed logistics to be managed as a core competency. Physical distribution was a likely candidate for elevated status in firms where customer service was critical to overall success (Figure 17-4). The automotive business was an example where materials management often increased in operational authority and responsibility because inbound materials and production were a major portion of product cost. Thus, the focal group that was elevated to higher prominence in stage 2 organizations typically depended on the nature of the enterprise's primary business.

As with stage 1, the stage 2 organizations did not achieve fully integrated logistics. This time failure to synthesize logistical management into an integrated system was due in part to a preoccupation with specific functions, such as order processing or purchasing, which were perceived as essential to traditional operations. A second limiting factor to total integration was the lack of cross-functional logistical information systems. As a general rule, organization integration was directly related to the firm's information system capability.

A significant point about stage 2 organization is that integrated physical distribution and/or materials management began to gain acceptance among financial, manufacturing, and marketing counterparts. The other corporate officers viewed these integrated organizations as something more than purely reactive efforts aimed at cost reduction or containment. In the stage 2 organization, it was common for the integrated unit to become a primary contributor to business strategy. Stage 2 organizations remain throughout industry today and represent a common approach to logistical facilitation.

Stage 3 Organization

Stage 3 organizations emerged in the 1980s as the logistical renaissance began. This organization structure sought to unify all logistical functions and operations under a single senior manager. Stage 3 organizations, having the comprehensive nature illustrated in Figure 17-5, were and continue to be rare. However, the trend at the stage 3 level of organization structure was clearly to group as many logistical planning and operational functions as practical under single authority and responsibility. The goal was the strategic management of all materials and finished product movement and storage to the maximum benefit of the enterprise.

The rapid development of logistical information systems provided an impetus for stage 3 organizations. Information technology became available to plan and operate systems that fully integrated logistical operations. Several aspects of the stage 3 organization justify further discussion.

First, each area of logistics—purchasing, manufacturing support, and physical distribution—is structured as a separate line operation. The lines of authority and responsibility directly enable each bundle of supportive services to be performed as part of an overall integrated logistical effort. Since areas of operation responsibility are well defined, it is possible to establish manufacturing support as an operation unit similar to purchasing and physical distribution. Because each unit is operationally self-sufficient, each can maintain the flexibility to accommodate critical services required by its respective operational area. In addition, since overall logistical activities can be

FIGURE 17-5

Stage 3 logistical organization

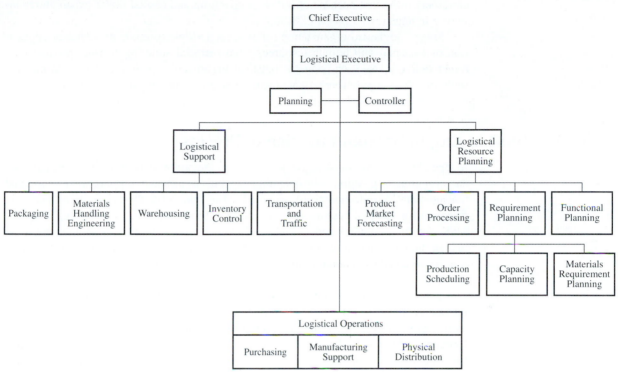

planned and coordinated on an integrated basis, operational synergies between areas can be exploited.

Second, five capabilities grouped under logistical support are positioned as operational services. This shared service orientation is the mechanism to integrate logistical operations. It is important to stress that logistical support *is not* a staff organization. Rather, the group manages day-to-day logistics work, which is structured with matrix accountability for direct liaison between physical distribution, manufacturing support, and purchasing operations.

Third, logistical resource planning embraces the full potential of management information to plan and coordinate operations. Order processing triggers the logistical system into operation and generates the integrated database required for control. Logistical resource planning facilitates integration. Logistical resource plans are based on product/market forecasting, order processing, and inventory status to determine overall requirements for any planning period. On the basis of identified requirements, the planning unit operationalizes manufacturing by coordinating production scheduling, capacity planning, and materials requirement planning.

Finally, overall planning and controllership exist at the highest level of the stage 3 organization. These initiatives serve to facilitate integration. The planning group is concerned with long-range strategic positioning and is responsible for logistical system quality improvement and reengineering. The logistical controller is concerned with measurement of cost and customer service performance and provision of information for managerial decision making. The development of procedures for logistical controllership is one of the most critical areas of integrated logistical administration.

The need for accurate measurement is a direct result of increased emphasis placed on continuous improvement in customer service performance.[3] The measurement task is extremely important because of the large operating and capital dollar expenditures involved in logistics.

Stage 3 logistical organization offers a single logic to guide the efficient application of financial and human resources from material sourcing to final product customer delivery. As such, stage 3 logistical organization positions a firm to manage trade-offs among purchasing, manufacturing support, and physical distribution.

Stage 4: A Shift in Emphasis from Function to Process

Independent of functional aggregation or disaggregation, it is clear that organizations are struggling to position their operating capabilities to better support process-oriented management. As one observer concluded, "The search for the organization perfectly designed for the 21st century is going ahead with the urgency of a scavenger hunt."[4] McKinsey consultants Frank Ostroff and Doug Smith proposed an architecture to illustrate how the functional hierarchical vertical organization could transition toward a process-oriented horizontal organization. The Ostroff/Smith model is presented in Figure 17-6.

The concept of the 21st century organization is envisioned as the result of three factors: (1) the development of a highly involved work environment with self-directed work teams (SDWT) as a vehicle to empower employees to generate maximum performance; (2) improved productivity that results from managing processes rather than functions (this notion has always rested at the core of integrated logistics); (3) the rapid sharing of accurate information that allows all facets of the organization to be integrated. Information technology is viewed as the load-bearing structure of the new enterprise, replacing organizational hierarchy.

The essence of the argument for radical restructuring is that the traditional evolutionary concept of organization change is not sufficient to stimulate major breakthroughs in service or productivity. Rather, traditional organization change shifts or realigns operating structure without serious redesign of the basic work process. Because such restructuring typically assumes that functional organizations will continue to perform basic work, little or no difference in actual practice results. In essence, companies are refocusing old business practices rather than designing new, more efficient processes.

The challenges of managing logistics as a process are threefold. First, all effort must be focused on value-added to the customer. An activity only exists and is justified to the extent it contributes customer value. Therefore, a logistical commitment must be motivated by a belief that customers desire a specific activity to be performed. Logistical mangers must develop the capacity to think externally. Second, integrating logistics as part of a process requires that all skills necessary to complete the work be available regardless of their functional organization. Organizational grouping on the basis of selected function can artificially separate natural work flows and create bottlenecks. When horizontal structures are put in place, critical skills need to be positioned

---

[3]Performance Measurement is discussed in greater detail in Chapter 19.

[4]Thomas A. Stewart, "The Search for the Organization of Tomorrow," *Fortune,* May 18, 1992, pp. 91–98.

FIGURE 17-6

From vertical to horizontal organizations

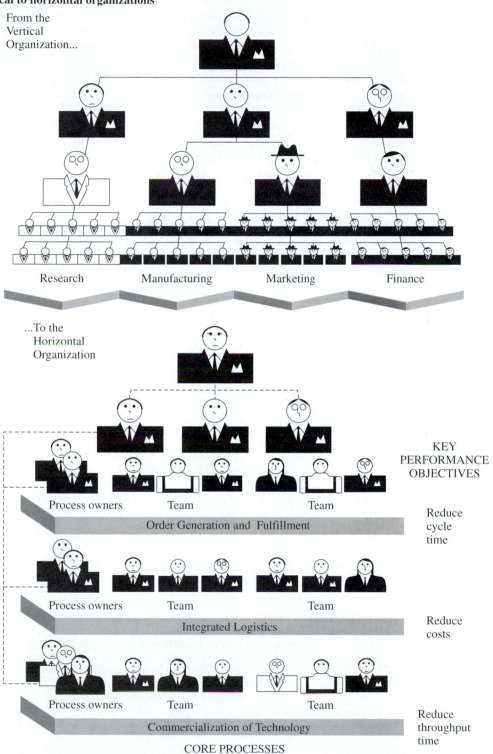

From the
Vertical
Organization...

Research   Manufacturing   Marketing   Finance

...To the
Horizontal
Organization

KEY
PERFORMANCE
OBJECTIVES

Process owners   Team   Team

Order Generation and Fulfillment

Reduce
cycle
time

Process owners   Team   Team

Integrated Logistics

Reduce
costs

Process owners   Team   Team

Commercialization of Technology

Reduce
throughput
time

CORE PROCESSES

Source: Thomas A. Stewart, "The Search for the Organization of Tomorrow," *Fortune,* May 18, 1992, p. 96.

and made accessible to assure that required work is accomplished. Finally, work performed in a process context should stimulate synergism. With systems integration, the design of work as a process means that overall organizational trade-offs are structured to achieve maximum performance for minimum input investment.[5] Industry Insight 17-1 discusses the concept of developing a process reposition.

The radical changes proposed by a shift from a functional to a process orientation have mixed messages for managers involved in logistics. On the positive side, general adoption of a process orientation builds upon the basic principles of systems integration. At the core of integrated logistics is a commitment to functional excellence which contributes to process performance. A general shift to managing logistics as a process means that it will be positioned as a central contributor to all initiatives that focus on new product development, customer order generation, fulfillment, and delivery. The overall trend of process integration expands the operational potential and impact of logistics.

Less clear is a full understanding of how processes themselves will be performed and managed. The most advanced logistical solutions observed during the past decade have combined organization form and best-practice performance to manage the overall logistics process using a modified hierarchical structure. The concept of matrix organization has emerged as a common structure to facilitate horizontal management.[6] The availability of superior information to operationalize a matrix approach relaxes dependence on a rigid formal organization structure. In terms of architecture for a logistical organization, the critical questions are: (1) How much formal hierarchical structure can and should be retained while seeking to enable and encourage a process orientation? and (2) How can an organization be structured so that it can manage a process as complex as global logistics without becoming overly bureaucratic? To address these questions, managers need to fully understand the potential of stage 5, which advocates information-driven logistical networks that integrate across organization boundaries.

Stage 5: Virtuality and Organization Transparency

It is highly unlikely that the attention being given to process will end management's quest for ideal logistical organization. While several different scenarios concerning the organization of the future are technologically feasible, one of the most intriguing is speculation that formal hierarchical command and control organization structure will be replaced with an informal electronic network often referred to as a *virtual organization*.[7] The adjective *virtual* implies underlying existence without formal

---

[5]Michael Hammer and Steven Stanton, "How Process Enterprises Really Work," *Harvard Business Review,* November/December 1999, pp. 108–17.

[6]Matrix organization structure is further developed later in this chapter on pages 535–537.

[7]For more detail and examples of virtual organizations, see: Charles C. Snow, Raymond E. Miles, and Henry J. Coleman Jr., "Managing 21st Century Network Organizations," *Organizational Dynamics* 20, no. 3 (Winter 1992), pp. 5–20; Walter Kiechel III, "How We Will Work in the Year 2000," *Fortune* 127, no. 10 (May 17, 1993), pp. 38–52; Joan Magretta, "The Power of Virtual Integration: An Interview with Dell Computer's Michael Dell," *Harvard Business Review,* March/April 1998, pp. 73–84; Nicholas G. Carr, "Being Virtual: Character and The New Economy," *Harvard Business Review,* May/June 1999, pp. 181–86; William H. Davidrow and Michael S. Malone, *The Virtual Corporation: Structuring and Revitalizing the Corporation for the 21st Century* (New York: Harper Business, 1992); John A. Byrne, "The Virtual Corporation: The Company of the Future Will Be the Ultimate in Adaptability," *Business Week,* February 8, 1993, pp. 98–102; and Kevin P. Gayne and Renee Dye, "The Competitive Dynamics of Network-Based Businesses," *Harvard Business Review,* January/February 1998, pp. 99–109.

INDUSTRY INSIGHT 17-1   A NEW WAY TO MANAGE PROCESS KNOWLEDGE

For most of the past decade, a team of researchers at the MIT Sloan School of Management in Cambridge, Massachusetts, has been quietly laboring on a Herculean task—to document, in meticulous detail, every major business process. The Process Handbook Project, as the effort is called, has succeeded in creating an electronic repository of information on more than 5000 processes and activities, together with a suite of sophisticated software programs for navigating and manipulating the data.

Now MIT is making the process repository and software available to companies everywhere by licensing them to start-up firm Phios Corporation. Phios plans to commercialize the research in two ways. First, it will help individual companies develop their own proprietary versions of the repository, providing an easy way to store, organize, and share diverse information such as process maps, procedure manuals, images, software programs, and Web links. Second, it will put the general process repository on the World Wide Web, giving managers access to a wealth of knowledge on process design.

Thomas W. Malone, a professor at the Sloan School and cofounder and chairman of Phios, believes that process management tools are becoming increasingly important. "Electronic commerce, outsourcing, and enterprise software systems are all forcing companies to rethink the way they organize work," he says. "Companies need to be more creative and flexible in managing their processes—and that requires a much more systematic approach to capturing and disseminating process knowledge."

One company that's already using the software to manage its process knowledge is Dow Corning. The company found, in the course of installing an SAP system, that it lacked a consistent way to document all its process designs and share that information throughout its organization. It is using the Phios software to create interlinked maps of its key processes, which have proven invaluable in designing and rolling out the new system. The company is also moving ahead with plans to store its process repository on its intranet. Anyone in the company will be able to quickly learn the steps involved in any process, find links to detailed process guidebooks and policy statements, check measures of process performance, and share ideas for improving process designs.

Much of the power of the Phios process repository lies in its unique two-dimensional structure, which organizes information according to both process parts and process types. A user exploring the general process of selling a product, for example, can move vertically through the database to gain more detailed information about the process's component parts, or subactivities. The user can also move horizontally to study more specialized types of the process, such as selling over the Internet or selling financial services. By making it easy for users to move in both directions through the process repository, Phios's software can spur creative thinking about new ways to do work.

One large services company used the repository to generate fresh ideas for restructuring its hiring processes. The company was growing rapidly in a tightening labor market, and it was having trouble bringing qualified new people on board, so it used the repository to explore the hiring processes of other companies, both inside and outside its industry. When it discovered that Marriott used an automated telephone system to screen job applicants, it realized that it could use a similar process for certain entry-level positions.

The company also looked at analogues to the hiring process. In the repository's classification scheme, "hiring" is a specialized form of the more general process of "buying." When exploring different buying processes, the company found a description of General Electric's Internet-based purchasing system, which enables buyers to efficiently find and compare different suppliers. The services company realized that a similar electronic clearinghouse might be a productive way of locating and evaluating potential employees. It also considered the possibility of setting up an online bidding system for jobs, as electronic auction houses like Onsale have done for products.

The value of well-managed process information will only grow in the future, according to Malone. "As the boundaries between functions and companies crumble, the old organizational chart loses its usefulness as a management tool," he says. "In tomorrow's companies, executives will likely depend on richly detailed process maps to guide their managerial and strategic decision making."

Source: Nicholas G. Carr, "A New Way to Manage Process Knowledge," *Harvard Business Review,* September/October 1999, pp. 24–25.

---

recognition.[8] In other words, a virtual organization, whether it is a total enterprise or a specific core competency, would exist as a provider of integrated performance but not as an identifiable unit of formal organization structure. In the case of logistics, key work teams may be electronically linked to perform critical activities in an integrated fashion. These work teams could be transparent in terms of the formal organization structure of their membership; that is, formal organization charts may not be related to actual work flow. (In fact, logistics organizations of the future could be characterized by functional disaggregation throughout the organization to focus on work flow rather than structure.)

The concepts of virtuality and transparency have far-reaching implications for long-standing organizational concepts such as centralization and decentralization:

> To meet customer requirements for speed and response, authority needs to be pushed down the organization. Strategic direction can be expected to originate at headquarters. Operational adaptations will increasingly be made on the front lines. Frontline managers will be increasingly expected to refine strategy and apply it directly to operations. Centralization and decentralization will increasingly become meaningless terms. Organizations of the future will seek to capture the best of centralization and decentralization without commitment to either concept.[9]

To fully exploit the benefits of information technology, a major structural and philosophical shift must take place. Command and control structures have a significant historical precedence in business that is difficult to change. In fact, some believe such radical change can only be accomplished if the original organization solutions are completely abolished or disintegrated. In other words, the change cannot be made by simply modifying the existing organization structure.[10]

The idea behind disaggregation is that the power of information technology will allow integrated management and performance of logistics work without grouping or aggregating functions into a formal organization unit. The responsibility for performing logistics work should ideally be organizationally positioned with users. The *user,* in this sense, is the organization that requires transportation, warehousing, inventory, or any other logistics service to complete its mission. Making those who perform the logistical services an integral part of the user organization has potential to increase relevancy and flexibility. In essence, ultimate empowerment would result. Each organization throughout an enterprise would perform its required logistical services. The disintegration paradigm is based on the belief that logistical functionality need not be

---

[8]Webster's Dictionary defines virtual as "being such in essence or effect though not formally recognized or admitted."

[9]Donald J. Bowersox, et al., *Logistical Excellence: It's Not Business as Usual* (Burlington, MA: Digital Press, 1992), pp. 173–74.

[10]Christopher Meyer and David Power, "Enterprise Disintegration: The Storm Before the Calm," *Commentary* (Lexington, MA: Temple, Baker and Sloane, 1989).

organizationally assigned to a special command and control structure to efficiently and effectively coordinate performance.

There are many arguments counter to functional disaggregation. First and foremost is the danger that disaggregation will create a danger of reverting to a functional fixation or myopia characteristic of fragmented logistics (pre-stage 1 organization). A second concern is that critical scale and scope in logistical operations will be lost and result in diseconomies. Finally, standardization and simplification of work may decrease if similar types of work are spread throughout user organizations without formal feedback mechanisms.

While the above arguments are not exhaustive, they are characteristic of the concerns managers have about abandoning formal integrated organizations. The key to improved performance is the realization that relevancy and flexibility may be increased by creating an electronic network to facilitate logistical coordination as contrasted to reliance on formal organization structuring. Actually, the information technology did not exist when the paradigm of functional organization grouping was launched in an effort to achieve integration requirements. Because of the newness of the ideas, it is difficult to perceive how a stage 5 organization could be managed.

From a technological perspective, it is reasonable to assume that the formal logistics organizations we know today may not continue to exist in terms of current command and control arrangements. Integration will increasingly be achieved via electronic connectivity and networking of logistics work on an informal basis. Under such coordination, the essential aspects of integrated performance can be retained and scarce knowledge and expertise shared to achieve maximum standardization and simplification. *All* logistics work, regardless of when and where it is performed, can be captured as part of the informal logistics network. Sharing common information regarding requirements and performance metrics while retaining local control offers a logistical core competency that far exceeds today's best-practice model.

The logistics organization of the future is essentially what amounts to an *electronic keritsu*. Adopted from Eastern culture, the keritsu is a loosely affiliated group of business firms that share commonalities and are committed to cooperative behavior. The transparent logistical network organization can be viewed as a composite of affiliated business functions that are motivated and directed by common interest and goals. The informal network is facilitated by information sharing.

The jury is out concerning if and when the functionally disaggregated information coordinated network will become a realistic logistics organization solution. Research on best practice indicates that some firms are at the initial stages of linking disparate work electronically rather than physically or organizationally.[11]

The idea of a virtual organization is broader than simply creating structural transparency. The notion that entities can configure to achieve common goals and then disband has significance for the challenges of relationship management discussed later in this chapter. The aspects of virtuality that deal with a fluid and flexible group of firms working together to leverage their individual core competencies is having major impact on the future of logistical service suppliers. It gives substance to the idea of a disposable logistics competency that users can acquire when needed and then abandon when no longer required. The idea of disposable logistics has application in such areas

---

[11]Donald J. Bowersox, David J. Closs, and Theodore P. Stank, *21st Century Logistics: Making Supply Chain Integration a Reality* (Oak Brook, IL: Council of Logistics Management, 1999).

as special promotion, seasonality, and new product development and introduction. The fact that firms today constantly form and then dismantle alliances gives credibility to the notions of transparency and virtuality.

Issues and Challenges

The general management literature is filled with a litany of ever-emerging buzzwords and organizational concepts that are touted as paths to instant success. Given this continuous bombardment of new ideas, it becomes confusing for executives who are responsible for managing logistics to sort out and implement the proper balance of proven traditional organization concepts and a mix of new, innovative ways to improve logistical productivity and operational flexibility. The challenge is to differentiate concepts that satisfy the unique requirements of each particular organization from those that are simply fads, offering limited or no relevancy. This challenge is amplified by the discrepancies that exist between words and realities.

This section addresses three important considerations that a manager concerned with logistical organization architecture should carefully review: (1) new organization concepts that appear to have particular relevancy to logistics, (2) the impact that an overall business environment characterized by rampant change has on the logistics workplace, and (3) the challenges of managing organization change and transformation.

Concepts Having Logistical Significance

At the present time organization restructuring is focused on facilitating process goal attainment. For logistics this means that operational competencies need to focus on maximizing customer value. Information technology is creating the potential for logistical networks that transcend traditional lines of authority and responsibility. The potential exists to create transparent organizations that coordinate logistical work everywhere a firm does business. Instead of logistics being managed at a department headquarters or some plant, logistics organizations may extend throughout and permeate all user locations.

In light of where organization structure has been and where it might go, logistical managers need to assess those ideas that have the greatest applicability and are most likely to be implemented. Four general concepts appear to be particularly relevant: structural compression, empowerment, teaming, and learning.

Structural Compression

Many different terms and concepts have been used to capture highly visible aspects of organization change. Terms such as *downsizing, flattening, networking, clustering, right-sizing, delayering, reengineering,* and *nonhierarchical* are abundant in the popular managerial press. All of these ideas have one thing in common: the desire to structure organizations so they can perform required work better while using fewer human resources. However, what is at stake is broader than simply trying to do more with less. The nature of logistical work is changing, and it is only logical that organization structures must adapt to facilitate lean execution.

The motivation for logistical structural compression starts with the changing roles of the chief logistics executive. In an environment characterized by restricted head count and intensive asset control, the senior logistics executive is emerging as an integral part of the firm's continued struggle to gain and maintain customer loyalty.[12] In today's competitive environment, senior logistics executives may spend more than 50 percent of their time working directly with customers. This frontline commitment typically means performing as a member of a cross-functional or category team. While logistics managers may have traditionally visited with customers at the request of sales executives to explain performance failures, their current role is less that of a sacrificial lamb and more that of a planner of upcoming events or a provider of strategic vision. To achieve effective customer collaboration, logistics executives need to have direct access to all types and levels of information.

Change at the top typically results in change throughout an organization. For the most part, such change in logistical organizations has focused on restructuring and downsizing middle management. A great deal has been written about the changing needs of business in terms of white-collar information workers and their traditional contribution to data flow and control. The availability of transaction-based data warehouses means that time and personnel, previously used to analyze and format information, are no longer required. In fact, the delays encountered by such analysis cannot be tolerated in a time-based competitive environment. Elaborate internal clearance procedures to obtain operational information can no longer support the quick analytical trade-offs required today. Rather, information sharing needs to transcend all layers of the organization and be easy for appropriate personnel to access. It follows that the fewer the organization layers, the less chance of information delay, distortion, amplification, or omission.

Therefore, while restructuring typically means fewer people, the desire to change is also related to improving response speed and flexibility. The bureaucratic command and control organization structure that effectively served the needs of yesterday simply does not satisfy the requirements of the information age. Beyond determining the layers of management that offer the correct balance between effective supervision and desired agility, the changing of basic structure requires careful review of long-standing beliefs.

Matrix to Horizontal Structure.   As indicated earlier, the dominant organization structure in logistics for the past three decades has been based on aggregating functional groupings. Under a functional structure, logistical activities such as transportation and warehousing were organizationally grouped into clusters and related by direct lines of authority and responsibility. Such functional groupings typically utilize line command and control to allocate resources to operations.

As an enterprise begins to confront the challenge of process management, it becomes difficult and even undesirable to maintain the crystal-clear lines of authority and responsibility representative of functional organization structures. In a command and control structure, it is difficult to achieve the cross-functional flexibility required to satisfy unique customer requirements. One solution that mangers developed to resolve cross-functional operations is referred to as *matrix organization.*

In the original matrix organization, two senior managers shared overall responsibility for the enterprise. The first senior manager focused on financial aspects and was responsible for the profitability of specific organization units that were often structured around product categories, geographical proximity, or class of business. The

---

[12]Eugene Emerson Jennings, *How Managers Become Chiefs: Rules and Moves* (Okemos, MI: Mobility Study Institute, 1997).

Figure 17-7

The horizontal corporation: It's about managing across, not up and down

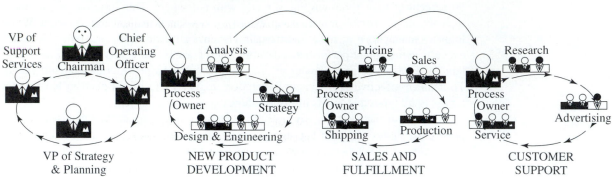

Source: Adopted from John Byrne, "The Horizontal Corporation: It's About Managing Across, Not Up and Down," *Business Week,* December 20, 1993.

second senior manager focused on resources and was responsible for the deployment of human and physical assets across organization units.

The matrix model of structuring authority and responsibility gained popularity in service organizations such as consulting and public accounting. Business managers were given full accountability for specific clients or projects and were assigned skilled personnel from resource pools on the basis of project requirements. While the skilled personnel were directly responsible to the resource manager, they were temporarily assigned to the business manager. The business manager had direct authority for work design, temporary assignment of functional staff, and project control. The business manager typically shared recommendations concerning promotion, salary increase, and other benefits for the skilled personnel with the resource manager. On completion of the project, skilled personnel would return to the functional pools for reassignment.

The potential of a matrix organization structure has gained renewed interest as managers struggle with the challenges of process management. Because the approach offers a way to share scarce assets and technical resources on a flexible basis, it reduces the potential duplication of highly skilled personnel across business units. An offsetting factor is that temporary personnel may not feel the same commitment that is characteristic of traditional functional organization arrangements.

The modern extension of the matrix approach to business structure is increasingly referred to as a *horizontal organization.* Similar to the McKinsey model discussed earlier, the horizontal organization is designed to facilitate process, not to perform tasks.[13] Figure 17-7 illustrates a horizontal organization, and Industry Insight 17-2 details the seven key elements of such an organization.

While the matrix organization of the 1980s is not identical to the horizontal corporation of the 1990s, several key concepts are similar. In subsequent parts of this chapter, other developments critical to horizontal management, such as teaming and learning, are discussed.

When restructuring an organization, the key question for the logistics manager concerns how innovative to make the new structure. Issues related to organization ca-

---

[13]See Thomas A. Stewart, "The Search for the Organization of Tomorrow," *Fortune* 125, no. 10 (May 18, 1992), pp. 92–98; and John A. Byrne, "The Horizontal Corporation: It's About Managing Across, Not Up and Down," *Business Week,* December 20, 1993, pp. 76–81.

Industry Insight 17-2 Seven Key Elements of the Horizontal Corporation

Simple downsizing didn't produce the dramatic rises in productivity many companies hoped for. Gaining quantum leaps in performance requires rethinking the way work gets done. To do that, some companies are adopting a new organization model. Here's how it might work:

1. *Organize around process, not task.* Instead of creating a structure around functions or departments, build the company around its three to five core processes and establish specific performance goals. Assign an "owner" to each process.

2. *Flatten hierarchy.* To reduce supervision, combine fragmented tasks, eliminate work that fails to add value, and cut the activities within each process to a minimum. Use as few teams as possible to perform an entire process.

3. *Use teams to manage everything.* Make teams the main building blocks of the organization. Limit supervisory roles by making the team manage itself. Give the team a common purpose. Hold it accountable for measurable performance goals.

4. *Let customers drive performance.* Make customer satisfaction—not stock appreciation or profitability—the primary driver and measure of performance. The profits will come and the stock will rise if the customers are satisfied.

5. *Reward team performance.* Change the appraisal and pay systems to reward team results, not just individual performance. Encourage staff to develop multiple skills rather than specialized know-how. Reward them for it.

6. *Maximize supplier and customer contact.* Bring employees into direct, regular contact with suppliers and customers. Add supplier or customer representatives as full working members of in-house teams when they can be of service.

7. *Inform and train all employees.* Don't just spoon-feed sanitized information on a "need to know" basis. Trust staff with raw data, but train them in how to use it to perform their own analyses and make their own decisions.

Source: John A. Byrne, "The Horizontal Corporation: It's about Managing Across, Not Up and Down," *Business Week*, December 20, 1993, pp. 76–79.

---

pacity, resource availability, critical knowledge and skill set requirements, economies of scale, and economies of scope serve to mediate the degree of desirable transition from vertical to horizontal management. The judgment of how horizontal to become will vary with every enterprise and will directly relate to the extent of information technology adoption.

Empowerment

To empower means to delegate. The delegation of authority is not a new management concept. What is new about contemporary empowerment is the extent to which employees are permitted and *expected* to make decisions related to performance of their assigned work.[14] Empowerment starts with availability and willingness of senior management to freely share relevant information.

The motivation behind empowerment is a belief that the overall effort to satisfy customers will be enhanced if frontline employees are permitted to take what in their

---

[14]Sharafat Khan, "The Key to Being a Leader: Company Empowerment," *Journal For Quality Participation,* January/February 1997, p. 23.

judgment is appropriate action. Such on-the-spot decision making can greatly speed up a firm's response to customer requests.[15]

In logistics, empowerment could range from accommodating all order requirements on a one-call basis to on-the-spot resolution of delivery discrepancies. What it all boils down to is trusting frontline employees to use sound judgement in dealing with day-to-day situations. Likewise, an empowered organization permits mid-level management to resolve problems and use proactive judgment. The extent to which an organization is empowered is reflected in response speed. A wide range of decisions does not need to transcend a business hierarchy for approval in an empowered organization. Employees are afforded maximum opportunity to perform their assigned work.

Empowerment in logistics takes on a special meaning. The multitude of details required to support the work of logistics makes it essential that frontline managers be positioned to complete all aspects of their respective work. If the essence of leadership is flexibility, then details of how work is ideally performed must be formalized through standardized methods and maximum simplification. By achieving such formalization, the foundation is established to capitalize on flexible operations to satisfy important customer requirements. Empowerment can be effective only in an organization that has fully established ways and means for gaining differential advantage.

Teaming

The concept of a **Self-Directed Work Team (SDWT)** has its origins in the cross-functional committee. The idea that multiple viewpoints are often better than one has long-standing roots in administrative practice. The idea of developing SDWTs, however, extended the power of group behavior in two important ways.

First, the SDWT is not typically structured for special assignment or problem solving. The original concept was that a committee would convene to review or evaluate a special situation, make recommendations, and then be dismantled. A similar expectation is common in special purpose work groups. In logistics, such special committees or work groups might be formulated to facilitate development of a new software application or to handle a unique requirement, such as selecting a new distribution warehouse location. In other situations, standing committees are structured to meet on a regular basis to perform some specified duties. For example, a standing committee might be assigned to perform audit and compensation reviews. In contrast, the SDWT is positioned as a permanent way to organize the performance of basic work. The team is an alternative to the more traditional departmental organization structure.

A second unique characteristic of an SDWT is the way its performance is planned and executed. The label *self-directed* means that the team membership is empowered to do whatever it takes to most effectively and efficiently perform designated work. A characteristic of a disciplined work team is that the members develop individual and mutual accountability. The idea is to focus the team on performance of cross-functional work. A group of highly motivated workers selected to represent different skills and knowledge would, on the surface, appear to have greater synergistic potential than a traditional vertical organization consisting of workers with a permanent su-

---

[15]For interesting discussions of empowerment, see: Chris Argyus, "Empowerment: The Emperor's New Clothes," *Harvard Business Review,* May/June 1998, pp. 98–105; and Suzy Wetlanfer, "Organizing for Empowerment: An Interview With AES's Roger Sant and Dennis Bokke," *Harvard Business Review,* January/February 1999, pp. 110–23.

TABLE 17-1   Not All Groups Are Teams: How to Tell the Difference

Work Group	Work Team
Strong, clearly focused.	Shared leadership roles.
Individual accountability.	Individual and mutual accountability.
The group's purpose is the same as the broader organizational mission.	Specific team purpose that the team itself delivers.
Individual work products.	Collective work products.
Runs efficient meetings.	Encourages open-ended discussion and active problem-solving meetings.
Measures its effectiveness indirectly through its influence on others (e.g., financial performance of the business).	Measures performance directly by assessing collective work products.
Discusses, decides, and delegates.	Discusses, decides, and does real work together.

Source: Jon R. Katzenbach and Douglas K. Smith, "The Discipline of Teams," *Harvard Business Review* 71, no. 2 (March/April 1993), p. 113.

pervisor. Part of the appeal of the team is its focus on process as contrasted to functional parochialism. Finally, a team approach provides the opportunity for the tasks involved to be guided by workers, as opposed to managers. Table 17-1 presents a summary of key differentials between working groups and teams.

Adopted from popular sports, the notion of a team is appealing because it implies that working together will create an end result greater than the sum of the skills of individual members. As you might expect, managers encounter problems in structuring effective SDWTs. One observer has gone so far as to conclude that "when managers try to form teams, they usually fail."[16] There are many reasons why SWDTs are unsuccessful. First, specific performance goals or challenges related to expected results are not always established. Teams need clear goals to establish directions, momentum, and dedication. Second, the role of individual accountability in the context of team performance is no always clearly defined. While the focus is the team, the individual participant is the building block to synergistic performance. Third, formation of teams often creates rivalries founded in turfism. All work is typically viewed as the rightful domain of some existing group or department. These traditional departments have an approach to doing work that each participant carries like baggage to the team. Fourth, how the team will work can become a matter of considerable debate. A lack of clear consensus or commitment to the team approach can result in such debate becoming dysfunctional, even to the extent that team members begin to work independently. Fifth, supervisors and managers often have problems letting teams perform without restrictions. Letting go isn't easy for managers who are used to operating under traditional supervisor/subordinate relationships. Problems related to managerial involvement can be magnified when team members are assigned from vastly different organizational units within an enterprise. The danger is that the agendas of the different employee parent units often hinder team performance. Perhaps the most difficult problem to resolve is compensation discrepancy. An individual team member may resent being expected to provide the same level of commitment or responsibility as

---

[16]Jon Katzenbach, "The Right Kind of Teamwork," *The Wall Street Journal,* November 9, 1992, p. A10.

another teammate who is receiving significantly higher compensation. While employees are motivated by a variety of factors, the need for comparative compensation levels is significant among peers performing at a similar level of empowerment.

The fact that significant changes are required in how work is structured to achieve major performance breakthroughs is acceptable to most managers and workers. To date, it appears that teams have greater success when given special achievement assignments as contrasted to the performance of continuous work. One reason for this may be the fact that permanent teams are not typically supported by development of performance measurement systems to gauge their progress toward goal achievement. To the extent that it requires a skunkworks environment for a team to excel, the potential of SDWTs is limited. The nature of work performed in logistics offers ample opportunity to apply team concepts. Selection and assembly of warehouse orders, receipt and processing of customer orders, and resolution of shipment quantity discrepancies are all areas where teams can provide productivity improvements. In contrast, the effective structure from a trucking viewpoint may be limited to a single driver or, at best, a two-person team.

The insights and potential achievements of SDWTs, as opposed to traditional committees, have appeal. The unleashing of creativity and the benefit of synergistic results are powerful motivators to encourage consideration of team structures. However, questions remain concerning the long-term viability of the *group* versus the *individual* in Western culture. Robert Bresticker warns that motivational concepts that work well in one society, such as Japan, may not be fully transferable to another part of the world:

> We should consider the possibility that the veneration of the "The Team" denigrates the American strengths of individuality and creativity. When we blindly copy the organization methods of our Asian competitors, we are playing on their home field and doom ourselves to second class status. By all means, we should take the best of their methods and join that to our strengths, as a multi-cultural workforce.[17]

The ultimate form of SDWT is an informal structure that emerges to address issues of common interest. This type of informal structure is referred to as *the community of practice.* Such communities represent employees who are informally bound by expertise and a shared passion for some form of achievement. The community of practice may focus on an operational problem or be linked by a mutual interest in developing a new perspective or strategy. Information technology offers the communication linkage to make communities of employees a powerful force without limits to geographical location or time. Table 17-2 provides a comparison of formal and informal teaming.

Patching/Coevolving

Complex, multiunit businesses face particular problems in stimulating cooperation across the varied businesses in which they compete. Yet when business units share some aspects of customers, products, technology, channels, or geography, cooperation may enable the firm to achieve significant synergy in developing efficiencies and/or effectiveness of operations. While many companies attempt to establish internal collaborations, two alternative approaches to developing internal cooperation are patching and coevolving.

---

[17]Robert B. Bresticker, *American Manufacturing and Logistics in the Year 2001* (Hoffman Estates, IL: Brigadoon Bay Books, 1992).

TABLE 17-2   A Snapshot Comparison

	What's the Purpose?	Who Belongs?	What Holds It Together?	How Long Does It Last?
Community of Practice	To develop members' capabilities; to build and exchange knowledge	Members who select themselves	Passion, commitment, and identification with the groups' expertise	As long as there is interest in maintaining the group
Formal Work Group	To deliver a product or service	Everyone who reports to the group's manager	Job requirements and common goals	Until the next reorganization
Project Team	To accomplish a specified task	Employees assigned by senior management	The project's milestones and goals	Until the project has been completed
Informal Network	To collect and pass on business information	Friends and business acquaintances	Mutual needs	As long as people have a reason to connect

Source: Reprinted with permission from Etienne C. Wenger and William M. Snyder, "Communities of Practice: The Organizational Frontier," *Harvard Business Review,* January/February 2000, p. 142.

Patching focuses on flexibility in organization. With patching, corporate-level executives take the responsibility of keeping the corporation aligned with constantly changing markets and customers. However, whereas traditional corporate managers see structure as relatively stable and efforts at reorganizing the corporation are seen as long-term changes, patching assumes that structure is temporary and that constant evolution is necessary to keep pace with constantly changing markets. It can take the form of adding, splitting, transferring, exiting, or combining parts of different business units.[18] For example, when Johnson & Johnson saw that hospital customers were forced to deal independently with many different business units, it created a new business, J&J Hospital Supply, that cut across its internal units to present one face to the customer.

Coevolving is a somewhat different strategy that relies on managers of independent business units seeking opportunities to collaborate that will be mutually beneficial yet independently rewarding.[19] Any established link between business units is assumed to be temporary and will be dropped when it no longer makes business sense. It relies on teams of business unit heads establishing links between the units that will be rewarding to the individual businesses. For example, a joint promotion and combination package of a Gillette razor with Right Guard deodorant might require collaboration between the two business unit executives for a 2- or 3-month period that ceases when the promotion period ends. Coevolving involves teamwork, frequent meetings, and communication among business unit executives; however, there is no attempt to force joint or collaborative programs for their own sake. Instead, executives are rewarded for their individual business unit's performance.

Each concept represents an approach to building internal collaboration beyond SDWTs. Patching and coevolving are broad concepts that may or may not initially involve logistics operations, but any form of collaboration will sooner or later impact a firm's logistical support of business strategy.

---

[18]Kathleen M. Eisenhardt and Shona L. Brown, "Patching: Restitching Business Portfolios in Dynamic Markets," *Harvard Business Review,* May/June 1999, pp. 72–83.

[19]Kathleen M. Eisenhardt and D. Charles Galunic, "Coevolving: At Last, A Way to Make Synergies Work," *Harvard Business Review,* January/February 2000, pp. 91–101.

Learning

Organizational learning is a relatively new concept in management. While learning has always been a recognized attribute for individual workers and managers, its extension to the overall organization introduces significantly different challenges and potential benefits. Some say that the primary challenge for senior management is to promote and nurture the organization's capacity to improve and innovate. In this sense, learning becomes the unifying force for the organization, replacing control as the fundamental responsibility of management.[20]

There can be little debate that today's logistical executives and workers need to become better educated to cope with challenges embodied in the widespread change discussed throughout this text. The ability to manage processes and avoid pitfalls of steep organization hierarchies means that all employees at all levels need to enhance their capacity to learn. This capacity for rapid learning may be the essential difference between winners and losers.

However, learning involves more than developing new individual skills and knowledge to achieve superior results. An organization needs to develop the capacity to retain experience and pass it along through generations of workers and managers. Far too often critical knowledge based on invaluable experience is lost to an organization when an employee retires or otherwise departs. Thus, learning in the broadest sense involves programs and devices to retain and share knowledge. Once again, the power of information technology seems to be the saving grace.

Online transaction systems can be designed to *window* or display critical *databanked* experience to assist workers who are empowered to make decisions. The key to effective flexible logistics lies in the capability to hypothesize and evaluate alternative operating scenarios. The point is that learning must transcend technique to encompass use of information. To benefit from experience an organization must learn how to retain it and make it available to others. Finally, learning has a direct relationship to individual careers and the more general topic of loyalty, which is developed in more detail in the next part of this chapter. Industry Insight 17-3 shows how information technology is altering the workplace and sums up many of the issues discussed in this section.

Careers and Loyalty

One author has referred to the state of affairs in industry as the new Darwinian workplace.[21] The challenge for both workers and managers is a growing belief that old and well-established career paths no longer exist. The most highly publicized impact of change is the decline of middle management as a result of the evolving flat nature of the enterprise. However, less publicized change and career modifications are also taking place at top management and frontline work levels.

In previous times, new employees could be given a fairly detailed map illustrating how their career path would develop if they performed to expectations. From entry level to at least upper middle management, the assumption was that as employees demonstrated an ability to learn the prerequisite skills and demonstrate dedication to the enterprise, they would be rewarded with promotions to positions leading to in-

---

[20]Morten T. Hanson, Nitin Nohria, and Thomas Tierney, "What's Your Strategy For Managing Knowledge," *Harvard Business Review,* March/April 1999, pp. 106–16.

[21]Stratford Sherman, "A Brave New Darwinian Workplace," *Fortune* 127, no. 2 (January 25, 1993), pp. 50–56.

INDUSTRY INSIGHT 17-3 WHEN INFORMATION TECHNOLOGY ALTERS THE WORKPLACE . . .

Managers must

1. Instill commitment in subordinates, rather than rule by command and control.
2. Become coaches, training workers in necessary job skills, making sure they have resources to accomplish goals, and explaining links between a job and what happens elsewhere in the company.
3. Give greater authority to workers over scheduling, priority setting, and even compensation.
4. Use new information technologies to measure workers' performance, possibly based on customer satisfaction of the accomplishment of specific goals.

Workers must

1. Become initiators, able to act without management direction.
2. Become financially literate, so they can understand the business implications of what they do and changes they suggest.
3. Learn group interaction skills, including how to resolve disputes within their work group and how to work with other functions across the company.
4. Develop new math, technical, and analytical skills to use newly available information on their jobs.

Source: James B. Treece, "Breaking the Chains of Command," *Business Week,* Special Edition on The Information Revolution, 1994, pp. 112–14.

---

creased compensation and added responsibility. However, the security that was once an integral part of career development no longer exists in most corporations, particularly those shattered by repeated efforts to reconfigure organization structures.

In today's enterprise, employees at all organization levels must assume full responsibility for their individual careers. This means continuous learning to develop skills that fit ever-changing job requirements. Skills for the future will be based much less on specialized knowledge and focus far more on capabilities related to analysis, integration, motivation, and creativity. The capability to think critically and innovatively will be considered a more attractive attribute than the ability to perform a specific task. The reason is obvious—the task may become obsolete overnight.

Each new wave of organization delayering is typically concluded with management assurance that necessary restructuring is now completed and no further layoffs or cutbacks are anticipated or planned. Such statements are translated by those who have jobs at the fringe of the cutback to mean they have survived another wave of layoffs and are safe until the next round hits. No one, senior managers or otherwise, really knows what the ultimate organization structure will be or what this structure will require in terms of human resources. As a result, it can be expected that employees at all levels will be quick to change jobs and employers will not hesitate to improve their status if they see an opportunity. Thus, the future is likely to see fewer managers who spend their careers in one or even a few firms. Unless management can rekindle loyalty throughout the organization, external mobility will increasingly become the career path of the future.

Enter, the challenges of learning! A solution for dealing with rapidly changing career requirements is to regenerate loyalty through continuous learning. One way for a logistics organization to keep its outstanding employees is to demonstrate a willingness to invest in their education. As an employee, if your learning is expanding in terms of depth and scope of knowledge, then the dangers of personal obsolescence decline. A person's career has always been a race between obsolescence and retirement. The essence of the problem is that the speed of the race has accelerated to the point where learning cannot be left to chance. Employees who are motivated and supported in continuous education are both more valuable and more marketable. The key to rebuilding loyalty is expanding commitment to individual worth. Such commitment demonstrates loyalty to the employee and encourages reciprocal loyalty for the enterprise. Industry Insight 17-4 illustrates this commitment.

Managing Organization Change

A final topic of concern to logistics managers is how to deal with change. It is one thing to decide what should be done. It is an entirely different thing to get it done. Once again, logistics managers cannot expect to find a blueprint to guide them. As a general rule, they are involved in three primary types of change.

First, there are issues related to strategic change. This involves the implementation of new and improved ways to service customers. The topic of strategic change management has been dealt within several different places throughout the text.

The second type of change concerns modifications in a firm's operational structure. On the basis of strategic considerations, logistics executives are constantly engaged in modifying where products are positioned, how customer requirements are handled, and so forth. Such operational reengineering represents a great deal of the change that must be managed to keep a firm's capabilities in line with its strategic requirements.

The third type of change concerns human resource structure. As the mission and scope of logistics change, managers have traditionally found it difficult to alter organization structures in a timely manner. Research clearly illustrates that organization change is frequent.

It is critical to avoid a quick-fix mentality. The prevailing command and control structure has survived for centuries—it need not all be dismantled overnight. The key is development of a change model that charts a meaningful and believable course of transition. As noted earlier, managers should use caution in trying to accelerate the transition of logistical organization structures through the five evolutionary stages discussed earlier in this chapter. While it may be possible to accelerate change, it appears that trying to skip what research indicates is the natural evolution of an organization can be highly dangerous and may result in aborted restructuring attempts. Therefore, despite the appeal of changing quickly, real success may be enhanced by proceeding with care.

A final consideration concerning change is an organization's capacity to absorb new and challenging ways to improve performance. While all of the desired change is taking place, the day-to-day business still needs to be run. Though some advocate radical change, it does not appear to fit logistical organizations very well.

The notion of radical change is not new or unique. Despite the fact that knowledge expands rapidly, associated skills and accepted practices change at a much slower pace. Joseph Schumpeter envisioned a need for what he labeled *creative destruction*.[22] Peter Drucker has warned that firms must develop skills for systematic

---

[22]Joseph A. Schumpeter, *Capitalism, Socialism and Democracy,* 6th ed. (London: Urwin Paperbacks, 1987).

INDUSTRY INSIGHT 17-4 STAYING POWER HAS REWARDS— AND A PRICE TAG

Nancy P. Karen, 46, is pretty sure her job won't be destroyed. In her 24 years with the company, she has been an energetic workaholic in the critical area of information systems. As director of the company's personal computer network, Karen is facing new and tougher demands as a result of management's efforts.

She joined New York Telephone in 1969 during the company's big bulge in hiring, often referred to as "the service glut." To meet explosive growth, the company hired tens of thousands of people in the late 1960s and early 1970s. Karen, a Vassar college graduate with a degree in mathematics, was one of 103,000 employees at New York Telephone in 1971. Today, NYT has about 40,220 people. Working in a regulated monopoly, she felt a sense of comfort and security that now seems a distant memory. "Downsizing was totally unheard of," she says. "Just about everybody here started with the company at a young age and retired off the payroll."

Management's plan—and Nynex's earlier efforts to slash the payroll—have changed all that. Of the 79 people who report directly to Karen, 59 have already seen colleagues forced off the payroll in previous rounds of cutbacks. Her department is likely to suffer a 30 percent reduction in staffing. "When they started talking about another round of downsizing, people were a little more anxious because they felt they were already stretched thin. Now we'll have to learn to work smarter and completely change the way we do things."

Working smarter also means working harder—much harder. She once directly supervised 26 people, instead of a current 79, and she used to work more normal hours as well. No longer. Karen now puts in 50 to 60 hours a week, from 8 A.M. to 7 P.M. every weekday, at Nynex's White Plains, New York, office. Wherever she goes these days, she carries a beeper and a cellular phone and checks her voice mail every hour. "It's a different mentality," she says. "My weekends and holidays are not reserved." On a recent biking vacation through California's wine country, she called the office at least once a day from "every little town." Since Karen is single, "nobody complains about my work hours," she says.

Nynex didn't push Karen into her new and grueling pace completely unprepared. The company dispatched her to the local Holiday Inn in early 1993 for a workshop on culture change put together by Senn-Delaney Leadership, a Long Beach, California, consulting firm. She was skeptical at first. "To me, it was yet another program," she says.

Surprisingly, Karen left a believer. The sessions—dubbed Winning Ways—are an effort to inculcate the new values and skills that Nynex believes it needs to make management's reengineering changes take hold. It's a quick-and-dirty roundup of today's managerial commandments, stressing teamwork, accountability, open communications, respect for diversity, and coaching over managing.

Although impressed by how the sessions encouraged employees to speak more freely to each other, Karen saw her share of nonconverts at the initial 2 1/2-day meeting. "Some people come back to work unchanged," she says. "But there's a big middle section that seems willing to change, and then there's a small percentage at the top that's very enthusiastic about it."

Not that Karen, who earned an MBA from Columbia University on the company's tab in 1981, doesn't have some big worries about the change effort. One of them is that the downsizing will get ahead of the company's ability to figure out ways to get the work done more efficiently. She's also worried that the company will lose expertise and talent. That would mean that she and other managers won't have enough of the right people to accomplish the tasks placed before them. "It's not going to work perfectly," she says. "There will be cases when the downsizing occurs before the reengineering."

Despite the increased workload and her concern over employee morale, Karen considers herself lucky. "This is a wonderful challenge," she says. "I'm looking at a task of building a new organization in the next six months to a year. I have the chance to test myself as I've never been tested before."

Source: John A. Byrne, "The Pain of Downsizing," *Business Week,* May 9, 1994, p. 67.

abandonment and build into their fundamental structure a mechanism for managing change. The problem in part is magnified by the fact that most significant changes do not result from self-improvement initiatives. Rather, radical improvements are typically generated by external creativity. This prompts the belief among some experts that massive change can be achieved only by total destruction of existing structural arrangements. In the final analysis, the tempo of change a firm can accommodate remains unique to each organization. How much change an organization can absorb requires precise calibration. Typically, it is less than most change managers gauge it to be and actual change takes longer than anticipated.

Relationship Management

Throughout the text, the importance of collaborative relationships as an integral aspect of supply chain management has been stressed. Table 17-3 summarizes the topical coverage of issues related to relationship management that have been discussed in previous chapters. At this point, it is appropriate to discuss special considerations related to managing across organization boundaries. The critical question is how internal and external efforts should be developed, organized, and managed to achieve desired performance objectives.

Developing Collaborative Relationships

Despite the large number of firms seeking to create relationships, the majority of managers report that organizations do not have clear policies or guidelines for implementing or measuring performance of such arrangements.[23] While trade and academic pub-

TABLE 17-3   Topical Coverage of Issues Related to Relationship Management

Chapter	Topic
1	Integrated Management
	Collaboration
	Enterprise Extension
	Multifunctional Outsourcing
	Implementation Challenges
	Leadership
	Loyalty and Confidentiality
	Measurement
	Risk/Reward Sharing
4	Relation Collaborative Arrangements
	Administered Systems
	Partnerships and Alliances
	Contractual Systems
	Joint Ventures
6	Supply Chain Competitiveness
	Risk
	Power
	Leadership
9	Collaborative Planning, Forecasting, and Replenishment

---

[23]Donald J. Bowersox, David J. Closs, and Theodore P. Stank, op. cit., p. 109.

lications offer some guidelines concerning what these relationships should seek to achieve, most articles are very general. However, six concerns have been identified as critical to the development of successful relationships: (1) channelwide perspective, (2) selective matching, (3) information sharing, (4) role specification, (5) ground rules. and (6) exit provisions.

Several reasons for failure have also been identified: (1) fuzzy goals, (2) inadequate trust, (3) lip-service commitment, (4) human incompatibility, (5) inadequate operating framework, and (6) inadequate measurement. While the list is interesting, it fails to go beyond description and does not specify underlying reasons for failure.

In an effort to better understand the anatomy of what makes for a successful collaborative relationship, in-depth case studies were completed with grocery manufacturing firms that are generally recognized as leaders in interorganizational arrangements.[24] The alliances investigated included relationships with material suppliers, logistical service providers, and merchandisers. Guidelines were developed concerning initiating an alliance, implementing an alliance, and maintaining alliance vitality. While the focus was specifically on alliances, the logic can be extended to any successful collaborative relationship.

Initiating Relationships

The alliances studied were typically initiated by the firm that was the "customer" in the relationship. One potential explanation for this pattern is the exercise of buying power. In a buyer/seller relationship, the seller will often implement reasonable changes at the request of its customer to facilitate interorganizational exchange. Also, when a seller's personnel initially approach a potential customer about forming an alliance, the suggestion does not carry the same weight and impact as when the suggestion is generated within the buying firm's organization.

Some alliances do show some anomalies to this pattern. In some cases the seller actually sparked the initial deal by planting the seed as far as conceptualizing the viability of an alliance. When the customer was ready to form the alliance, it initiated more detailed discussion.

Another critical consideration during the development of a collaborative relationship is the need for the initiating firm to perform an in-depth assessment of its internal practices, policies, and culture. The initiating firm should evaluate its ability to make any necessary internal changes to implement and support a successful relationship.[25] For example, in manufacturer/material supplier alliances, the manufacturers had to examine their ability to redefine the importance of purchase price. Buyers needed a method to incorporate the intangible benefits of an alliance in competitive evaluations. The key for the buyer was the evaluation of total cost of ownership, not strictly purchase price.

Another internal assessment includes the ability to truly empower the key alliance contacts to manage the relationship. For example, manufacturers needed to honestly assess the level of operational and strategic integration they could foster with service suppliers. Integration that generated the type of competitive advantage envisioned at the alliance's initial design, such as increased productivity of rapid response to

---

[24]This section is adapted from Judith M. Schmitz, Robert Frankel, and David J. Frayer, "ECR Alliances: A Best Practice Model," Joint Industry Project on Efficient Consumer Response, Grocery Manufacturers Association, Washington, D.C., 1995.

[25]For an in-depth discussion of internal assessment, see: Clifford F. Lynch, *Logistics Outsourcing: A Management Guide* (Oak Brook, IL: Council of Logistics Management, 2000), pp. 37–38.

customer orders, could be achieved only through extensive information sharing. The questions to be addressed concern the level of systems capability, data collection, analysis, performance measurement, and training that was necessary to enable the information to be shared in a timely and accurate manner.

Integration capability also needs to be evaluated if the alliance involves a number of partner plants, warehouses, and/or stores that operate under different conditions, capabilities, or competitive requirements. This is especially important for firms that operate multiple distribution centers and/or store locations. A key concern in this situation is the ability for internal units to utilize common operating practices and compatible information systems. The flexibility to adapt to meet specific market-based requirements is important to long-term viability.

Implementing Relationships

The key to a successful implementation is choosing a partner wisely. The partners should have compatible cultures, a common strategic vision, and supportive operating philosophies. It is not necessary that organization cultures be identical. Rather, the strategic intentions and philosophies must be *compatible* to ensure that core competencies and strengths are *complementary.*

For example, manufacturers initiated alliances with service suppliers in part to achieve improved warehousing operations, transportation reliability, and/or increased consolidation programs that support their particular strategic competitive advantage in the marketplace. Although the service suppliers are leaders, manufacturers may have a more sophisticated conceptualization and operationalization of quality, performance measurement standards, and expertise. The attraction between the partners is based, to a considerable degree, on the service suppliers' ability and willingness to provide creative, innovative operational and information-based solutions to the manufacturer's problems and on the service suppliers' desire to internalize the quality and performance measurement expertise that are the hallmark of the manufacturer. In this sense, the alliance partners' operating philosophies support and complement each other, in particular by enhancing their common strategic vision of improving systemwide logistics processes.

The alliances should start on a small scale to foster easily achievable successes or early wins. It is important that such early wins be acknowledged to motivate key contacts and build confidence concerning alliance performance. For example, in the manufacturer/material supplier alliances, starting small meant that investments were not initially made in information technology. Manual communication systems were sufficient and provided the opportunity for key contacts. A critical issue is to implement the alliance in its simplest form and then fine tune the arrangement with technological sophistication when improvements will add substantial value.

Maintaining Relationships

Long-term continuity is dependent on three key activities: (1) mutual strategic and operational goals, (2) two-way performance measurements, and (3) formal and informal feedback mechanisms.

Strategic and operational goals must be mutually determined when the alliance is implemented. This proposition has been discussed extensively in the academic and business press and appeals to common sense. It is perhaps less well understood that these goals must be tracked, reviewed, and updated frequently to gain improvements over the long term. For example, if a manufacturer develops a new product, a mutual goal must be set with customers concerning that product's position, especially its market launch. This goal must include consideration of the merchandiser's critical role in new product introduction and acceptance.

Goals should be translated into specific performance measures that can be continually tracked. The performance measurements used and the measurement frequency should be jointly determined. Also, the measures should be two-way. Oftentimes, performance measures between manufacturers and material suppliers focus specifically on the suppliers' performance attributes, such as on-time delivery and quality. One of the alliances studied developed a joint measure of success—total systems inventory. The manufacturer acknowledged that it was important for both partners to reduce inventory, not just the manufacturer. Manufacturers have historically accomplished reductions by pushing inventory back upstream on material suppliers. The measure of total systems inventory includes consideration of both partners to ensure that reductions are real and benefit both parties.

Feedback on performance can be provided through formal and informal methods. Annual reviews are formal assessments of alliance performance. These reviews typically involve top managers and focus primarily on examining and updating strategic goals. Quarterly or monthly reviews are not as formal as annual assessments and usually do not include top managers. They focus on tracking and reviewing strategic goals and operational performance. When used, the reviews enable changes in operating practice to be made to achieve strategic goals and create an avenue for continuous improvement projects to be identified.

Weekly/daily reviews may also occur on an informal basis. These reviews are managed by the key contacts and are intended to solve specific problems and identify potential opportunities for improvement. They are critical to resolving or avoiding conflicts and allow key contacts to develop close working relationships. Although the process is typically informal in nature, the resolution mechanisms may be quite detailed. For example, when a partnered manufacturer and service supplier do not operate on the same physical site, the involved partners may have specific lists of contact personnel for the plant and the service supplier's customer center or warehouse facility.

Developing Trust

It is clear that no *real* collaboration can exist in supply chain relationships without meaningful trust. While a powerful firm may be able to influence the behavior of a less powerful organization, the change in behavior may be temporary and certainly entered into unwillingly. Research has also shown that consistent use of coercion by one organization ultimately leads the vulnerable firm to seek alternative supply chain relationships.[26] Further, the fundamental premise of collaborative relationships is that supply chain management requires firms to work together to find ways to increase the value delivered to end customers.

But trust is an elusive concept that means different things to different people. So two questions must be answered. First, in a supply chain context, what is trust? Second, how can organizations build trust among each other?

---

[26]Nirmalya Kumar, "The Power of Trust in Manufacturer-Retailer Relationships," *Harvard Business Review*, November/December 1999, p. 98.

Reliability and Character-Based Trust

It is clear that trust has more than one dimension. While several typologies of trust exist, the most meaningful way to understand trust in supply chain collaboration is to distinguish between reliability-based trust and character-based trust.

Reliability-based trust is grounded in an organization's perception of a potential partner's actual behavior and operating performance. Essentially, it involves a perception that the partner is willing to perform and is capable of performing as promised. If supply chain participants cannot rely on partner performance as promised, all efforts to develop collaborative relationships fail. Simply put, a firm that is perceived as incapable of delivering as promised will also be perceived as being unreliable and therefore unworthy of trust in a relationship.

Character-based trust is based in an organization's culture and philosophy. Essentially, it stems from perceptions that supply chain partners are interested in each other's welfare and will not act without considering the action's impact on the other.[27] When this aspect of trust is developed, participants do not feel vulnerable to the actions of one another. Trusting partners believe that each will protect the other's interest. For example, a manufacturer who shares its plans for new product introductions or promotion with a retailer trusts that the retailer will not share that information with a competitive supplier. Likewise, sharing of production schedule information with a supplier of component parts will only occur when a manufacturer has trust that the information will be used appropriately.

It is clear that reliability-based trust is necessary to the formation of collaborative relationships in supply chains, but it is not a sufficient condition. For example, a partner who frequently threatens to punish and consistently follows through with that punishment can be said to have reliability. It is not likely, however, to be trusted in character.

Trust clearly develops over time and repeated interactions among organizations. In particular, character-based trust evolves when partners perceive that each acts fairly and equitably with the others. Notions of character-based trust are especially relevant when one supply chain partner is clearly more powerful than the others are. In such situations, it is dependent upon less powerful firms' perception of justice in prior interactions. Justice, in turn, has two components of interest: distributive justice and procedural justice.

Distributive Justice.   Distributive justice depends upon how the risks, benefits, and rewards of supply chain participation are shared. In effect, it has to do with how equitably supply chain participants perceive they are compensated for their functional performance. Such actions as forcing a supplier to take ownership of inventory or unilaterally reducing allowable margins in a distribution channel are likely to lead to perceptions of inequality and a lack of justice. Trust is not likely to be developed in such circumstances.

Procedural Justice.   Procedural justice, on the other hand, is related to the manner in which problems and disputes among supply chain participants are resolved. When a powerful firm unilaterally imposes its will on less powerful organizations, the

---

[27]Nirmalya Kumar, op. cit., p. 95.

effect is to destroy, or at least lessen, trust. When issues are openly discussed and a mechanism exists for consideration of all parties' points of view, firms can trust their interests will be considered. Conflicts are resolved through open discussion, negotiation, and such procedures as mediation or arbitration. For example, several manufacturers like Caterpillar have developed dealer councils which oversee implementation of new dealer-related policies and are used to resolve conflicts between a specific dealer and the manufacturer. Such approaches are more likely to be perceived as procedurally just than approaches that rely purely on one party's power.

Building Trust in Relationships

To build trust first requires that a firm demonstrate reliability in its operations, consistently performing as promised and meeting expectations. As noted above, however, reliability is only one aspect of building trust.

The second key requirement for building trust is full and frank sharing of all information necessary for the effective functioning of the relationship. In fact, information sharing and communication have been stressed throughout the text as the foundation for effective collaboration. Companies that hoard information or fail to disclose vital facts are not likely to be trusted.

Related to information sharing is explanation. Sometimes a company, due to competitive pressures, may be required to undertake actions that its supply chain partners may perceive as threatening. For example, a manufacturer opening new distribution channels might threaten existing retailers. Just such a situation arose when John Deere introduced the Sabre line of lawn tractors and recruited Montgomery Ward and other independent dealers, bypassing its traditional network. In such situations, trust may be maintained through thorough explanation of the rationale and business case that drove such a decision. Unfortunately, John Deere implemented its policy without such explanation and then was put in a position of trying to justify its decision after the fact. Considerable damage to its dealer relationships resulted.[28]

In the final analysis, trust must be earned and learned. Time provides new situations and circumstances for partners to assess reliability and character. Industry Insight 17-5 describes the relationship and development of trust between TRW, a manufacturer of automobile components, and Mollart, a small supplier in the United Kingdom.

In many ways the entire subject of supply chain management is also a discussion of relationship management. The text has focused on issues related to logistical processes in the supply chain and managing these processes across company boundaries. Unique operating relationships among supply chain participants differ significantly in their intensity and extent of real collaboration. While legal contracts and joint ventures may characterize some of these interactions, partnerships and alliances represent the most intense forms of informal relationships. Power, leadership, conflict, cooperation, risk, and reward are all critical issues in relationship management. Resolution of these issues, however, ultimately depends upon the development of trust among supply chain participants.

---

[28]David A. Aacker, "Should You Take Your Brand to Where the Action Is?" *Harvard Business Review,* September/October 1997, pp. 135–43.

INDUSTRY INSIGHT 17-5 MARRIAGE OF CONVENIENCE

TRW Steering Systems is a subsidiary of TRW, an American-owned multinational company. Mollart is a supplier of gun-drilling tools and services based in suburban Surrey, UK. These companies have forged a relationship based on trust and confidence that has brought Mollart to South Wales as the first tenant of TRW's new supplier park, which means that it is now a critical second-tier supplier to automotive assemblers in the UK and globally.

A key component of a steering system is the rack bar—a steel bar about a meter long with a rack at one end that engages with the steering column pinion. Along about three-quarters of the axis of this bar, a thin, deep, accurate hole has to be drilled.

Mollart, a family firm founded in the 1920s, has long specialized in deep hole, or "gun," drilling. Its relationship with TRW Steering Systems began 10 years ago when it eased TRW's peak capacity problems. Initially at a rate of 100 per week, this built up to 7500 a week by 1997—a significant proportion of TRW's weekly output of between 26,000 and 30,000 components.

But the material flow—from British Steel in Sheffield to TRW to Mollart in Chessington and then back to TRW—was not only wasteful but made fine control and rapid response impossible. So, Mollart moved to the Neath Vale Supplier Park and started production there in March 1998. It is machining bars for Honda, Rover, and Land Rover product, with plans to raise production to 13,000 units a week—half of TRW's total requirement. Mollart's intention is to do 60 percent of its business with TRW and 40 percent for other customers.

Mollart has taken a big risk with no guarantees; it has no unique design or manufacturing capability to lock the customer in and is a minnow compared with its (currently) sole customer. Why, then, does the relationship work so well? Largely, it is a tribute to TRW's attitude toward its suppliers. "We have a safety-critical product, so we have to select suppliers carefully," states Roger Llewellyn, TRW's group purchasing manager. "Moreover, external suppliers account for 52 percent of the product, so our own lean production, however good, can only address 48 percent of the problem."

TRW has supplier development teams based on the principles of kaizen—continuous improvement—and the Toyota Production System. They teach suppliers about synchronous manufacturing, eliminating batch-and-queue and other techniques, and suppliers are included on TRW's internal courses, which emphasize features such as teamworking and single-piece flow.

For Mollart and TRW's other 21 core suppliers whose product changes if the TRW platform changes and which account for 80 percent of spending, Llewellyn says, "We are totally transparent. We open our books in front of them and vice versa. I know their costs, cycle times, everything, and they know mine. Everyone has to be extremely ethical in a relationship based on trust, but information has never been abused. I want all my suppliers to be successful, to make a profit and to share in savings."

Llewellyn continues, "We market test all the time. I need to know that I am dealing with the right gun-driller on a total cost basis, but an existing supplier like Mollart will see the results of genuine quotations. I can't tell them how the other company does it, but we will help them with value engineering and so on. I want to see people looking at process and securing continuous improvement, not shaving margin to retain business."

Source: Sam Tulip, "Marriage of Convenience," *Supply Management,* May 27, 1999, pp. 36–7.

Summary

Logistics is undergoing massive change. New concepts and ideas concerning how the best organizations achieve logistical goals appear daily. The challenge is to sort through the best of time-proven practices and merge them with the most applicable new ideas and concepts.

A careful review of logistics organization development suggests that most advanced firms have evolved through three stages of functional aggregation. The evolution started from a highly fragmented structure in which logistical functions were assigned to a wide variety of different departments. For over four decades firms have been grouping an increasing number of logistical functional responsibilities into single organization units. The typical format for aggregation was the traditional bureaucratic organization structure. The objective was to aggregate functions in an effort to improve operational integration.

The advent of management focusing on critical processes began to usher in what is referred to as horizontal organizations. Today, leading-edge firms are beginning to experiment with stage 4 organizations as they shift from functional to process management.

There is increasing evidence that a fifth stage of organization may be emerging. Stage 5 adopts the use of information technology to implement and manage logistics as a transparent organization structure. While stage 5 structural arrangements remain more conceptual than real, the required information technology is available today. The concept has particular appeal to the management of logistics, which involves substantial challenge in terms of time and geographical scope of operations.

A number of significant issues and challenges face logistics organizations today. Structural compression, horizontal organizations, empowerment of frontline employees, development of formal work teams and changing the nature of these teams in response to changes in the environment, and extending learning throughout the organization are all major managerial challenges faced in logistics as they are faced in all other functions in the organization. Of particular concern has been the erosion of loyalty by employees to the firm and by the firm to employees. Because of this erosion managers can no longer count on remaining with a firm for a long period and firms may lose their best executives to other companies. Thus, learning on the part of both managers and organizations is critical to long-term success.

Perhaps the most difficult job of all is managing change in the organization. Whether the change is strategic, involving fundamental new processes, operational, or only in personnel, managers must develop new skills that allow them to implement change without disrupting the focus of the organization.

In addition to managing the internal organization, supply chain executives are intimately involved in managing relationships among organizations. Initiating, implementing, and maintaining relationships with suppliers and customers are highly dependent upon the existence of trust among those firms. While reliability is a critical aspect of trust, ultimate success in relationship management will depend upon evaluation of character as firms make decisions concerning which supply chains they choose to participate in.

Challenge Questions

1. What is the functional aggregation paradigm and why is it important?
2. Compare and contrast the three stages of functional aggregation.
3. Discuss the three challenges logistics faces as it manages on a process, rather than a functional, basis. Describe each challenge and give an example of how it may be overcome.
4. What is meant by the term "structural compression"? How does this term affect logistics?

5. What is a horizontal company and how would this type of company be organized? What are the strengths of this type of organization structure?

6. Describe a situation where empowerment has been used. What are the benefits and drawbacks to empowerment in the situation?

7. Describe why teams are being formed more frequently in business today. What are some of the special considerations required for a team to be successful?

8. Defend a position on the following question: Does radical organization change require disintegration of existing structures?

9. Describe four reasons why collaborative relationships fail. How can these failures be avoided?

10. Distinguish between reliability and character-based trust. Why is character-based trust critical in collaborative relationships?

CHAPTER

18 PERFORMANCE AND FINANCIAL ASSESSMENT

Creating competitive advantage through high-performance supply chain logistics requires integrated measurement systems. The old adage, If you don't measure it, you can't manage it, holds true for logistical activities both internal to an organization and externally with supply chain partners. For this reason, a framework for performance and financial assessment must be established.

Measurement System Objectives

Effective measurement systems must be constructed to accomplish the three objectives of monitoring, controlling, and directing logistical operations.

Monitoring is accomplished by the establishment of appropriate metrics to track system performance for reporting to management. For example, typically metrics are developed and data gathered to report basic service performance related to fill rates and on-time deliveries and for logistics costs such as transportation and warehousing. *Controlling* is accomplished by having appropriate standards of performance relative to the established metrics to indicate when the logistics system requires modification or attention. For example, if fill rates fall below standards, logistics managers must identify the causes and make adjustments to bring the process back into compliance. The third objective, *directing,* is related to employee motivation and reward for

FIGURE 18-1

Shareholder value model

FIGURE 18-1

Shareholder value model

performance. For example, some companies encourage warehouse personnel to achieve high levels of productivity. They must be paid for 8 hours of work, based on standard measures of picking or loading. If the tasks are completed in less than 8 hours, they may be allowed personal time off.

An overriding objective of superior logistical performance is to improve *shareholder value.* A comprehensive measurement system must therefore address the critical points of impact on shareholder value. Figure 18-1 provides a framework that considers both operational excellence and asset utilization in logistical performance. On the operational excellence dimension, key metrics focus on improved accommodation of customers through increased customer success and on lowest total cost of service.

Asset utilization reflects effectiveness in managing the firm's fixed assets and working capital. **Fixed capital** assets include manufacturing and distribution facilities, transportation and materials handling equipment, and information technology hardware. **Working capital** represents cash, the inventory investment, and differential in investments related to accounts receivable versus accounts payable. In particular, by more efficiently managing the assets related to logistics operations, the firm may be able to liberate assets from the existing base. This freed capital is known as *cash spin,* which can be used for reinvestment in other aspects of the organization.[1] Overall asset utilization is particularly important to shareholders and to how the firm is viewed by financial markets.

Logistics Performance Assessment

A system for logistics performance assessment first requires a functional perspective. In addition to basic functional performance, improved methods for measurement of customer accommodation are receiving increased attention in many organizations. Measurement of integrated supply chain performance poses a major challenge for contemporary management. Benchmarking is a fourth concern in logistics assessment.

---

[1]See Chapter 1, p. 23.

TABLE 18-1   **Typical Performance Metrics**

Cost Management	Customer Service	Quality	Productivity	Asset Management
Total cost	Fill rate	Damage frequency	Units shipped per employee	Inventory turns
Cost per unit	Stockouts	Order entry accuracy	Units per labor dollar	Inventory levels, number of days supply
Cost as a percentage of sales	Shipping errors	Picking/shipping accuracy	Orders per sales representative	Obsolete inventory
Inbound freight	On-time delivery	Document/invoicing accuracy	Comparison to historical standard	Return on net assets
Outbound freight	Back orders	Information availability	Goal programs	Return on investment
Administrative	Cycle time	Information accuracy	Productivity index	Inventory classification (ABC)
Warehouse order processing	Delivery consistency	Number of credit claims	Equipment downtime	Economic value-added (EVA)
Direct labor	Response time to inquiries	Number of customer returns	Order entry productivity	
Comparison of actual versus budget	Response accuracy		Warehouse labor productivity	
Cost trend analysis	Complete orders		Transportation labor productivity	
Direct product profitability	Customer complaints			
Customer segment profitability	Sales force complaints			
Inventory carrying	Overall reliability			
Cost of returned goods	Overall satisfaction			
Cost of damage				
Cost of service failures				
Cost of back order				

Functional Perspectives

Research over a period of years suggests that functional measures of logistics performance can be classified into these categories: (1) cost, (2) customer service, (3) quality, (4) productivity, and (5) asset management.[2] Table 18-1 provides an overview of measurements related to each of these five areas of concern.

Cost

The most direct reflection of logistics performance is the actual cost incurred to accomplish specific operations. As shown in Table 18-1, **cost performance** is typically

---

[2]Donald J. Bowersox et al., *Leading Edge Logistics: Competitive Positioning for the 1990s* (Oak Brook, IL: Council of Logistics Management, 1989); World Class Logistics Research Team at Michigan State University, *World Class Logistics: The Challenge of Managing Continuous Change* (Oak Brook, IL: Council of Logistics Management, 1995); Donald J. Bowersox, David J. Closs, and Theodore P. Stank, *21st Century Logistics: Making Supply Chain Integration a Reality* (Oak Brook, IL: Council of Logistics Management, 1999).

measured in terms of total dollars spent on each function. Thus, it is common to monitor and report cost data for specific logistics functions such as warehousing, outbound transportation, inbound transportation, and order processing. Such categories may be further fine-tuned and cost data reported for individual activities such as warehouse picking, order loading, and the like.

It is also common to monitor and report cost data as a percentage of sales or as a cost per unit of volume. For example, transportation cost is frequently expensed as a percentage of dollar sales volume and as the number of dollars spent per order delivered. Warehouse cost may also be reported as a percentage of sales and cost of individual activities reported such as the picking cost per item or loading cost per order. Such measures, when compared to historical levels or performance standards, provide critical information regarding the potential need to take corrective action. When considering the number of different specific logistics activities, ranging from entering an order to picking an item to unloading a delivery vehicle, and the number of different ways in which volume can be measured, ranging from sales dollar to number of orders to pounds of product, a rather lengthy list of possible cost metrics could be generated. The key is for logistics executives to identify the most appropriate metrics for their organization and consistently apply them over time to control and direct the activities.

Table 18-1 also shows other measures related to the cost of logistical performance such as direct product profitability, customer profitability, and cost of service failures. In fact, most firms recognize the importance of these measures but currently lack the information necessary to accurately assess these costs. Accurate measurement in these critical dimensions requires a level of sophistication in accounting data that has just recently become available. Activity-based costing is discussed later in this chapter as a means to more accurately assess the cost related directly to customers and products.

Basic Customer Service

In Chapter 3, the elements of basic **customer service** were identified as availability, operational performance, and service reliability. An effective basic service platform requires specific metrics for assessing performance in each dimension.

Availability is typically reflected by an organization's fill rate. It is critical to note, however, that fill rate may be measured in a variety of ways:

$$\text{Item fill rate} = \frac{\text{Number of items ordered by customers}}{\text{Number of items delivered to customers}}$$

$$\text{Line fill rate} = \frac{\text{Number of purchase order lines ordered by customers}}{\text{Number of purchase order lines delivered complete to customers}}$$

$$\text{Value fill rate} = \frac{\text{Total dollar value of customer orders}}{\text{Total dollar value delivered to customers}}$$

$$\text{Order fill rate} = \frac{\text{Number of customer orders}}{\text{Number of orders delivered complete}}$$

Clearly, the order fill rate (also known as orders shipped complete) is the most stringent measure of a firm's performance relative to product availability. In this metric, an order that is missing only one item on one line is considered to be incomplete. It is also common for companies to track specifically the number of stockouts encountered and number of back orders generated during a time period as indicators of availability.

Operational performance deals with time and is typically measured by average order cycle time, consistency of order cycle time, and/or on-time deliveries. *Average order cycle time* is typically computed as the average number of days (or other units of time) elapsed between order receipt and delivery to customers. *Order cycle consistency* is measured over a large number of order cycles and compares actual performance with planned. For example, suppose average order cycle time is 5 days. However, if 20 percent were completed in 2 days and 30 percent in 8 days, there is great inconsistency around the average. In situations where delivery dates or times are specified by customers, the most stringent measure of order cycle capability is *ontime delivery,* the percentage of times the customer's delivery requirements are actually met.

Quality

Performance relative to service reliability is generally reflected in an organization's measurement of **logistics quality.** As Table 18-1 shows, many of the quality metrics are designed to monitor the effectiveness of individual activities, while others are focused on the overall logistics function. Accuracy of work performance in such activities as order entry, warehouse picking, and document preparation is typically tracked by computing the ratio of the total number of times the activity is performed correctly to the total number of times it is performed. For example, picking accuracy of 99.5 percent indicates that 99.5 out of every 100 times, the correct item(s) were picked in the warehouse.

Overall quality performance can also be measured in a variety of ways. Typical measures include damage frequency, which is computed as the ratio of the number of damaged units to the total number of units. While damage frequency can be measured at several points in the logistics process, such as warehouse damage, loading damage, and transportation damage, it frequently is not detected until customers receive shipments or even some point in time after receipt. Therefore, many organizations also monitor the number of customer returns of damaged or defective goods. It is also common to measure customer claims for credit.

Other important indicators of quality performance relate to information. Many organizations specifically measure their ability to provide information by noting those instances when information is not available on request. It is also common to track instances when inaccurate information is discovered. For example, when physical counts of merchandise inventory differ from the inventory status as reported in the database, the information system must be updated to reflect actual operating status. Additionally, the occurrence of information inaccuracy should be recorded for future action.

Productivity

Productivity is a relationship, usually a ratio or an index between output of goods, work completed, and/or services produced and quantities of inputs or resources utilized to produce the output. Productivity is thus a basic concept. If a system has clearly measurable outputs and identifiable, measurable inputs that can be matched to the appropriate outputs, productivity measurement is quite routine. However, it can be difficult and frustrating if (1) outputs are hard to measure and input utilization is difficult to match up for a given period of time; (2) input and output mix or type constantly changes; or (3) data are difficult to obtain or unavailable.

Generally, as Table 18-1 shows, logistics executives are very concerned with measuring the productivity of labor. While the labor input can be quantified in many ways, the most typical manner is by labor expense, labor hours, or individual employees. Thus, typical labor productivity measures in transportation include units shipped or delivered per employee, labor dollar, and labor hour. Warehouse labor productivity may be measured by units received, picked, and/or stored per employee, dollar, or hour. Similar measures can be developed for other activities, such as order entry and order processing. It is also common for managers to set goals for productivity improvement and compare actual performance to goal, or at the very least to prior year performance.

Asset Management

Asset management focuses on the utilization of capital investments in facilities and equipment as well as working capital invested in inventory. Logistics facilities, equipment, and inventory can represent a substantial segment of a firm's assets. For example, in the case of wholesalers, inventory frequently exceeds 80 percent of total capital. Asset management metrics focus on how well logistics managers utilize the capital invested in operations.

Facilities and equipment are frequently measured in terms of capacity utilization, or the percentage of total capacity used. For example, if a warehouse is capable of shipping 10,000 cases per day, but ships only 8000, capacity utilization is only 80 percent. It is also common to measure equipment utilization in terms of time. Logistics managers are typically concerned with the number or percentage of hours that equipment is *not* utilized, which is measured as equipment *downtime*. Downtime can be applied to transportation, warehouse, and materials handling equipment. These measures indicate the effective or ineffective utilization of capital asset investment.

Asset management measurement also focuses on inventory. *Inventory turnover rate* is the most common measure of performance. Throughout the text, improved inventory turnover has been stressed as a critical focus of logistical management. It is important to understand how firms specifically measure inventory turnover rate. In fact, three specific metrics exist, each of which is used by different types of firms:

$$\text{Inventory turnover} = \frac{\text{Cost of goods sold during a time period}}{\text{Average inventory valued at cost during the time period}} \qquad (1)$$

$$\text{Inventory turnover} = \frac{\text{Sales revenue during a time period}}{\text{Average inventory valued at selling price during time period}} \qquad (2)$$

$$\text{Inventory turnover} = \frac{\text{Units sold during a time period}}{\text{Average unit inventory during the time period}} \qquad (3)$$

The vast majority of firms use (1) to calculate inventory turnover rate. However, some retail organizations use (2). In fact, either of the two ratios should yield approximately the same result. Any differences in the two calculations would result from changes in the amount of gross margin (the difference between sales and cost of goods sold) during the time period.

The third approach, using units rather than dollars, is particularly applicable to products whose cost or selling prices change significantly during a relatively short time. For example, inventory turnover of gasoline, which changes in cost and sales almost daily, would most appropriately be measured by computing units of gasoline sold and units of inventory rather than dollars of any kind.

As a final note on computation of turnover, it is critical that average inventory be determined using as many data points as possible. For example, suppose a company had no inventory at the beginning of the year, bought and held a large quantity for 11 months, then sold all inventory before end of year. Using only the beginning and ending inventory positions, average inventory would be zero and turnover infinite. Clearly, this would be misleading to management.

Inventory investment can also be tracked in terms of the amount which is available to meet forecasted sales volume and is expressed as the *days of supply*. For example, if sales are forecast at 100 units per day and 5000 units are in inventory, the firm has 50 days of supply on hand.

Of major interest to senior executives is *return on assets* and *return on investment*. Rate of return is of such importance that it is discussed in considerable detail later in this chapter.

Most organizations have substantially improved their functional measurement systems over the past 10 years.[3] The number of specific metrics has increased, and the quality of information has improved. Much of the improvement in information quality can be attributed to improved technology. Years ago measurement of on-time delivery typically did not actually monitor delivery receipt by the customer. Most firms had no mechanism to capture information concerning when customers received orders. Instead, they typically measured on-time shipment by discerning if the order was shipped on time. It was assumed that if shipments left the supplier's facility "on-time," then they also arrived at customer facilities "on-time." Thus, the transportation delivery aspect of the order cycle was ignored. Today, using EDI linkages, satellite, and Internet tracking, many organizations monitor whether orders actually arrive at the customer location on time.

Today, many firms have focused increased attention on alternative methods of measuring their ability to accommodate customer requirements. They recognize that traditional customer service metrics are actually internally focused rather than customer-focused. For example, fill rate metrics do not really reflect customer needs; they only reflect the supplier's point of view. Improved metrics focusing on customers are needed. A further requirement is for metrics which reflect process performance in addition to functional performance.

Measuring Customer Accommodation

Chapter 3 suggested that basic logistical service performance is necessary but is not sufficient for firms that are truly committed to excellence in logistics operations. As a result, an additional set of metrics is required for companies that strive to move beyond provision of basic service to customers. Measurement of perfect orders, absolute performance, and customer satisfaction are three approaches adopted by some organizations as part of their commitment to supporting customer requirements. The ultimate in accommodation, customer success, has no specific metrics but remains as the goal for firms committed to supply chain relationships.

Perfect Orders

The perfect order concept was introduced in Chapter 3 as an indicator of an organization's commitment to zero-defect logistics. Delivery of perfect orders is the ultimate measure of quality in logistics operations. A perfect order measures the effectiveness of the firm's overall integrated logistical performance rather than individual functions. It measures whether an order proceeds flawlessly through every step—order entry, credit clearance, inventory availability, accurate picking, on-time delivery, correct invoicing, and payment without deductions—of the order management process without fault, be it expediting, exception processing, or manual intervention.[4] Table 18-2

---

[3]Donald J. Bowersox, David J. Closs, and Theodore P. Stank, op. cit.

[4]William C. Copacino, "Creating the Perfect Order," *Traffic Management,* February 1993, p. 27.

Table 18-2   Dimensions of the "Perfect Order"

Correct order entry	Timely arrival
Correctly formatted EDI and transaction codes	Shipment not damaged
	Correct invoice
Items are available	Accurate overcharges
Ship date allows delivery	No customer deductions
Order picked correctly	No errors in payment processing
Paperwork complete and accurate	

Source: Donald J. Bowersox, David J. Closs, and Theodore P. Stank, *21st Century Logistics: Making Supply Chain Integration a Reality* (Oak Brook, IL: Council of Logistics Management, 1999).

expands on these dimensions of the perfect order. In fact, customers may consider as many as 20 different logistic service elements to assess a perfect order. From a measurement perspective, perfect order performance is computed as the ratio of perfect orders during a given time period to the total number of orders completed during that period. Today, with some exceptions, even the best logistics organizations report achieving only 60 to 70 percent perfect order performance. There are simply so many things that can go wrong with an order!

Absolute Performance

Most basic service and quality measures, and even perfect order measures, are aggregated over many orders and over a period of time. The problem some executives report with these "on average, over time" measures is that they tend to disguise the organization's real impact on its customer base. These executives feel that such measures can actually result in a feeling of complacency within the firm and that it is more appropriate to track **absolute performance** as close to real time as possible. The absolute approach provides a better indication of how a firm's logistical performance really impacts customers. For example, managers may feel that 99.5 percent on-time delivery represents excellent performance. As an executive of a large delivery company said, "To us, 99.5 percent on-time delivery would mean that on a typical day, over 5000 customers received late orders. We can't feel good about having that kind of impact on that many customers." This firm, and many other companies seeking to achieve maximum impact in the market, monitors absolute rates of failure and success as well as the more typical ratio and percentage metrics.

Customer Satisfaction

The ultimate judge of how well an organization accommodates customer expectations and requirements is the customer. All of the internally generated statistics related to basic service, perfect order, or absolute performance may be internal indicators of customer accommodation, but to quantify satisfaction requires monitoring, measuring, and collecting information from the customer. While a comprehensive discussion of interview and survey research methodology is beyond the scope of this text, typical satisfaction measurement requires careful investigation of customer expectations, requirements, and perceptions of firm performance related to all aspects of logistics operations. For example, the typical survey measures customer expectations and performance perceptions regarding availability, order cycle time, information availability, order accuracy, problem resolution, and other aspects of logistics quality. It is useful to gather information concerning customers' overall feelings of satisfaction in addition to their assessment of specific logistics activities. Additional questions may be included to capture customer perceptions of competitor performance. Only through collecting data from customers can real satisfaction be assessed! Further, efforts to enhance customer success can only be measured from the customer's perspective.

Supply Chain Comprehensive Metrics

The contemporary focus on overall supply chain performance and effectiveness demands metrics that provide an integrated perspective. This perspective must be comparable and consistent across both firm functions and supply chain institutions. Without integrated measures, managers in different functions and in different firms may have different perspectives concerning actual logistical performance. Specific measures to consider are cash-to-cash conversion time, supply chain inventory days of supply, dwell time, on-shelf in-stock percentage, total supply chain cost, and supply chain response time.

Cash-to-Cash Conversion

The cash-to-cash conversion concept was introduced in Chapter 1.[5] It is a measure of an organization's effective use of cash. While inventory is typically reported as a current asset on the balance sheet, the reported dollar value may not be a valid indicator of the organization's true asset deployment. Some inventory may have been delivered to customers who, because of trade credit terms of sale, have not yet paid for related invoices. Conversely, an organization may owe its suppliers for products or components which are in its possession. Cash-to-cash cycle time is the time required to convert a dollar spent on inventory into a dollar collected from sales revenue. It can be measured by adding a firm's days of supply of inventory and its days of accounts receivable outstanding, subtracting the days of trade accounts payable outstanding. Consider a hypothetical retailer that maintains a 30-day supply of inventory, has 30 days' trade credit from suppliers, and sells to end consumers in cash-only transactions. This firm theoretically has a cash-to-cash cycle time equal to zero because it sells and collects from end customers just as its payment is due to suppliers. More importantly, the firm's actual investment of money in inventory is zero, regardless of what the balance sheet says.

Cash-to-cash cycle time is not solely impacted by logistics, although logistics is an important aspect. It is a measure of internal process because it includes a component of marketing—customer pricing and terms of sale—as well as a component from procurement—supplier pricing and terms. It offers an integrated perspective of the organization's real commitment of financial resources in the inventory asset.

Supply Chain Inventory Days of Supply

Traditional measures of inventory performance, turnover and days of supply, focus on individual firms. From a supply chain perspective the flaw in these measures is that one firm may improve its performance by simply shifting inventory to its suppliers or to customers. Supply chain inventory days of supply is focused on total inventory at all locations and is typically defined as the total finished goods inventory at all plants, distributions centers, wholesalers, and retailers expressed as the calendar days of sales

---

[5]See Chapter 1, p. 22.

available based on recent sales activity. This measure may be further extended to include raw materials and components held by manufacturing plants and suppliers. These unfinished inventories are converted to equivalent units of finished goods and included as part of the true total supply chain inventory. This measure, when adopted by all members of a supply chain, provides the focus of integrated operations. Several examples of integrated supply chain efforts to reduce total days of supply have emerged in recent years. As one example, the Efficient Consumer Response (ECR) initiative in the food industry was prompted by a study which found that in many supply chains for consumer-processed food, there existed over 120 days' supply of finished goods inventory being held by manufacturers, wholesalers, and retailers.

Dwell Time

Dwell time is another metric reflecting overall supply chain performance in managing assets. Inventory dwell time is the ratio of the days inventory sits idle in the supply chain to the days it is being productively used or positioned.[6] While it is sometimes necessary for inventory to sit idle for reasons of quality control or to buffer uncertainty, extended dwell time reflects the potential magnitude of nonproductive inventory. Dwell time can also be computed for other assets, especially transportation equipment. For example, railcar utilization can be measured by computing the number of days a rail car sits idle and empty versus the number of days it is loaded with freight. Reducing asset dwell time is a key objective for many logistics executives. Assets that sit idle are not contributing to productivity in the organization.

On-Shelf In-Stock Percent

Ultimately, a key objective of all participants in a supply chain is to have products available when and where end customers are ready to buy. Individual firm metrics related to fill rates at distribution centers or to retail stores provide little assurance that products are available for consumer selection when a consumer is in a store. For example, at any given point in time during a typical week, a supermarket is out of stock of 8 percent of the items that should be on the shelf. For this reason, in some supply chain relationships, a critical measure of overall performance is the on-shelf in-stock percent, the percentage of time that a product is available on the shelf in a store. The rationale is that consumers typically cannot or will not select and buy an item that is not easily available on the store shelf. Increasing the on-shelf in-stock percent benefits all members of the supply chain, not only the retailer. Industry Insight 18-1 presents more detail regarding supermarket on-shelf inventory performance. While it focuses on the retail impact, consider also the impact on suppliers when their products are not on the shelves at the time consumers want to buy.

Total Supply Chain Cost

Much of the discussion of cost thus far has focused on an individual firm's logistics costs. Figure 18-2 illustrates the fact that total supply chain cost is the aggregate of costs across all firms in the supply chain, not an individual organization. This perspective is absolutely critical to effective supply chain management. Focusing on a single firm's cost may lead to suboptimization and attempts by one company to shift cost to another. If the objective in supply chain management is to reduce *total* cost, it is reasonable to assume that one organization may actually experience increased cost as oth-

---

[6]See Chapter 1, p. 22.

INDUSTRY INSIGHT 18-1 OUT-OF-STOCKS PROVE COSTLY

Out-of-stocks cost retailers more than 15 percent of potential sales on advertised items and reduce potential consumer purchases by an average of 3.1 percent during the average shopping trip. And on a typical afternoon, 8.2 percent of items are not available to consumers. These were some of the conclusions reached in an extensive out-of-stock study conducted by Andersen Consulting, Chicago, for the Coca-Cola Retailing Research Council.

The report tracked 700 items at 650 stores operated by six chains. The month-long audit focused on eight categories in the frozen food, dairy, and grocery departments. Overall, 48 percent of the items were out of stock at least once during the month.

Faced with out-of-stocks, shoppers do not buy alternative items on that trip 34 percent of the time. About 50 percent of the time, the store loses the sale completely. The rest of the time, outs put retailers at risk because the purchase is delayed until the next shopping trip, the study said. Even worse, out-of-stocks erode consumer loyalty and cost retailers between 0.3 and 0.5 percent of their customer base annually. In fact, 50 percent of the 900 consumers interviewed for the study said they would consider switching stores if three or four items they intended to purchase were routinely out of stock.

Most retailers realize that the majority of outs result from gaps in their own business systems, with direct store delivery vendors contributing to the problem, according to the study. Store ordering problems related to everyday volume account for 54 percent of the out-of-stocks. Promoted item forecasting and ordering account for another 19 percent of outs on warehouse-supplied items, the study said. Shelf capacity that cannot handle everyday volume within a store's existing order cycle accounts for another 16 percent of outs, while failure to restock shelves with available inventory accounts for 8 percent of outs on warehoused items.

Source: Anonymous, "Out-of-Stocks Prove Costly," *Frozen Food Age,* March 1996, p. 4.

FIGURE 18-2

Total supply chain cost

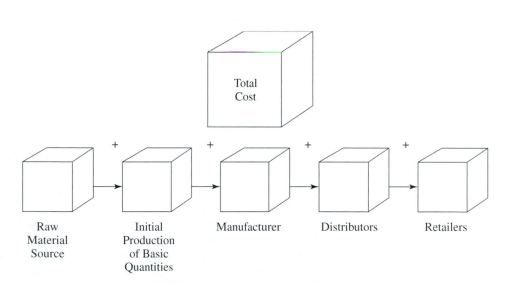

ers in the supply chain experience reductions. As long as the total reductions in cost are larger than the cost increase for one supply chain member, the supply chain as a whole is improved. It is then incumbent upon those companies whose cost is reduced to share benefits to fairly compensate those whose cost is increased. This willingness to share benefits and risks associated with changes in operational integration is the essence of true supply chain management.

Supply Chain Response Time

An interesting and extremely meaningful metric for comprehensive supply chain performance is **Supply Chain Response Time (SCRT).** SCRT is computed as the amount of time required for a firm to recognize a fundamental shift in marketplace demand, internalize that finding, replan, and adjust output to meet that demand. For example, in the auto industry, when it was discovered that demand for sport utility vehicles was extremely high, it took *several years* for the auto companies to develop sufficient production and capacity, rearrange supplier relationships, and meet consumer demand. In most instances, developing an actual metric for SCRT would be a theoretical approximation rather than a real measure. Nevertheless, it is extremely useful for supply chain executives to think in terms of how long it would take for an entire supply chain to ready all activities from raw material sourcing to final distribution when demand for a product is significantly greater (or less) that anticipated.

Benchmarking

A discussion of **benchmarking** was first introduced in Chapter 17 in relation to logistics process reengineering. Benchmarking is also a critical aspect of performance measurement that makes management aware of state-of-the-art business practice. Many firms have adopted benchmarking as a tool to assess their operations in relation to those of leading firms, both competitors and noncompetitors, in related and nonrelated industries. While benchmarking performance metrics has become a fairly standard practice, many firms do not benchmark processes.

A critical aspect of benchmarking is the choice of whom to benchmark. Many firms compare performance of internal business units involved in similar operations or located in different regions. For example, Johnson & Johnson, with over 150 different business units, has ample opportunity for internal benchmarking. Since business units in large diversified corporations are often unaware of what occurs in other units, internal benchmarking provides a way to share knowledge as well as improve performance.

Internal benchmarking, however, provides little information concerning performance relative to competition. A firm may be lagging competition and not be aware of it. Information about competitor performance can be used to identify where improvement is most needed; however, it is extremely difficult to capture information about competitors' operational processes.

Nonrestricted benchmarking involves efforts to compare both metrics and processes to best practices, regardless of where the relevant practice is found. It does not restrict sources of information to any particular company or industry. Nonrestricted benchmarking is grounded in the philosophy that is possible to learn from organizations in unrelated industries which have outstanding performance or use innovative approaches. L. L. Bean, the mail and catalog company, has been benchmarked in order fulfillment processes by firms from such diverse fields as food, personal care, and electronics.

Benchmarking is an important tool in the performance assessment system of an organization. In a study of best-practice supply chain companies, it was found that those firms which perform at high levels of supply chain capability are much more likely to be involved in benchmarking activity than firms which demonstrate average supply chain capability.[7] Table 18-3 shows the results of the research related to bench-

---

[7]Donald J. Bowersox, David J. Closs, and Theodore P. Stank, op. cit., p. 96.

TABLE 18-3   **Performance Benchmarking Differential**

Performance Dimension	Percent of High Index Achieving Firms	Percent of Average Index Achieving Firms
Customer Service	92.5	56.0
Cost Management	80.0	47.1
Quality	70.0	31.0
Productivity	77.5	38.5
Asset Management	55.0	25.8

Note: All differences are statistically significant at the .05 level.

Source: Donald J. Bowersox, David J. Closs, and Theodore P. Stank, *21st Century Logistics: Making Supply Chain Integration a Reality* (Oak Brook, IL: Council of Logistics Management, 1999), p. 97.

marking. It is clear that benchmarking is considered an essential aspect of measurement by leading organizations.

Financial Assessment

In today's corporate environment, logistics executives must be positioned to demonstrate how supply chain practices and processes affect the overall financial health of the organization. Traditional performance assessment does not describe achievement in the financial language spoken at the board level. Measurement systems must enable logistics managers to link supply chain performance directly to financial results. To do so effectively, logistics managers must be well grounded in three fundamental tools of financial assessment: financial budgeting, costing methodologies, and the strategic profit model.

Financial Budgeting

A financial budget is a plan for expenditures anticipated to be made during a time period. As such, it becomes the foundation for achieving logistics cost control. The vast majority of the cost measures identified in the previous discussion must be compared with budgeted expenditures as a basis for control. Four basic types of budgets are used in logistics financial controllership: fixed-dollar, flexible, zero-level, and capital. The first three types are used to control operational expenditures. The last type is used to fund major adjustments in logistical system design such as facilities, equipment, or information technology applications.

Fixed-Dollar Budgeting

A **fixed-dollar budget** is an estimate of functional expense for anticipated logistical activity. Examples of functional expenses include transportation, warehouse labor, and customer service. Given a sales volume projection, the budgeting process seeks to identify a realistic expenditure level to achieve performance goals. The purpose of a finalized budget is to provide a basis for comparison and control. For example, budgeted costs for a specific month or year-to-date operating plan can be evaluated in terms of planned to actual expenditure. The fixed budget is rarely used because it does not consider the influence of environmental changes, such as sales volume less than or greater than forecasted.

Flexible Budgeting

A **flexible budget** offers a way to accommodate unexpected increases or decreases in volume during an operating period. Normally, a flexible budget is structured on a standard cost basis. A *standard cost* is typically defined as an expected norm. Standard costs can be developed to measure a variety of logistical activities, such as receiving and putting away, order selection, packing, and transportation. The process of developing standard costs should be a coordinated, interdepartmental effort that involves logistics, accounting, and industrial engineering personnel. The authorized expenditure level is then compared on the basis of the standard cost measure multiplied by the anticipated activity level. Thus, budgeted expenditures automatically adjust to the anticipated activity level. Although flexible budgeting is preferable to fixed budgeting, it is necessary to have a high degree of sophistication to implement the process. Disciplined cost tracking and complex information systems are required to monitor activity levels and costs.

Table 18-4 illustrates a flexible budget with variances for major logistics activities. The initial budget for both line items and categories is illustrated in columns A_1 and A_2. The budget is developed using forecasted operating levels and standard costs. Forecasted operating levels are specified in terms of anticipated unit weight or order volume. Table 18-5 illustrates the calculation of the flexible budget figure for the transportation line item, which is calculated to be $12,150 at a sales volume of $126,000.

Column B of Table 18-4 is the allowable budget amount based on actual activity level. Since actual net sales were only $112,000, the transportation standard allowed is 0.89 ($112,000/$126,000) of the original budgeted amount, or $10,800.

Column E of Table 18-4 is the actual amount expensed in each category for the budget period. The difference between the original budget amount (column A_2) and the actual amount (column E) is known as the *budget variance*. Variances may be attributed to a combination of ineffectiveness and inefficiency. Variances due to ineffectiveness may result from the fact that net sales are less than anticipated. Since the activity level was 89 percent of anticipated sales, the amount budgeted for the variable cost categories in 89 percent of the original budget. For transportation, the effectiveness variance is $1350. This is calculated by subtracting the $10,800 budgeted at the actual volume level from $12,150 budgeted at forecasted volume. In addition, a $1000 efficiency variance exists because actual transportation expense was only $9800 instead of the $10,800 allowable at the actual sales volume. Note that the allocations for the assignable fixed costs do not change.[8]

Variances due to inefficiency may be attributed to performance of required activities at a level above or below standard cost. A negative variance occurs when an activity has been completed at greater than standard cost. In Table 18-4, the transportation category illustrates a positive efficiency variance of $1000 since actual expenditures were $9800 versus the allowable $10,800 in the flexible budget. The warehouse handling category illustrates a negative efficiency variance of $1000 dollars because actual expense of $4600 is greater than it should have been for the actual sales activity.

The concept of flexible budgeting allows management to examine a range of activity levels. Depending on the particular activity levels that actually occur, managers are able to utilize predetermined standard cost measures to decide what the relevant costs should have been and to analyze the reasons for differences.

---

[8]The concept of direct and indirect costs is discussed later in this chapter.

TABLE 18-4 Example of Flexible Budget

	(A₁) Line-Item Budget	(A₂) Category Budget	(B) Budgeted Expense & Actual Sales Achieved	(C) Variance Due to Ineffectiveness/Activity Level Above (Below) Budget	(D) Variance Due to Inefficiency/Performance Above (Below) Standard	(E) Actual Results
				Variation from Budget		
Net Sales		$126,000	$112,000	$14,000	—	$112,000
Cost of Goods Sold						
Raw materials	$22,050		$19,600	$2,450		
Variable manufacturing costs	40,950		36,400	4,550		
Total Cost of Goods Sold		$ 63,000	$ 56,000	$ 7,000	—	$ 56,000
Manufacturing Contribution		$ 63,000	$ 56,000	$ 7,000	—	$ 56,000
Variable Marketing and Logistics Costs						
Order processing	4,050		3,600	(450)	400	3,200
Sales commissions	6,750		6,000	(750)		6,000
Transportation	12,150		10,800	(1,350)	1,000	9,800
Warehouse handling	4,050		3,600	(450)	(1,000)	4,600
Total Variable Marketing/Logistics Costs		$ 27,000	$ 24,000	($ 3,000)	$ (400)	$ 23,600
Customer Segment Contribution Margin		$ 36,000	$ 32,000	($ 4,000)	$ 400	$ 32,400
Assignable Fixed Costs						
Inventory carrying	2,500		2,500			2,500
Product advertising	5,500		5,500			5,500
Salaries	2,000		2,000			2,000
Total Assignable Fixed Costs		$ 10,000	$ 10,000			$ 10,000
Customer Controllable Margin		$ 26,000	$ 22,000	($ 4,000)	$ 400	$ 22,000

TABLE 18-5   Flexible Budget Computation for Transportation

Sales level	$126,000
Based on average of ($) per pound	$10.00
Sales level (pounds)	12,600
Standard cost for transportation	$12,150
Standard cost for transportation per pound	$0.964

Zero-Level Budgeting

Zero-level budgeting is usually used to facilitate operational control in two forms. At a line management level, a typical zero budgeting process starts without authorized funds at the inception of budget planning. Funding is developed in a *zero up* manner. That is, funds are justified on the basis of planned activity levels and associated or standard cost performance. The expenditure of each dollar must be judged in accordance with the anticipated benefits. A second zero-level budgeting form is used to identify and commit staff activities. **Zero-level staff budgeting** assigns all costs necessary to perform a range of support services for functional units. Each functional unit must then justify the utilization of the support staff. Both types of zero-level budgeting seek to tie operational expenditures to specific tasks and to improve the basis for managerial review and control.

Capital Budgeting

Capital budgeting specifies the amount and timing of significant financial investments for logistics resources. Major logistical system changes may be initiated, continued, or completed during any specified operating period. Most such changes extended over several operating periods. These changes might require expenditure authorization for construction of a new facility, installation of a new order processing system, or purchase or lease of transportation equipment. When major system changes are planned, the capital budgeting process is straightforward. The expenditure is researched, and, if justified, the necessary funding is approved.

A more difficult situation occurs when capital investment is required for research and development. At inception, such expenditures are nearly impossible to justify on a cost/benefit basis and thus are typically allocated over a number of future time periods.

A *creeping* capital deployment can occur when day-to-day operations result in unplanned expenditures. For example, logistical operations may experience unplanned inventory buildups. While annual inventory increases may not seem significant at the time, inventory turnover may decline substantially over a number of years. This leads to a creeping increase in the capital committed to inventory. If such trends in capital investments are not rigorously monitored, a substantial unplanned capital commitment may result.

A final note on capital budgeting concerns identification of which costs are tied to specific capital investment decisions. The typical capital budgeting process considers only those investments that require new capital. If planned system modifications can be achieved that result in operational savings without new capital commitment, they are not typically subjected to the rigid controls of the capital budgeting process.

Logistical Implications

The budget development and approval process is critical in logistical administration. In particular, senior logistics executives must be concerned with total system performance rather than individual budgets of specific functions. Development of an integrated budget that assesses total system performance provides senior management with an estimate of expenditures required to achieve operating objectives and provides the basis for financial performance measurement.

Budget requests by individual line managers typically exceed the level of funding senior management desires to authorize. This is understandable because no individual manager is positioned to envision the total system. A tendency also exists to view requirements in any specific activity on a unit-cost basis. A bias toward unit costs often encourages actions resulting in efficiency in one area without full appreciation of the impact on other areas. For example, a traffic manager held responsible for achieving lowest possible transportation unit cost could be motivated to select low-cost transport without necessary consideration of on-time performance.

Why are individual managers asked to formulate budget requests if such deficiencies and misallocations can result? The answer is twofold. First, it is essential that individual managers participate in budget formulation to gain a complete understanding of and take ownership responsibility for the integrated system performance. Budget formation is one of the most potent training and control tools available to senior management. Second, individual unit managers are often aware of items that must be considered in a specific operating plan but do not come to the attention of senior management. Logistics management interaction is essential to the development and implementation of realistic but demanding budgets.

Cost/Revenue Analysis

The achievement of logistical integration requires the establishment of a cost/revenue analysis framework. Traditional accounting practices make such a framework difficult for logistics executives. Contribution margin and full-costing methodologies have been supplemented by the use of Activity-Based Costing (ABC) as the most promising way to identify and control logistics expenses.

Public Accounting Practice

The two main financial reports of a business enterprise are the **balance sheet** and the **income statement.** The balance sheet reflects the financial position of a firm at a specific point in time. The purpose of a balance sheet is to summarize assets and liabilities and to indicate the net worth of ownership. The income statement reflects the revenues and costs associated with specific operations over a specified period of time. As the name *income* implies, its purpose is to determine the financial success of operations. Logistical functions are an integral part of both statements; however, the primary deficiency in determining logistical costing and analysis is the method by which standardized accounting costs are identified, classified, and reported. Unfortunately, the conventional methods of accounting do not fully satisfy logistical costing requirements.

The first problem results from the fact that accounting practice aggregates costs on a standard or natural account basis rather than on an activity basis. The practice of grouping expenses into natural accounts such as salaries, rent, utilities, and depreciation fails to identify or assign operations responsibility. To help overcome the natural account aggregation, it is common for statements to be subdivided by managerial or organizational areas of responsibility within an enterprise. Internal income statements generally classify and group expenses along organization budgetary lines. Thus, costs are detailed by managerial responsibility. However, many expenses associated with logistical performance cut across organization units. For example, efforts to reduce inventory will reduce inventory carrying cost, but they may also lead to more back orders, which would increase total transportation cost. The result is deficient data for integrated performance measurement.

A somewhat overlapping deficiency of accounting involves the traditional methods of reporting transportation expenditures. It remains standard practice in retail accounting to deduct inbound freight expense from gross sales as part of the cost of goods to arrive at a gross margin figure. Outbound freight, on the other hand, is generally reported as an operating expense. However, the problem extends beyond *where* freight is accounted for and reported. In many purchasing situations, freight is not reported as a specific cost. Many products are purchased on a delivered price basis, which includes transportation cost. Most progressive procurement procedures require that expenses for all services, including transportation, be *debundled* from the total purchase cost for evaluative purposes.

A final deficiency in traditional accounting practice is the failure to specify and assign inventory cost. The deficiency has two aspects. First, full costs associated with the maintenance of inventory, such as insurance and taxes, are not identified, resulting in an understatement or obscurity in reporting inventory cost. Second, the financial burden for assets committed to material, work-in-process, and finished goods inventory is not identified, measured, or separated from other forms of capital expense incurred by the enterprise. In fact, if a firm deploys internal funds to support inventory requirements, it is likely that no capital expenses will be reflected by the profit and loss statement.

To remedy these shortcomings, several modifications to traditional accounting are required to track logistical costs. In particular, the two largest individual expenses in logistics—transportation and inventory—have traditionally been reported in a manner that obscures their importance rather than highlighting them. Although the situation is improving, routine isolation and reporting of logistical costs is not standard practice in most organizations.

To control cost and improve operational efficiency, it is necessary to properly identify and capture all relevant cost information in a manner that is meaningful to decisionmakers. Logistical costing must also provide those executives with the information to determine whether a specific segment of business such as a customer, order, product, channel, or service is profitable. This requires the matching of specific revenue with specific costs.

Effective costing requires identification of the specific expenses included in an analysis framework. Two frameworks which each have numerous proponents are the *contribution approach* and the *net profit approach.*

Contribution Approach

A pure **contribution approach** requires that all costs be identified as fixed or variable according to the cost behavior. **Fixed costs** are those that do not directly change with volume of activity. In the short term those costs would remain even if volume were reduced to zero. For example, the cost of a delivery truck is fixed. If the truck cost $40,000, the firm is charged $40,000 (or the appropriate depreciation) whether the truck is used for 1 or 1000 deliveries. **Variable costs** are those costs that do change as a result of volume. The gasoline required to operate a delivery truck is variable: total gasoline cost depends upon how frequently and how far the truck is driven.

It is also necessary in contribution analysis to specify which are direct costs and which are indirect costs. **Direct costs** are those that are specifically incurred due to the

TABLE 18-6   Contribution Margin Income Statement for Two Customers

	Hospital	Retailer	Total
Revenue	$100,000	$150,000	$250,000
Less: Variable Cost of Goods Sold	42,000	75,000	117,000
Variable Gross Profit	58,000	75,000	133,000
Less: Variable Direct Cost	6,000	15,000	21,000
Gross Segment Contribution	52,000	60,000	112,000
Less: Fixed Direct Costs	15,000	21,000	36,000
Net Segment Contribution	$37,000	$39,000	76,000
Less: Indirect Fixed Costs			41,000
Net Profit			$25,000
Net Segment Contribution Ratio	37%	26%	30.4%

existence of the product, customer, or other segment under consideration. If that segment were eliminated, the direct cost would no longer exist. All variable costs can be directly traced to specific products, customers, channels, and the like. Some fixed costs may also be direct, if they exist to logistically support a specific business segment. For example, a warehouse facility may be constructed specifically to support a specific product line or major customer account. **Indirect costs** exist due to more than one segment of business and would continue to exist even if one specific segment were eliminated. Thus, a warehouse that maintains multiple product lines would continue to operate even if one product line was discontinued. In this case, the warehouse is *indirect* to the products.

Income statements in the contribution method of analysis can be prepared that identify profitability for each segment by determination of fixed, variable, direct, and indirect costs. Table 18-6 provides a hypothetical example of such income statements for a firm analyzing profitability of two customers, a hospital and a retailer. Variable costs of goods sold are directly related to the product mix sold in each customer segment; it includes only direct labor, materials, and supplies. All factory overhead costs are treated as indirect costs in the contribution margin approach. Variable direct costs include such items as sales commission, discounts, certain logistics costs related to servicing each customer, and any other expenses that vary directly with volume sold to each customer. Fixed direct costs include any other costs that can be traced directly to the specific customer. Such costs *might* include certain aspects of sales, salaries and expenses, advertising, transportation, warehousing, order processing, and other logistical activities. The key is that these expenses must be directly attributable to those customers. Indirect fixed costs includes all expenses that cannot easily be traced to a specific segment. Many of these may also be logistics-related costs. For example, shared warehouse, transportation equipment, and other jointly used resources should be specified as indirect costs.

In Table 18-6, both customers are covering direct costs and making a substantial contribution to indirect fixed cost. The hospital, however, has a substantially higher percentage net segment contribution than does the retailer—37 percent versus 26 percent. A large portion of this difference is attributable to the difference in variable gross profit of 58 percent versus 50 percent. This difference suggests that analysis of the product mix for the retailer should be conducted to determine whether emphasis should be placed on a more profitable mix. Elimination of the retailer would be a clear mistake, however, as the hospital customer would then have to bear all of the indirect fixed cost, resulting in a net loss of $4000.

Net Profit Approach

The **net profit approach** to financial assessment of segments requires that all operating costs be charged or allocated to an operating segment. Proponents of this approach argue that all of a company's activities exist to support the production and delivery of goods and services to customers. Furthermore, in many firms most costs are, in fact, joint or shared costs. To determine the true profitability of a channel, territory, or product, each segment must be allocated its fair share of these costs. In the previous example, allocating indirect fixed cost on the basis of sales volume would result in the hospital being charged with 40 percent, or $16,400, and the retailer 60 percent, or $24,600. The net profit of serving the hospital would then be reported as $20,600. The net profit from the retail customer would be reported as $14,400.

Clearly, significant problems arise in determining how to allocate indirect costs on a fair and equitable basis. Proponents of the contribution margin approach contend that such allocations are necessarily arbitrary and result in misleading financial assessment. They point to the use of sales volume as a typical basis for allocation of expense and the inherent bias in such an approach. For example, the retailer above accounts for 60 percent of total sales volume but does not necessarily account for 60 percent of the expense of advertising, warehousing, order processing, or any other shared activity. It may account for much more or less of each expense category, depending upon circumstances that are not at all related simply to sales volume.

Net profit proponents argue, however, that the traditional notions of fixed and variable cost and direct and indirect cost are too simplistic. Many of the so-called indirect fixed costs are not, in fact, indirect or fixed at all. These expenses rise and fall, depending upon demands placed upon the business by the various operating segments.[9]

Activity-Based Costing

As a partial solution to the problem of arbitrary allocations, **Activity-Based Costing (ABC)** suggests that costs should first be traced to activities performed and then activities should be related to specific product or customer segments of the business.[10] Suppose, for example, the order processing expense is basically a fixed indirect cost in our hypothetical example, amounting to $5000. Allocating this expense to the two customers based on sales volume results in a charge of $2000 to the hospital and $3000 to the retailer. However, it is likely that the hospital places very many orders during the year, each of a small quantity, while the retailer may place only a few large orders. If the hospital placed 80 orders and the retailer placed 20 orders, an ABC approach would charge the hospital with 80 percent or $4000 and the retailer with 20 percent or $1000 of the order processing expense. Applying similar logic to other indirect fixed costs by identifying the activities and drivers of cost could result in further refinement of customer profitability. Industry Insight 18-2 tells the story of a wholesaler who has

---

[9]B. Charles Ames and James D. Hlavacek, "Vital Truths about Managing Your Costs," *Harvard Business Review* 68, no. 1 (January/February 1990), p. 144.

[10]For information, see Ronald L. Lewis, *Activity-Based Costing for Marketing and Manufacturing* (Westport, CT: Quorum Books, 1993); John K. Shank and Vijay Govindarajan, *Strategic Cost Management: The New Tool for Competitive Advantage* (New York: Maxwell Macmillan International, 1993); and Robert S. Kaplan and H. Thomas Johnson, *Relevance Lost: The Rise and Fall of Management Accounting* (Boston: Harvard Business School Press, 1987).

Industry Insight 18-2 A Full Measure of Customer Service

Torrington Supply Co. knows exactly how much profit it is making on its customers and sales thanks to the inquisitive minds of Chairman and CEO Joel Becker and Chief Financial Officer David Petitti, who can pinpoint to the dollar what percentage of gross margin on the average sale is profit or loss for any given customer. And they are able to use those numbers to improve profitability for both Torrington and the customer.

Becker confesses to spending what he considers "an inordinate amount of time" putting together a comprehensive profitability analysis system. He is convinced that the key to successful distribution is knowing where the profit comes from and, by extension, where Torrington should concentrate its efforts. "With some customers you make money; with some you lose money. Knowing which is which is the name of this game."

Becker realized that that kind of real time information about a customer's net profitability would be very helpful to Torrington's inside sales staff as they took orders. Once they had the data, they were shocked to discover that some of the company's "best" customers were also among its biggest profit drains.

Becker points to one customer who was buying more than $200,000 in materials from Torrington every year and paying in less than 29 days. Torrington was earning a gross profit of almost 20 percent on these orders. "Yet we were losing a fortune on him!" Becker says.

The problem was that Torrington was making less than $3 a line—$21 per order—on this customer. "There is a fixed cost associated with every single order," Becker says. "What matters is the gross profit per order, not the individual gross profit per line item. We actually make the lowest gross profit percent on our most profitable customers. The secret is the size of the order."

Becker decided that the best approach to take with such a delicate situation was the direct route. Armed with the profitability report, he called on the owner and the operations manager of the customer company. "I told them, 'You're a great customer,'" he recalls. "'You've been doing business with us for a long time, and we love you. But we need you to do something if we're going to continue to do business. We need you to help us reduce our transaction costs.' And I specifically listed what I thought they could do."

The customers themselves were surprised. They realized that placing so many orders was undoubtedly costing them money, as well. They were happy to work with Torrington to reduce their shared business costs.

"They now place all their orders electronically," Becker says. "Most customers are surprised at the activity levels their business requires of us. It's a real win–win."

So far Becker has had these conversations with only those customers with significant opportunity for improvement. "I review the details of their activity with us over the last 52 weeks— how much business they've done; the gross profit we earned; the number of lines, invoices, returns, deliveries, counter pickups, direct shipments, everything. They forget about our costs for what they require of us. But when they see all this, they respond very well."

Source: Marjie O'Connor, "A Full Measure of Customer Service," *Supply House Times,* December 1999, pp. 44–49.

used ABC to determine customer profitability and more effectively manage its operations.

Logistical Implications

Identifying the activities, related expenses, and the drivers of expense represents the biggest challenge in an ABC approach. Order processing cost may be related to the number of orders in one company and to the number of lines on orders in another company. Warehouse picking expense may be related to the number of items picked in one company and to the number of pounds in another. Transportation might be related to number of deliveries for one firm and number of miles driven for another. According to proponents of this activity-based costing method, only two types of costs should be excluded from allocation to segments. First, excess capacity cost in a firm should not be charged to a segment. Thus, if an order processing system could process five million orders per year but is only utilized for four million orders, the excess capacity should not be charged to any segment. Similarly, if a warehouse and its employees could handle 100,000 shipments but are only used for 80,000, the excess capacity is a cost of the time period rather than a cost attributable to an existing operating segment. All other costs, however, can and should be traced through an activity-based system.[11]

Much of the distinction between the contribution margin and net profit approaches to segment cost analysis is disappearing as analysts are developing better approaches to identify expense behavior. Advocates of direct costing and contribution margin probably go along with the tracing of costs to segments based on activities performed, as long as the basis for tracing reflects the *real* cost of the activity. Historically, their argument has been based on the fairness and appropriateness of the allocation method. Even the most avid proponent of full costing, on the other hand, would not argue in favor of arbitrary allocation of cost. The development of better ABC systems has the potential for ultimately resolving this controversy, which has existed in marketing and distribution for a number of years.

Strategic Profit Model

While costing and profitability assessment are important aspects of financial controllership, the most critical measure of strategic success is **Return on Investment (ROI).** There are two ways of viewing ROI. The first is **Return on Net Worth (RONW),** which measures the profitability of the funds that the owners of the firm have invested in the firm. The second is **Return on Assets (ROA),** which measures the profitability generated by managing a firm's operational assets. While owners and investors are most likely interested in RONW, ROA offers a measure of how well management is utilizing assets to earn profits.

Figure 18-3 presents the **Strategic Profit Model (SPM),** with hypothetical data. The SPM is a tool frequently used to analyze ROI in a business firm. In fact, the SPM is a tool that incorporates both income and balance sheet data and demonstrates how these data relate to each other to result in ROA.

One of the primary benefits of the SPM is that it shows very clearly that a key financial objective of the firm is to achieve and increase ROA. Too often, managers focus on more limited objectives. For example, sales management may focus on sales as the primary objective of the business and, therefore, will base decisions on sales volume. Logistics managers may focus on cost minimization or turnover and feel that decisions must be based on reducing expense or increasing the firm's efficient utilization of assets. The SPM demonstrates that there are two fundamental ways in which a firm can increase return on assets: managing net profit margin and/or managing asset turnover. Logistics operations have a significant impact on both.

Net Profit Margin

Defined as a percentage, **net profit margin** is net profit divided by net sales. Going beyond this simple expression, however, net profit margin actually measures the proportion of each sales dollar that is kept by the firm as net profit. For example, the hy-

---

[11]For a discussion of ABC in logistics decision making, see Matthew J. Liberatore and Tan Miller, "A Framework for Integrating Activity-Based Costing and the Balance Scorecard into the Logistic Strategy Development and Monitoring Process," *Journal of Business Logistics* 19, no. 2 (1998), pp. 131–54.

FIGURE 18-3
Strategic profit model

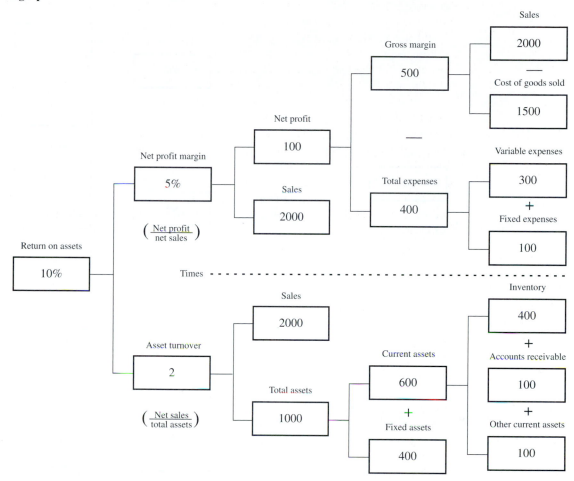

pothetical firm has a net profit margin of 5 percent; this simply means that $.05 out of every $1 represents net profit to the company. It is important to note that net profit margin is also divided into a number of specific components. These components are sales volume, cost of goods sold, and operating expenses. For a full evaluation of whether the firm's net profit margin is adequate, and whether it might be improved, it is necessary to investigate each component to determine whether an increase or decrease in any one component or in any combination of components might lead to improved net profit margin performance.

Asset Turnover

Asset turnover is the ratio of total sales divided by total assets. Asset turnover actually measures the efficiency of management in utilizing assets. It shows how many dollars in total sales volume are being generated by each dollar that the firm has invested in assets. For example, the hypothetical company with an asset turnover ratio of 2:1 is generating $2.00 in sales volume for each dollar it has invested in assets. As Figure 18-3 illustrates, there are a number of assets used to generate sales. The most

Strategic profit model (inventory reduction)

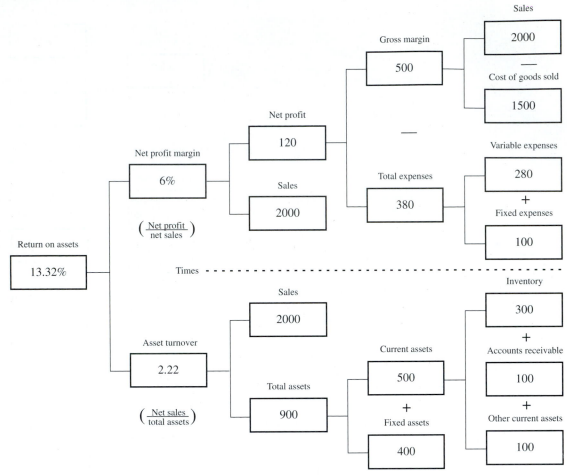

important are inventories, accounts receivable, and fixed facilities. Inventory is a particularly important asset to many firms because it is typically one of the largest areas of asset investment. Thus, it is common in logistics to focus specifically on the management of the inventory turnover ratio.

Applications of the SPM
The SPM can be used for many different types of logistical analysis. Two of the most common are the impact of changes in logistical activities or processes on ROA and analysis of segmental ROA.

Inventory Reduction Example.   Figure 18-4 illustrates a recomputation of ROA assuming that the hypothetical firm was able to accomplish an inventory reduction of $100. The most obvious impact of this inventory reduction occurs through the reduction in the inventory asset from $400 to $300. A corresponding change in total

TABLE 18-7   CMROI for Two Products

	Product A	Product B
Sales	$100,000	$50,000
Cost of Goods	60,000	35,000
Gross Margin	40,000 (40%)	15,000 (30%)
Direct Expense	25,000	9000
Contribution Margin	15,000 (15%)	6000 (12%)
Average Inventory	40,000	10,000
CMROI	37.5%	60%

assets results in a new asset turnover rate of 2.22 versus the base case of 2.0 times. It is assumed, for explanatory purposes, that sales volume remains the same.

However, a reduction in average inventory also has an impact on operating expenses. Inventory carrying costs, discussed in Chapter 10, should be reduced as well. In this example, assuming an inventory carrying cost of 20 percent, the expense reduction amounts to $20, increasing net profit to $120, and net profit margin to 6 percent. The combined profit margin and asset turnover impact of inventory reduction result in an increase in ROA from 10 percent to over 13.3 percent. No wonder so many organizations are focusing on methods to improve inventory management!

The simplifying assumption of no change in sales could be subjected to further examination by using the SPM. A variety of scenarios regarding potential changes in volume, expenses, and investments can be proposed and analyzed. In fact, the SPM framework is very adaptable to a spreadsheet model, which allows investigation and analysis of many different changes in logistics operations and their projected impact on ROA. Changes in facility structure or methods with projected changes in expenses, asset investment, and sales level can be analyzed to project impact on ROA.

Segmental Analysis.   The SPM, in conjunction with concepts discussed in the section on cost/revenue analysis, can also be used to examine the return on assets generated by various customer or product segments of a business. Table 18-7 provides a sample calculation of **Contribution Margin Return on Inventory Investment (CMROI)** for two products. Contribution margin for each product is calculated using only those expenses directly traced to each product.

No indirect costs are allocated. Similarly, asset investments directly attributable to specific products should be identified. In this case, the only direct asset investment is inventory investment. Notice that product B has lower gross margin and contribution margin but actually provides a substantially higher return because of its low average inventory investment. In other situations, for example, analysis of customer return on assets, accounts receivable and other direct asset investments attributable to specific customer should be included.

Other segment profitability and ROI analysis can be conducted using the SPM framework. It requires careful thought and identification of those costs and asset investments traceable to specific segments. With this approach, the logistics executive has a powerful and useful tool for identifying how logistics process, activities, and decisions impact the financial objectives of the organization.

Logistical Implications

One problem faced by logistics executives is that typical approaches to logistics performance assessment are not generally expressed in terms that are meaningful to other senior executives. For example, transportation expense per mile, warehouse picking expense, and cost-related metrics are extremely meaningful in terms of managing those specific activities but are somewhat obscure to executives in finance and marketing. The SPM framework is a very useful tool for relating logistics activities to the overall financial objectives of the organization. It provides a mechanism to trace specifically how changes in logistics' assets or expenses relate directly to measures, which are more meaningful to other executives: measures such as profit margin, asset turnover, and return on assets.

Summary

Effective management of logistics operations and supply chain integration requires establishment of a framework for performance assessment and financial controllership. This framework provides the mechanism to monitor system performance, control activities, and direct personnel to achieve higher levels of productivity.

Comprehensive performance measurement systems include metrics for each of the logistics functions. Five critical dimensions of functional performance must be addressed: cost, customer service, quality, productivity, and asset management. Leading firms extend their functional measurement systems to include metrics focused on their ability to accommodate customer requirements. These include measures of absolute performance rather than average performance, perfect orders, end-consumer focused measures, and customer satisfaction. To aid in achievement of supply chain integration, leading firms have instituted a set of across-firm metrics such as inventory days of supply, inventory dwell time, cash-to-cash cycle time, and total supply chain cost.

Effective logistics contollership requires knowledge of three critical tools. The first is financial budgeting. Budgeting provides the foundation for control of logistics cost. A budget represents management's estimate of the costs and resources required to achieve logistical objectives. Four types of budgets are used in logistics controllership: fixed-dollar, flexible, zero-level, and capital. The second tool is cost/revenue analysis. Traditional accounting practices are typically inadequate for logistics costing. Effective decision making requires that management be able to match revenues with expenses incurred to service specific customers, channels, and products. Contribution margin and net profit represent two alternative formats for cost/revenue analysis. Activity-based costing provides management the ability to more specifically trace logistics expenses to the segments that generate revenue. The third tool for controllership is the strategic profit model. This model provides managers the ability to assess the impact of logistics decisions on profitability, asset utilization, and return on assets. It also provides the ability to more accurately assess segments in terms of profit and return on investment.

Challenge Questions

1. Briefly discuss the three objectives for developing and implementing performance measurement systems.

2. Compare and contrast the various metrics for product availability. Why is the order fill rate considered the most stringent metric?

3. Is the ideal of a perfect order a realistic operational goal?

4. Why is it important that a firm measure customer perception as a regular part of performance measurement?

5. Why are comprehensive measures of supply chain performance, such as total supply chain cost, so difficult to develop?

6. Why is flexible budgeting a more valuable tool for logistics managers than fixed-dollar budgeting?

7. Compare and contrast the contribution approach with the net profit approach in cost/revenue analysis.

8. Do you believe that activity-based costing represents an equitable basis for allocating indirect expenses?

9. Suppose you have been asked by a firm to assess the impact on return on assets of outsourcing transportation. Currently the firm uses a private truck fleet and is considering a switch to a third-party transportation company. Which aspects of the strategic profit model would be affected?

10. How can the strategic profit model be integrated with cost/revenue analysis for the purpose of analyzing the return on assets from servicing a specific customer account?

19 DIMENSIONS OF CHANGE

This concluding chapter is focused on the future of logistics in supply chain management. The discussion commences with a brief look at the environment that logistical managers will face during the next decade. As the future develops, it now appears that ten megatrends will drive changes and transformations necessary to enable firms to achieve superior performance. Each trend is developed in terms of anticipated impact on emerging logistical management priorities, and the discussion concludes with a review of associated risks. The epilogue provides your authors' concluding comments.

Looking Toward the Next Decade

Given the extreme changes that have occurred in logistical management concepts and practices during the past several decades, an appropriate question is, What can we expect to happen as the world moves forward during the next 10 years? The primary determinant of the shape and form of future logistical requirements will be the nature of demand that needs to be serviced.

The logistical renaissance developed a sound foundation to guide logistics managers. While significant lessons have been learned over the past decades, the process of change is far from finished. The globalization of business promises to offer new and unique challenges for the logistical competencies of most firms. Few will be able to escape the impact of a global economy. Challenges will also increase in the environmental aspects of logistics, often referred to as *green* issues. The full ramification of long-term cradle-to-cradle responsibility for the environmental impact of all products and services is just emerging. Finally, firms can fully expect that customers making major business commitments to supply chain partners will expect nearly perfect logistical performance. Even in today's operational environment, firms that build strong customer and supplier relationships must be committed to operational excellence. Tolerance for logistical error will become even less in the future.

Current projections are that the gross domestic product of the United States will exceed $12 trillion by the year 2010. Significant growth is projected in both goods and services. However, most futurists predict that the United States and most of the industrialized world will increasingly become service-oriented economies. In comparison to today, a significantly larger share of the world's total population will seek participation in the good life possible in the new millennium. Logistical systems of the future will face complex and challenging performance requirements. Even more so than today, logistics will be required to support multiple-product distribution to globally dispersed heterogeneous markets.

Barring a catastrophic event, it is difficult not to expect a world population exceeding eight billion people by the year 2025. To put this population growth into perspective, at a bare minimum it will be necessary to provide logistical support for one additional person for every four in the world today. People in general will increasingly have resources to participate in economic growth. However, significant differences are expected in lifestyle and related social priorities. Evidence suggests that consumers of the future will demand services and conveniences contained in the products they purchase. For instance, such items as frozen meat might well be precooked and ready for consumption when bought. To the extent that this service/convenience pattern accelerates, more value will be added to the typical product before it begins the logistical process. To support this trend, the complexity of the total manufacturing/marketing system will increase.

The priority placed on development of integrated management skills rests on the contribution that superior logistics performance can make to business success. A firm can achieve sustainable competitive advantage when important customers perceive that it has the capabilities to logistically outperform competitors. A prerequisite to strategic logistics is the development and implementation of supply chain integration. Managing logistics on an integrated basis is becoming increasingly relevant for the following reasons.

First, there is considerable interdependence between areas of logistical requirements that can be exploited to the advantage of an enterprise. The idea of a *total* movement/ storage system offers efficiency and synergistic potential. Throughout the logistical system, management is faced with ever-increasing labor costs. Since logistical work is among the most labor-intensive performances within an enterprise, logistics managers must develop methods to substitute capital for labor-intensive processes. Complete integration increases the economic justification for substituting capital for labor.

Second, a narrow or restricted functional approach may create dysfunctional behavior. The potential exists that concepts relevant solely to market distribution, manufacturing support, or procurement can create diametrically opposite operational priorities and goals. The failure to develop integrated logistical management creates the potential for suboptimization.

Third, the control requirements for each individual aspect of operations are similar. The primary objective of logistical control is to reconcile operational demands in a cross-functional manner focused on overall goals.

A fourth reason for the integration of logistical operations is an increasing awareness that significant trade-offs exist between manufacturing economies and marketing requirements and that these can be reconciled only by a soundly designed logistical capability. The traditional practice of manufacturing is to produce products in various sizes, colors, and quantities in *anticipation* of future sale. The *postponement* of final assembly and initial distribution of products to a later time when customer preferences are more fully identified can greatly reduce risk and increase overall enterprise flexibility. Innovative new systems are emerging to make use of logistical competency to increase responsiveness and reduce the traditional anticipatory commitment and risk of business.

A final, and perhaps the most significant, reason for integration is that the complexity of future logistics will require innovative arrangements. The challenge for the new millennium is to develop *new ways* of satisfying logistical requirements, not simply using technology to perform *old ways more efficiently*. While this is similar to the challenge faced in the 1990s, the stakes are getting higher. In the world of the future, leading firms can be expected to increasingly use integrated logistical competency to gain differential advantage. The broad-based achievement of integrated logistical management will remain a prerequisite for such innovative breakthroughs.

The combined impact of these factors is that logistics will increasingly be managed on an integrated basis. However, the job of reengineering logistics as an integrated process is far from completed. Research continues to point out that a significant number of firms worldwide have only made limited progress toward logistical integration. Approximately 10 percent of North American firms have achieved a level of integration that facilitates their use of logistical competency to gain and maintain customer loyalty. Events of historical significance—like the radical restructuring of Eastern Europe; the decomposition of communism in the Soviet Union; and even the rapid adoption of the Internet as a mechanism for communication—serve to underline the increasing importance of logistics to all aspects of society. In many ways, these events highlight just how demanding logistical requirements are and how challenging they are capable of becoming. The reality is that a great deal of work remains to make the full potential of the logistics renaissance an everyday reality.

Ever present in future society will be the continued problems and pressures of energy and ecology. The dependence of the logistical system on a ready supply of energy is and will continue to be a critical concern. The cost of energy remains significant in the logistical sector and will continue to be so for the foreseeable future. From an ecological viewpoint, continued pressures will exist to reduce the negative impact of logistics on the environment. These pressures reflect socially worthwhile goals, although compliance will be costly. It can be anticipated that ecological considerations will eliminate some current logistical practices such as specific types of packaging material. Finally, it is clear that selected raw materials will from time to time be in relatively short supply.

Ten Megatrends[1]

As leading firms transform their supply chain capabilities to accommodate the transition from an industrial to an information technology-driven society, these megatrends

---

[1]Adapted from Donald Bowersox, David Closs, and Theodore P. Stank. "Ten Mega-Trends That Will Revolutionize Supply Chain Logistics," *Journal of Business Logistics* 20, no. 2 (2000), pp. 1–16.

imply substantial change in logistics practices. The change must occur both within and among supply chain partners as they struggle to establish efficient, effective, and relevant product/service solutions for end customers. The transitions underlying some of the megatrends represent the challenges of the emerging decade for logisticians and supply chain executives and identify the direction for change.

Customer Service to Relationship Management

Customer relevancy will increasingly become the key strategic commitment of leading corporations. While traditional customer service focuses on achieving internal operating standards, a truly relationship-driven supply chain focuses on establishing customer success. For many customers, such operating features as cycle time compression, exact-point-in-time delivery performance, and perfect order-to-delivery may be the prime drivers of supplier acceptability. In contrast, other customers may not be willing to shoulder the cost of day-to-day six-sigma logistics support. Their preference may be for a high level of average logistical support fortified by responsive logistical recovery when and where needed. Supply chains designed to achieve unique customer value propositions have the potential to turn commodities into value-added solutions. Given an understanding of what drives end customer purchase behavior, a supply chain based on relationships has the greatest potential to result in unique logistical solutions that are simultaneously effective, efficient, and relevant. This implies that firms will likely participate in multiple supply chains to support different customers.

Although most firms have not achieved the desired level of closeness with customers, it is the most advanced of the megatrends. Leading firms increasingly recognize that success hinges on establishing intimate relationships with key customers. Intimate relationships enable firms to generate unique and profitable product/service offerings for their preferred customers. This, of course, is in direct contrast to principles of mass marketing, and it is certainly cost-prohibitive to all but the most narrowly defined market niche firms. Managers seeking to achieve this level of intimacy with customers must assess their firm's resources relative to the needs and desires of *select individual* customers. Then the firm can deploy its resources and capabilities to perform customer-valued activities and services that competitors cannot match at all or at a reasonable cost.

There are two shifts that must take place for firms to evolve along this continuum. First, firms seeking to develop strong customer relationships should recognize that all customers do not have the same service expectations and do not necessarily want or deserve the same overall level of service. They must, therefore, identify core customers best suited to be their business clients and then meet or exceed expectations by providing unique value-added services. These services may include assignment of specific focus teams to identify, design, implement, and refine specialized and synchronized offerings. Additionally, firms must develop the ability to satisfy not only existing needs but also those that may emerge. By continuously matching service capabilities with changing customer expectations, providers can stay ahead of competition.

Second, firms seeking to enhance customer relationships must develop operating systems capable of quickly reacting to change rather than depending upon anticipatory deployment of inventory to handle planned requirements. This is facilitated by gathering and exchanging information throughout the supply chain as contrasted to guessing what may happen. The focus must be on efficient and effective accommodation of unique customer requests as well as on the ability to react to unexpected operational circumstances. These capabilities enable firms to capitalize on uncertainty to enhance customer satisfaction. Some approaches that facilitate flexibility include providing frontline employees with the authority to approve special customer requests, automatically accommodating stockouts through multiple service locations, and implementing preplanned solutions. Another critical enabler of flexibility is routinization and simplification of fundamental work to minimize effort expended on handling day-to-day details and free resources to deal with unexpected events. Judicious employment of form and time postponement also contributes to a firm's ability to respond to unknown or unplanned circumstances.

Adversarial to Collaborative Relationships

In most business relationships today, suppliers sell to customers. Often there is considerable conflict in these buyer/seller arrangements as each party seeks the best financial deal. Neither side fully trusts the other. Vendors must guess customers' needs since specific demand or planning information is not shared. In such situations, the potential for achieving overall operating efficiency is limited as firms maneuver for short-term benefits at the expense of their trading partners. The concept of integrated supply chain management, however, highlights the leveraged benefits of firms collaborating to achieve common goals. The notion of focused collaborative arrangements, coupled with true cradle-to-grave accountability, is revolutionizing the way that firms work together to streamline the distributive process. The potential for increased overall efficiency as a result of reduced work duplication and redundancy is astounding.

Developing collaborative behavior has been the subject of substantial discussion. These behaviors, however, are not well defined in most firms. Managers at many firms feel that behavioral change is extremely difficult to achieve. Often they find themselves talking about collaboration much more than they actually practice it.

There are three shifts that must occur to enhance firm collaboration. First, collaborative relationships must encourage the mutual trust and value needed to develop and sustain coordinated operations and strategies. True collaboration is not dominated by or self-serving to one party in the arrangement; there must be a shared vision and objectives among customers and suppliers about interdependency and principles of collaboration. Efforts to achieve objectives must focus on providing the best end customer value regardless of where along the supply chain the necessary competencies exist. This perspective is key to long-term supply chain viability.

Second, rules and agreements should clarify leadership roles and shared responsibilities, delineate guidelines for sharing proprietary planning and operational information, and create financial linkages that make firms dependent on mutual performance. They also should encourage risk and benefit sharing by detailing how rewards and penalties are to be apportioned across partner firms. Such sharing reflects commitment to the belief that individual firm performance is linked to overall supply chain performance. In addition, formal guidelines that define joint operating policies and procedures for handling both routine and unexpected events should be derived.

Finally, to be truly effective, collaborative arrangements also must be highly sensitive to the potential negative aspects of interlocking agreements. Specifically, participating firms must be willing to address difficult issues related to relationship deintegration far in advance of the actual need to dissolve a supply chain arrangement. Although most collaborative relationships are voluntary and, in effect, can be dissolved at any point, setting formal exit procedures is advisable to prevent disputes over assets. A clause relating to duration and termination of the relationship ensures that it does not outlive its usefulness to the participants.

Forecast to Endcast

The ability to share both operational and strategic information is a key characteristic of collaboration. As noted earlier in the text, operations in the prevailing distribution model are driven by forecasts. In essence, many firms continue to forecast activity levels and events that other participants in the supply chain already know. At the center of collaborative management is the ability to jointly develop supply chain plans to best serve end customers. In addition to sharing information itself, cooperating firms must redesign products, processes, and facilities to fully take advantage of the power of quality information. While forecasts will remain an important step in planning future activity and gauging requirements, they should not be used to direct day-to-day operations. A concerted effort must be made to reduce the number and horizon of forecasts.

The shift from forecasting to endcasting is receiving a great deal of attention now as a result of the **Collaborative Planning, Forecasting, and Replenishment (CPFR)** initiative. Improved forecasts are a widely acknowledged means to enhance supply chain performance, and there is some empirical evidence that they also reduce supply chain cost. While the concept is reasonably simple, its implementation continues to be difficult. The difficulty is due to suspect proof, lack of systems support, and lack of trust.

Many managers are suspicious of the measurements and environmental controls used in current examples highlighting the benefits of CPFR arrangements. Credibility of such practical experiments and managerial confidence in the results could be enhanced with greater control. Firms and researchers need to work together to design and complete experiments that will build the necessary credibility.

There also needs to be further information system development to facilitate the interfaces between the CPFR Internet-based exchanges and current planning systems. These system capabilities have been developed, but their implementation and refinement have not been as fast as desired due to the resources invested in implementing systems such as enterprise resource planning.

Finally, there is the trust factor that has limited other aspects of supply chain integration. Lack of trust between supply chain partners reduces the willingness to share tactical and strategic information such as forecasts, promotions, and product development plans. Enhanced trust will take experience and time. While considerable progress has been made, complete transformation will require greater support and confidence.

Experience to Transition Strategy

For years, the so-called experience curve has dominated strategic responses to market and competitive situations. Firms based their strategies on concepts that had achieved past success. Increasingly, however, firms confront unique situations about which they have zero or limited experience. For example, it is becoming common for firms to employ solely contracted resources (possibly including consigned inventories) for many supply chain activities. Most firms have limited experience in establishing and managing these relationships. A second example is the increasing focus on achieving reduced or negative cash-to-cash cycles. Today, new competitors have achieved success in traditional supply chains using a combination of e-commerce and direct logistics to operate on less than zero capital investment. This shift in measurement and practice has forced many firms to design and manage in uncharted waters. The point is that all the experience in the world concerning how the traditional logistics model works is of very little value in developing a strategy to confront this new competitive pattern.

During periods of intensive change, previous experience and existing infrastructure are typically among the most difficult barriers to overcome. Firms increasingly confront the need to reinvent processes that are performing adequately when assessed historically, but in fact are being dramatically outperformed by solutions tailored to new competitive conditions. Three changes must occur to facilitate the shift from an experience- to a transition-based strategy.

First, fundamental total cost-to-serve frameworks must be identified, documented, and refined. Through experience, most managers have created business models regarding the processes they manage. While these models are sometimes comprehensive, in many cases they are limited in scope and perspective. As a result, the decisions weigh heavily on past limited experience. In the future, new business models must include the organizations, activities, resources, and relative parameters of the expanded enterprise.

Second, managers need to develop skills in solving case situations outside their traditional experience base. This should include analysis of situations involving "fictional" products and markets where managers must rely on the application of concept rather than historical practice.

Finally, managers must develop expertise in the application and interpretation of decision support tools that are becoming more crucial in the conceptualization and evaluation of supply chain alternatives. Effective decision support system applications provide a broader range of nontraditional experiences for the manager of the future. The capability to identify new strategic patterns, accurately assess their likely performance, and manage continuous transition is becoming the leading-edge model.

Absolute to Relative Value

The key to long-term success is doing the things that attract and maintain the most profitable customers *and* doing them well. A traditional success measure has been absolute market share typically measured in gross sales dollars. A more sophisticated approach to measuring success may be the relative share a supplier enjoys in terms of key customer success and resulting profitability—the difference between revenues and cost. Many firms act to increase sales in response to market pressures only to find that escalating costs associated with the increased sales fully erode the marginal profits. The notion of relative value is to grow a larger share of the *profitable* revenue available in a business arrangement by a willingness to perform a broader range of value-added services while enhancing marginal profitability.

Some enlightened firms are beginning to accept and exploit this shift. They realize that efforts focused on serving profitable accounts can yield enhanced returns compared to those obtained by offering mediocre service to a wide range of customers. Such "average" service may oversatisfy some customer segments while undersatisfying other segments willing to pay more for better service. Often the result is loss in both revenue and profit in these marginal accounts. Thus, the true measure of successful growth may not be the absolute size of dollar sales but the relative share of sales received for value rendered. While there are many changes that must occur for this trend to materialize, there are two that are particularly critical.

To begin with, a wider implementation and acceptance of activity-based and segmental costing is required. Logistics information systems capable of accurately tracking cost components, assigning them to the correct segments, and producing credible reports for senior management must be employed. Sales and marketing involvement must be secured, as they have to accept the principle that more sales and revenue do not necessarily mean higher firm profitability. Logistical practices such as multicustomer transportation consolidation, cross-docking, mixing in-transit, and other operational innovations that improve efficiency and enhance relative value must be adopted.

Additionally, the financial markets must begin to place more emphasis on profit than on market share. While earnings per share and profitability are very important measures of performance, the financial markets do place some emphasis on share. This forces senior management to maintain share even when the marginal share is not profitable. Visionary firms are beginning to recognize this change, but the focus on relative value will evolve quite slowly as it requires major paradigm shifts. The concept is easy to understand; its implementation, however, requires major changes in management philosophy.

Functional to Process Integration

One of the oldest and potentially most productive trends is the continued migration from functional to process integration. While the work of logistics itself has remained relatively the same over the past decade and will continue to remain the same during the next 10 years, what has and will continue to change rapidly is how we view work. As pockets of power and control developed within organizations, the traditional notion of a department became synonymous with being departed from the rest of the organization. While departments may remain the preferred method of managing work, the reality is that process-oriented, self-directed work teams are increasingly the solution for significant breakthroughs in efficiency. Managers realize that functional excellence is only important in terms of the contribution functions make to the processes they serve. In terms of organization structure, the concept of functional departments is as obsolete as punch cards are to information technology.

The validity of trading costs among functional areas to benefit total cost is beyond question. Information technology extensions such as ERP are starting to support more sophisticated costing approaches, lessening the difficulty of measuring across functions. While there has been substantial progress, major opportunities to shift to the process focus remain.

First, while purchasing, production, logistics, and marketing functions have each been integrated within their individual processes, there has been less progress integrating between these areas. This divide is recognized by most managers. Further integration across a firm's major functional boundaries is the first step toward additional process integration.

Second, there must be substantial advancement of process integration with external supply chain partners, particularly with service providers. This requires more consistency in the definition, execution, and measurement of supply chain processes to establish common language and expectations.

Third, most employees will do what they are measured on and what they are paid to do. The challenge is to convert metric and reward structures from department-related budgets to coordinated process-related incentives. The reality and potential of meaningful metrics based on one plan, which in turn is based on one forecast, will increasingly become reality. There has been substantial progress in this area, but more opportunities remain as additional cost information and accuracy will lead to more refined processes with reduced duplication.

Vertical to Virtual Integration

Historically, firms have tried to reduce supply chain conflict by owning consecutive levels in the business process. Henry Ford's original business strategy is a legendary attempt at using ownership to achieve vertical supply chain integration. Ford's dream was full ownership and management of the entire value-creation process in order to reduce waste and increase relevancy. Ford's rubber plantations, ships, and foundries converted raw iron ore to a finished car in 7 days.

The problem with vertical integration is that it requires tremendous capital investment and an incredibly complex organization structure. Re-creating Henry Ford's vertical supply chain is infeasible today. Firms, therefore, must harness the expertise and synergy of external supply chain partners to achieve success. Virtually integrating operations with material and service suppliers to form a seamless flow of internal and external work overcomes the financial barriers of vertical ownership while retaining many of the benefits.

While many manufacturing and retail firms have traditionally worked with third-party logistics providers to handle physical movements of products, there is a growing trend to outsource knowledge processes as well. Staff and process design activities are being outsourced to consultants. Information design, collection, maintenance, and analysis are outsourced to information integrators. Knowledge specialization will increasingly become an activity considered for outsourcing by the virtual enterprise. The benefits of outsourcing such competency to focus on core business requirements will continue to drive firms from vertical to virtual integration. While most firms have taken initial steps toward virtually integrating their supply chains, relatively few firms have achieved full-scale implementation.

To move to virtual integration, three shifts must occur. First, managers who interface with material and service suppliers must learn how to manage assets and activities that they do not directly control and cannot directly see but whose performance they can and must monitor to ensure success. These suppliers represent a firm's extended family and will contribute as much to the future success or failure of the supply chain as any internal department. A firm's management strategy must reflect the recognition that a supply chain is only as strong as its weakest supplier link.

Second, supply chain partners must have a common vision of the total value-creation process as well as shared responsibility for achieving it. Firms must carefully identify and select partners with complementary visions, strategies, and operational capabilities. Partners must interface their operations in ways that reduce duplication, redundancy, and dwell time while maintaining synchronization. Additionally, firms must spread the risks and rewards of collaboration to solidify goal attainment. Evolving the structures to facilitate virtual integration is neither easy nor quick.

Finally, firms must extend management practices beyond suppliers to include suppliers' suppliers. Suppliers' views on resource needs and constraints, threats, opportunities, and weaknesses must be considered when setting goals, objectives, and action plans as they play increasingly vital and irreplaceable roles in creating end-customer value.

Information Hoarding to Sharing

Implicit in several of the megatrends is the need for supply chain participants to share information. The shift from a need to know mentality to relevant information sharing is a difficult transition for old school managers. Most, with years of experience in the trenches, have learned the hard way that information is power. It is becoming increasingly clear, however, that those who hoard information can only exploit it—they cannot leverage it. The immediate gains that are generated from such information hoarding pale in comparison to the cost savings and enhanced service that progressive firms find attainable through sharing relevant information with supply chain partners. The open deployment of information across the supply chain is the catalyst that enables effective integration.

Currently, the shift from information hoarding to information sharing is dependent upon technology. Primarily, the ease of use and low cost of the Internet are driving rapid change. This is presenting a difficult transition for managers who are measured and rewarded on traditional metrics for the following reasons.

First, effective information sharing is heavily dependent on trust beginning within the firm and ultimately extending to supply chain partners. Managers are slowly learning to share information although some still believe that sharing forecasts, sales, inventories, costs, and promotional or development plans will compromise their organization's competitive position. This is particularly frustrating when a manager's view of the organization encompasses only his or her own specific functional department. For this reason, information is often not shared among departments of the same operating unit. If managers do not share internally, it is doubtful that they will share information with supply chain partners.

The scope of shared information usually expands as trust is established. Initially, such tactical data as short-term forecasts and inventory availability may be provided to facilitate resource planning and product flow. Once the benefits of tactical sharing are realized, firms tend to become more open to sharing sensitive information on costs, product development plans, and promotional schedules. The automotive industry is a prime example of firms designating tier one lead suppliers that in turn coordinate and sequence the work of secondary suppliers. This supply chain strategy has significantly reduced cost and time of automobile assembly. Such benefits are totally dependent on information sharing. Eventually, long-term plans and strategies are revealed to develop and integrate logistics processes and resources across the supply chains.

Second, many organizations will not share forecast or planning data under any circumstances while others have adopted the practice of selling it to a third-party provider of competitive data such as Nielson or Information Resources (IRI). Some retailers, for example, view point-of-sale data as a valuable commodity they own and from which they can extract a profit. This is a short-term mentality. Managers must begin to realize that the efficiencies obtained through information sharing substantially exceed the profits resulting from the sale of such information.

Third, organizations that view information as a key resource manage its exchange in a confidential manner to reduce conflict when conducting business with competing suppliers or in serving competing customers. For example, a number of manufacturers have established separate cross-functional teams to serve competing mass merchants. The teams include personnel from both organizations in such areas as sales, marketing, finance, and logistics. Increasingly, shared confidential information is required to plan joint operations. To ensure that confidentiality is maintained, there must be credibility and trust between supply chain partners.

Finally, information sharing may take many forms. The most comprehensive is the exchange of data files and provision of direct access to databases. Shared employees, although not yet common, extend the process by providing a managerial conduit through which information flow among organizations can be coordinated and translated. Information also can be shared through third-party logistics suppliers who assign dedicated employees to shipper locations to ensure coordination. A substantial increase in information sharing is critical to enhanced supply chain integration and performance. Despite the historical inhibition, firms must begin to extend their willingness to share.

Training to Knowledge-Based Learning

In the foreseeable future the logistics process will remain human-centric. Effective management of the logistics process, however, is complicated by the fact that over 90 percent of all logistical work takes place outside of the vision of any supervisor. No other employees within the typical business enterprise are expected to do so much critical work without direct supervision as those who make logistics happen. For example, an unsupervised truck driver performs almost all the value created by moving a product from a shipping location to a customer destination. Truck drivers, in fact, may spend more time face-to-face with key customer representatives than any other company employee. The truck driver may not even be an employee of the firm that is making the shipment to the customer. Other examples include customer representatives and inventory planners. There is a critical need in these areas for employees who understand supply chain dynamics and can use information-based tools to develop and implement effective strategies.

While many enlightened executives acknowledge that this megatrend is one of the most critical they face, practice indicates that not much progress is being made. Those trying to implement knowledge-based learning are having problems finding the time and the appropriate methods to effectively train employees. Training time is difficult to find due to the manpower reductions that have been forced on most firms. It is difficult to find the appropriate training approaches as they must integrate across a number of functional areas and incorporate multiple technologies. The challenges of effective human resource management are being complicated by increased globalization. There are significant changes needed to achieve an environment of knowledge-based learning.

To begin with, senior management must improve capabilities to manage a diverse workforce. Training must shift from emphasizing individual employee skill training to developing knowledge-based learning. This means that skill development must be placed in the context of the overall process in terms of objectives, dynamics, and measurements. For example, truck drivers certainly must be skilled in all facets of driving. However, they also need to possess knowledge concerning how they fit into the logistical process and how to access expert data warehouses, tracking capabilities, and adaptive decision support systems to resolve and prevent operating problems. Some forms of knowledge generation are as simple as learning how to cooperate. Others may require astute skills to identify emerging trends or observe competitive superiority.

In addition, it is becoming increasingly clear that firms must build the knowledge capabilities of key managers and planners. These individuals must be provided the education and experience that enable them to build an understanding of the risks and benefits inherent in supply chain integration and the relationships between supply chain partners. In a world where all logistics and supply chain employees are relatively high-paid specialists, the firms that develop and maintain broad-based supply chain managers will exploit the winning formula.

Managerial Accounting to Value-Based Management

For decades firms have been managed by the numbers. Over the last 10 years, however, managers have become sufficiently aware of the limitations of generally accepted accounting procedures to be willing to spend significant resources on managerial accounting methods such as activity-based costing. These methods improve managers' understanding of the dynamics of integrating internal and external functional activities. They also provide the metrics managers need to support strategic and tactical decisions.

Today managers seek to extend measurement to assess how their work drives stakeholder value. Recent developments, driven in part by widespread adoption of economic value-added (EVA) and market value-added (MVA), are resulting in integrative frameworks to implement value-based management. Value-based management is closely related to the basic paradigm shift toward financial sophistication. In fact, value management is appropriately viewed as the implementation of financial sophistication. The key is to identify and support activities that create value as contrasted to those that only increase revenue or decrease cost.

This megatrend has long been recognized as particularly relevant for operational managers. Unfortunately, it has taken a considerable amount of time and effort to gain senior management's attention. Current initiatives to link operations to value-based performance are facilitated by commitment to ERP implementation. The trend is likely to take off now that supply chain management concepts are receiving increased acceptance by the financial community.

Although the drive toward value-based management remains in its infancy, managers are increasingly forced to demonstrate how supply chain practice and process changes can affect the overall financial health of their enterprise. Traditional performance measures do not describe achievement in the financial language spoken in the executive suite. Measurement systems must enable managers to link supply chain performance directly to financial performance.

There are three transformations required to apply value-based management. First, firms must identify and assign the benefits of specific initiatives to the appropriate supply chain partner. Activity-based costing approaches provide one way for firms to measure performance across functional areas and focus on benefits associated with a specific activity or process. Total cost and activity-based methods enable firms to pinpoint the profitability of specific products, customers, and supply chains, as well as project cost/revenue outcomes for different programs and strategies. These approaches enable managers to set goals for specific actions and programs and to measure achieved performance. They have the potential to relate customer sales and profitability based on exact costing of ordering practices and delivery expectations. This precise cost information can be used to modify supply chain practices. For example, managers can work with specific customers to develop new routines that simplify and streamline order placement, resulting in better service as well as lower cost.

Second, there must be a change in the way benefits are measured. A few firms have adopted a comprehensive value model that incorporates operational excellence and asset utilization perspectives to assess value-based management decisions. Key operational excellence metrics focus on increased customer service and lowest total cost of ownership. The combination allows the supply chain to respond more precisely to specific customer needs. Customer service measurement is associated with revenue and is assessed by developing a set of shared cross-functional and cross-organizational measures to guide and monitor work performed by multiple supply chain partners as they add value for the end customer. Lowest total cost of ownership incorporates all basic product costs as well as all supply chain costs related to inventory financing, acquisition, processing, movement, storage, handling, and delivery.

Asset utilization measures a supply chain's effectiveness in terms of fixed assets and working capital. Fixed assets include manufacturing and distribution facilities, transportation and materials handling equipment, and information technology hardware. Working capital reflects the supply chain's inventory investment and the differential investment in accounts receivable relative to accounts payable. Overall asset utilization is a particularly important measure of firm and overall supply chain performance as viewed by the financial market.

Finally, firms must alter performance achievement reporting. EVA has become an increasingly popular indicator of financial performance. EVA monitors the level of value created by a firm. It allows stockholders to determine whether management is creating or destroying wealth. EVA is calculated as annual operating profit after tax, minus a cost of capital charge. The measurement is a reminder to companies that a short-term increase in the share price of stock is not a justification for revenue growth at any cost. Rather, earnings growth should be faster than new capital expansion. The theory is that no matter how good the numbers look, a company is not creating value to stockholders until it provides a profit greater than its cost of capital.

Associated Risks

Transformations associated with the ten megatrends highlighted above should enhance supply chain performance over the next decade. They also, however, introduce some risks that merit consideration as change is contemplated: (1) dependence on real time connectivity, (2) channel balance of power, (3) vulnerability of global operations, and (4) vulnerability stemming from strategic integration, information sharing, and technology investment.

First, real time connectivity enables reduced supply chain uncertainty and inventory. Lack of inventory buffers, however, reduces availability of critical items when communication or transportation systems fail to perform at anticipated service levels. Second, while there has been a significant shift in distribution channel power from manufacturers to retailers, it is still reasonably balanced. Increased Internet usage has helped to maintain that balance. Continued consolidation of megaretailers, however, could shift that balance. Third, global operations introduce substantial supply chain vulnerability. In addition to distance and time, global operations introduce significant diversity in the political, legal, labor, cultural, and economic environment. This vulnerability reduces firm control and frequently removes managers from their areas of competency. The result is enhanced potential for supply chain failures. Finally, the enablers of collaborative supply chain approaches expose the firm to considerable risk. High-profile failures of strategic partnerships have contributed to managers' reluctance to share information. The significant technology investment required to link far-flung markets and operations has also posed a significant risk that many firms have been unwilling to take. Until believable returns on technology investments can be documented, many firms will remain on the sidelines of meaningful change.

Despite the risks, most executives will be challenged to undertake substantial supply chain logistical change. Unfortunately, few managers have been trained in change management and most have limited experience with successful change. It is important that executives understand the dynamics of change and take steps to self-develop their change management knowledge and skills. The education process starts with understanding the basic challenges of change.

The first challenge of supply chain change is that a business process that provides some level of performance is almost always in place. Rarely does change management commence from ground zero. Supply chain change improves a process or practice that isn't broken and, in the minds of some, doesn't need to be fixed. The second challenge is that successful supply chain logistical change requires comprehensive, long-term leadership and planning. Typically, logistics operating policies, procedures, and systems are developed at different times and motivated by different circumstances to solve a particular need. Although each may be an appropriate solution, the supply chain that results typically lacks integration and cohesiveness.

Finally, supply chain logistical change requires the alignment of operations outside the direct control of a specific executive and often outside the firm itself. It is estimated that as little as 20 percent of the scope of a typical logistical change initiative is within the direct control of a firm's logistics organization. The remaining 80 percent typically involve the responsibilities of managers from other business areas. Thus, logistical change leaders must sell ideas and serve as cross-functional catalysts. Managing change through others is a difficult task that logistics leaders need to master.

Epilogue

In the final analysis, the logistical management challenge is to rise above traditional incremental thinking in an effort to help capture and promulgate the need for businesses to reinvent what they are all about. What they should be about is very simple—servicing customers. While it is sometimes hard to comprehend why, the fact is that most business firms are in need of significant reengineering to reposition resources to most effectively and efficiently accomplish this basic goal. For a host of reasons, complexity dominates the modern enterprise. Reinvention of a business is all about simplification and standardization. It is all about getting back to basics. Logistics is basic.

The logistics manager of the future will be much more of a change agent and much less of a technician. The challenge of change will be motivated by the need to synchronize the speed and flexibility of logistical competency into the process of creating customer value. Technology and technique will not be limiting factors. If no new technology is invented for a decade or more, we will still not have fully exploited what is currently available. The techniques being promoted as new ways to improve productivity are for the most part old and quite adequate to perform—costing, time-based competition, ABC inventory analysis, continuous replenishment, quick response, segmentation, and so forth. What is new is that today's manager is using information technology to make them work.

Of course, the challenge to reinvent the enterprise is not the sole responsibility of logistics, but it *is* a responsibility of logistical managers to participate in the process, especially those who direct global operations, have stewardship for extensive capital and human resources, and facilitate the actual delivery of products and services to customers. The logistical executive of the future will not be able to neglect responsibility for contributing to and participating in the change management required to reinvent the enterprise.

To this end, authors typically collect quotations and statements that they feel capture the meaning and intensity of their message. To the logistics manager of today and tomorrow who will face the challenges of change, we offer the following quotes as a source of compassion and inspiration:

Concerning Change: Logistics Is Not an Ordinary Occupation

Experience teaches that men are so much governed by what they are accustomed to see and practice, that the simplest and most obvious improvements in the most ordinary occupations are adapted with hesitation, reluctance and by slow graduations.

Alexander Hamilton, 1791

Concerning Organization: It Is a Matter of Perspective

We trained hard . . . but it seemed that every time we were beginning to form up into teams we would be reorganized. I was to learn later in life that we tend to meet any new situation by reorganizing; and a wonderful method it can be for creating the illusion of progress while producing confusion, inefficiency and demoralization.

Petronius, 200 B.C.

Concerning New Ideas: Every Dog Has Its Day

One may even dream of production so organized that no business concern or other economic unit would be obligated to carry stocks of raw materials or of finished goods . . . picture supplies of every sort flowing into factories just as machines are ready to use them; goods flowing out to freight cars and trucks just pulling up to shipping platforms; merchandise arriving at the dealer's shelves just when space was made available . . . under such conditions the burden of expense and risk borne by society because of the stocks necessary to the production process would be at a minimum.

Leverett S. Lyon, 1929

Concerning Appreciation: What Have You Done for Me Lately?

The Logistician

Logisticians are a sad and embittered race of men who are very much in demand in war, and who sink resentfully into obscurity in peace. They deal only in facts, but must work for men who merchant in theories. They emerge during war because war is very much a fact. They disappear in peace because peace is mostly theory. The people who merchant in theories, and who employ logisticians in war and ignore them in peace, are generals.

Generals are a happily blessed race who radiate confidence and power. They feed only on ambrosia and drink only nectar. In peace, they stride confidently and can invade a world simply sweeping their hands grandly over a map, pointing their fingers decisively up terrain corridors, and blocking defiles and obstacles with the sides of their hands. In war, they must stride more slowly because each general has a logistician riding on his back and he knows that, at any moment, the logistician may lean forward and whisper: "No, you can't do that." Generals fear logisticians in war and, in peace, generals try to forget logisticians.

Romping along beside generals are strategists and tacticians. Logisticians despise strategists and tacticians. Strategists and tacticians do not know about logisticians until they grow up to be generals—which they usually do.

Sometimes a logistician becomes a general. If he does, he must associate with generals whom he hates; he has a retinue of strategists and tacticians whom he despises; and, on his back, is a logistician whom he fears. This is why logisticians who become generals always have ulcers and cannot eat their ambrosia.

Author and date unknown

Cases for Part I—Integrative Management

Case 1   Integrated Logistics for DEP/GARD
Case 2   Woodmere Products
Case 3   Zwick Electrical
Case 4   Alternative Distribution for SSI

Cases for Part IV—Network Design

Case 5   A System Design Assessment at Westminster Company
Case 6   Michigan Liquor Control Commission
Case 7   W-S-P Chemical Company
Case 8   Western Pharmaceuticals (A)
Case 9   Western Pharmaceuticals (B)

Cases for Part V—Supply Chain Management

Case 10   Customer Service at Woodson Chemical Company
Case 11   Performance Control at Happy Chips, Inc.
Case 12   Change Management at Wilmont Drug Company
Case 13   Supply Chain Management at Dream Beauty Company

Case 1: Integrated Logistics for DEP/GARD

Steve Clinton

Tom Lippet, sales representative for DuPont Engineering Polymers (DEP), felt uneasy as he drove to his appointment at Gard Automotive Manufacturing (GARD). In the past, sales deals with GARD had proceeded smoothly. Oftentimes competitors were not even invited to bid on the GARD business. Mike O'Leary, purchasing agent at GARD, claimed that was because no competitor could match DEP's product quality.

But this contract negotiation was different. Several weeks before the contract renewal talks began, O'Leary had announced his plan to retire in 6 months. GARD management quickly promoted Richard Binish as O'Leary's successor. Although Binish had been relatively quiet at the previous two meetings Lippet sensed that it would not be business as usual with Binish. While the contract decision ultimately depended upon O'Leary's recommendation, Lippet felt Binish might pose a problem.

Binish, 35, had worked for a Fortune 500 firm following completion of his undergraduate degree in operations management. While with the Fortune 500 firm Binish had become extensively involved with JIT and quality programs. He had returned to school and earned an MBA with a concentration in purchasing and logistics. Eager to make his mark, Binish had rejected offers to return to large corporations and instead accepted GARD's offer in inventory management.

GARD, an original equipment manufacturer (OEM) for U.S. auto producers and aftermarket retailers, makes a wide variety of plastic products for automobiles and light trucks. Examples of GARD products are dashboards, door and window handles, and assorted control knobs. When Binish began working with GARD's inventory management he applied the 80/20 rule, illustrating to management that 80 percent of GARD's business was related to 20 percent of its product line. Over the next 3 years, as contracts expired with customers and suppliers, Binish trimmed GARD's product line. GARD management was impressed with the positive impact on GARD's profits as unprofitable contracts and products were discarded. A trimmer product line composed primarily of faster-moving products also resulted in higher inventory velocity.

So, when O'Leary announced his retirement plans, management immediately offered Binish the position. After taking a few days to review GARD's purchasing practices Binish felt he could make an impact. He accepted management's offer. As he learned his way around the purchasing department Binish tried to stay in the background, but he soon found himself questioning many of O'Leary's practices. He particularly disdained O'Leary's frequent "business lunches" with long-time associates from GARD suppliers. Despite these feelings Binish made an effort to not be openly critical of O'Leary. Such efforts did not, however, prevent him from asking more and more questions about GARD's purchasing process.

O'Leary, for his part, felt his style had served GARD well. Prices were kept low and quality was generally within established parameters. Although O'Leary typically maintained a wide network of suppliers, critical materials were sourced from a limited number of them. In those cases contract bids were a ritual, with the winner known well in advance.

DEP was one such winner. Its polymers were a critical feedstock material in GARD's manufacturing process. When O'Leary began sourcing from DEP nearly 15 years ago, there was no question that DEP polymers were the best on the market. GARD's production managers rarely complained about production problems caused by substandard polymers. O'Leary reasoned that the fewer complaints from manufacturing, the better.

"Hi, Tom! Come on in! Good to see you. You remember Richard Binish, don't you?" Lippet's spirits were buoyed by O'Leary's cheery greeting.

"Absolutely! How are you, Richard? Coming out from the old horse's shadow a bit now?"

This case was prepared for class discussion. Actual facts have been altered to maintain confidentiality and provide an enhanced business situation.

Binish politely smiled and nodded affirmatively. Light banter continued as the three moved down the hallway to a small conference room.

"Well, great news, Tom! DEP has the contract again!" O'Leary paused, then continued, "But there's going to be a slight modification. Instead of the traditional 2-year contract we're only going to offer a 1-year deal. Nothing personal, just that management feels it's only fair to Richard that these last contracts I negotiate be limited to a year. That way he doesn't get locked into any deals that might make him look bad!" O'Leary roared with laughter at his last comment.

"It is certainly no reflection on DEP," Richard interjected. "It simply gives me a chance to evaluate suppliers in the coming year without being locked into a long-term contract. If my evaluation concurs with what Mr. O'Leary has told me about DEP I see no reason that our successful relationship won't continue."

"Entirely understandable," replied Tom as his mind pondered the meaning of Binish's *evaluation*. "I'm confident you'll find DEP's service and product every bit as good as Mike has told you."

Following the meeting O'Leary invited Lippet to join him for a cup of coffee in GARD's lunchroom. Binish excused himself, saying he had other matters to attend to.

As they enjoyed their coffee, O'Leary sighed. "You'll be seeing some changes coming, Tom. The best I could do was get you a year."

"I'm not sure I understand. As far as I know GARD's never had a major problem with DEP's products."

"We haven't," O'Leary replied. "At least not under the guidelines I hammered out with management. But there will be some changes by next year."

"Such as?"

"Well, you remember when I started buying from DEP? You were the leaders, no question about it. Now I knew some other suppliers had moved up since then but I figured, hey, if it ain't broke don't fix it! As long as DEP's price was in line, I knew I wouldn't have any troubles with manufacturing. Less headaches for me. Now it turns out that Binish has some other ideas about purchasing. I can tell you for a fact that he's sampled several lots of DEP feedstock. He's also invited other potential suppliers to submit samples. The long and short of it is that there's not much difference between DEP and the competition in terms of product."

"I still don't clearly understand the problem, Mike."

"In Binish's terms, product merely becomes a 'qualifying criterion.' If everyone's product is comparable, especially in something such as polymer feedstock, how do you distinguish yourself? Binish claims companies will need to demonstrate something called 'order winning criteria' to get our business in the future."

"I still don't see a problem. We have our reviews with GARD every year. Our service performance has always been found to be acceptable."

"True. But acceptable according to my guidelines. Let me throw a number at you. On average GARD schedules delivery 10 days from date of order. I count on-time delivery as plus or minus 2 days from scheduled delivery date. That's a 5-day service window. GARD's minimum service threshold within this 5-day window is 95 percent. DEP had a 96.2 percent record last year using my window. Do you know what Binish is talking?"

"Probably 3?"

"Exactly. And do you know what DEP's performance is if we use a 3-day service window?"

"No, Mike, I really don't."

"Well, Tom. Sorry to tell you it's 89.7 percent. Worse yet, with Binish not only will the window decline but also the threshold level will be bumped up to 96 percent. And, that's only going to be for the first 3 years after I retire. After that Binish is shooting for same-day delivery only with 96.5 percent service capability. Right now using same day DEP only has 80 percent flat. You aren't even close to being in the game."

"So we've got a 1-year contract essentially to demonstrate that we can deliver service as well as product?"

"You understand the problem now."

TABLE 1   **Performance Statistics of Compound Suppliers**

Supplier	Chemical Compounds					
	A	**B**	**C**	**D**	**E**	**F**
Company 1	60%	60%			15%	15%
	3–8 days	2–9 days			5–8 days	6–9 days
	93%	94.5%			92%	94%
Company 2	25%	25%	15%	15%		
	4–6 days	3–4 days	2–4 days	2–4 days		
	95%	96%	98%	98.7%		
Company 3	15%	15%			25%	25%
	2–5 days	2–4 days			5–9 days	4–6 days
	95.5%	98%			97.5%	98.7%
Company 4			60%	60%		
			4–9 days	2–9 days		
			96.5%	97%		
Company 5					60%	60%
					4–7 days	4–6 days
					98.3%	97%
Company 6			25%	25%		
			3–6 days	3–5 days		
			98.4%	96%		

Entries list percentage of business, delivery time from order, and fill rate, respectively.

Polymer feedback production requires a mixture of chemical compounds. DEP's manufacturing process relies heavily on six principal compounds (A–F). DEP's current procurement policy is to source each of these compounds from three sources determined through an annual bidding process. Typically the firm with the lowest price is considered the best bid. The top bid receives 60 percent of DEP's business while the other two firms receive 25 percent and 15 percent, respectively. Management feels this policy protects DEP from material shortages and unreasonable price increases. Table 1 indicates the current compound suppliers and their performance statistics (percentage of business, delivery time from order date, fill rate).

DEP currently uses the following performance criteria:

1. Delivery of A: On-time considered 4 days from date of order ± 2 days.
2. Delivery of B: On-time considered 4 days from date of order ± 2 days.
3. Delivery of C: On-time considered 4 days from date of order ± 2 days.
4. Delivery of D: On-time considered 5 days from date of order ± 2 days.
5. Delivery of E: On-time considered 6 days from date of order ± 2 days.
6. Delivery of F: On-time considered 6 days from date of order ± 2 days.
7. Minimum acceptable fill rate on all compounds is 92 percent.

The manufacture of polymer feedstock is highly standardized. DEP has continually invested in technologically advanced manufacturing equipment. As a result, DEP can quickly change processes to manufacture different polymers.

To avoid material shortages and thereby maximize production, DEP normally maintains a 7-day supply of each compound. An earlier attempt at JIT manufacturing was abandoned after DEP experienced material shortages and production shutdowns. As a result, the manufacturing department is opposed to any reimplementation of JIT-type concepts.

The manufacturing department is electronically linked to the procurement and marketing/sales departments. Marketing/sales receives customer orders by phone or facsimile. The orders are then entered into the information system. This allows manufacturing to monitor incoming materials shipments as well as schedule production runs. Under this system most customer orders are produced within 6 to 8 days of order.

Following production, orders are immediately sent to a warehouse a short distance from DEP. At the warehouse shipping personnel verify manufacturing tickets, match the manufacturing ticket with the purchase order, and prepare shipping documents. Once the shipping documents are completed, the order is prepared for shipment (e.g., palletized, shrink-wrapped, etc.) and labeled. Once a shipment is labeled, delivery is scheduled. Three to 6 days normally elapse from the time an order leaves manufacturing until it is shipped from the warehouse.

Physical distribution is divided between the private DEP truck fleet and common carriers. The majority of DEP's customers are within a 200-mile radius. DEP trucks service these customers via twice-a-week delivery routes. Customers beyond this delivery zone are serviced through common carriers; delivery time fluctuates according to location and distance but rarely exceeds 6 days from time of shipment.

Questions

1. Diagram the DEP/GARD supply chain. What stages are adding value? What stages are not?

2. Using the primary DEP suppliers (60 percent of business), what is the minimum performance cycle for the supply chain diagrammed above? What is the maximum?

3. Can the performance cycle be improved through the use of the 25 percent and 15 percent suppliers? What trade-offs must be made to use these suppliers?

4. If you were Tom Lippet, what changes would you make in DEP's operations? Why? What problems do you foresee as you try to implement these changes?

5. Assuming you can make the changes mentioned in question 4, how would you "sell" Richard Binish on DEP's next bid? What will likely be "qualifying criteria" and "order winning criteria"? Will these change over time? What does this suggest about supply chain management?

Case 2: Woodmere Products

Judith M. Schmitz

John Smith had just returned from what may prove to be one of his most important sales calls. John, a sales representative for a top furniture manufacturer, had been meeting with a representative from HomeHelp, a major home decorating retailer. It seems the buyer, Nan Peterson, and the product team she heads had just returned from the annual Council of Logistics Management Conference. At the conference, Nan's team had attended several sessions on time-based logistics strategies. Even though Nan and her team had just been exposed to the new strategies, they felt it had the potential for significant competitive advantage in their industry.

At the meeting with John, Nan explained that HomeHelp is an entrepreneurial company that encourages product teams to try new products and channel relations. The few rules a team has to follow are simple: (1) deal only with manufacturers (no independent distributors are contacted)

This case was prepared for class discussion. Actual facts have been altered to maintain confidentiality and provide an enhanced business situation.

and (2) keep costs low and service high. The second rule highlights HomeHelp's basic business philosophy. HomeHelp is a design and home decorating retail chain that follows the warehouse club format. As such, a premium is placed on maintaining low overhead to support an everyday low price (EDLP) strategy. Service is also a premium since HomeHelp targets two distinct customer segments: do-it-yourself consumers, who need special in-store guidance; and interior decorators, who need speedy checkouts and convenient delivery or pickup.

Nan explained that the team has been considering applying time-based logistics strategies to furniture. Such an arrangement had the potential to improve product availability for in-store customers while reducing overall inventory. HomeHelp's close relationship with professional decorators required continued attention to improve its profitability and to ensure long-term growth. Interior decorators need convenient and exacting service, and HomeHelp feels that time-based logistics applied to furniture could be an important step to improving profitability.

HomeHelp's main concern is that the furniture industry as a whole appears to be trailing other industries in terms of sophisticated logistics operations. For example, the furniture industry has invested little in information technology and maintains high inventories throughout the channel, including at the retail level. The results other firms reported for their innovative logistics applications gave HomeHelp a new insight into how an alliance with a furniture manufacturer might create a best practice distribution system with lower costs and less inventory.

Nan told John that his company, Woodmere, had the potential to achieve an exclusive distribution arrangement with HomeHelp if the two companies could create time-based logistical capability. Woodmere was chosen since the business press had recently featured articles on its new organization plan that focused on channels of distribution and leading-edge logistics strategies. In addition, Woodmere was beginning to invest in information technology. Nan felt both companies should be able to reduce overall channel costs and offer customers superior product availability. Her specific request was for John to formulate a tentative proposal within 3 weeks to strike while the iron was hot. Nan knew the timing and unexpected opportunity created a great challenge for Woodmere, but she explained that HomeHelp strives to remain leading edge. Furthermore, HomeHelp wants to increase annual growth to 20 percent and feels that furniture offers the best opportunities. As such, top management attention is on this potential business arrangement.

As John walked to his regional sales manager's office, it was hard to conceal his excitement. The potential agreement HomeHelp offered was enormous. However, the effort required to get all groups at Woodmere involved would be great. The first step was to convince top management of the unique opportunity so that a team could be formed to create the proposal HomeHelp was expecting.

John's boss, Frank Harrison, was on the phone as John walked in. John carefully planned his words while Frank finished his conversation. As Frank hung up the phone, John blurted out, "We've got the potential for an exclusive with HomeHelp, but they want a customized delivery system. The proposal's due in 3 weeks. I think we need the top brass in on this one. It's big."

Frank's reply was typical. "It's not April 1 again already, is it John? What's the problem with our current system? Three weeks! It will never happen." After John explained the meeting with Nan, Frank got on the phone to arrange a senior management review. Surprisingly, a business planning meeting was scheduled for the coming Friday. Frank and John could get on the agenda under new business. What a break! It was Wednesday and John began to reorganize his calendar to concentrate on the Friday meeting.

The first item John focused on was researching HomeHelp. He discovered that HomeHelp operated over 200 warehouse-style stores in 18 states with the average store being over 100,000 square feet and offering 25,000 different products. Typical sales breakdown is 50 percent wallpaper and draperies, 25 percent accessory pieces, 20 percent lighting and electrical fixtures, and 5 percent furniture. The potential for growth in furniture was clear. Furniture included fabric-covered items such as sofas, loveseats, and reclining chairs as well as wooden products such as tables, dinettes, and end pieces. HomeHelp was the industry leader with 10 percent of the $120 billion home decorating retail market. Forecasts indicate that the market will reach $150 billion by 2006. Industry observers predict that HomeHelp is positioned to enjoy up to 20 percent of total industry sales.

HomeHelp is dedicated to service. In-store classes illustrate design techniques, repair and installation procedures on wallpaper, drapes, and lighting and electrical fixtures. The classes are taught by HomeHelp's employees, most of whom are retired or part-time professional decorators and contractors. HomeHelp provides installation service in a majority of its stores as well as professional decorating services. Both services are offered on a fee basis.

Forty percent of HomeHelp's sales involve professional decorators. The remaining 60 percent come from do-it-yourself consumers. The professional segment is quite large, and HomeHelp works closely with this group to meet service requirements. Affiliated professionals, called Propartners, have separate checkout lanes, a commercial credit program, and delivery services. Currently, Propartners customers purchase only 10 percent of HomeHelp's home furniture. Nan feels that this low sales level results from two factors. First, the delivery service offered by HomeHelp is contracted out to local moving companies, with the cost to HomeHelp passed on to the customer. Delivery for a piece of furniture typically adds 8 percent to the price HomeHelp charges for the product. This increase makes the overall price of purchase within $10 to $30 of the price charged by the competition, which offers free delivery. The close price range, accompanied by the psychological effect of free delivery, prompts many Propartners customers to purchase furniture elsewhere. While not a major concern, the use of moving companies sometimes also creates delays so delivery promises are not always met.

Second, each HomeHelp store's inventory is restricted to display items plus a limited stock of fast-moving products. Typically, only 7 percent of all customer orders can be filled from store inventory. As such, if a store does not have a specific piece of furniture, an order for the item is forwarded to a regional warehouse where the item is taken from inventory and sent to the store the following day. Furniture is available for delivery or customers can pick it up 2 days after the original order, assuming the regional warehouse has stock. If the regional warehouse is out of stock, the piece is typically not available for shipment or pickup for 5 to 7 days because an interfacility transfer or manufacturer shipment is required.

Since many Propartners are working on remodeling/redecorating projects, unexpected problems and delays can easily cause schedule changes. On a day-in and day-out basis, the exact time of furniture delivery and installation is difficult to accurately gauge. Propartners would like to be able to place an order 48 hours (or less) before the expected completion to reduce cost of rescheduling. Working on shorter timetables would improve their efficiency and cash flow and is perceived by Propartners as a major benefit. Currently, Propartners buy mostly from independent distributors who have more flexible delivery programs.

Friday's meeting was long. Frank and John weren't scheduled to present until near the end and they hoped it wouldn't run overtime, forcing them to be rescheduled. Finally, it was their turn. Frank started the presentation and discussed how long and hard a struggle it had been to develop a relationship with HomeHelp. Then John spoke of the benefits. He built on the need to develop new business relationships because Woodmere was involved in an alliance with a retailer in financial trouble. This retailer, Happy Home & Living, had historically accounted for 25 percent of Woodmere's sales, but this figure was dropping dramatically. Happy Home & Living's erratic purchases were creating undercapacity in Woodmere's manufacturing facilities.

Furthermore, HomeHelp had a relationship with decorators, a customer group that Woodmere had been targeting under its reorganization plan. Woodmere's image was as a value leader— good quality furniture at a low price. Attracting professional decorators to its products would definitely enhance Woodmere's image. Furthermore, Woodmere hoped to have some direct contact with professional decorators to get firsthand information on upcoming fashion trends.

Finally, an exclusive arrangement with HomeHelp appeared critical for the future. Home furniture manufacturing is heavily consolidated among a few key players, meaning stiff competition. While the home decorating industry remains heavily fragmented, HomeHelp is a leader and appears positioned to grow faster than competitors. Even though HomeHelp currently only has 10 percent of the market share, they have unlimited growth potential and are often referred to as the Wal★Mart of the home decorating industry.

Reaction from senior management was mixed. While many were excited about the potential, they were also cautious. The long-term relationship with Happy Home & Living that had prospered for 50 years was clearly becoming a potential problem for Woodmere. Relying on Happy

Home & Living had created a false sense of security, and when Happy Home & Living suffered financially during the recessions of the eighties, Woodmere also suffered. Furthermore, Happy Home & Living's reputation as a quality retailer was beginning to decline. In fact, it was getting the reputation for providing low-quality, outdated products. Top management was afraid to launch another close relationship that tied Woodmere's success to another company. Frank responded that HomeHelp had achieved at least 10 percent growth each year for the last 15 years, even through the recessions. The main reason for this growth was its advertising strategy, which convinced consumers who couldn't afford a new home that they could afford to remodel/ redesign their current one.

Another concern was the shift in traditional operations necessary to support a customized delivery system. While no concrete evidence was available on the exact requirements of customized delivery, it was still apparent that the service being requested was unique and nontraditional and might require major reorganization and financial investment. Also, several board members wondered how traditional customers, not interested in time-based logistics, would benefit. Their specific concern was that the commitment to HomeHelp would increase the overall cost of doing business with all customers. In short, some customers would be overserviced at a cost penalty. John agreed these were serious concerns, but reminded the group of the potential benefits that could result from a successful shift to time-based logistics. Not only was the exclusive agreement with HomeHelp important, but this "test case" with a major retailer could forge a leading-edge path for Woodmere, resulting in difficult-to-duplicate competitive advantage. Furthermore, John was convinced that HomeHelp would make a move to time-based logistics in the furniture segment with or without Woodmere. After extended discussion, the group decided to assign a task team, with John as the leader, to take the steps necessary to determine if an arrangement with HomeHelp was in Woodmere's best interest and, if so, to develop the requested business proposal. The proposal would need approval before the presentation to HomeHelp. A special review meeting was scheduled in 2 weeks.

First, John felt the team had to detail Woodmere's current operations. Then, an appropriate time-based system would need to be defined and compared to current operations to isolate changes necessary to offer excellent service support. A modified system would also need to be outlined and the cost and benefits determined. The issue of coexistence of current and time-based response capabilities was also a concern.

Current Operations

Woodmere currently has two manufacturing facilities and six regional distribution centers. One manufacturing facility is located in Grand Rapids, Michigan, while the other is in Holland, Michigan. The Grand Rapids facility produces fabric-covered items, such as sofas, cushioned chairs, and recliners. The plant in Holland produces wooden items, such as tables and end pieces. The six distribution centers are located throughout the United States with one adjacent to the manufacturing facilities. Orders are received from customers electronically as well as by phone through sales representatives. Only 40 percent of Woodmere's customers are electronically linked to the ordering system.

Woodmere's manufacturing facilities forecast sales to create the production schedule. Forecasts are locked in 6 weeks prior to assembly. Three of the distribution centers carry a full line of product inventory and seek to maintain a minimum on-hand quantity for each product. When inventory hits the predetermined minimum, a restock order is sent to the appropriate manufacturing facility. The other distribution centers stock only the fast-moving products. When a customer order is received it is assigned to the distribution center closest to the customer. If the product ordered is not available, the required item is transferred from the closest distribution center that has the required stock. If multiple products are ordered, the original order is held until the out-of-stock item is available to ship so customers receive all requirements in one delivery. No shipments are sent directly from the manufacturing plant to the customer; all orders are processed through a distribution center.

Woodmere's customers are dealers at the retail level who maintain their own inventory of Woodmere's products. When customers' inventory is low, they place replenishment orders.

These orders are transmitted to Woodmere's designated distribution center. Distribution centers review their orders nightly in an effort to consolidate truckloads and schedule efficient delivery routes. When a full load is available, orders are assembled and loaded to facilitate sequenced delivery. Typical order cycle time is 3 to 6 days when inventory is available at the initially assigned distribution center. Interfacility inventory transfers typically add 2 to 3 days to the order cycle. When an item is backordered to a manufacturing plant, 8 to 12 more days are added to the order cycle. When factory backorders are required, a partial order may be sent to the dealer or retailer; however, no firm policy exists concerning when to ship and when to hold partial orders. Currently Woodmere uses a national for-hire carrier to handle all its outbound deliveries to customers and interfacility movements between distribution centers. This carrier is already working with food and clothing customers that operate on a time-based logistics system.

Time-Based Logistics

John felt it was important for the task team to talk with a representative from another company concerning its experience with time-based logistics. John contacted an old college roommate working at JeanJean, a clothing manufacturer, to see if he could help. John's old roommate, Phil Williams, arranged for John's team to visit JeanJean to discuss QuickJeans, its proprietary time-based system.

In JeanJean's system, retailers play a major role. When a product sells in a retail store, the bar code on that product is scanned, and the POS information is transmitted electronically to Jean-Jean. POS data detail the size, color, and style of product sold and are transmitted directly to JeanJean's manufacturing facilities where they are used to derive production schedules in response to consumer sales. Rapid movement of information replaces the need to forecast. To the Woodmere team, it looked as though information was being traded for inventory. Product replenishment was exact and done within days of the sale depending on each retail store's volume. For example, high-volume stores receive daily replenishment shipments whereas lower volume retail outlets are served less frequently. The time-based system was flexible and able to accommodate a variety of different replenishment styles based upon individual retail customer requirements.

This type of system reduces response order cycle time and inventory. Since delivery is tied to actual sales, consumer trends are responded to quickly, reducing obsolescence. Furthermore, daily or weekly replenishment cycles allow the retail outlet to carry significantly less inventory while improving stockout performance. JeanJean was also able to reduce inventory by 20 percent by timing production to POS data. This reduction was even more impressive when JeanJean explained that its sales increased by 25 percent. Even though transportation cost doubled, it was more than justified by the savings in inventory and the benefits of knowing for sure that product was needed to service customers.

The QuickJeans solution was technology-driven. EDI used to transmit POS data and bar codes were essential to making the system work. EDI was also utilized for invoicing and payments, advanced shipment notification, and delivery verification. This reduction in paperwork and clerical tasks benefited both JeanJean and its customers.

To implement QuickJeans, JeanJean had to change its fundamental business processes not just with its customers but also within its manufacturing plants. Flexible manufacturing required quick product changeovers to be fully responsive to the POS data. Furthermore, the ability to produce small runs of necessary product was a key requirement.

The management at JeanJean pointed out that one of the most difficult parts of implementing time-based logistics was the sales decline that resulted from "deloading the channel." This "sales hit" was created by the false sense of expected sales and anticipatory inventory that resulted from manufacturing according to forecast, not to actual need. JeanJean had to wait until inventory at the retail stores, retail warehouses, JeanJean warehouses, and manufacturing facilities moved through the channel system before QuickJeans began to work and show the expected benefits. This created tension among JeanJean's top management because it was a cost not originally expected when they bought into the QuickJeans program.

The main cost to implement QuickJeans was the investment in technology. For example, JeanJean invested over $1 million in scanners, lasers needed to make distribution operations fast

FIGURE 1

**QuickJeans:
A time-based logistics
system**

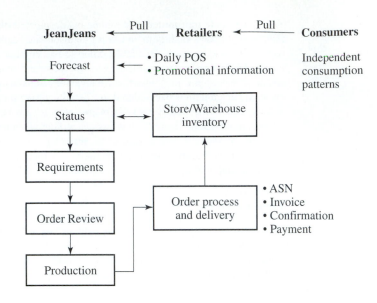

and efficient, and ticket printers to label products with retailers' unique bar codes. Key retailers spent close to the same amount to purchase new equipment to scan the bar codes. This investment was not a one-time deal, either. The need to reinvest to upgrade technology has remained constant from the start. Some retailers, especially locally owned stores, didn't want to participate in QuickJeans because of the initial investment. However, the retailers that participated were so pleased that most have placed JeanJean on their preferred supplier list.

JeanJean provided John's team with a flowchart of its QuickJeans operation as shown in Figure 1. The chart shows that daily transmission of POS data, as well as any promotional specials, is provided by the retailer. This information is used to calculate an initial production schedule. Inventory already on-hand in JeanJean's warehouse as well as in its retail customers' storage areas is subtracted from the schedule, creating production requirements for all JeanJean's products. These requirements are reviewed by an order specialist, who creates a final production schedule that is transmitted to the appropriate manufacturing plant. This order specialist also manages orders from retailers that are not involved in QuickJeans. All products are bar coded after manufacturing as required. Delivery is initiated by an electronic Advanced Shipping Notification (ASN) to tell the retailer what products are on the way. Delivery is direct to the retail store unless an alternative delivery site is specified. When the order is received at the designated location, the bar code is scanned and compared to the ASN and invoice. If the information matches, the retailer pays the invoice electronically.

The Proposal

John's team was finally ready to present its time-based delivery system to top management and they hoped the proposal would be accepted. The presentation to HomeHelp was scheduled in 3 days. The Woodmere task team had worked hard and was confident their proposal had strong selling features for both Woodmere and HomeHelp. The special meeting with top management was called to order.

The task team called the project "Customized Distribution: Creating Time-Based Customer Response" and began discussing how the proposal was developed, including the meeting with JeanJean. The team felt that Woodmere could benefit greatly from accepting the HomeHelp challenge.

Each HomeHelp store will transmit POS data on furniture sales at the close of each day. HomeHelp will not carry any Woodmere inventory in its regional warehouses and will carry only a limited amount of furniture and display items in each store. The POS transmission will include furniture items actually sold from inventory at the store and the furniture ordered, but not in stock. The POS transmission will be sent to a central information service. The information service will sort the POS data and compare them to inventory on hand at each Woodmere distribution center. Furniture in stock will be consolidated, while those items that are not in stock will be added to the production schedule and manufactured the next day. After manufacturing, the products will be delivered to the distribution center where initial consolidation of in-stock items will occur, and the entire order will be shipped out to the customer. After shipment, the on-hand quantities at the distribution centers will be examined to determine if a replenishment needs to occur. If the on-hand quantity is too low, a replenishment order will be sent to the appropriate manufacturing plant.

Questions

1. What are the major business propositions for Woodmere and HomeHelp to consider in evaluating this proposal? Is time-based logistics the right strategy for each company?
2. What are the benefits and barriers (short- and long-term) to this proposal for both Woodmere and HomeHelp? What other factors need to be considered?
3. If you were Woodmere's top management, what suggestions would you make to improve the current proposal for long-run viability?
4. If you were HomeHelp would you accept or reject the proposal? Why?

Case 3: Zwick Electrical

Steve Clinton

"Did the consultants come up with anything?" asked Wilton Zwick.

His brother, Carlton, nodded affirmatively. "There are several possible alternatives. In terms of alliances it looks like they have identified two potential partners. Here, take a look for yourself."

Wilton quickly scanned the report's front page. "Hmm, Asea Brown Boveri and Siemens?"

Carlton and Wilton Zwick are, respectively, president and vice president of Zwick Electrical Incorporated (ZEI), a privately held company. Carlton joined ZEI in 1983 after earning a marketing degree. After receiving an engineering degree in 1975 Wilton spent 4 years with an electrical-products division of a major firm in Pittsburgh. He then joined ZEI in late 1989.

ZEI began operations in 1952 when Gunther Zwick, Carlton and Wilton's father, opened for business in Cleveland, Ohio. In the early years ZEI's product line was limited to electric motors and parts. The company gradually expanded its product line to include power transformers, high-voltage switchgear, and metering devices. By the mid-1960s ZEI had added production facilities in Cincinnati, Ohio, and Louisville, Kentucky.

In 1978 gaps in ZEI's product line prompted the elder Zwick to purchase EL Transmission and Power (ELTP), a Memphis-based power transmission equipment company. Although ELTP's Memphis headquarters was closed, ZEI retained the Memphis distribution center and engineering department. ELTP's manufacturing plants in Chattanooga (Tennessee), Springfield (Missouri), and Shreveport (Louisiana) continued operations under ZEI.

During the 1980s no further acquisitions were made. The plants in Cincinnati and Chattanooga were significantly expanded to handle ZEI's increasing business. Minor renovations were made in the Cleveland and Springfield facilities.

This case was prepared for class discussion. Actual facts have been altered to maintain confidentiality and provide an enhanced business situation.

Although business took a sharp downturn in the early 1990s ZEI management remained optimistic about the future. At Wilton's urging the engineering staffs were increased and plans were made to build a modern facility in the Southeast. In 1994 ZEI opened a new plant and distribution center in Greenville, South Carolina. This plant specializes in power transformers and high-voltage switchgear.

In 1998 Gunther retired from ZEI. At that time he appointed Carlton as president of ZEI and Wilton as executive vice president. In reality Carlton is in charge of everything except product design. Wilton oversees product design and consequently works closely with the engineering and production departments.

Following the downturn of the early 1990s ZEI enjoyed modest growth until 1999. The American power business, plagued by overcapacity, had stagnated. It became obvious that ZEI's Cleveland, Louisville, and Shreveport plants were seriously outdated. A decision was made in 2000 to renovate Shreveport and close production facilities in Cleveland and Louisville.

This decision was particularly difficult for Carlton to accept. Carlton believed that ZEI could not expect loyalty from its workers unless it demonstrated concern for their welfare in difficult times. Wilton, although sympathetic to the plight of the workers, had been watching European and Japanese firms erode American's market share in the power business. He felt that ZEI must remain competitive. If that meant closing noncompetitive facilities, then so be it.

At this time the Zwick brothers also decided ZEI needed to aggressively pursue international markets. ZEI had sporadically exported in the past—but only if a foreign customer initiated the contact. Electing for a more proactive posture, ZEI entered into an agreement with an export management company, Overseas Venture Management (OVM).

OVM acts primarily as a manufacturer's representative for ZEI in Western Europe. OVM receives a commission on each sale of ZEI product plus a fixed rate for representing ZEI at European trade fairs. In 1998, the first year of the agreement, OVM sales represented less than one-half of 1 percent of total ZEI sales. That figure improved to slightly more than 1 percent in 1999.

The Zwick brothers were generally pleased with OVM's performance. Although OVM sales in 2000 and 2001 represented less than 3 percent of total ZEI sales, trade fair appearances had generated considerable interest in ZEI's line of power semiconductors (electronic switching devices for high-voltage transmission). In fact, power semiconductors represented 70 percent of ZEI's European sales in 2000 and 2001. In particular, the rebuilding of Eastern Europe offered a potentially lucrative power semiconductor market. OVM sales were expected to increase modestly in 2002.

Future growth in Europe was threatened, however, by stagnant economies and the fear of "Fortress Europe." In 1987 European leaders agreed, through the Single European Act, to create a single, integrated market. This borderless Europe opened protected markets, creating a large regional trading bloc. Some business analysts predicted that this trading bloc would erect trade barriers designed to protect European-domiciled companies, thus leading to "fortress" mentality.

Troubled by such predictions abroad and eroding market share at home, ZEI sought the advice of an international consulting firm. In initial discussions with the consultants the Zwick brothers had underscored three primary objectives:

1. *Maintain ZEI's access to international markets as regional trading blocs develop.* The Zwick brothers believe several of their products could attain substantial success abroad.

2. *Increase international sales of ZEI products at a greater pace than OVM had attained.* ZEI would like international sales to be 15 to 20 percent of company sales by 2006. The Zwick brothers doubt a manufacturer's representative will be able to produce that level of sales.

3. *Find complementary product lines from overseas suppliers to add to ZEI's U.S. product line.* Product development costs hamper ZEI's efforts to develop complete product lines in-house. Evidence suggests that ZEI is losing business to domestic and foreign competitors that offer more complete product lines. Many of those competitors enjoy substantially lower product development and production costs by developing and sourcing products from lower cost countries.

As the dialogue with ZEI continued, the consultants identified several areas of concern. First, despite ZEI's nearly 5-year relationship with OVM, the level of international business savvy within ZEI was quite low. Second, neither Zwick brother indicated any desire to relocate outside the United States. Third, the Zwick brothers were so accustomed to making their own decisions the consultants wondered how effectively they would work with an outside organization. Of course, the consultants also realized that foreign competition and sliding profits had convinced many American companies to reexamine the way they did business.

With that in mind, the consulting firm has suggested that ZEI consider, as one alternative, entering into a business relationship with either Asea Brown Boveri (ABB) or Seimens AG.

ABB

"I'd rather be roughly right and fast than exactly right and slow.
The cost of delay is greater than the cost of an occasional mistake."
—Percy Barnevik, president and chief executive, ABB

Guided by that kind of thinking, Percy Barnevik, in 1992, fashioned a merger between two prominent European firms: Asea AB (Sweden) and BBC Brown Boveri Ltd. (Switzerland). In typical Barnevik style the merger was quietly initiated and quickly concluded, deftly avoiding possible delays from government, union, or shareholder opposition. The result of this Swedish–Swiss merger, ABB, found itself with 180,000 employees and annual sales of about $18 billion.

Effective October 1, 1993, ABB reorganized into four business segments (power plants, power transmission and distribution, industrial and building systems, and transportation) and three economic regions (Europe, the Americas, and Asia Pacific). Each business segment is composed of distinct business areas (BAs). Under the new alignment ABB has 50 BAs. The bulk of its revenues is still generated by the power-related business segments. Chief competitors—GE (U.S.), Siemens (Germany), Hitachi and Mitsubishi (Japan)—have all diversified away from the power industry.

History. Prior to the merger, Asea AB and BBC Brown Boveri Ltd. were widely regarded as national industrial treasures in their respective countries. Each firm had earned that respect by developing and supplying products for nearly a century.

Brown Boveri, primarily a manufacturer of heavy-duty transformers and generators, had large customer bases in Germany and the United States. But the engineer-led firm had been experiencing declining profits since the late 1970s. An analyst's report identified "empire-building" subsidiaries as a major problem. Lacking a clear corporate strategy, many Brown Boveri subsidiaries independently engaged in R&D, marketing, and production. Such duplicative costs contributed to dividend-free years in 1986 and 1987.

In the late 1970s Asea AB was slowly growing, a dominant force in the Swedish electrical engineering and power plant market. That changed in 1980. Barnevik took over the firm and began to behave in a very un-Swedish manner. First order of business? Slash overhead at Asea headquarters. In the first 100 days, Barnevik reduced Asea's main office staff from 1,700 to 200. (This was to become a Barnevik trademark. In subsequent acquisitions the first order of business was always the severe reduction of headquarters personnel.) Responsibility was shifted downward as numerous profit centers, with specific target goals, were established. Throughout the 1980s other Scandinavian firms were acquired (Stromberg, Finland; Flotech, Denmark; Elektrisk Bureau, Norway) in an effort to widen Asea's electromechanical product line as well as its distribution channels. Further expansion took Asea beyond Europe to Asia and North America. In 8 years Barnevik tripled Asea's sales and increased earnings fivefold.

While on this acquisition/growth binge Barnevik was contemplating the future European landscape. A borderless Europe would open protected markets. For Asea that meant an opportunity to wrest part of the power plant market away from domestic firms. This realization eventually led Barnevik to approach Brown Boveri. The Asea/Brown Boveri merger, domiciled in Zurich, Switzerland, became official January 5, 1993.

After the merger Barnevik rationalized or streamlined the ABB workforce and then launched a series of acquisitions. In 1994 ABB entered a joint venture with Italy's state-owned Finmeccanica and completed a buyout of Westinghouse Electric Corporation's U.S. power transmission and distribution business. The following year saw ABB (1) assume control of Combustion Engineering, an American boiler and nuclear plant builder; (2) move into Eastern Europe with a majority position in Zamech, a Polish turbine maker; and (3) establish links with an electrical-equipment supplier, Bergmann-Borsig. In 1993 ABB acquired Bergmann-Borsig and continued its aggressive investment in Central and Eastern Europe by entering into approximately 30 joint ventures. By 2000, ABB held roughly 1,300 subsidiaries spread across Europe, Asia, North America, Latin America, Africa, Australia, and New Zealand. In 2001, it was reported that ABB would expand further into Asia and Eastern Europe.

ABB: Organization.   To control this far-flung network ABB employs a matrix organization, divided by products and geography. The four major product lines are subdivided into BAs. Each BA manager is responsible for setting a global strategy for that product line. That responsibility includes setting and monitoring factory cost and quality standards, allocating export markets among the BA factories, and personnel management and development.

Within each of the three primary geographical regions ABB is divided by country. Country managers deal with national and local governments, unions, laws, and regulations. They operate traditional, national companies. But the country managers also work across BAs by coordinating all operations within their assigned country. It is this latter role that links business segments and attempts to create an efficient distribution and service network across product lines.

At a still lower level is the company manager. This person is responsible for a single facility and its products. The company manager reports to two bosses: the BA manager and the country manager.

This matrix organization creates what Barnevik prefers to call a "multidomestic" rather than a multinational company. It is, in Barnevik's opinion, the multidomestic firm that can truly "think global, act local." Company managers are usually nationals of the country in which they are employed. Naturally they are familiar with the local customs and marketplace, but they are also forced to think globally because of the BA manager's global strategy (i.e., export markets) for the domestically produced goods. As a consequence, ABB plants typically produce a variety of products for the local market and a narrower line for export. The narrower line reflects the particular specialty or core product of the plant. Barnevik notes that this strategy forces a plant to be flexible to meet specific local needs while still producing internationally competitive products for export.

For the matrix system to work Barnevik tries to "overinform." Information is continually disseminated in face-to-face meetings between executive committee members and business area, country, and company managers. But it is Abacus, ABB's management information system, that ties the highly decentralized company together. Abacus provides centralized reporting to ABB's 1,300 subsidiaries and 5,000-plus profit centers.

In addition to traditional financial performance measures Barnevik reviews aggregated and disaggregated results by business segments, country, and companies. It is within this latter information that Barnevik discerns trends and problems. With little fanfare, the situation is discussed with appropriate ABB personnel. A course of action is quickly planned and implemented.

Siemens AG

Siemens, a German company, has 15 business segments: power generation, power transmission and distribution, industrial and building systems, drives and standard products, automation, private communication systems, public communication networks, defense electronics, automotive systems, semiconductors, medical engineering, passive components and electron tubes, transportation systems, audio and video systems, and electromechanical components. In addition, a 1990 merger with Nixdorf resulted in the formation of Siemens Nixdorf Informationssysteme AG (SNI). SNI, the second largest computer company in Europe after IBM, is a separate legal entity.

History. In 1847 Werner Siemens and J. G. Halske formed Siemens & Halske (S&H) to manufacture and install telegraphic systems. The company was successful and within 10 years found itself constructing an extensive telegraph system in Russia as well as developing the first successful deep-sea telegraphic cable.

Spurred by such accomplishments S&H diversified into other products. By the latter 1800s S&H had become involved in telephones, electrical lighting, x-ray tubes, and power-generating equipment.

Growth continued into the 1900s until the outbreak of World War I. With civilian demand dampened, S&H sought military contracts. During the war the company supplied the German military with communication devices, explosives, rifle components, and aircraft engines. Defeat of the German state carried a penalty for S&H. Its assets in England and Russia were seized by the respective governments. Despite such losses S&H continued operations, concentrating on electrical manufacturing. In 1923 S&H began producing radio receivers. Soon thereafter the firm once again moved into international markets, setting up an electrical subsidiary in Japan and developing hydro projects in Ireland and the Soviet Union.

War again interrupted S&H's business. During World War II S&H devoted the majority of its manufacturing capacity to military orders. The company's electrical skills were utilized in the development of an automatic-pilot system for airplanes and the German V-2 rocket. As a result, S&H factories were frequently targeted for Allied bombing raids. After the Soviet army gained control of Berlin in 1945, S&H's corporate headquarters was destroyed.

Following World War II S&H relocated its headquarters to Munich. By the early 1950s S&H was again producing a variety of products for consumer electronics, railroad, medical, telephone, and power-generating equipment markets. S&H established an American subsidiary in 1954. By the end of the 1950s S&H had broadened into data processing and nuclear power.

In 1966 S&H underwent a major reorganization. All subsidiaries were brought under the direct control of the parent company. In turn, the parent company reincorporated and emerged with a new name, Siemens AG.

By the 1970s Siemens had once again become a respected international competitor in electrical manufacturing. Siemens displaced Westinghouse as the world's number-two electrical manufacturer. This pitted Siemens against number-one General Electric in numerous markets in the 1970s through the 1990s.

Despite a series of acquisitions and mergers in the 1980s Siemens remains a Eurocentered organization. Sales in 1999 show that 75 percent of Siemens' sales occur in Europe, with 46 percent of that amount in Germany alone.

Siemens: Organization. From 1847 until 1981 a Siemens family member controlled day-to-day operations at Siemens. That changed with the retirement of Peter von Siemens in 1981. Since that time the company has been directed by non-Siemens family members.

Siemens corporate structure is based on the concept of decentralized responsibility. This philosophy is supported by a flat hierarchy and, consequently, short decision-making paths. Management believes that decentralized organization guarantees maximum market responsiveness in today's competitive environment.

The corporate structure is characterized by three primary divisions: groups, regional units, and corporate divisions and centralized services. The groups comprise the previously mentioned 15 business segments as well as several legally independent business entities (e.g., SNI). Headed by a group president, who has worldwide responsibility for their business activity, each group is intended to act as a stand-alone business, resembling an independent company.

The role of a regional unit is to implement the business goals of a group. The regional unit must encourage maximum local entrepreneurial responsibility while ensuring that local units understand each group's overall strategy. In most cases the regional unit deals directly with local subsidiaries.

The utilization of corporate divisions and centralized services is intended to separate staff functions from service units. Within the corporate divisions there are five main corporate departments: finance, research and development, human resources, production and logistics, and planning and development. These departments provide general guidelines and serve as a coordinating function in their particular area. This coordinating function supports each group's business while keeping Siemens' overall strategic goals in mind.

Having finished the consultant's report, Wilton Zwick leaned back in his chair and wondered about ZEI's future. He realized that ZEI's decision would, in large measure, determine the company's future. A misstep at this juncture might be disastrous. A correct decision, however, could launch a new era of growth and prosperity.

Questions

1. At what stage of global operations are ZEI, ABB, and Siemens? Justify your answer.
2. Beyond a simple sales perspective, why might ZEI want to consider greater international activity?
3. From a ZEI perspective what advantages and disadvantages do ABB and Siemens offer?
4. Alliances with ABB and Siemens are only one alternative contained in the consultants' report. What other alternatives do you think the report might contain?
5. What course of action do you think ZEI should pursue? Why?

Case 4: Alternative Distribution for SSI

Judith M. Schmitz

Sugar Sweets, Inc. (SSI), was considering ways to increase market coverage and sales volume on its candy and snack products. Historically, the majority of SSI products were sold to consumers through various grocery and convenience stores. Vending machines and institutional sales, such as airports, represent the remaining consumer market segments. The selling environment for candy and snack foods was becoming increasingly competitive and traditional channels of distribution were being distorted, especially in the grocery and convenience trade.

Grocery and convenience stores were traditionally serviced through distributors known as candy and tobacco jobbers. These distributors purchased SSI products in large quantities and then sold them to retail stores for sale to consumers. The number of candy and tobacco jobbers was decreasing, which was distorting the traditional distribution channel. Two factors were causing this distortion. First, the wholesaler and distributor industry in general was going through consolidation as large distributors continued to get larger and more profitable, while smaller and less profitable distributors either were bought up or closed. Second, the popularity of warehouse club stores threatened candy and tobacco jobbers. Small mom-and-pop grocery or convenience stores were able to purchase many products they needed at these warehouse clubs at the same price or less than what the distributors offered. Furthermore, the warehouse clubs provided a one-stop shopping experience so that the grocery stores could purchase a wider range of products at the club store than was sold by any one candy and tobacco distributor. For example, a club store may offer a narrow selection of the most popular SSI products as well as its competitor's products, while an individual distributor may handle SSI products exclusively. While SSI encouraged grocery and convenience stores to carry its products, regardless of whether these stores purchase products from distributors or club stores, there was a concern about how the products were serviced. Distributors provide a significant benefit in that they carry a broader line of SSI products than most club stores. Also, some candy and tobacco jobbers visit their retail customers regularly to ensure the stores remain stocked with a large variety

---

This case was prepared for class discussion. Actual facts have been altered to maintain confidentiality and provide an enhanced business situation..

TABLE 1   Alternative Distribution Concept

What is it?

• A unique new concept for distributing and selling SSI snack foods through new retail outlets to broaden market coverage.

How does it work?

• Display units of popular snack foods are provided to retail outlets for direct purchase by consumers.

• Fast-selling items are easily restocked by telephone order with an 800 number and rapid small package delivery service.

What are the special features?

• Minimal effort is required on the retailers' part since the popularity of well-known SSI brands makes selling easy.

• Freshness is guaranteed by direct shipment from SSI's warehouses through rapid delivery service.

• Incremental money is made by selling high profit "impulse" snack foods to customers at no risk since SSI will remove slow-moving products at no cost to the retail outlet.

---

of fresh product. In this sense, candy and tobacco jobbers provided a marketing service for SSI that is not achieved with club stores.

As such, SSI began looking for an alternative channel system that would not only increase market coverage in light of the new competitive environment but also provide the important marketing service to ensure a large variety of fresh product available for consumers. To accomplish this, SSI questioned the reliance on its traditional marketing channel, as well as the typical outlets through which its products were sold. Andy Joslin, the vice president of integrated logistics, had an idea. Andy began to focus on new retail outlets where SSI products could be sold and how these sales could be uniquely managed via a new channel arrangement. It was determined that direct store delivery of SSI products could be handled by using telemarketing for order processing and small package delivery. The notion was that any retail outlet that had sufficient counter space and high customer traffic was likely to sell high-impulse snack items such as SSI products. Examples of potential retail outlets that traditionally did not carry snack items included dry cleaners, barbers and beauty shops, hardware stores, and drinking establishments. The concept is summarized in Table 1.

The alternative distribution plan offers various benefits. First, it is a unique selling concept in that it provides retailers a way to increase their business through incremental sales of snack products with little risk of cannibalization by other retail outlets due to the impulse nature of the product. Furthermore, retailers are not required to make a significant capital investment to try the concept and there is little risk to the retailer if the plan fails. SSI will provide countertop units or shelving to display the products for sale and will suggest pricing for maximum sales volume and profit. The alternative distribution concept benefits SSI as well by providing market growth and exposing its products to a wider range of customers. Also, SSI will have direct contact with retailers, providing a great opportunity for testing and tracking new products while ensuring timely delivery.

One potential drawback is that the retailers may feel the incremental revenue received is insufficient, which will dissuade product reordering. Also, retailers may have pilferage problems that would discourage their participation. Finally, the arrangements could threaten candy and tobacco jobbers that rely on similar retail accounts. Resentment from candy and tobacco jobbers could potentially result in decreased service to grocery and convenience stores.

From initial interviews with target retailers, SSI became convinced the alternative distribution concept had merit. The next step was to evaluate whether the idea was a viable business decision in terms of retail interest versus actual participation. An internal operating plan for managing the alternative distribution program would also need to be devised to identify and determine the internal costs and potential profit.

TABLE 2   Retail Characteristics

Sales Regions	Total Number of Target Retailers
Eastern	320,000
Midwestern	290,000
Western	210,000

Percent of retailers for initial contact: 20%.

Projected retailers who will participate after initial contact: 30%.

Retailers who will continue after 6-month trial period: 55%.

Expected average retail sales transactions: $1.40 per customer purchase.

Expected average unit sale: 1.12 units per customer purchase.

Expected average customer traffic/retail store: 100/day.

Expected average number of customers who will purchase product: 10%.

TABLE 3   Initial Display and Product Package Characteristics

	Large	Small
Weight	25 lbs.	14 lbs.
Cubic Feet	2.75	2.00
Product Included	24 lbs.	12 lbs.
Cost of Display Unit	$35	$18
Units of Product	180	92
Production Costs	$190	$98

Retail Interest.   The research summarized in Table 2 illustrates important considerations for retail sales. Fifteen types of retail stores were targeted for participation, and 30 product lines were considered for distribution. Estimates concerning expected retail participation and sales were a critical part of business viability. To start, SSI estimated it could contact only 20 percent of all target retailers. The remaining retailers would be approached after a 1-year test period if the alternative distribution program was successful.

Two types of display units were designed as well as two reorder packages. An initial order would include two boxes shrink-wrapped together. One box would hold the product and the other would hold the display unit. Table 3 provides display and product package characteristics. Reorder packs would contain the same product weight and units as shown for the initial order.

Operating Procedures.   Two logistics networks are under consideration for the new channel. Both networks facilitate direct retail customer contact: no distributors are included in the channel. One network uses three distribution centers while the other uses four. Service for the first network is estimated at 2 to 4 days, with some outlying areas serviced in 5 days. Service through the second network is estimated at 1 to 3 days and to outlying areas in 4 days. The number of outlying areas is reduced under the second network. Table 4 compares the costs of both networks.

The information flow would start with order entry at the telemarketing department. Retail orders would be transmitted to the appropriate distribution center and compiled each night. Orders would be picked and packed, then delivery would be arranged based on the aforementioned service levels.

TABLE 4   Operating Costs per Order

Costs	Three Distribution Centers	Four Distribution Centers
Handling	$3.00	$3.00
Storage	.11	.21
Transportation of average package	6.25	5.90
Ordering costs/order	.75	.75
Total logistics costs/order	$10.11	$9.86

Summary.   Before SSI can determine whether the alternative distribution concept should be initiated, it must analyze the information gathered and project the potential sales and profits. Profits must be determined for SSI as well as for the retail customers. If retailers do not make sufficient incremental profit, it is unlikely they will continue participating in the plan. A team has been assigned to perform the data analysis. Andy Joslin has identified five questions he feels are critical for the team to analyze. These questions are provided below.

Questions

1. Determine the total number of retailers in the program initially as well as after the trial period.

2. Determine what the average retailer will sell on a daily basis as well as annually. Provide sales in terms of unit and dollar amounts. (Assume 260 business days per year, with 5 business days each week.)

3. Translate the annual sales for an average retailer into the number of large packs that retailers will order per year. Repeat for the small pack order. (Round if necessary.) Include the initial order in the calculation.

4. SSI would like to determine its potential sales for the first year on the basis of the information in question 3. However, there is some concern that the estimate of average retail sales is too high. SSI assumes only 40 percent of the participating retailers will actually achieve the average sales and reorders (this group is designated as high performers). Twenty percent of the retailers are expected to have medium performance success and will only sell/reorder 75 percent of the average suggested order. Low-performing retailers represent the remaining 40 percent and will achieve half the sales/reorder expected on average. Calculate the orders (separate initial and reorder quantities) for the 6-month trial period if 45 percent of retailers exclusively order/reorder large packs and the remaining retailers exclusively order/reorder small packs. Calculate the second 6 months accounting for the dropout. (Round if necessary.) Assume the "performer" ratios remain the same after the trial period (i.e., 40 percent are average performers, 20 percent sell 75 percent of the average, and 40 percent sell 50 percent of the average.)

5. Assume retailers pay $205 for a large pack (initial or reorder) and $115 for a small pack. On the basis of the first year's sales calculated in question 4, determine the profit to SSI if three distribution centers are used. Repeat for the four-distribution center network. Which network, if either, should be used? What factor(s) aside from cost/profit might influence the network decision?

Case 5: A System Design Assessment at Westminster Company

David J. Closs and Christopher Kitchen

Westminster Company is one of the world's largest manufacturers of consumer health products; its distinctive name and company logo are recognized throughout the world. Originally founded as a family-owned pharmaceutical supply business in 1923, the company's corporate headquarters are still located in a scenic town of 60,000 people in the northeast United States. Westminster also maintains regional offices in Europe, Latin America, and the Pacific Rim to support overseas manufacturing and distribution.

Westminster's domestic operations consist of three separate sales divisions—each of which manufacture and distribute its own product line. Decentralized divisional management is a proud historical tradition at Westminster. According to President Jonathan Beamer, it is a process that requires and encourages responsibility and self-ownership of the work process and provides the key component of corporate success. Westminster's products are marketed through a network of diverse retailers and wholesalers. Trade Class as a percent of sales is 37 percent grocery, 31 percent drug, 21 percent mass merchandise, and 11 percent miscellaneous.

Westminster Today

Pressure from domestic and global competitors, as well as large domestic Westminster customers, has recently forced the company to reevaluate its current distribution practices. In particular, attention has focused on the changes which will be required to effectively compete in the marketplace of the twenty-first century.

Westminster just concluded several months of extensive research which focused on customers' primary logistics concerns for the future. The research findings addressed a variety of issues, but two key topics were identified: customer composition and customer service requirements.

The most significant trend with regard to customer composition over the past decade has been the evolution of the company customer base into either very large or very small accounts. This development is expected to continue at a comparable pace in the foreseeable future; however, the major shift in the mix of accounts is not expected to dramatically alter the historical composition of product sales. Approximately 50 percent of domestic consumer sales volume is concentrated within 10 percent of Westminster's customers. What may affect the composition of product sales to large retail accounts is the rapid growth of private-label nonprescription drugs and consumer health products. Cost-efficient private-label manufacturers offer large retail accounts higher profit margins, willingness to quickly change or customize products, and the ability to appeal to increasingly price-conscious consumers. Specifically, the private-label health and beauty aids business totaled sales of $3 billion in 2000.

Research findings have confirmed top management's belief that these large accounts generally possess an intense commitment to increasing their firm's logistics efficiency. To maintain and increase the percentage of sales volume Westminster derives from these important customer accounts, the company has identified several key customer service concerns. These concerns specifically address the second issue of customer service requirements. Company research has also concluded that the formulation of supply chain partnerships between Westminster and its large customers has now become a competitive necessity. In many instances, powerful retailers now demand such arrangements and oftentimes have the leverage to dictate the conditions of the arrangements. Westminster will have to maintain considerable flexibility to accommodate different solutions for a variety of large, powerful customers. Ideally, Westminster would like to establish a position of leadership within these partnership arrangements where practical.

Westminster is well aware that successful retailers and wholesalers are heavily focusing strategic effort on more timely, efficient, and accurate inventory positioning. Many large firms have identified supply chain management techniques as a primary tool in achieving successful inventory management and improving overall financial performance. "I visualize three important changes for our operations with regard to large accounts," says Alex Coldfield, Westminster vice president of logistics. "First, traditional inventory replenishment procedures will be replaced by POS driven information systems. Customers will transmit daily or biweekly product sales movement to us in order to ensure timely inventory replenishment and allow production to be scheduled according to sales-driven forecasts rather than marketing forecasts. We will also establish and utilize customer support 'work-teams' that operate on-site with key customer accounts to better manage ordering and distribution. Second, order cycle times will have to be reduced from current levels. Large accounts will increasingly demand two rather than one delivery per week. In addition, many large accounts want to simplify their manufacturing contacts and are questioning why we cannot provide consolidated order shipment from our three consumer product divisions when cost reductions are achievable. The demand for direct store delivery (DSD) may also significantly increase. Third, products will increasingly have to meet specific customer requirements, such as assembly of individual store shipments, and customized inner packs and display units. Bar codes will have to utilize industry standards such as UCC 128. Invoicing and payment, particularly with regard to promotional allowances and discounts, will become paperless transactions conducted via EDI. Our pricing will evolve to reflect services provided, rather than purely traditional logistical order fulfillment, transportation, and handling."

For the balance of Westminster's customers, distribution service will be provided much as it is today. Although other customers may not be willing or able to initiate such close working relationships, they will be entitled to a high standard of basic service that provides timely and consistent performance. For these accounts, purchase price will remain the priority, although there will be some increased pressure for improved order fill rates and decreased cycle times. Traditional purchase order invoicing and payment will also remain the rule.

In response to the issues raised by company research, CEO Wilson McKee directed the company's executive management committee to organize a logistics taskforce. The taskforce, which includes top-level managers from each division's functional departments, has been directed to identify potential changes within the three domestic sales divisions' networks that will achieve improved distribution performance and responsiveness.

Westminster's Distribution Network.   Table 1 outlines Westminster's existing distribution network for the three domestic consumer sales divisions. Each division consists of a number of company-owned-and-operated manufacturing plants and distribution facilities. Table 2 presents a number of key demand and inventory statistics for the facilities.

Each manufacturing plant produces SKUs unique to that particular facility. All SKUs are distributed on a national basis. Due to significant capital outlays and fixed costs associated with each manufacturing plant, the logistics taskforce has already eliminated the possibility of relocating any manufacturing facilities from their present locations.

Manufacturing plants must route products through a distribution center before final delivery to a retail or wholesale customer. Any distribution center may be utilized within its own division. Distribution centers may ship product to any region of the country; however, customers are typically serviced by the closest distribution center based on Westminster's regional boundaries. Transfer shipments between distribution centers are also permissible.

Most shipments from manufacturing plants to distribution centers are delivered via motor carrier on a TL basis. Air freight may be utilized for emergency shipments, but also must pass through a distribution center before delivery to a final destination. Most shipments between distribution centers and retail or wholesale customers are delivered by motor carrier on an LTL basis and vary in size from a few pounds to nearly truckload quantities. Table 3 illustrates the three domestic sales divisions' shipments by typical weight brackets and the number of bills of lading issued within each bracket. The first weight bracket (0–70 pounds) represents shipments typically delivered by small parcel carriers; the majority of these shipments represent order fulfillment of back-ordered SKUs. Approximately 67 percent of all shipments are 500 pounds or less.

Distribution center locations are based upon both market and production factors. The majority of distribution centers are strategically located throughout the country to service geographic

TABLE 1 Westminster Company Facility Locations

Division A

Manufacturing Plants	Percentage of Total Pounds Produced	Distribution Centers	Percentage of Total Pounds Shipped
Los Angeles, CA	53%	Newark, NJ	28%
Atlanta, GA	24	Atlanta, GA	31
Jacksonville, FL	23	Dallas, TX	41

Division B

Manufacturing Plants	Percentage of Total Pounds Produced	Distribution Centers	Percentage of Total Pounds Shipped
Philadelphia, PA	39%	Philadelphia, PA	78%
Newark, NJ	37	Los Angeles, CA	22
Atlanta, GA	24		

Division C

Manufacturing Plants	Percentage of Total Pounds Produced	Distribution Centers	Percentage of Total Pounds Shipped
Chicago, IL	75%	Newark, NJ	38%
Houston, TX	10	Chicago, IL	54
Trenton, NJ	15	Los Angeles, CA	8

TABLE 2 Westminster Customer Demand 1992

Characteristics	Division A	Division B	Division C
Total Demand (000,000 lbs)	150	72	60
Sales ($000,000)	475	920	271
Cases (000,000)	13.2	8.5	9.8
Shipments (000)	80	88	73
Lines Ordered (000)	1,060	683	340
Inventory Turns P/Yr	6.5	10.8	7.2
Total SKUs	1,260	430	220

TABLE 3 Shipment Profiles

Shipment size	Percent of Weight	Percent of Shipments
Package delivery	6	25
< 500 lb	8	22
500 < size ≤ 2,000 lb	13	20
2,000 < size ≤ 5,000 lb	18	15
5,000 < size ≤ 10,000 lb	22	10
> 10,000 lb	32	8

TABLE 4   Westminster 2000 Distribution Costs ($000,000)

	Division A	Division B	Division C
Transportation			
Transfer freight	4.2	3.2	2.8
Customer freight	9.9	8.3	8.5
Total Transportation Costs	14.1	11.5	11.3
Warehousing			
Storage & handling	6.2	4.4	3.2
Fixed	2.3	1.6	4.2
Total Warehousing Costs	8.5	6.0	7.4
Total Distribution Costs	22.6	17.5	18.7
Average Number Days Transit Time (DC to customer)	2.8	2.9	2.3

TABLE 5   Hourly Wage Rate for U.S. Cities

City	Wage Rate ($)	City	Wage Rate ($)
Chicago, IL	$16.20	Laredo, TX	13.63
Seattle, WA	17.87	El Paso, TX	13.63
Buffalo, NY	15.59	Dallas, TX	13.78
Syracuse, NY	15.59	Detroit, MI	19.38
Pittsburgh, PA	16.96	Los Angeles, CA	16.96
Atlanta, GA	12.72	Minneapolis, MN	16.96
Houston, TX	15.14	Denver, CO	16.96
Phoenix, AZ	12.87	Memphis, TN	12.57
Kansas City, MO	15.90	New York, NY	15.14
Philadelphia, PA	15.75	San Francisco, CA	17.87

territories that contain the strongest demand for Westminster products. Demand patterns for consumer products follow major population centers and are generally consistent across the country for all three divisions. Several distribution centers are located near manufacturing plants to reduce transportation costs.

Table 4 lists the current system's transportation and warehousing costs for each of the three divisions. Freight rate classification for product shipments is different for each of the three divisions. Division A freight has a rating of class 60; Division B freight has a rating of class 70; and Division C freight has a rating of 200. Transfer freight costs are based on TL rates from the manufacturing plants to the distribution centers. Customer freight costs are based on LTL shipments from distribution centers to retail and wholesale customers. Average transit time (in number of days) from the distribution centers to the customer is the shipment time from the point an order leaves the distribution center's loading dock until it reaches a customer. Any potential systems redesign must consider the effect of labor costs. Table 5 lists average hourly wage compensation for a number of major U.S. cities.

The logistics taskforce is presently considering these three options or alternatives:

1. Consolidating the current three distribution systems to a single distribution system serving all three companies, using fewer warehouses than are currently being used.

2. Using public or third-party warehousing and third-party transportation rather than the current system network.

3. Continuing with the current arrangement as is.

Questions

1. What effects would the two new alternatives have on transfer and customer freight costs? Why?

2. What effects would warehouse consolidation have on inventory carrying costs, customer service levels, and order fill rate?

3. How are warehousing costs affected by the decision to use public or private warehouse facilities? What effect would this have on handling, storage, and fixed facility costs?

4. What effect would shipping mixed shipments from consolidated distribution centers have on shipment profiles?

5. What factors should be taken into consideration when determining the appropriate number of warehouses?

6. What selection criteria should be used when evaluating a service provider's (public or third-party warehouse, or third-party transportation provider) ability to meet critical logistical requirements?

Case 6: Michigan Liquor Control Commission

On a Friday afternoon in October 2000, Joseph Duncan, a third-year distribution systems analyst for the Michigan Department of Commerce, was sitting at his office desk reading through some background material on distilled liquor distribution in Michigan. Prior to his current position, Joseph had worked as a distribution analyst in private industry for several years after graduating from a large midwestern university with a degree in materials and logistics management. His direct supervisor, Donna Mills, had given Joseph his next assignment earlier that day. "Be prepared to head up a project team and prepare a proposal on distilled liquor distribution," Donna said, "We'll meet Wednesday afternoon at 2:00 P.M. to lay out an initial plan." This was Joseph's first "lead" project assignment, and although he was unfamiliar with the topic, he was excited about the opportunity to demonstrate his ability. He placed the background material in his briefcase and decided to reexamine it at home over the upcoming weekend.

History of Michigan Liquor Distribution System

In the early 1900s, brewers in Detroit were the dominant force in the state due to efficiencies of size, new bottling technology, and local "option laws," which restricted or outlawed in-county production. This created a sharp division between outstate and Detroit brewers and prevented the formation of a strong state liquor association. Prohibition forces also benefited from this divisiveness; by the year 1917, Michigan had 45 dry counties. Michigan enacted a statewide prohibition on liquor in May 1918, approximately 18 months prior to passage of federal Prohibition (the 18th Amendment). By the late 1920s and early 1930s, significant pressure existed throughout the country to repeal Prohibition. In early 1933, Congress passed a bill authorizing 3.2 percent beer. In the same year, a similar bill was considered in Michigan and along with it, the introduction of a state board which came to be known as the Michigan Liquor Control Commission (MLCC). In April 1933, Michigan became the first state to ratify the repeal of federal prohibition and the present-day liquor distribution system was designed and put into place.

A bill for beer and wine (defined legally as under 21 percent alcohol by volume) was passed that allowed distribution from brewers and wineries to private wholesalers who then resell to retailers. However, all distilled "spirits" (defined legally as over 21 percent alcohol by volume) were to be purchased by the State of Michigan. Michigan "come-to-rest" laws required that any distilled liquor moving through or stored in state bailment warehouses must be handled by state employees. Package liquor sales were allowed through any hotel or established merchant. Many of the merchants were druggists who also had the right to dispense "medicinal" liquors as well as valid medical prescriptions. A local option was also set up to provide for on-premise consumption.

The State of Michigan's decision in 1933 to exercise public, rather than private control over distilled liquor distribution was due to a variety of reasons. First, Michigan's geographical proximity to Canada made politicians familiar with Ontario's system of monopoly control. Second, there was a strong influence of "dry" sentiment and a fear of bootlegging, which was common during Prohibition years. Third, druggists exerted considerable political influence at the time and were positioned to benefit from state control. Finally, the state believed government control would protect the public from middleman profiteering and excessively high private enterprise pricing.

Currently, Michigan is one of 18 states in the United States that completely controls the wholesale distribution of distilled liquor between distillers and retail licensees. The remaining 32 states utilize an "open" private license system in which the state government is not involved in wholesale distribution at all.

In 1993, Michigan and many other states throughout the country faced the problem of rapidly increasing costs of government services and strong citizen resistance to any tax increases to provide those services. Unlike nearly all other Michigan government functions, the control and distribution of liquor generates a considerable general revenue contribution for the state. Distilled liquor tax contributions go directly to the General Fund in the Executive Budget for running the State of Michigan. At present, taxes of 11.85 percent are assessed on the full price of liquor as follows: 4 percent for excise taxes, 6 percent for a Michigan school-aid fund, and 1.85 percent on packaged liquor.

Public sensitivity toward liquor as a social issue and its ability to provide the state with significant revenue make liquor control a high-profile government activity. Under a recent directive from the governor, all state functions must be examined to determine how state government efficiency could be improved. Despite the contribution of current operations, considerable room for improvement appears to exist. For example, even in light of technological improvements and the addition of more modern facilities, the cost of liquor distribution has continued to increase. Specifically, administrative cost as a percentage of sales has risen 121 percent over the past 11 years, while the number of inventory turns has decreased from 6.7 to 5.5.

The Liquor Distribution Process

Distilled liquor distribution in the State of Michigan during the fiscal year 2000-2001 involved the shipment of 6.97 million cases of liquor to retail markets, and generated $515.0 million in revenue for the state. After purchase costs and operating expenses, the net contribution to the state came to $61.5 million. The state also realizes roughly $50 million per year from taxes on distilled liquor.

Contributions from the sale of distilled liquor are generated in the following manner: the state buys liquor directly from a distiller at a delivered price of, for example, $10.00 per bottle. Then, the state factors in transportation and other costs and marks up the $10.00 bottle a state mandated 51 percent to $15.10. Retailers buy liquor from the state at a 17 percent discount off the "markup" price, and in this example would pay a wholesale price of $12.53. Thus, the state markup (51 percent) and retail gross profit margin (17 percent) are fixed by Michigan law. The net result is that consumers pay the same retail price for distilled liquor everywhere throughout the state. The state-imposed taxes of 11.85 percent are assessed on the $15.10 price and collected by the retailer upon sale to consumers.

FIGURE 1

MLCC distribution network

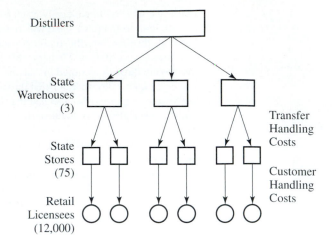

Distillers

State Warehouses (3)

State Stores (75)

Retail Licensees (12,000)

Transfer Handling Costs

Customer Handling Costs

• Off-premise (packaged)
• On-premise (by glass)

Any alteration of Michigan liquor distribution must consider potential effects on liquor prices at the retail level. In terms of consumer purchase behavior, liquor quantity is generally price inelastic. The price elasticity of liquor sales with respect to total expenditures is, however, fairly elastic. These conditions imply that as prices are raised, consumers will generally purchase the same quantity of liquor but will shift their consumption to cheaper brands. This shift reduces projected consumer expenditures and tax revenues. If system changes require that prices be raised, the effect on tax revenues could be detrimental.

Currently, distilled liquor is distributed through a two-tier network consisting of three state-owned-and-operated warehouses, 75 smaller second-tier state warehouses (known as "state stores"), which function as wholesale outlets, and 12,000 retail licensees serving the consuming public throughout the state (see Figure 1). Licensees are divided into two categories of approximately 6,000 members each: (1) on-premise bars, restaurants, and hotels that serve liquor by the glass and (2) off-premise package liquor dealers/stores. The package liquor dealers represent a wide variety of businesses, ranging from traditional liquor or party stores to large retail grocery superstores like Meijer, Inc. The first 600 retail licensee outlets were authorized in 1934 and have steadily increased to their current level. The number of state stores has remained fairly constant over the years and most of the original 75 stores are still in their original cities.

The cost to operate the current distribution network is approximately $20 million per year. Average distilled liquor inventory within the 75 second-tier warehouses is $25 million. Inventory carrying cost is assumed to be 15 percent and is considered a conservative estimate compared to figures used in private industry liquor analysis.

Distillers ship their products to the three state-owned-and-operated warehouses based on state-suggested shipping quantities. The distillers are charged a handling fee for storage of their product because the State of Michigan does not take title to the liquor until it has been shipped from the three warehouses to one of the state stores. The process of title transfer in the system is essentially a consignment arrangement. Under consignment, a product is sent to a sales agent (in this case, the State of Michigan) for sale or safe-keeping. From the State of Michigan's perspective, the consignment arrangement reduces inventory ownership risk and inventory carrying costs because the state does not take title until retail licensee demand is established. This operational arrangement was implemented several years ago; however, distillers circumvented the state's fiscal efforts by sufficiently raising prices to cover their increased storage costs. No direct shipments are made from the three state-owned-and-operated warehouses to retail licensees. Transhipment among the three state-owned-and-operated warehouses and the state stores is

FIGURE 2

The three operating districts for Michigan's liquor distribution network.

TABLE 1   MLCC District Operating Characteristics

	District 1	District 2	District 3
Population	4,363,850	4,267,531	334,518
(% of state)	(48.7%)	(47.6%)	(3.7%)
Cases Sold of Distilled	3,945,441	2,749,611	286,013
Liquor (% of state)	(56.6%)	(39.9%)	(4.1%)
Fixed Cost of District Warehouse	$924,542	$576,294	$93,825
Variable Cost per Case at Warehouse	$0.41	$0.35	$1.48
Warehousing Cost per Case	$2.20	$3.91	$13.13
Average Fixed Cost per State Store	$163,810	$65,274	$54,341
Variable Cost per Case per State Store	$1.37	$1.43	$3.64
Number of State Stores	12	46	17

minimal. Licensees place their orders weekly through a centralized order processing system and may either pick up an order in person or have it delivered by common carrier. The only exception to this delivery system occurs in the Detroit metropolitan area, where state delivery service is mandated from the largest state store to all its retail licensees.

Geographically, Michigan's liquor distribution network is broken down into three operating districts. Figure 2 illustrates the districts which each contain one of the major state-owned-and-operated warehouses. The Lincoln Park warehouse serves the Detroit area (District 1); the Lansing warehouse serves the western and central portion of the state (District 2); and the Escanaba warehouse serves the northern portion, or Upper Peninsula, of the state (District 3). District population, case liquor sales, and facility costs are shown in Table 1.

While the state does not directly pay the cost of inbound freight from distillers, research indicates that the cost is approximately $1.00 per case. Transfer freight is defined as freight movements from and between the three state-owned-and-operated warehouses to the 75 state stores. Customer freight is defined as freight movements between state stores and a retail licensee. Transfer and custom freight charges are listed in Table 2.

TABLE 2   MLCC Transfer and Custom Freight Charges

	District 1	District 2	District 3
Transfer Freight (per case)	$0.35	$0.28	$0.60
Customer Freight (per case)	$1.00	$0.40–0.70 (south) $1.10–1.30 (north)	No service available; "pickup" only

FIGURE 3

Michigan distilled spirits consumption (1993–2001)

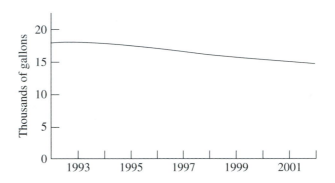

Current Issues

Redesigning the liquor control system in Michigan is not a new idea. Lawrence Desmond, business manager for the MLCC, says "When you talk about the liquor commission you're really talking about two distinct aspects. One is a regulatory agency that enforces the state's liquor laws. The other is the fact that we're the state's sole wholesaler of spirits, and along with our licensing process, we directly contribute to the state's general fund." The subject of system redesign has been raised numerous times for a variety of reasons, and many powerful economic and political special interest groups have strong opinions on the two issues of liquor enforcement and sales and licensing.

Liquor enforcement is a highly sensitive social issue. From 1992–2000, nationwide per capita consumption of distilled liquor declined about 3 percent per year. Michigan sales figures mirror the national trend (see Figure 3). Increased public awareness of alcohol abuse has been heightened through the efforts of the distillers and brewers, government agencies, and groups such as Mothers Against Drunk Driving (MADD). Antialcohol groups such as MADD argue that the state's highly controlled system contributes to strong enforcements of liquor violations, and thereby acts as a deterrent to alcohol abuse. "Alcohol is a problem-causing narcotic drug, and we need to retain as much control as possible," says Reverend Allen West of the Michigan Council on Alcohol Abuse and Problems.

The chairperson and the five commissioners of the MLCC are appointed by the governor of Michigan. Given the nature of the political process, the MLCC and its licensing procedures have historically been subject to frequent charges of political patronage, graft, and corruption by whichever political party is out of power in the state legislature. The MLCC employs approximately 620 people and a considerable number of the positions are well-paying, low-skill jobs. Although the population of Michigan is concentrated in the lower third of the state, many of the MLCC positions are located in geographically remote areas where it is unlikely that employees would be able to secure similar, private sector jobs if system redesign eliminated their positions. Also, approximately 500 MLCC employees are represented by United Auto Workers local unions. Teamsters Union delivery firms with long-term contracts for hauling liquor also exist, especially in the Detroit metropolitan area.

A number of state budget analysts and legislators, as well as academic and professional consultants, believe that the state liquor distribution system is considerably less efficient than private industry. They argue that, for example, mandated state delivery contracts and state employees with little job performance incentive hinder productivity improvement.

Lower volume retail licensees fear that redesigning the current system may hinder their ability to purchase small quantities of liquor, particularly if minimum order sizes or delivery freight breaks are instituted. They believe that changing the current setup will severely disadvantage them relative to larger, high-volume chains and retailers. Jerry Faust, spokesperson for a state organization representing retailers says, "If the system ain't broke, don't fix it." Many consumer advocates argue that the current distribution system of state-set, single pricing at all retail outlets provides consumers with an economically equitable system.

Challenges of System Redesign

Before leaving the office, Joseph outlined two general objectives of distribution network redesign: (1) increase the state's return from liquor distribution by reducing distribution costs and inefficiencies and (2) improve inventory management by utilizing Management Information Systems (MIS) to further increase efficiency. He also identified four specific objectives: (1) maintain the current service level; (2) increase inventory turns; (3) decrease administrative costs; and (4) maintain the current level of control over a highly sensitive socioeconomic policy area.

Joseph realized he would need to contact a variety of people upon his return to work on Monday in preparation for Wednesday's meeting. He sketched out plans to meet with representative MLCC staff and operations personnel, MIS staff, external industry experts in liquor and custom delivery operations, and academics in marketing and logistics at the nearby state university.

Joseph decided that any changes in distilled liquor distribution would have to reflect key operational issues of pricing, service level, projected retail sales and tax impact, direct delivery from distillers to major chain warehouses, and delivery cost considerations—not to mention a host of economic and political special interest group concerns. He began to realize that the topic of liquor distribution in Michigan was a much more complex issue than it had seemed a few hours earlier.

Questions

1. What alternative designs for distilled liquor distribution in Michigan might be considered? Explain the rationale for your suggestions.

2. Discuss the benefits and risks of alternative designs for distilled liquor distribution. Which political, economic, geographic or special interest group considerations would exert the strongest influence on system redesign?

3. Are the historical conditions which the current liquor distribution system is based upon still important today? What, if any, other factors exist that require consideration?

4. Does an inherent social conflict exist when state governments rely upon tax contributions from liquor sales to fund educational programs?

5. How would you organize the final report on distilled liquor distribution in Michigan if you were Joseph Duncan?

Case 7: W-G-P Chemical Company

John White, vice president of distribution for W-G-P Chemical Company, was preparing for the annual strategy review session conducted by the firm's executive committee. He was charged with the task of evaluating his firm's physical distribution costs and customer service capability for his firm's packaged dry and liquid agricultural chemicals.

Figure 1

**W-G-P chemical
channel flow**

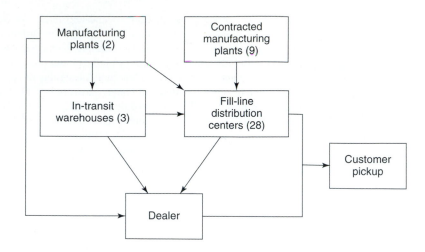

W-G-P Distribution Systems

Figure 1 outlines the existing physical distribution system for W-G-P Chemical Company. Four types of facilities: (1) two continuous, company-owned manufacturing plants; (2) nine seasonal contracted manufacturing plants; (3) numerous in-transit distribution centers; and (4) 28 full-time distribution centers. Growing environmental activism has influenced management to reject any relocation of the manufacturing plants. W-G-P distributes 129 different products or SKUs on a national basis. For distribution considerations, the products may be grouped into two different categories. Category A consists of 13 SKUs of a product called *Prevention*. The sales of *Prevention* are highly seasonal and account for 85 percent of W-G-P's total revenue. The 116 Category B products (called *Support*) sell throughout the year but also have a seasonal pattern similar to that of *Prevention's* sales. Although the sales volume of Category B is only 15 percent of W-G-P's total revenue, this group of products contributes approximately 30 percent of total before-tax profits. The typical end user of W-G-P's products purchases a variety of both A and B products. In many cases, the products are used jointly in agricultural applications. W-G-P's total product line is marketed through a network of agricultural dealers. The company sells to the dealers, who then resell the products to farmers. The typical dealer provides farmers with a broad line of products, including those that are directly competitive with W-G-P products. Historically, farmers tend to purchase both A and B products 1 to 2 weeks before field application. Application occurs at different times in different parts of the country and is directly related to the intensity of rainfall. Thus, W-G-P's products must be available precisely when the farmers need them. Likewise, the quantity needed per acre varies depending on the rainfall received in an area. Therefore, although W-G-P produces *Prevention* and *Support* all year, sales to farmers take place during a very short time period. Farmers' requirements vary in time and duration of use throughout the country.

To even out physical distribution to dealers across the year, W-G-P offers discount incentives and warehouse allowances to dealers who purchase at least 90 days in advance of estimated application dates. This early-order program accounts for 30 to 40 percent of the total annual sales of *Prevention* and *Support*. For the dealer, placing an early order means taking an inventory position on *Prevention* in advance of farmer purchases. However, since both *Prevention* and *Support* products are available, in effect, the early-order warehouse allowance means a special discount of the *Support* products which sell all year. To avoid abuse of the program, W-G-P requires that a proportional amount of *Prevention* products accompany each order. W-G-P also agrees to accept returns up to 15 percent of the total quantity of early-ordered *Prevention* products. The return policy requires a refund of the full purchase price providing dealers repay the return freight to W-G-P's warehouse.

The advantages afforded W-G-P through the early-order program are two-fold.

1. W-G-P can schedule shipments at its convenience to achieve the lowest possible transportation cost.
2. Dealers are given an additional discount if their own transportation equipment is used to pick up early orders, provided the cost is less than transportation paid for by W-G-P.

Seasonal sales, those sales which dealers buy within 90 days of estimated application dates, account for 60 to 70 percent of sales. Thus, to a significant degree, seasonal sales volume depends on W-G-P's ability to deliver products rapidly. During the seasonal period, dealers expect *Prevention* and *Support* to be available for pickup at distribution centers within a few hours of order placement. During this period, approximately 50 percent of the dealers pick up products. When transportation is arranged by W-G-P, dealers expect overnight delivery. Although the service level required during the seasonal period is high, these sales are very profitable for dealers because the farmers who purchase the products are willing to pay the full retail price. The capability to provide products during the application period is one of the most important criteria dealers use when selecting a chemical firm. Historically, sales have been concentrated in eight midwestern states which account for 80 percent of annual revenue. A summary of 1997 data is presented in Table 1.

The distribution pattern for W-G-P products is relatively simple. Two company-owned manufacturing plants are located in Alabama and Louisiana. The Alabama plant produces *Support,* while the Louisiana plant produces both *Prevention* and *Support.* Both facilities are continuous-process plants, and their location at deepwater ports facilitates economical inbound raw material movement. The nine contracted seasonal manufacturing plants have passed the environmental audits and are strategically located at key transportation gateways.

The three in-transit warehouses are utilized because the manufacturing plants have only enough storage space for 2 or 3 days' production. Table 2 lists the in-transit facility locations.

In terms of total system, the in-transit warehouses have three functions: (1) to provide storage until forward shipments are required; (2) to postpone the risk of advance shipments; and (3) to provide a combination of transportation rates that are lower to field distribution centers than the sum of published rates into and out of the in-transit warehouse. In a sense, the in-transit warehouses are economically supported by special transportation rates. All warehouses and distribution centers in the W-G-P system are public facilities. Therefore, W-G-P's costs are based

TABLE 1 Annual Sales, 1997

Dollars	525,146,747
Weight (lb.)	242,717,768
Cubic Feet	26,887,513
Cases	2,912,753
Product Lines per Order	25,392
Orders	19,139

TABLE 2 In-Transit Warehouses

Birmingham, AL

Memphis, TN

Alexandria, LA

TABLE 3   Warehouse Locations

Indianapolis, IN	Brooklyn Center, MN
Memphis, TN	Rockford, IL
Ennis, TX	Memphis, TN
Alexandria, LA	Phoenix, AZ
Fresno, CA	Orlando, FL
Baton Rouge, LA	Milwaukee, WI
West Helena, AR	Goldsboro, NC
West Sacramento, CA	Des Moines, IA
Greenville, MS	Decatur, IL
Weslaco, TX	Columbia, SC
Omaha, NE	Pennsauken, NJ
Evansville, IN	Houston, TX
Albany, GA	Lubbock, TX
Montgomery, AL	Charlotte, MI
Birmingham, AL	Lima, OH
Kansas City, MO	

---

on volume throughput and duration of storage. The 28 full-line distribution centers are primary facilities from which dealers are served. Although some early orders are shipped directly from plants and in-transit warehouses to dealers, they represent less than 10 percent of the annual tonnage shipped to dealers. Ninety percent of all tonnage is either shipped from or picked up by dealers at the full-line distribution centers. Table 3 provides a list of distribution center locations. Replenishment of distribution center inventories is primarily on an allocation basis controlled by central inventory planning. All orders are processed in an online basis at the central office after they are received over a telecommunications network. The elapsed time from order entry to shipment release from the distribution center is less than 24 hours. The primary method of shipment from plants to in-transit warehouses and distribution centers is motor carrier.

The System Review

A primary objective of the physical distribution system review is to evaluate the cost and service levels of the existing program in comparison with alternative methods of operation. Despite relatively smooth operations, the fact remains that at the end of each application season, many dealers' requirements have not been satisfied, while other dealers have returned inventory. Thus, sales are lost that could have been enjoyed if products had been available to the dealers in need. A critical element of customer service is forward inventory availability to accommodate customer pickup. In preparing the study, John White asked the Accounting Department to provide standard costs. The following standards were developed:

1. Order processing at a standard fixed cost per month with a variable cost per order.
2. Inventory at before-tax cost of 18 percent per annum of average inventory per field warehouse location.
3. Handling and storage at actual local cost for each existing and potential facility. Appropriate storage rate applicable at in-transit warehouses.
4. Inbound transportation from plants and in-transit warehouses to field warehouses based on point-to-point rates.

The cost for the reference year 1997 are contained in Table 4.

TABLE 4   Distribution Cost, 1997

Storage	$ 3.1 Million
Handling	$ 1.3 Million
Ordering	$ 3.5 Million
Average Inventory Level	$90.0 Million
Transportation to Warehouse	$ 2.3 Million
Transportation Transfer between Distribution Centers	$ 1.2 Million
Transportation to Customers	$ 5.6 Million

Questions

1. What is the total distribution cost for W-G-P Chemical Company? What is the cost per pound, cubic foot, case, line, and order? How can these measures contribute to the distribution review process?

2. On a map, plot the distribution facilities and network for W-G-P Chemical Company. What product and market characteristics can help explain this distribution structure?

3. What alternative methods of distribution should W-G-P consider for *Prevention* and *Support*?

4. Discuss the rationale for:
   A. The early order program,
   B. Customer pickup policies,
   C. Use of public versus private warehouse facilities.

Case 8: Western Pharmaceuticals (A)

David J. Closs and Christopher Kitchen

George Castro has a lot to be proud of. His company, Western Pharmaceuticals, has just merged with the largest producer of over-the-counter (OTC) cold remedies on the East Coast. The merger with Atlantic Medical should guarantee coast-to-coast market penetration for both Western Pharmaceutical's upset stomach products and Atlantic Medical's cough syrups. George has been selected to serve as CEO of the newly formed United Pharmaceuticals and is rapidly becoming recognized as being one of the top Mexican-American business leaders in the country.

History

Western Pharmaceuticals was founded by George's grandfather in postwar Los Angeles. Tony Romero's reputation for hard work combined with his strong pharmaceutical background made the introduction of his first antacid tablet an unqualified success in the booming downtown area. The company grew quickly and soon became the largest producer of antacid tablets in central and southern California.

George's father, Rudy, married into the Romero family in 1961. Although not a pharmacist, Rudy received a degree in urban planning from Pepperdine University. After many heated discussions with his new son-in-law, Tony acted on Rudy's advice to expand the company outside of the congested Los Angeles city limits. Tablet production would then take place in tiny Ontario, some distance to the east of LA. The urban site, conveniently located in proximity to several major freeways and a railhead, would serve only as a distribution center.

Rudy's suggestion to separate production and distribution worked. Ontario offered markedly lower rent and labor costs than Los Angeles but was close enough to the city to prevent any significant inconveniences. Additionally, allowing the Los Angeles site to focus only on production led to significant economies. Western Pharmaceutical flourished.

Upon his father-in-law's recommendation, Rudy enrolled in business school and received his MBA from California State University at Los Angeles in 1968. Rudy was subsequently appointed executive vice president of Western Pharmaceuticals and quickly focused on expanding and diversifying the company. Aside from seeking new products, Rudy recognized the importance of a viable distribution system to market penetration. A second distribution center was constructed in Indianapolis, and Western Pharmaceuticals began to move eastward. By 1972, Western Pharmaceuticals had a dominant position in the Northwest, Utah, Idaho, and New Mexico and was making significant inroads in Colorado. Upon Rudy's recommendation, Tony pursued the acquisition of Central Solutions, a small midwestern outfit that manufactured liquid antacids. Although Central Solutions was a struggling company, its acquisition allowed Western Pharmaceuticals to diversify into the liquid market. More importantly, Western obtained distribution centers in Omaha, Nebraska, and New Brunswick, New Jersey. Midwestern and East Coast market share and profits followed.

George started working part-time as a warehouseman in the Los Angeles distribution center in 1978. After graduating from UCLA in 1982, George worked as a production manager at the Ontario site. By the time George earned his MBA in 1986, Western Pharmaceuticals had conquered the majority of the West, Midwest, and East Coast and was now eyeing the South. In 1988, Western Pharmaceuticals opened its newest distribution center near Atlanta's inner beltway. Construction of the Atlanta site made access to the South and Southeast significantly more efficient, and market share increased accordingly.

By 1996, Western Pharmaceuticals was recognized as a "cash-cow" in the stomach upset industry. No longer an innovator, Western Pharmaceuticals had well-recognized products that retained their market share through creative and aggressive advertising campaigns. Rudy, now president of the company, was content to leave the company in its current state. This led to some amount of disagreement between him and his son. George, always the go-getter, had developed an aggressive reputation within the company and frequently encouraged his father to extend their product offering.

George became the president of Western Pharmaceuticals after his father's retirement in mid-2000, and immediately began his pursuit of acquisitions. Atlantic Medical offered everything that he felt Western Pharmaceuticals needed to guarantee its continued success. First, the company offered cold remedies, something that Western had considered but never pursued. Second, the company had key East Coast distribution centers in Mechanicsburg, Pennsylvania, and Atlanta, Georgia. George was convinced that the successful merger of the companies would guarantee nationwide success in the OTC market for antacids and cough syrups.

Present

The newly formed United Pharmaceuticals comprises six factories and eight distribution centers and produces six products (A–F) with nationwide market penetration. Now that the company has achieved a coast-to-coast presence, George is looking internally for further efficiencies. Namely, based on production and handling costs—inbound, outbound, and service costs—are all of the distribution centers necessary?

Table 1 lists the premerger, Western Pharmaceuticals plants and distribution centers. Table 2 lists the premerger plants and distribution centers for Atlantic Medical.

Table 3 lists the production capability and percent of volume for each plant.

Even though both firms utilize contract warehouse facilities, there are fixed costs incurred for each facility due to management and technology. Each distribution center operates with fixed costs of $300,000. The handling cost at each distribution center is estimated at $1.00/cwt. The handling cost covers the labor and equipment required to receive shipments from plants, put-away, order picking, and truck loading.

TABLE 1　Western Pharmaceuticals' Current Plants and Distribution Centers

Plants	Distribution Centers
Columbus, OH	Atlanta, GA
Omaha, NE	Indianapolis, IN
Ontario, CA	Los Angeles, CA
South Bend, IN	Omaha, NE
New Brunswick, NJ	

TABLE 2　Atlantic Medical Plants and Distribution Centers

Plants	Distribution Centers
Buffalo, NY/Toronto, ONT	Atlanta, GA
Newark, NJ	Mechanicsburg, PA
Sparks, NV	

TABLE 3　Plant Production Profile

Plant	Products Produced	Source Division	Percent of Sales Weight Represented by Product
Ontario, CA	A	WP	48
Columbus, OH	B	WP	6
South Bend, IN	C	WP	4
Omaha, NE	D	WP	7
Newark, NJ	E	AM	11
Buffalo/Toronto, ONT	E	AM	10
Buffalo/Toronto, ONT	F	AM	14

For accounting and inventory carrying cost purposes, each pound of inventory is valued at $5/lb. Finished goods inventory turns in the distribution centers has historically been 3.5 turns annually for Western Pharmaceuticals and 3.0 turns annually for Atlantic Medical. Each product at the distribution centers is typically replenished on a biweekly basis.

Table 4 lists the current service areas for each division and state. While there are numerous exception shipments, each state is generally served by its assigned distribution center.

At this time, the production capacity of the combined firm is 100 percent utilized. As a result, it is not possible to shut down any production capacity. It is possible, however, to shift capacity around to different plants for a one-time charge of $500,000. This covers the cost to prepare the new site, tear down the equipment, transfer it, set it up, and recalibrate it at the alternative plant location. With the exception of product E scale economics don't allow any other products to be produced at multiple plants.

Customer satisfaction requires that all products for a single customer be shipped from a common distribution center. This implies that shipments cannot be made directly from any plants.

TABLE 4 Historical Service Areas

State	AM Service Location	WP Service Location
AL	Atlanta	Atlanta
AR	Atlanta	Atlanta
AZ	Sparks	Los Angeles
CA	Sparks	Los Angeles
CO	Sparks	Omaha
CT	Mechanicsburg	New Brunswick
DC	Mechanicsburg	New Brunswick
DE	Mechanicsburg	New Brunswick
FL	Atlanta	Atlanta
GA	Atlanta	Atlanta
IA	Mechanicsburg	Omaha
ID	Sparks	Omaha
IL	Mechanicsburg	Indianapolis
IN	Mechanicsburg	Indianapolis
KS	Mechanicsburg	Omaha
KY	Mechanicsburg	Indianapolis
LA	Atlanta	Atlanta
MA	Mechanicsburg	New Brunswick
MD	Mechanicsburg	New Brunswick
MI	Mechanicsburg	Indianapolis
MN	Mechanicsburg	Omaha
MO	Mechanicsburg	Omaha
MS	Atlanta	Atlanta
MT	Sparks	Omaha
NC	Atlanta	Atlanta
ND	Mechanicsburg	Omaha
NE	Mechanicsburg	Omaha
NH	Mechanicsburg	New Brunswick
NJ	Mechanicsburg	New Brunswick
NM	Sparks	Los Angeles
NV	Sparks	Los Angeles
NY	Mechanicsburg	New Brunswick
OH	Mechanicsburg	Indianapolis
OK	Atlanta	Omaha
OR	Sparks	Los Angeles
PA	Mechanicsburg	New Brunswick
RI	Mechanicsburg	New Brunswick
SC	Atlanta	Atlanta
SD	Mechanicsburg	Omaha
TN	Atlanta	Atlanta
TX	Sparks	Los Angeles
UT	Sparks	Omaha
VA	Mechanicsburg	New Brunswick
VT	Mechanicsburg	New Brunswick
WA	Sparks	Los Angeles
WI	Mechanicsburg	Indianapolis
WV	Mechanicsburg	New Brunswick
WY	Sparks	Omaha

The integrated firm has operationalized this policy by requiring that each state be assigned to only one distribution center source. The firm also requires that 95 percent of the volume be within 2 days' transit of the servicing distribution center. This effectively means that 95 percent of the volume must be within 750 miles of the servicing distribution center.

The accompanying Excel spreadsheet contains three worksheets. The first "Weight by State" lists the number and total weight of the current shipments going to each state. The volume is broken down into LTL and TL shipments and includes a standard mixture of all products. For products that have multiple production sites, each distribution center is sourced from the nearest plant. The second worksheet "Customer Rates" contains the LTL and TL rate (per CWT.) from each distribution center to the major city representing each state. These rates are based on the discounted zip-to-zip rates provided by Western Pharmaceutical's major carrier. The third worksheet "Inbound" provides the inbound TL rates from each plant to each distribution center. These rates are also in $/CWT.

Case 9: Western Pharmaceuticals (B)

David J. Closs

Once George has initiated the supply chain design project (see Western Pharmaceuticals (A)), his next task is to investigate the firm's inventory management capability relative to the refined supply chain. The integration of the Western Pharmaceutical and Atlantic Medical distribution systems requires a refinement of the firm's inventory management system.

Although the firm wants to have a comprehensive inventory analysis, the information available is limited due to the merger and a simultaneous move to an ERP system. In fact, in terms of quickly available data, there is only a limited sample from the Atlantic Medical sales and inventory records. For a sample of 100 SKUs, the database includes the average and standard deviation of weekly sales, average order cycle time (OCT), replenishment order quantity (OQ), and the average inventory. Based on history, the current standard deviation in the replenishment cycle time is 1 week. The sales, order quantities, and inventory are recorded in cases. The historical information is provided for each of the three existing distribution centers.

Atlantic believes that the historical case fill rate is 95 percent but they are not really sure.

Questions

1. What should the case fill rate be for each product given the current uncertainty levels and order quantities and how does the calculated aggregate case fill rate differ from the historically observed level?

2. What are the safety stock and average inventory levels for each product and in aggregate necessary to achieve 95 percent case fill rate for each product? To what extent do the actual inventory levels deviate from the theoretical inventory levels? What conclusions can you draw from the differences?

3. What is the inventory carrying cost impact for increasing the case fill rate from the current level of 95 percent to 99 percent? Assume an annual inventory carrying cost of 20 percent. Assuming that 5 percent of potential sales is lost due to stockouts (100 – 95 percent) and that there is a 25 percent margin on the average item (COGS = 75 percent), would you recommend that the service level be increased? Justify your answer.

4. What would be the impact on inventory and service of consolidating all of Atlantic Medical stock into a single facility? Apply both the square of *n* and item level approaches. The square root of *n* should be applied to aggregate inventory values for a total of all products. The item level approach combines the averages and standard deviations used for the individual sites into the demand and standard deviation representing a single site. The weekly average for the combined site is

the sum of the weekly averages. The combined weekly standard deviation is computed as: $\sigma_c = \sqrt{\sigma_1^2 + \sigma_2^2 + \sigma_3^2}$

where:

σ_c = Combined weekly standard deviation; and

σ_i = Weekly standard deviation for distribution center i.

Discuss the differences between the two approaches. What is the reason for these differences?

Case 10: Customer Service at Woodson Chemical Company

From the perspective of Melinda Sanders, the problems of Woodson Chemical Company (WCC) were straightforward and easily identifiable. Solutions, however, appeared to be far more difficult and complex. Sanders had just turned 29 years old and was in her sixth year of employment with WCC. After graduating from a top university in the western United States with an MBA in marketing, she had steadily progressed through a series of positions in marketing, sales, and distribution operations. Her current position is lead distribution planner in the Chemicals and Performance Products Division of WCC North America.

The most recent WCC North America customer service report revealed that "customers continually give the company average-to-poor marks in customer service performance. In particular, customers express extreme dissatisfaction with the order-information process." Sanders was of the opinion that the more WCC sales and distribution systems were expanded, the more management and communication bottlenecks seemed to be created. She was also well aware that the issue of order information status was problematic throughout all of WCC's North American operations. Each division had been hard at work over the past 18 months developing and instituting a variety of software packages aimed at improving its service performance. During a recent meeting with Barry McDonald, WCC North America Chemical and Performance Products Director of Customer Service, Sanders had been given a copy of a report regarding projected directions and importance ratings of customer service requirements in the chemical industry. The report stated:

> customers specifically desire instantaneous access to real-time order information status. This information accessibility is necessary throughout the supply chain—from the customer's initial inquiry to production status, shipment loading, and arrival at the final destination. A critical goal is to be able to both commit and monitor inventory from the point in time an order is placed. While the goal of integrated logistics is a major goal for many chemical companies, efforts are frequently being hindered by inadequate information systems and organization structural design.

Woodson Chemical Company

WCC was founded in 1899 by Alexander Woodson. The company originally was located in southeast Texas; in the early 1960s the corporate headquarters were moved to St. Louis to capitalize on the city's central geographic location. Approximately one-third of WCC's business is conducted overseas. Most arrangements are wholly-owned subsidiaries; there are few industrialized countries in the world where WCC does not have some manufacturing or sales presence. WCC North America, a wholly-owned subsidiary of Woodson Chemical Company, is the sixth largest chemical company in North America, and produces a diversified range of chemicals used as raw materials for manufacturing in the food, personal care products, pharmaceuticals, pulp and paper, and utility industries.

The company operates four product groups which are broken down into three divisions (see Table 1). Division 1 comprises chemicals and performance products, which are mainly used as raw materials in the manufacture and/or processing of consumer products. Division 2 is composed of two product groups: plastic products, and hydrocarbons and energy. Plastic products

TABLE 1   WCC Sales 1997–2001 ($000,000)

Division	1997	1998	1999	2000	2001
1: Chemicals and Performance Products	$3,630	$3,785	3,562	$3,165	$3,130
2: Plastic Products,	4,857	4,896	5,174	4,775	4,701
Hydrocarbons and Energy	1,051	1,243	1,547	1,353	1,214
3: Consumer Specialties Medical Health Agriculture					
Consumer Products	2,120	2,387	3,537	3,838	4,184
Total	$11,658	$12,311	$13,820	$13,131	$13,229

are utilized in numerous markets such as packaging, automotive, electrical appliances, building and construction, housewares, recreation, furniture, flooring, and health care. The hydrocarbons and energy group is concerned with the purchase of fuels and petroleum-based materials as well as the production of power and steam used to manufacture WCC's plastics, chemicals, and metals. Division 3 comprises consumer specialties, which serve the food care, home care, and personal products markets.

In terms of functional support, each division maintains its own marketing, manufacturing, logistics, and administrative departments. Currently, divisional information processing responsibilities for customer service, transportation, and warehousing are provided by the logistics group. Information processing responsibility for finance and accounting are provided by the administration group. Figure 1 presents the organization structure for WCC North America's operations.

Across the four product groups, performance has varied considerably over recent years. Although chemical and performance product sales have been declining or flat, increased volume and profit improvement is projected due to growth opportunities. In Division 2, plastic products has exhibited reduced sales; although moderate growth is attainable, prices are projected to remain under pressure due to a weak global economy and considerable industry oversupply. Hydrocarbons and energy sales have declined significantly in the past 3 years; although feedstock and energy purchase costs have been reduced, lower sales have more than offset procurement savings. Industry overcapacity remains a severe problem; additional capacity coming online in developing industries in Korea and China will only exacerbate the situation. Consumer specialties continues to exhibit very strong sales gains, particularly in medical and health and consumer product categories. Agricultural sales are relatively unchanged. Steady growth for consumer specialties is projected to continue, although perhaps not at the rapid rate of the past 5 years.

A significant concern of WCC management are the major cost and expense areas of distribution and marketing (see Table 2). The company has made considerable progress in reducing the cost of purchased raw material inputs, but other category expenses are increasing at a rate in excess of sales.

Industry Background

Chemical manufacturing has historically been a very cyclical industry; recessions and periods of slow economic growth typically depress chemical industry sales for several years at a time. As economies begin to rebound, manufacturing picks up and chemical production often leads the U.S. economy into a recovery period.

The chemical industry's attempts to alter its strategic planning with regard to markets and strategy are changing. The expansion of a global economy and leading-edge chemical technology have dramatically altered the manner in which the chemical industry operates today. In the past, a large, fully integrated chemical company with control of raw materials, economies of scale, and modern plants possessed significant cost advantages that could eliminate marginally efficient chemical producers throughout the world. Today, such a strategy is easily negated. The

636

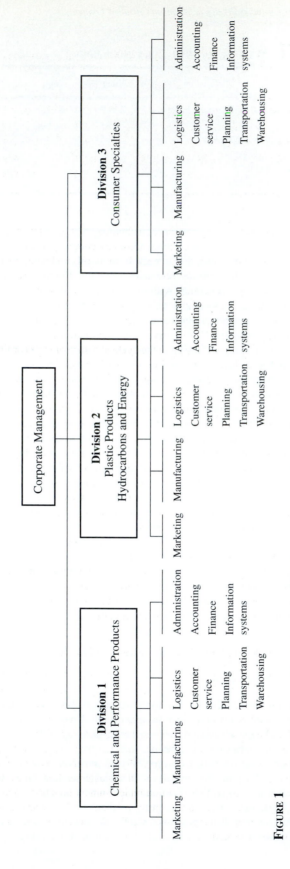

FIGURE 1
Woodson Chemical Company—North American Division organization structure

TABLE 2   Selected WCC Operating Costs and Expenses—1988–2001 ($000,000)

	1997	1998	1999	2000	2001
Costs of Goods Sold	$6,864	$7,335	$9,125	$8,863	$8,893
Research and Development	540	611	795	811	902
Promotion and Advertising	291	346	447	505	557
Selling and Administrative	1,138	1,231	1,459	1,527	1,630
Total	$8,833	$9,523	$11,826	$11,706	$11,982

availability of cutting edge chemical technology that goes into building premier chemical plants can make a low-cost producer out of most any company that can structure an arrangement for a constant supply of chemical feedstock from an oil-producing country. Contemporary competitive advantage is typically derived from a focused market position, good raw materials supply without the heavy investment required in a completely vertically integrated structure, and a lean efficient organization structure. Industry leaders must maintain efficient resource and organization structure while they leverage their technological expertise across as many chemical applications as possible. In addition, many chemical manufacturers are diversifying into specialty chemicals in an attempt to balance the cyclical nature of their earnings.

Faced with mounting pressure to become increasingly globalized, especially during difficult economic conditions, chemical industry information systems leaders are scrambling to implement more cost-efficient and effective strategies to track and share business information. Angela Lowrey, director of WCC North America's Information Resources Planning, says, "better logistics information across business divisions is integral to instituting a strategic business plan. With current spending on computer information systems accounting for approximately 2% of corporate revenues, [business] information is a premium commodity and a potential strategic asset that many firms in our industry are just beginning to recognize."

The determination of where to focus chemical operations is also becoming increasingly complex as the geographic nature of the industry changes economically. Uncertainty in Eastern Europe, rapid growth in the Pacific Rim, and potential markets in Latin and South America and the Caribbean have upset the traditional patterns of global chemical manufacturing. Very high research and development costs are necessary to maintain a steady stream of high-margin, new products. Environmental problems and liability issues are a significant concern for the chemical manufacturing industry. Although compliance with increasingly stringent emission controls has improved the relationships among chemical manufacturers, government, and public interest groups, the transportation and handling of hazardous materials remains a high-profile issue, particularly in North America and Western Europe.

WCC North American's Distribution Network

WCC North America produces and sells more than 1,500 products in many different formulations, packaging containers, and labeling arrangements. The products are manufactured at one or more of the 22 manufacturing locations in the USA, and are distributed through 5 WCC distribution centers to field warehouses and then to 325 stocking points (cooperatives and dealers). Table 3 lists the WCC manufacturing plants and distribution centers located in North America.

Chemical manufacturing does not maintain significant levels of WIP (work-in-process) inventories and managing them is typically not difficult. However, managing finished goods inventories is a considerable problem. Short customer lead times, high customer service levels, large manufacturing and distribution replenishment quantities, and long manufacturing and distribution lead times require that many products be in inventory when customer orders are received. The size and complexity of the WCC distribution network makes distribution management complex and difficult.

TABLE 3   WCC North America's Distribution Network

Manufacturing Plants	Distribution Centers	
Schaumburg, IL	Gary, IN	Reno, NV
Los Angeles, CA	Omaha, NE	Louisville, KY
Harrisburg, PA	Spokane, WA	Shreveport, LA
Memphis, TN	Denver, CO	Charlotte, NC
New Orleans, LA	Little Rock, AR	Omaha, NE
Shreveport, LA	Raleigh-Durham, NC	
St. Louis, MO	Morristown, NJ	
Houston, TX	Toledo, OH	
Lubbock, TX	Wilmington, DE	
Tulsa, OK	Jacksonville, FL	
Montgomery, AL	Billings, MT	

Field Warehouses (as necessary) Primary public facilities

Dealers and Cooperatives Contractual throughout North America

According to Melinda Sanders, WCC's management structure does not match up well to the company's needs of supply chain management. Recently, however, the company has begun to implement an integrated logistics system to coordinate planning, purchasing, manufacturing, marketing, and distribution functions. Increased attention has been directed to the problems of providing manufacturing with the necessary information to determine the level of individual SKU production (via MRP) as well as how much and where to deploy products (via DRP). Improved communication among marketing, manufacturing, and distribution has led to better forecasts of IT customer demand.

However, although each division of WCC is beginning to operate in a more integrated manner, each division continues to maintain separate responsibility for customer orders and information status. Each division also designs, plans, and executes its manufacturing, warehousing, picking, and loading activities. The majority of warehouses utilized are public facilities. Transportation is provided by common and contract carriage and railroad. A significant portion of WCC's product moves by rail; in fact, WCC owns and operates a sizeable private railcar fleet due to the specialized nature of its products. The link between transportation and customer service is a vital component at WCC. "Logistics at WCC North America's Chemicals and Performance Products Division is a competitive tool," says Logistics Manager Michael Davidson. "I make sure that we always have more than enough carriers on our inbound and outbound traffic lanes to keep product moving throughout our system."

Traditionally, a general level of attention to customer service was acceptable but as WCC restructured its divisional operations by product grouping and, in particular, diversified into specialty chemicals, the requirements across divisions have become very differentiated. The complexity of customer service is additionally complicated because each division serves a considerable number of common customers, many of whom are high-volume, key accounts. WCC North America's decentralized divisional structure has historically allowed each division to provide tailored, high-quality customer service to meet the differentiated and demanding requirements of WCC customers. The ability to tailor such services is considered a competitive strength at WCC. Sales, marketing, and cost control efforts are becoming increasingly customer responsive—the level of focus is now not only division-specific but also individual customer account-specific. In particular, the Consumer Specialties Division serves a highly time-sensitive market that includes many powerful, large retailers and mass merchandisers.

Melinda Sanders and her staff have a meeting scheduled tomorrow morning with Douglas Liddell, vice president of WCC's Corporate Information Systems Group, to discuss the direction of WCC North America's Chemicals and Performance Products Division. Sanders strongly believes that any investment in information systems should directly support a specific business strategy. The question is, which investments should be made and what exactly should WCC's strategy be?

Questions

1. What is the critical issue(s) confronting WCC North America?
2. What changes, if any, should be initiated to address the critical issue(s)?
3. Identify the risks and benefits of your proposed changes from the perspective of (a) WCC North America corporate management; (b) WCC North America line distribution management; (c) WCC North America customers.
4. What would be the impact on WCC North America operations if the proposed changes were successfully implemented?
5. What changes, if any, would you recommend in WCC North America's information processing arrangements?
6. Is Melinda Sanders in a position to properly understand WCC North America's problems? Why or why not?
7. Do you think WCC North America's current situation is applicable across its global operations? How, if at all, does it change the nature of the problem?

Case 11: Performance Control at Happy Chips, Inc.

Wendell Worthmann, manager of logistics cost analysis for Happy Chips, Inc., was faced with a difficult task. Harold L. Carter, the new director of logistics had circulated a letter from Happy Chips' only mass merchandise customer, Buy 4 Less, complaining of poor operating performance. Among the problems cited by Buy 4 Less were: (1) frequent stockouts (2) poor customer service responsiveness and (3) high prices for Happy Chips' products. The letter suggested that if Happy Chips were to remain a supplier to Buy 4 Less, it would need to eliminate stockouts by: (1) providing direct store delivery four times per week (instead of three) (2) installing an automated order inquiry system to increase customer service responsiveness ($10,000.00) and (3) decreasing product prices by 5 percent. While the previous director of logistics would most certainly have begun implementing the suggested changes, Harold Carter was different. He requested that Wendell prepare a detailed analysis of Happy Chips' profitability by segment. He also asked that it be prepared on a spreadsheet to permit some basic analysis. This was something that Wendell had never previously attempted, and it was needed first thing in the morning.

Company Background

Happy Chips, Inc., is the fifth largest potato chip manufacturer in the metropolitan Detroit market. The company was founded in 1922 and following an unsuccessful attempt at national expansion has remained primarily a local operation. The company currently manufactures and distributes one variety of potato chips to three different types of retail accounts: grocery, drug, and mass merchandise. The largest percentage of business is concentrated in the grocery segment, with 36 retail customer locations accounting for 40,000 annual unit sales and more than 50 percent of annual revenue. The drug segment comprises 39 customer locations which account for 18,000 annual unit sales and more than 27 percent of annual revenue. In the mass merchandise segment, Happy Chips has one customer with three locations that account for 22,000 annual unit sales and almost 22 percent of annual revenue. All distribution is store-direct, with delivery drivers handling returns of outdated material and all shelf placement and merchandising.

TABLE 1   Income Statement

Income	
Net Sales	$150,400.00
Interest and Other Income	3,215.00
	153,615.00
Cost and Expenses	
Cost of Goods Sold	84,000.00
Other Manufacturing Expense	5,660.00
Marketing, Sales, and Other Expenses	52,151.20
Interest Expense	2,473.00
	144,284.20
Earnings before Income Taxes	9,330.80
Income Taxes	4,198.86
Net Earnings	5,131.94

TABLE 2   Annual Logistics Costs by Segment

Cost Category/Segment	Grocery	Drug	Mass Merchandise
Stocking Cost ($/Delivery)	$1.80	$1.20	$2.80
Information Cost (Annual)	1,000.00	8,000.00	1,000.00
Delivery Cost ($/Delivery)	5.00	5.00	6.00

Recently, Happy Chips has actively sought growth in the mass merchandise segment because of the perceived profit potential. However, while the company is acutely aware of overall business profitability, there has never been an analysis on a customer segment basis.

Performance Statistics

Wendell recently attended a seminar at a major midwestern university concerning activity-based costing. He was anxious to apply the techniques he had learned at the seminar to the current situation, but was unsure exactly how to proceed. He did not understand the relationship between activity-based costing and segment profitability analysis, but he knew the first step in either is to identify relevant costs. Wendell obtained a copy of Happy Chips' most recent income statement (Table 1).

He also knew specific information concerning logistic costs by segment (Table 2).

All deliveries were store-direct with two deliveries per week to grocery stores, one delivery per week to drug stores and three deliveries per week to mass merchandisers. To obtain feedback concerning store sales, Happy Chips purchased scanner data from grocery and mass merchandise stores at an aggregate annual cost of $1,000.00 per segment. The drug store segment required use of handheld scanners by delivery personnel to track sales. The cost of delivery to each store was dependent on the type of vehicle used. Standard route trucks were used for drug stores and grocery stores, while extended vehicles were used to accommodate the volume at mass merchandisers.

Trade prices for each unit were different for grocery ($1.90), drug ($2.30), and mass merchandise ($1.50) customers. Wendell was also aware that Buy 4 Less required Happy Chips to cover the suggested retail price with a sticker bearing its reduced price. The machinery required to apply these labels had an annual rental cost of $5,000.00. Labor and materials cost an additional $.03 per unit.

Conclusion

As Wendell sat in his office compiling information to complete the segment profitability analysis, he received several unsolicited offers for assistance. Bill Smith, manager marketing, urged him not to bother with the analysis:

Buy 4 Less is clearly our most important customer. We should immediately implement the suggested changes.

Steve Brown, director of manufacturing, disagreed. He felt the additional manufacturing cost required to meet Buy 4 Less' requirements was too high:

We should let Buy 4 Less know what we really think about their special requirements. Stickers, of all things! What business do they think we are in?

The sales force had a different opinion. Jake Williams felt the grocery segment was most important:

Just look at that volume! How could they be anything but our best customers?

The broad interest being generated by this assignment worried Wendell. Would he have to justify his recommendations to everyone in the company? Wendell quietly closed his office door.

Based on the available information and his own knowledge of ABC systems, Wendell Worthmann needed to complete a segment profitability analysis and associated spreadsheet before his meeting with Harold in the morning. With all these interruptions, it was going to be a long night.

Questions

1. What is the difference between activity-based costing and segment profitability analysis? How would you counter the arguments by other managers concerning the most attractive segments? Using relevant costs provided above, determine the profitability for each of Happy Chips' business segments.
2. Based on your analysis, should Happy Chips consider the changes desired by Buy 4 Less? Why or why not?
3. Should Happy Chips eliminate any business segments? Why or why not?
4. If the price to mass merchandise stores were to increase by 20 percent, would that change your answer to the previous question?
5. Are there factors other than segment profitability that should be considered? If so, what are they?

Case 12: Change Management at Wilmont Drug Company

As Charlie Smith, vice president of logistics at Wilmont Drug Company, headed down the corridor toward the conference room, he once again reviewed events of the past several months. After a decade of unprecedented sales growth, wholesaler Wilmont Drug experienced its fifth consecutive quarterly loss in March 2001. While revenue continued to grow, albeit at a much slower rate than the previous decade, expenses had outpaced sales. The company's approach to high-service wholesaling, which had been the cornerstone of its national growth strategy, had fallen into disfavor with some outspoken shareholders.

Founder and former president Robert H. Wilmont, Sr., advocated a strategy of low price, no frills service, supported by a drastic cost reduction initiative. As the company's primary shareholder, he was an influential individual whose support would be critical to any revitalization plan. John W. Brown, the current president of Wilmont Drug, had successfully established leadership at his previous employer in the computer industry by implementing a high-service strategy similar to the one in place at Wilmont Drug. He recommended the company "stay the course," because revenue growth would eventually return to previous levels and eliminate the current losses.

Charlie Smith was a realist. He knew that strategic change was necessary, but disagreed with the drastic shift being advocated by the company's founder. A high-service wholesaling strategy had served the company well during its growth period, but ever-increasing customer demands made high service on a universal basis very costly. While studying for his MBA in logistics at a major midwestern university, Charlie was introduced to the concepts of segmentation and selective determination of service levels. Over the summer, Charlie developed a four-stage plan for reorienting the company based on these concepts. He now had to convince Bob Wilmont, John Brown, and the senior management team assembled in the conference room, that his plan could work if given the chance.

Company Background

Wilmont Drug Company, the second largest wholesaler of drugs and ethical pharmaceuticals in the United States, was founded by Robert H. Wilmont, Sr., in 1948. At first, the company prospered as a small regional wholesaler serving drug stores and hospitals in the northeastern United States. In the ensuing decades, Wilmont Drug grew primarily by acquisition. By 1970, the company had acquired three additional warehouses and reached $10 million in sales. By 1978, sales exceeded $250 million and coverage extended as far west as Ohio. In spite of a general decline in wholesaling across the United States, Wilmont Drug continued to expand. The company achieved national distribution in 1985, with the purchase of Jones Drug Company, then the seventh largest drug wholesaler in the United States.

Wilmont Drug was able to offer consistent and dependable overnight delivery service, despite significant operational differences between the networks of the acquired companies. As the company grew, the development of customer-specific service offerings by geographic market was viewed as a unique strength. Creative solutions to customer requirements rapidly expanded the service base and made Wilmont Drug the preferred supplier for many national chains. However, with this uniqueness came difficulties. When revenue growth began to decline in the early 2000s, the inefficiency of the extensive service offerings combined with the lack of operational consistency led to consecutive quarterly losses.

Wholesaling

The problems experienced by Wilmont Drug Company were not unique to the drug industry. Based on changes brought about by transportation deregulation and improved technology, wholesalers across the United States were being forced to reexamine traditional supply chain roles. The basic cost/service relationship changed in favor of companies with both efficient and effective customer service strategies. The notion of high-performance wholesaling, which focuses on clear delineation of customer needs and provision of differentiated service, emerged as a logical strategic alternative.

Charlie Smith recognized this shift in wholesaling and chose to make it the focus of his revitalization plan. He believed that by developing and implementing a high-performance wholesaling strategy before the competition, Wilmont Drug would be able to define the competitive structure of the drug industry and lock-in the most attractive customers.

Revitalization Plan/Change Management Model

With these goals in mind, Charlie drafted the following memorandum to John W. Brown, president of Wilmont Drug Company, detailing his proposed revitalization plan and associated change management model:

Memorandum

Date: September 1, 2001

To: John Brown

From: Charlie Wilson

Re: Change Management Model to Revitalize Wilmont Drug Company

The following model and discussion detail a plan to propel Wilmont Drug Company to the forefront of the wholesale drug industry. I hope you will give this plan your most serious consideration and let me know when you would like to discuss its potential implementation.

The plan has an expected time span of 5 years. While some aspects of implementation can be completed simultaneously, the first two stages must be completed prior to launching the market extension and creation phases of development. See the accompanying diagram.

Change Management Model

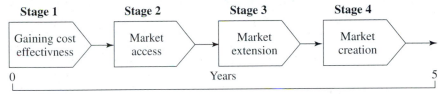

Cost Effectiveness

During the cost effectiveness stage, the objective is to achieve operational control necessary to support segmentation strategies. It is essential that basic services be provided at a consistently high level of performance and in a cost-effective manner. To gain cost-effectiveness requires that supplier, product, and facility rationalization be completed. Typical key services used by all areas are centralized to achieve economies of scale and standardization of business processes. Such standardization is required to gain the operational competence and credibility necessary to move forward.

Market Access

This aspect of implementation consists primarily of customer segmentation. Selected customers are identified and operations are focused to position Wilmont Drug as the preferred supplier to those customers targeted as high potential buyers. Emphasis in this stage of implementation is on high-quality basic service to selected customers. The segmentation plan should be as simple as possible.

Market Extension

Market extension involves programs to increase business penetration to selected customers. It consists of continuous improvement of basic service toward zero-defect performance and the introduction of value-added services to solidify and expand business relationships with top customers. Value-added innovations include extensive use of bar coding, computer linkages, vendor-managed inventories, business consulting, and other programs designed to improve customer operating efficiency and increase their overall market presence. Such value-added services can only be offered to customers who are willing to commit to extended business arrangements.

Market Creation

The final stage of strategic implementation consists of implementing programs to expand the profitability and competitiveness of top customers and to assist them in developing business growth strategies. To gain share in a low-growth market, a wholesaler must facilitate growth in customer market share. Implementation of joint systems that leverage the combined resources of the wholesaler and selected customers are a key consideration.

The foundation of the strategic change management model proposed by Charlie Wilson depends upon full implementation stage 1, gaining cost effectiveness and stage 2, market access. For the most part, these stages require managerial brute force implementation and continuous reinforcement of initiatives designed to standardize operating processes and service offerings. By achieving the first two stages of the model, a business is positioned to exploit a leadership position. Success is highly unlikely in stage 3 unless the foundation of the first two stages is in place. Stage 3, market extension, and stage 4, market creation, represent increased penetration of target customer relationships. Unlike the first two stages, these stages are customer-specific. Therefore, associated initiatives can be implemented simultaneously, rather than sequentially. Once a customer is firmly established in the stage 3/4 category, significant improvements can be projected in sales penetration, quality of transactions, and deployment of assets.

After reviewing the memorandum, John Brown was skeptical of the plan. He had never personally been involved in such an initiative. Nevertheless, he recommended that Charlie present the revitalization plan and associated change management model to the entire senior management team.

Conclusion

Charlie sincerely believed that improving the firm's performance would take considerable time and effort on the part of both senior and middle management. He also believed the vast majority of managers had neither the training nor the work experience to manage such initiatives. He expected strong resistance from the senior management team. While he had prepared responses to all anticipated questions, an implementation plan detailing specific actions remained to be developed.

Charlie Wilson paused outside the conference room. He recognized the revitalization plan and change management model he was about to propose would significantly alter the destiny of Wilmont Drug Company. If senior management agrees with his plan, the question remains whether middle management will accept the challenge of implementing change of this magnitude. Charlie took a deep breath and entered the conference room.

Questions

1. Discuss the internal and external influences which impacted Wilmont Drug's need to reorient the company.
2. Critically evaluate the revitalization plan and change management model proposed by Charlie Smith. Can you suggest any changes?
3. Would your evaluation change if Wilmont Drug Company had significant international business operations? Why or why not?
4. Using the model provided or your own change management model, develop a detailed implementation plan for reorienting the company.

Case 13: Supply Chain Management at Dream Beauty Company

Dream Beauty (DB) Company is a manufacturer of consumer beauty supplies and cosmetics. Based out of Money City, Nevada, the company services its customers across the U.S. Recently, a supply chain expert was elected to the board of directors. With his insight into supply chain operations, heightened attention was turned toward that area. The costs in this area have been increasing, and management became very concerned about the issue. The company annual sales reached $130,000,000 for the first time since inception. Management believed that some of the increase in supply chain costs may be attributed to additional sales, but they were confident that other factors existed that needed to be addressed. The situation had management's full attention, especially since supply chain costs (and savings for that matter), flow directly to the bottom line.

DB supplies its products through three distinct channels: retail stores (direct), convenience stores, and mass merchants. Each channel is considered an independent profit center with full financial responsibilities for income statement and balance sheet. From DB sales, retail accounted for 50 percent, convenience stores for 30 percent, while mass merchants picked up the remaining sales. Cost of goods sold accounted for 40 percent of sales. All three channels seem to be profitable, and contribute equally to DB, according to the company's cost accountant.

The order fulfillment cycle at DB consists of four areas:

	Total Cost
Order Processing	$10,000,000
Packaging	8,000,000
Labeling	2,000,000
Delivery	$30,000,000
Total Supply Chain-Related Costs	$50,000,000

The total order fulfillment averages 3 days. All orders are processed through a central location, and delivered from distribution centers located across the U.S. Usually retail and convenience store orders are shipped unlabeled on standard nonmixed pallets. Mass merchants, on the other hand, have placed a lot of pressure on DB and want the company to take an active role in helping them manage their inventory. To accommodate this channel, DB has assumed some of the jobbers' functions in the store and started labeling the orders for mass merchants. To accomplish that, the company recently purchased a labeling machine that can process labels at a speed of 30 labels/second. The machine's historical value was determined to be $10,000,000. The company usually depreciates similar equipment on a straight-line basis over a period of 5 years.

The company has a discount policy for all three channels that it services. The net is due in 30 days. While this policy is explicitly stated on all DB's invoices, retail stores are the only ones that pay according to invoice terms. Mass merchants usually pay within 15 days, while convenience stores usually pay within 45 days. The company's cost accountant reported that all sales were sold on credit. Cash sales and C.O.D. sales were rare; therefore, they can be ignored for the purpose of this analysis. DB does not engage in any barter transactions.

The company received a total of 3,600 orders. Retail orders amounted to 1,000; convenience stores to 2,500; and mass merchants had 100 orders. Each order has a corresponding delivery that is usually completed within the 3-day fulfillment cycle. The company's practice has been to allocate logistics-related costs to its three channels based on their relative percentage of sales volume. The orders were shipped in 2,000 packages, with retail accounting for 800 packages, convenience stores for 1,100 packages and mass merchants for 100 packages. Packaging cost is estimated to be the same regardless of size. To service these orders, the company has maintained an inventory safety stock so that it can meet the level of service that it promises its customers (the 3-day fulfillment cycle). It is estimated that the company holds an average of 90 days' inventory for retail, 60 days' inventory for convenience stores, and 40 days' inventory for mass merchants. The company's cost accountant estimated the total carrying costs of inventory to be approximately 15 percent of total average annual inventory. These costs also include the cost of capital.

The company's customer base in convenience stores includes 13 different stores located in major U.S. cities. Table 1 provides a breakdown of sales per store, as well as the number of orders, and packages for each store.

Historically, DB has offered its customers a level of service that is of the highest standards. One of the fulfillment managers has been quoted, "We do not discriminate between customers; our 3-day fulfillment cycle in my opinion is becoming an industry benchmark, and I like it that way. I do not think that our strategy should change in that regard."

The board has some second thoughts about this strategy, and what type of value-added it is generating to the company.

On your first day, you get accustomed to your surroundings, and you become familiar with the computer system. On your second day, the vice president for supply chain (and your hiring

TABLE 1

Store Name	Sales	Orders	Packages
Love Your Style	$5,000,000	300	50
Looking Good	$1,500,000	75	10
Wild by Nature	$3,000,000	200	100
Beautyss Bliss	$10,000,000	450	150
Cosmo Naturelle	$3,500,000	60	30
Beautee Fatale	$1,000,000	100	100
La Belle Femme	$5,000,000	200	20
Le Beau Monsieur	$2,500,000	320	200
Fruity Beauty	$1,500,000	120	120
Tuti Fruity	$2,000,000	250	200
L'Air Du Jour	$1,000,000	150	75
Make-up Galore	$2,000,000	175	10
Nuttin' Homely	$1,000,000	100	35

manager) comes up to you. He proceeds to brief you on a high-level meeting that he just concluded with the top brass at the company. He states that management wants to know why supply chain costs seem skewed, as well as a full analysis of the three logistical channels that the company employs. Management would like you to answer the following questions:

1. Analyze the way that current costs are being allocated; what potential changes can you recommend to make the system more efficient and more accurate?
2. What is the profitability level and return on investment by distribution channel, both under the current and the recommended allocations?
3. What are your recommendations regarding the company policy of offering all its customers the same service level (3-day fulfillment cycle)?

Note: The company's cost of capital for both borrowing and lending can be estimated at 9 percent. Ignore tax effects on all transactions.